THEODERIC THE GREAT

THEODERIC THE GREAT

King of Goths, Ruler of Romans

HANS-ULRICH WIEMER

Translated by John Noël Dillon

Yale
UNIVERSITY
PRESS
New Haven & London

Published with assistance from the foundation established in memory of Henry
Weldon Barnes of the Class of 1882, Yale College.

The translation of this work was funded by Geisteswissenschaften International—
Translation Funding for Work in the Humanities and Social Sciences from Germany,
a joint initiative of the Fritz Thyssen Foundation, the German Federal Foreign Office,
the collecting society VG WORT and the Börsenverein des Deutschen Buchhandels
(German Publishers & Booksellers Association).
Originally published in Germany as *Theoderich der Grosse*, by Hans-Ulrich Wiemer,
© Verlag C.H.Beck oHG, München 2018.
English translation copyright © 2023 by Yale University.

Yale University Press books may be purchased in quantity for educational, business, or
promotional use. For information, please e-mail sales.press@yale.edu (U.S. office) or
sales@yaleup.co.uk (U.K. office).

Set in Electra and Trajan types by IDS Infotech Ltd.
Printed in the United States of America.

Library of Congress Control Number: 2022936919
ISBN 978-0-300-25443-3 (hardcover : alk. paper)
ISBN 978-0-300-27991-7 (paperback)

A catalogue record for this book is available from the British Library.

10 9 8 7 6 5 4 3 2 1

In memory of Wolf Liebeschuetz (1927–2022)

CONTENTS

Contents

Abbreviations

To save space in the notes and bibliography, the abbreviations listed here are used to designate book series, which appear in roman type, and a selection of major, usually multi-volume editions, the titles of which appear in italics.

ACO	*Acta Conciliorum Oecumenicorum*
ACW	Ancient Christian Writers
AE	*L'année épigraphique*
Agath. *Hist.*	Agathias, *Historiae*
Agn.	Agnellus, *Liber Pontificalis ecclesiae Ravennatis*
Ambr. *Ep.*	Ambrose, *Epistulae*
Ambr. *Spir.*	Ambrose, *De spiritu sancto*
Ambr. *Virg.*	Ambrose, *De Virginibus*
Amm.	Ammianus Marcellinus, *Res gestae*
Anon. Val.	*Anonymus Valesianus*
Anth. Lat.	*Anthologia Latina*
Anthim.	Anthimus, *De observatione ciborum ad Theodoricum regem Francorum epistula*
App. Maxim.	*Appendix Maximiani*
AQDGMA	Ausgewählte Quellen zur Deutschen Geschichte des Mittelalters
Arat. *Hist. Apost.*	Arator, *Historia Apostolica*
ARC	Accademia Romanistica Costantiniana
Auct. Haun.	*Auctarium Prosperi epitomae chronicon Hauniense*
Auct. Haun. ord. post.	*Auctarium Hauniense ordo posterior*

Auct. Haun. ord. post. margo	*Auctarium Hauniense ordinis posterioris margo*
Auct. Haun. ord. pr.	*Auctarium Hauniense ordo prior*
Auct. Marcell.	*Auctarium Marcellini comitis*
Auct. Prosp. Vat.	*Auctarium Prosperi epitomae chronicon Vaticanae*
Aug. *Civ.*	Augustine, *De civitate dei*
Aug. *Ep.*	Augustine, *Epistulae*
Aux. *Ep.*	Auxentius, *Epistola*
Avell.	*Collectio Avellana*
Avit. *Ep.*	Avitus, *Epistulae*
BAug	Bibliothèque Augustinienne
BGL	Bibliothek der griechischen Literatur
BKV²	Bibliothek der Kirchenväter, 2. Reihe
Boeth. *Cons.*	Boethius, *Consolatio Philosophiae*
Boeth. *In categ. comm.*	Boethius, *In categorias Aristotelis commentarii*
Boeth. *In Cic. top.*	Boethius, *In Ciceronis topica commentarii*
Boeth. *Mus.*	Boethius, *De musica*
Boeth. *Tract.*	Boethius, *Tractatus theologici*
BPS	*Die Briefe der Päpste und die an sie gerichteten Schreiben von Ninus bis Pelagius II (vom Jahre 67–590)*, ed. S. Wenzlowsky, 7 vols. (Kempten, 1878–1880)
BT	Bibliotheca Teubneriana
C. Eur.	*Codex Euricianus*
C. Sirm.	Constitutiones Sirmondianae
Caes. *Ep.*	Caesarius of Arles, *Epistulae*
Caes. *Serm.*	Caesarius of Arles, *Sermones*
Caes. *Test.*	Caesarius of Arles, *Testamentum*
Cand. *Frag.*	Candidus, *Fragmenta*
Cass. *Anim.*	Cassiodorus, *De anima*
Cass. *Chron.*	Cassiodorus, *Chronica*
Cass. *Ex. Ps.*	Cassiodorus, *Expositio psalmorum*
Cass. *Inst.*	Cassiodorus, *Institutiones divinarum et humanarum litterarum*
Cass. *Lib.*	Cassiodorus, *Libellus*

Cass. *Or.*	Cassiodorus, *Orationes*
Cass. *Orth.*	Cassiodorus, *De orthographia*
Cass. *Var.*	Cassiodorus, *Variae*
Cass. Epiph. *Hist.*	Cassiodorus and Epiphanius, *Historia ecclesiastica tripartita*
CCCM	Corpus Christianorum. Continuatio Mediaevalis
CCH	*La colección canónica hispana*, ed. G. Martínez Díez and F. Rodríguez, 6 vols. (Madrid and Barcelona, 1966–2002). Page references are also provided to the more accessible edition by José Vives, ed., *Concilios Visigóticos e hispano-romanos*, España cristiana: textos, 1 (Barcelona and Madrid, 1963)
CCL	Corpus Christianorum. Series latina
CFHB	Corpus fontium historiae Byzantinae
Chron. Caes.	*Chronica Caesaraugustana*
Chron. Gall.	*Chronica Gallica*
Chron. Gothan.	*Historia Langobardorum codicis Gothani*
Chron. Pasch.	*Chronicon Paschale*
Chronicon ad annum 724	*Chronicle to the Year 724*
Chrys. *Hom.*	John Chrysostom, *Homiliae*
CIL	Corpus Inscriptionum Latinarum
CISAM	Centro italiano di studi sull'alto medioevo
CJ	*Codex Justinianus*
Coll. Aug. c. Pasc.	*Collatio Augustini cum Pascentio*
Conc. Agath.	*Concilium Agathense a. 506 habitum*
Conc. Araus.	*Concilium Arausicanum a. 529 habitum*
Conc. Arel.	*Concilium Arelatense a. 524 habitum*
Conc. Aurel.	*Concilium Aurelianense a. 511 habitum*
Conc. Carp.	*Concilium Carpentocratense a. 527 habitum*
Conc. Epaon.	*Concilium Epaonense a. 517 habitum*
Conc. Gerun.	*Concilium Gerundense a. 517 habitum*
Conc. Mass.	*Concilium Massiliense a. 533 habitum*
Conc. Tarrac.	*Concilium Tarraconense a. 516 habitum*
Conc. Tolet. II	*Concilium Toletanum II a. 531 habitum*
Conc. Tolet. III	*Concilium Toletanum III a. 589 habitum*
Conc. Vas.	*Concilium Vasense a. 529 habitum*
Cons. Const.	*Consularia Constantinopolitana*

Const. Porph. Cer.	Constantine Porphyrogenitus, *De Cerimoniis*
Const. Sirm.	Constitutiones Sirmondianae (the "Sirmondian Constitutions")
cos.	consul (followed by the year in which the office was held)
CSCO	Corpus Scriptorum Christianorum Orientalium
CSEL	Corpus Scriptorum Ecclesiasticorum Latinorum
CSHB	Corpus Scriptorum Historiae Byzantinae
CTh	*Codex Theodosianus*
CUF	Collection des Universités de France (Collection Budé)
Cyr. *Cat.*	Cyril of Jerusalem, *Catecheses*
Damasc. *V. Isid.*	Damascius, *Vita Isidori*
Dex. *Frag.*	Dexippus, *Fragmenta*
Dionys. Exig. *Praef.*	Dionysius Exiguus, *Praefatio*
Drac. *Satisf.*	Dracontius, *Satisfactio*
Ed. Theod.	*Edictum Theoderici*
Einhard *V. Karoli*	Einhard, *Vita Karoli Magni*
Ennod. *Carm.*	Ennodius, *Carmina*
Ennod. *Dict.*	Ennodius, *Dictiones*
Ennod. *Ep.*	Ennodius, *Epistulae*
Ennod. *Libell.*	Ennodius, *Libellus adversus eos qui contra synodum scribere praesumpserint*
Ennod. *Opusc.*	Ennodius, *Opuscula*
Ennod. *Pan.*	Ennodius, *Panegyricus*
Ennod. *V. Ant.*	Ennodius, *Vita Antonii*
Ennod. *V. Epif.*	Ennodius, *Vita Epiphanii*
Ep. Arel.	*Epistulae Arelatenses*
Ep. Austr.	*Epistolae Austrasicae*
Ep. Theod. Var.	*Epistulae Theodericianae Variae*
ERPG	*Epistolae Romanorum pontificum genuinae* . . ., vol. 1 [no more appeared], *A S. Hilaro usque ad S. Hormisdam*, ed. A. Thiel (Braunsberg [Braniewo], 1868)
Eug. *V. Sev.*	Eugippius, *Vita S. Severini*
Eun. *Frag.*	Eunapius Sardianus, *Fragmenta*
Eus. *Hist.*	Eusebius, *Historia Ecclesiastica*

Eus. *V. Const.*	Eusebius, *De vita Constantini*
Eust. Epiph. Frag.	Eustathius of Epiphania, *Fragmenta*
Eutr.	Eutropius, *Breviarium*
Evagr. *Hist.*	Evagrius Scholasticus, *Historia ecclesiastica*
Exc. Sang.	*Excerpta Sangallensia*
Fasti Vind. post.	*Fasti Vindobonenses posteriores*
Fasti Vind. pr.	*Fasti Vindobonenses priores*
FC	Fontes Christiani
FCHLR	*The Fragmentary Classicising Historians of the Later Roman Empire*, vol. 2: *Eunapius, Olympiodorus, Priscus and Malchus*, ed. R. Blockley (Liverpool, 1983)
FCPS	Fathers of the Church; Patristic Series
Felix III *Ep.*	Pope Felix II, *Epistulae*
Felix IV *Ep.*	Pope Felix IV, *Epistulae*
Ferr. *Ep. dogm.*	Ferrand of Carthage, *Epistula dogmatica adversus Arrianos aliosque haereticos*
Ferr. *V. Fulg.*	Ferrand of Carthage, *Vita Fulgentii*
FHistLA	*The Fragmentary Latin Histories of Late Antiquity (AD 300–620): Edition, Translation and Commentary*, ed. L. van Hoof and P. van Nuffelen (Cambridge, UK, 2020)
FIRA	*Fontes iuris Romani antejustiniani*, ed. S. Riccobono et al., 2nd ed., 3 vols. (Rome, 1968)
Frag. Laur.	*Fragmentum Laurentianum*
FSI	Fonti per la storia d'Italia
Fulg. *Ad Thras.*	Fulgentius of Ruspe, *Ad Thrasamundum*
Fulg. *De fide*	Fulgentius of Ruspe, *De fide sive de regula fidei*
Fulg. *Dicta reg. Thras.*	Fulgentius of Ruspe, *Dicta regis Thrasamundi et contra eum responsionum liber unus*
Fulg. *Ep.*	Fulgentius of Ruspe, *Epistulae*
Gaud. *Serm.*	Gaudentius of Brescia, *Sermones*
GCS	Die griechischen christlichen Schriftsteller
Gelas. *Ep.*	Gelasius, *Epistulae*
Gelas. *Frag.*	Gelasius, *Fragmenta*
Gelas. *Tract.*	Gelasius, *Tractatus*
Gest. sen. a. 438	*Gesta senatus Romani de Theodosiano publicando a. 438*

GL	*Grammatici Latini*, ed. H. Keil, 8 vols. (Leipzig, 1855–1880; repr. Hildesheim, 1981)
GLQGM	*Griechische und Lateinische Quellen zur Geschichte Mitteleuropas bis zur Mitte des 1. Jahrtausends u.Z.*, ed. J. Herrmann and G. Perl, 4 vols. (Berlin, 1988–1992)
Greg. Magn. *Dial.*	Gregory the Great, *Dialogi*
Greg. Magn. *Ep.*	Gregory the Great, *Epistulae*
Greg. Thaum. *Ep. can.*	Gregory Thaumaturgus, *Epistula canonica*
Greg. Tur. *Glor. conf.*	Gregory of Tours, *Liber in gloria confessorum*
Greg. Tur. *Glor. mart.*	Gregory of Tours, *Liber in gloria martyrum*
Greg. Tur. *Hist.*	Gregory of Tours, *Historiae*
Hdt.	Herodotus, *Historiae*
Herod.	Herodian, *Historiae*
HJ	*Regesta pontificum Romanorum*, ed. K. Herbers and P. Jaffé, 2 vols. (Göttingen, 2016–2017)
Horm. *Ep.*	Pope Hormisdas, *Epistulae*
HRG	*Handwörterbuch der deutschen Rechtsgeschichte*, ed. A. Erler et al., 5 vols. (Berlin, 1971–1998)
Hyd.	Hydatius Lemicus, *Continuatio chronicorum Hieronymianorum*
IJudOr I	*Inscriptiones Judaicae Orients*, vol. 1, *Eastern Europe*, ed. D. Noy, A. Panayotov, and H. Bloedhorn (Tübingen, 2002)
IJudOr III	*Inscriptiones Judaicae Orientis*, vol. 3, *Syria and Cyprus*, ed. D. Noy and H. Bloedhorn (Tübingen, 2004)
ILCV	Inscriptiones Latinae Christianae Veteres
ILER	*Inscripciones Latinas de la Espana Latina; antología de 6800 textos*, ed. J. Vivés. (Barcelona, 1971–1972)
ILS	*Inscriptiones Latinae Selectae*, ed. H. Dessau, 3 vols. (Berlin, 1892–1916)
InscrIt	Inscriptiones Italiae
Isid. *Etym.*	Isidore of Seville, *Etymologiae*
Isid. *Hist. Goth.*	Isidore of Seville, *Historia Gothorum Vandalorum et Sueborum*

JE	*Regesta pontificum Romanorum*, vol. 1, A S. *Petro ad a.* *MCXLIII*, ed. P. Jaffé and P. Ewald, 2nd ed. (Leipzig, 1885)
Jer. *Ep.*	Jerome, *Epistulae*
Jer. *Quaest. hebr. in Gen.*	Jerome, *Liber hebraicarum quaestionum in Genesim*
JIWE	*Jewish Inscriptions of Western Europe*, ed. D. Noy, 2 vols. (Cambridge, UK, 1993–1995)
JK	*Regesta pontificum Romanorum*, vol. 1, A S. *Petro ad a.* *MCXLIII*, ed. P. Jaffé and F. Kaltenbrunner, 2nd ed. (Leipzig, 1885)
Joh. Ant. *Frag.*	John of Antioch, *Fragmenta*
Joh. Bicl. *Chron.*	John of Biclaro, *Chronica*
Joh. *Cass. Coll.*	John Cassian, *Collationes*
Joh. Diac. *Ep. ad Senarium*	John the Deacon, *Epistula ad Senarium*
Joh. Lyd. *Mag.*	John the Lydian, *De magistratibus populi Romani*
Joh. Nik.	John of Nikiu, *Chronicle*
Joh. Ruf. *Pleroph.*	John Rufus, *Plerophories*
Jord. *Get.*	Jordanes, *De origine actibusque Getarum*
Jord. *Rom.*	Jordanes, *De summa temporum vel origine actibusque gentis Romanorum*
Jos. Styl.	Joshua the Stylite, *Chronicle*
KFHist	Kleine und fragmentarische Historiker der Spätantike
L. Burg.	*Leges Burgundionum (Liber Constitutionum)*
L. Rom. Vis.	*Lex Romana Visigothorum*
L. Vis.	*Leges Visigothorum*
Lat. reg. Vand.	*Laterculus regum Vandalorum et Alanorum*
Lat. reg. Vis.	*Laterculus regum Visigothorum*
LCL	Loeb Classical Library
Leo *Ep.*	Leo the Great, *Epistulae*
Leo *Serm.*	Leo the Great, *Sermones*
Leo Mars. *Chron.*	Leo Marsicanus, *Chronicon Casinense*
Lib. gen.	*Liber genealogus*
Lib. Hist. Franc.	*Liber Historiae Francorum*
Lib. *Or.*	Libanius, *Orationes*
Lib. pont.	*Liber Pontificalis ecclesiae Romanae*
Libt. *Brev.*	Liberatus of Carthage, *Breviarium*

Macr. *Sat.*	Macrobius, *Saturnalia*
Malal.	John Malalas, *Chronica*
Malch. *Frag.*	Malchus, *Fragmenta*
Malch. *Test.*	Malchus, *Testimonia*
MAMA	Monumenta Asiae Minoris Antiqua
Mar. Avent.	Marius of Avenches, *Chronicon*
Marc. Com.	Marcellinus Comes, *Chronicon*
Mart. Cap.	Martianus Capella, *De nuptiis Mercurii et Philologiae*
Maxim. *Eleg.*	Maximianus, *Elegiae*
Merob. *Carm.*	Merobaudes, *Carmina*
MGH.AA	Monumenta Germaniae Historica. Auctores Antiquissimi
MGH.Cap.	Monumenta Germaniae Historica. Capitularia Regum Francorum
MGH.Ep.	Monumenta Germaniae Historica. Epistulae
MGH.GPR	Monumenta Germaniae Historica. Gesta Pontificum Romanorum
MGH.LNG	Monumenta Germaniae Historica. Leges Nationum Germanicarum
MGH.SRG	Monumenta Germaniae Historica. Scriptores Rerum Germanicarum
MGH.SRL	Monumenta Germaniae Historica. Scriptores Rerum Langobardicarum et Italicarum
MGH.SRM	Monumenta Germaniae Historica. Scriptores Rerum Merovingicarum
MGH.SS.rer. Germ.	Monumenta Germaniae Historica. Scriptores Rerum Germanicarum in usum scholarum
MHS.SC	Monumenta Hispaniae Sacra. Serie canónica
MST	Medieval Sources in Translation
Not. Gall.	*Notitia Galliarum*
Nov. Just.	*Novellae Justiniani*
Nov. Maior.	*Novellae Maioriani*
Nov. Sev.	*Novellae Severi*
Nov. Theod.	*Novellae Theodosii*
Nov. Val.	*Novellae Valentiniani*
Olymp. *Frag.*	Olympiodorus, *Fragmenta*
Origo gent. Lang.	*Origo gentis Langobardorum*
Oros. *Hist.*	Orosius, *Historia adversus paganos*

P.Ital.	*Die nichtliterarischen lateinischen Papyri Italiens aus der Zeit 445–700*, ed. J.-O. Tjäder, 3 vols. (Lund and Stockholm, 1954–1982)
P.Marini	*I papiri diplomatici raccolti ed illustrati*, ed. G. Marini (Rome, 1805)
P.Vic.	"Un nuovo papiro latino del VI secolo," ed. T. de Robertis, A. Ghignoli, and S. Zamponi. In *De la herencia romana a la procesal castellana: Diez siglos de cursividad*, ed. María Carmen del Camino Martínez (Seville, 2018), 11–28 (text on 19–20).
Pall. *Agric.*	Palladius, *Opus agriculturae*
Pall. *Hist. Laus.*	Palladius of Helenopolis, *Historia Lausiaca*
Pan. Lat.	*Panegyrici Latini*
Pasch. Camp.	*Paschale Campanum*
Paul. Diac. *Lang.*	Paul the Deacon, *Historia Langobardorum*
Paul. Diac. *Rom.*	Paul the Deacon, *Historia Romana*
Paul. Nol. *Carm.*	Paulinus of Nola, *Carmina*
Paul. *Sent.*	Paulus, *Sententiae*
PCBE II	Prosopographie chrétienne du Bas-Empire, vol. 2: *Prosopographie de l'Italie chrétienne*, ed. C. Piétri and L. Piétri, 2 vols. (Paris, 1999)
PCBE IV	Prosopographie chrétienne du Bas-Empire, vol. 4: *Prosopographie de la Gaule chrétienne*, ed. L. Piétri and M. Heijmans, 2 vols. (Paris, 2013)
Pelag. *Ep.*	Pope Pelagius I, *Epistulae*
Petr. Chrys. *Serm.*	Petrus Chrysologus, *Sermones*
PG	Patrologia. Series Graeca, ed. J.-P. Migne (Paris, 1857–1867)
Philost.	Philostorgius, *Historia ecclesiastica*
Phot. *Cod.*	Photius, *Codex*
PL	Patrologia. Series Latina, ed. J.-P. Migne (Paris, 1844–1855, 1862–1865)
PLRE I	*Prosopography of the Later Roman Empire*, vol. 1: AD 260–395, ed. A. H. M. Jones, J. Martindale, and J. Morris (Cambridge, UK, 1972)
PLRE II	*Prosopography of the Later Roman Empire*, vol. 2: AD 395–527, ed. J. Martindale (Cambridge, UK, 1980)
PLRE III	*Prosopography of the Later Roman Empire*, vol. 3: AD 527–641, ed. J. Martindale, 2 vols. (Cambridge, UK, 1992)

PO	Patrologia Orientalis
Polem. *Brev.*	Polemius Silvius, *Breviarium temporum*
Polem. *Lat.*	Polemius Silvius, *Laterculus*
Prisc. *Fig. num.*	Priscian of Caesarea, *De figuris numerorum*
Prisc. *Frag.*	Priscus of Panium, *Fragmenta*
Proc. *Aed.*	Procopius, *De aedificiis*
Proc. *Bell.*	Procopius, *Bella*
Proc. *Hist. Arc.*	Procopius, *Historia arcana*
Prosp. *Chron.*	Prosper Tiro, *Epitoma chronicorum*
Ptol. *Geogr.*	Ptolemy, *Geographia*
RAC	Reallexikon für Antike und Christentum
RE	Pauly-Wissowas Realencyclopädie der classischen Altertumswissenschaften
RGA	Reallexikon der Germanischen Altertumskunde
RIC	Roman Imperial Coinage
RICG	*Recueil des inscriptions chrétiennes de la Gaule, antérieures à la Renaissance carolingienne*, ed. H. I. Marrou. Paris 1975–present (ongoing)
Rur. *Ep.*	Ruricius of Limoges, *Epistulae*
Rut. Nam.	Rutilius Namatianus, *De reditu suo*
Salv. *Gub.*	Salvian of Marseille, *De gubernatione dei*
SC	Sources chrétiennes
SEG	Supplementum epigraphicum Graecum
Sev. Ant. *C. imp. gram.*	Severus of Antioch, *Contra impium grammaticum*
SHA	Scriptores historiae Augustae
Sid. *Carm.*	Sidonius Apollinaris, *Carmina*
Sid. *Ep.*	Sidonius Apollinaris, *Epistulae*
Simpl. *Ep.*	Pope Simplicius, *Epistulae*
Socr.	Socrates Scholasticus, *Historia ecclesiatica*
Soz.	Sozomen, *Historia ecclesiastica*
Strab.	Strabo, *Geographia*
Suppl. Ital.	Supplementa Italica
Symm. *Ep.*	Quintus Aurelius Symmachus, *Epistulae*
Symm. pp. *Ep.*	Pope Symmachus, *Epistulae*
Symm. *Rel.*	Quintus Aurelius Symmachus, *Relationes*
Syn. *Ep.*	Synesius, *Epistulae*
Tac. *Ann.*	Tacitus, *Annales*

Tac. *Germ.*	Tacitus, *Germania*
Thdt. *Hist.*	Theodoretus, *Historia ecclesiastica*
Them. *Or.*	Themistius, *Orationes*
Theod. Lect.	Theodorus Lector, *Historia ecclesiastica*
Theoph.	Theophanes, *Chronica*
ThLL	Thesaurus linguae Latinae
TTH	Translated Texts for Historians
V. Abb. Acaun.	*Vitae Abbatum Acaunensium*
V. Apollinaris	*Vita Apollinaris Valentinensis*
V. Caes.	*Vita Caesarii episcopi Arelatensis*
V. Eptadii	*Vita Eptadii presbyteri Cervidunensis*
V. Floridi	*Vita S. Floridi*
V. Hilari	*Vita Hilari abbatis Galeatensis*
V. Lupi	*Vita Lupi episcopi Trecensis*
V. Marciani	*Vita Marciani Oeconomi*
V. Melaniae.gr.	Gerontius, *Vita Melaniae graeca*
V. Melaniae.lat.	Gerontius, *Vita Melaniae latina*
V. Sigismundi	*Passio S. Sigismundi regis*
V. Symeonis. syr.	*Vita Symeonis syriaca*
V. Vincentii	*Passio S. Vincentii Aginnensis*
Vict. Tunn.	Victor of Tunnuna, *Chronica*
Vict. Vit. *Hist.*	Victor of Vita, *Historia persecutionis Africanae provinciae*
Vigil. *Ep.*	Pope Vigilius, *Epistulae*
WGRW	Writings from the Greco-Roman World
Zach. *Hist. eccl.*	Zacharias of Mytilene, *Historia ecclesiastica*
Zon.	Zonaras, *Epitome Historiarum*
Zos.	Zosimus, *Historia Nova*

FOREWORD TO THE ENGLISH EDITION

The first edition of this book was published in German by C. H. Beck (Munich) in 2018. International research on Theoderic and the Goths, late antique Italy, and the Age of Migrations has been extraordinarily productive in the five years that have passed since then. For this English edition, I have thoroughly revised the notes, corrected errors, supplemented the source material, and added references to current scholarly literature; the bibliography has thus become considerably longer, albeit still not exhaustive. I also have improved coordination between the text and endnotes. This edition should thus be the one to which scholars turn for research purposes. The text remains largely unchanged, but I have supplemented some chapters to state my arguments more clearly. The manuscript was completed in early 2021; it thus was not possible to incorporate literature that appeared subsequently.

The German edition of this book was the product of over a decade of work on the subject that began in Zurich in 2005. My research subsequently received important impetus from the research group on "communities of violence" (*Gewaltgemeinschaften*) at the Justus Liebig University, Giessen, and was generously sponsored by a research fellowship at the Historisches Kolleg in Munich. The fact that this English edition is more than merely a translation of the German original is due above all to John Noël Dillon. He not only translated the German text into English with great care, profound expertise, and a fine feeling for language, but also, with his indefatigable search for clarity and precision, helped make the translation in many places more limpid and concise than the original. He also translated quotations from the Latin and Ancient Greek sources into English as precisely and elegantly as the originals permitted. Not many an author will be so fortunate as to find a translator like him.

I received inspiration and support from many quarters while writing this book; it would take up too much space to thank everyone by name, but there are three people whom I would like to single out here: Stefan von der Lahr, the friend and reader of the German edition; Trutz von Trotha, the *spiritus rector* of the research group in Giessen; and Noel Lenski, who gave me his advice and help when I needed it most. I am delighted that the English edition is being published by Yale University Press, where I have had the pleasure of collaborating with an understanding editor in the person of Heather Gold. The Geisteswissenschaften International foundation funded the translation, for which I owe it my profoundest gratitude. Bojana Ristich was an outstanding copyeditor, both diligent and thoughtful. Kai Preuß supported me by reading and correcting the text. The German edition of this book was dedicated to Wolf Liebeschuetz, a great scholar who became my model and teacher through his works. Since he died on July 11, 2022, the English version is now dedicated to his memory.

Hans-Ulrich Wiemer

TRANSLATOR'S NOTE

Oddly enough, I first met Hans-Ulrich Wiemer in Knoxville, Tennessee, where we both had traveled from our respective homes—paradoxically, mine in Germany and his in the United States—to attend a conference in 2009. I had come with a contingent of scholars from Heidelberg, where I was a post-doc at the time, while Professor Wiemer was a Gerda Henkel Fellow at Brown. I knew him then as an especially rigorous and sophisticated ancient historian, whose outstanding work on late antique acclamations had been a valuable resource for my own project on Constantine the Great. I was both flattered and excited when he reached out to me a decade after our ways had parted to inquire about translating his magnificent book on Theoderic the Great. I have thoroughly enjoyed our collaboration, and I hope that that scholarly *Freude* filters through to our English readers.

A German book originally intended for a German audience, *Theoderich der Grosse* could not become *Theoderic the Great* without a series of small but significant modifications. Theoderic is wrapped up in the historical ethnic and nationalist discourses of Germany and the German people. Thus, although I translated the text indeed as faithfully and accurately as possible, I occasionally elaborated on German terms derived from these discourses (e.g., "Volksseele," "Germanentum") to elucidate their subtle, sometimes highly fraught, connotations for an English-speaking, or rather non-German, audience. In such cases, I included the original German terms in parentheses to signal their cultural specificity to the reader. Chapters 3 and 13, in which historical views on Theoderic in Germany are discussed, were the most affected by these light editorial interventions.

Theoderic and his successors spoke Gothic, issued texts in Latin, clashed with Germanic kings, and had diplomatic dealings with the Greek-speaking

Eastern Roman Empire. Rendering proper names derived from these disparate cultures and the languages they spoke proved complicated. As a general rule, I used conventional Anglicized forms insofar as they exist. Hence, the Frankish king "Chlodwig" in German becomes "Clovis" in English, and his wife "Chrodechilde" becomes the more familiar "Clotilde." The names of other, less famous historical actors are relatively more fluid in English than in modern German, which favors transliteration of the original language. I tried to adopt the most or at least the more common variant and use it consistently. Some are traditional Latinizations; others are not.

A final departure from the German original concerns the identity of the "Romans." In the German original, Professor Wiemer uses the term *"römisch"* flexibly to designate the population of the city of Rome, ethnically "Roman" subjects of Theoderic's kingdom, persons and things "of Rome," as well as the emperor and people of the Eastern Roman Empire, who indeed both considered and called themselves "Romans" (*Rhōmaioi*). This last usage proved especially troublesome. In translating, "Eastern Roman" often was more cumbersome and obtrusive in English than *"römisch"* or *"oströmisch"* were in German, and it felt increasingly jarring with the passage of time in the absence of a "Western Roman" counterpart. After discussing the matter, we decided to adopt the conventional label "Byzantine" to avoid awkwardness and especially any confusion between the Romans of Rome and Italy and those of the empire of Justinian (*Romani* and *Rhōmaioi*, as it were). This greatly simplified the translation of chapter 12, on the Gothic War, in which the Goths' "Roman" collaborators, the "Roman" senate, and Eastern "Romans" and their "Roman" emperor were all major players.

I converted conventional abbreviations for classical authors and their works to the Latinized English forms where these differed from the German version (e.g., "Jer." vs. "Hieron." for Jerome). Although the updated bibliography retains the basic format of the German edition, I have added quotation marks and revised the punctuation with an American audience in mind; it would have taken great effort for little gain to supply given names and publishing houses for every entry.

Chapters 1–7 were translated somehow during the COVID-19 pandemic and the political turbulence of the latter half of 2020, and chapters 8–13 *melioribus auspiciis* in the first half of 2021. It would be trite to thank my wife, Professor Yii-Jan Lin (Yale), here, as if she graciously kept house while I led a scholar's life. Instead, I want to thank her for the sacrifices she makes from *her* career as we raise our two wonderful (and sometimes wonderfully frustrating) boys, John and James, together while we both keep learning and writing. As I type these words, tomorrow is our tenth anniversary. Thank you, JanJan.

John Noël Dillon

Approaching Theoderic the Great

1. RAVENNA, LATE FEBRUARY, 493

The year 493 got off to a bad start for the inhabitants of Ravenna. The city was cut off from the outside world. Food was scarce and for many had become exorbitantly expensive. People had begun to eat everything they could chew, even weeds and leather.

Malnourishment and sickness carried off the elderly and children. The reason for their plight was the war that Kings Odoacer and Theoderic were waging against one another for supremacy in Italy. At the time, it was already going into its fourth year. Odoacer had been bested by Theoderic in open battle near Verona in September 489. He then retreated to Ravenna because the city was considered impregnable on account of its location: in a lagoon surrounded by swamps.

A counteroffensive launched by Odoacer in August 490 failed when the king was again defeated in open battle on the Adda (Addua) River near Milan. In July 491 he attempted to break out but again was unsuccessful. After that, neither he nor his people left the city again. The siege had lasted now over two years, and since August 492 it had become impossible to receive supplies even by sea. Theoderic had stationed a fleet of light warships — so-called *dromones* — at Porte Lione, six miles north of Ravenna; these blockaded the harbor. A severe earthquake made everything even worse. The situation of the people of Ravenna was desperate.[1]

A glimmer of hope returned in February 493 because the generals had begun to negotiate. Theoderic, however, set a condition for ceasing hostilities: Odoacer had to deliver his son Thela as hostage; in return, Theoderic would guarantee Odoacer's personal safety. Odoacer accepted; Thela was handed over on

Fig. 1. Map of Ravenna and environs circa 1600. Copperplate engraving by
Francesco Bertelli. Courtesy Visualizzare Ravenna, Interuniversity Center e-GEA.
http://www.visualizzareravenna.it/cartografia.

February 25. The next day, Theoderic and his men withdrew to the port of Classe,
which lay only a few kilometers from Ravenna's walls. Intense negotiations ensued
in the following week; messengers repeatedly went back and forth between
Ravenna and Classe. John, the Catholic bishop of Ravenna, went with his entire
clergy to Classe, singing psalms and bearing candles, censers, and bibles. There he
threw himself at Theoderic's feet and humbly begged for peace. An agreement was
finally reached; in the future, Theoderic and Odoacer would rule the Western
Roman Empire jointly, and they swore a treaty to that effect. The gates of Ravenna
were then opened; Theoderic entered the city on March 5, 493.[2]

The people of Ravenna breathed a sigh of relief: the war was over; food could
be delivered to their city again. Henceforth, two kings would rule together in
Italy in harmony—that at least was the hope. Theoderic and Odoacer now both
lived in Ravenna, albeit not in the same palace, and they visited one another
frequently in the following days. But the peace lasted no more than ten days
before Odoacer, who was sixty years old at the time, was struck down unawares
during a visit to a palace called the "Lauretum" ("Laurel Grove"). The perpetrator was some twenty years younger than his victim; it was none other than

Theoderic himself. A Byzantine chronicler describes the sequence of events as follows: when Odoacer entered the palace, two of Theoderic's men approached him as supplicants and grasped him by the hands, making escape or resistance impossible. Then men armed with swords rushed in from side rooms but did not dare kill Odoacer themselves. For this reason, the chronicler continues, Theoderic himself approached and killed the king with a single sword stroke, slicing him apart from collarbone to hip. Odoacer is reported to have cried, "Where is God?," to which Theoderic supposedly answered, "That is exactly what you did to my relatives!" As Odoacer collapsed, dead, Theoderic added, "There wasn't a single bone in this wretch!"[3]

Of course, we cannot be certain that these words were really said as such; our witness — John of Antioch — was writing more than a century after the events; from where he got his information is unknown. We thus cannot rule out that John's source may have freely invented the details. It is also possible, though, that Theoderic himself spread the story. That would at least explain why Theoderic blamed the dying Odoacer of having committed violence against unnamed relatives of his: the claim would justify the murder since taking revenge was regarded as a moral obligation at the time. There is no doubt, however, that Theoderic broke his oath by killing Odoacer with his sword. The Byzantine chronicler's report is confirmed by several independent accounts that were composed much earlier, around the middle of the sixth century. From these witnesses, we learn that Odoacer's murder was only the opening act of a carefully planned massacre of his followers inside and outside Ravenna. Odoacer's brother Hunwulf, who had fled into a church hoping to receive asylum, was also eliminated; so they did not have to enter the sanctuary, Theoderic's men shot him down with arrows. Odoacer's son Thela and his wife Sunigilda were initially spared, but later also killed, when Thela, who had been banished to Gaul, escaped custody to return to Italy.[4]

March 493 was by no means the first time that Theoderic had slain an adversary with his own hand. At roughly the age of eighteen, the king had killed the Sarmatian king Babai at Singidunum (Belgrade) during a campaign he was personally leading; Theoderic would later count the years of his reign as Gothic king as beginning with this victory in 471. In 482, he killed the Gothic leader Rekitach, whose following was scarcely smaller than his own, at Boniphatianae, a suburb of Constantinople; he ran Rekitach through with his sword as the latter went from the baths to a banquet. In the following years, he often charged into battle at the head of his troops, killing many of the enemy with his own hand.[5]

Who was this Theoderic, who had won sole power over Italy and Dalmatia, the remnant of the Western Roman Empire, by eliminating Odoacer and his followers? The man we call Theoderic, following the linguistic conventions of our Latin sources, was born in Pannonia (Hungary) in the early 450s, perhaps in 453. He was the son of a Gothic king named Thiudimir (Theodemir), who came from the family of the Amals. Theoderic's very name is program matic: in Gothic, he is called Thiudareiks, which combines *thiuda*, which basically means "people," and *reiks* (pronounced *rix*), a word that is cognate with the Latin word for king, *rex*, but in Gothic generally means a leader. "Theoderic" (Thiudareiks) thus means "Ruler of the People." Thiudimir had two brothers, Valamir and Vidmir, who, like himself, each led an independent group of Gothic warriors as king. All three of them had shaken off Hunnic rule after the death of Attila and allied themselves by treaty with the Roman emperor Leo (457–474) in return for annual payments. When this treaty was struck, presumably in 461, Theoderic was surrendered as a hostage; hence he spent his youth at the imperial capital on the Bosporus. He did not return from Constantinople to the Goths in Pannonia until 471. He quickly won their respect with his successful campaign against Babai and his Sarmatians. When Thiudimir died in 474, his followers recognized Theoderic as their new leader. By this time, Thiudimir's Goths had already left Pannonia and were in Macedonia. In the Balkans, they had to contend for the next few years with another group of Gothic warriors living in Thrace (modern Bulgaria) whose ruler was also named Theoderic. To avoid confusion, modern scholars usually call him by his cognomen, Strabo ("the Squint-Eyed"). Both Theoderics relied on warriors who, together with their families, lived off booty and extorted payments; both sought to be recognized by the Eastern Roman emperor because that status brought with it major material benefits and symbolic advantages. The emperor, in turn, tried to maintain his independence by playing the Gothic leaders against one another. This power struggle was waged on the back of the Roman provincial population as the fortune of war constantly changed sides. Hence the size of both warrior bands and their leaders' power fluctuated wildly.[6]

The two warrior bands at last merged when Strabo died after falling from his horse in 481. Theoderic now became the *magister militum* ("master of soldiers") of the Roman emperor Zeno (474–491); killed Rekitach, Strabo's son, with Zeno's consent in 482; and even held the office of Roman consul in 484; although it had long ceased to have any real power, the consulship still conferred great prestige. Theoderic's good understanding with Zeno, meanwhile, was short-lived. He soon rebelled again against his imperial master; in 487, he pillaged right up to the walls of Constantinople itself, even cutting off its water supply. In the following year, Theoderic and Zeno agreed that the king and his people would march on Italy, where he would depose Odoacer, who had ruled there as king since 476. If Theoderic should succeed, he himself would rule there until the emperor arrived. When he clove Odoacer's torso asunder in mid-March 493, he may have believed he had achieved this goal. Shortly thereafter, he had his followers hail him as king in Ravenna. The story soon began to circulate that the massacre had been purely an act of self-defense because Odoacer himself had been plotting to take Theoderic's life.

These events give depth to the figure of Theoderic, although we have no insight into his inner world for lack of suitable sources. The king was a warlike ruler, a "warlord" who fought alongside his men in the front rank and proved that he could take on any adversary. This behavior met the expectations of those who obeyed him because to them the only acceptable ruler was one who possessed strength and agility, courage and endurance—in a word, a formidable warrior. Like his father Thiudimir, Theoderic won his position as king as a successful leader of warriors, and his personal prowess in battle went far to help him defend this position against others' claims. In the world in which Theoderic grew up, a man's worth was measured by what he could do in battle. Boldness and victory brought honor; cowardice and defeat, disgrace. In a speech in praise of the king, a Catholic clergyman named Ennodius puts the following words in Theoderic's mouth, which he supposedly told his mother Ereleuva before battle with Odoacer (Ennod. *Pan.* 43):

> You know, mother, you who are famous among all peoples on account of the honor of your offspring, that at the time of my birth you, in your fertility, brought forth a man [*vir*]. The day has come on which the field shall declare the sex of your son. I must take up arms so that the renown of our ancestors does not perish on account of me. We lean on the titles of our parents in vain if we are not bolstered by our own. I see my father before my eyes, whom fortune never made a subject of ridicule in battle, who made her favorable to himself as he compelled success with strength.

Again, there is no guarantee that Theoderic actually said these words or something like them at the time. Nonetheless, they illustrate quite nicely the code of honor that the king and his warriors followed. A warlord who wanted to be certain of his armed following could not rest on his ancestors' laurels, even if he was the son of a king; he had to prove by dint of arms that he was at least an equally worthy warrior. The pressure on the leaders to prove themselves was especially high because there were always others who believed they were just as capable and were merely waiting for the king to show weakness. In Theoderic's youth, at least four Gothic kings ruled over the territory between Lake Balaton and the Black Sea. Let's see what Ennodius has to say; he has Theoderic win

the battle at Verona single-handedly so to speak (Ennod. *Pan.* 45): "The multitude of the slain immediately heralded your arrival: the vastness of the slaughter
announced its author. But still they had their usual means of escape. They
abruptly took up the wings that fear provided and chose to perish in headlong
flight out of fear of death." The literary stylization of the passage is obvious:
Theoderic appears in the guise of an epic hero whose martial valor decides
battles. More than a thousand years earlier, Homer had described the heroes
Hector and Achilles in a strikingly similar way. What makes Ennodius' depiction of Theoderic so remarkable is its implicit assumption that the king would
have wanted to be praised as a hero. The Catholic clergyman adopted classical
epic models in his depiction of Theoderic because the Gothic king, like
Homeric heroes, obeyed a code of honor that revolved around prowess in combat. This code of honor did not necessarily require one to slaughter every enemy
without mercy. Theoderic is said to have spared the life of a Bulgarian king (his
name is unknown) who surrendered after he was defeated in battle. What mattered above all was the ability to impose one's will through physical force and to
ward off attacks on one's own body. That was also important because a warrior's
honor also depended on whether he could answer violence that had been
inflicted on others, whether his relatives or his followers, with violence in
return. Warriors who were unable to take vengeance swiftly lost face; for a
leader, revenge was an imperative of maintaining power, indeed even of self-
preservation. Ennodius captured the king's self-conception in this point as well:
he explains that the murder of Theoderic's relatives was his reason for going to
war against Odoacer. According to this account, the conquest of Italy was a
campaign for vengeance.[7]

If we observe Theoderic against this background, we can understand better
why the king liked to hear from those praising him that the large number of
corpses showed the enemy that he was approaching: he viewed killing enemies
with his own hands as proof of his ability to rule. That attitude stood in marked
contrast to the Roman emperors of his day. Sure, emperors like Zeno, Anastasius
(491–518), and Justinian (527–565) had people executed, killed, or secretly eliminated whenever they considered it expedient. But they left the killing to others,
both in war and in peace. By definition, the Eastern Roman or "Byzantine"
emperor was victorious and all-powerful, but his acceptance among his subjects
was not predicated on his personal ability as a soldier.[8] He appointed generals to
lead campaigns against the enemies of the emperor and took care not to sully
himself with the blood of those killed. For Theoderic, in contrast, the power to
annihilate an opponent with physical force was part of the role he had to play
as a ruler if he hoped to be successful; it reinforced his prestige among his

friends and followers and spread fear and dismay among his enemies. In this respect, Theoderic was like other barbarian rulers of the day, not least his own victim Odoacer, who in 477 had personally killed a certain Brachila in Ravenna "to instill fear of him in the Romans," as one source puts it. The Burgundian prince Gundobad made a name for himself at a young age by beheading Emperor Anthemius (467–472) in 472. After he became king of the Burgundians, he personally killed his brothers Chilperic and Godegisel, along with their families. The Frankish king Clovis was especially violent. He is said to have mercilessly slaughtered everyone who posed even a remote threat, including his closest kin. He laid low the Frankish kings Sigebert and Ragnarchar with an ax; he had other rivals killed by his men. When a warrior dared to criticize the king publicly, Clovis split his skull from behind before the entire army.[9]

But the successful "warlord" was only one side of Theoderic. If the king had known nothing other than fighting and warfare, he could hardly have successfully ruled over Italy for so long after he seized power with the help of his army in a devastating war. In fact, after eliminating Odoacer, Theoderic reigned virtually unchallenged for over three decades, until he finally died of natural causes in Ravenna on August 30, 526. That would not have been possible without the support of key players in the land he had conquered. To get an impression of how this transformation took place, we will put ourselves in the city of Rome in early 500, when the population was expecting the arrival of the king. Almost exactly seven years had passed since Odoacer had been eliminated.

2. ROME, EARLY 500

When Theoderic came to Rome in early 500, it had been a quarter-century since a ruler had resided within the walls of the "Eternal City." Julius Nepos had been elevated to emperor of the Western Roman Empire in June 474 but soon left the city for Ravenna. By 475, he had fled to Salona (Solin) in Dalmatia, where he hoped in vain until his death in 480 that he might return to his realm as emperor. Odoacer, in contrast, who had ruled Italy as king since 476, does not seem to have ever visited Rome. He preferred to reside in Ravenna, where he ultimately met his end thirteen years later. Theoderic also stayed exclusively in northern Italy in the early years of his reign, predominantly in Ravenna it would appear. Now, however, in early 500, he made ready to pay a visit to the city on the Tiber to celebrate his thirtieth jubilee, his *tricennalia*, as king.

The disasters of the fifth century had left Rome reduced to a fraction of its former population, but it was still the largest city of the western Mediterranean with an unparalleled collection of plazas, buildings, and artworks. Above all, though, Rome remained the stage where the public life of the richest and most powerful men of Italy played out. It was here that the senate still met and here where its members lived. Rome was also the location of the episcopal see that enjoyed the highest prestige among Catholic Christians outside the emperor's territory and controlled the graves of the apostles Peter and Paul, pilgrimage sites of unique significance. In short: the representatives of the two most important powerbrokers of Italy were waiting for the king in Rome: the senators and the successor of St. Peter. It was an opportune moment for such a visit: in the preceding years, a policy had taken shape that was based on the cooperation of the king and Italian elites; senators and bishops made themselves available to the king and were entrusted with important tasks. In 497, the emperor in distant Constantinople had also at last recognized Theoderic as ruler of Italy. At the beginning of 499, his position was so secure and his prestige so high that the Roman clergy and senate called on him to arbitrate a schism over the simultaneous election of two popes on November 22, 498. Theoderic thus assumed the role that the emperors had come to play since Constantine the Great, despite the fact that his own Christian confession was considered heretical by the men who had summoned him as arbiter. Theoderic decided in favor of Pope Symmachus (498–514) because he had been elected first (if only by a few hours) and by a larger number of people, and the defeated Pope Laurentius yielded to the king's decision and vacated the Throne of Peter. In this way, the danger of a schism was averted and the unity of the Church restored. When Pope Symmachus gathered the Catholic Church of Italy together in St. Peter's in March 499, the clergymen shouted no fewer than thirty times: "Hear, Christ! Long life to Theoderic!" (*Exaudi Christe! Theoderico vitam!*).[10]

A year later, the Romans were awaiting the arrival of the king with bated breath as he made his way with his retinue from Ravenna to Rome along the Via Flaminia. Imperial visits required careful preparation; little was left to chance. The rooms of the palace were readied and decked out; cellars and kitchens were filled. Lodgings were needed for the men and stalls for the animals. Even if the Romans had not had such an eminent visitor in a very long time, they were perfectly aware of how crucial it was that the first encounter with a ruler went well. The ruler's entrance into the city was a ritual that took several hours. If he visited on the occasion of a jubilee, it stretched out to several days. Since Rome had but seldom been an imperial residence in a long time, a kind of protocol for the emperor's arrival, the *adventus Augusti*, had evolved. The population came to meet the ruler not as an anonymous mass, but rather as a body divided into its constituent parts, the senate and people of Rome (*senatus populusque Romanus*), whereby the senators were subdivided into their own different ranks of *illustres*, *spectabiles*, and *clarissimi* ("illustrious," "admirable," and "most renowned," in descending order of eminence). The social hierarchy and harmonious coexistence of the whole population were carefully orchestrated. The ruler was received with devotion and studied jubilation, as well as with petitions and requests. A ruler who valued his subjects' support went along with this ritual by showing himself to be merciful and benevolent.

Theoderic's entry into Rome, with few but significant exceptions, indeed followed the same protocol as the visits of Roman emperors in the first half of the fifth century had done. Pope Symmachus, the entire senate, and a mass of people came forth far from the city to meet the king and received him with loud cries of joy. Christian emperors had always been welcomed that way. Now, however, it was not a senator but rather the pope who headed the reception committee. This change of protocol highlighted the increased importance of religious leadership. Before Theoderic crossed the Pons Aelius built by Hadrian and set foot in the city, he stopped at the basilica on the Vatican sponsored by Constantine the Great and paid his respects at the grave of the Apostle Peter. The Christian emperors of the fifth century had likewise done so, although they first visited St. Peter's after they had entered Rome, not before. The fact that Theoderic followed their example was a carefully calculated gesture that was appreciated all the more so since the religious community to which he belonged did not recognize Symmachus as the bishop of Rome and successor of Peter at all.

The king's procession passed along on a predetermined route to the Forum Romanum; he passed through the triumphal arches of Constantine and Titus; passed basilicas, temples, and countless statues along the Via Sacra; and finally reached the senate house, the Curia, where a senator (whose name is unknown to us) delivered a panegyric in honor of the distinguished guest. Theoderic then proceeded to a place called Ad Palmam ("at the palm tree") and delivered a speech to the Roman people. This address, which was called an *adlocutio*, was also part of the traditional reception ritual that had been performed on the visits of Roman emperors to Rome since time immemorial. Theoderic, who presumably spoke Latin on this occasion so that his audience could understand him, solemnly promised to preserve intact everything that Roman rulers of the past (*retro principes Romani*) had decreed. And the king did not merely make vague promises, but also announced specific measures, especially in regard to the food supply for the common people, which we will discuss below.

While Theoderic was delivering his address, a Catholic clergyman named Fulgentius happened to be listening in the crowd. He had left North Africa to escape persecution by Thrasamund (496–523), king of the Vandals, and come to Italy, where Catholics had nothing to fear. His biographer emphasizes the

Fig. 2. Old St. Peter's in the year 1611 (drawing by Domenico Tasselli): the observer enters the atrium and sees the vestibule. akg-images/Rome/Old St. Peter's/Atrium.

celebratory mood that prevailed at that time throughout the city: the senate and people were overjoyed at the presence of King Theoderic. At Theoderic's address, he saw "the nobility, the glory, and the order of the Roman Senate [*curia*] adorned according to its distinct grades" and heard the acclamations of a "free people" (*liber populus*). Fulgentius, however, his biographer assures us, refused to let the glorious pomp of this world impress him and told his brothers, who were present, "If earthly Rome dazzles with such splendor, how marvelous must heavenly Jerusalem be!"[11]

Fulgentius' biographer here makes him unwillingly bear witness to the emotional power of a profane ritual. He had in fact not yet experienced the climax of the festivities when he spoke (unless the statement was purely fictional), and we may doubt whether he, being a clergyman, took part in the ensuing ceremony. After Theoderic had visited the senate house and addressed the people at Ad Palmam, the solemnities entered their third phase, which had been assimilated to the celebration of a triumph. First, while the Roman people cheered, Theoderic entered the palace on the Palatine, vacant since 475, but where

Roman emperors had lived for centuries. A ruler would now reside here again for the next six months. The king subsequently staged chariot races in the Circus Maximus, which still drew the masses, even if the population of Rome was no longer large enough to fill all the rows. We may imagine Theoderic in the loge where the emperors once had sat. The spectacle lasted from morning to evening; at least twenty-four races were held. Whether Theoderic also staged the beloved battles of man against beast (*venationes*) in the context of his *adventus* festivities is doubtful. Senators are known to have held animal hunts in the Amphitheatrum Flavium—since the High Middle Ages usually known as the Colosseum—throughout Theoderic's reign, but the king himself made no effort to hide his dislike of this form of popular entertainment; perhaps he therefore struck this item from the program of events.[12]

Over the course of this complex ritual, a concept of power emerges that was based on the cooperation of the Gothic king with the bishop and senate of Rome. Theoderic played the part that the Roman emperors had played before him. He first met the pope as the successor of Peter, then the senators and the people of Rome at various places in such a way that met their high expectations—in St. Peter's, in the Curia, in the Forum Romanum, in the Circus Maximus, and perhaps also in the Amphitheatrum Flavium. This ritual, in which every inhabitant of Rome was somehow involved, demonstrated the harmony between Theoderic and his Roman subjects in a way that squared perfectly with Roman tradition.

The harmony between Theoderic and the Romans would have been short-lived, of course, had he merely fobbed them off with symbolic gestures and ephemeral tokens of favor. That, however, was not the case. He honored individual senators by awarding them offices and ranks. The senator Liberius, who had served Theoderic for years as the head of the most important civil ministry, the praetorian prefecture, and now was leaving office, received the highest rank that a subject could hold, that of *patricius*. He was replaced as prefect by Theodorus, a scion of the most powerful family in Rome, the Decii. Most importantly, however, Theoderic gave the Romans permanent subventions of a material nature. He had the public treasury (*aerarium publicum*) supply 120,000 bushels (about 1,000,000 liters) of grain annually to the common people and the poor. About one-seventh of this amount was to be distributed to the beggars who gathered daily around St. Peter's. This measure reduced the susceptibility of the food supply to weather- and climate-related fluctuations and the dependence of the poor on the generosity of individual senators. The distribution of meat was probably also supposed to be subsidized by the treasury in the future. The revenue of the wine treasury (*arca vinaria*), however, was to be used to repair the palace and the city walls. Lastly, the senators were relieved of the burden of financing expensive games, for which the treasury now also provided annual resources. This funding excluded animal hunts, however. It was probably these privileges that inspired the Romans to give Theoderic the epithet of a "new Trajan," an emperor (98–117) who had done more for the city of Rome than any other. Nothing shows more clearly how important these measures were to the Romans than the fact that the king was formally petitioned to have the promises that he had made the people in his address at Ad Palmam inscribed on a bronze tablet and put on public display. And so it was done.[13]

Theoderic met the Romans in the year 500 like a Roman emperor. The senate and people of Rome reciprocated by showing him due gratitude. The senate had a gilt statue of the king erected as a visible and permanent testament to it. Looking back from 519, the senator Cassiodorus praised the king's conduct in the highest tones: "In this year, our lord King Theoderic, desired by the wishes of all, came to Rome. He treated his senate with remarkable affability, gave provisions of grain to the Roman plebs, and subsidized the marvelous walls with a massive amount of money to be expended annually."[14] Reading this paean, we get the impression that the transformation of the warrior king, who had slain Odoacer with his own hands seven years earlier, into the successor of the Western Roman emperors was complete. But looks deceive. Although our sources almost completely block out the king's Gothic retinue, we can still see that Theoderic entered Rome as a Gothic king whose power was not at all derived solely from the support of the Roman elite. Theoderic's non-Roman, warrior side was also conspicuous during his visit to Rome, beginning with the official occasion for it: the thirtieth anniversary of his accession to power, which was styled his *tricennalia* according to Roman tradition. But Theoderic had ruled Italy not thirty years but merely seven. The count of his regnal years began with his victory over the Sarmatian king Babai, long before his arrival in Italy, a time when Theoderic was merely one of several leaders of Gothic warrior bands in the Balkans. By Roman reckoning, the date of his *tricennalia* was nowhere close to the year 500. The celebration of the *thirtieth* anniversary of his accession at this date could be justified only by the tradition of the warrior band with which the king had conquered Italy. A dynastic marriage also took place during the six months that Theoderic spent in Rome: Theoderic gave his sister Amalafrida in marriage to Thrasamund, king of the Vandals, from whom Fulgentius had fled to Italy. We unfortunately have very little information about the circumstances of this union. As it seems, Thrasamund sent a delegation to ask for Amalafrida's hand. Theoderic assented and sent his sister with a strong military retinue—no fewer than 1,000 bodyguards and 5,000 retainers—to North Africa. Even if the wedding was apparently celebrated in Carthage, the Vandal delegation must have raised eyebrows in Rome. The marriage created family ties between Theoderic and the grandson of Gaiseric, the king who had ravaged the Western Roman Empire like no other. Gaiseric (428–477) had captured Rome in May 455 and let his soldiers plunder it for fourteen days. However much as a Roman Theoderic might carry himself in Rome, his kinsmen came from the families of barbarian kings. He himself had long been married to Audefleda, a sister of the Frankish king Clovis. Of his two daughters from his first marriage, he gave one— Ostrogotho—in marriage to Sigismund, king of the Burgundians, and the other—Thiudigotho—to Alaric, king of the Visigoths, a successor and namesake of the king who on August 24, 410, had conquered Rome—which till then had defied all enemies for eight hundred years—and let his soldiers sack it for three days. The day of his departure was celebrated in Rome decades later; the traumatic event had not been forgotten even in Theoderic's day.[15]

Theoderic's Gothic retinue appears only once in accounts of his visit to Rome, but that tells us nothing of its real visibility and significance. For the Romans, the Goths around the king must have been impossible to miss. If Theoderic wanted to receive communion, he could not go to one of the many churches under the authority of the bishop of Rome. He had to seek out one of the few churches where clergymen of his confession—called Arians by their enemies—were permitted to celebrate mass. He presumably left the palace on the Palatine in the company of his coreligionists and proceeded to the *ecclesia Gothorum* ("church of the Goths") in the Subura, today know as Sant'Agata dei Goti, the apse mosaic of which the *magister militum* Ricimer (d. 472) had funded. The king himself drew attention to his retinue by holding a trial against a certain Odoin, a member of his court, in the Sessorian palace near the Church of Santa Croce in Gerusalemme and condemning him to death by beheading. Odoin was accused of planning an attack on Theoderic. We no longer can tell what really lay behind the charges. What is striking, at any rate, is that Theoderic condemned Odoin to be executed in the Roman way, by beheading, and had others carry out the sentence. Also in this respect, the king acted according to the proverb, "When in Rome, do as the Romans do."[16]

Theoderic's very appearance revealed that he was no emperor. The king indeed used some insignia of his royal status that had also been used by Roman emperors. He notably wore purple garments adorned with gems on ceremonial occasions. But Theoderic dispensed with the symbol of an emperor *par excellence*, the diadem, a circlet decorated with one or more jewels. Ennodius describes his appearance in the year 507 as follows (Ennod. *Pan.* 90–91): "Your stature is such as would reveal a ruler by its height. The snow of your cheeks

Fig. 3. Medallion of Morro d'Alba, obverse. By courtesy
of the Ministry of Cultural Heritage and Activities and
for Tourism—Museo Nazionale Romano (Rome).

harmonizes with their blush; your eyes radiate constant serenity. Your hands are
such as repay rebels with destruction and your subjects with the honors they
wish for. Let no man claim you are unseasonably coiffed because what diadems
accomplish for other rulers, nature has wrought for my king with the help of
God." A unique find, a gold medallion discovered in a grave near Morro d'Alba
in the province of Ancona in 1894, enables us to understand this indistinct
image more clearly. The medallion, equivalent to three gold coins (*solidi*) in
weight and value, was reworked as a disc brooch. Its obverse bears the only
contemporary likeness of Theoderic that can be identified with certainty. The
medallion was probably minted in the same year that Theoderic visited Rome,
perhaps in Rome itself, and distributed to his retinue. Such gifts (*donativa*,
"donatives") in the form of precious metals had long been customary in the
Roman Empire, and Theoderic continued this tradition. Normally, however,
Theoderic always put the likeness of the Byzantine emperor on the coins
minted in his kingdom. He broke this rule for a special issue that was intended
for a unique event and for a limited number of loyal servants.

On the obverse, we see a frontal view of the king. He is wearing a cuirass with a cloak (*paludamentum*) draped over his shoulders; it is pinned together by a brooch on his right. His right hand is raised in a gesture of speaking (*adlocutio*); in his left, he holds an orb surmounted by a small statue of Victory (*victoria*), who is extending the king a wreath. The legend reads, REX THEODERICVS PIVS PRINC(EPS) I(NVICTV)S: "King Theoderic, pious and invincible prince." On the reverse, we see Victory again, surrounded by the legend VICTOR GENTIVM: "Conqueror of (non-Roman) peoples." At first glance, the iconography looks thoroughly Roman. The cuirass and general's cloak, the *adlocutio* gesture, the orb, Victory—all of these were familiar from the coins of Roman emperors. And yet Theoderic stands out as a post-Roman ruler not only on account of his title, *rex* ("king"), but also on account of his hair: Roman emperors did not let their hair grow down over their ears. His facial hair also broke with the conventional appearance of Roman emperors, who usually were depicted either clean-shaven or with a full beard. Theoderic, in contrast, wore a mustache (*barba Gothica*) like his victim Odoacer.[17]

3. FROM WARLORD TO RULER OF THE GOTHS AND ROMANS?

The episodes narrated above paint a striking contrast: here the Gothic "warlord," there the ruler of the Goths and Romans. This contrast points to a tension that followed Theoderic his entire life. The questions that arise from it constitute the subject of this book: How did this transformation take place, and how profound was it? Where did Theoderic and his followers come from? How did they come to Italy? Equally urgent is the question of how this Gothic military commander succeeded in establishing a kingdom over Goths and Romans in Italy— once the nucleus of the Roman Empire—that remained stable for three whole decades and could be transferred to his underage grandson Athalaric on his death in 526. Why were the native elites—senators, municipal notables, and bishops— willing to accept the conqueror as their ruler? What form did the coexistence of the Gothic warrior band that accompanied Theoderic to Italy and the king's new Roman subjects take? What effects did his reign have on the Goths and Romans? And finally, we cannot avoid the question of what Theoderic wanted and what he achieved: did the king have something like a political agenda? What areas did he want to change, and what means did he employ to do so?

Modern scholars down to the present day interpret the reign of Theoderic in Italy predominantly as an almost seamless continuation of Roman traditions. This approach can be traced back to Theodor Mommsen, the founding father of late Roman studies, who argued that Theodoric ruled in Italy as a kind of governor for the Byzantine emperor; he carried the title *patricius* as the holder of this office. The ancient historian Wilhelm Ensslin, who published what remains the standard biography of Theodoric in 1947, took a similar view. In Ensslin's eyes, Theodoric was "the last of the Germanic leaders, who, touched by the spirit of Rome, marshaled the power of a Germanic people and dedicated himself on behalf of the ancient Roman world." The king was "a German (*Germane*) and remained so in his innermost essence in spite of everything," but his policy sought to preserve the Roman state and Roman culture; he aspired to be "not the new founder of the state" but rather "the preserver of an ancient legacy." The interpretation of the medievalist Herwig Wolfram, which gained wide popularity through his "ethnography" of the Goths, published in 1979 and appearing in several new editions since then, was likewise based on constitutional legal categories. In contrast to Mommsen and Ensslin, Wolfram interprets Theodoric's kingdom as a synthesis of Roman and non-Roman ("gentile") components, a *sui generis* creation; but Wolfram still regards the Roman structures and elements of Theodoric's Italian kingdom as dominant: it supposedly was an immediate continuation of the kingdom of Odoacer and the Western Roman emperors. The "Roman" interpretation of Theodoric has recently been taken to extremes in the theory that Theodoric was virtually a Western Roman emperor in Italy. According to this view, Theodoric restored the Roman Empire in the West, which he ruled as *princeps Romanus*. This book takes a different approach. It proceeds from the conviction that the willingness of Theodoric's subjects to accept him as ruler cannot be derived from a single, unified notion of legitimacy, whatever its nature or definition. The conglomeration of subjects Theodoric ruled as king in Italy was characterized by a high degree of social inequality and great cultural, religious, and ethnic diversity: Gothic warriors and Roman senators, municipal notables, craftsmen and merchants, peasants and shepherds, *coloni* (unfree peasants) and slaves, bishops and clergymen of two different Christian confessions, as well as Jewish communities. The answer to the questions of why accept Theodoric as ruler, why support him, or at least tolerate him, was different for each of these groups.

Theodoric's image in modern scholarship is characterized by a second basic feature: his reign is normally judged very positively. Ensslin lauded Theodoric as "provided with all the qualities of a true king"; he followed a peaceful foreign policy that strove to preserve what he had achieved and a domestic policy that was a blessing to his subjects. His economic policy benefited the "productive classes," he mastered the difficult situation of the coexistence "alongside and for

one another" of Gothic warriors and Roman civilians, and he sponsored magnificent buildings. For those reasons, his reign was a "golden age" for Italy. We
frequently encounter similar verdicts even today. Wolfram credits Theoderic
with a "policy of mediation between Romans and Goths, Catholics and Arians,
Latin and barbarian culture"; he praises the king for his "sound" economic
policy, for "modernizing Roman imperial law," and for an "intensive, albeit
restorative building policy." Others go so far as to attribute the project of a multicultural society to Theoderic. The latest monograph about Theoderic trans-
lates the paeans that contemporaries sang to him into modern scholarly prose
without the least critical scrutiny; hence Theoderic supposedly invested vast
sums in rebuilding Italian and Gallic cities, sparking a period of economic and
cultural prosperity lasting until it was brutally cut short by Justinian's recon-
quista. This book tells a different story.[18]

THEODERIC IN THE EYES OF CONTEMPORARIES

1. LOOKING GLASS OR DISTORTING MIRROR? LITERATURE AS A HISTORICAL SOURCE

The past is that which no longer exists. It can be observed only insofar as it has left traces behind; the study of history is the search for such traces. But only those who have an idea of what they are looking for can find something; only those who ask questions receive answers. It is the historical question that transforms traces of the past into sources of history. Still, something more is needed: the interpretation of the sources must satisfy certain rules if it aspires to be authoritative. These rules are determined by the nature of the material that serves as a source: it can be artifacts like buildings, graves, or tools or texts of the most diverse genres, from funerary inscriptions to sales contracts to historiographical works. Legal forms and conventions, semantic fields, names of persons and places, urban layouts and pictorial motifs—everything can become a source if it can be interpreted in response to a specific question. No matter how different the material might be, a rigorous methodological interpretation always requires us to re-create the context in which each source originated. We must ask who left the traces behind and why and how they did so; we have to explore their intentions and functions, their purposes, means, and meanings.

These questions apply to the study of every past, no matter how recent or remote. When the traces of the past we are studying have entirely or largely vanished from our everyday world—and that undoubtedly includes Theoderic— we face especially great challenges because the sources we have available to reconstruct the person and times of our subject derive from contexts with which we are no longer familiar.

In these circumstances, evidence in the form of texts is extremely important. More written sources survive for Theoderic and his Goths than for any other leader or state of his time, excepting the Roman Empire itself. Among these written sources, it is texts, which we may designate "literature" according to contemporary understanding, that take precedence for their length and informational value. They are linguistic works of art that are influenced by both formal conventions and the individual creative will of their authors. Whether writing letters or drafts of speeches or even composing narrative accounts of past events or the description of foreign peoples, late antique authors followed models that were thought to possess timeless authority, even if they had been written centuries earlier, in pre-Christian times. Historiography, epistolography, and rhetoric were regarded as literary genres that were defined by a long tradition; whoever claimed to be educated, therefore, tried to meet the expectations of the audience of such texts. The *Panegyricus* by the Catholic clergyman Ennodius, which we have already encountered several times, illustrates especially well how literary sources can adequately be understood only if we also carefully consider the circumstances of their production and reception. The word *panegyricus* literally means a "speech delivered at a festival/feast" (in Greek, a *panēgyris*, πανήγυρις), but in Late Antiquity the label was also applied to encomia—"panegyrics"—that were not delivered at a formal occasion but rather were merely disseminated in writing. If the panegyric to Theoderic was delivered as its title claims—"In the name of the Father, Son, and Holy Spirit, here begins the panegyric to the most merciful King Theoderic, delivered by Ennodius, a servant of God"—we can no longer determine the occasion and its ceremonial context. It was written, at any rate, in the year 507, probably in its first half.

Ennodius describes Theoderic in this panegyric as an educated ruler who had made Roman culture his own: he is a Christian who worships the supreme deity. He has no need to wear the diadem of an emperor, because he is equal to any and all other rulers even without this emblem, particularly since he descends from the royal family of the Amals. He liberated Italy from the tyrant Odoacer, thereby restoring the country's freedom (*libertas*); now he rules as king of the Romans and Goths by grace of God. Ennodius portrays Theoderic as an unstoppable warrior and an undefeatable king, surpassing even Alexander the Great himself—an account of Theoderic's heroic feats takes up a majority of the speech. Although he had his Gothic generals carry out military operations since becoming ruler of Italy, he was always still with them in spirit. With the help of his Goths, Theoderic protected Italy from all external threats, thereby ensuring peace in the land. Indeed, he had even restored its old borders

by reconquering the city of Sirmium (modern Sremska Mitrovica) on the
Danube, which had previously belonged to the Western Roman Empire. In
Theoderic's kingdom the rule of law as set down in statutes—a state of affairs
called *civilitas*—prevails, and even the Goths bow down to it. For, according to
Ennodius, Theoderic also possesses all the virtues that a ruler in peace needs:
he is wise, just, and generous; he confers offices only on those who deserve
them; and he rewards those who deliver panegyrics in his honor. All Italy flour-
ishes under his rule; its ruined cities are rising up to new glory; Rome is rejuvenated. A new golden age (*aureum saeculum*) has dawned![1]

It goes without saying that these claims cannot be taken at face value. They
abound in commonplaces that appear, in this or in similar form, in countless
panegyrics delivered in honor of Roman emperors. That would neither have
surprised nor bothered a contemporary audience: everyone who composed a
speech praising the emperor submitted to the basic rule that only and always
positive things would be said. But the conventions of the genre were not limited
to the prohibition of open criticism. Careful assessment and measured judgment were also at odds with the expectations placed on the authors of panegyrics. A large repository of themes, motifs, and arguments had been compiled
that one could recycle in endless variation when praising an emperor. These
genre-specific topoi sketched a concept of an ideal ruler; in detail, however, the
content was not at all set in stone but could vary considerably within certain
limits. Hence a speech like the panegyric to Theoderic did not merely repro-
duce some set of instructions or requirements, but rather interpreted Theoderic's
reign from the point of view of a specific person or group of persons. The author
used the ruler's self-representation as a reference point but still formulated his
own claims and wishes, albeit in an indirect and abstract way.

In the case of the panegyric to Theoderic, it was not easy to overcome the
cultural and social gap between the author of the speech and the object of his
praise. Ennodius was only fifteen or sixteen years old when Theoderic came to
Italy; he was born in southern Gaul, presumably in Arles, in 473 or 474. He
descended from a senatorial family and took pride in that fact all his life.
Orphaned at an early age, he was raised by his sister. After her death, he was
taken in by a well-to-do family in Liguria. At the latest in 495, Ennodius joined
the clergy. He initially belonged to the clergy under the bishop of Ticinum
(Pavia), Epiphanius, whose *vita* he later wrote. After a few years, prior to 499, he
transferred to the clergy of Milan, to which he belonged until approximately
513–515. While in Milan, Ennodius composed an extensive literary oeuvre, the
majority of which has survived. In addition to the panegyric to Theoderic and
the *vita* of Epiphanius, it includes eight other prose texts of miscellaneous con-

tent (*opuscula*), twenty-eight speeches intended primarily for school use, 297 letters, and 172 poems, partly spiritual and partly secular in nature. During the so-called Laurentian Schism, Ennodius sided with Pope Symmachus, whom he supported with a pamphlet against his opponent; he was one of the people who could rejoice when Theoderic had the "anti-pope" Laurentius deposed in 506. Between late 513 and summer 515, Ennodius was consecrated bishop of Ticinum; he held this office until his death on July 18, 521. During his episcopate, he traveled twice to Constantinople as an envoy of Pope Hormisdas (514–523) and played a key part in the restoration of church unity between Rome and Constantinople, which had been broken since 484 in the so-called Acacian Schism. Ennodius' epitaph survives and leaves no doubt as to what was important to him: it celebrates his noble ancestry, his education and eloquence, his generosity (which manifested itself particularly in church buildings), and his engagement on behalf of the faith that the Apostle Peter had professed.[2]

There thus were many things that separated the author and his addressee and subject: as a clergyman, Ennodius belonged to the Catholic Church of Italy; the king was a layman, and, moreover, as an "Arian," he practiced a form of Christianity that the Catholic Church considered heretical. Ennodius descended from the senatorial nobility and remained closely connected to it all his life; he thus was a Roman. The king was a Goth and had seized power over Italy as the leader of a Gothic army. Theoderic was beholden to the ideal of a warrior king; for Ennodius, three factors determined the value of a man: the right faith, aristocratic ancestry, and the internalization of the values and contents of Latin education.

Hence, the panegyric to Theoderic tells us little if we should want to know how Theoderic became king, how he defeated Odoacer, or what measures he took as king of Italy. It reveals much to us, however, about how Theoderic presented himself to the traditional elites of Italy and how they reacted. The panegyric to Theoderic shows us the discursive strategies that enabled Roman senators and clergymen to come to terms with the rule of a Gothic king: they largely ignored Theoderic's past as the leader of a warrior band in the Balkans and passed over his "heretical" faith in silence. Instead, they praised his prowess as a warrior and general, because it guaranteed peace for Italy, and emphasized his readiness to accept all the duties that had once been the responsibility of the emperors to fulfill. Senators and clergymen could rest easy: this king respected them, their ideals, and their privileges; he also knew how to keep a tight grip on his army.

Contemporaries did not expect the author of a panegyric to lay bare his innermost thoughts when he celebrated a ruler; we likewise should not take every word of the panegyric to Theoderic to reflect Ennodius' personal convictions. Yet there can be no doubt that Ennodius was speaking in earnest when he praised Theoderic's reign as a blessing for Italy because he expressed the same sentiment elsewhere, even where there was no reason to tell the king what he wanted to hear. Theoderic was the *dominus libertatis*, the "master of liberty" in Ennodius' eyes, a ruler who ensured the survival of the cultural tradition and social order with which Ennodius wholly and completely identified. The fact that Theoderic was a "heretic" was a blemish to which Ennodius could turn a blind eye because Theoderic did not insist on actively propagating his own faith and decided in favor of the group to which Ennodius himself belonged in his rare intervention in internal Catholic affairs.[3]

Since rhetoric has long been stigmatized in German- and English-speaking lands as mendacious frippery—and Ennodius' overwrought, opaque, and baroque style, overloaded as it is with figures of speech, severely tests the patience of modern readers—his testimony has had little influence on the image scholars have painted of Theoderic since the early nineteenth century. The evidentiary value of a text known to modern scholars as the *Anonymus Valesianus* (because it was first published in 1636 by the French scholar Henri Valois) has been rated much more highly. The author and title of this work are unknown. To be precise, it is actually two texts that happen to be transmitted together: the first concerns Constantine the Great; the second, Theoderic. In this book, whenever I mention the *Anonymus Valesianus*, I always mean the second part.[4]

The *Anonymus Valesianus* presents many mysteries. The place and date of its composition are uncertain and disputed. Most scholars presume that the unknown author wrote in the middle of the sixth century, after Theoderic's death, which he mentions, but prior to the demise of the Gothic kingdom in Italy, about which he says nothing at all; he potentially wrote in Ravenna, which again came under the Byzantine emperor's control in 540. He was a Catholic Christian at any rate, well informed about events in the Byzantine Empire, and took great interest in Theoderic's legal relationship to the emperor. In contrast to the writings of Ennodius, his work is not written in an idiom that one laboriously had to learn at school, far removed from everyday speech, but rather in a language that linguists have denoted "Vulgar Latin." His account is erratic, his sentence structure clumsy, and the logical connection between his thoughts often obscure. The text defies categorization in any of the literary genres of Classical Antiquity, although there are echoes of Suetonius' *Lives of the Twelve Caesars*. The *Anonymus Valesianus* is, moreover, highly heterogeneous in form and content.

The text begins in the year 474, at the accession of the last Western Roman emperor recognized by the East, Julius Nepos. It then narrates the events that led to Odoacer's abolition of the position of Western Roman emperor, as well as his origins and reign, while constantly also noting contemporaneous events in the Eastern Roman Empire. This account takes up about a quarter of the text (§ 36–48). Theoderic comes to the fore only afterward, when Emperor Zeno commissions him to march on Italy to depose Odoacer (§ 49). Anonymus then describes the two kings' battle for supremacy in Italy in great detail (§ 50–56). He mentions that Theoderic was recognized only hesitatingly by the Eastern Roman Empire but then proceeds to give a very positive account of Theoderic's reign in Italy (§ 59–73); the heart of the account consists of his visit to Rome in the year 500 (§ 65–70). The author makes use of topoi that served to evoke a "golden age" in panegyrics: gold and silver were as safe in the countryside as behind city walls, city gates were never shut, grain and wine cost only a fraction of what had been customary at other times, and so on. One central passage states:

> Hence he was renowned and well-intentioned in all things, reigning thirty-three years. In his time, Italy experienced prosperity for thirty years, so much so that even travelers were unmolested. He did nothing wrong. Thus he governed two peoples at the same time, Romans and Goths. Although he himself belonged to the Arian sect, he did not try anything against the Catholic religion. He ordered that the civil service [*militia*] for the Romans continue as under the emperors. While lavishing gifts and grain, although he found the public treasury exhausted, he restored it by his labor and made it rich. He gave circus games and amphitheater spectacles, so that the Romans called him Trajan or Valentinian, whose eras he imitated, and he was regarded by the Goths as the strongest king in every way on account of the edict he issued for them.[5]

The religious and ethnic difference between the author and his subject is clearly indicated in this text. Despite that, however, the first thirty years (493–523) of Theoderic's reign—beginning not with the victory over Babai, but rather with the overthrow of Odoacer—are depicted as remarkably prosperous. The following statements reinforce this impression until the author turns his gaze to the Eastern Roman Empire (§ 74–79). In the concluding part of the text (§ 80–96), however, the verdict about Theoderic is turned almost completely on its head: on account of the devil's influence, the good king whose reign was a blessing to Italy transforms into an enemy of the True Faith and the Romans, who has senators arbitrarily executed and persecutes the Catholic Church; God's just punishment therefore overtakes him before he can realize his plan to deprive the Catholics of Italy of all their churches.[6]

This about-face has bothered modern readers so much that some have suspected a different author composed the conclusion. But this assumption is
undermined not only by the fact that the paean to Theoderic just cited implicitly excludes the last three years of his reign (523–526); the abrupt change of a
wise and just king into a bad one was also a familiar theme to Christians who
knew their Bible: 1 Kings tells how, in his old age, wise King Solomon himself
turned his back on God under the influence of his women. Modern scholars
have normally regarded the negative conclusion as less credible than the rest of
the text; the devil has lost his place in our secularized understanding of history.
The positive image of Theoderic in the middle of the text, in contrast, has seldom received as much critical scrutiny as seems appropriate. The obvious use
of panegyrical topoi alone should put us on the alert: the extremely positive
overall characterization of Theoderic's reign reproduces panegyrical commonplaces that correspond to the king's own representation and derive from a discursive system that cannot serve as the basis of modern judgments. The same
thing could be said of virtually every emperor, if and as long as he was accepted.
We should be wary of the fact that the specific details of the positive part relate
to the narrow time window around Theoderic's visit to Rome in 500, while the
generalizing negative verdicts are bolstered by anecdotes and apothegms the
original context of which remains obscure.

Anonymus thus does not at all give us an undistorted view of historical reality, even though its narrative has sometimes seemed naive to modern readers
and been treated as credible for that very reason. Still, it is remarkable that an
author who was writing after Theoderic's death and was probably a subject of
Emperor Justinian describes Theoderic's reign as predominantly beneficial and
does not question his legitimacy. That fits well with the assumption that
Anonymus was writing during or after Justinian's reconquest of Italy because
after the war the emperor implicitly confirmed all of Theoderic's acts and thus
retroactively recognized his reign as legitimate once more.[7]

Whereas Anonymus composed his account in a language and form that
flouted the rules of classical Latin biography and historiography, Procopius saw
himself as a representative of a time-hallowed tradition of Greek historiography
founded in the fifth century BCE by Herodotus and Thucydides. Procopius
may have been born around the year 500; he thus was over a generation younger
than Theoderic. He came from Caesarea Maritima, the capital of the province
of Palaestina Prima (in modern Israel). He served the Byzantine general
Belisarius as a counselor (*assessor*) from 527 to 540 or 542 and accompanied him
in that capacity on his campaigns against the Persians, Vandals, and finally the
Goths in Italy. Procopius held the senatorial rank of *spectabilis* and ultimately,

it seems, became a member of the senate of Constantinople. In 551, he published an account, in seven books, of the wars that Justinian had waged against the Persians, Vandals, and Goths; since his account is divided according to theaters of war—the Roman East, North Africa, Italy and the West—the individual books are often cited as the "Persian War," "Vandalic War," and "Gothic War," but in reality they are successive parts of a single historiographical work that extended right down to the present. A few years after 551, Procopius appended an eighth book to this work in which later events were added; his account of the West extends to the end of the year 552. While writing *The Wars of Justinian* (*Bella*), Procopius also composed a work known as the *Secret History* (*Historia arcana*), so titled because Procopius declined to publish it in his lifetime (hence its Greek title, *Anekdota*, "unpublished material"). As he explains in the introduction, Procopius wanted to lay bare everything that he had had to suppress in his *Wars* for fear of reprisals. The *Secret History* thus was conceived as a complement and corrective to the *Wars of Justinian*. In reality, the *Secret History* is a hateful tirade against Emperor Justinian, who is called the "prince of demons." Procopius' reputation as a historian has also suffered in modern times because he later wrote a panegyrical text about Justinian's building projects that has also survived. In this text, Procopius praises the emperor beyond measure, just as the genre called for.[8]

Procopius' historical works stand in a tradition that was already a thousand years old when he began to write in the mid-540s. Procopius inserted himself in this tradition by adopting the language and style, narrative techniques, and way of thinking of the authors who had founded historiography as a literary genre; the works of Herodotus and Thucydides served him both as a standard and as a model. Procopius' decision to adopt this classicizing form of depicting past events entailed that he abstain from Christian interpretive models but not that he embrace the old gods, as most scholars previously believed and occasionally still assume today. At a time when large segments of the population of the Roman Empire anxiously wondered how near the coming of the Last Judgment was and Christian theologians imputed all earthly events to God's divine plan, authors like Procopius tried to make sense of human actions without implicating the will of God. To do so, he drew on the categories of ancient popular philosophy that provided a kind of template for interpreting and assessing human actions. According to this scheme, good rulers possessed the four cardinal virtues of valor, justice, prudence, and wisdom; bad rulers were cowardly, unjust, lavish, and stupid. In Procopius, this rough explanation of actions is paired with the naive belief that the righteous cause always prevails. This belief may have been challenged by the extremely vicissitudinous events of the Gothic

War, which still had not been won a decade and a half since it began, but it was never shaken to its core; hence it caused internal narrative contradictions. When the historian found himself at a loss to explain the events, he enlisted fate (*tyche*), conceived as blind chance, to close the analytical gap.

Like the characterization of persons, the depiction of foreign peoples was also heavily influenced by clichés. When depicting peoples who seemed exotic, Greco-Roman historiography made use of conventional patterns of perception, interpretation, and composition: the historian inquired about their homes and origins, language and appearance, physical and mental faculties, ways and customs. The range of conceivable answers, meanwhile, was limited by axiomatic assumptions. These clichés or topoi enabled one to come to grips with the present by tracing back what was new to what was already familiar, indeed often interpreting new phenomena as virtually "the eternal recurrence of the same." Classicizing historians of the sixth century still drew a basic distinction between the cultural world they identified with the Roman Empire and the world of the barbarians, although they described their own culture no longer as Greek but as Roman. The barbarian, however, was a second-class human being; he was unruly and immoderate, wavered between savage cruelty and cowardly submissiveness, could check neither his appetite nor his sex drive, and was incapable of acquiring higher education. Political moves and maneuvering by non-Roman actors thus tended to be viewed as indicative of a defect of character, of treachery. Classicizing historiography also entailed identifying the peoples that featured in present events whenever possible with those that were already known to the "classical" authors. For example, all the peoples who cropped up along the lower Danube could be called Scythians because Herodotus had once placed a people or rather a group of peoples of that name in the region. These ethnographic conventions limited the scope of what was conceivable and reinforced popular prejudices, but they did not completely obscure the unique features of foreign peoples, with whom the Romans often had close ties, after all. Authors noted features that differentiated certain peoples from others and called them by the names in common use in Late Antiquity if it seemed reasonable or unavoidable to do so. Procopius did not have the slightest intention of describing foreign cultures from an insider's point of view, but rather viewed them primarily as potential enemies or allies of the emperor. By no means, however, is his view of barbarian peoples and rulers entirely negative; moreover, he attentively registers differences in their political system, their weaponry and equipment, and their style of combat.

All this must be borne in mind when reading Procopius' *History of the Wars* as a source for the history of Theoderic and the Goths in Italy. His ethnographic mindset is particularly conspicuous in the introductory account of the Goths as part of a large family of "Gothic peoples," which also includes the Vandals, Visigoths, and Gepids. Procopius identifies these peoples with the Sauromatae (Sarmatians) and Melanchlaines of Herodotus while adding that other authors equated them with the Getae, who had also been mentioned by Herodotus. In his view, all of them descended from the same people but had received different names from their leaders over time. In accordance with this ethnographic mindset, he derives their common ancestry from a set of shared characteristics: all "Gothic peoples" in his opinion are tall and stately; their skin is white, and their hair is blonde. Moreover, they all speak the same language, which he calls Gothic, and they all adhere to the same faith—namely, the teachings of Arius. They originally had lived on the far side of the lower Danube but later gradually penetrated deep into the Roman Empire, doing so for the first time in the reign of Emperor Arcadius (395–408).[9]

The subject of Procopius' *History of the Wars* is not the kingdom of Theoderic in Italy, but rather the war that Justinian waged against his successors. Theoderic's reign therefore is discussed only in the author's introduction to his account of this war. Procopius narrates the deposition of the last Roman emperor in Italy, Romulus, by Odoacer and the latter's conflict with Theoderic, who marched on Italy at the behest of Emperor Zeno to overthrow a "tyrant." A detailed account of the siege of Ravenna down to Odoacer's murder is followed by a general assessment of Theoderic's reign, part of which it is worthwhile to quote in full (Proc. *Bell.* 5, 1, 26–28):

> He declined to usurp either the garb or the name of "emperor of the Romans" [Greek: *basileus tōn Rhomaiōn*] but rather continued to be called *rex*—that is what the barbarians conventionally call their leaders. He ruled over his subjects, however, endowed with all the things that befit a natural ruler [*basileus*]. He paid exacting attention to justice and maintained the laws on a firm foundation; he kept the land safe from the surrounding barbarians and exemplified the pinnacle of prudence and valor. And he did almost no wrong to his subjects personally or tolerated anyone else who attempted to do so, with the exception that the Goths divided among themselves the share of the land that Odoacer had given to his soldiers.

Procopius concludes this exceedingly positive assessment by remarking that while Theoderic may have been a tyrant in name, he was a true *basileus* in reality and in no way inferior to anyone who had achieved fame with this title. The Goths and the Italians (*Italiōtai*)—in Procopius, "Romans" (*Rhōmaioi*) are subjects of the Eastern Roman, i.e., Byzantine, emperor—accordingly loved him.

The historian plays on the many meanings of the Greek word *basileus*, which could indicate the Roman emperor or indeed any monarch who was recognized as legitimate and therefore not a tyrant. According to Procopius, Theoderic was born to rule: he possessed all the virtues a ruler needed, although his legitimacy was dubious. Procopius of course qualifies his praise of Theoderic by noting that the king unjustly put two high-ranking senators, Symmachus and Boethius, to death at the end of his thirty-seven-year reign (calculated from 489 to 526). He adds, however, that Theoderic regretted this mistake but died immediately afterward.[10]

The standards that Procopius applies to the reign of Theoderic are essentially the same as those used by the author of the *Anonymus Valesianus*: the presence or absence of the virtues of a ruler and recognition by the Eastern Roman emperor. Both authors omit the final years of his reign from their laudatory overall assessment, but only Anonymus also mentions Theoderic's measures against the "True Faith." Despite the fact that a detailed treatment of Theoderic's reign lay outside the scope of his *History of the Wars*, Procopius covers this theme a second time by making it the subject of speeches that he puts in the mouths of protagonists of his narrative. In keeping with classical tradition, his work includes numerous speeches and letters that are often arranged in pairs; they are partly based on historical information, partly fictional. One such pair of speeches is dedicated to the Goths' claim to rule over Italy; it occurs in the context of negotiations between the Gothic king Vitigis and the Byzantine general Belisarius. Procopius has the Gothic delegates speak first. They explain that Theoderic had toppled the tyrant Odoacer at the behest of Emperor Zeno, who gave Italy to the Goths as their permanent possession. They then declare (Proc. *Bell.* 6, 6, 17–19):

> Thus seizing power over Italy, we preserved the laws and government no worse than any who have ruled as emperor, and not a single law [*nomos*], written or unwritten, was ever issued by Theoderic or any of his successors. As concerns the worship of God and belief, we have been so respectful of the Romans [*Rhōmaioi*] that, to this very day, no Italian has changed his faith, whether willingly or unwillingly. Nor has there been any persecution of the Goths who have changed theirs. And indeed we have held the sacred places of the Romans [*Rhōmaioi*] in the highest honor. No one who has sought refuge in one of them has suffered violence at the hands of any man. Indeed, they themselves have continued to hold the public offices, in which the Goths have no share.[11]

As in the *Anonymus Valesianus*, this passage depicts Theoderic's rule as exercised in legal form over both Goths and Romans. The toleration of the Catholic faith and the Roman monopoly on high offices both recur here. Procopius refuses to make any explicit comment on the Gothic delegates' argumentation. The depiction of Theoderic's reign also goes uncontested in Belisarius' rebuttal. The general contents himself with formulating the emperor's legal position: Theoderic may have eliminated Odoacer at Emperor Zeno's behest, but that did not give him the right to claim Italy permanently for himself. He thereby had become a tyrant.

Procopius wanted to write the history of a war in the style of the classical Greek historians. He was extremely well qualified to do so since he had taken part in this war personally until Belisarius' recall in the year 540. During this time, he worked in the headquarters of the Byzantine army, where the enemy was carefully studied. He undoubtedly had known and spoken with Goths personally—delegates, prisoners, and deserters. Although he covered the period thereafter no longer as an eyewitness and participant, he was well situated in Constantinople to obtain information about the war. In some respects, his history resembles a journalistic account that follows the course of events at close hand without knowing the outcome. His account is detailed and lively down to the year 540 but often brief and dry thereafter. Procopius' opinion of the protagonists and the purpose of the war also wavers significantly. The euphoria over apparent victory in 540 quickly gave way to disillusionment. The longer the war dragged on, the more Procopius doubted whether the Byzantine victory that he had constantly hoped for would prove to be a boon to the inhabitants of Italy.

Despite his positive opinion of Theoderic, Procopius never fundamentally questioned the Byzantine emperor's claim to Italy. He viewed the Goths as barbarians and was convinced that Gothic warriors were no match for the elite soldiers of the emperor with respect to their technology and tactics. According to his account, they could neither capture a city by storming the walls nor withstand the onslaught of the emperor's mounted archers. The Goths also lacked the necessary know-how for naval combat in Procopius' view. Procopius consequently explained setbacks in the Italian theater as caused by mistakes on the Byzantine side, in particular the emperor's failure to pay the soldiers their wages. His opinion of the Gothic warriors improved, however, when they began to enjoy success again under King Totila after 542. Totila is the first successor of Theoderic to whom Procopius frequently ascribes positive traits. In his account, the king stands out not only for his personal valor, but also for his mercy and justice; against this background, Justinian's officials, whom Procopius accuses of greed and cruelty, contrast all the more unfavorably. Totila's demise is depicted sympathetically. Teia, finally, the last Gothic king in Italy, was an utterly fearless warrior who was second to none of the ancient heroes of antiquity in military prowess.[12]

2. TESTIMONY OR REPRESENTATION? ROYAL CORRESPONDENCE IN CASSIODORUS

As different as Ennodius, Anonymus, and Procopius are as authors, the texts they composed all depict Theoderic from the outside; no matter how close to or how far from their subject they stand, their perspective is always that other people had on the king. The king's self-representation is at best reflected only indirectly in these texts. For this reason, it is a special stroke of good luck that no fewer than 240 texts survive that were composed in the king's name. They were not formulated by the king himself; he always entrusted this task to educated Romans. But they nonetheless may be considered personal testimonia insofar as in every single case he is named as the person responsible for their content; for the recipients, they counted as the king's word. This extensive corpus of official texts, most of which are stylized as letters from the king to specific addressees, enables us to describe the way in which Theoderic communicated both with his subjects and with other rulers more exactly than we can do for any other contemporary barbarian ruler. Any interpretation, however, first has to acknowledge the elementary fact that the overwhelming majority of these texts—235 out of 240—were written by one and the same man, who held several high offices under Theoderic and also played an important political part under his first successors. This man is well known to us; his full name was Flavius Magnus Aurelius Cassiodorus Senator. Modern scholars call him Cassiodorus for short, while he himself preferred the name Senator.

That was no coincidence. Cassiodorus was the descendent of senators and himself reached the highest offices available to this rank. His father before him had already enjoyed a brilliant political career. He successively served as the head of two of the three financial ministries located at the court: first as *comes rerum privatarum* ("count of private property"), who oversaw the administration of royal property, and then as *comes sacrarum largitionum* ("count of the sacred largesses"), whose job was to ensure that the king's coffers were always filled with silver and gold. The ruler whom Cassiodorus' father served was no longer a Roman emperor; he was a barbarian king—in fact, no other than the Odoacer who deposed the last emperor in Italy, Romulus, in the year 476. Cassiodorus' father defected to Theoderic, however, when the latter arrived in Italy with his army in 489. The victorious king rewarded him by placing him in charge of the most important civil ministry in Italy, the praetorian prefecture, and then conferred on him the highest rank that the Roman Empire had at the time, that of *patricius*.[13]

Cassiodorus began his career as his father's adviser while the latter served as praetorian prefect, from 503 to 506. He was not yet thirty years old when he caught Theoderic's attention with a panegyric he delivered for him. In 506, he was appointed to one of the highest offices at court, that of *quaestor palatii* ("quaestor of the palace"), the official responsible for composing royal communiqués. He held this office for five years, until 511. In 514, Theoderic awarded him the extraordinary honor of giving his name to the year as "sole consul" (*consul sine collega*). After that, Cassiodorus retreated from the public eye and lived a life of private *otium* ("leisure") befitting his high rank for over a decade.

In the final years of Theoderic's reign, however, Cassiodorus returned to hold high office at the king's court yet again. As *magister officiorum* ("master of offices"), he was responsible for directing the chancelleries attached to the court that handled the king's correspondence with his administrators and subjects. As an acknowledged master of the late Roman chancellery style, he simultaneously supported the *quaestor palatii* in formulating royal pronouncements. Cassiodorus did not leave this office until 527, after the kingdom had passed to Theoderic's grandson Athalaric in 526. Theodoric's daughter Amalasuintha, who acted as regent for her underage son Athalaric, reactivated Cassiodorus in 533, appointing him praetorian prefect. In this position, Cassiodorus served no fewer than three Gothic rulers who succeeded one another: first Athalaric and his mother Amalasuintha; then, after Athalaric's death, Amalasuintha and Theodahad during their joint rule. Cassiodorus remained in office after Theodahad had Amalasuintha imprisoned and then executed in 535, and he was also retained by his successor, Vitigis, after Theodahad was overthrown and killed in late 536. At this time, the war that Emperor Justinian was waging to reconquer Italy was already in full swing. Cassiodorus did not leave the service of the Gothic kings permanently before the end of 537. After the capitulation of Ravenna in 540, he moved to Constantinople. There he began a new chapter of his life. He remained an active author, but he only composed texts intended for spiritual edification and instruction. We will discuss those in greater detail below.[14]

In the meantime, Cassiodorus published a collection of official letters that he had composed on behalf of and largely also in the name of the Gothic kings. This collection is divided into twelve books and is titled *Variae* ("letters of various content"). The first five books contain letters that Cassiodorus wrote in the name of Theoderic; books 6 and 7 contain *formulae*—that is, templates for regularly recurring official acts; books 8–10 contain letters that Cassiodorus wrote in the name of Theoderic's successors down to Vitigis. The last two books collect letters that Cassiodorus wrote in his own name as praetorian prefect from 533 to 537. All in all, the collection consists of nearly 500 letters, including letters to foreign rulers, instructions to officials, judicial decisions, and legal rulings, as well as numerous letters that were sent to high officials on the occasion of their appointment and to other addressees, especially the senate. The circle of recipients includes Romans and Goths, the senate and individual senators, civil officials, military commanders and units, and ecclesiastical dignitaries, as well as barbarian kings and Byzantine emperors.[15]

Cassiodorus himself states in the foreword to the *Variae* that he had published the collection at the insistence of his friends, so that his selfless labors for the common good not be lost to posterity. In particular, they had given him three reasons as to why it was indispensable to publish the work: first, the letters he had composed could instruct others eager to dedicate themselves to the commonwealth (*res publica*); second, they would ensure that the senatorial offices and ranks that the kings had conferred would not be forgotten; and third, they would preserve a reflection of his own personality. The collection thus was published at a time when Cassiodorus had not yet abandoned all hope of further cooperation between the Gothic kings and Roman senators and looked back at his labors in their service with hardly concealed pride. The selection and arrangement of the letters he included in the collection, moreover, reveal that he strove to depict Theoderic's reign as an uninterrupted continuation of Roman institutions and norms under a Gothic king. It was his firm conviction, in turn, that these institutions and norms were anchored in a transcendent world of eternal values that were not susceptible to human intervention. Insofar as the collection presents the Gothic kingdom as governed by ideal principles, it not only reproduces the king's self-representation, but also defends the author's own political engagement: serving an excellent ruler who adapted to Roman tradition was honorable even for a (S)enator.

The nature of the surviving tradition entails that we know the royal chancellery, with very few exceptions, exclusively from letters that Cassiodorus composed as a high official and included after his service in a collection that he intended to serve as a kind of apologia for his active participation in the reign of the Gothic kings in Italy. This observation, of course, by no means changes the fact that, with slight modification—the omission of greetings and dating formulae—the letters contained in the collection preserve the original wording of royal letters. Cassiodorus himself explains in a second foreword that since he had spoken with the king's mouth in the preceding ten books, he added the final two so that his own personality would not remain unknown.

Cassiodorus' job as the author of royal letters consisted in dressing the political will of the Gothic kings in a linguistic form that corresponded to the tradition of the late Roman chancellery. This chancellery style, which had defined the pronouncements of Roman emperors and officials, is characterized by long, complicated sentences, impersonal constructions, and a predilection for substantives instead of verbs. This idiom followed rhetorical models and was far removed from the Latin of everyday life. It accordingly was not easy to understand even for educated contemporaries.

Another peculiarity of the chancellery style was that the authors of official documents normally adopted a four-part structure. An introduction or preface (*prooemium*) that set forth general principles was followed by a "narration" (*narratio*) of the facts of the case at hand, which was followed in turn by the ruler's substantive decision or decree (*dispositio*). The conclusion (*conclusio*) consisted of penalty clauses, warnings, and publication instructions. This basic structure reflects the fact that the pronouncements of late antique emperors frequently contain prolix discourses on principles and values that applied to the ruler and/ or his subjects; in other words, they instructed and admonished. In contrast to modern laws, which are written in a legal language that strives for precision and brevity, the pronouncements of late antique rulers by no means served exclusively—and often not even primarily—to codify norms. On the contrary, they were a communications medium between rulers and subjects that served to reinforce common values by the constant repetition of truisms.

It was Cassiodorus' ambition to command this style in such a way that his contemporaries would appreciate it as literary brilliance. He aspired to be a virtuoso, not a bureaucrat. In accordance with the mannerist tastes of his age, he sought to avoid everything plain and informal; he hunted instead for unanticipated expressions, piling up literary figures like antitheses and paradoxes, aphorisms and metaphors, similes and puns. The genre of the letter, which constitutes a major part of the Latin literature of Late Antiquity, served him as a model in terms of both form and content. In keeping with the didactic and parenetic tendencies of late antique legislation, the royal will as expressed by Cassiodorus is usually formulated very succinctly, while the instruction and exhortation of the addressees often takes up far more space. In some letters, these learned excursuses make up almost the entire text.

Anyone who reads the *Variae* as a source for the policy of the Gothic kings cannot avoid the question of how much a hand Cassiodorus had in formulating royal pronouncements. We unfortunately do not know how exact his instructions as the king's "mouthpiece" were. Decisions and decrees by the king were obviously predetermined for him, as probably also were key concepts of the king's self-representation that we encounter in other authors and in other media. The linguistic form and also many of the sentiments in the introductory, admonishing, and moralizing passages of the *Variae*, in contrast, undoubtedly stemmed from Cassiodorus himself. In this regard, the king relied on the political acumen of his quaestor and the vigilance of his courtiers.

The mannerist style of the *Variae* raises a second problem, however: that of their reception by different groups of addressees. It is easy to see why educated Romans appreciated receiving letters from a Gothic king that were formulated in literary style if we consider the value that Roman senators still attached to a classical education, even in the sixth century. What about addressees, however, who lacked this education or even had, at best, an imperfect command of Latin, like many Goths? How did the message contained in the letters reach them?

An example can illustrate the issue: it is a kind of circular letter that was sent before the beginning of the Gallic campaign in the summer of 508 (Cass. *Var.* 1, 24). The inscription or address reads "King Theoderic to all the Goths." The paragraph that follows combines the message that the king had decided to send an army to Gaul with an exposition of his reasons for doing so; this is the *prooemium*:

> Goths need only be informed of battles rather than urged, because for a warlike race it is a joy to be tested: he who desires the glory of valor shuns no labor. And therefore, with the help of God, through whom all things prosper, we have resolved to dispatch an army to Gaul for the common good, so that both you may have an opportunity for advancement and we may be shown to have conferred on deserving people what we have already granted. Laudable bravery is hidden by peace, and when it lacks the occasion to prove itself, the light of one's merits is totally hidden.

The actual message is succinctly stated in the second paragraph; this is the *dispositio*:

> And therefore we have seen to it to advise you through our agent [*saio*] Nandus that you are to mobilize for an expedition in the name of God, adequately supplied in the customary way with weapons, horses, and all necessary provisions, on the coming 8th day before the kalends of July [i.e., June 24, 508], so that you may demonstrate that the courage of your fathers resides in you and successfully execute our command.

A cumbersome exhortation to bravery follows in the third and final section, this time addressed to the leaders of the young Gothic warriors. An analogy from the animal kingdom is intended to lend it emphasis; this is the *conclusio*:

> Educate your young men in the science of war: under your leadership, let them see what they might strive to pass down to future generations. For what is not learned in youth remains unknown in ripe old age. Even hawks, whose sustenance always comes from prey, push their newborn offspring, weak with their newness, out of their nests so that they do not grow accustomed to soft repose. They beat with their wings those that linger, force their tender chicks

to fly, so that they may become such as their dutiful mother might take pride in. You, though, whom both nature has raised tall and whom love of repute has made bold, strive to leave behind such sons as it is known your own fathers had in you.

This letter—technically, marching orders for a military campaign—evidently presumes the availability of people capable of putting the content into words that Gothic warriors could understand. That will normally have been done in the Gothic language. Embellishments that had nothing to do with the subject, such as the comparison of the Gothic leaders to hawks, which derives from Cassiodorus' fondness for examples from the animal kingdom, may have been dropped in the process. The letter does not, however, contain all the information that the addressees needed to execute the command that they were to march on June 24, 508, such as the route they were supposed to take and the destination they were supposed to reach. This information was transmitted by other means, in the form of written rosters and itineraries or oral instructions. Letters to Gothic addressees thus often represent but one aspect of a communications process that had to be multimedial and also often bilingual but which is no longer tangible in all its aspects for us.

We normally cannot precisely determine Cassiodorus' share in the intellectual content of a royal letter. Despite that, it is appropriate to emphasize the basic fact that Theoderic and his successors decided to continue the style of communication between ruler and subjects that the Western Roman emperors had cultivated and which accorded with the cultural self-conception of Roman elites. The fact that a man like Cassiodorus was commissioned repeatedly, for years at a time, to draft royal pronouncements not only attests to the respect and confidence that he enjoyed at court, but also reflects a political decision: to rule Italy in a way that enabled the traditional elite to collaborate with the new lords of the land.

—————————◆•◆—————————

WHO WERE THE OSTROGOTHS?

1. GERMANS, GERMANI, AND GOTHS: TRADITIONAL INTERPRETATIONS

Let's take up the thought once more: that which has left no traces behind has been irretrievably lost. The remains of the past become sources of historical information, however, only when we ask them questions. What questions we ask depends on what we feel is significant. In that sense, it is fair to say that we can understand what once existed only by relating it to the present because it is only with respect to the present that we can determine what is or is not significant. Historical research therefore is shaped by cultural conditions that are subject to change. The intellectual resources we marshal to answer historical questions are likewise not the same everywhere and at every time. In order to comprehend and depict the past, we need to interpret actions and construe contexts by conjecturing about intentions and causes, relying on concepts of meaning and causal models. Historiographical concepts and models therefore are closely linked to cultural imprints and needs, as well as to material interests and political options. It is impossible to write history without attributing meaning to events. Historiography thus provides an orientation for one's actions and evaluates political power and social inequality. In the postmodern age, as the diversity of cultural standards and norms is greater and their change more rapid than ever before, it is not especially hard for those striving for the advancement of knowledge in their own generation to recognize how contingent on the times the questions and concepts of earlier generations were.

We have to recall these commonplaces particularly in the case of Theoderic and the Goths because this subject has long been a major factor in the national self-conception of the German people and has at times become highly politicized.

In Germany, Theoderic was regarded as belonging to German history until well into the twentieth century. The Gothic ruler was considered a Germanic *Volkskönig* ("king of the people") who founded a short-lived but glorious kingdom in Italy. This idea can still be found outside academia. Goths, Germani, Germans — these three terms are treated like synonyms in this view. The idea is based on a syllogism: the Goths were a Germanic people — Germani; the Germani were the first Germans; ergo, the Goths must also have been Germans. In point of fact, scholars routinely called the Goths a "German tribe." As a "German tribe," however, the Goths were part of the German people in its earliest, Germanic stage of development.

An example might suffice: the long-standing standard reference work on Germanic research (and indispensable even today) by Ludwig Schmidt discusses the subject under the title *History of the German Tribes down to the End of the Period of Migrations* (*Geschichte der deutschen Stämme bis zum Ausgang der Völkerwanderung*). Schmidt's "classic" was conceived in Wilhelmine Germany and published before the outbreak of World War I; a revised edition was produced under the Third Reich. The interpretive tradition it represented lived on under the Federal Republic of Germany, as we may infer from the fact that the book was reprinted unaltered in the late 1960s. Outside the historical disciplines, in the media and in the popular imagination, the equation of "German" and "Germanic" persists even today.

In the nineteenth century, as modern historiography was taking shape, this identification was based on the idea that the German people possessed an ancient and indestructible essence that had been formed in time immemorial and survived down to the present day despite all subsequent changes. It was taken for granted that every people — every *Volk* — was a living organism with an individual soul — a *Volksseele* — and a unique collective character (*Volkscharakter*). Terms related to this idea thus pervaded the contemporary historical discourse. Scholars were convinced that in order to find the essential traits of the German *Volk* in their purest form, they needed to get as close as possible to their very origin. They therefore searched for these origins in "Germanic Antiquity" because it was the Germanic people, the Germani, after all, from whom the present-day Germans descended. The Germani were the ancestors of the Germans.[1]

The roots of the idea that a generic Germanic people shared essential traits extend far back into the past, to Classical Antiquity. The Roman senator and historian Tacitus had grouped the inhabitants of the lands beyond the Rhine and Danube, and thus the territories of Central Europe outside the Roman Empire, under the label Germani. In a monograph published in CE 98 under the title *On the Origin and Abode of the Germani* (*De origine et situ Germanorum*) —

today, however, usually called Tacitus' *Germania*—Tacitus described the
Germani as an uncorrupted but primitive people who were distinguished by
shared traits yet also divided into a plethora of tribes. Moreover, he named the
territory in which he situated this people *Germania*.[2]

Tacitus' *Germania* was destined to have a massive influence, but it was felt
only after long delay. The text was hardly read in Late Antiquity and the Middle
Ages. The only manuscript that survived the Middle Ages (at Hersfeld Abbey)
was not rediscovered until the middle of the fifteenth century. Soon afterward,
however, Tacitus became the star witness in a dispute over the value or worthless-
ness of the German nation that was raging between learned friends of Classical
Antiquity—the "humanists"—during the Renaissance and Reformation. With
Tacitus' *Germania*, the pro-German side believed it could prove that qualities
like love of liberty, courage, loyalty, and strict morals had always or at least had
once been intrinsic in the Germans. The reception of the *Germania*, which had
been virtually forgotten for more than a millennium, was a crucial factor in the
broad identification of ancient Germanic peoples with the Germans in the early
modern period. Consequently, the humanist Sebastian Münster (1488–1552), a
professor in Basel since 1529, declared in his *Cosmographia* (1544) that German
history stretched back two thousand years.[3]

In the Age of Revolution and Restoration in Europe, this idea of Germanic-
German continuity coalesced with a romantic conception of a people—a
Volk—to become the defining paradigm of historical research. Whereas the
humanists had relied almost exclusively on the works of Greek and Latin
authors, a new discipline, *Germanische Altertumskunde* (literally, the "study of
German antiquity"), attempted to glimpse the earliest period of Germanic/
German history by interpreting texts in Germanic languages as expressions and
reflections of the "soul of the Germanic people" (*germanische Volksseele*). The
founders of this innovative scholarly approach were Jacob Grimm (1785–1863)
and Karl Müllenhoff (1818–1884). The Germanists investigated legal terms and
customs, personal and place names, fairy tales and heroic sagas. They discovered the *Nibelungenlied*; the *Poetic Edda*, a collection of songs about gods and
heroes put in writing in Iceland in the thirteenth century; and the *Prose Edda*,
a roughly contemporary handbook for court poets (*skalds*) that contains, among
other things, a systematic depiction of Old Norse mythology. These texts, which
were composed in the High Middle Ages, were interpreted as echoes of much
older, pre-Christian conditions and ideas and taken as evidence of the "character of the Germanic people" (*germanischer Volkscharakter*).[4]

Now all peoples who spoke a language that could be classified as Germanic on
account of its morphology and semantics were considered Germani. This new

definition—which remains in use today in the field of linguistics—resulted in a vast expansion of the spatial and chronological range of the term "Germanic." If we regard the so-called First Germanic Consonant Shift (also known as "Grimm's Law") as the starting point of the Germanic languages, we can speak of Germanic peoples from the middle of the first millennium BCE on, a much earlier date than that reported by Greek and Latin authors. More importantly, however, the philological study of the Germanic peoples also included Scandinavia, which lay beyond the horizon of Tacitus and most other ancient authors. Scholars anticipated profound insights into *das Germanentum* ("Germanness") from studying this Scandinavian legacy—especially the two *Eddas* and the *Sagas of Icelanders*—because they were convinced that the "Germanic essence" had survived intact in these regions for a much longer time than on the continent because they were Christianized at a much later date. Everything Christian was considered non-Germanic, if not outright *un*-Germanic.

The science of history and *Germanische Altertumskunde* did not remain the only disciplines that grappled with primitive Germanic/German history. In the early twentieth century, prehistoric archeology joined them as the third and youngest member of the group. The founder of this new field, Gustaf Kossinna (1858–1931), named it "German Prehistory" to distinguish it from Classical Archeology, which was concerned with the remains of Greek and Roman art and culture. Kossinna and his students viewed the archeological investigation of the Germanic peoples as an "eminently national science," as he declared in the title of his oft-reprinted programmatic textbook. Prehistory promised to give direct access to the Germanic early history of the German people. Its proponents wanted to rid themselves of the deceptive pictures that Greco-Roman authors had painted of the Germanic peoples, and they were no longer content to draw uncertain inferences about original conditions from Germanic texts of a much later date. They now intended to investigate what their forebears themselves had left behind: tools and jewelry, graves and cemeteries, dwellings and settlements. Material culture was considered the key to the "Germanic essence."

These scholars operated on the presumption that the territory in which a homogeneous material culture existed corresponded to the settlement area of a specific ethnic group. Hence it was theoretically possible to link a "cultural province" (*Kulturprovinz*), as defined by certain features of its material culture, to a specific "people" (*Volk*) or tribe (*Stamm*) whose name was known from written sources. Depending on the features that were chosen as the "key fossils" (*Leitfossilien*) of these cultural provinces, links could be made that extended far beyond the horizon of ancient authors and even far beyond the linguistic definition of "Germanic." On the one hand, ancient authors attest far more names of peoples than the number of "cultural groups" that archeologists were able to discover, and, vice versa, the boundaries drawn by archeologists often did not correspond with those found in ancient ethnography. On the other hand, though, Germanic prehistory stretches from an archeological perspective back to the third millennium BCE, while Germanic does not appear as a language until two and a half thousand years later. So now there were three different concepts of the Germanic people, each one devised in an entirely different way and impossible to reconcile with the others: that of the ancient authors, that of linguistics, and that of archeology.[5]

The rise of prehistory to an established academic discipline took place at a time when the public discourse about Germanic peoples had long been driven by racial ideas, and racist beliefs resonated ever more strongly. Kossinna argued that the primary purpose and specific achievement of prehistoric archeology was to prove that the unique "cultural level" (*Kulturhöhe*) of the Germans was a "product of ancient Germanic racial excellence" (*Schöpfung altgermanischer Rassentüchtigkeit*). In 1940, Kossinna's student and successor, Hans Reinerth (1900–1990), produced a three-volume *Prehistory of the German Tribes* (*Vorgeschichte der deutschen Stämme*) under the auspices of the Amt Rosenberg, the office responsible for the ideological education of the Nazi Party, headed by Alfred Rosenberg. In the field of German studies, Otto Höfler (1901–1987), an Austrian philologist and ethnologist supported by Heinrich Himmler and his Ahnenerbe ("Ancestral Heritage Organization") set the tone at this time, distilling from the Icelandic myths essential traits of the Germanic peoples that were virtually indistinguishable from the self-image of Nazi organizations like the Schutzstaffel: creative political power, manifesting itself in male secret societies (*Männerbünde*) and in sacred kingship; the "ecstatic enhancement of life" (*rauschhafte Lebenssteigerung*); and the "highest regard for a man capable of defending himself" (*höchste Wertschätzung des wehrhaften Menschen*). Now "racial doctrines" (*Rassenlehren*) also infiltrated historiographical research on the Germanic peoples. The influential ancient historian Wilhelm Weber (1882–1948) actively promoted this pseudo-scientific approach. His pupil Gerhard Vetter investigated *The Ostrogoths and Theoderic* (*Die Ostgoten und Theoderich*) in the light of the "race theory" (*Rassenkunde*) of Nazi ideologue Hans F. K. Günther (1891–1968). He came to the conclusion that "extensive daring and the desire to acquire riches," as well as the "power to persevere," were "fundamental traits of Gothic nature."[6]

"Racial" approaches were never completely accepted by academic Germanic scholars, even during the Third Reich. After its catastrophic demise, they were summarily dropped. The theory of continuity, however—the idea that German history had ancient Germanic roots and that the analysis of medieval institutions therefore had to begin with the *Germania* of Tacitus—persisted much longer in disciplines dedicated to the European Middle Ages, down to the 1980s, when the generation of historians whose intellectual formation had taken place in the 1920s and 1930s finally stepped aside. The groundwork for this break with the hitherto dominant theory had long since been laid.

In 1961, the medievalist Reinhard Wenskus (1916–2002) developed a new, dynamic understanding of the origin of ethnic groups that stripped the continuity theory of its basis. Wenskus showed that common ancestry—that is, actual biological kinship—was not normally a factor in the creation of ethnic identity in premodern times, and indeed it was not even necessary, despite the fact that the members of ethnic groups believed in it or at least claimed to do so. Common ancestry, according to Wenskus, is the intellectual form with which early societies imagined their own genesis and reproduction, but it is not a feasible model if we want to understand how a society really emerged and why it often also soon disappeared again. The *gentes* of the Age of Migrations were heterogeneous and unstable; very often, they were ephemeral entities that arose from the merger of different groups under common leaders before normally quickly falling apart again. The number of ethnic groups that have survived for centuries is relatively small. According to Wenskus, a group became stable and consolidated when it broadly accepted belief in its common ancestry; Wenskus used the term *Stammesbildung* ("tribe building") for this process. The term *Stammesbildung* was soon felt to be old-fashioned, however, and was replaced by the neologism "ethnogenesis." The question that scholars tried to answer, however, remained basically the same: when, how, and why did it come about that a group of people viewed themselves as sharing common ancestors?

The insight that ethnic identity is a social construct has since become generally accepted in the historical disciplines. The idea that the Germanic peoples were a group with common ancestry and unchanging essential traits that split into a plethora of tribes has been abandoned; the theory of Germanic continuity is obsolete. Scholars, moreover, have rightly pointed out that the term "ethnogenesis" is also misleading since a group's description of itself in ethnic terms is a product of continuous interaction and communication and thus results from a process that never comes to an end. Admittedly, this consensus is primarily negative: we believe we know today what a people is *not*. It is still disputed, however, as to how belief in common ancestry comes about and on what it is based. Wenskus himself thought features such as a common language, customs, and conventions were secondary; in his view, what mattered was the existence of groups of people who could pass down traditions suited to generating belief in common ancestry. Wenskus used the term *Traditionskern* ("tradition nucleus") to designate such groups, thinking primarily of noble families that produced kings. This conception of ethnogenesis also underlies the interpretation of the history of the Goths developed by the medievalist Herwig Wolfram (b. 1934) since the 1970s. In his view, Goths were those who attached themselves to a noble family that called itself Gothic, no matter what their followers' origins actually were. Accepting this argument entails identifying the royal families of the Amals and Balts as the bearers of Gothic identity.[7]

In contrast to this interpretation, other scholars argue that Gothic identity was based on a set of traits that were difficult for individuals to acquire or change: shared experiences; a common language; common customs and conventions; and, after conversion to Christianity, the common adherence to a form of Christianity labeled Arianism, persecuted as heretical in the Roman Empire since the reign of Emperor Theodosius I (379–395). According to this interpretation, Gothic identity was rooted in the daily life of broad segments of the population and thus easy for outsiders to perceive. This view does not presuppose that the set of traits on which Gothic identity was based was and remained the same at all times and places; it does, however, imply that Gothic identity was more than allegiance to a Gothic leader.[8]

Controversy continues to rage over the origins and substance of Gothic identity today primarily because ethnicity itself—self-attribution to an ethnic group—is very difficult to detect in our sources. We usually are dealing with descriptions produced by outsiders. Personal testimony, strictly speaking, is completely lacking. Ethnic identity, however, is a protean phenomenon; it can manifest itself in many ways, and every single trait is multivalent. The traits that a given group of people regard as indicators of their identity always depend on their social and cultural context; that is no less true of ethnicity than of any other form of identity. This problem is even more acute for early societies because it is often difficult to determine how widespread the ethnic designations that we find in the sources really were among the peoples in question and how binding they were for their members.

The deconstruction of the old, essentialist concept of a people has demolished many old certainties and toppled whole theoretical edifices. Today, outside of linguistics, the concept of "Germanic" has dropped out of use almost completely because it has been stripped of nearly all the meanings with which it had once been invested. The sole common trait of all Germanic "tribes" that can be identified empirically is the fact that they spoke a language that—by modern linguistic criteria—can be classified as Germanic. This commonality was not lost on Roman observers either: the historian Procopius states that the Goths,

Visigoths, Vandals, and Gepids spoke one and the same language — although he calls it Gothic, not Germanic. There are also good reasons to assume that, prior to the Second Germanic Consonant Shift (which began around 600 but did not conclude until two centuries later), speakers of the Germanic languages could, with some patience, still make themselves understood, as, for instance, is the case today with speakers of Spanish, Italian, and French. Cultural knowledge thus could spread especially quickly in this milieu because it did not need to overcome high linguistic barriers.[9]

This common language, however, determined neither the political behavior nor the self-conception of the people designated Germanic from a linguistic perspective. As far as we can tell, political alliances between peoples and kings that were Germanic in a linguistic sense were never justified on the grounds that the peoples in question were related to one another. Those who spoke a form of Germanic did not believe in common ancestry for that reason; nor did they call themselves by a name that would have reflected their speaking a common language. Even Tacitus' concept of the Germani, which Germanic scholars invoked for centuries, hardly fits the self-conception of the peoples beyond the Rhine and Danube that it was supposed to cover. Tacitus' spatial concept of the Germani did not even carry the day in Greco-Roman ethnography. Even under the Roman Empire, Greek authors still placidly continued to distinguish between Celts along the Rhine and Scythians along the Danube. In Late Antiquity, Tacitus' concept of the Germani became almost completely obsolete and appeared at most only as an antiquarian reminiscence. Byzantine historians like Procopius and Agathias used the term Germani as a name for the Franks. In their eyes, the Goths belonged to the Scythian family of peoples. They also sometimes used the term "Gothic peoples" to indicate the similarity of several peoples who are regarded as Germanic by modern scholars. The word *Germanus* does not occur in the vocabulary of Theoderic's chancellery. Nor did any other Germanic king ever use the word to describe himself.[10]

In spite of all these reservations, however, we cannot expect the Germanic peoples to vanish from the scholarly discourse entirely, not least because the concept has firmly taken root outside of academia. Whoever continues to use it, however, should bear two things in mind: (1) *Germanus* and "Germanic" are categories taken from modern scholarly disciplines, not from the self-conception of the people that they are intended to designate; and (2) which traits define Germani or "Germanness" depends entirely on the scholarly discipline using the term. Linguists understand the term "Germanic" differently from historians and archeologists. In historiography, at any rate, the term "Germanic" creates more confusion than order. Scholars working on the history of the Goths would do well to avoid it.[11]

2. GOTHS, VISIGOTHS, AND OSTROGOTHS: JORDANES, CASSIODORUS, AND GOTHIC HISTORICAL CONSCIOUSNESS

Anyone who explains that Theoderic was a Germanic ruler thus is not really saying much at all because the concept "Germanic" as it is used today tells us nothing about the king's own self-conception or how he was perceived by others. But that does not mean that the question of the ruler's ethnic identity is moot. There is no doubt that Theoderic considered himself one of the Goths over whom he ruled as king. Who were these Goths, then, and why are they also called Ostrogoths?

In the scholarly literature, it is customary to distinguish between Visigoths and Ostrogoths. The Visigoths were the Goths who sacked Rome in 410 under the leadership of King Alaric I and subsequently settled in Aquitania (southwestern France) in 418. Their kings' domain subsequently came to extend over large sections of Gaul and Hispania. When Theoderic became sole ruler in Italy in 493, the "Visigothic" king Alaric II (484–507) ruled Gaul up to the Loire and the Cottian Alps and considerable parts of Spain. After Alaric II suffered a devastating defeat against the Frankish king Clovis in 507, these Goths were largely driven out of Gaul, but they held their ground on the Iberian Peninsula, where a Gothic kingdom existed until the early eighth century. "Ostrogoths," in contrast, is the name modern scholars give the Goths who did not join Alaric I's Italian campaign and were living in the Balkan Peninsula at the peak of the power of Attila the Hun. There is little reason to object to this terminology, provided we are aware that we are dealing with modern constructs. But how did contemporaries describe Gothic identity?[12]

Theoderic himself proclaims through Cassiodorus that he ruled over Goths and Italians in Italy, Gaul, and Hispania, but he left no doubt that he himself was a Goth. The term "Ostrogoth" used by modern scholars, however, was unknown to the royal chancellery. The Goths on the Iberian Peninsula, whom modern scholars normally call Visigoths, are likewise almost always simply called Goths. A particular name for them—*Wisigothae*—appears only in the diplomatic correspondence that Cassiodorus conducted in Theoderic's name before the "Visigothic" king Alaric II lost the Battle of Vouillé and with it his life in 507. Since Theoderic took his place as king soon afterward, the royal chancellery no longer needed to draw a terminological distinction between the Goths in Italy and those on the Iberian Peninsula. They were all considered members of one Gothic people. That did not change until after Theoderic's death (526), when the Goths on the Iberian Peninsula refused to recognize Theoderic's grandson Athalaric, who was elevated as his successor in Ravenna, as their king, and instead put their kingdom in the hands of a different grandson—named

Fig. 4. Signet ring of Alaric II with the inscription
ALARICVS REX GOTHORVM. © Kunsthistorisches
Museum, Vienna.

Amalaric. The two kingdoms now were officially separate, and every Goth had
to decide to which of the two Gothic peoples he henceforth wished to belong.
From that moment on, there were incontrovertibly two and only two Gothic
peoples, but both of them still called themselves "Goths" plain and simple.[13]

Theoderic's chancellery treated all Goths under his rule as members of a
single people, regardless of where they lived. Be that as it may, the notion that
the Goths in Hispania and those in Italy were one people that had originally
constituted a unit and later went separate ways is not a modern construct. This
notion was already common in the sixth century. It appears in the work of the
Byzantine historian Procopius, who distinguishes between Visigoths and Goths,
although he also counts other ethnic groups as "Gothic peoples." The idea also
appears in a curious work that was composed in 551 or 552—after Theoderic's

death but before the death of the last Gothic king in Italy. It is known today by the title *Getica*, although the complete title is *On the Origin and Deeds of the Getae* (*De origine actibusque Getarum*). The author, Jordanes, had served as the secretary of a *magister militum* with a barbarian background but later set out on a new life dedicated to God; whether as a clergyman or layman is unknown. He himself mentions a conversion (*conversio*) that gave his life a new purpose. Jordanes wrote, probably in Constantinople, as a subject of the Byzantine emperor Justinian, but he calls himself a Goth. Like many barbarians who served in the emperor's armies, he had a twofold identity, in this case Gothic-Roman. Jordanes recounts that the Goths had originally lived in Scandinavia before settling on the opposite shore of the Baltic Sea. When they continued southward to the coast of the Black Sea, they split into two groups that initially remained neighbors. One lived in the west and so was called the Vesegothae; the other lived in the east and bore the name Ostrogothae. Both lived for years under the rule of their respective royal families, the Vesegothae under the Balts and the Ostrogothae under the Amals.[4] These two Gothic populations were not permanently separated until the reign of the Roman emperor Valens (364–378). The separation was caused by the advance of the Huns into the Goths' settlement areas between the Don and the Danube; to escape the Huns, the Vesegothae crossed the Danube and, after various trials and tribulations, settled in Gaul and Hispania. This kingdom, ruled by the Balts, however, collapsed with the death of Alaric II in 507. The Ostrogoths, ruled by the Amals, in contrast, fell under the Huns' power and could not free themselves until Attila's death in 453. Theoderic succeeded his father as the ruler of these Goths, who had settled in Pannonia after Attila's death. He marched on Italy with them and founded a kingdom there that he fused with that of the Vesegothae after the death of Alaric II. In Jordanes' account, the Goths under Theoderic's reign thus experienced a kind of reunion after a long separation.

This view of Gothic history is not Jordanes' own invention. For the distinction between Vesegothae and Ostrogothae, he refers to a mysterious historian named Ablabius, who is known to us solely because Jordanes cites him several times. Jordanes, moreover, explains in the preface to the *Getica* that the work was not at all a creative endeavor but rather merely an epitome of a much more detailed *Gothic History* (*Historia Gothorum*) by Cassiodorus, supplemented by material that he had found in other authors. In fact, after his conversion, Jordanes composed two historiographical texts simultaneously in a short time. He started composing a "world history" titled *On the Sum of Time or the Origin and Deeds of the Roman People* (*De summa temporum vel origine actibusque gentis Romanorum*), usually called the *Romana* for short. It is a typical chronicle that views the history of the world from creation to the present as a succession of world empires (*translatio imperii*) that are defined by a ruling people: the Assyrians come first, followed by the Medes, Persians, Ptolemies, and finally the Romans, whose empire will endure until the Last Judgment. The narrative is driven by a pessimistic worldview: if the reader considers the misery of different peoples, Jordanes explains in the preface, he will free himself of love of the world and turn his thoughts to God. At the end of the work, Jordanes lists all the defeats, rebellions, and sacks that the Roman Empire had suffered in the recent past and compares its condition to a tragedy: whoever observes its history will learn how the Roman Empire came into being, how it subjugated the world, and how it gradually lost its power under incompetent leaders.[15]

While Jordanes was working on his *Romana*, however, a friend approached him with a request to make an epitome of the twelve books by Senator—meaning none other than Cassiodorus Senator, the author of the *Variae*—about the origin and deeds of the Goths. Jordanes accordingly stopped working on the *Romana*, borrowed Cassiodorus' *Gothic History* for three days, and composed the *Getica*. In the preface to this work, he says the following about the reason and way it came about:

> Although I wanted to coast along the shore of the calm sea in a little boat and catch tiny fish, as someone said, from the lagoons, you compel me, brother Castalius, to set sail for the deep. And dropping the little project I have in my hands—namely, the *Epitome of the Chronicles*—you urge me to compress in this one little booklet, in my own words, the twelve volumes of Senator *On the Origin and Deeds of the Goths*, proceeding from the past to the present through their generations and kings. Quite an unbending command, as if imposed by one unwilling to recognize the burden of this task. Do you not also see that my feeble breath cannot fill the magnificent trumpet of his speech? And on top of every other burden, there is the fact that I have no access to those books so that I might follow his thought. But, to be honest, I obtained the books to reread over three days as a favor from his steward. I do not recall their wording, but I think I remember the thoughts and events described in full. I added to these some corresponding material from Greek and Latin histories, including the beginning and end and many things in the middle in my own words.[16]

This personal account raises a series of questions that have been answered in the most diverse ways. Is the *Getica* really nothing more than an epitome of Cassiodorus' lost *Gothic History*? Or is Jordanes hiding his light under a bushel in his preface? In other words: how much Cassiodorus is lurking in Jordanes'

Getica? This question is also very important because both works discussed the same topic but in different historical contexts and with different means and for different ends.

When Jordanes wrote the *Getica* (circa 551–552), he did so as a subject of Emperor Justinian who viewed himself as a Goth and regarded the history of the Gothic kingdom in Italy as over. He had no agenda that could have been translated into active policy but rather merely wanted to show that cooperation between Goths and Romans in the past had benefited both sides as long as each respected the other. Cassiodorus, in contrast, was a Roman through and through and wrote his *Gothic History* at the behest of King Theoderic. The work, titled *Historia Gothica* or *Historia Gothorum*, was finished and known to Roman senators by 533 at the latest. Cassiodorus' *Gothic History* was many times more detailed that that of Jordanes, who compressed twelve books into one. Cassiodorus' own statements about the contents of the work indicate that it covered the origin, dwelling places, and customs (*origo, loca, mores*) of the Goths. It is also clear that in recounting the origins and deeds of the Goths, he placed special emphasis on their kings. His work listed seventeen generations of Amal kings down to Theoderic's grandson and successor Athalaric, attributing a specific virtue to each one.[17]

This same genealogy of the Amals appears in Jordanes. Scholars previously believed that it derived from a centuries-old oral tradition, and they used this hypothetical tradition to underpin the theory that the Amals had constituted the *Traditionskern* that had made Gothic ethnogenesis possible. In reality, this genealogy is a product of dynastic propaganda that was fabricated in Theoderic's kingdom to protect his right to sole rule over the Amals against rival claims. Theoderic's own grandfather was already a shadowy figure for contemporaries, and it is highly unlikely that several kings from the Amal family had succeeded one another before Theoderic. The genealogy was artificially extended with the inclusion of people who were not Amals at all and other mythical or even fictitious figures so the Amal line could top the sixteen kings who succeeded one another in Latium prior to the founding of Rome according to Roman tradition. Cassiodorus' *Historia Gothica* thus was a historical work with close ties to Theoderic's court that legitimated the Amals' rule over the Goths by projecting it back into the remote past.[18]

We can still observe this tendency in many passages of Jordanes. He not only repeats the official genealogy of the Amals, but also has only praise for kings from this house, constantly celebrating their valor and courage. Jordanes also refers to a calculation that marks the year 510/11 as the two-thousandth of Gothic history. This year can only have been chosen because that was when Theoderic

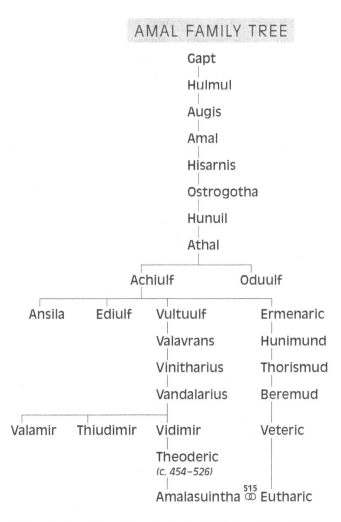

Fig. 5. Jordanes' genealogy of the Amals. © Peter Palm, Berlin.

became king of the Visigoths; year 2,000 of Gothic history was the year in which the Visigoths and Ostrogoths were reunited after long separation. The narrative itself makes precisely this point, as the separate history of the Visigoths ends with the death of Alaric II. Jordanes must have found this narrative in Cassiodorus because, by the time he was writing, the Visigoths and Ostrogoths had long since gone their separate ways again. The theme fits Theoderic's day but not that of his successors.[19]

Proving Theoderic's dynastic legitimacy was not the only narrative goal
Cassiodorus pursued in his *Historia Gothica*. He was much more at pains to
demonstrate the venerable antiquity and high civilization of the Goths. This
narrative objective can be explained by the audience for whom Cassiodorus was
writing: Roman senators. Great antiquity was regarded as valuable per se in
ancient ethnography; the further back in time the history of a people reached,
the better. How, though, could he give the Goths a history that could compete
with that of the Greeks and Romans? The prevailing view was that Rome was
founded in 753 BCE; the Trojan War was dated far earlier, in the twelfth century BCE. The Goths, though, are not mentioned in ancient historiography
until the third century CE.[20]

An easy solution was close at hand. Ancient ethnographers tended to identify
peoples whose names sounded similar, especially if they appeared in roughly
the same territory. Now the historian Herodotus had mentioned a people called
the Getae living on the lower Danube in the fifth century BCE. Hence the
most obvious course of action was to equate the Goths with these Getae.
Cassiodorus was not the first to hit on this identification. We find it in much
earlier authors, as well—in Jerome, Augustine, and Orosius. For Cassiodorus,
though, this identification had the invaluable advantage of enabling him to
extend the history of the Goths to pre-Christian times. He gained an extra millennium of Gothic history in this way since every mention of the Getae in
ancient authors could now be interpreted as testimony about the Goths.[21]

Cassiodorus made ample use of this material. The work begins with a long
section on the origins of the Goths (§ 4–46). This section contains descriptions
of the lands near which the Goths supposedly once lived: Britain, the mysterious island of Scandia in the far north, and a land called Scythia that bordered
the Black Sea. He tells of the Goths' journey from the north to the Black Sea
and of the Gothic sages Zalmoxis, Zeuta, and Dicineus, who introduced the
Goths to philosophy at an early date. That is why they were always better educated than other barbarians and hardly inferior to the Greeks themselves.[22]

A long section on the history of the Goths since their migration to the lower
Danube follows, concluding with the onslaught of the Huns (§ 47–130). This
account begins long before the founding of Rome and confirms the bold thesis
that the history of the Goths stretched back to the middle of the second millennium BCE. According to Jordanes, the Goths battled—always victoriously, of
course—against Egyptian pharaohs, the Amazons, and Greek heroes from the
days before the Trojan War. They defeated Persian kings and the generals of
Alexander the Great. The Romans appear quite late in this account, and Jordanes
emphasizes that the Goths always loyally supported legitimate emperors like

Constantine and Theodosius the Great. This second part concludes with a depiction of the vast Gothic empire that extended from the Crimea to the Danube under a king named Ermanaric before it collapsed in the Hunnic assault.

The third part of the *Gothic History* (§ 131–246) then covers the deeds of the Goths who fled westward from the Huns, ultimately settling in Aquitania. It recounts the struggle against Attila the Hun in detail and concludes with Alaric II, the king of the Goths in Gaul and Hispania — and Theoderic's predecessor there — killed in 507. The fourth and final part (§ 246–314) tells the story of the Goths from whom Theoderic's army descended down to the author's own time, the year 552.

Even if we often cannot determine whether Jordanes himself had personally read an author he cites or only knew him at second hand from Cassiodorus, there is no denying that his depiction of the early history of the Goths is a farrago derived predominantly from works of ancient historiography, ethnography, and geography. The list of authors cited by name stretches from Latin authors of the early Principate like Livy and Tacitus to the Athenian Dexippus, who wrote a work about Rome's wars against the barbarians on the lower Danube (the Scythians) in the late third century CE, to Latin and Greek historians of the recent past like Priscus, Symmachus, and Ablabius. This modus operandi perfectly matches the profile of an author like Cassiodorus, who was very well read and enjoyed showing it off.[23]

But not everything that Jordanes tells us about the Goths came from the works of other ancient authors. On close inspection, elements come into relief that had never previously appeared in the ethnographic tradition. These remnants consist in part of the non-Latinized names of kings, peoples, and places that are completely foreign to other ancient authors. Some appear in catalogue-like lists; others are mentioned in isolation. Some of these kings have stories connected to them; others are merely names in Jordanes. Some also do not fit into the Amal genealogy, although they apparently were very well known. Jordanes traces the ancestors of one such king back four generations.[24]

This pre-ethnographic material also includes Germanic names and terms that Jordanes interprets for the reader, such as *haliurunnae* for "sorceresses" or *anses* for "demigods." He also explains that Scythia was called *Oium* in Gothic and that the Goths lived by rules called *belagines*. The audience of an ethnographic text would likewise not have expected an etymology of the name of the Gepids ("sluggish") or the family name Balt ("bold"). Vice versa, Jordanes attributes venerable antiquity to the term *capillati* (referring to the Goths' military haircut), which was commonly used in Theoderic's kingdom.[25]

Accounts of the Goths' usually victorious battles against other barbarian peoples at places far beyond the horizon of ancient Greco-Roman historiography attest to a specifically Gothic historical consciousness: victory over the Ulmerugi and Vandals in a land called Gothiscandza, the Spali in Scythia, the Gepids with King Fastida, the Heruli of King Alaric, the Vandals under King Vismar, and the Antes under King Boz. These stories always preserve the name of the victorious king and the name of the defeated people, and in some cases also that of their leader, but virtually no other circumstantial information. The historical context remains in the shadows; the chronology is vague or arbitrary. Ermanaric, the "great king" (that is what his name means), in contrast, can be dated quite precisely because the Roman historian Ammianus Marcellinus wrote about him. His name, however, was connected to the painful memory of subjugation by the Huns, which profoundly affected the Goths. The account of the Goths' Scandinavian origin, however, is unprecedented in ancient literature; precisely for that reason, we may recognize it as a Gothic creation.[26]

Where does this pre-ethnographic material come from? Cassiodorus cannot have invented it; it contains too many things that an educated Roman would have found abstruse and irrelevant because they had no place in a Roman worldview. But there was no historiographical tradition in Gothic. The collective memory of Gothic groups was based on oral transmission. Jordanes mentions several times that the Goths sang songs about the deeds of their ancestors; in one passage, he explicitly states that the memory of the victory over the Spali was preserved in Gothic songs. Since the Goths did not preserve the memory of their common past in written texts, their collective memory stretched hardly further back than the memory of their oldest members. Whatever happened more than three generations in the past was forgotten entirely or transformed into heroic songs that lacked a clear chronology.[27]

Thus around the year 500, the only thing to report about Theoderic's grandfather Vandalarius, the "Vandal-fighter," was that he was the son of Vinitharius, the "Wend-fighter." Vinitharius, however, was already a legendary figure: the Hunnic king Balamber who supposedly defeated him never existed. The Goths apparently were quite confident in their information about their own origins. They told stories about the distant past that explained how everything had begun. But a vast gulf lay between this primitive time and the recent past, which among the Ostrogoths hardly extended further back than the generation of Theoderic's father. This gap was filled with stories that were more or less free-floating in time.[28]

The structure of the Goths' historical consciousness is typical for societies with a low degree of literacy and lacking anything resembling historiography. Scholars have determined in the past few decades how a historical consciousness based on oral tradition ("oral history") can satisfy a collective need to give meaning and direction to one's actions. We can also easily see in the case of the Goths that stories of a great migration, brave kings, and glorious victories reinforced the solidarity of warrior bands and validated fundamental norms. The Goths delighted in the praise of their warlike virtues and were more than happy to hear the tale of how their ancestors once crucified Boz, the rebellious king of the Antes, together with his sons and seventy nobles "to terrify the subjugated." Since contemporary witnesses provide the only control for this kind of historical consciousness, it is especially prone to distortion and indeed even the complete loss of the memory of events. In reality, Theoderic's Goths knew little about their remote past; what they thought they knew was often an inextricable tangle of tradition and invention. Events that had taken place before the middle of the fifth century CE had already largely faded from memory; names, places, episodes were passed down without context and were accordingly vulnerable to manipulation. Cassiodorus thus had little difficulty in dating the reign of the Amals to hoary antiquity.[29]

3. THE GOTHS IN SCYTHIA AND THE ROMAN EMPIRE: CONFLICT AND COOPERATION

If the traces of a pre-ethnographic Gothic tradition preserved by Jordanes permit us to infer how the Goths in Theoderic's kingdom viewed their past, the belief that they descended from a common ancestor in the remote past must have been widespread among them. Theoderic's Goths told themselves that their ancestors had once lived in the far north and migrated from there to the shores of the Baltic and then to the Black Sea. From there, they had been driven out by the Huns.

It is another question as to what facts lie behind this story. Archeologists have not found any remains between the Oder and Vistula that clearly point to the immigration of a large population; the so-called Wielbark culture (named after a find-site in northeastern Poland) developed undisturbed by outside influences since the first century BCE. Many archeologists, however, then see clear evidence that the bearers of the Wielbark culture gradually left the territory between the Elbe and Vistula and moved south to Volhynia, Ukraine, and Moldavia, where an archeological culture known as the Chernyakhov culture (named after a find-site near Kiev) appeared in the early third century. ("Sântana de Mureş culture," named after a site in Transylvania, is also sometimes used.) Like the Wielbark culture, the Chernyakhov culture, which comprises over 2,000 find-sites between the Danube and the Dnieper, stands out from its neighbors above all for the coexistence of cremation and inhumation and the absence of weapons in the graves of males. If we combine this finding with the observation that the name "Goth," which was used in various forms (*Gotones* or *Gutones*) for a people in the vicinity of the Vistula in the early imperial period, appears in the third century as the name of warrior bands on the lower Danube, we gain another argument in support of the theory of Gothic migration. This theory is reflected in maps, which use arrows to give the impression they are depicting the migration of whole populations.[30]

It is disputed whether this impression is accurate. In principle, the dissemination of crafting techniques and cultural practices can be explained not only by migration, but also by diffusion. Small groups of people suffice as mediators. Even if the migration of large populations from the Baltic to the Black Sea really occurred, that by no means entails that they viewed themselves as part of one and the same people, the Goths. Archeological finds say nothing about how such populations might have been organized. Written sources tell us merely that the people who lived in the vicinity of the Vistula in the early imperial period received names from others that are closely related to the name of the Goths.

It is therefore difficult to judge what connections there may have been between the Goths of the third century CE and their early imperial namesakes. It recently has been proposed that the Goths coalesced as an ethnic group with a collective consciousness and continuous history only in the third century CE and that their interaction with the Roman Empire played a major part in this process. But this model also remains hypothetical. Proponents of a late ethnogenesis are just as unable to produce conclusive evidence as those who presume some form of continuity with the Goths who dwelt on the Vistula. The only thing that seems certain is that there is no basis for a narrative account of Gothic history prior to the third century. In that sense, this time is and remains prehistory.[31]

The history of the Goths cannot be told until the Romans perceived them as dangerous neighbors and they duly became the subject of contemporary historical works—the original texts of which, however, have been entirely lost. What survives consists merely of meager and often confused notes at second and third hand, the context and chronology of which are often unclear and controversial. In the year 238, one anonymous author of the late fourth century writes, Gothic warriors conquered the city of Histria on the Romanian coast of the Black Sea. He also reports that a Gothic army led by Argaith and Guntheric conducted raids around the year 249. The anonymous author's source appears to be the Greek history of Rome's Scythian Wars by the Athenian Dexippus, who covered these events in detail.

We are also indebted to Dexippus for our relatively good information about Gothic raids under Emperor Decius (249–251).[32] According to his account, a multiethnic coalition under Gothic leadership broke through Rome's frontier defenses on the lower Danube in the year 250, attacking the provinces of Dacia, Moesia Inferior, and Thrace. A band of Gothic warriors advanced into Dobruja and laid siege to Marcianopolis (in northeastern Bulgaria) but then moved on after ransoms had been paid. A second Gothic army, led by a king named Cniva, unsuccessfully attacked Novae (Svishtov) and then marched on Philippopolis (Plovdiv) by way of Nicopolis ad Istrum (Nikyup). On the way there, Cniva's warriors encountered a Roman army at Beroea (Stara Zagora) led by Decius and inflicted a devastating defeat on it. They then successfully stormed Philippopolis and butchered its inhabitants.[33]

From fragments of Dexippus that could be deciphered only recently, we learn that King Cniva distinguished himself in these battles by conducting a nighttime assault on the city walls with about 500 select warriors. From the same source, we learn that the other Gothic army was led by a man named Ostrogotha, who was anything but pleased by Cniva's success; his followers praised Cniva to the heavens, even celebrating him in song, while they accused Ostrogotha himself of weakness and inefficacy. He therefore concluded that he had to justify himself before the Gothic army (*koinon*) and so decided to lead his warriors—allegedly some 50,000 men—in an attack on Decius' troops. The rest of the narrative is lost, but what is clear is that the Gothic warriors spent the winter on Roman soil. When in early 251 they made their way to transport their booty back across the Danube, Decius saw a chance to wipe out the stain of the previous year but suffered a devastating defeat in battle at the Abrittus in Dobruja. A large part of the Roman army was annihilated; the emperor himself vanished without a trace. A more impressive demonstration of Gothic strength could scarcely be imagined.[34]

While these Goths attacked via the land route into Thrace, others took part in raids by sea. These naval campaigns apparently began in the year 255. Attacks on the cities of Pityus (Pizunda) and Trapezus (Trabzon) took place in the years 255 and 256 respectively. In 257, the raiders reached Bithynia and the Propontis, devastating the cities of Chalcedon, Nicomedia, Nicaea, Apamea, and Prusa. After a decade of peace, a second wave followed in the year 268. This time, a large fleet steered for the cities on the west coast of the Black Sea. After assaults on Tomi (Constanța), Marcianopolis, Cyzicus, and Byzantium failed, the Gothic fleet split into three groups. One set its sights on Thessalonica; the second laid waste to Attica. The third group went the farthest: it sailed around the southern coast of Asia Minor as far as Rhodes and Cyprus, attacking several coastal cities in its path. In some places, the Goths penetrated deep into the hinterland and made away with rich booty, both in the precious objects they

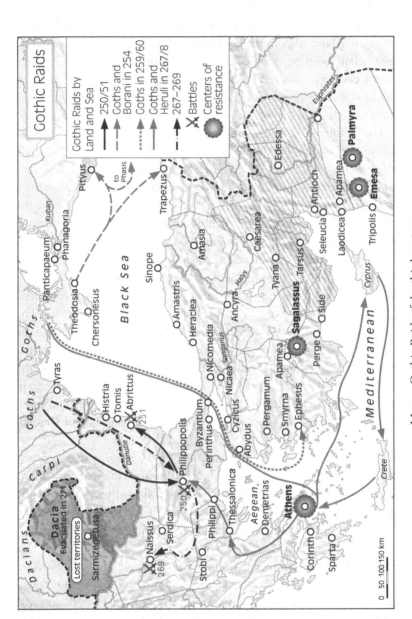

Map 1. Gothic Raids of the third century.

seized and in the people they abducted. Roman countermeasures soon commenced. Emperors Gallienus (253–268) and Claudius II (268–270) inflicted heavy losses on the retreating Goths. Claudius, who won a victory over the Goths at Naissus (Niš in modern Serbia) in 269, became the first Roman emperor to receive the victory epithet of *Gothicus maximus* from the senate, apparently shortly after his death the following year. The Romans now officially distinguished between Germani and Goths; the victory epithet *Germanicus maximus* had long been customary and continued to be conferred.[35]

In 270, the Goths yet again crossed the Danube and pushed into Thrace, capturing the cities of Anchialos (on the Black Sea coast of Bulgaria) and Nicopolis ad Istrum. In the following year, however, Emperor Aurelian (270–275) launched a counteroffensive and defeated the Gothic king Cannabaudes. Aurelian then shifted the frontier with *barbaricum* back to the Danube, evacuating the province of Dacia in modern Transylvania. The far bank of the Danube thereby became the *ripa Gothica* ("Gothic bank") to the Romans. Attacks by sea on targets along the Turkish shore of the Black Sea are mentioned for the last time for 276.[36]

This chronicle of military encounters leaves no doubt that armies in which Gothic leaders and warriors played a major part became a dangerous adversary of the Roman Empire in the latter half of the third century; indeed, Cniva and his army had vanquished an emperor. Goths appear as partners in apparently *ad hoc* multiethnic coalitions for military operations. In addition to the Goths, the Heruli, Carpi, Peucini, Burgundians (?), and Borani ("people of the north"?) are mentioned. A permanent political order that encompassed all Goths did not exist; instead, a variety of leaders competed with one another. Ostrogotha and Cniva both fought against the soldiers of Emperor Decius, but they also were rivals. Some of these leaders are styled *basileus* or *rex* in Greek and Latin sources, indicating a monarchic position that could be translated as "king"; others are not. Their sphere of action was vast and presupposes formidable organizational capabilities. The Goths' maritime raids set out from the Crimea and the Taman Peninsula; these apparently amounted to joint ventures with Greek maritime cities, which put their nautical expertise and infrastructure at the Goths' disposal.[37]

By no means were all Goths enemies of Rome. On the contrary, many Goths entered the emperor's service individually or in groups. In his trilingual *Res Gestae* at the Ka'ba-ye Zartosht at the Naqsh-e Rustam compound (near Persepolis in the Iranian province of Fars), the Persian great king Shapur I includes both Germani and Goths among the auxiliary troops that the Roman emperor Gordian III deployed against him in 238. Since mercenaries usually returned to their homeland, loan words for mercenary service, pay, and the military haircut entered the Gothic language from Latin at an early date.[38]

The Goths figure far more prominently in historical sources for the fourth century. Now the Romans drew a distinction within the overarching ethnic group named the Goths between two peoples called the Tervingi and Greutungi. As early as 291, an orator delivering a panegyric to Emperor Maximian describes the Tervingi as a part of the Goths. The territory of the Tervingi bordered the empire and appears to have extended down to the Dniester. The Greutungi lived to the east, their settlement area stretching to the Don. These names were coined by speakers of a Germanic language, presumably Goths, because they can be derived from Germanic: "Greutungi" means "shore-dwellers," and "Tervingi," perhaps "forest people," though the precise meaning is disputed. The Tervingi also, however, called themselves the Vesi, a name that has nothing to do with the direction west but rather means "the noble ones." Jordanes interprets the ethnic name Ostrogothae, which is first attested in the fourth century, as "eastern Goths"; if that is correct, those who bore it received it from others, perhaps from the Tervingi. It is more probable, however, that Ostrogothae is a name the Greutungi took for themselves because Ostrogotha was the name of a Gothic leader in the middle of the third century, as we have seen. The ethnic name Ostrogothae apparently means "glorious Goths."[39]

The Romans knew very little about the Greutungi since a vast distance separated them from the empire. Still, they had heard of a Greutungian kingdom ruled by a king named Ermanaric. They had more detailed information, however, only about the Tervingi, who were in close contact with the empire. Hence almost all remarks made by ancient authors refer to them, even when they are speaking generally about Goths or Scythians.[40]

During the Tetrarchic Period (293–305), when the Roman Empire was ruled by four emperors acting broadly in harmony on their respective fronts, the lower Danube could be considered pacified; in 297, Gothic auxiliary troops accompanied Emperor Galerius on his campaign against the Persians. After the abdication of Emperors Diocletian and Maximian (305), however, the Tetrarchic system rapidly collapsed. The Tervingi found themselves in the crossfire of the civil wars that ensued. Constantine the Great (306–337) had seized power as a usurper in the extreme northwest of the empire, in Britain. In 312, he expanded his territory to include Italy and North Africa; in 316, he added most of the provinces in the Balkans, which until then had been subject to Licinius, the emperor of the eastern half of the empire. The task of guarding the Danube frontier thus fell to Constantine, and he was more than happy to do it since victories over barbarians reinforced his subjects' acceptance of his rule. When a Gothic king named Rausimod attacked the provinces on the lower Danube, Constantine marched to meet him, although by doing so he infringed on Licinius' territory. In Constantine's second war against Licinius, which ended in total victory in 324, strong bands of Gothic warriors stood on the defeated emperor's side. Constantine took on the victory epithet *Gothicus maximus* and pursued a policy of strength against the Danubian barbarians afterward, too. In 328, he had a stone bridge built over the Danube, linking the city of Oescus (Gigen) with the bridgehead Sucidava on the far bank. In 332, he supported the Sarmatians in a war against the Goths, defeated the latter, and forced the Gothic kings Aoric and Araric to agree to a treaty whereby they acknowledged the suzerainty of the emperor and pledged to provide troops, if needed; in return, they were promised the annual payment of subsidies.[41]

With the treaty of 332, a phase of cooperation between the Tervingi and the empire commenced that would continue largely undisturbed for a generation. The Goths repeatedly provided troops for the Persian War of Emperor Constantius II (337–361) and sold captives to Galatian slave traders. When Emperor Julian launched an offensive against the Persian Empire in 363, Gothic warriors accompanied him on the march to Ctesiphon in modern Iraq.[42]

The importation of Roman goods increased during these decades, and service for the emperor introduced a large amount of Roman coins to the Goths' territory. The cultural influence of Rome also intensified. As early as 325, at the Council of Nicaea (Iznik), over which Constantine the Great presided, a bishop bearing the Greek name Theophilus is recorded as responsible for Gothic territory (*Gothia*). In the 340s, a man named Wulfila worked in this capacity until he was expelled by Gothic potentates, probably in 348. He had been consecrated by Bishop Eusebius of Nicomedia, who was close to the imperial court, baptizing Constantine shortly before the emperor's death in 337.[43]

Soon after Julian's death, military conflict broke out again, unleashed by a Roman civil war. In 366, the Tervingi provided an auxiliary contingent of 3,000 men to Procopius, a relative of Julian's, who had risen up in Constantinople against Emperor Valens. By the time they reached their rendezvous, though, Valens had already defeated the usurper; he then seized on the support of the Tervingi for Procopius as a pretext for war. In 367, the emperor crossed the Danube on a ship-bridge near the fortress of Daphne in Dobruja and penetrated into Gothic territory. But the Goths had fled before his anticipated attack, and he was unable to lure them into open battle. Instead the Romans plundered the land and enslaved the part of the defenseless population that could not flee to safety in time. A flood of the Danube prevented Valens from continuing the offensive in 368, but in 369 a Roman army again crossed the Danube (this time, at Noviodunum ad Istrum) and advanced into Gothic territory. Again, no battle took place: the army of Tervingi, led by Athanaric, retreated before the emperor's advancing troops. Valens had to content himself with thoroughly devastating the Goths' land. The Romans spent the winter of 369–370 back on imperial soil. When the Goths, who were now suffering from famine on account of the devastation, sent envoys to petition for peace, the emperor gladly accepted. The payment of subsidies to the Tervingi ceased, and trade across the border was limited to two places. The treaty nonetheless also benefited the Goths, who were released from the obligation of providing auxiliary troops to the emperor.[44]

The Roman offensives of the years 367 and 369 awakened in the Goths a need to separate themselves more pronouncedly from the empire. Goths who had adopted the emperor's religion now were suspected of sympathizing with the enemy. In 372, Athanaric ordered all Tervingi to sacrifice to their ancestral gods; whoever refused would be forced to do so. The political unity of the Tervingi soon splintered in a civil war, leading to the secession of a group led by Fritigern. The Tervingi thus had already been weakened when the onslaught of the Huns' mounted warriors reached them in 375. The Huns had already shattered the Greutungian kingdom of Ermanaric; Athanaric tried in vain to stop their advance at the Dniester before retreating to a position between the Pruth and the Danube.[45]

The greater part of the Tervingi, however, had lost confidence in Athanaric and turned to new leaders. Under the joint leadership of Alavivus and Fritigern, they occupied the far bank of the Danube and sent envoys to petition the emperor—then residing in faraway Antioch—for permission to settle in the empire. Valens accepted since settling barbarians on imperial soil gave him soldiers, taxpayers, and additional income: subjects of the empire were obligated to provide recruits, and this duty was converted into cash payments if no levy was held. Hence barbarians had often been permitted to settle in the past, indeed sometimes outright encouraged to do so. In 376, however, the situation spun out of control. Many more Goths than expected crossed the Danube—men, women, and children—and the local Roman authorities were unable to disarm them. The immigrants also were not provided with sufficient sustenance; they thus were left to the mercy of unscrupulous businessmen who demanded inflated prices. They began to plunder Roman estates, in the process turning into a marauding army under Fritigern's leadership.[46]

This army rapidly grew as it received reinforcements from several sides: Greutungi under the leadership of Alatheus and Saphrax and the confederation of Farnobius, dominated by Taifal warriors, had crossed the Danube despite

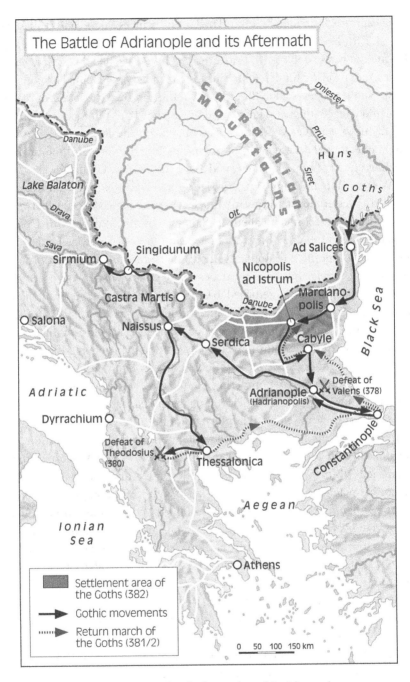

Map 2. The Battle of Adrianople and Its Aftermath.

being expressly forbidden to do so. The Gothic princes Suerid and Colias, who had already been received in the empire and had wintered at Adrianople (Edirne), now also defected to Fritigern. The horde avoided the walled cities of Thrace and instead plundered the villages; the raiders were joined by numerous Goths who had been sold to the Romans in the past by slave traders or recently by their own tribesmen and now seized the chance to regain their freedom.[47]

This news was received with grave concern on the Roman side. Emperor Valens interrupted his war against the Persians, sent the generals Profuturus and Traianus ahead of him to Thrace, and asked his nephew Gratian, then ruler of the Western Roman Empire (367–383) for support. Gratian's general Richomer duly led a Western Roman army to Thrace, where he joined forces with Traianus and Profuturus at a place called Ad Salices ("By the Willows") in Dobruja. Fritigern had entrenched his army in a wagon fort not far away. Despite their numerical inferiority, the Roman generals moved to attack in hope of seizing the enemy's booty, but they were beaten back and had to take refuge in Marcianopolis; Richomer returned to Gaul. Now the Roman generals changed tactics; they tried to contain the Goths in the Haemus Mountains and starve them out. Fritigern responded by inducing Alans and Huns to cross the Danube and join him as allies, promising rich booty. The Roman generals then dropped their plan and sounded the order to retreat; freed of confinement, the barbarians now resumed their plundering campaigns. The warrior band around Farnobius, however, suffered a devastating defeat. Farnobius himself was killed, and his warriors were settled as farmers in northern Italy.[48]

In early 378, the Romans set out to put an end to the enemy invasion once and for all with the combined might of the Eastern and Western Empires. Valens left Antioch, where he had spent the winter, and personally took command. He reached Constantinople in late May 378; in mid-July, he marched toward Adrianople with an army that was at least 30,000 men strong. Gratian first had to beat back an Alamannic invasion of Alsace early in the year, but he too was now leading the field army of the Western Empire eastward at a forced march. Fritigern recognized the danger and decided to offer battle to Valens before the armies could join forces. On August 7, a messenger from Gratian arrived at Valens' headquarters bringing news of the victory over the Alamanni and urgently asking him not to begin the battle against the Goths before the Western Roman army had arrived.

The question of why, after intense debate in his war council, Valens decided to reject this request already preoccupied contemporaries; since Valens' scouts reported that the enemy numbered no more than 10,000 men, he may have seriously underestimated their strength. The desire to avoid sharing the glory of victory may also have played a part, particularly since Gratian could claim victory over the Alamanni for himself alone. The fact that Fritigern had a presbyter declare the next day that he would keep eternal peace if the emperor gave him the province of Thrace, with its cattle and crops, may have confirmed the emperor in this opinion; at any rate, he rejected the offer. Fritigern, of course, had his own reasons for delaying the start of the battle: he was waiting for the return of Alan and Greutungian cavalry, who had kept apart from the main army. They had not yet come back when the Romans set out in the early morning of August 9 toward the Gothic wagon fortress, an eight-hour march away. When they made visual contact, the sun was already at its zenith.

Fritigern sent envoys yet again, and now Valens was suddenly prepared to negotiate—but events spiraled out of control. As a Roman envoy was on his way toward enemy lines, two Roman cavalry units attacked, only to be driven back. Then the Alan and Greutungian cavalry appeared on the battlefield and joined the fight. After that, there was no stopping. Thus began the Battle of Adrianople, which has often been considered an epoch-making event, the beginning of the Age of Migrations—the *Völkerwanderung*. It ended as darkness fell in an utter rout of the Roman troops, who were exhausted by their eight-hour march and struggled under the weight of their armor in the burning summer heat; about two-thirds of them were slaughtered. The emperor himself also lost his life; his body was never found.

At the Battle of Adrianople, a Roman army comprised primarily of infantry was defeated by a multiethnic coalition of warriors dominated by Goths, at the head of which stood Alan and Greutungian cavalry. The Roman historian Ammianus Marcellinus, on whose detailed account (composed around the year 390) all modern reconstructions are based, compares the battle to the defeat that Rome had suffered against Hannibal at Cannae half a millennium before; in the same breath, looking back at barbarian attacks of the past, he expresses the hope that Romans would overcome the invaders this time, too, if only they would remember their old virtues. The historian celebrates the determination of the general Julius, who ordered the summary execution of every Goth to be found in Asia Minor at the time of the battle after he received news of the defeat at Adrianople. Ammianus could not foresee that the Romans would never successfully drive out or subjugate the invaders completely. In fact, after unsuccessfully attempting to storm walled cities, Fritigern's army broke up into its constituent parts. Individual groups pushed westward to the Julian Alps; others crossed the eastern Balkans as far as Macedonia.[49]

Emperor Theodosius I, an experienced general who was elevated to emperor of the Eastern Roman Empire on January 19, 379, scored some initial successes in Thrace. In 380, however, he suffered a defeat and thereafter proved unable to land any decisive blows, although he took many Goths into his service. The fact that Athanaric, who had remained on the far side of the Danube in 376, now sided with the emperor did nothing to change things; the Gothic leader was received in Constantinople on January 11, 381, but died there just two weeks later.[50]

In the end, Theodosius had no choice but to permit Fritigern's Goths, whom he could not defeat, to settle on imperial soil under the terms of a treaty. The Goths now were obligated to provide troops for the emperor, in return for which they were guaranteed annual payments. Most importantly, however, these Goths were recognized as a closed confederation that was permitted to negotiate with the emperor and to appoint its own leaders. This treaty created a new legal status, the holders of which modern scholars have called *foederati* because they were bound to the Roman Empire by treaty (*foedus*). The people in question were barbarians who settled on imperial soil as subjects of the emperor but were not considered Roman. This status was the germ of the Germanic kingdoms that would arise on Roman soil after 382. At the time, of course, this development still lay far in the future, well beyond contemporaries' field of view. Themistius, an orator with close ties to the court, hailed the *foedus* of 382 as the beginning of the integration of Gothic warriors into the world of Roman culture.[51]

4. FARMERS, WARRIORS, AND "JUDGES": THE POLITICAL AND SOCIAL CONSTITUTION OF THE GOTHS IN THE FOURTH CENTURY

Modern scholars often call Athanaric, the man who had led the Tervingi in the 360s and died in Constantinople in 381, a king. Contemporary sources, however, do not use one of the Latin or Greek equivalents of "king" or "emperor" to describe his position: they call him "judge" (*iudex*). At the time, however, "judge" was also the general term for a provincial governor appointed by the emperor. What contemporaries wanted to express with this title was the fact that Athanaric did not hold his position of leadership for life and could not simply pass it down to an heir. An elective monarch with limited powers apparently ruled the Tervingi at this time; in Gothic, he was presumably designated with the word *kindins*. The *kindins* ruled at the behest of a larger group of powerful men who bore the title of *reiks*. This title is related to *rex*, the Latin word for king, but in Gothic it meant a powerful man and so could be applied to a group of persons.[52]

What, though, was life like for those who chose Athanaric to lead them? Archeological finds shed light on their settlement forms and economy. Since the early twentieth century, several hundred cemeteries and settlements have been discovered, some of them only a few kilometers apart; settlement density thus appears to have been quite high. Villages normally were located above rivers or streams; with the exception of the coast of the Black Sea, they were entirely unfortified. Villages usually were laid out in parallel series of houses, collectively covering a surface of 10–35 hectares. Buildings of stone and public spaces were unknown. Houses varied greatly in size and construction but can be assigned to two basic types: the pit house (in German, *Grubenhaus*) and the stable house (*Wohnstallhaus*). Gothic pit houses were sunk in the earth, leaving only a small part projecting aboveground; they were only 5–16 square meters large and thus accommodated only a few people. Stable houses were ten to twenty times larger; the floor was at ground level, and the interior was often divided into living quarters and a stable.

Villagers made their livelihood from agriculture. They planted varieties of grain and kept herds of domesticated animals, large and small, as well as horses; hunting was only marginally important. There also were specialized crafts, especially smithing and pottery. Tools—such as plowshares, sickles, knives— and weapons—shield bosses, lances, arrowheads—were made of iron. Roman coins poured into the land in large quantities but were not used as a means of payment for everyday transactions; rather they were hoarded as precious objects. The volume of trade in areas near the border was large; finds of tableware (*terra sigillata*) and transport containers for wine and olive oil (*amphorae*) indicate that by no means were only luxury goods imported, but so and especially were goods for mass consumption. With wine came Greco-Roman drinking customs: the Latin word for "reclining" (*cubitus*) was used in Gothic to designate a dinner party. Everyday communication took place without writing. The Goths knew of written symbols—so-called runes—but used them only for magical and cultic purposes. A lance point found at Kovel (Ukraine) bears the inscription *tilarids* or "target rider," apparently describing the weapon as a rider rushing toward its target. A gold ring found in Pietroasa (Romania) bears a runic inscription that should probably be interpreted as stating "hereditary property of the Goths, consecrated (and) inviolable."[53]

The close ties between the Goths and the Roman Empire are the reason why a text survives from the late fourth century that gives us a unique glimpse inside a Gothic village: the *Martyrdom of Sabas the Goth* composed after a Gothic Christian named Sabas was martyred on April 12, 372, at the age of thirty-eight. Christians close to him wrote a Greek account of his life and death dedicated

to God. This account is stylized as a letter from the Church of God in Gothic
territory (*Gothia*) to the Church of God in Cappadocia, where Sabas' remains
found their final resting place. It serves to justify why Sabas deserved to be
revered as a martyr by depicting him as courageously confessing his faith in
times of persecution and joyfully dying for it; when Gothic nobles (*megistanes*)
wanted to force the Christians to eat sacrificial meat, the pagan villagers tried to
protect their Christian neighbors from the persecutors with a ruse, serving them
meat that had not been slaughtered in the sacred ritual. Sabas, however, refused
to go along with the plan and instead cried out that whoever ate of that meat
could not be a Christian. Sabas was then driven out of the village but soon
returned and was welcomed back. When yet another order to sacrifice was
issued, the pagan villagers wanted to swear an oath that no Christians lived
among them, but Sabas again thwarted them by confessing Jesus Christ before
the village assembly. A few days later, a certain Atharid, the son of a man of
royal rank (*basilikos*), came to the village with a band of "robbers": they seized
Sabas and a presbyter named Sansalas (who also lived in the village), tortured
them, and finally drowned them in the Buzău, a tributary of the Siret. The
account ends with the notice that Sabas' remains were transported across the
Danube into the Roman Empire and ultimately brought to Cappadocia.[54]

The *Martyrdom of Sabas* casts before our eyes a tightly knit village community that has its own assembly and attempts to protect its Christian members
when Gothic nobles order everyone to eat sacrificial meat. The order to partake
in the sacrifice is not enforced until men sent by these nobles enter the village
from the outside and take action against the objectors. Christians were a small
minority in this village, which is never mentioned by name, but they were
treated as part of the community, even though they were in touch with Christians
in the Roman Empire; the priest Sansalas had fled to Roman territory to escape
persecution and had just returned to the village a few days before his arrest.

From archeology and hagiography emerge the contours of an agrarian society of sedentary farmers and livestock breeders with a village settlement structure. How, then, did this society generate the enormous military potential that
Gothic warrior bands represented as early as the middle of the third century?
That can only be explained if not all Goths were preoccupied with the production of food, objects for everyday use, and tools. There was a warlike nobility
that lived off the dues that their dependents paid. Free men gathered around
these noblemen and were prepared to follow them provided that they were
appropriately hosted and received a share in the booty from campaigns. A
nobleman's power was measured by the number of followers he could muster,
and that number in turn depended on how many followers a nobleman could

entertain and provide with booty. Since the latter point depended crucially on personal prowess, as well as luck, the boundary between nobles and common free men may have been porous. The outcome of a campaign decided whether a nobleman might defend or reinforce his position as a warlord or whether he died or was abandoned by his men. This form of community building was described by Tacitus, but it is by no means peculiarly Germanic as earlier scholars once believed. On the contrary, it has existed in many warlike societies of Europe, Asia, and Africa.[55]

When a majority of the Tervingi asked to be allowed into the empire in 376, there were already many Christians among them. Before the Battle of Adrianople, Fritigern sent a priest to Valens as a negotiator. The majority, however, appear to have adhered to a polytheistic religion about which we know very little. Not even the names of the gods worshipped by the Goths have been transmitted; only a war god, called Tius in Germanic (surviving in the word "Tuesday"), can be inferred with certainty. At any rate, there also were religious specialists ("priests"), ritual forms of predicting the future, and sanctuaries. They also obviously had festivals. The most important sacred act was animal sacrifice with an ensuing meal. It is striking that inhumation and cremation appear side by side in Gothic cemeteries; the cult of the dead thus did not follow a uniform pattern. The graves of men do not contain weapons and contain few burial items of any kind; women, in contrast, were often buried with clothing accessories such as belt buckles, brooches, and jewelry.[56]

Christianity reached the Goths by many paths. The most effective intermediaries were Christians from Asia Minor who were carried off to Gothic territory on the plundering raids of the mid-third century. Wulfila himself, the bishop in Gothic territory mentioned above, was descended from these captives. When Wulfila was expelled from Gothic territory, probably around 348, he found a new home near the Danube on the territory of the city of Nicopolis. There, a community gathered around him that still existed in the sixth century: Jordanes calls them the "lesser Goths" (*Goti minores*). Wulfila took part in a major church council in Constantinople in 360 as the bishop of these Goths living within the empire, but he remained in touch with the Goths living beyond the Danube all his life. Wulfila preached in Gothic, Latin, and Greek and left behind treatises and commentaries in all three languages. His most significant accomplishment was a translation of the Bible into his countrymen's language; parts of this Bible translation, which definitely included the New Testament and probably also the Old, have survived.[57]

The task Wulfila set himself was extraordinarily difficult. Since there had never been any long texts in Gothic, he first had to develop a script that was suitable for this purpose. He thus became the inventor of the Gothic script, which he developed from the Greek alphabet. His goal was to translate the Hebrew and Greek texts that told of the fate of the people of Israel, the appearance of the Messiah in Palestine, and the proclamation of Christ's Good News in the Roman Empire into a language that was used as a means of oral communication by people who lived in completely different social and cultural conditions. Wulfila had to find Gothic words for unfamiliar ideas and foreign institutions. He thus creatively enriched the Gothic language, thereby opening up new means of expression to all people who spoke or understood Gothic; at the same time, he facilitated the spread of the Christian message among people who had no part in the Greek and Latin education of the Roman Empire. Wulfila's Bible translation was adopted by all Germanic-speaking peoples, receiving the status of a canonical text. Soon after the invention of the Gothic script, theological texts began to be composed in Gothic. Profane literature, in contrast, was never produced in Gothic.[58]

When Sabas lost his life during the persecution of 372, there already were established Christian communities with ecclesiastical offices in Gothic territory beyond the Danube. They maintained connections with one another and also with the Roman Empire. At that time, however, Christians still remained a minority. Scholars dispute when and how Christianity became the majority religion of the Tervingi. Some are of the opinion that this transition did not take place until after the Tervingi set foot on imperial soil. It is more probable, however, that a large part of the Tervingi had voluntarily embraced Christianity several years earlier. In the aforementioned civil war between the Tervingi, Fritigern, Athanaric's adversary, had received support from the Romans; in order to confirm and reinforce this relationship, he and his followers adopted Emperor Valens' religion. Valens, however, adhered to a Christian confession that his theological adversaries labeled "Arian" and which modern scholars call "Homoean," because it defines the relationship between God the Father and God the Son by the adjective *homoios* ("equal"). This Homoean confession was the official confession of the Imperial Church at the time and remained so until the end of Valens' reign.[59]

The Tervingian majority must have embraced Christianity within a very short time because they and all other peoples who converted to Christianity in the fifth century adopted the religion in the Homoean form that was condemned as heresy in 381 at the insistence of Emperor Theodosius, in power since 379. Since the Tervingi now clung to a confession that was persecuted in the empire after the emperors turned their backs on it, they also constituted a self-contained Christian religious community that had its own priests and used

Gothic as its cult language. A church in the sociological sense thus came into being that did not make common cause with the bishops whom the emperors recognized and supported but instead bore the mark of a Gothic cult community, even if it understood itself—like all Christian churches—as "catholic" (in the sense of "universal").

Settling on imperial soil unleashed profound transformations among the Goths; that is undeniable. The course and speed of these transformations, however, are difficult to estimate. Christianity apparently spread rapidly among the Tervingi and was transmitted from them to other Gothic groups. What specific consequences adopting Christianity had, however, is beyond our knowledge. It is not unreasonable to assume that Gothic warriors viewed Jesus Christ as a god who gave one victory over the enemy in battle; the same is true of the emperor's army and court. This belief was presumably combined with hope of protection from sickness and death. It is hard to imagine, however, that Gothic warriors knew what to make of the New Testament's commandment to love one's neighbor. Their code of honor corresponded to the Old Testament principle of an eye for an eye, a tooth for a tooth. The selection and interpretation of biblical texts must have taken that into account. There are no sources, however, that give us insight into how the Gospel was preached among the Goths.

Well into the twentieth century scholars believed that the Goths and other Germanic peoples decided in favor of Homoean Christianity because its theology suited the religious worldview of the Germani; the form of Christianity they adopted was thus called "Germanic Arianism." That interpretation was based on two assumptions: first, that Homoean theology emphasized the human nature of Jesus Christ to a degree that almost stripped him of his divinity, and second, that this emphasis accorded with the spiritual needs of "Germanic nature." This hypothesis, which was misused under the Third Reich as a specious justification for a "German Christianity," is untenable not only because "Germanic nature" has long since been exploded as a chimera; it is, moreover, misconceived because, for Homoean theologians, Jesus Christ was nonetheless God, Lord of mankind and creator of the world, despite being subordinated to God the Father. The problem of how the human and divine natures of Jesus could be reconciled does not appear to have preoccupied Homoean theologians either then or later.[60]

It is still undeniable that moving to imperial territory promoted the hierarchization of the Goths. Gothic chiefs could acquire greater resources and build greater followings with the empire's cooperation than before. The distance between leaders and followers grew, and competition between the leaders intensified. The mobilization of large groups of people, moreover, went hand in hand with their militarization; the number and clout of the warriors within each group increased. Most significant, however, whole new ethnic groups and political confederations emerged in the aftermath of the Battle of Adrianople. The Tervingi dissolved; their members followed various new leaders and lost the memory of having once belonged to a single tribe. They were replaced by a multitude of Gothic groups, of which the group that was settled in Thrace under the treaty of 382 was just one. The Greutungi also ceased to exist as an ethnic group after the attack of the Huns; their name disappears in the early fifth century. What survived was an awareness of having once belonged to a larger community that was called the Goths.

4

FROM ATTILA TO THEODERIC: THE OSTROGOTHS IN THE BALKANS

1. GOTHS AND HUNS

The warrior confederation that helped Theoderic conquer Italy from 489 to 493 consisted—so we read in Jordanes—of the eastern branch of the Gothic people. According to his account, the Goths had split into two parts several centuries earlier and, under pressure from the Huns, had also become separated spatially in the 370s: Theoderic's Goths, accordingly, were the descendants of the Goths who settled beyond the Dniester in the fourth century and had since then been ruled by kings from the Amal house. In reality, the genesis of the warrior confederation over which Theoderic became king was much more complicated. The Amal dynasty cannot be traced back farther than the middle of the fifth century; its history begins in the empire of Attila the Hun.

The first credible mention of the Amals relates to the events of the year 447. It was then that Attila, the king of the Huns, invaded the Eastern Roman Empire at the head of a multiethnic army and defeated the imperial field general Arnegisclus at the River Utus (Vit) in the province of Dacia Ripensis (northern Bulgaria). He and his warriors then swept across the Balkan Peninsula, burning and looting, advancing as far as Thermopylae in central Greece, where the Persians and Greeks had done battle a thousand years before. Attila and his followers stormed more than seventy cities on this campaign, winning rich booty. It was an opportune moment: the Eastern Roman Empire faced simultaneous threats on several borders. Emperor Theodosius II (408–450) thus saw no alternative but to satisfy all of Attila's demands. He bound himself by treaty to surrender all Hunnic defectors, to dispense outstanding subsidy payments totaling 6,000 pounds of gold, and to pay an annual subsidy of 2,100 pounds of gold

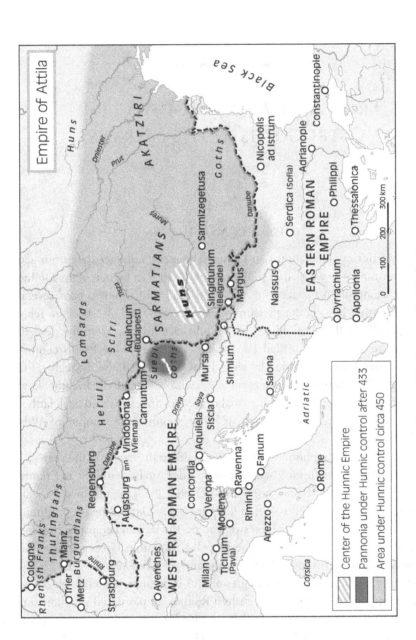

Map 3: The Empire of Attila the Hun.

thereafter. In addition to Attila, two other leaders distinguished themselves on this successful campaign: Ardaric, the king of the Gepids, and Valamir, an uncle of Theoderic the Great who led a band of Gothic warriors at the time. Both men led warlike peoples, were Attila's vassals, and followed him on his campaigns.[1]

When Attila marshaled his warriors against the Western Empire four years later, after the new Eastern Roman emperor Marcian (450–457) canceled the agreed payments in 448, Ardaric's Gepids and Valamir's Goths were again among his followers. Attila's army advanced down the Rhine as far as Cologne, then turned toward the west and passed through Tournai, Amiens, and Paris en route to Orléans. Also on this campaign, numerous cities were taken and plundered along the way. The advance then ground to a halt because in the meantime the imperial general Aëtius had assembled a multiethnic army of his own around a core of Visigoths and Alans. Thus two armies composed of many different peoples met on the Catalaunian Plains in 451, somewhere between Châlons-en-Champagne and Troyes. Alongside the Roman soldiers of the Western Roman emperor Valentinian III (425–455) fought Visigoths under their king, Theoderic I (419–451), and Alans under their king, Sangiban, as well as numerous smaller contingents, including Franks and Burgundians. In Attila's army, Gepids and Goths are mentioned by name in addition to the Huns, but many other peoples were also involved. Jordanes reports that Attila stood at the center of his lines with the boldest of the Huns, while "many different peoples" (*nationes*) whom he had subjugated made up the wings. Among them, the Ostrogothic army led by the brothers Valamir, Thiudimir, and Vidimir was particularly prominent. According to Jordanes, "that most courageous and renowned king" Ardaric was also present with an "innumerable band" of Gepids; he and Valamir were among the Hunnic king's closest confidants and were unshakably loyal. Attila thus had no compunction about sending them into battle against "their kin," the Visigoths. Even two generations later, the Neoplatonist philosopher Damascius still considered Valamir "one of Attila's men."[2]

The Ostrogoths completely justified the Hunnic king's trust in them in battle: although Attila's army was sorely pressed during the hours-long carnage, they bravely stood their ground and one of them, a certain Andag, later boasted that he had struck down the Visigothic king Theoderic with his own hand. News of Theoderic's death spread like wildfire and saved Attila from defeat because the Visigothic army hastened home to ensure the succession of Theoderic's son Thorismund. Even if the "Battle of the Catalaunian Plains" was not decisive, it was subsequently regarded as a Visigothic victory over Attila when Theoderic the Great ruled Italy. In reality, the king of the Huns broke off his campaign and returned with his vassals—including Valamir, Thiudimir, and Vidimir—whence he came, to the vast steppe beyond the Danube, the Great Hungarian Plain.[3]

In Jordanes' account of the Battle of the Catalaunian Plains, the Ostrogoths appear as a mobile warrior band that maintained a relationship of subordination and cooperation with Attila. In 447 and 451, they traversed wide expanses of Europe in the Hunnic king's retinue—from the Aegean to the Atlantic—traveling thousands of kilometers in a short time; they apparently were mounted warriors like the Huns themselves. Jordanes mentions three leaders—the brothers Valamir, Thiudimir, and Vidimir—but he emphasizes that Valamir had seniority and ascribes the title of king to him alone. It is difficult to say what the precise nature of the three brothers' relationship was. Valamir's brothers, at any rate, had followings of their own and enjoyed remarkable autonomy. We can only speculate about the origins of this group of warriors. Be that as it may, there is reason to believe that Valamir did not inherit his position of leadership from his father but rather acquired it only a few years beforehand in a fight for supremacy. It also is unclear where exactly these Goths made their home. Perhaps their families still resided east of the Carpathian Mountains; it is also possible, however, that they had already settled between Lake Balaton and the Sava River, where they chose to stay after Attila's death in 453.

The heart of Attila's empire at the time lay in the Puszta between the Danube and the Carpathian Mountains, a steppe-like grassland that presented favorable conditions for mounted warriors. There Attila gathered his army early in the year, there lay the graves of his family, and there at least one of his "residences" was located. The king was constantly on the move and seldom stayed in one place long; his "court" was often nothing more than a tent city. Attila, however, also had "residences" at fixed locations that he visited relatively often. We can get a quite precise idea of the appearance of such "residences" because an account of an Eastern Roman delegation that visited Attila in 449 happens to survive. The author, the historian Priscus of Panium, was personally present. Even though the place where Priscus met Attila is disputed—some scholars place it farther east, in Greater Wallachia (Muntenia)—his account is very informative: Attila's "residence" was a large village with a single stone building, a bathhouse that one of Attila's confidants had had built by a captured Roman architect:

> And crossing several rivers, we arrived at a very large village in which Attila's house was said to be more prominent than all his others elsewhere. It was assembled of smoothed wooden planks and surrounded by a wooden fence,

not for security but rather to enhance its magnificence. After the king's house, the house of Onegesius was also stately and also had a wooden fence, but unlike Attila's it was not adorned with towers. There was, however, a bath not far from the fence that Onegesius, the most powerful man among the Scythians [that is what Priscus calls the Huns here] had had built with stone imported from Pannonia. The barbarians who live in this part of the world have neither stone nor trees but use imported materials.[4]

After the peace of 448, Attila was at the zenith of his power. He had eliminated his brother Bleda in 445 and absorbed his followers. Since then, his power stretched over the vast majority of all the Hunnic warrior bands in Europe, from Ukraine in the east to Walachia as far as the Little Hungarian Plain in the west. This "empire" had no fixed borders; it extended as far as people obeyed the king. His power was felt most intensely where the king himself was present and waned with growing distance from him. There were not many things people would have put past Attila in the year 449; his plans preoccupied minds deep inside Western Europe: a delegation of Western Romans who met with Priscus' own delegation at Attila's "court" believed that Attila really might march against the Persians on his next campaign, although they also feared an attack on the Western Roman Empire. Two years later, a Frankish petty king approached the king of the Huns seeking help against his brother.[5]

Attila's power was based on the obedience of many different peoples who all had one thing in common: a warlike mentality and way of life. His core followers were the Huns who had advanced from the Eurasian steppes into the lower Danube in the 370s. They were nomads, moving with their herds from pasture to pasture. Their way of life and customs were the opposite of what educated Romans considered culture. In their eyes, the Huns lived like wild animals who had no share in the achievements of civilization and who, moreover, spoke an incomprehensible language. They did not even have a roof over their heads but rather lived on horseback, surviving exclusively on meat and dairy products. They had no laws and gave no mercy. Nomads had been described in this way since the time of Herodotus, who had told of the Scythians, a horse-riding people from beyond the Danube, a millennium earlier. On top of it all, the Huns practiced a religion that Christian theologians regarded as empty superstition at a time when ever more people were converting to Christianity in the Roman Empire.[6]

The arrival of the Huns unleashed terror not only on the inhabitants of Roman cities, but also on Gothic farmers; no doubt, it was enhanced by stereotypes and prejudices, but it was by no means unjustified. The Huns who crossed the Dniester in 370 were not peaceful nomadic shepherds in search of new pastures but rather mounted warriors who had no qualms about seizing by force whatever they needed or desired. Their nomadic, pastoral economy created slim surpluses at best and was always threatened by unfavorable terrain, bad weather, and disease; the Huns were also incapable of producing luxury goods on a large scale. By invading the settlement areas of sedentary farmers, these mounted warriors could obtain, by means of predation and extortion, food and prestige objects that they were unable to produce themselves. The special strength of the Huns' mounted warriors stemmed from the fact that they had mastered both the art of riding and of archery. They attacked by surprise and retreated as suddenly; they thus were hard for their enemies to catch. They shot highly accurate arrows, fletched with three feathers, from horseback; a shot could still be fatal even at a distance of over fifty meters. This power derived from the way their archers' bows were made of elastic wood reinforced with plates of bone at the ends and in the middle—so-called composite or reflex bows.

When companies of Hunnic riders penetrated Gothic territory, they swept over those in their way without an identifiable plan but with great energy, killing and abducting people, driving off their livestock, and plundering their settlements. Several Gothic leaders tried to resist, only to fail. Ermanaric, king of the Greutungi, chose suicide; his successor, Vithimir, fell in battle. At last, a section of the Goths fled across the Danube onto imperial soil, where they set in motion the events that led to the Battle of Adrianople. Others stayed beyond the river and submitted. It was from the Goths who fell under the power of the Huns at that time that the groups we call the Ostrogoths emerged.[7]

The Hunnic warriors who drove the Goths across the Danube and into the Roman Empire in 376 did not constitute a permanent political confederation; it was a coalition of independent groups that quickly disintegrated. It was not until the end of the fourth century that a Hunnic leader appears to have united a large number of such groups under his power for a relatively long time. In the year 400, a certain Uldin appears on the lower Danube as the ruler of the Huns; he held his own for several years but then was defeated in battle in 408 and vanished without a trace. The next attempt to create a major Hunnic power falls in the 420s: at that time, two brothers gathered a large number of Hunnic warrior bands around themselves. One was named Octar (or Optar?), and the other Rua (or Ruga), although he also is sometimes called by the diminutive Ruila or Rugila. Octar died on campaign against the Burgundians—allegedly bursting asunder after a decadent meal. Rua, however, managed to force Emperor Theodosius to pay 350 pounds of gold in annual subsidies. This time, the warrior confederation outlasted its founder's demise. After Ru(g)a died in 434, power passed to the sons of his brother Mundzuk, Attila and Bleda, but it was divided: one part of the warrior bands who had hitherto followed Ru(g)a now answered to Attila, the other to Bleda. The two kings were independent but made common cause against the Roman Empire. This division came to an end in 445, when Attila killed Bleda; he subsequently extended his power over the tribes that had hitherto been under his brother's control. He thereby became the first ruler to unite under his command most, albeit probably not all, of the Hunnic warrior bands.[8]

Now by no means all the warriors who fought for Attila were Huns. The leaders of many other peoples who did not view themselves as Huns had pledged allegiance to Attila and had been confirmed in their positions in return. These peoples included Alans, Sciri, Heruli, Rugi, Gepids, and Goths. Generally speaking, these peoples had not at all joined the Huns voluntarily. In the case of the Goths, it is explicitly attested that they fought the Huns with all their might. There is also evidence that many Goths disliked the Huns, indeed even hated them. Jordanes tells us that according to Gothic tradition, the Huns had been sired by unclean spirits with Gothic sorceresses; these sorceresses bore the Gothic name *haliarunnae*, which was derived from *halja*, "beyond." From a Gothic perspective, then, the Huns were relatives but twisted beings and ultimately creatures of the underworld. This resentment ran deep: in the late 460s, more than a decade after Attila's death, a Roman general warned the Goths, who were then waging war against the emperor together with the Huns, to beware being enslaved by their own allies: if the Goths received land from the emperor, it would benefit the Huns rather than themselves because the Huns did not practice agriculture but instead would treat the Goths as slaves and force them to feed their masters. Moreover, the Goths, he claimed, would be breaking an oath they had sworn generations ago to escape from their alliance with the Huns. This warning proved to be so compelling that the Goths turned their weapons against the Huns in their own ranks. Only after the imperial troops joined battle, killing Goths and Huns indiscriminately, did both groups realize they had been tricked and fled together.[9]

Though Hunnic rule may have been a curse for many, warlords could gain significant advantages by cooperating with Hunnic rulers. That was as much true for the Gepid king Ardaric as it was for Valamir and his brothers Thiudimir and Vidimir. They served as Attila's followers by putting their warriors at his disposal and going to war with him. In return, they were included in Attila's inner circle, received a share of the glory and booty, and were richly rewarded. Attila's successes raised their own standing in the eyes of their followers and put them in a position to obtain prestigious luxury goods and to give gifts of their own. The possession of such prestige objects—especially precious clothing and jewelry—indicated a person's status. Attila's inner circle wore silk robes, carried gilt ceremonial swords, and dressed their horses in tack adorned with gold and gems. And just as Attila secured his followers' loyalty by generously rewarding them, they in turn dedicated a large part of their resources to the same purpose: to satisfy their followers and increase their number as much as possible. Of course, the followers themselves were entitled to their own share of the booty; they were not completely dependent on what their leaders handed down to them. But when the booty was divided, the lion's share went to the leaders. The king of the Huns himself lived humbly: his clothing was simple, his diet frugal. The king probably distributed most of the 6,000 pounds of gold that he had received from Theodosius II according to the treaty of 448 to settle accounts with his circle of followers. The redistribution of these resources served in turn to enable them to preserve and enhance their own positions.[10]

Attila depended on his followers' loyalty to an especially high degree because he did not possess an administrative apparatus that might have operated on his behalf; his "empire" made do without bureaucracy. Attila surrounded himself with an inner circle of retainers who could intercede on his behalf anywhere and at any time—the historian Priscus calls them his *logades*, his "select men." These men made up the functional elite of Attila's empire and were totally dependent on the king's personal trust. Onegesius, mentioned above, was especially close to Attila; he was the king's right hand. There was, however, no permanent division of governing responsibilities independent of individuals, whether in terms of geography or competence: Attila's empire had neither offices nor provinces. It thus likewise lacked an apparatus to collect taxes. Attila did not receive regular taxes in fixed amounts from the Huns or any of his other subjects. His "chancellery" consisted of a handful of Romans who had joined his service; these secretaries maintained Attila's correspondence and served as interpreters in negotiations with the Greek-speaking imperial court in Constantinople. According to Priscus, three languages were spoken at Attila's "court": that of the Huns, that of the Goths, and that of the "westerners" (*Ausonioi*)—that is, Latin. Gothic served as the general lingua franca among Attila's Germanic followers. Greek, in contrast, was seldom used among Attila's followers because it was spoken only by captives from the Greek-speaking part of the Roman Empire; and since most of these captives were ransomed, only a few were forced to stay with Attila.[11]

This personal rule over so heterogeneous a conglomeration of armed followers without the support of an institutional framework was by its very nature precarious. Attila was forced to ensure that new victories continuously bolstered his prestige and provided a constant flow of booty, ransoms, and tribute. This

vital prerequisite, however, soon faltered: in 450, Theodosius II, who had promised to pay Attila 2,100 pounds of gold annually, died. His successor, Marcian,
refused to abide by the treaty any longer. Attila therefore turned to the Western
Roman Empire, but his campaign in Gaul failed to produce the necessary
results; the spoils fell far short of expectations. In 452, the king of the Huns led
his warriors to northern Italy and sacked Aquileia, Milan, and Ticinum. When
his army was decimated by famine and disease, however, he was forced to turn
back before he could break the resistance of the Western Roman emperor;
again, he was unable to satisfy his followers' material interests. When Attila yet
again celebrated a wedding in early 453, his aura of invincibility had been tarnished. On the day after the feast, the king was found dead in his chambers; he
had been asphyxiated in his sleep by a severe nosebleed. No sooner had his
corpse been laid to rest than the struggle for the succession broke out. Jordanes
reports the following about it (Jord. *Get.* 259):

> The sons of Attila, of whom there was virtually an entire people on account
> of the wantonness of his lust, demanded that the peoples be divided equally
> between them, so that lots would be cast for warlike kings with their peoples
> like household slaves. When Ardaric, the king of the Gepids, found out
> about this, outraged that so many peoples were being treated as if they were
> the basest of chattels, he became the first to rebel against the sons of Attila
> and wiped away the disgrace of servitude inflicted on him with his subse
> quent good fortune. He released not only his own people by his secession,
> but also all the others who were equally oppressed because all men eagerly
> take up something that is being dared for the common good.

By a river called the Nedao in Pannonia, which we cannot precisely locate
today, the anti-Hunnic coalition led by Ardaric met the sons of Attila, probably
in 454. By no means did Attila's sons lead only Huns into battle, but also other
peoples who still adhered to them after Attila's death. The battle ended in glorious victory for Ardaric's army; more than 30,000 Huns and their followers, with
their allied peoples, are said to have perished. Ellac, Attila's oldest son, also lost
his life. There were also many Goths among the dead: Valamir and his brothers
fought for, not against, Attila's sons by the Nedao. Cassiodorus and, following
him, Jordanes took great pains to gloss over this embarrassing fact, but they
nonetheless did not dare dispute that the glory of freeing the Goths from the
Hunnic yoke belonged to Ardaric and his Gepids.[12]

After the defeat at the Nedao, the kingdom of the Huns collapsed. The political map of the middle and lower Danube was redrawn. According to Jordanes,
the Gepids settled in Dacia—he probably means the area between the Tisa,

Danube, and the Eastern Carpathians—the Sarmatians, near the city of Castra Martis (northern Bulgaria); the Sciri, Sadagari, and some Alans, in the provinces of Scythia Minor and Moesia Inferior; and the Rugi, in Thrace. They all requested and received permission to settle on Roman soil from the Eastern Roman emperor; even a portion of the Huns who submitted to Roman rule was admitted (in the province of Dacia Ripensis).

After Attila's sons had been defeated at the Nedao, the Ostrogoths also broke with them. Like so many others, Valamir and his brothers sent envoys to Marcian with the request that he direct them to a settlement area. The emperor granted their request by assigning them Pannonia, a territory that they had perhaps already seized in the past. According to Jordanes, their lands were circumscribed by the Danube in the north, by Dalmatia in the south, by Noricum in the west, and by the province of Moesia Superior in the east. This territory stretched from Lake Balaton to the Sava River, encompassing the late Roman provinces of Valeria, Pannonia Secunda, and Savia, and it also contained the old imperial residence of Sirmium in modern Serbia.[13]

A treaty of alliance (*foedus*) was struck, obligating Valamir's Goths to provide troops for the emperor; they thereby acquired the status of what modern scholars call *foederati*. In return, the emperor agreed to pay Valamir 300 pounds of gold annually—a seventh of the amount conceded to Attila in 448. Thiudimir and Vidimir were evidently also included in the treaty since the three brothers subsequently rose up against the emperor together. With this treaty, the history of the Gothic warrior confederation of which Theoderic the Great ultimately became the leader really and truly begins.[14]

Admittedly, this warrior confederation did not include all the Goths who lived along the lower Danube and had been under Hunnic rule. There were several groups of Goths in the Balkans at the time: the so-called lesser Goths (*Gothi minores*), who had gathered around the exiled Gothic bishop Wulfila a century earlier, had settled near the city of Nicopolis ad Istrum, some thirty kilometers south of the Danube. They were regarded as peaceful herders and farmers. Warrior bands under their own leaders also emerged from the disintegration of the empire of the Huns operating in the Thracian Plain south of the Haemus Mountains. One group was led by a *rex Getarum* named Bigelis, about whom we know only that he was killed between 466 and 471. A certain Ullibus, killed in the late 460s for rebelling against the emperor, remains an equally shadowy figure. At roughly the same time, the Goths Anagast and Ostrys held high military command in Thrace, yet also appear to have maintained followings of their own. It was from these groups that a second major Gothic warrior confederation coalesced under unified leadership by the year 473 in a process that remains obscure. Since this group operated in Thrace, it is convenient for us to distinguish between "Pannonian" and "Thracian" Goths, even if both were Ostrogoths as Jordanes understood the term.[15]

2. THE GOTHS IN PANNONIA (454–473)

From the time that Valamir and his brothers struck a treaty with Emperor Marcian, the history of the Ostrogoths can be shaped as a coherent narrative in which the Pannonian Goths played a decisive part. Once Valamir and his brothers had become political players who commanded the Romans' attention, the historical tradition becomes richer. What Jordanes now tells us about the Ostrogoths is in much greater detail. There also are some fragments of Priscus. First and foremost, however, we have at our disposal a contemporary source in Greek for the period from 474 to 480: the historian Malchus of Philadelphia, who paid close attention to relations between the Eastern Roman Empire and the Goths on the Balkan Peninsula. Although Malchus' history survives only in the form of quotations and paraphrases, it gives us insight into the inner makeup of these Gothic groups that is impossible to obtain for the preceding period.[16]

According to Jordanes, the Pannonian Goths lived in three zones: Thiudimir, by Lake Balaton; Vidimir, southeast of him; and Valamir, the farthest to the east. It is impossible to say where and how the Goths settled in this territory, whether they made their homes inside cities, either entirely or in part, or outside them in the countryside. Be that as it may, there were several Roman cities in their settlement area, even a former imperial residence in Sirmium. There also were fortresses of considerable size; the walls of the late Roman fort of Keszthely-Fenékpuszta, located fifteen kilometers south of Lake Balaton, enclosed an area of about fifteen hectares.[17]

Jordanes does not say anything about the nature of their settlements, and archeologists have been helpless to produce material evidence of the Goths' presence in Pannonia. At any rate, the division of territory suggests a high degree of autonomy, even if Valamir enjoyed precedence as king. In fact, Valamir initially had to defend his newly acquired independence alone. When the sons of Attila were hunting down their former followers "like runaway slaves" (*velut fugacia mancipia*), he had to fight off their attack without his brothers' help; he crushed the Huns so decisively with a small force that the survivors took refuge beyond the Dnieper. That may have happened in 455 or 456.[18]

The story of Theoderic's birth was later connected to Valamir's victory over the Huns: Valamir was said to have immediately sent a messenger to his brother Thiudimir; the messenger learned there that a son named Theoderic had been

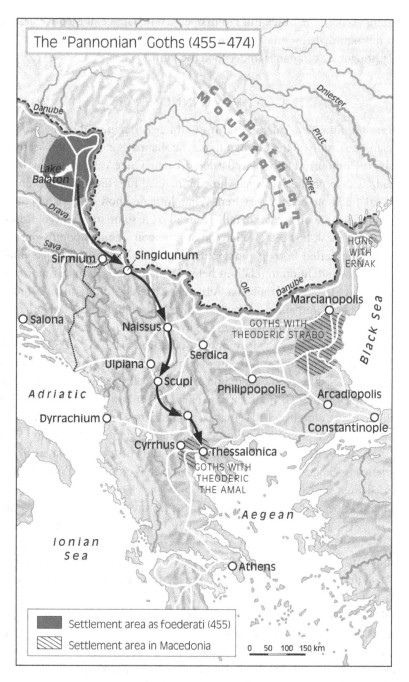

Map 4. The "Pannonian" Goths, 455–474.

born to Thiudimir on that very day. Coincidences make a strong impression but can also be easily constructed when you are dealing with people whose dates of birth are difficult or downright impossible to pinpoint. This case is also probably a construction intended to link Theoderic's birth to a significant event. In all likelihood, the future king was probably born somewhat earlier, in 453 or 454. His mother, Ereleuva, was allegedly not Thiudimir's wife but rather a concubine. If that is true, the low status of Theoderic's mother did not do him any harm. His name itself proves that he was equal in his father's eyes: "Theoderic" means "Ruler of the People" in Gothic. Thiudimir intended great things for his sons; he named his second son Theodemund, "Protector of the People." Naming conventions in the preceding generation did not betray such ambitions: Thiudimir means "Famed among the People," Valamir means "Famed in Battle," and Vidimir means "Famed in the Forest." Any Gothic warrior who thought highly of himself might claim such qualities.[19]

Theoderic's childhood was spent at a time of violent conflicts between non-Roman groups attempting to fill the power vacuum created by the collapse of Attila's empire. The former Roman provinces on the middle Danube were a fiercely contested corridor that neither the Western nor the Eastern Roman Empire could effectively control. Holding one's own here was no easy task. Valamir and his brothers could not count on the faraway Eastern emperor because Marcian's successor, Leo, again canceled the agreed subsidies at the beginning of the 460s. Valamir and his brothers responded by sending envoys to Constantinople, but they were turned away. The Pannonian Goths were even more dismayed when they observed that their kin in Thrace still received their annual payments. Valamir and his brothers had no intention of tolerating this degradation. They led their warriors into the Roman Balkans and plundered and devastated numerous cities and vast tracts of land until Emperor Leo announced through ambassadors that he was prepared to resume paying the subsidies as agreed. Priscus gives the following account of the event:

> When the Scythian Valamir broke the treaty and laid waste to many Roman cities and territories, the Romans sent envoys to him who rebuked him for the rebellion and stipulated that they would pay him 300 pounds [of gold] per year so that he would not ravage the land again. He had said that his people had risen up for war for want of necessities.[20]

Priscus' report shows how the act of plundering Roman cities and territories was perceived in the Eastern Roman Empire: as rebellion against the emperor. It also makes clear, however, how dependent the Goths were on booty and subsidies because they did not produce enough food themselves. Valamir justified his actions with the argument that his people were driven to war by want. Warlords have often resorted to such arguments.

The Pannonian Goths' renewed treaty of alliance with the emperor entailed that they surrender a hostage of royal descent. The then seven-year-old son of Thiudimir was chosen; Valamir himself apparently did not have a son. Thus Theoderic came to the imperial city on the Bosporus as a child; he lived there a full ten years. Constantinople, the permanent residence of the Eastern Roman emperors since 395, was at the time the largest city in the entire Mediterranean where hundreds of thousands of people of the most diverse origins, speaking a wide variety of languages, lived together in close quarters. Greek was usually the language of everyday communication, but Latin remained the language of the imperial administration and the army. Although no surviving sources give us reliable information about Theoderic's youth, the young Goth's experiences here undoubtedly left a lasting impression on him and gave him insight into matters from which his father's generation had been excluded. In Constantinople, Theoderic learned to read and write not only Latin, but also perhaps elementary Greek. He became acquainted with the forms of imperial representation and the modes of communication between emperor and subjects at an early age. He also became familiar with the complicated hierarchy of the court, which manifested itself in a multilevel system of ranks and titles. And he also encountered the prejudices that could be mobilized against any and all those who did not descend from Roman stock and adhered to a faith that the majority of the urban population regarded as heretical.[21]

Lastly, however, a young man in Constantinople who surveyed his surroundings with a sharp eye could also observe at that time that while in theory the emperor was both just and all-powerful, *de facto* he was dependent on his ministers and unscrupulous in his methods. A bitter power struggle was raging in the 460s between Leo and his supreme military commander Aspar. Flavius Ardabur Aspar—his name in full—was the son of a general of Alan background and led a retinue of Gothic followers. Aspar had been a major player in Eastern Roman politics since the 420s; in the 450s, he helped two of his former soldiers ascend the throne: Marcian in 450 and Leo in 457. He was supported in his current power struggle by his son Ardabur, who was made consul in 447 and held the position of *magister militum* of the East from 453 to 466. One contemporary observer reports that he and his father were revered "like emperors" in the territories under their command. Aspar could also count on two more younger sons: Patricius, who was made consul in 459, and Herminericc, who held the office in 465. Aspar, who was striving to attain the imperial purple for his family, seemed to have finally realized his dream when Leo named

Patricius *Caesar* in 470, thereby designating him his successor. A year later, however, the emperor had Aspar, Ardabur, and Patricius treacherously murdered in his palace; Hermineric escaped the massacre only because he was not in Constantinople at the time. An entire family of military men of "barbarian" background that had seemed to be on the cusp of seizing the empire itself was extinguished at a stroke.[22]

Theoderic did not forget this experience. Thirty years later, he warned the bishops of Italy not to create an ominous precedent by citing a remark Aspar had made in the senate of Constantinople, probably before the death of Emperor Marcian (457): when the general was asked whether he himself wanted to be emperor, he said, "I fear a convention in the empire might be established on account of me" (*timeo, ne per me consuetudo in regno nascatur*). Theoderic accordingly highlighted the Alan general as a model of shrewd self-restraint, as the man who willingly declined to become emperor in order to prevent his example from inspiring others and plunging the state into civil war.[23]

The Pannonian Goths' treaty of alliance with the emperor was probably renewed in the year 460 or 461. Since the subsidies granted by the emperor would not suffice, however, the Goths intended to generate additional income from raiding their neighbors. First, they attacked the Sadagari in "inner," western Pannonia. During this campaign, however, the Huns, under the leadership of Dengizich, one of Attila's sons, attacked the city of Bassiana (near Sirmium), which lay in Valamir's territory. His Goths thereupon turned back and inflicted a crushing defeat on Dengizich's Huns; in the Goths' collective memory, this battle marked their final liberation from Hunnic rule. Soon afterward, a Suebian raid that passed through Thiudimir's territory en route to Dalmatia on the Croatian Adriatic coast unleashed a series of military events. As the Suebi, who had stolen the Goths' herds, made their way back, Thiudimir offered battle at Lake Balaton, defeated them, and forced the king, Hunimund, to surrender. His submission was sealed by a special form of adoption: Thiudimir adopted Hunimund as his "son-in-arms" by solemnly conferring on him military arms, binding him to devotion toward his "father." The king of the Suebi, however, was unwilling to play along in this role for long and found allies against the Pannonian Goths in the Sciri. In battle against this Suebian-Scirian coalition, Valamir died a hero's death, pierced by enemy spears. In Theoderic's empire, however, the battle was nonetheless considered a Gothic victory: the story was that the Goths had avenged Valamir's death by slaughtering almost all the Sciri.[24]

After Valamir's death, Thiudimir was elevated to king of all Pannonian Goths. We do not know whether he won over all Valamir's followers or only a part. Unified leadership was desperately needed because the Goths' conflict with the Suebi had escalated into a struggle for their very survival. Hunimund still refused to concede defeat; he subsequently assembled an even greater anti-Gothic coalition. Now Sarmatians, Gepids, Rugi, and others joined Hunimund's Suebi; the Sciri, too, led by Edica and his son Hunwulf, wanted to get back at the Goths and obtained military support from the emperor to do so. Yet again, the place where the two armies met can no longer be identified; the River Bolia is otherwise unknown. The outcome of the battle, though, was decisive and ensured that the Pannonian Goths remained the most significant non-Roman power on the Middle Danube.[25]

In the aftermath, Thiudimir now plagued the Suebi in their settlement area beyond the Danube. When he returned in triumph to Pannonia—potentially in the year 470 or 471—he found his son Theoderic, whom Emperor Leo had sent home bearing rich gifts after he had spent ten years as his hostage. The seventeen-year-old made it immediately clear that he was willing and able to follow in his father's footsteps. He is said to have raised 6,000 followers without his father's knowledge and set out on a campaign against the Sarmatian king Babai, who had seized control of the city of Singidunum not long before. The young prince defeated Babai, killing him with his own hand; he then plundered his lands and people. He brought Singidunum under his own power. With this victory over Babai, Theoderic sent a clear message: even though he had been a hostage in Constantinople for ten years, he could stand his ground in battle, just like his father and uncle. In the eyes of Gothic warriors, that also qualified him to rule over them. Theoderic himself dated the beginning of his reign to the year of his victory over Babai.[26]

As long as the fight against the anti-Gothic coalition lasted, Thiudimir's position of leadership remained undisputed. Soon afterward, however, the brothers must have fallen out because they agreed to leave Pannonia in opposite directions. Jordanes reports the following about this incident:

> As the booty taken from neighboring peoples here and there declined, the Goths began to suffer from a lack of food and clothing; peace began to be burdensome to men to whom war had long provided their sustenance, and all of the Goths approached King Thiudimir and begged him with a great cry to lead the army in whatsoever direction he wished. After summoning his brother and drawing lots, he urged the latter to enter the part of Italy where Glycerius was then ruling as emperor; he himself, being stronger, would go to the stronger kingdom of the east, which he then did.[27]

Why Thiudimir and Vidimir parted ways remains unclear to us. Both men potentially no longer saw any future for themselves in Pannonia. It no longer seemed possible to obtain sufficient sustenance there, and perhaps it never had been. If the Goths practiced agriculture in Pannonia, it did not suffice to guarantee their survival. Vidimir, however, did not find a livelihood in Italy; he had hardly arrived there before he himself perished. His homonymous son, who succeeded him, was persuaded by gifts to depart for Gaul after unsuccessful battles against Glycerius. His warriors merged there with the Visigoths. Thiudimir's Goths meanwhile set out to the southeast and soon reached lands that belonged to the Eastern Roman Empire.[28]

The almost twenty-year history of the Pannonian Goths (454–473) is typical in more ways than one of how non-Roman confederations coalesced and dissolved again in these turbulent times. An original group of three largely autonomous Gothic warrior bands linked by a shared ruler became two when one of the three leaders died. The two remaining bands first operated jointly but then parted ways and became separated from each other by a vast spatial distance. Soon thereafter, one of them lost its independence as it was absorbed by a larger group so that in the end only one independent band remained: Thiudimir's Goths.

The Pannonian Goths in this period appear as a coalition of groups of people who had a high potential for violence and used it with single-minded determination to obtain resources. Military operations took the form of raids that produced booty, plunder, and ransoms and were not always led by the kings personally. It is incidentally reported that the Goths advanced as far as Carinthia in the early 470s, besieged the city of Teurnia, and did not depart until a large amount of clothing that had been collected for the poor was delivered to them. In addition to goods taken by force and extorted services, yearly payments were also important, and the Goths used violence to force the Romans to pay them. Among the Ostrogoths, the ability to employ violence was not only a means of generating income, but it was also a source and measure of social recognition. The Gothic code of honor demanded prowess in battle. That is reflected in their naming conventions: many Ostrogothic personal names allude to skill as a warrior. Every man who aspired to be accepted as a leader had to meet these expectations.[29]

The Pannonian Goths thus were the same kind of social group as the Huns; they could also be designated a "community of violence." Such a social group is characterized by the fact that its genesis and reproduction depend critically on its ability to employ violence. But there were also considerable differences between the Goths and the Huns. Their manner of fighting was different, for one: Gothic mounted warriors did not use the Huns' composite bow but rather carried long lances. Hence the lance was considered the characteristic weapon of the Goths and the arrow that of the Huns. The Goths also battled on foot.

They knew how to handle a sword, but they were hardly experts at archery, let alone users of composite bows.

The supposed "Hunnification" of the Goths is a chimera of modern scholarship. Undoubtedly a number of Goths adopted the fighting style of the mounted nomadic peoples—in German, scholars call this their *Verreiterung*, their "riderization"—but this change took place earlier, on the steppes of southern Russia, and it did not follow the Hunnic model. The Pannonian Goths may have been mobile warriors, but they were not nomads who followed their herds from pasture to pasture. They also kept animals, but they were not fundamentally averse to agriculture like the Huns. They viewed sedentary life as a desirable goal. They settled in places where there were Roman cities; by the year 450, these cities may not have functioned as local administrative units anymore, but they still remained settlement and economic centers. We also may presume that the Goths did not entirely forget the artisanal knowhow of the Chernyakhov culture after they crossed the Danube. There may have been craftsmen among the Pannonian Goths who could forge iron, work leather, and make pottery, even if they evidently could not completely satisfy demand. The Goths had been familiar with Roman institutions for generations; they had established close ties to the Roman world long before the Huns reached Europe. They also were ultimately more able and willing to adapt to ancient urban culture because Christianity had already spread among the Goths before they crossed the Danube, and soon afterward broad segments of the population had converted. At least a majority of Pannonian Goths were Homoean Christians, whereas Attila and the Huns were pagans from a Christian perspective. Christian priests were part of Theoderic's wandering army.[30]

3. GOTH AGAINST GOTH: THE STRUGGLE OF THE TWO THEODERICS (473–484)

A new phase in the history of the Goths we call Pannonian commenced in the year 473. One part of them, led by Vidimir, went west, first to Italy and then to Gaul, where they were subsumed by the Visigoths. The other part, led by Thiudimir, also left Pannonia; they, however, set out to the southeast. The convoys must have been endless: thousands of men, women, and children on wagons, on horseback, on foot. Thiudimir led his people on the main road to Naissus; there they split into two groups. First, Theoderic advanced by way of Ulpiana to Stobi (in modern north Macedonia); both cities were captured. From there, he marched on to Thessaly, sacking and plundering the cities of Heraclea Lyncestis and Larissa on the way. Theoderic's father then marched on

Thessalonica, the largest city in the region, and began to besiege it. Emperor Leo took up negotiations to prevent the city from falling; a treaty was the outcome. Thiudimir's Goths received land in the bountiful Macedonian region of Eordaia, which they had occupied before the end of 473; the cities of Cyrrhus, Pella, Europa, Petina (Pydna), Mediana (Methone), and Bcroca are mentioned. It is not known whether the newcomers were quartered in the cities or on their territory; they will hardly have been received with open arms since they settled there at the natives' expense. Several years later, word that the Goths were coming caused a panic in Thessalonica, the capital of the province of Macedonia Prima. Thiudimir died of an illness in Cyrrhus not long after arriving in Macedonia, but he had already designated Theoderic his heir. It is astonishing that Theoderic indeed succeeded Thiudimir unopposed, even if he had already distinguished himself as a general. At the age of twenty-one, he was now the sole ruler of a confederation of people that counted several thousand warriors — perhaps 10,000 — and their families.[31]

The challenges he faced were immense. Time would tell whether he could satisfy his followers' ambitions by settling permanently in Macedonia. As a matter of fact, the Goths did not put down roots there. Two years later, they had already left Macedonia; in 476, they were several hundred kilometers to the north, near the city of Novae on the bank of the Danube. The exact circumstances are unknown, but a glance at the overall political situation explains why the treaty of 473 swiftly became irrelevant. It was right at this moment that developments unfolding at breathtaking speed made a complicated situation even more explosive.[32]

When Thiudimir led his Goths from Pannonia to Macedonia, he pushed into a territory that belonged to the heartlands of the Eastern Roman Empire. He thereby came into direct competition with the "Thracian" Goths, who had operated for years in the hinterland of Constantinople; they had recently come under unified leadership and were receiving subsidies as *foederati*. They were led by a man named Theoderic, like the son of Thiudimir, but modern scholars usually call him by his sobriquet Strabo. This Theoderic was not one of the Amals, as has been assumed despite Jordanes' explicit evidence to the contrary. His father bore the Latin name Triarius but is otherwise unknown. Strabo was, however, linked by marriage to the powerful general Aspar, who had numerous Goths among his retainers. A sister or aunt of Strabo was Aspar's third wife; this union produced a son with the Gothic name Hermineric (Ermanaric). When Aspar was overthrown and killed in 471, Strabo rebelled against Emperor Leo, marched on Constantinople, was beaten back, and then devastated cities in Thrace. Leo finally relented, conferred the highest military office in the empire on Strabo—that of supreme commander at court (*magister militum praesentalis*)—promised to pay him 2,000 pounds of gold annually—that is, almost as much as to Attila in 448—and nominated him supreme commander (*autokrator*) of the Goths as such. This extremely advantageous treaty for Strabo was struck in the same year that Thiudimir's Goths advanced on Thessalonica from Naissus. Thiudimir was still far removed from such a comfortable position even after settling in Macedonia; he neither held high office nor received a comparable amount of subsidies (if any at all).[33]

It was a whole new ballgame after Emperor Leo died on January 18, 474. His successor was the Isaurian Zeno, a high general who had been one of Aspar's enemies. Zeno initially reigned jointly with his underage son, Leo II, and alone after the latter's death in November 474. He had many enemies at court. In January 475, he fled Constantinople to his Isaurian home to escape a conspiracy hatched by members of the imperial family. From January 475 to August 476, Basiliscus reigned in Constantinople; he was the brother of Verina, Leo's widow, who had personally been involved in the conspiracy. Zeno successfully returned, however, because the generals Illus and Armatus, who had been tasked with fighting the fugitive emperor in Isauria, defected to his side. Basiliscus was deposed after twenty months in power; he was thrown in prison and left there to starve. Thereafter, Zeno was again the sole ruler of the Eastern Roman Empire, but his status in Constantinople remained precarious even afterward.[34]

The power struggle at the imperial court forced the Theoderics to decide whose side they should take. Strabo decided in favor of Basiliscus. This mistake cost him dearly: Zeno deposed Strabo after he returned and now made Theoderic general. He thereby now also received regular payments for his followers. Strabo tried in vain to win back Zeno's favor, but the emperor explained that the treasury lacked the funds to support two armies of Gothic *foederati* in addition to regular Roman troops. This state of affairs dictated the behavior of the two Theoderics over the following years: both tried to win the emperor's recognition for themselves and their people; integration was their preferred means of reinforcing their position of leadership and guaranteeing that their followers were provided for. The emperor, in turn, tried to exploit the competition between the two Gothic warrior confederations for his own purposes, playing their leaders off against one another. He of course also had to take into consideration the conflicts in which he was involved with members of the Roman elite in his immediate vicinity.[35]

At first, Theoderic appeared to emerge from this tug-of-war as the clear winner. He was not only appointed supreme commander at court, but also was adopted by the emperor as his son-in-arms, just as his father Thiudimir had once adopted the king of the Suebi, Hunimund. But the understanding was short-lived. When Strabo managed to win additional followers despite losing his status as *foederatus*, Zeno commissioned Theoderic to smash this dangerous threat and promised him substantial support with regular troops. after leaving Marcianopolis in Thrace, where he was at the time, in order to march against Strabo, Theoderic was joined by 2,000 cavalry and 10,000 infantry at the Haemus Mountains; farther to the south, near Adrianople, 6,000 more cavalry and 20,000 infantry joined him. Theoderic thus set his warriors in motion and marched to the Haemus Mountains, but he did not find the support promised by the emperor. Instead, Strabo and his people were waiting for Theoderic's army at Mount Sondis. They conducted raids and stole each other's herds and horses but did not join battle. Strabo urged Theoderic to end this fight against his kinsmen, and under the pressure of his followers, Theoderic agreed. Malchus reports that men and women stridently urged Theoderic to come to terms with Strabo, or else they would leave him and follow their own best interests. In the end, a meeting between the two Theoderics took place: they agreed not to wage war against each other, and both sent envoys to the emperor. Theoderic demanded land and grain for the winter; Strabo, the restoration of the status he had held under Emperor Leo.[36]

From Zeno's position, the alliance of the two Theoderics was extremely dangerous. He immediately promised Theoderic a sizeable reward of 1,000 pounds of gold and 10,000 pounds of silver and the hand of an emperor's daughter, Anicia Juliana (daughter of Olybrius), in the event that he defeated Strabo. When Theoderic refused, Zeno declared war on him. At the same time, he made peace with Strabo and now reappointed him *magister militum praesentalis*. He also told Strabo that he would pay him subsidies and provide support for an army of 13,000 soldiers.[37]

The years from 478 to 483 were extremely difficult for Theoderic. He had gone from serving as the highest-ranking official in the empire to being declared a public enemy (*hostis publicus*) and lost any and all claims to material support. His ability to feed his followers was now acutely threatened and his authority as their leader in jeopardy. Since he had no success in an attack on the Long Walls of Constantinople, he led his people out of Thrace to Macedonia. He laid waste to Stobi, then proceeded to Heraclea Lyncestis during the year 479. From there, he reached Dyrrachium (Durrës) in the province of Epirus Nova (Albania) on the coast of the Ionian Sea. When the news spread that Theoderic and his Goths were approaching, the population—including the garrison—abandoned the city in flight.[38]

Map 5. The "Pannonian" and "Thracian" Goths, 474–483.

During this time, Theoderic repeatedly conducted negotiations with the emperor. While the king was in Heraclea, the general Adamantius traveled as imperial envoy to meet him; he was supposed to present Theoderic with an offer to settle with his people in the city of Pautalia in the province of Dacia Mediterranea (in southwestern Bulgaria). But the meeting never took place because the king set out for Epirus before Adamantius could reach him. Soon afterward, Theoderic gave the emperor his own proposal: he would come to Thrace with 6,000 warriors in early 480 to annihilate Strabo's Goths if the emperor would reappoint him general and receive him in Constantinople as a Roman citizen. But he was also prepared to move his army to Dalmatia to restore the Western Roman emperor Julius Nepos, who had been driven out of Italy in 475, if the emperor so wished.[39]

These negotiations broke down, however, because, at the same time, the general Sabinianus launched a surprise attack on the baggage train and rear guard of Theoderic's army. Theoderic's brother and mother narrowly escaped, but some 2,000 wagons and more than 5,000 of his people fell into Roman hands. Malchus describes the episode as follows:

> Someone told Sabinianus that the barbarians were overconfidently making a leisurely descent from Candavia, and so were their baggage-carriers, most of their wagons, and the rear guard, where Theodemund, Theoderic's brother, and their mother were, and that there was a good chance they might capture most of them. He drew up his cavalry with himself and sent a large number of infantry on a roundabout way through the mountains, telling them in advance when and where they should appear. . . . He attacked them at dawn as they were already under way. When Theodemund and his mother saw the attack, they quickly broke away and fled to the plain. And they immediately destroyed the bridge they crossed (it spanned a deep gorge over which the road ran); that made it impossible for those who had descended to the plain to pursue them, but it also made it impossible for their own people to escape, so in desperation they advanced to join battle with the cavalry despite their small number. When the infantry appeared overhead, however, as planned, they turned and fled. And some rushed at the cavalry; others dashed at the infantry. And Sabinianus captured their wagons, of which there were 2,000, more than 5,000 prisoners, and a large amount of booty. After burning some of the wagons on the mountain because they would have been too hard to drag over such steep cliffs, he marched back to Lychnidus.[40]

The loss of his baggage train was a heavy blow for Theoderic; with it, his warriors lost most of their possessions and many family members. The fact that Theoderic was nonetheless able to remain king is a testament not only to his people's high degree of loyalty, but is also a result of the fact that no concentrated effort was made against him. Emperor Zeno may have taken up the war against Theoderic again, but he soon had to turn his attention to other tasks because he had to defend himself yet again against a usurper. This time, Marcian, a son of Emperor Anthemius, attempted to seize the throne. He assembled troops in the middle of Constantinople in late 479 and led them in an attack on the imperial palace. Although the revolt quickly collapsed, it weakened Zeno's position in the capital. Most importantly, however, it caused Zeno to break with Strabo for good since the latter had taken sides with Marcian. Although Strabo came too late to support Marcian against Zeno, he had to be persuaded with pleas and gifts to withdraw his warriors from the walls of Constantinople. The emperor responded by dismissing him as general and replaced him with an Isaurian he considered to be more trustworthy, Illus' brother Trocundes. Zeno's attempt to play Theoderic and Strabo off against one another had utterly failed; the emperor had now made enemies of both Gothic leaders.[41]

The political situation in the years 480–482 can only be described as chaotic. Theoderic's Goths operated in the southwestern Balkans; in 482, they devastated Macedonia and Thessaly again and plundered the provincial capital of Larissa. Strabo attacked Constantinople again in 481, apparently planning to cross the Bosporus, but then he turned around and led his people toward Greece. He had just advanced past Philippi in Macedonia when he fell from his horse at a place called Stabula Diomedis ("Diomedes' Stables") and impaled himself on a lance. The successful leader's sudden death unleashed a power struggle among his aspiring successors until Strabo's son Rekitach decided the issue in his favor by murdering his paternal uncles. While this dispute over who would lead still raged, however, this "community of violence" was virtually crippled. Theoderic again gained the upper hand.[42]

How he did so has not been preserved. The emperor, who tried to win Theoderic's allegiance again after Strabo's death, apparently played a key part. In 483, Theoderic was appointed *magister militum praesentalis* for the second time and was also designated consul for the year 484. Thiudimir's son thus received the highest distinction that a subject of the Roman emperor could obtain; on top of that, an equestrian statue of the Gothic king was erected in front of the palace. Last of all, the emperor permitted his new supreme commander to settle his Goths in the provinces of Dacia Ripensis and Moesia Inferior. Zeno needed Theoderic because he was preparing to do battle with his Isaurian *magister militum* Illus, who was in Antioch and commanded the Roman army of Oriens. In the same year that Zeno appointed Theoderic *magister militum*, he had dismissed Illus, but the latter refused to vacate his post.[43]

Theoderic knew how to turn the emperor's difficulties to his own advantage. During the year 484, with the emperor's blessing, he personally murdered Rekitach, his great rival's son, in broad daylight. The vast majority of Rekitach's followers subsequently went over to Theoderic's side. And so, for the first time, the two great Gothic warrior confederations on the lower Danube that had emerged from the collapse of the empire of the Huns were united under a single leader. After 484, Theoderic was by far the most powerful leader of a barbarian military confederation in the territory of the Byzantine emperor. He may have had at least 20,000 warriors under his command and had achieved what his father had always dreamed of: he was *magister militum praesentalis* and Roman consul; his army could lay claim to payment and provisions from the emperor.[44]

4. FAILED INTEGRATION (484–488)

The agreement between Theoderic and Zeno barely lasted a year. The emperor mobilized an army after Illus installed two pretenders one after the other, first Marcian and later Leontius. Zeno summoned Theoderic's Goths for the campaign. The armies met near Antioch (Antakya) in September 484; Illus was defeated and fled with his adherents to the Isaurian mountains, where he held out until 488. Theoderic and his Goths, meanwhile, were dismissed after the battle; the emperor was allegedly no longer sure whether he could trust his supreme general. The Gothic king retreated to Novae, which had served him as a residence of sorts since at least 483. A civilian settlement with municipal status had grown up outside the gates of a legionary camp on the bank of the Danube in the third century; a bishop for the city is attested from the middle of the fifth century. Until the 430s, the camp was provided with food from the Aegean region; the officials that oversaw the supplies (*primipilarii*) erected three bronze statues there in the years 430–432. Later, the civilian population moved inside the walls of the camp. By the end of the fifth century, Novae was a fortified city that had several churches, including a triple-naved basilica measuring forty-six meters long and twenty-four meters wide with an adjoining episcopal residence. An imposing building with rooms grouped around an inner court with two colonnades may have served as Theoderic's "palace."[45]

Theoderic and his people, however, did not settle down here either. The payments to his army apparently were soon stopped or made irregularly. Theoderic was plundering Thrace again already by 486, openly rebelling against the emperor. In the following year, Theoderic and his army marched on Constantinople, laid waste to its suburbs, and cut off an aqueduct that brought drinking water to the city. The Gothic king refused to leave until Zeno surrendered a sister of Theoderic's (who had lived up to that time as a hostage at the court of the empress) and paid a considerable sum of money.[46]

They at last found a way out of the intractable situation. During the year 488, Zeno and Theoderic agreed that the king would march on Italy and eliminate Odoacer, who had ruled there since 476, when he had deposed Emperor Romulus. If Theoderic succeeded, he would rule Italy in lieu of Zeno until the latter could come there himself. For this mission, Theoderic was rewarded with the office of *magister militum* and the rank of *patricius*.[47]

The sources attribute the initiative for this agreement to Theoderic or Zeno, depending on whether they want to derive Theoderic's right to rule from the emperor's mandate or not. After Theoderic's death, this question became extremely important, but in 488 it was immaterial since both sides viewed the agreement as advantageous. The emperor had given up hope of integrating Theoderic and his warriors permanently into the Byzantine Empire; he therefore seized the opportunity to remove an uncontrollable military power far from the walls of Constantinople. He was taking little risk: if Theoderic failed, everything in Italy stayed the same. If he was victorious, one barbarian ruler would simply replace another. The stakes were much higher for Theoderic when he decided to lead his followers to Italy to wage war on Odoacer. The idea was not new to him: he himself had brought it up in the year 479. The fact that he was prepared to act on it nine years later shows that he had come to regard his attempt to secure a place for himself and his people in Emperor Zeno's territory definitively as a failure. Victory over Odoacer offered the prospect of rule over Italy and permanent access to the resources of a rich land. Moreover, the undertaking could be justified as vengeance for his kinsmen whom Odoacer had killed. But Theoderic's followers and their families must also have shared the view that there was nothing left for them in Thrace. They left everything behind to try their luck in a faraway land, where an armed enemy waited for them — whom it would be the first order of business to defeat.[48]

The decision taken by Theoderic's Goths in the year 488 was only reasonable: in the fifteen years since they had left Pannonia, they had lost every tie that once bound them to the soil. While the Goths probably had still practiced agriculture in Pannonia, albeit with inadequate harvests, they had since largely abandoned the life of sedentary farmers and herders. All their efforts to settle permanently, in the provinces of Macedonia Prima, Epirus Nova, and Dacia Ripensis, had failed. Theoderic's host consisted of uprooted people who had covered vast distances with their families and all their belongings, often had no roof over their heads, and not infrequently went hungry. Even after Theoderic united the two largest warrior confederations in the Balkans under his leadership in 484, the economic existence of this community of violence remained precarious. The emperor paid subsidies only irregularly; booty, protection money, and ransoms brought in high income on a short-term basis but never lasted. The predatory economy was an economy of scarcity.

5

THE PATH WEST: THE CONQUEST OF ITALY

1. COLLAPSE, DECAY, OR TRANSFORMATION? THE FALL OF THE ROMAN EMPIRE IN MODERN HISTORIOGRAPHY

On August 23 of the year 476, troops that had sworn allegiance to Emperor Romulus proclaimed an officer with a barbarian background named Odoacer their king. Odoacer then led this army against his commander, Orestes, whom he defeated and killed at Placentia (Piacenza) on August 28. Exactly one week later, on September 4, he entered Ravenna. There, he killed Paulus, Orestes' brother, and declared that Emperor Romulus, Orestes' young son, had been deposed. He subsequently sent Romulus into retirement in Campania with a generous pension. Since Romulus remained the last Roman emperor in Italy, this event has an undeniably high symbolic value. Even today, in many people's minds, Romulus' deposal by Odoacer evokes the fall of a world empire, and the year 476 continues to be regarded as a watershed between epochs. The question of the causes of the "fall of the Roman Empire" has preoccupied European historians since the Renaissance.[1]

Anyone who would like to understand how barbarian kings could come to rule Italy instead of Roman emperors is well advised to cast a glance at the research history because the question of the real significance of the year 476 has been debated for over two hundred years. It still is impossible to avoid the classic work published in six volumes by the English scholar Edward Gibbon (1737–1794), *The History of the Decline and Fall of the Roman Empire* (1776–1788). Gibbon indeed viewed the year 476 as a watershed in the history of the Roman Empire. He regarded the disappearance of the Roman emperor in the West, however, only as one step of a secular process that continued for over a millennium, from the "golden age" of the Antonines (96–192) to the capture of

Constantinople by Sultan Mehmed II in 1453, which ended the empire in the east. As a proponent of the Enlightenment and an admirer of ancient culture, Gibbon interpreted this process as the disintegration of an empire that had secured peace and the rule of law and as cultural regression. Hence he conceived of his subject as the *Decline and Fall of the Roman Empire*, and this formula has had a profound impact on European historical consciousness. The "fall of Rome" continues to serve as the classic example of the collapse of an empire.

Scholars of the nineteenth and twentieth centuries unabashedly described this process as the "decline of the ancient world" when they wanted to indicate that its consequences extended far beyond the political; in this regard, the Marxist Ludo Moritz Hartmann (1865–1924) was no different from the Social Darwinist Otto Seeck (1850–1921). The negative connotations of terms like "decline" and "fall" were hardly questioned, while there was a broad consensus that Greco-Roman antiquity was the intellectual foundation of Europe and the Western world. This conviction translated into the lens through which scholars viewed the transition from Antiquity to the Middle Ages: they investigated the ways in which the "legacy of Antiquity" was transmitted, measuring kingdoms and rulers according to the contribution they made to preserve what they considered to be a legacy of enduring value. Western Europe, the "West," served as the focal point of this perspective; hence scholars turned their attention not to the survival of the Roman Empire in the east but rather to its disappearance in the west, which was equated with the end of Antiquity itself. Even when the concept of "Late Antiquity" emerged between the two world wars, it initially designated only the last phase of Roman history. It was not until the 1960s that "Late Antiquity" became the name of a historical era that extended beyond the borders of the Roman Empire in time and space.[2]

The question of the nature of the transition from Antiquity to the Middle Ages, in contrast, had always been controversial. Did it happen quickly or slowly, continuously or in fits and starts? When did it begin and when did it end? Whereas the Wilhelmine ancient historian Seeck dated the "decline of the ancient world" (as he titled his magnum opus, *Geschichte des Untergangs der antiken Welt*) to the year 476, the Viennese medievalist Alfons Dopsch (1868–1953) took the view, shortly after World War I, that the thread of continuous cultural development in Europe remained unbroken from Caesar to Charlemagne. Shortly before World War II, the Belgian medievalist Henri Pirenne (1862–1935) took the same position, arguing that it was not the Germanic invasions but rather the spread of Islam that destroyed the cultural unity of the Mediterranean world.[3]

The causes of the fall of the Roman Empire were also the subject of controversy: what part did external factors play, and what part did internal factors play?
Did the Roman Empire succumb to an onslaught of outside enemies and foreign peoples—Huns and Germans in the west, Persians and Arabs in the east?
Or did civil war and social unrest cause it to collapse? Did intellectual stagnation
and moral decline rob the empire of its resiliency? Had political despotism and
social evils extinguished all its patriotism and fighting spirit? Still other scholars
believed that soil exhaustion and climate change, population decline, "miscegenation," or the "eradication of the best" were responsible for the decline and fall
of Rome. All these questions were vigorously debated, often in deliberate reference to contemporary events, because the fall of the Western Roman Empire
was viewed as an ominous precedent for Europe and the Western world.[4]

At the same time, however, the subject continually challenged historians to
test new methods, questions, and theoretical models. Fundamental historiographical questions were always up for debate; scholars clashed over the relationship between specific military and political decisions and actions, on the
one hand, and long-term economic, social, and cultural developments on
the other, and they discussed the problem of historical continuity—that is, the
question of whether it is possible to conceive of long historical processes and to
distinguish individual phases in their development and, if so, how. At the same
time, until after the end of World War II, historians routinely adopted metaphors from the fields of biology and medicine (such as sickness, age, and death)
and terms like "decadence" or "disaster."[5]

Talking about the decline and fall of the Roman Empire, as historians of
previous generations did as a matter of course, has become problematic in the
age of multiculturalism. Scholars have not only long since lost their faith in
Classical Antiquity as a model, but they also generally try to avoid passing judgment on cultural phenomena; instead of speaking of "decline and fall," for
some time scholars have preferred to speak of the "transformation" of the
Roman world. The perspective from which scholars view Late Antiquity has
also shifted: today Late Antiquity is usually understood to be a distinct era
between Greco-Roman Antiquity and the European Middle Ages. Its spatial
and chronological boundaries shift dramatically from one scholar to the next,
but they always extend beyond the year 476. According to one view, the Prophet
Muhammad and the Umayyad caliphs are no less a part of Late Antiquity than
Roman emperors like Constantine the Great and Justinian. This school, which
drew key impetus from the oeuvre of the ancient historian Peter Brown (*1935),
defies categorization according to the established and traditional subdisciplines
of ancient history. Brown's and his followers' efforts to reach an understanding

of Late Antiquity free of value judgments goes hand in hand with a focus on cultural developments that took place over the *longue durée*.[6]

This paradigm shift has also affected the assessment of the changes unleashed by the decline of imperial power in the West. Whereas earlier scholars presumed that migrating peoples destroyed the empire, contemporary scholars who emphasize transformation focus instead on phenomena and processes that might be characterized as cooperation, integration, and acculturation. From this perspective, the disappearance of the empire looks like a superficial event that barely touched the underlying economic, social, cultural, and even administrative structures—it was "an imaginative experiment that got a little out of hand," as the Canadian medievalist Walter Goffart (*1934) put it.[7]

Justified objections have meanwhile been raised against this way of seeing things. Two aspects in particular warrant emphasis here. First of all, the replacement of the Roman emperor by barbarian kings was a process that was accompanied by a high amount of violence, as the medievalist Peter Heather (*1960) has stressed. The decline of imperial power was a consequence of constant foreign and civil wars, usurpations, and invasions. Barbarian kingdoms could take root on imperial soil precisely because the Roman Empire proved incapable of controlling large groups of armed immigrants. Certainly, forms of integration and acculturation emerged between natives and newcomers in these new kingdoms, but their specific forms were determined by the fact that the newcomers wielded military power. Hence they normally enjoyed a very strong negotiating position when it came time to distribute power and resources.[8]

Second, the Roman Empire was much more than a mere political idea that underwent manifold metamorphoses and renaissances, from Charlemagne to Moscow as the Third Rome. It was an institution that was intimately linked to political, social, and economic realities. As the British medievalist Chris Wickham (*1950) emphasizes, the emperor constituted the pinnacle of an apparatus that was capable of collecting taxes and dues from almost all his subjects. For premodern conditions, the late Roman state was an astonishingly effective machine for extracting and allocating resources. This redistribution had significant economic and social consequences; it financed the army, the court, and the bureaucracy, thereby creating privileged spaces and classes. The social status of Roman subjects was intimately linked to the duties they performed in the emperor's service; the two highest senatorial ranks—that of *vir spectabilis* and *vir illustris*—could be obtained only either by holding an office that conferred these ranks or by receiving them directly from the emperor as a privilege. This form of elite-building rewarded the expensive and time-consuming acquisition of cultural knowledge with lucrative prizes: anyone who wanted to hold high office in the Roman Empire did not need specialist knowledge but rather education (and good connections). The Later Roman Empire was administered by people who had acquired cultural knowledge from the mastery of classical texts. The way they spoke and wrote proved that they were members of a small elite of educated men, and it distinguished them from the common rabble in city and country. Almost everywhere, the disintegration of the Western Roman Empire into different kingdoms not only simplified and weakened state structures, but also undermined the importance of secular education. At the same time, the spaces in which people communicated and acted shrank. The decline of imperial power thus resulted indirectly in the reduction and, at least for elites, the regionalization of social life.[9]

The importance of the questions of how and why the Western Roman Empire fell thus extends far beyond the history of a political institution. Although there is broad consensus over the events, despite many fuzzy details, the number of answers is legion. Connections and causes continue to be vigorously debated, and no end to the discussion is in sight. At the death of Theodosius the Great in the year 395, the territory ruled by the Roman emperors still stretched to the Rhine in the west and as far as Britain in the north. Eighty-one years later, there was no longer an emperor in the heartland of the Roman Empire. How was that possible? It is especially disputed as to whether internal or external factors were primarily responsible for the empire's collapse. In simple terms: did pressure on the borders become so great that the empire no longer could withstand it? Or had its internal ability to resist declined? Did the empire collapse primarily on account of domestic conflicts that played out in the form of civil war?

Both these basic positions still have advocates, but in reality the range of opinions is much more nuanced. Even those who stress the primacy of internal factors — "internalists" — normally do not deny that forces affecting the empire from the outside also played a major part. Vice versa, those who believe the crisis was triggered by external factors — "externalists" — do not dispute that external pressures unleashed internal conflicts, which in turn influenced the way the Romans responded to threats from outside. The gap between the internalists and externalists is by no means as wide as it may seem in light of their sometimes biting polemic. It also is by no means impossible to bridge because the boundary between the inside and outside of the Roman Empire frequently shifted as imperial structures disintegrated and often no longer could conclusively be identified. There thus is a broad consensus that internal and external factors operated in constant alternation. The question of why the Roman Empire fell revolves around a process that is far too complex for a single cause to explain it satisfactorily, whatever form that cause might take.

2. CRISIS AND RETREAT: THE LAST
EMPERORS IN THE WEST

If we wanted to give a synopsis of the end of the Western Roman Empire, the best place to begin would be the death of Julian the Apostate, who died on campaign against the Persians on June 26, 363. The Roman Empire at the time stretched from Hadrian's Wall in the northwest to the Euphrates in the southeast; on the European continent, the Rhine and Danube were regarded as the borders that separated the empire from *barbaricum*. It stayed that way until the death of Theodosius the Great. Since March 28, 364, however, this empire was ruled almost constantly by several emperors, called "Augusti" (singular: "Augustus"), who were equal in rank. It was on that date that Valentinian I (364–375) appointed his brother Valens co-emperor; thereafter, each of them ruled one half of the empire and also resided there, Valens in the east and Valentinian in the west. From now on, the Eastern and Western Empires were separate entities, each with its own court, its own army, and its own administration. Legislation may have been issued in the name of both emperors, but every law issued by one emperor had to be confirmed by the other before it went into force in his half. The emperors nonetheless viewed each other as colleagues ruling over the Roman Empire, which was conceived as a unit encompassing both parts, and they appointed consuls for the entire Roman Empire. A common currency and common citizenship bound them together economically and socially.[10]

This state of affairs was temporarily suspended in 394, when Theodosius crushed the usurper Eugenius, who had ruled the West since 392 as the puppet of the Frankish *magister militum* Arbogast. This reunification of the two halves of the empire lasted only a few months, however, because Theodosius died on January 19, 395. After his death, the Western and Eastern Roman Empires again went their separate ways because the emperor left behind two sons who already held the rank of Augustus, even if they had not yet ruled in their father's lifetime. The older son, Arcadius (born ca. 377), took the eastern half of the empire; the younger one, Honorius (born in 384), took the western half. The border between them ran, in Africa, near the Greater Syrtis between Tripolitania and Cyrenaica; and in Europe, through the middle of modern Serbia and Montenegro, between the diocese of Illyricum (including Dalmatia and the Pannonian provinces), which belonged to the praetorian prefecture of Italy and hence to the Western Roman Empire, and the praetorian prefecture of Illyricum, which had belonged to the Eastern Roman Empire since 395.[11]

Under the Theodosian dynasty, which ruled in the east until 450 and in the west until 455, the institutional separation of the western half, the *pars occidentalis*, and the eastern half, the *pars orientalis*, became entrenched, even if the idea that they were two halves of one Roman Empire persisted. Each half normally acted independently and pursued its own interests, even at the expense of the other. Of course, the Western Roman Empire soon ceased to be an equal partner, as the western emperors increasingly lost control of the provinces of their half of the empire in the first half of the fifth century. The erosion of the Western Roman Empire began in Gaul and Britannia. Imperial troops evacuated Britannia after 410. Gothic, Vandal, and Alan warriors roamed Gaul since 407; in 418, the Goths settled with their families in Aquitania, while the Vandals and Alans marched on to Hispania. When the Vandals crossed to Morocco in 429 and conquered western North Africa within a decade, the Western Roman emperor lost some of the richest provinces of the Roman Empire. The Western Empire shrank, losing the greater part of its financial resources. The military might that the Western emperors had at their disposal was reduced proportionally because armies cost money.[12]

The imperial monarchy in the west thus developed in a completely different way than it did in the east. A key distinction is the relationship between the emperor and the military. Under Theodosius' sons, both the Eastern and Western Roman Empires transitioned from a mobile monarchy that stayed in close contact with the troops to a distant, sedentary monarchy. This transition was accompanied by a demilitarization of the role of the emperor himself, as command of the armed forces was relinquished to generals. The Eastern Roman emperors hardly left Constantinople for the next two hundred years, while the Western Roman emperors usually resided in Ravenna or Rome after the year 408 and likewise steered clear of military operations. In the west, however, the emperors became ever more dependent on their high-ranking generals, the *magistri militum*, to whom the soldiers showed more loyalty than to their nominal employers. This development began in the Western Empire even prior to 395—the aforementioned *magister militum* Arbogast had driven the underage Emperor Valentinian II (367–392) to his death and replaced him with Eugenius. After Theodosius' death, this trend gained momentum, and for the first time all the troops of the field army were placed under a single supreme commander; the young Western Roman emperor Honorius (395–423) remained in the shadow of his *magister militum* Stilicho until 408, when he at last fell victim to court intrigue. Stilicho potentially managed to combine the office of supreme commander at court (*magister militum praesentalis*)—which until then had entailed command over a single, if particularly powerful, army—with supreme commander over all the field armies (*comitatenses*) of the Western Roman Empire, which is attested for this office from roughly the year 420. This "generalissimo" bore the title of *magister militum et patricius* ("master of soldiers and patrician").[13]

Map 6. The Western Roman Empire in the Year 475.

The Western Roman emperors resisted the dominance of their supreme military commanders, but they were not equal to the fight. Honorius managed to eliminate Stilicho, but he then became no less dependent on his *magister militum* Flavius Constantius, a Roman from Naissus who held the office for eleven years (410–421) and was even formally recognized as co-emperor shortly before his death. Under Valentinian III, who received the status of Augustus at the age of six, real power lay in the hands of Aëtius for more than twenty years, from 433 to 454. Aëtius was a Roman from Durostorum in the province Moesia Inferior on the lower Danube; he held the office of consul no fewer than three times—until the emperor himself personally drew his sword and killed him in the year 454. Valentinian had intended to strike a blow for his freedom with that murder, but he too failed to achieve his goal: he was cut down by one of Aëtius' retainers (*buccellarius*) at a parade on the Campus Martius in Rome in 455, and no one lifted a finger to defend him. Thus ended the Theodosian dynasty in the west, which had met its end in the east five years earlier with the death of Theodosius II. No western emperor subsequently succeeded in transferring power to a descendant. The last emperors of the Western Roman Empire could no longer assert their right to rule because they had descended from emperors. They thus lost an argument that might have motivated their subjects to obey their commands if they proved unable to fulfill the expectations placed on them. The weaker a ruler was, the more important was his subjects' belief in his legitimacy by birth. The successors of Valentinian III desperately needed such legitimacy for precisely that reason. Emperors followed one another in quick succession, none of them ruling longer than five years—Petronius Maximus for only two months (455), Eparchius Avitus for a year (455–456), Majorian for four years (457–461), and likewise Libius Severus (461–465). The most powerful man since 457 was Ricimer, the son of a Suebian father and a Visigothic mother who were both of royal descent; he held the office of supreme commander from 457 to 472 and installed and deposed several emperors during that time. He died of natural causes in 472 after defeating Emperor Anthemius in a civil war.[4]

Another reason why the Western emperors became ever more dependent on their generals was that the soldiers who made up the heart of the field armies had often been socialized outside the empire. They had grown up in an environment in which the forms of communication and interaction practiced by civilian elites and the political traditions of Rome meant very little. They often did not even have Roman citizenship; in the eyes of the civilian elites of the Roman world, they were barbarians, even if they served the emperor. Their world was the military, and they gave their loyalty less to the faraway emperor than to the generals who commanded them. The *magistri militum*, who stood at the top of the military apparatus, thus could mobilize their soldiers against the emperor, if necessary. The emperor could not rule against their will and had to win their assent before appointing high court officials. Of course, not even these genera-lissimos were all-powerful; they could not completely control either the emperor or the court. Even if they sometimes ruled the empire *de facto*, their supremacy lacked a basis in law; *de jure*, all power still emanated from the emperor, who was entitled to depose his officials at any time he pleased. But merciless compe-tition raged at the imperial court, not infrequently playing out with murder and homicide. Since the headquarters of the army was normally physically distant from the court, the *magistri militum* were at a disadvantage in exerting personal influence on the emperor compared to key court officials and courtiers. Only a few, like Stilicho, Flavius Constantius, and Aëtius, could maintain their pre-eminence for several years, and even fewer left office alive.

When Libius Severus died of natural causes on November 14, 465, the impe-rial throne remained vacant for a year and a half. Then, three miles outside Rome on April 12, 467, a man dispatched to the west by Emperor Leo was ele-vated to emperor: Procopius Anthemius. He had arrived in Portus, Rome's port, with an Eastern Roman fleet just a few weeks earlier. Anthemius was a high-ranking member of the Eastern Roman senate and son-in-law of the Eastern emperor Marcian; he had been consul in 455 and had led Eastern troops against the Pannonian Goths as *magister militum*. Soon after his arrival, the wedding of Ricimer and Alypia, Anthemius' daughter, was celebrated with great fanfare; the marriage was intended to bind the *magister militum* especially closely to the new imperial house. At the ceremonies in early 468, the newly appointed con-sul Sidonius Apollinaris gave voice to the hope that Anthemius would free the Western Empire from its most dangerous external threat, the kingdom of the Vandals, with the energetic support of the Eastern Empire. As a matter of fact, even before Anthemius was sent to the west, a joint land and naval operation had been planned. Leo invested vast sums in the undertaking: 65,000 pounds of gold and 700,000 pounds of silver. In early 468, an Eastern Roman army set out westward from Libya on the land route to Tripolitania. At the same time, troops under the command of the *magister militum* Marcellinus drove the Vandals out of Sardinia and secured Sicily. The Eastern Roman fleet, com-manded by Basiliscus, Leo's brother-in-law, was supposed to deliver the main blow, but this plan fell completely apart. The fleet was almost totally annihi-lated fifty miles off Carthage. With that, the entire expedition failed.[15]

Anthemius never recovered from this catastrophic failure. In 470, Ricimer rebelled against his imperial master and father-in-law; he left Rome with 6,000 sol-diers and traveled to northern Italy. Epiphanius, bishop of Ticinum, tried to avert the impending civil war by serving as mediator, but he did not have lasting success.

In the fall of 471, Ricimer marched on Rome, where Anthemius had resided since his elevation; he seized Portus and blocked all access to the city. The siege lasted nine months. The population was starving; after Ricimer elevated the senator Anicius Olybrius to counter-emperor in April 472, the people split into two hostile camps that fought one another. Ricimer's troops finally penetrated into the city itself in July; he allowed them to plunder twelve of its fourteen regions. Anthemius fled to the church of St. Chrysogonus in Trastevere, disguised as a beggar, but he was discovered and beheaded. His assassin, the Burgundian prince Gundobad, was destined to take Ricimer's place not long thereafter; Ricimer survived Anthemius by only twenty days. Anicius Olybrius thereupon conferred the position of *magister militum* on Gundobad. Then Olybrius also died, sixteen days after Ricimer.[16]

No one in this situation could have prevented Gundobad from seizing the purple for himself. He decided, however, to transfer that role to the commander of the imperial bodyguard (*primicerius domesticorum*), Glycerius, who was elevated to emperor on March 3, 473. Soon thereafter, Gundobad laid down his office as *magister militum* and returned to the kingdom of his uncle Chilperic, whom he succeeded in 480. Glycerius held on as emperor for barely a year. His downfall was orchestrated by Julius Nepos, who had served as Emperor Leo's *magister militum Dalmatiae* and was married to a niece of the empress Verina. Nepos sailed with a fleet for Portus, had Glycerius dragged out of the palace on June 19, 474, and consecrated bishop of Salona. He himself was crowned emperor soon afterward. But Nepos' day in the sun was also of short duration: while the emperor resided in Rome, his *magister militum* Orestes rebelled. Nepos fled to Ravenna and traveled from there by ship to Salona, where Glycerius (whom he had deposed) was still serving as bishop. Nepos resided there until he was murdered in 480, in the palace that Emperor Diocletian (284–305) had once built as his residence for retirement.[17]

Orestes, in turn, had just as little interest in becoming emperor as his predecessors Ricimer and Gundobad. He instead had intended the role for his young son Romulus, who was proclaimed emperor in Ravenna on October 31, 475. He thus re-created the arrangement whereby the imperial monarchy and the military leadership were separate. Of course, now these two parts were played by father and son.[18]

3. A BARBARIAN AS RULER OF ITALY: KING ODOACER (476–493)

The soldiers who proclaimed Odoacer their king on August 23, 476, were not Romans. The sources mention Alans, Heruli, and Sciri, as well as "some Gothic peoples." Odoacer forthwith led this army against Orestes, who had supreme command of Romulus' army. Orestes was defeated at Placentia on August 25, captured, and killed. Odoacer then proceeded to Ravenna, where Orestes' brother Paulus had barricaded himself with the child emperor. After Odoacer had also killed Paulus, he ended Romulus' reign, sending him into retirement with a pension of 6,000 gold coins per year. Romulus withdrew "with his relatives" to the villa Castellum Lucullanum near Naples, which the senator Lucullus had built to support his luxurious lifestyle half a millennium before. Romulus appears to have lived there into Theoderic's reign, if he is the homonymous man whose property the king confirmed between 507 and 511. There were no more emperors in Italy after Romulus was deposed, although Julius Nepos—who had fled to Salona—still insisted that he was the rightful ruler of the Western Roman Empire.[19]

A situation like this had occurred many times since the end of the Theodosian dynasty. After Eparchius Avitus was deposed on October 17, 456, it took almost half a year before Majorian was elevated emperor of the Western Roman Empire, and it took another eight months before Majorian received the rank of Augustus, on December 28, 457. The interregnum that began with the death of Libius Severus on November 14, 465, lasted significantly longer. His successor, Anthemius, did not ascend the throne until a year and a half later, on April 12, 467. And four months passed between the death of Anicius Olybrius on November 2, 472, and the accession of Glycerius. Since real power in the meantime lay in the hands of the *magistri militum*, people were used to emperors being abruptly proclaimed and disappearing again just as quickly, and they had learned that the Roman Empire would not sink into anarchy right away just because the imperial throne was vacant for a while. Emperors might come and go, but the Western Roman Empire abided—or so it seemed.

Odoacer did what no one before him had done and what many had not even dared to think: he induced the Roman senate to send a delegation to Constantinople to declare that the Western Roman imperial monarchy had been abolished. The Byzantine historian Malchus describes this unprecedented act as follows:

> When Augustus, the son of Orestes, heard that Zeno had recovered control over the east, having driven Basiliscus out, he forced the senate to send a delegation to Zeno to indicate to him that they did not require their own imperial monarchy, but rather a shared sole emperor would suffice for both parts. Odoacer had been chosen as capable of saving their affairs, as he was endowed with both political and martial acuity. And they asked Zeno to send him the rank of *patricius* [by letter] and to entrust him with the government of Italy.[20]

This Western Roman delegation thus did not balk at declaring to the Eastern emperor that the Western Empire no longer needed an emperor because the senators had chosen a clever and capable man in Odoacer, who had already proven that he was able to protect their interests; Zeno should confer the title of *patricius* on Odoacer and transfer the administration of Italy to him. Apparently, they meant the position of *magister militum*, which in the Western Empire was linked with the rank of *patricius*, presumably with some additional powers, especially the right to appoint civil officials. The facts were undeniable: Odoacer had decided to abolish the position of the Western Roman emperor, and the senate was prepared to support his decision. To prevent the slightest misunderstanding, the envoys delivered to the emperor all the insignia of the Western Roman emperor; such symbols of imperial power were no longer needed in Italy when there was only one Roman emperor who resided in Constantinople. How had such a radical break with tradition become possible?[21]

If we recall the special relationship between emperors and their supreme military commanders that took shape over the course of the fifth century, we can understand how the imperial monarchy had come to be a burden on the *magistri militum*. The factual and spatial separation of military power and the imperial government practically invited people to play the emperor off against the supreme commander. The court and the army could seldom be found in the same place, and the generals had to prevent courtiers and civil officials from gaining the emperor's confidence or turning him against themselves in their absence. To do so, however, required close monitoring, which was difficult to put into practice. Moreover, there was always the risk that the emperor might become discontent with permanently playing the part of a mere figurehead; he might try to strip his supreme commander of power and rule independently. That prospect threatened the generals with the loss of power and the whole country with civil war. Hence it is easy to understand why Odoacer might have hit on the idea of ruling over what remained of the Western Roman Empire without an emperor and also why the Western senators might have seen some appeal in it. But it is well known that there is a long way from an idea to reality; what had at most merely been considered Odoacer actually carried out.[22]

But who was this Odoacer, and why had an army of barbarians in the middle of Italy proclaimed him their king? Odoacer was born in 433 and grew up in the retinue of Attila the Hun. His father, Edica, was Thuringian by birth and enjoyed great prestige as a warrior. He had been admitted to the exclusive circle of Attila's *logades*, the military-political elite of the kingdom of the Huns. Indeed, he had acquired the prominent and influential position of Attila's bodyguard. At Attila's court, Edica had gotten to know Orestes, Romulus' father, who was serving as the Hunnic king's secretary at the time; they both traveled to Constantinople as envoys in 449. When the Eastern Roman court had tried to induce Edica to assassinate Attila, Edica pretended to go along with the plan but revealed it to Attila on his return.[23]

After the collapse of the kingdom of the Huns, Edica and his son Hunwulf sought a place among the Sciri; both of them attained leading positions. They were part of the coalition of Suebian, Sarmatian, Gepid, and Rugian kings that were crushed by Theoderic's father Thiudimir at the Battle of the Bolia in 469. Edica may have been among the fallen then; he is not mentioned afterward. His son Hunwulf, however, went to Constantinople and entered the emperor's service. With the patronage of Armatus, the nephew of Empress Verina, he rapidly rose through the ranks; by 477, a year after Emperor Romulus was deposed, Hunwulf was already *magister militum* for Illyricum, at the very time when Theoderic and his Goths were active in the region. Later, after Odoacer became king, Hunwulf also moved to Italy; he led a campaign against the Rugi for his brother in 488.[24]

Odoacer had the same mother as Hunwulf, a Scirian woman whose name is unknown to us; his name is Germanic, like that of his brother, and means "He Who Watches over His Property." In the sources, Odoacer is called a Scirian, a Rugian, or a Goth. This ambiguity is not surprising since Odoacer was a product of the multiethnic leadership of the empire of the Huns. He had served many masters before he went to Italy. When and why he came there, though, is uncertain. What is clear is that on the way there, he met a man named Severinus in Noricum (Lower Austria). Severinus enjoyed great prestige on account of his ascetic way of life; after the holy man's death it was said that he had prophesied to Odoacer, who was still wearing shabby clothing at the time, that he would someday be king. But the source does not give a date for their encounter or reveal where Odoacer was coming from at the time. Some scholars identify him with a leader of Saxon pirates called Adovacrius, who captured the city of Angers around 463 and lost it again several years later to the Frankish king Childeric. If that is right, Odoacer must have become separated from his father and brother and traveled to northern Gaul years before the Battle of the Bolia. It is more probable, however, that these are two different persons. If that is the case, then the first datable mention of Odoacer refers to the siege of Rome by Ricimer in 471–472. Odoacer was in league with Ricimer against Emperor Anthemius at the time. He was subsequently admitted to the imperial bodyguard; perhaps soon afterward, he even became the commander of this prestigious and influential unit as *comes domesticorum* but this is uncertain.[25]

A single account gives us information about the circumstances in which Odoacer was proclaimed king; it comes from Procopius and so was written several generations after the events. He writes:

When Zeno was emperor in Byzantium, Augustus held power in the West, whom the Romans called by the diminutive "Augustulus" because he had become emperor while still a boy, while his father Orestes, a most astute man, administered the empire for him. Some time previously, the Romans had induced Sciri and Alans, as well as some other Gothic peoples, to become allies. . . . The more the barbarians flourished among them, the more the prestige of the Roman soldiers declined, and under the euphemistic name of alliance they were tyrannized violently by infiltrators. And so they wantonly forced the Romans to do many things against their will and finally demanded that the Romans share all the cultivable land of Italy with themselves. They ordered Orestes to give a third of it to them, but when he resolutely refused to do so, they promptly killed him. There was a man named Odoacer among them, however, then serving as one of the emperor's bodyguards, who agreed that he would do what they ordered if they would put him in power. Thus seizing tyrannical power [*tyrannis*], he did no other wrong to the emperor but instead let him live out the rest of his days in a private capacity. And after granting the barbarians a third of the cultivable land and having won their firmest loyalty in this way, he ruled as tyrant for ten years.[26]

Procopius reports that Sciri, Alans, and "some other Gothic peoples" proclaimed Odoacer king because, in contrast to the *magister militum* Orestes, he was prepared to satisfy their demand for land in Italy. Other sources mention the Heruli or a mysterious people named the Turcilingi instead or in addition to these peoples. However this information should be reconciled, it was a single army made up of several groups that were defined by ethnic criteria, so different "peoples." This army had joined the regular Roman units and apparently largely displaced them; at any rate, that would explain why Orestes was helpless to resist Odoacer for long.

According to Procopius, the barbarians demanded no less than a third of the cultivable land in Italy, but that can hardly be correct. The soldiers made up only a fraction of the population and probably had no interest in lands far removed from their theater of operations in northern Italy. It is very plausible, however, that Romulus' barbarian soldiers wanted to become landowners. Land was the most secure and the most prestigious source of income in all premodern societies. Money payments could be stopped at any time. The legally certified possession of land, in contrast, decoupled the military's economic basis from the whims of imperial politics, guaranteed steady income, and conferred great social prestige. Romulus' barbarian army only had to look to Gaul or North Africa to see how groups of warriors could transform into landowners if they had the state on their side. Two generations earlier (418), the Roman general Constantius had settled the Goths under King Wallia in Aquitania, granting them two-thirds of the land. After 455, the Vandal king Gaiseric distributed wide tracts of the province of Africa Proconsularis in modern Tunisia to his Vandals. There thus is no good reason to doubt the basic accuracy of Procopius' report, as scholars have sometimes done.[27]

Land distribution in grand style was impossible without diminishing the property of the old owners. Expropriation came at the expense of local elites, whose estates were concentrated on the territory of a city, and also at the expense of senators, whose estates were scattered across several provinces. Anyone who distributed land to soldiers inevitably faced fierce resistance. Orestes therefore shrank from granting his soldiers' demand for land. Odoacer was chosen king because he did not share these reservations. Of course, he can hardly have been the only "officer" who was prepared to champion the soldiers' interests. The fact that Odoacer was chosen would be easier to understand if as *comes domesticorum* he was the commander of the imperial bodyguard. Majorian (457–461) and Glycerius (473–474) both had held this prestigious office, which was close to the throne, before they were elevated to emperor. Since we have no information about Odoacer's position, this remains speculation. Odoacer was proclaimed king by a motley army; he thereafter bore the title *rex*, which was not specified further in reference to a territory or a particular group of people. Since the soldiers who had elevated him to king were members of different ethnicities and he himself had no obvious, firm connection to a single ethnic group on account of his own vicissitudinous history, it was neither feasible nor sensible to tie his status as king to any one ethnicity. Odoacer was a king like the Vandal Gaiseric or the Visigoth Euric (466–484), but in contrast to them he could not rely on a relatively homogeneous warrior confederation that had existed prior to his accession and was dedicated to him by reason of shared experiences, victories, and defeats. Odoacer's army could not be defined as a people. His power rested on the support of a multiethnic confederation of warriors whose loyalty depended solely on his ability to meet their expectations. Odoacer did not enjoy the prestige of a successful general and also could not build on established cooperation and tried and tested loyalties. It thus is not surprising that his rule was contested by men from within his own ranks. In 477, the king killed a man named Brachila for opposing him. Brachila is described as a "nobleman" (*vir nobilis*) and apparently held a military command as a *comes*. The following year, Odoacer had a man named Adaric, who had rebelled against him, killed together with his brother and mother. There thus were men who believed that they were no less suitable and qualified to rule than Odoacer.[28]

Odoacer's relationship with the Eastern Roman emperor was as undefined as his status as king. As we have seen, shortly after his elevation he had a senatorial delegation ask Zeno to entrust him with the administration of Italy. This request, however, was not granted. At the same time that the delegation of Western Roman senators was working on Odoacer's behalf in Constantinople, a delegation from Julius Nepos was also on hand to congratulate Zeno on the occasion of his victory over Basiliscus. They asked Zeno in particular, however, to make it possible for Julius Nepos to return to Italy by providing him with money and soldiers.

The emperor was confronted by an impossible dilemma: if he granted Odoacer his wish, he would have to abandon Julius Nepos. That would have seriously damaged Zeno's reputation because Julius Nepos had become Western Roman emperor with the assistance of his predecessor Leo and so had always been recognized by Constantinople instead of Romulus. If Zeno granted Julius Nepos his request, however, then he would have to divert resources to him that he could hardly afford to lose so soon after Basiliscus' attempted putsch and risked letting Italy slip out of his grasp completely. Zeno tried to avoid making a decision by giving both sides an answer that could be interpreted as affirmative: he informed the delegation from the Western Roman senate that Julius Nepos should receive a warm welcome on his return to Italy. He informed Odoacer himself that he had done well to receive the rank of *patricius* from Nepos; Zeno would have personally conferred it on him if Nepos had not anticipated him, he claimed: "He praised him for making such a start of protecting the order that befitted the Romans and he [Zeno] believed that he [Odoacer] would quickly receive the emperor who had honored him in such a way if he were to do what was right."[29]

This answer poses a riddle for modern scholars: if Nepos had indeed conferred the rank of *patricius* on Odoacer, how could Odoacer declare that the West no longer needed a new emperor? That was precisely the position that Nepos claimed for himself. Or did the emperor simply act as if Odoacer had voluntarily submitted to Nepos' authority and the latter had taken him into his service? In that case, the emperor would have been lying to the face of both delegations. The problem becomes even more baffling when Malchus ends his account with the remark that Zeno addressed Odoacer as *patricius* in the letter he sent him. That cannot have meant the same thing that Odoacer understood by that term. Zeno wanted precisely *not* to give Odoacer the status of a "generalissimo" and governor of Italy. Apparently, Zeno used the word *patricius* merely as a title, without any powers, as was conventional in the Eastern Roman Empire. It is doubtful that Odoacer was satisfied with that. At any rate, he never bore the title of *patricius*; his own chancellery styled him *rex*, and his subjects called him *rex* or *dominus* ("master").[30]

As long as Julius Nepos lived, no Eastern emperor could recognize Odoacer without losing face. On May 9, 480, however, Julius Nepos was murdered by two of his own followers in his country estate near Salona; they allegedly acted on behalf of Glycerius, who had deposed Nepos as Roman emperor six years beforehand and had subsequently been consecrated bishop of Salona. In the same year, a member of the Western Roman senate was appointed consul again, and the highest civil authority of the Eastern Roman Empire, the praetorian prefecture based in Constantinople, included the incumbent of its Western counterpart in its dating formula. In Rome, years were indicated by the regnal years of Zeno and Odoacer, who were both called *domini* and thus placed on equal footing. Apparently, Constantinople had come to terms with Odoacer's reign, at least at first.[31]

In Theoderic's Italy, Odoacer was considered a tyrant. The defeated and executed enemy served as a dark foil for the brilliant image of the victor in Ennodius' panegyric to Theoderic. The clergyman depicts Odoacer as a cowardly and wily weakling who was afraid of his own soldiers and as a robber who enriched himself at his subjects' expense so as to indulge his profligacy without restraint. Everything was for sale during his reign; merit went unrewarded, and all Italy was brought to its knees. In the *Vita* of bishop Epiphanius of Ticinum, Ennodius describes Odoacer as the instrument of the devil. This image cannot be taken at face value. Whether an emperor was good or bad was not determined until after his death: if his successor had come to power by defeating the deceased emperor in battle, he normally fell victim to the verdict that he had ruled contrary to law and above his station—as a tyrant. Critics could turn to a rich store of standard accusations to tarnish his memory, the *topoi* of tyranny. Hence it is with good reason that modern scholars are skeptical of Ennodius' statements and usually give a much more positive assessment of the first barbarian ruler of Italy. It is not infrequently said that Odoacer's reign anticipated Theoderic's kingdom in all essential points.[32]

This view, however, needs to be corrected, even though it is not at all so easy to describe Odoacer's domestic policy in detail for lack of relevant sources. The civil institutions of the Roman state undeniably continued to exist: the central "ministries" located at the imperial court and the provincial offices continued to be filled with members of the Roman elite. Taxes and dues were still collected in the usual way, and justice was still administered according to the laws issued by the Roman emperors. The only institutional innovation that we can identify is the separation of the administration of the ruler's personal private property (*patrimonium*) from that of imperial property (*res privata*)—that is, attached to the institution of the monarchy rather than to the person of the monarch. Henceforth, the *comes rei privatae* was no longer responsible for the ruler's personal property but rather a *vicedominus* ("vice-master") who was appointed by the king. This reform was prompted by Odoacer's decision to split off parts of his territory, including Sicily and Dalmatia (reconquered in 481), from the imperial provincial system and to administer them as his own private property. The number of domains owned directly by the ruler thus grew significantly.[33]

Such a high degree of institutional continuity was possible because the small but rich and powerful Italian elite, which had the senate in Rome to represent its interests, was prepared to cooperate with the barbarian king. Odoacer confirmed the senators' privileges and even granted them additional freedom of action. The urban prefect (*praefectus urbi*), who was appointed for an indefinite term by the ruler, was joined by the highest-ranking ex-consul as "head of the senate" (*caput senatus*). He also owed his position to the ruler but held it for life. Rome again became the preferred stage for senators to profile themselves: the two bottom rows of seats in the Amphitheatrum Flavium (i.e., the Colosseum) were inscribed with the names of senators who presented themselves to the *populus Romanus* at the battles between man and beast (*venationes*) held there.[34]

For the majority of the population, for craftsmen and merchants, for peasants free and unfree, one thing mattered more than anything else: the burden of taxes and dues they had to pay to the central administration. Odoacer made few changes here too. Thirty years after Odoacer's death, delegates from two otherwise unknown communities complained before Theoderic that the burden of their land tax had been increased although their territory had not become more prosperous. Theoderic then instructed the praetorian prefect Faustus Niger not to exact more from these communities than what they had paid under Odoacer. Ennodius reports that Odoacer also reined in his praetorian prefect Pelagius when the latter threatened to ruin the landowners of Liguria by forcing them to sell their products to the state at reduced prices. Finally, if we look at Odoacer's personnel policy, we again find no evidence that supports the allegation that Italy in his reign was governed by men who received their offices through corruption and arbitrarily bled the taxpayers dry. Not a few of these men—including the praetorian prefect Liberius—were retained by Theoderic and continued their careers under his rule.[35]

With respect to the Catholic bishops of Italy, in contrast, Odoacer adopted a completely new position. Never before had the ruler of Italy not belonged to the Christian church that they represented. Odoacer was a Homoean; that is, he adhered to a form of Christianity that its opponents viewed as a dangerous heterodoxy—"Arianism." Of course, we do not know how close Odoacer's relationship with the Homoean church was. Pope Gelasius I (492–496) claimed after the king's death that he had resisted orders from Odoacer that targeted Catholicism, but he does not mention any particulars. If Odoacer had tried to spread his personal confession among his subjects, he hardly would have escaped accusations of being a persecutor, at least posthumously. As far as we can tell, the king treated the Catholic bishops of Italy with respect; he permitted the bishop of Rome to hold synods in the "Eternal City." The Catholic bishops nonetheless had to adjust to an unfamiliar situation. Since Odoacer adhered to a different confession, they did not have any pastoral or doctrinal authority over him. They had to justify their wishes with arguments that were acceptable across confessional boundaries. And they definitely could not hope that the ruler would support them in the battle against heterodoxy. Pope Felix III (483–492) could not hail Odoacer as the "protector and defender of the right faith," as he had done with Emperor Zeno, until he steered a collision course with Zeno and the bishops of the imperial church in 484, excommunicating Acacius (471–489), patriarch of Constantinople. After that, Felix was very appreciative of the fact that Odoacer had no intention of executing Zeno's religious policy in his territory.[36]

In some corners of modern scholarship, the year 476 is considered an epoch-making caesura. This view is already found, however, in a Latin chronicle that originally extended from 395 to 518 and was later continued to 534. Its author, Marcellinus Comes, had served the future emperor Justinian in the 520s as a legal adviser. For the year 476, Marcellinus writes,

> Odoacer, king of the Goths, took Rome. Odoacer killed Orestes immediately. Odoacer condemned Augustulus, Orestes' son, to exile in the Lucullanum, a fortified place in Campania. The western empire of the Roman people, which the first of the Augusti, Octavian Augustus, began to rule in the seven hundred ninth year since the founding of the city, perished with this Augustulus, in the five hundred twenty-second year of the rule of deceased emperors. Thereafter the kings of the Goths held Rome.[37]

This depiction, obviously, was composed two generations after the events, when contemporaries in the Eastern Roman Empire began to deliberate whether Italy should remain separate from the empire permanently. They justified the emperor's claim to rule Italy by tracing the power of the Gothic kings back to Odoacer's usurpation. However, in other chronicles that rely on a common source presumably composed shortly after the events in northern Italy, Romulus' deposition and the commencement of Odoacer's reign are registered so matter-of-factly that they give the impression that nothing had changed beyond the identity of the ruler.

Map 7. The Kingdom of Odoacer, 476–489.

It is doubtful, though, that we can conclude that contemporaries barely noticed the fall of the Western Roman Empire. Granted, almost nothing changed for working people in the cities and countryside. They may not have cared whether the ruler of Italy was a Roman emperor or a barbarian king. The same may be true of the bishops of small country cities. Pope Felix III, however, was very well aware of the fact that the situation of his church had dramatically changed. He wrote to Emperor Zeno in 483: "In you alone survives the name/ might of the time-honored empire" (*unicum in te superest prisci nomen impe-rii*). We may doubt whether the senators knew what they were getting into when they agreed in 476 to abolish the imperial monarchy of the Western Roman Empire. There were no relevant experiences to draw on: Odoacer's rule was an unprecedented experiment for all parties involved. At any rate, they believed he could stop the endless series of civil wars and would ward off foreign enemies. But an uneducated soldier of barbarian background, who did not even know how to write, hardly lived up to the senatorial ideal of a ruler. They could appar-ently live with that as long as Odoacer kept the peace inside and outside Italy.[38]

Odoacer's foreign policy enjoyed only moderate success. Right at the begin-ning of his reign, he had to concede Provence to the Visigothic king Euric. That was a heavy blow for senators who had relatives and property in this wealthy province. The following year, the king was able to make up for this embarrassment by inducing King Gaiseric to restore Sicily, which had fallen under Vandal rule a few years before, in return for annual tribute. Since Sicily was critical to the food supply of the city of Rome after the provinces of North Africa had been torn from the Romans' grasp, and because it was also a center of senatorial landed property, this treaty benefited senators both directly and indirectly. After Julius Nepos' death, Odoacer himself marched with an army into Dalmatia, where he defeated and killed a certain Ovida, who had risen up to become the local ruler there. With that victory, he was able to expand his kingdom by no small extent, although he did not permit senatorial governors to administer the conquered territory but rather sent appointees who answered directly to him.[39]

Odoacer's relationship with the emperor still lacked a clear definition after 480; it thus remained tense and prone to turbulence. It seems significant that the usurper Illus sought Odoacer's support against Emperor Zeno in 484 by sending the failed usurper Marcianus to Italy as an envoy. Vice versa, Zeno was rumored to have incited the Rugi, who had supported Zeno against Illus, against Odoacer a few years later. After the collapse of the empire of the Huns, these Rugi had settled on the north bank of the Danube opposite the province of Noricum Ripense (the area between the Danube and the Eastern Alps). They had provided troops for Emperor Majorian in 458 and fought in vain against the Pannonian Goths at the Battle of the Bolia in 469. After the Goths abandoned Pannonia in 473, the Rugian king Flaccitheus was able to extend his domain across the Danube to the neighboring Roman province, whose inhabi-tants had to pay tribute. Since the Roman central administration had already evacuated the area, the population was left to fend for itself. In this context, the ascetic Severinus of Noricum emerged as a monastic founder and advocate for the Roman provincials. Probably in the year 475, Feletheus, also known as Feva, succeeded his father Flaccitheus as ruler of the Rugi. Both men are said to have valued Severinus' counsel, although they did not share his Catholic confession. If we are to believe Severinus' *Vita*, which was composed in the kingdom of Theoderic a full generation later, it was on account of the holy man's intervention that Feletheus made his soldiers spare the Roman provincials. At Severinus' request, he allegedly forbade his wife Giso to force Catholics to be rebaptized in the Homoean church. We may doubt, however, that Severinus' advocacy was always so effective. No sooner was Severinus dead (482) than Feletheus' brother Ferderuch plundered a monastery in Favianis (Mautern).[40]

This Rugian kingdom on the Danube met its end when, in the winter of 487, Odoacer marched from Italy to Lower Austria, crossed the Danube, and defeated Feletheus. The king, his wife, and part of the Rugian army were captured and brought back to Italy. Frideric, Feletheus' son, managed to escape with some of the Rugian warriors. When he returned the following year, Odoacer again sent an army across the Danube, but this time it was commanded by his brother Hunwulf. Hunwulf drove Frideric out and ordered the Roman inhabitants of both provinces of Noricum to relocate to Italy. The *Vita* of Severinus reports that all the Romans abandoned their cities on the banks of the Danube and moved to Italy, where they were settled in all its regions. The exhumed corpse of the holy man took the same route: after temporarily residing in Ravenna, Severinus found a new resting place in Lucullanum near Naples — the same place where former emperor Romulus had taken up residence after he was deposed in 476. It is, of course, unlikely that the province was completely evacuated; presumably some of the Roman population stayed behind.[41]

Undoubtedly, Odoacer no longer considered it possible or practical to defend this province beyond the Alps with his troops. He may have had a variety of reasons for concluding so. He probably anticipated that he would be the target of an attack undertaken at the behest of the Eastern Roman emperor. Odoacer had tried to prove his loyalty to Zeno after defeating Feletheus by sending him a portion of the booty, as the emperor's generals usually did. But the gesture fell flat: the emperor was no longer willing to tolerate Odoacer's rule over Italy. At approximately the same time that Odoacer's *comes* Pierius was organizing the resettlement of the Roman population of Noricum Ripense, Zeno commissioned Theoderic, who had caused him so many problems since his accession, to eliminate Odoacer and to rule in lieu of the emperor in Italy until he could come personally.[42]

4. A STRUGGLE FOR RAVENNA: THEODERIC VS. ODOACER (489–493)

In the fall of 488, some 100,000 people—men, women, and children—made ready to follow their leader Theoderic from Novae to Italy. The road ahead of them was over 1,000 kilometers long, and only about half of it ran through territory that obeyed the emperor. They would need months to reach their destination and would be exposed to the rigors of winter virtually unprotected. Attacks by enemy warrior groups could be expected along the way. In Italy, they were awaited by an enemy whose dangerousness was difficult to assess. It was a leap into the unknown. Everyone who followed Theoderic to Italy burned all his bridges behind him. Understandably, not every Goth who lived in the Balkans at that time wanted to make the journey. Some preferred to try their luck in the emperor's service. It is explicitly reported that a group of about 3,000 Goths living on the Crimea rejected Theoderic's invitation to follow him to Italy.[43]

Be that as it may, the core of the armed people who followed Theoderic to Italy consisted of the Goths who had been unified under his leadership since the death of Strabo (481). Several thousand of them had already been following their king for fifteen years, had celebrated victories and suffered defeats, and had shared trials and labors with him. Others had joined only a few years before, but they were no less proud of the fact that they were Goths. The Rugi who had fled with Frideric to Novae to escape Odoacer's troops also joined the undertaking. It has been conjectured that warriors of other backgrounds also took part, and some have gone so far as to describe Theoderic's army as "multiethnic." But there is no solid evidence for such claims. Theoderic's army was, at heart, a Gothic army.[44]

When Theoderic gave the signal to march, he must have set in motion some 20,000 riders and several thousand oxcarts. The column may have been several kilometers long. Our sources, regrettably, give us little to fire our imagination. Procopius tersely reports that Theoderic marched to Italy with the Gothic people; they put women and children in wagons and loaded them with as many of their belongings as possible. Ennodius drapes their hardships and dangers in flowery turns of phrase: wagons served as houses; all the necessities of life were transported on them. Not even the route they took is known, although every indication suggests that Theoderic led his people from Novae on the Roman military road along the Danube. After Singidunum, the most important stops along the way would have been Oescus, Ratiaria, Bononia, and Viminacium (Kostolatz).[45]

The emperor's reach at the time extended only as far as Singidunum. Since Zeno had commissioned Theoderic to attack Odoacer, he may have ensured that supplies were provided along the road for this traveling people; they otherwise would have had to be requisitioned from the provincial population. Zeno had conferred the title of *patricius* on Theoderic, after all, prior to his departure for the west. These supplies, however, cannot have been especially copious because Theoderic's people suffered hunger when they left Eastern Roman territory. Beyond Singidunum lay the territory of the Gepids, a warlike people that had shaken off the emperor's control and fought many a battle against the Goths. The Gepids controlled the road that ran from Sirmium up the Sava past Siscia (Sisak) and Neviodunum (Dmovo) to Emona (Ljubljana). Their leader, Thraustila, feared for his authority and his people's belongings if he permitted such a large army to pass; he therefore refused Theoderic passage. At a river called the Ulca, which should probably be identified as the Vuka, flowing into the Danube at Vukovar, in eastern Croatia, a battle took place between Thraustila's Gepids and Theoderic's Goths in the dead of winter 488–489.[46]

We can no longer reconstruct the course of the battle. Ennodius describes the events in his panegyric to Theoderic almost two decades later in the style of a heroic epic: the Goths had to wade through the Ulca to attack the Gepids standing on the opposite bank, but they at first were driven back. As ever more Goths fell and defeat seemed imminent, Theoderic leapt into the thick of the battle. Briefly addressing his men, he rushed headlong into the fight and routed the enemy almost single-handedly:

> As a torrent devastates crops, as a lion devastates flocks, so did you devastate [the enemy]. No one who met you could resist or escape your pursuit. You were transported everywhere as the spears ran out, yet your rage still grew. The Gepids' situation was immediately reversed: the victors could be seen to scatter as the tables were turned. For you, venerable one, who had first sought out the savor of battle unaccompanied, drove forward fortified by thousands. A multitude of the enemy was slaughtered, until the coming night snatched some few away, and then the vast storehouses full of the resources of cities were reached. They were enough not only to satisfy one's needs but even to please the discriminating palate of a gourmand.[47]

Although this account tells us little about the course of the battle, it nevertheless reveals that the victory at the Ulca played a prominent part in the Goths' collective memory and Theoderic's self-representation: the king lived up to his reputation as an irresistible warrior, even if this time he could not claim the prestige of personally striking down the enemy leader. The account also unintentionally reveals that Theoderic's situation before the battle was critical: "The clash with the enemy conquered hunger," Ennodius says. Although Thraustila's Gepids were not the only foes Theoderic's Goths had to overcome on their way to Italy, their advance was unstoppable after the victory at the Ulca. The road to Italy lay open.[48]

We know next to nothing about how Odoacer prepared for the coming attack. If he tried to win allies, his effort was not crowned with success. He apparently planned to intercept Theoderic on the border of his kingdom. To that end, he established a fortified camp at Pons Sontii, a bridge over the Isonzo near the mouth of the Frigidus (Vipava). There, where Emperor Theodosius had defeated Eugenius with Gothic troops in 394, Odoacer's men would now await Theoderic's army and prevent it from crossing the Isonzo. Theoderic and his army crossed the Julian Alps into northern Italy in the summer of 489 and reached the Isonzo valley in late August. The king let his men and their mounts rest for a few days. On August 28, he gave the order to attack and routed Odoacer's army. Odoacer retreated to Verona, where another battle took place hardly a month later, September 27–30, 489.[49]

Again, the only detailed account is found in Ennodius' panegyric to Theoderic. It is introduced with scenes typical of ancient epics: the sun rises; the hero dons his armor; he addresses his close kin as he goes forth into battle. In Ennodius, however, Theoderic bids farewell to his mother and sister, not his wife and child like the Trojan hero Hector in Homer's *Iliad*. The king acknowledges his obligation to preserve and increase the glory of his ancestors with his own deeds and hastens into battle on horseback as the balance seems already to be tipping in his enemies' favor. Again, Theoderic's arrival turns the tide: the enemy breaks and flees before him; the waters of the Adige run red with the blood of the dead; the battlefield is strewn with corpses. It goes without saying that this report also cannot be taken at face value, and yet it still betrays how Theoderic wanted himself to be seen: as a hero that no one could resist.[50]

In reality, the victory was important but by no means complete: Odoacer yielded the battlefield to Theoderic but successfully escaped with part of his army. He made haste back to Ravenna, where he arrived on September 30, three days after the battle. Theoderic, meanwhile, marched from Verona to Milan, which opened its gates to him. Here he was visited by Epiphanius, bishop of Ticinum. Odoacer's *magister militum* Tufa defected to Theoderic with his troops soon afterward. Theoderic graciously received the defector and immediately ordered him to besiege his former master in Ravenna. Tufa did as instructed, proceeded to Faventia (Faenza) accompanied by men from Theoderic's retinue (*comites*), and put Ravenna under siege. Theoderic already looked like the certain victor to many observers.[51]

How Odoacer slipped out of the noose around his neck is not entirely clear. He is reported to have visited Tufa in Faventia, after which the latter pledged his loyalty again and surrendered Theoderic's followers to him. Now Odoacer launched a counterattack, advancing on Milan from Cremona. He won back the city and reprimanded its inhabitants; Bishop Laurentius was taken into custody. Theoderic retreated to Ticinum, where he camped for a while.[52]

Now at the latest Odoacer broke with the policy he had followed hitherto with respect to Emperor Zeno and elevated his son Thela to Caesar. The report of this action is transmitted without date or context and is accordingly problematic. But it shows that Odoacer intended to reinaugurate the Western Roman imperial monarchy that he had declared superfluous fourteen years earlier by creating an emperor, even if only with the title of Caesar. That can only have been registered as usurpation in Constantinople.

At this juncture, Odoacer seems to have decided to mint coins bearing his image and name, something no Germanic king had done before him. The issue in question consists of silver coins weighing half a *siliqua* (about a gram). As we can tell from the reverse type, they were minted in Ravenna. The obverse shows Odoacer in a cuirass with a general's cloak. He has long hair and a beard but no imperial insignia. The legend also lacks a title; it reads *Fl(avius) Odovac(ar)*. *Flavius* was not a family name but rather a status indicator for all those who were in the emperor's service. Odoacer's legitimacy remained undefined, his relationship to the emperor ambivalent to the very end.[53]

The war that Theoderic waged against Odoacer in northern Italy invited neighboring rulers to capitalize on the situation. The Burgundian king Gundobad led a plundering army back to the land he had left fifteen years earlier, when he had laid down his office as Emperor Glycerius' *magister militum*. His warriors won rich booty in Liguria and carried off thousands of captives back to their kingdom. Vandalic warriors attacked Sicily at probably the same time. In this situation, Theoderic managed to win the support of the Visigothic king Alaric (484–507). Did he benefit from the fact that the part of the Pannonian Goths that had gone to Italy with Vidimir in 473 had soon afterward been received in the kingdom of Alaric's father Euric? At any rate, Alaric dispatched an unknown number of warriors to northern Italy to support Theoderic in his fight against Odoacer. Odoacer thereupon broke off the siege of Ticinum and returned to Milan. At the Adda River on August 11, 490, they met again in open battle. Odoacer appears to have put his *comes domesticorum* Pierius in command this time. Both sides suffered heavy losses, but the victory was Theoderic's. Pierius fell in battle; Odoacer retreated again to Milan. Although Ennodius passes over the Battle of the Adda in silence, Theoderic's victory must have made an impression because soon afterward the highest-ranking senator, Festus, put himself at Theoderic's disposal. He accepted the

Fig. 6. Silver coin (half-*siliqua*) of Odoacer, obverse and reverse
(significantly enlarged). Obverse: bare-headed, draped and
cuirassed bust of Odoacer, right; reverse: monogram of Odoacer
within wreath. British Museum, London, Great Britain © The
Trustees of the British Museum/Art Resource, NY.

task of traveling to Constantinople to petition Emperor Zeno to confer a royal
vestment on Theoderic but waited in vain for an answer.[54]

In the meantime, Theoderic pursued his defeated enemy and established a
fortified camp south of Ravenna at a place known as the "pine grove" (*Ad
Pinetum*), cutting off the city from its connections to the interior. Thus began
the two-and-a-half year siege of Ravenna, which was described at the beginning
of this book. On July 10, 491, an attempt to make a sally failed; Odoacer attacked
Theoderic's camp with his Heruli at night but was beaten back; his *magister
militum* Libila perished in the fighting. Odoacer did not dare to leave the pro-
tective walls of Ravenna after that. He could only hope that Tufa might relieve
him. This hope was in fact encouraged when the Rugian king Frideric, who
was quartered with his people in Ticinum, took sides with Tufa for unknown
reasons. The two kings could not, however, come to an agreement to lead their
troops together to Ravenna; they soon fell out and fought a bloody battle in the
Adige valley between Verona and Tridentum (Trient) in the winter of 492–493
in which thousands lost their lives, including Tufa himself. Since Theoderic
had obtained ships in the meantime, with which he had blockaded Ravenna by
sea, the situation for the besieged became desperate.[55]

Odoacer initiated negotiations through the Catholic bishop John in February
493 and concluded a treaty on February 25. The two kings agreed to rule Italy
jointly. It is doubtful whether Theoderic ever intended to honor this treaty. His
goal was to enter Ravenna without storming the city. His wish was granted on

March 5. Only a few days later, he broke the oath he had sworn with Odoacer that he would abide by the treaty and killed Odoacer with his own hands. The attack had been carefully planned: while Odoacer met a miserable end in the palace, Theoderic's followers dashed forth to kill Odoacer's armed retinue, who had gathered in the city with their families. The onslaught struck them too like a bolt from the blue. A horrific massacre ensued; it is not known how many were able to escape their pursuers. Odoacer's own family was not spared: his brother Hunwulf, who had sought asylum in a church, was killed with arrows; his wife Sunigilda was thrown into prison, where she starved to death. Only Odoacer's son Thela initially escaped with his life; he was banished to Gaul but later also killed, allegedly because he had made preparations to return to Italy. Odoacer's body was buried outside the city walls near a Jewish synagogue.[56]

For the inhabitants of Italy, the massacre of Ravenna meant the end of a civil war that had ravaged wide expanses of the countryside. Our sources depict the horrors of the war only to magnify the victor's glory; they mention the suffering of the civilian population at best only in passing. Scattered reports allow us to guess, however, how devastating the war had been, and not only in northern Italy. Ennodius remembered the death and destruction, hunger, and distress many years later. The two warlords' armies lived off the countryside for these four-and-a-half years; they requisitioned and plundered. In Ticinum, where Theoderic's Goths and Frideric's Rugi were initially quartered, the inhabitants had to vacate their dwellings and houses to make room for the uninvited guests, who spread fear and terror even as Bishop Epiphanius worked to rein in their wanton violence. The rural population of northern Italy, where the major battles were fought, fled for their lives. Many of those whose homes had been destroyed by the war came to Rome in the hope that the Church could and would provide for the penniless refugees. The conquerors' raids, however, extended as far as central and southern Italy. Pope Gelasius I lamented that the provinces neighboring Rome had been devastated by barbarian raids and military operations; the province of Tuscia (Toscana) was hit hardest. Abduction was the order of the day during the war, as captives were either sold into slavery or released for ransom. The number of people who were captured and kidnapped must have been in the tens of thousands. And Theoderic's warriors of course not only made prisoners of enemy combatants; Epiphanius of Ticinum was celebrated for persuading the king to allow captured Romans to return home and not to mistreat captive barbarians.[57]

The war between Odoacer and Theoderic was a traumatic event for the population of Italy. They had not experienced a war of this length and destructive force since the days of Alaric I. Shortly before the end of the war, a prophesy made the rounds in Campania that the arrival of the Antichrist was at hand. The new ruler's first decree seemed to confirm the fear that he would mercilessly settle the score with all of Odoacer's partisans. By a decree that was posted generally, Theoderic deprived all who had not joined him by the end of the war of the right to dispose of their property. This measure cut wealthy Italians to the quick, especially senators, who hoped to transfer their property to their descendants and relatives; in their eyes, Theoderic's decree meant no less than the loss of their right to Roman freedom (*Romanae libertatis ius*). They resolved to send two bishops, whom Theoderic already knew personally—namely, Laurentius of Milan and Epiphanius of Ticinum—to ask the king to retract the measure. Theoderic actually relented; he was not willing to declare a general amnesty, but he limited his sanction to those persons he regarded as "instigators of evil" (*malorum incentores*). These people were to be banished, while all the others would get off scot free. The court official responsible for royal letters, the *quaestor sacri palatii* Urbicus, was ordered to publish this limited amnesty under the label of a "general indulgence" (*generalis indulgentia*). Ennodius attributes the retraction of the original decree to Epiphanius' intercession. In reality, though, Theoderic may not have genuinely intended to take drastic action as it first appeared. He wanted to demonstrate his power to the senators but also create a situation in which he could show mercy, provided they proved to be compliant. By rescinding punishment that he himself had imposed at his new subjects' request, he pried from them the assent that he urgently needed to put the power he had seized by military means on a lasting foundation.[58]

As a matter of fact, Theoderic soon took further measures intended to win over the inhabitants of Italy. He commissioned the bishops Victor of Turin and Epiphanius of Ticinum to petition the Burgundian king Gundobad to permit all refugees or prisoners who had come into his kingdom to return to Italy, and he made funds available for this purpose. Their release would serve as a kind of bride-gift for Theoderic's daughter Ostrogotho, who had been engaged to Gundobad's son Sigismund shortly beforehand. Victor and Epiphanius thus traveled to Lyon, where Gundobad resided, and obtained his agreement: refugees would be free to return home while prisoners could be ransomed. Ennodius says over 6,000 people were permitted to return without ransom; he does not, however, state for how many a ransom was paid. The money that the bishops had received from Theoderic, at any rate, was not sufficient because they also solicited donations from Bishop Avitus of Vienne and the Roman Syagria, who lived in Lyon.[59]

Not two years later, Theoderic remitted two-thirds of the land tax owed by the war-ravaged province of Liguria after a delegation led by Epiphanius had petitioned him. The king was following an established pattern with this decision as well: Roman emperors in comparable cases had also not infrequently been willing to forego a portion of tax revenues.[60]

Theoderic had launched his war against Odoacer on behalf of Emperor Zeno; that mission was to overthrow Odoacer and then rule Italy in the emperor's place until he himself could come in person. Zeno had conferred on Theoderic the office and title of *patricius*. Hence when the king arrived in Italy, he already possessed a legitimate right to rule that had been conferred on him by the emperor. Nonetheless, in the fall of 490, after he had defeated Odoacer at the Adda and had trapped him in Ravenna, he sent a delegation to Constantinople led by Festus, the highest-ranking senator and consul of 472, to ask the emperor to confer a "royal vestment" (*vestis regia*) on Theoderic. The purpose of this request does not emerge from the account of the episode in the *Anonymus Valesianus*. Theoderic must have already possessed symbols of his status as Gothic king. Did he want to receive the insignia of a client king from the emperor? Or does the expression *vestis regia* mean the costume of a "vice-emperor"? The only thing that seems certain is that Theoderic's wish was still unfulfilled when Zeno died on April 9, 491. He was succeeded by the court official (*silentiarius*) Anastasius, who was already over sixty years old. It was not certain whether Anastasius might have felt obligated to honor his predecessor's agreement with Theoderic. Theoderic therefore sent envoys to Constantinople again, this time headed by Faustus Niger, consul of the year 490. The *Anonymus Valesianus* claims that the delegation set out from Ravenna before news of Zeno's death had arrived, but that makes no sense, particularly since Faustus Niger did not return until after victory over Odoacer. He probably set out as soon as it became evident that Odoacer would probably not be able to break out of the siege of Ravenna—hence in the summer of 492. He did not return until Odoacer was dead.[61]

The reason why Faustus stayed so long in Constantinople was apparently because Emperor Anastasius was unwilling to recognize the treaty concluded with his predecessor until Theoderic successfully completed his mission. When Theoderic agreed to rule Italy jointly with Odoacer in March 493, he himself was guilty of ignoring the treaty. The fact that he killed his co-ruler Odoacer shortly thereafter did not undo the breaking of his oath. Soon afterward, a ceremonial act that was interpreted as "usurpation of monarchy" (*praesumptio regni*) in Constantinople strained his relationship with the emperor even further. The *Anonymus Valesianus* reports, "When he entered Ravenna and killed Odoacer, the Goths confirmed Theoderic as their king without waiting for the new emperor's order."[62] The significance of this act is disputed. Why was

Theoderic confirmed as king at this point in time? Theoderic himself dated the beginning of his reign to his victory over King Babai in the year 471. Since 474, moreover, he had been recognized as king of all the Goths who had previously followed his father. And Strabo's Thracian Goths had also subsequently submitted to his rule. Some scholars think that the act of confirmation in Ravenna was necessary because Theoderic had been recognized as king only by the Pannonian Goths up to that point. In their opinion, this act first made him king of all the warriors who conquered Italy with him. This view is contradicted, however, by the fact that the Thracian Goths had already recognized Theoderic as king several years before his mission to overthrow Odoacer. Moreover, it is difficult to see how the act constituted "usurpation" if it merely concerned Theoderic's relationship with his army. The accusation presumes that Theoderic claimed rights to which he was not entitled, from an Eastern Roman perspective, as long as Anastasius had not confirmed the treaty he had struck with Zeno. Jordanes, in fact, says that Theoderic put on a "royal mantle" (*regius amictus*) after murdering Odoacer, "as if he already was the ruler of Goths and Romans." Accordingly, he had himself proclaimed king in Italy and thus king over Goths and Romans. Since this right had been conferred on him before he had set out for Italy, he hardly can have viewed it as usurpation. It is equally unlikely that he believed he needed a constitutive act to receive the right to rule Italy like an emperor; if that had been the case, he would have had Romans participate. He did not need the office and title of a *patricius* for that; henceforth, the title *rex* sufficed. In point of fact, the king had already exercised rights that none of the emperor's officials possessed by issuing a general amnesty for the majority of Odoacer's followers; pardoning whole groups of people was an imperial prerogative.[63]

At the end of four-and-a-half years of warfare, Theoderic had more pressing problems than the legal definition of his relationship with the Eastern Roman emperor. If he hoped to consolidate his rule over Italy, he needed the support of the secular and ecclesiastical elites of the country, especially its bishops and senators. To accomplish that, he had to adapt to these groups' ideas of a good ruler. Above all, though, he had to live up to the expectations of the warriors to whom he owed his victory over Odoacer. They had suffered trials, withstood dangers, lost family and friends; now they wanted to receive their due reward. They demanded a carefree livelihood for themselves and their families. Meeting these demands could suffer no delay: if Theoderic gambled away the favor of his Goths, his power was gone. His first priority, therefore, was to grant their wishes without inciting his new subjects against him.

6

THE CONSOLIDATION OF POWER

1. THEODERIC'S GOVERNING STRATEGY: INTEGRATION THROUGH SEPARATION

In March 493, Theoderic had achieved the goal he had set himself in coming to Italy in August 489: he had eliminated Odoacer and shattered his army. Now Theoderic was the sole and absolute ruler of the land over which Roman emperors had reigned for almost five hundred years. In the thrill of victory, he had his followers proclaim him king. Theoderic's power at this moment depended on the loyalty of the men who had come to fight with him in Italy. They had risked their lives for Theoderic and expected to be rewarded. Hence Theoderic's first and most urgent concern was to provide for the economic well-being of the army to which he owed his triumph over Odoacer. But Theoderic was also well aware that a regime based solely on naked force seldom endures; if he wanted to rule a land like Italy permanently, he needed the support of the people who possessed wealth and social capital there. Only if these key players were prepared to accept a Gothic king as their ruler could Theoderic consolidate his power. The key players in Italy, however, came from two different, albeit variously interconnected, milieus: the secular and the ecclesiastical elite. On one side were the Roman senators: they were the richest men in Italy, their properties were scattered over several provinces, and they had a kind of representative body in the form of the Roman senate. On the other side were the bishops of the Catholic Church. They held office within a framework that was normally limited to the territory of a city, but they constituted a network that spanned all Italy, with nodes in Rome, Milan, Ravenna, and Aquileia. Any man at the head of 20,000–25,000 warriors who wanted to rule millions of subjects had to win over the senators and Catholic bishops of Italy. The vast population of the cities and countryside—the slaves and dependent farmers; the craftsmen and traders; the widows, orphans, and beggars—did not constitute an independent social force; they hardly took part at all in what happened at the top of the state as long as it had no perceptible impact on their everyday lives.[1]

Theoderic thus faced the twofold task of retaining the loyalty of the warriors who had come with him to Italy and simultaneously motivating the native Italian elites to cooperate. It was no easy dilemma to solve: his warriors wanted a reward that would guarantee them a comfortable livelihood. Theoderic could satisfy their demands only by mobilizing vast resources, inevitably clashing with the interests of Italian elites, who expected to keep their material property, legal privileges, and social prestige. Matters were complicated further by the fact that Theoderic and the vast majority of his warriors adhered to a religious community that the Catholic clergy of Italy considered heretical. Theoderic's Goths were distinct from native Italians not only on account of their military function, but also because of their religion.

Theoderic's dilemma after victory over Odoacer was daunting but promised great rewards: if he solved it, he would rise to become the richest and most powerful ruler in the part of the Mediterranean world that had once comprised the Western Roman Empire. By the standards of the day, Italy was still a wealthy country despite the devastation of the fifth century. The profits of agriculture and industry still sufficed to finance the lavish lifestyle of urban elites, as well as the imperial court, the army, and the provincial and civil administration. For premodern conditions, the late Roman state was an astonishingly effective machine for extracting and allocating resources. It collected taxes and dues from every free inhabitant of Italy and was capable of organizing the transportation of goods and persons over great distances. Of course, native Italian elites had to cooperate with Theoderic for this bureaucratic apparatus to function smoothly. If they were willing to lend his regime their active support, he had the chance to control sums of regular income the likes of which his ancestors had never even dreamed of.[2]

Theoderic maintained his control of Italy virtually uncontested for over thirty years, until his death in 526; indeed, because he successfully solved the dilemmas sketched above, he even extended his power to southern France and the Iberian Peninsula. Probably in the very first years of his reign in Italy, Theoderic developed a governing strategy that, from a modern observer's point of view, can be distilled into the formula "integration through separation." The king transformed the mobile warrior coalition he had led to conquer Italy into a standing army. For that purpose, he furnished the soldiers of his army landed estates that produced enough revenue to guarantee them a comfortable livelihood. Anyone who belonged to this *exercitus Gothorum* ("army of Goths") was obligated to perform military service for the king, as soon as and for as long as he was able. The army thus was equivalent to the Goths in Theoderic's kingdom, insofar as they were male and able to fight. They thereby constituted a military elite that was, moreover, defined in ethnic terms. The official equation was as follows: whoever bore arms for the king was a Goth; only Goths bore arms for the king. The royal chancellery incessantly pronounced that Theoderic ruled over two peoples, over Goths and Romans. The Goths' job was to defend the kingdom from internal and external threats; the Romans', to enjoy the peace and punctually pay their taxes.

This official categorization reduced a complex ethnic situation to a simple and contradictory antithesis: Goth or Roman; there was no third option. In reality, however, men served in Theoderic's army who did not, or at least did not exclusively, view themselves as Goths. This was especially true of the Rugi, who were jealous of their autonomy even in Theoderic's kingdom and refused to tolerate mixed marriages. Then there were the Breones, a warlike tribe based in Tyrol; they controlled the Brenner Pass and were impossible to disarm. Herulian and Gepid warriors were also subsequently admitted to Theoderic's kingdom, although we do not know whether they were integrated into the *exercitus Gothorum* like the Rugi or remained separate bands. In isolated cases, even Romans who enjoyed Theoderic's confidence were entrusted with military responsibilities.[3]

But the official categorization "Gothic" was by no means imposed on Theoderic's army arbitrarily. On the contrary, the heart of his army really consisted of men who were proud to be Goths. They were bound to one another by their shared experiences and traditions, by their language, customs, and conventions. Vice versa, by no means did all the inhabitants of Italy attach the same value and meaning to the label "Roman." Slaves, for example, and the religious minority of Jews had no place in this binary scheme. Senators with proud pedigrees traced their families back to famous magistrates of the Roman Republic—a past that meant nothing to dependent farmers and slaves. Anyone in Italy who did not live in Rome, moreover, belonged to a municipal community with its own institutions and traditions that differed from those of the Roman Republic and Roman Empire. Yet the native population of Italy—with the exception of slaves—still constituted a legal unit insofar as all free inhabitants fell under the jurisdiction of Roman law.[4]

In order to place his power in Italy on a firm footing, Theoderic had to transform the Gothic "community of violence" into an ethnically defined class of landowners who performed mandatory military service. His warriors thus assumed a responsibility on behalf of the commonwealth that was intended to make them both indispensable and permanently and conspicuously distinct from the Roman civilian population. To the secular and ecclesiastical elites of Italy, what mattered most was that the king did not fundamentally change the traditional structures of the late Roman civil administration. Theoderic left the existing provincial and central administrations as he found them and retained the personnel that they employed. In this way, a kind of dual state came into being: on the one hand, there was the civil administration, which was organized according to the late Roman model. Its personnel consisted exclusively of Romans who spoke Latin. The central administration had authority over Theoderic's Goths only insofar as they were obligated to pay taxes and dues. On the other hand, there was the Gothic military administration. Its personnel were recruited from the army, and it had judicial competence for Goths. The military administration became involved with Romans only when the latter had disputes with Goths.[5]

Theoderic's governing strategy thus was by no means calculated to fuse the Goths and Romans into a single people, as scholars have occasionally believed. The Gothic king was not trying to bring about the cultural assimilation and social fusion of conquerors and conquered, not even at the level of elites, as, for instance, Alexander the Great had done. On the contrary, Theoderic was striving to build a barrier between the conquerors and the native inhabitants of Italy by dividing his subjects into two peoples that performed different tasks and played different parts: the Goths as warriors, the Romans as civilians.[6]

Since only sporadic information survives about Theoderic's government from the years prior to Cassiodorus' quaestorship (506), we cannot follow the evolution of this strategy in detail. It was already full-fledged when Cassiodorus began as quaestor to dress the maxims of Theoderic's policy in solemn language. There are several indications, however, that the king made fundamental decisions shortly after defeating Odoacer. The warriors to whom Theoderic owed his victory wanted him to provide for them. This task could brook no delay.

We have already seen that Theoderic's warriors came to Italy with their wives and children, some 25,000 men with their families. A majority of them had seldom lived long in a single place, and many had spent years crisscrossing the Balkans with Theoderic. They had hardly even practiced agriculture, let alone a trade, during this time. When they arrived in Italy, their personal possessions amounted to what they could carry on their backs or load in a wagon—clothing and weapons, objects for everyday use, jewelry and other valuables. Anyone who counted as somebody also owned horses, animals, and slaves. Theoderic's warriors had suffered trials and tribulations for him and risked their lives in battle against Odoacer; not a few of them had perished in the process. Those who lived to behold the victory now demanded their reward. They were not about to accept a short-term service relationship for an annual salary that could be canceled arbitrarily like that of the emperor's soldiers, who were sometimes deployed thousands of kilometers away at his command. Theoderic's warriors wanted a comfortable and crisis-proof livelihood for themselves and their families — and they wanted that security for the rest of their lives. The best material guarantee of a livelihood under contemporary conditions was land ownership. Obviously, Theoderic's warriors were not thinking of beating their swords into plowshares; they wanted to live off of rent, just as Roman aristocrats had done since time immemorial. Gaiseric's army had also realized this dream, receiving land in the richest province of Roman North Africa (Africa Proconsularis) after 455. A generation later, the same demand had been made in Italy and was satisfied by Odoacer.[7]

Theoderic thus ensured the material existence of his Goths by settling them as landowners in Italy. Since no direct accounts of this fundamental process have come down to us, there are major gaps in our knowledge of how it played out. Modern scholars previously disputed even whether Theoderic had made his warriors into landowners at all. In this view, Theoderic's warriors did not receive estates that they could use as they pleased but rather only a share in the land tax that estates paid to the imperial fiscus. Individual estates, so the argument goes, were assigned to individual Goths and now had to pay the portion of their revenues that had previously gone to the fiscus instead to their Gothic "guests" (*hospites*). Since this would have amounted merely to a reallocation of state resources, the cost of providing for the barbarian warriors would have fallen exclusively on the fiscus, while the income of Roman landowners would not have shrunk at all, and that would also supposedly explain why the measure was implemented without provoking any discernible resistance.[8]

This view has notable advocates but is untenable for several reasons. First and foremost, Theoderic's warriors wanted to be immune to political vicissitudes and fiscal slumps. Contemporary sources moreover explicitly mention the physical division of land between Goths and Romans. Cassiodorus, for example, celebrates the senator Liberius, who was entrusted with the task of executing the measure in Theoderic's name and on his behalf, in the following words:

> We are pleased to report how he [Liberius] united both the possessions and the hearts of Goths and Romans in the assignation of thirds [*tertiae*]. For despite the fact that men customarily clash because they are neighbors, the sharing of estates [*communio praediorum*] appears instead to have given

them reason for harmony: so it has happened that each of the two peoples [*utraque natio*], while living together, has come to one and the same wish. Behold a new and altogether laudable deed: the mutual goodwill of the owners [i.e., both Goth and Roman] has stemmed from the division of land; the friendship between the peoples [*populi*] has grown because of losses, and a defender has been acquired in part of the land [*pars agri*] so that the security of the property may be preserved intact.[9]

Even though Cassiodorus is at pains to highlight the blessings of the "division of the land" between Goths and Romans in this letter to the senate and only alludes in passing to the fact that the Roman landowners had suffered losses, his wording leaves no doubt that Theoderic's Goths now owned land that had formerly belonged to Romans, thanks to the measures implemented by Liberius. That is precisely why Cassiodorus argues that the Romans had acquired Gothic "protectors," who defended everyone's property from external threats. We find similar euphemisms in a letter from Ennodius addressed to Liberius himself: "It is thanks to you, after God, that we are able to acknowledge our riches free from care in the presence of the most powerful and all-conquering lord: the wealth of subjects is safe when the emperor has no needs. What of it then that you enriched those countless throngs of Goths with an abundant grant of estates [*praedia*], while the Romans scarcely noticed? The victors desire nothing more, and the conquered felt no loss."[10] Ennodius likewise concedes that the Romans suffered losses from the "grant of estates" (*praediorum conlatio*), although, to compliment his addressee, he quickly adds that they had hardly noticed. By the same token, Ennodius also indicates that the victorious Goths could easily have demanded more. The message was clear: we Romans have you to thank, Liberius, for letting us off so easy.

Theoderic's Goths became the owners of estates that had previously belonged to Romans; that much is certain. Very little is known, however, about how this division of land was carried out. Theoderic seems to have issued a general decree relatively soon after his victory over Odoacer; the aforementioned Liberius was appointed to implement it. Liberius was a young senator who did not belong to any of the major senatorial families. He had, however, previously served Odoacer, and after the latter's defeat, Theoderic entrusted him with the highest office of the civil administration, that of praetorian prefect. Liberius carried out his delicate mission to Theoderic's complete satisfaction; when he left office in the year 500, he was awarded the title of *patricius*. Now Liberius was not physically present everywhere Gothic warriors were installed in their new property; he was represented locally by officials of the prefecture called *delegatores*; they gave the recipients certificates (*pittacia*) detailing their title of ownership. Only Goths who could produce such a certificate were subsequently considered the rightful owners of the lands they occupied.[11]

Cassiodorus says that the Goths were assigned "thirds" (*tertiae*). This term apparently refers to the distribution ratio used on the estates where Gothic warriors were settled. That settlement area by no means covered all Italy comprehensively. Theoderic's Goths were settled predominantly in the northern half of the Italian peninsula. Gothic settlements were concentrated in the Po Valley, the Cottian Alps, and central Italy. Strategic considerations may have played a decisive part in the land allocation because the Gothic warriors' estates and the garrisons where they served could not be separated by too great a distance. The garrisons were concentrated in the north, on the Adriatic coast, and along the Via Flaminia, which linked Rimini to Rome. Southern Italy and the island of Sicily were protected by some garrisons as well, but they were entirely or at least largely exempt from the land redistribution. Nor does it appear that any Gothic families were settled in the provinces beyond the Alps: Raetia I, Raetia II, and Noricum Mediterraneum. Theoderic also does not appear to have settled Goths in Provence after he integrated it into his kingdom.[12]

The land division thus affected the provinces of Italy to widely varying degrees. The unevenness of the burden was potentially compensated by a special tax, also called the *tertia*, that only landowners who did not surrender land were required to pay. It is attested only in the kingdom of Theoderic; hence he must have introduced it. We can only speculate as to who had owned the land that was transferred to Theoderic's warriors. It is clear, however, that senators also had to make sacrifices. They were able to ensure that at least their possessions on Sicily, which were especially extensive and profitable, remained undiminished. Procopius reports that "the Romans" asked Theoderic not to station any large garrisons in Sicily "so that nothing might impede their freedom and prosperity," and he supposedly granted their wish. These negotiations were undoubtedly spearheaded by senators who wanted to be spared Gothic neighbors as much as possible. Perhaps Theoderic made the loss of their land more palatable by abolishing a tax on senatorial property that had been levied since the days of Constantine the Great, the *collatio glebalis*, although it is not known for certain whether this tax might already have lapsed. Municipal elites, whose economic survival likewise depended on landed property, also hardly came out unscathed. In contrast to senators, however, they had no leverage for negotiating special conditions. On top of their land, that of Odoacer's supporters who had been killed or banished after Theoderic's victory could also be distributed among the Goths. And finally, it also cannot be ruled out that municipal land was included in the distribution.[13]

Map 8. Gothic Garrisons in Italy.

If we take a look at the Gothic side of the process, the conspicuous gaps in the tradition are especially painful: no source reveals whether the Goths were all treated equally in the distribution—that is, whether every one of them had a claim to the same number of estates of the same size and quality. It is beyond doubt that Theoderic's personal relations received privileged treatment. His sister Amalafrida left behind extensive properties after her death; his nephew Theodahad is reputed to have owned the better part of Etruria. Only sparse information is available for the property holdings of Goths who did not belong to the royal family. It is inconceivable, however, that Goths who excelled common warriors in valor and prestige, and so had gathered their own followings, were placed on an equal footing with their followers in the land distribution.[14]

The Goths were not an egalitarian community already on arrival in Italy, even if their hierarchies were relatively flat and permeable in comparison to those of late Roman society. By no means every Goth had the resources to equip himself as a mounted warrior. Many needed horses and weapons to be provided to them or fought on foot with sword and bow. There thus was something like a Gothic aristocracy, but it does not come to the fore in the sources until after Theoderic's death. This social stratification of the Goths is reflected in Procopius' terminology: the Greek historian uses adjectives like *logimos* ("prestigious," "notable"), *dokimos* ("excellent," "esteemed"), and *aristos* ("eminent," "noble") to differentiate between different degrees of excellence and honor among the Goths. At the other end of the spectrum were Goths who had lost their freedom and come under the power of other Goths. It thus is very probable that distinctions were made in the land distribution, depending on the merits individual Goths had earned from their king and how much he depended on their loyalty. The land distribution thus may very well have reinforced and intensified existing social hierarchies.[15]

We also know virtually nothing about how the Goths used their estates. Since grown men were obligated to do military service and a large part of them actually had to be mustered to man far-flung garrisons and forts, they will hardly have preoccupied themselves with the oversight of agricultural industries. They presumably left that to free or unfree stewards, unless they rented their land out to tenant farmers; the Roman aristocracy did the same thing. Be that as it may, the Goths in Italy were not normally absentee landlords who hardly ever set eye on their properties. There is clear evidence that the wives and children of Gothic warriors lived on the land. These families were thus really present on the landed property of the head of the household. Other Goths, of course, may have established their households within the confines of municipal settlements, especially those Goths to whom proximity to the king was of great importance.[16]

2. A PEOPLE OF WARRIORS: THE GOTHIC ARMY

Theoderic's Goths come into clear view in the sources for us only as warriors. That is not a coincidence: it was the king's will that they should play precisely that part. As a people of warriors, the Goths were to defend Theoderic's kingdom against outside threats. This military function served to justify why the king raised a small but armed minority up as the second pillar of his regime alongside the great majority of Roman civilians. To maintain this arrangement, it was necessary to ensure that the warriors he led to Italy did not lose their formidable military prowess by adapting to their unwarlike environs. The Romans of Italy, who had once repelled Hannibal and defeated Hellenistic kings, had forgotten how to fight long ago. In Theoderic's day, it did not make military sense to levy armies of men who plied a different trade in their everyday lives, as had been customary under the Roman Republic. Civilians were permitted to bear arms only in narrowly defined cases or exceptional circumstances. Romans were not supposed to wear a cuirass or helmet or carry a shield or lance in Theoderic's kingdom. Trained specialists waged the wars of the fifth and sixth centuries. Contemporary armies were much smaller than those of the Roman Republic, and it was no longer the infantry that decided battles but the cavalry. To field such armies, generals needed men with intensive, constant training to do battle on horseback.[17]

Roman emperors obtained most of their cavalry from outside their own territory. The mounted warriors with whom Theoderic had conquered Italy, however, were Goths like himself and part of his kingdom's military elite. Some of them may have fought on foot with bow and arrow, sword, javelin, and spear, but the heart of his army consisted of mounted warriors who had learned how to deal lethal thrusts and blows with lance and sword from the back of a galloping horse. Body armor, shields, and helmets served to protect them from being wounded or killed in turn. Battles were decided by close combat, even if they were often preceded by protracted barrages of arrows. Since the opposing side could only be weakened, not routed, in this fashion, sooner or later a full-on attack ensued. In single combat, Gothic warriors tried to strike at the right moment with sword or lance while never exposing their own bodies to attack. They aimed for the parts of the body that were not protected by armor: the legs, shoulders, neck, and face. They needed strength, agility, and skill, qualities predicated on natural talent but also such that could be perfected and maintained only with constant training. A mounted warrior, however, not only had to master his own weapons, but he also had to become one with his horse if he wanted to capitalize on the additional strength and speed that his mount gave him. Since stirrups were not in use, the heft that a mounted warrior could put into a lance thrust depended on how well he could stay on his horse purely with the strength of his legs. Moreover, he had to train his horse so thoroughly that it subordinated its will completely to his own and shunned no danger; only then could his mount become an obedient instrument of violence. Although the demands made of foot soldiers were not as high, they also needed special skills that had to be acquired and constantly practiced. Collective success and individual survival in battle were closely tied to one's physical constitution: it mattered how well a soldier could handle a sword, throw a spear, and shoot an arrow. The force and accuracy of slashes and stabs, throws and shots, decided over life and death.

The arms and fighting style of Gothic warriors in Theoderic's day hardly differed from those of imperial soldiers. The most significant difference was that the skill of shooting arrows accurately from the back of a galloping horse was much less widespread among Gothic warriors than among the emperor's elite mounted soldiers. The Goths left the long-range combat that conventionally preceded open battle to archers from the infantry. But otherwise Theoderic's warriors were hard to tell apart from the emperor's soldiers by appearance because they were armed in the same way and neither side wore uniform clothing or armor. There thus was no specifically Gothic armor and weaponry. Even the magnificent (and in some cases, gilded) riveted helmets that have been found in Italy were not a distinctive feature of Gothic troops, although helmets of this type were undoubtedly worn by prominent Goths.[18]

Theoderic's army consisted of warriors who had been accustomed to using weapons since childhood. A Goth was considered an adult as soon as he was a full-fledged warrior. His service to the king ended when he could no longer fight. Theoderic intended his Goths to continue to cultivate this lifestyle in Italy. The royal chancellery never tired of invoking the Goths' martial excellence. In the muster for the Gallic campaign of 508, Cassiodorus claims that a "warlike tribe" (*stirps bellicosa*) enjoyed being tested in battle. A few years before Theoderic's death, Cassiodorus introduced a directive to the praetorian prefect Abundantius as follows: "Let our youths [*iuvenes*] show in war what they have learned on the training grounds of valor [*gymnasium virtutis*]. Let the school of Mars send forth its swarms: he who has grown accustomed to training in peace will fight for fun."[19] Theoderic thus expected his Goths to be ever ready for battle, and their military successes during his reign and fierce resistance to Justinian's elite soldiers under his successors show that he was not disappointed. The zeal with which the Goths cultivated their warlike lifestyle impressed Theoderic's Roman subjects. Ennodius praised the king for keeping the peace by ensuring that his Goths incessantly trained for war:

Under your very eyes, you have the untamed youth practice for war amid the blessing of peace. The might of your victorious hordes stands firm, and already more have grown up. Their muscles are hardened by hurling missiles, and they perform the deeds of brave men while they play. As if in a spectacle, they act out what will suffice as valor in the future. While flexible spears are hurled with children's throwing-straps, while bows—the daily death of people—shoot further into the distance, the whole circuit of the city walls is trampled by the likeness of battle. This image of battles prevents dangerous real ones from arising.[20]

The psychological impetus behind this lifestyle was a pronounced warrior ethos. The Goths judged the value of a man by his ability as a warrior and even paid respect to the enemy if he proved valorous in battle. The valor of the emperor's soldiers, who put up a fierce fight before the walls of Rome and ultimately perished, won the astonished admiration of their enemies, Procopius tells us. The Goths attentively registered feats of valor, wounds in battle, and heroic deaths. Cassiodorus celebrates the Gothic nobleman Tuluin by claiming that the wounds he had received from enemies in battle were indisputable proof of his deeds, which spoke for themselves; wounds were the "proper language of [military] excellence" (*propria lingua virtutis*). Since proving oneself in battle was the foremost way of demonstrating male excellence, duels were regularly fought before battles by warriors who volunteered to answer a formal challenge to single combat. These warriors seized the opportunity to distinguish themselves before a large audience of their peers because they believed they could obtain the greatest glory in this way. Both sides accepted this ritual without considering the psychological effects that the defeat of their comrade-in-arms might have on the collective. The battlefield transformed into a stage; the enemy armies became the spectators of a performance with a lethal outcome. Only afterward did the actual battle commence.[21]

The tactical structure of the armies that battled one another in the sixth century was fairly unsophisticated and apparently as flexible as the command structure. The Gothic army was divided into nominal units of a thousand men. The leader of such a "thousand" was styled the *millenarius*, which was derived from the word *millenus* (a thousand each). It must be stressed that the actual strength of these units could be far lower. It is not certain whether these "thousands" were themselves divided into smaller units, but there is good evidence to suggest that such subdivisions were made *ad hoc*. Military ranks or service grades remain a mystery; the commanders of divisions bore the unspecific title of *dux* ("leader," whence the word "duke"); those of forts and garrisons, the equally unspecific title of *comes* ("companion," whence the word "count").

Hence a fixed and precisely graduated hierarchy of ranks, as the late Roman legions still observed, simply did not exist in the Gothic army any more than it did among the emperor's elite troops. Military commands were held by men who had distinguished themselves through their accomplishments and who enjoyed Theoderic's trust; such persons were chosen as needed and did not hold an established service grade or rank. Since the king no longer commanded his armies personally after becoming sole ruler of Italy, he relied on the loyalty of his generals. That was not without risk for the leader of a warrior people: success on the battlefield conferred prestige and could kindle aspirations to rule. "You long were victorious in every battle in person; now you begin to have victors in your service," Ennodius declares in his panegyric, with a fine feeling for the problem of victories that others won on Theoderic's behalf. To avoid the impression that he was praising the victorious general Pitzia at the king's expense, he puts an address to the army in Pitzia's mouth that demonstrates his unconditional loyalty: they all were fighting at the king's command, indeed virtually before his very eyes, because no deed would remain hidden from him.[22]

In Theoderic's kingdom, the Goths were subject to a separate administration that stood alongside the Roman civil administration. The king deployed officials who were given the general title of *comites Gothorum* to the places where Goths were settled or stationed. The competence of this official, who served without a colleague, was normally limited to the territory of a city (*civitas*). The name for each of these officials thus consisted of the title of *comes* and the name of the city where he was stationed. Such *comites* are attested in Reate (Rieti) and Nursia (Norcia), Novum Comum (Como) and Ticinum, Marseille and Avignon, and on the island of Krk/Veglia off the coast of Dalmatia. Of course, there also were *comites* who were responsible for larger areas or even for entire provinces, although their official titles followed the pattern described above. Hence the *comes* of Naples was also responsible for monitoring the Campanian coast, and the *comes* of Syracuse was responsible for all Sicily. The *comites Gothorum* were supposed to adjudicate disputes between Goths in their cities and were Goths themselves. Disputes between Goths and Romans also fell under their jurisdiction.[23]

In a model pronouncement to inform the population of a city of the appointment of such a *comes Gothorum*, we read:

Since We know, by the grace of God, that Goths live mixed among you, We have deemed it necessary to appoint so-and-so, *vir sublimis*, who has hitherto been proven to be of upright character, as *comes* for you so that no unruliness should arise among partners, as customarily happens. He shall resolve disputes between two Goths according to Our edicts, and if a suit should perchance arise between a Goth and a Roman, he shall consult a Roman jurist and decide it in equitable fashion. Cases between two Romans, however, will be heard by the Roman judges [*cognitores*] whom We are dispatching throughout the provinces. In this way, every person will retain his own particular laws [*sua iura*] and, with this variety of judges, one justice will embrace all. Thus both peoples [*utraeque nationes*] shall enjoy sweet leisure [*otium*] in shared peace [*pax communis*] with God's blessing.

Know, however, that We have one and the same affection equally for all, but he who cherishes the laws by moderating his wishes will commend himself to Our mind more so. We have no love for anything not civic-minded [*incivile*]: We detest wicked pride and its agents. Our Piety curses the violent. The laws, not arms [literally, *brachia*], shall prevail in disputes. For why should they seek violent redress when they demonstrably have courts at hand? It is for this reason that We grant boons to judges, for this reason that We retain so many offices with sundry emoluments: so We may prevent anything that might lead to hatred from sprouting among you.

May one and the same wish in life enfold you, who notably share one and the same empire. Let each people hear what We love. Just as the Romans are your neighbors on your possessions, so may they be joined [to you] also in love. And as for you, Romans, you ought to love the Goths with great enthusiasm, for they make your peoples numerous in peacetime and defend the entire Republic in war. Therefore you should obey the judge We have appointed, so that you fulfill in every way whatever he should rule to maintain the laws, in such a way that you appear to have followed both Our command and your own benefit.[24]

This model pronouncement emphasizes the responsibility of the *comes Gothorum* for maintaining the peaceful coexistence of Goths and Romans, but it gives no detailed instructions as to how he should keep the peace among the Goths themselves. Other sources likewise betray little about how the *comites Gothorum* fulfilled their mandate. We know that they were supported by an official staff led by an officer styled the *princeps*, exactly like Roman governors. Like the chiefs-of-staff of the Palatine ministers and provincial governors, this *princeps* joined the staff from the outside; in contrast to them, however, he was not promoted from the ministry of the *magister officiorum*. Instead, he came from the staff that had formerly served the Roman *magister militum* but under Theoderic answered directly to the king. Cassiodorus preserves a model letter in which the royal chancellery recommends a Roman *princeps* to his Gothic superior. The recipient is urged to observe the old norms of Roman law and is reminded that the king has raised the Goths up so that they were not only trained in the use of arms, but were also moderated by equity: "This is what no other peoples can have; this is what makes you unique, if you, though accustomed to war, are seen to live under the law with the Romans."[25]

The fact that such instructions were considered necessary suggests that collaboration between a Gothic officer and judge and his Roman chief-of-staff did not always go smoothly. There are also some indications that the theoretically strict separation of competences between Roman governors and Gothic *comites* was not always respected in practice. That is precisely what the notables of the city of Syracuse accused the *comes* Gildila of neglecting: he allegedly usurped the right to decide legal disputes that should have been heard by Roman judges. Sometimes a *comes* was probably also directly asked to interfere since the parties to property disputes cared little about procedural rules. Thus we learn from a letter to Florianus, *vir spectabilis*—apparently a provincial governor—that a trial concerning an estate (*fundus*) of the Goth Matza had been heard in the court of the Gothic *comes* Anna. The losing, Roman, party was dissatisfied and wanted to appeal the ruling before the provincial governor. The Gothic party, however, which had prevailed in the first instance, thereupon went personally before the king. Theoderic ended the dispute by instructing Florianus to reject the appeal. Theoderic, incidentally, also reserved the right to disregard the principle that Gothic judges were competent only if at least one party was Gothic as he saw fit if he could delegate a trial to someone who enjoyed his trust. For example, he had the *comes* Marabad decide a dispute between two eminent Roman women of Provence and commissioned the *illustris femina* Theodegunda—who was apparently related to the Amals—to ensure that a ruling reached in a dispute between a Roman man and a Roman woman was enforced. This ruling, moreover, had been reached by judges whom Theodegunda herself had appointed.[26]

The *comites Gothorum* were appointed by the king and answered directly to him. Their office also conferred on them the rank of *vir spectabilis* or *vir illustris*; they thereby ranked higher than the curials of the cities in which they served. From the king's point of view, the *comites* derived their power from the commission he had given them and which he could take away again. In order to determine whether he really was able to exert this kind of control, we would have to know the criteria by which *comites Gothorum* were selected and how long they stayed in office. Little, however, is known about either of these points. The *comes* of Naples was appointed for a year, but this term may have been exceptional because the city was of great strategic importance. It is likewise difficult to generalize from the sparse information about the identity of the officeholders. Shortly before his death, Theoderic promoted a certain Quidila to leader (*prior*) of the Goths of Reate and Nursia, who had in fact nominated him. Quidila accordingly was known and congenial to the men whom he commanded. Theoderic's nephew Theodahad, in contrast, justified the appointment of a certain Wisibad *comes* of Ticinum with reference to his noble pedigree (*nobilitas*) and proven loyalty (*fides*). The man had distinguished himself decades earlier in the war against Odoacer.[27]

In the border provinces, the king installed officials whose title consisted of *comes* and the name of a province. They thus were collectively known as *comites provinciarum*. In contrast to the *comites Gothorum* of individual cities, however, these officials were equally competent for both Goths and Romans. The fundamental separation of the Gothic military administration and the Roman civil administration did not exist in this area. The *comites provinciarum* also controlled a staff that was headed by an officer appointed from the *officium* of the king. The distinction between the *comites* in the cities and their counterparts in the provinces should not, however, mislead us into concluding that their designation or specific competences followed a strict pattern: whereas the military governors of the provinces of Dalmatia, Savia, and Pannonia Sirmiensis were called *comites provinciarum*, the military governor of the two Raetic provinces was called *dux*. The nature of the responsibilities and size of the territories under the control of the *comites* of Naples and Syracuse, moreover, corresponded to those of *comites provinciarum*, although they took their titles from cities.[28]

It was the job of the Gothic *comites* in the territories of cities and border provinces to administer their districts according to the king's instructions and to ensure that his will was enforced where he could not personally be present. As a consequence of settling in Italy, the king could no longer maintain constant, close contact with his warriors as before. While Theoderic's Goths were wandering around the Balkans, his warriors had constituted a mobile camp in which they frequently encountered the king himself; in Italy, however, they were scattered across several provinces. The king now resided predominantly in Ravenna, Verona, and Ticinum and seems to have seldom left northern Italy. Personal encounters with their ruler became a rarity for most Goths; if they happened at all, they were of brief duration. In these circumstances, the king sought to prevent the growth of local concentrations of power that might elude his control. There was no guarantee that the *comites* he dispatched would always use their power in his interest, and it was also not a foregone conclusion that their commands would universally be obeyed. Theoderic therefore looked for and found additional ways to bind his warriors to himself. One such way was the promise of personal protection (*tuitio*) to Goths who lodged complaints about maladministration and abuses; the model letter used by the royal chancellery to grant such protection survives:

> It indeed seems superfluous to seek protection specifically from a prince whose mission is to defend all people generally. But because the detestable temerity of certain violent individuals troubles your peace, We are not averse to being moved by the complaints of the grieving to assume this pious role, so that what We wish to provide to all We should confer especially on a supplicant. And therefore We mercifully receive you, as you have been wounded by losses inflicted by certain persons, as you complain, into the camp of Our defense, so that you should appear to contend with your adversaries, not on the field of battle, but rather from the protection of the walls. Hence, though pressed by savage force, you are made a match for it by royal aid.
>
> Our Authority therefore grants you the protection of Our Name like an impregnable tower against lawless assaults [*inciviles impetus*] and harm from litigation, on the condition, however, that relieved of these presumptuous acts you yourself do not disdain to give a lawful response and appear to trample insolently on the public laws, you who formerly were oppressed by detestable audacity. And because Our order should have effective ministers and it is unbecoming a prince to declare something that cannot be realized, by virtue of the present command, loyalty and diligence will readily guard you, the one against the Goths, the other against the Romans. Because no one strives to defend what he is afraid may cause offense, while he fears that the generous master may become displeased.
>
> Therefore, enjoy Our mercy: rejoice in receiving this boon. If you are assailed with further lawlessness by anyone, it is your wishes about your enemies that will be granted.[29]

In order to make good on his promise to protect his subjects from the superior strength of their betters, the king needed helpers who were unswervingly loyal, mobile, and effective. For this purpose, Theoderic employed special agents who stood outside the official hierarchy and were permitted to intercede in his name anywhere and at any time. These agents bore the Gothic title of *saiones* and were Goths themselves; they only took action when Gothic interests were at stake. Their Roman counterparts were the *comitiaci*, who were likewise special agents authorized by the king to haul people to court who refused to appear. In contrast to the *saiones*, the *comitiaci* were Romans and responsible for Romans. In practice, though, the *saiones* and *comitiaci* not infrequently collaborated because the interests of Goths and Romans often overlapped.[30]

The king employed *saiones* to counteract the threat that he might become alienated from the people to whom he owed his kingdom. At the same time, the *saiones* and *comitiaci* served as tools he could use to put powerful private citizens and even civil and military officials in their place. The king could never be certain, though, whether those who sought his protection were really innocent victims as they claimed. Hence everyone to whom the king extended his protection through a *saio* was bound on oath to pay a penalty and damages if his adversary was disadvantaged by the unlawful actions of the *saio*.

Royal protection was also a two-edged sword for the king's subjects. Anyone who wished to avail himself of it first had to bring his request to the king's ear. To accomplish that, support at court was necessary, and that was hard to come by without effort and expense. The *saiones*, moreover—like all officials—charged fees (*sportulae*) for their services, and at twice the usual rate. And lastly, it was uncertain whether the king's protection, once it had at last been granted, would actually have the desired effect because in a majority of cases the goal was to facilitate a trial or execute a judgment in the first place. In the former case, it was impossible to know what the final verdict would be; in the latter, the petitioner had to trust that the *saio* dispatched by the king would be willing and able to assert himself against the defeated party. Whether that happened depended on the social status of the litigants and the agent in question. Since *saiones* were armed and could point to their royal commission, they had considerable leeway. It was not uncommon that *saiones* used force against those whom they actually were supposed to support. Theoderic threatened one such *saio* who abused his authority with the withdrawal of royal favor and the loss of his donative.[31]

Theoderic could dispense with helpers no more than any other ruler could, and yet he still had one way of preventing his personal connection to his army from breaking completely, despite the fact that he had relinquished command to others since becoming king in Italy: once a year, Theoderic summoned every Goth who was obligated to perform military service to the court—hence normally to Ravenna. He reviewed his warriors on this occasion. By dispensing praise and blame, greeting all, and speaking personally with individuals, he renewed his personal connection to them. Every Goth considered fit to serve received a donative of five gold pieces. Anyone who was no longer able to serve could be released from the obligation to appear at court for this muster, but he thereby lost his claim to the donative. A series of Gothic nobles also lived permanently at court; these "greater men of the house" (*maiores domus*) constituted a group of advisers and helpers alongside the traditional privy council staffed by Romans (the *consistorium*).[32]

Lastly, Theoderic reinforced the bond between himself and his warriors by providing less wealthy Goths with weapons and horses. The king bred and bought horses for his army in grand style and could turn to the state weapons factories of late antique Italy for a supply of arms. The *Notitia dignitatum*, a kind of government handbook from around the year 425, attests no fewer than seven arms factories (*fabricae*), almost all of which were specialized in the production of specific pieces of equipment. They were located in Cremona and Verona, Mantua and Lucca, Concordia and Ticinum. A factory in Verona also produced weapons and armor of all kinds. Even though we do not know whether all seven of these arms factories were still in operation under Theoderic, there is no question that he could turn to weaponsmiths (*armifactores*) who were under state supervision and received a government salary (*annona*) to equip his warriors. The king reserved the right to inspect the quality of their products personally.[33]

The extraction of the raw material iron was also under royal control; Theoderic instructed the *comes* of the province of Dalmatia to inspect the iron mines there; ore was needed for the production of weapons and agricultural implements. Weapons depots that enabled the king to equip his people as mounted warriors are also attested in Theoderic's kingdom. In this way, the king reduced the dependence of less wealthy Goths on their noble patrons while putting them under a greater obligation to himself.[34]

Theoderic almost always could count on his Goths when he summoned them to his standards during his reign of over thirty years: they fought for him against the Gepids in Serbia, against Clovis' Franks in southern France, against the Visigoth Gesalec, and finally against the Burgundians. Undoubtedly, not all Gothic nobles were equally satisfied with Theoderic's rule. In the year 500, Theoderic had the Gothic *comes* Odoin executed, but we know absolutely nothing about the background or aftermath of this event. Fourteen years later, the king killed the Gothic *comes* Petia with his own hands. If this Petia is identical with the general Pitzia, who had defeated the imperial general Sabinianus for Theoderic in 505—these are just two different ways of transcribing the same name—the murder had a political dimension; the victim would have been a potential rival. This identification, however, is not secure; moreover, it presumes that Theoderic posthumously rehabilitated Pitzia because Theoderic honored his memory at the end of his reign. At any rate, this conflict also had no repercussions that we can observe.[35]

Several factors explain Theoderic's success in neutralizing the centrifugal forces unleashed by the transformation of the Goths into a standing army and the transition to a sedentary regime. For one, he controlled vast resources that he could distribute among his followers. The Goths who followed Theoderic to Italy owed him their economic livelihood as landholders and continued to profit from his reign on account of the donatives he annually disbursed. After Theoderic brought the kingdom of the Visigoths under his control, he also distributed the taxes he collected there among the Goths in Hispania and Italy. Moreover, we can presume that Goths who had somehow proven themselves worthy were personally rewarded for their special merits. We incidentally learn, for instance, that Theoderic rewarded the Gothic general Tuluin with a gift of estates. As Theoderic's territory expanded over the years, the amount of income and resources at his disposal also increased, making their redistribution a powerful instrument of government.

Theoderic could also capitalize on the prestige he enjoyed on account of his unparalleled success. The conquest of Italy alone must have seemed like the realization of a distant dream to those among his followers who had served Theoderic's father or Theoderic Strabo. The Italian campaign of Theoderic's uncle Vidimir in 473 had been a pathetic failure. Theoderic, in contrast, turned a mobile group of warriors that had experienced highs and lows together, and even threatened to disintegrate at times, into the military basis of a great kingdom, all while making those who loyally served him wealthy and respected. His series of successes remained unbroken even afterward: at his death, Theoderic controlled an empire that stretched from Portugal in the west to Serbia in the east. A king like Theoderic had no equal, many, if not most, of his Goths may have thought.[36]

Theoderic's army was composed of warriors with wives and children. Since the latter also counted as Goths, the army was considered the armed part of the Gothic people. As long as Theoderic was wandering around the Balkans with his Goths, these woman and children lived in immediate proximity to their husbands and fathers. They rode horses or wagons on the march, accompanied by men who were supposed to protect them from enemy attacks, although they were not always successful. In one attack in 478, imperial troops seized no fewer than 2,000 wagons and 5,000 people. When Theoderic could not lodge his people in cities, the men, women, and children camped together in the open country. After they settled in Italy, the lifestyle of Gothic women changed radically as their husbands became landowners. Gothic families now appear to have frequently lived on estates that belonged to the husbands and fathers. There, they often had to make do without the head of the household since the Gothic men were regularly separated from their families on military service. It is not known whether Gothic women took on the role of the lady of the house in the sense that they personally preoccupied themselves with agricultural operations.

The wives of Gothic warriors were not Amazons. Their life cycle revolved around marriage and motherhood. Gothic warriors and their wives were bound to one another by a long-term, socially recognized relationship that created obligations on the part of the spouses both toward one another and toward their children. Monogamy was the rule. It would be mistaken to infer from that, however, that Gothic warriors were always faithful to their wives. Unconditional faithfulness toward one's spouse was a female virtue among the Goths, just as it was for large parts of Roman society. Tacitus had declared that "adultery" (*adulterium*) was extremely rare among the Germani so as to condemn the—in his view—lax morals of Roman wives by comparison. Adultery was defined as sexual intercourse by a man with the wife of another man; hence the Roman moralist added that when adultery occurred among the Germani, the husband of the adulterous wife punished her severely without delay.[37]

The social status of Gothic women depended on that of their parents and husbands. The wives of Goths of senatorial rank also held this rank. They were able to acquire property through inheritance, particularly if their husbands and fathers owned estates in Italy. That had repercussions on their marriage behavior: as long as Theoderic's Goths were wandering around the Balkans, there were only movable goods to inherit; heiresses who could make their grooms wealthy were a rare commodity outside the family of the Amals. In Italy, there soon were good and bad matches for Goths who wanted to be somebody. Vice versa, soon marriageable girls, divorced women, and widows were competing on the marriage market. When large estates were at stake, the king himself probably arranged marriages that served his interests; that at any rate is attested for Theoderic's successors Theodahad and Ildebad.[38]

Before they settled in Italy, the cohabitation of men and women among the Goths was regulated by unwritten norms about which we know little. After victory over Odoacer, Theoderic attempted to compel his Goths to follow the norms of Roman law; the behavior of spouses would now also be judged according to them. In an edict that appears to date from the first years of his reign in Italy, Theoderic declares adultery a capital crime: a man who had sexual intercourse with another's wife would be put to death along with the cheating wife; the same punishment would befall a man who made his house available for the perpetration of adultery, as well as anyone who convinced a woman to commit adultery. According to this definition, sexual intercourse with an unmarried woman was not adultery but at most fornication (*stuprum*), and then only if the woman involved was not a slave or disreputable in the eyes of the upper class. Theoderic thus recognized the double standard presumed in Roman law for the behavior of spouses. The king posed before Goths and Romans as the protector of marital morals; when he dealt with family affairs, he exhorted the women to marital fidelity and touted the virtues of modesty (*pudor*) and chastity (*castitas*). For Theoderic, there was no question that husbands were entitled and, in certain circumstances, obligated to punish their wives. The husband was the head of the household and, as such, responsible for the behavior of its members. When a judge banished a husband who had caught his wife's lover *in flagranti delicto* and killed him, Theoderic rescinded the verdict and declared the man free of all wrongdoing.[39]

Even though we know little about the daily life of Gothic women, it is clear that Gothic men and women were together for better and for worse; during their wanderings on the Balkan Peninsula, the Gothic women expressed their feelings vociferously at times when the whole group faced existential decisions. When King Vitigis capitulated to the imperial general Belisarius in 540, the Gothic women rebuked their husbands for cowardice. They evidently identified completely with the group to which they belonged.

The names of Gothic women indicate very clearly that they were regarded as part of the Gothic people. Among the Goths, men and women had only a single name to distinguish them from other people. These names were based on a deliberate choice by their parents; since the meaning of Gothic names was generally intelligible, they constituted a kind of catalogue of the values of the entire group. Among the Ostrogoths, the vast majority of men's and women's names are either derived from collective reference points like dynasty and people or refer to qualities useful in battle and on campaign. Gundihild, for instance, means "(female) warrior in battle"; Sendefara, "she who is setting out on a (martial) journey"; Rani(h)ilda, "she who fights with a lance." In contrast, women's names derived from the qualities "young" (*jung*), "beautiful" (*schön*), and "soft" (*sanft*), like those in the Western Germanic dialects, are lacking. The semantic range of Ostrogothic women's names differs from that of men's names only insofar as there are many men's names derived from predators like the wolf, boar, bear, eagle, and raven.

Wealthy Gothic women also expressed their status as members of the military elite with their clothing. Grave finds show that they wore expensive fibulae and belt buckles, as well as earrings, bracelets, chains of pearls, and rings. The fibulae used by the Goths to fasten garments can be assigned to various categories; the most magnificent are made of gilded metal and garnets in the form of a stylized eagle; hence they are called "eagle fibulae" (*Adlerfibeln*). A find made at San Domagnano in the Republic of San Marino at the end of the nineteenth century gives an excellent impression of such accoutrements: a grave was found to contain a pair of eagle fibulae, a pair of earrings, nine necklace pendants, a golden ring, and three belt-plates.[40]

Women used such jewelry as means of demonstrating their status. In this way, noble Gothic women highlighted the social distance between themselves

Fig. 7. Jewelry (eagle fibula) from the treasure of
San Domagnano (San Marino). © Germanisches
Nationalmuseum, Nuremberg.

and lower-class women, particularly other Gothic women. At the same time, costume differentiated the wives of Gothic warriors from Roman women whose fathers and husbands could only be civilians in Theoderic's kingdom. This context explains the choice of the eagle for female fibulae: in the late Roman world of the Goths, the eagle was primarily a military symbol; it adorned legionary standards, and it also stood for the victoriousness of the emperor. Gothic women who used eagle-shaped fibulae thus were appropriating a symbol that evoked power and strength. The eagle was by no means a Gothic symbol per se, as earlier scholars often assumed, and its meaning should also not be extrapolated from the mythology of medieval Scandinavia. In Gothic Italy, the eagle was a distinguishing token of women who wanted to advertise their status as members of a warrior elite.[41]

Gothic men distinguished themselves from their Roman counterparts first and foremost with their warrior lifestyle and military function. It was easy to tell at a glance who belonged to the *exercitus Gothorum* because the right to bear arms in public was a military privilege. Just as under the Roman Empire, civilians were forbidden to own and use weapons in Theoderic's kingdom except for hunting or self-defense. This ban applied particularly to lances, cuirasses, shields, and helmets and less so to javelins and swords. Theoderic made this ban even stricter, supposedly only permitting Romans to own knives. A weapons ban had already existed under the Western Roman emperors and is not specific to his kingdom as such; Justinian also issued a law prohibiting the possession of weapons. In Theoderic's kingdom, however, bearing arms marked the separation of two groups that were defined not only in functional but also in ethnic terms. There is good reason to believe that Theoderic's Goths also differentiated themselves from their Roman counterparts with their hairstyle. The name *capillati* indicates that the Goths liked to grow their hair down to their shoulders; on the evidence of the Morro d'Alba medallion, Theoderic himself sported a billowing mane. Since moustaches were unusual among the Romans, they were also regarded as a Gothic custom in Italy; Ennodius makes fun of a Roman who copied them.[42]

In addition to religion, which we shall discuss in greater detail below, language in particular created a barrier between Goths and Romans. The Goths' everyday language was and remained Gothic. We may presume, naturally, that there were many Goths living in Theoderic's kingdom who could, with some effort, make themselves understood in Latin. There also must have been Goths with extensive knowledge of the Latin language because officials in the civil and military administration conducted all their written correspondence in it. Hence every Gothic military unit needed at least one person who could translate the baroque Latin of the late Roman chancellery, which was difficult even for many Romans to understand, into Gothic. Individual bilingualism must also have been widespread in the clergy of Homoean communities, at least among presbyters and deacons, who viewed themselves in Italy as part of a "Church of the Gothic law." It is hard to imagine, however, that Gothic warriors attended the schools of Roman grammarians or rhetors. They had neither the time nor a reason to preoccupy themselves with this kind of education, even if the king probably did not forbid them outright to attend Roman schools, as Procopius claims. We hardly can assume that the Gothic nobility could read and write. The Gothic lady Hildevara indeed signed a donation in the year

523 in her own hand. Some thirty years later, however, the eminent Gothic lady
Ranilo and her no less distinguished husband Felithanc used a cross to sign an
instrument to convey fifty pounds of silver and parts of two estate complexes;
the eminent couple was illiterate.[43]

Vice versa, the Romans seldom learned Gothic. The fact that Theoderic's
Roman collaborator Cyprianus spoke Gothic and had his sons instructed in the
language was the exception to the rule, and Cassiodorus emphasizes it for precisely that reason. It moreover is no coincidence that Cyprianus was one of the
Romans who held several high offices at court because complete bilingualism
will have been much more common at Theoderic's court than elsewhere.
Theoderic's daughter Amalasuintha and other women from his family were
even taught Greek and Latin literature. Gothic men, in contrast, learned Latin
solely to make themselves understood in everyday life; for that, it sufficed to be
able to understand spoken Latin and to construct simple sentences. This form
of functional bilingualism harmonized perfectly with Theoderic's own views:
he had little love for his educated but unwarlike nephew Theodahad.[44]

The coexistence of Gothic warriors and Roman civilians held great potential
for conflict. The royal chancellery took pains to downplay the extent of the tension, but it still incessantly had to remind its addressees to obey the law. In a
letter to the Goths in Reate and Nursia, written soon after Theoderic's death,
Cassiodorus explains to the recipients quite bluntly that the Gothic-Roman
compromise not only required compliance with the law, but also was in their
own interest:

> For this is what adorns Our kingdom, what magnifies your reputation among
> peoples [*gentes*]: if you do such things as can be both agreeable to Us and
> most welcome to the Deity. Our enemies are conquered more mightily by
> good manners because those protected by the powers above cannot have
> fortunate adversaries. You fight effectively abroad while you strive to culti-
> vate justice in your homes. In this way two things are joined in mutual
> embrace: he who cultivates equity will have the fruit of victory. For what
> need drives you toward unjust acts, when both your own allotted lands
> [*sortes*] nourish you and Our gifts make you wealthy with God's help? For
> even if someone had reason to demand something, he should place his
> hopes rather in the prince's munificence than in the daring of [martial]
> prowess because it benefits you that the Romans are peaceful: while they fill
> our treasuries, they multiply your donatives.[45]

In this letter, as in many others, the royal chancellery presupposes a latent
tension between Roman civilians and Gothic warriors that could explode in

acute violence at any moment. There is evidence, in fact, that Gothic soldiers looted civilians. Quartering garrisons was unpopular; the movement of troops, feared. Theoderic's nephew Theodahad was notorious for seizing his neighbors' land on a whim, and his was not an isolated case. In an edict issued in the name of her son Athanaric soon after Theoderic's death, his daughter Amalasuintha censured the usurpation of others' property. This measure was not addressed exclusively against the Goths, of course; senators were prone to the same impulse to enrich themselves. But Goths who did so at the Romans' expense were no less unpopular; since they could be called to account only by their own kind, they were sometimes tempted to use violence against unarmed Romans to back up their claims. If charges were brought against them, they still could hope that the competent judge might be inclined to dismiss the case. In the province of Samnium, where many Goths lived, the Romans had so little confidence in the fairness of Gothic judges that the provincial assembly asked the king to commission someone he trusted to settle pending disputes between Goths and Romans. The regular authorities were apparently overwhelmed by the task. Theoderic dispatched a trusted Goth who had served him for many years to decide all the cases involving Goths and Romans.[46]

If Theoderic hoped to be accepted by both Goths and Romans, he had to ensure that abuses perpetrated against the civilian population remained within tolerable limits. The king thus strove to ensure that his army was always adequately provisioned and constantly called for discipline. He appeased his Roman subjects by providing monetary compensation to those who could prove that his troops had caused damage. In the early years of his reign, Theoderic published a collection of legal norms—the so-called *Edict of Theoderic*—that penalized violent crimes and property offenses in particular. The edict applied to all of Theoderic's subjects equally, both Goths and Romans. But in light of the circumstances, it must have been viewed as an effort to restrain the armed portion of the population that had come to Italy with Theoderic. He was especially inflexible when Goths refused to pay the land tax on their property. Refusing to pay taxes endangered the Gothic-Roman compromise because tax collection was the job of the civic authorities, who were liable to the imperial treasury for a sum fixed in advanced. If some taxpayers refused to do their duty, others were forced to take their place.[47]

If Theoderic wanted his Goths to adjust to Roman law, he had to suppress archaic forms of dispute resolution that are common in warrior societies. Every physical assault on property, life, or limb, every insult among warriors, demanded retaliation; vengeance was a point of honor. One way of ending the cycle of vengeance unleashed by such actions was the payment of punitive damages. This

custom was so entrenched in the kingdom of the Burgundians that the kings did
not even attempt to suppress it completely but rather merely tried to limit it. A
codification of royal norms compiled before 501 and repeatedly expanded thereafter, the so-called *Lex Burgundionum*, reveals that a defendant who was unwilling to acknowledge his guilt could still free himself of the accusation brought
against him by protesting his innocence under oath jointly with eleven relatives.
If his adversary rejected this procedure, however, he could challenge the defendant to single combat, the outcome of which decided the matter.[48]

Theoderic was unwilling to tolerate such forms of dispute resolution. His
Goths would no longer be able to ward off suits with the help of oaths sworn
with their kin or engage in single combat before the court. It was the express
wish of the king that they submit to the judgment of the *comes Gothorum* he
appointed. After the territory of Sirmium was integrated into Theoderic's kingdom, Cassiodorus held up the Goths as a glowing example for the "barbarians
and Romans" living there:

> Why do you resort to single combat [*monomachia*] when you do not have a
> venal judge? Set down your iron, you who have no enemy. You do nothing
> worse than to raise your arms against your kin, for whom you rather must die
> gloriously. What need has a man for a tongue if his armed hand pleads his
> case? Or how might one believe there is peace if there is fighting under a
> civil state [*sub civilitate*]? Imitate our Goths, who know to fight battles out-
> side and practice restraint inside. We want you to live the way you see our
> kindred flourishing by the grace of God.[49]

We may doubt whether Theoderic's Goths were really ready to give up every
form of self-help against real or alleged injustice. Blood feud demonstrably
remained imperative to protect one's honor. It is also indisputable, however,
that the king was unwilling to recognize the resolution of a dispute by oath or
single combat as binding. The royal chancellery, moreover, proclaimed the
unity of substantive law. Even if Theoderic's Goths enjoyed a privileged status,
since they could be tried only before Gothic judges, they were subject to the
same legal norms as the Romans. That may have remained purely theoretical
as long as disputes were kept between Goths: in that case, neither the parties nor
the judge may have insisted on applying Roman law, the complicated concepts
of which could be mastered only with the help of jurists. And at any rate, the
involvement of a Roman legal expert was required only when a Roman was one
of the litigants.[50]

Theoderic's ruling ideology was based on the notion that two peoples with
different responsibilities lived together peacefully and to their mutual benefit

under his regime. Gothic warriors and Roman civilians were regarded as the two pillars of his kingdom. The Goths in Italy actually maintained their status as a privileged warrior people down to the demise of the kingdom. Nonetheless, real life was obviously more complex than the discourse promoted by the royal chancellery. There were several reasons for this. First of all, the Goths' estates were scattered and surrounded by those of Roman landowners; that resulted in economic and social ties. Insofar as names permit us to draw inferences, mixed marriages between members of the Gothic army and Roman women definitely occurred. The military and civil administration were not strictly separated since a civil official, the praetorian prefect, was responsible for provisioning the army. It thus is not at all surprising that the prefect Liberius was also celebrated for his service to the military. The Goths in Italy also adopted cultural practices and military technologies for which they had had no use while they still lived as a wandering warrior people on the Balkan Peninsula. When Theoderic's Goths became sedentary in Italy, the Goths began erecting gravestones with Latin inscriptions for deceased family members. In the war against Justinian's army, the Goths made use of mobile siege towers and torsion siege engines, as well as armored cavalry horses. At the end of his life, Theoderic issued an order to construct a major fleet. A process of military acculturation was thus taking place.[51]

By conferring senatorial rank on the Goths whom he entrusted with military offices, Theoderic placed them on an equal footing with members of the Roman senatorial class. Some Goths even obtained the rank of *vir illustris*, which entitled them to admission to the senate itself. Only a single Goth is known to have actually become a member of the senate, however, and that case can be explained by special circumstances: soon after Theoderic's death, the veteran general Tuluin was admitted to the senate after he supported the accession of the underage Athalaric. Normally, Gothic nobles appear to have had no interest in moving their place of residence to Rome in order to lead the life of a Roman senator.[52]

Vice versa, Theoderic entrusted Romans with military responsibilities in individual cases. In the years 504 and 505, the Roman Cyprianus participated in campaigns against the Gepids and Bulgars and distinguished himself as a warrior; he later served at court as a *referendarius*, a kind of judicial liaison for litigants who sought redress directly from the emperor, and in 524–525 he became the director of one of the three central "financial ministries" as *comes sacrarum largitionum* ("count of the sacred largesses"). Cyprianus thus was one of the Romans who enjoyed Theoderic's complete confidence. He lived many years at court and held a prominent position there; his military employment thus remained limited to the beginning of his career.[53]

Social contact between Goths and Romans was especially intense at the king's court. Here, Roman senators and Gothic noblemen constantly rubbed shoulders. Anyone who wanted to make something of himself under Theoderic was well advised to cultivate the Goths whose counsel the king heeded. Theoderic also employed Romans in the area of the palace known as the "bed-chamber" (*cubiculum*), which was off limits to the public. In 510, he brought the eminent Roman woman Barbara to his court to tutor his daughter Amalasuintha. In addition to Gothic and Latin, Amalasuintha also spoke Greek; she thus must have received an education according to the Roman model. Theoderic's niece Amalaberga was also celebrated for her learning, although not for speaking multiple languages. Theoderic had no intention, however, of educating Gothic men according to the Roman model. Even though he some-times enjoyed lively discussions with Cassiodorus about natural phenomena — the explanation of which was considered a branch of philosophy — he thoroughly disapproved of his nephew Theodahad, who had dedicated himself to the study of Platonic philosophy and lived in Etruria like a Roman aristocrat, far from the army and court. Theoderic's closest advisers were Goths who had proven them-selves as warriors and were capable of holding military command.[54]

Theoderic was obviously not blind to the fact that the luxurious and cultured lifestyle of Roman senators certainly had its appeal for some Goths, just as vice versa some Romans envied the Goths' status as privileged warriors. But the king did not want to encourage these tendencies. The *Anonymus Valesianus* attri-butes the following aphorism to him: "The wretched Roman imitates the Goth, and the rich Goth imitates the Roman." This statement is anything but a call for mutual adaptation as some people have believed. If it were a broad policy, then each segment of the population's imitation of the other half would not be limited to poor Romans and rich Goths. The sentence rather laconically indi-cates precisely the behaviors that Theoderic did *not* want to be imitated. For him, Goths and Romans were peoples with specific, albeit complementary, roles; he did not want this ethnic division of labor to change in any way.[55]

3. WEALTH AND ANCESTRAL PRIDE: THE SENATE AND SENATORS

Any ruler who hoped to hold on to power in Italy for long needed the sup-port of local elites. The social group with the greatest influence was the sena-tors. That was not because the senate was involved in the government. The decision-making powers of the late Roman senate were narrowly circum-scribed; normally, the senate limited itself to confirming decrees composed at

court. The political significance of the senate in the age of Odoacer and
Theoderic derived from the fact that over the course of the fifth century, the
senate had become a kind of representative body for the wealthiest and most
powerful men in Italy. These men owned palatial houses in Rome and villas in
the provinces. These happy few, whose estates were usually scattered across
several provinces, owned the better part of Italy. Thousands of free and unfree
peasants worked their land; hundreds of slaves served in their houses. Their
clients included beggars, day laborers, artisans, clergymen, decurions (municipal council members), and senators. These men wielded immense social clout.

The Gallic senator Sidonius Apollinaris came to Rome in 467 with the goal
of obtaining an office that would confer the rank of *vir illustris*. When he began
searching for a patron to help him, he consulted the former urban prefect
Paulus and reached the following assessment of the situation:

> Indeed there were many men in the senate of exquisite wealth and lofty
> pedigree, venerable age and valuable counsel, high rank and equal worthi-
> ness, but with apologies to the rest, the two most preeminent consulars,
> Gennadius Avienus and Caecina Basilius, towered over all the others. In the
> most eminent [senatorial] order—excepting the prerogative of the armed
> branch—these men easily were princes second to the prince clad in purple
> himself. . . . Both of them, if by chance they emerged from their homes,
> were crowded by a throng of fawning clients in their path and around them.
> The hopes and attitudes of the retinues of these peers, however, were far dif-
> ferent: Avienus did everything he could to promote the careers of his sons,
> sons-in-law, and brothers, and because he was always tied up with the candi-
> dates from his own house, he was less highly effective at meeting the needs
> of those seeking office from outside. And in this regard the family of the
> Decii was preferred to that of the Corvini because what Avienus obtained for
> his own kin while wearing his belt of office, Basilius conferred on people
> outside his family without one.[56]

Sidonius Apollinaris knew what he was talking about; he duly became urban
prefect in the year 468. His testimony thus carries weight. The senate was an
assembly of wealthy men that was dominated by a small number of families.
Relatives, followers, and petitioners who were part of this clientele, or hoped to
be admitted to it, gathered around the heads of these families. Anyone who
hoped to achieve something was well advised to win their favor. The patronage
of these men also extended down to the lower classes. Ordinary people sought
out a senator's protection against the superior strength of highly placed people
with or without office and even in disputes with people of their own rank; they

needed advocates before the authorities and in court and material support
when in need. In return, patrons expected their clients to throng around them
in public and stand by if things became dangerous. It was no coincidence that
the instigators of riots and unrest were often sought among senators. Hence the
clergyman Fulgentius rejoiced when he heard that the *patricius* Theodorus had
converted to an ascetic life: just as the authority of the powerful inspired "many
brothers and friends, clients and subordinates, acquaintances and strangers" to
love the temporal world, his conversion would now inspire many to reject it.
That remained a pious wish, but it gives us an impression of how one assessed
the social clout of a *patricius*. Senators who had landholdings in the provinces
also exercised an overwhelming influence there. It was said of Cassiodorus'
father that he kept the province of Sicily from opposing Theoderic when he
invaded Italy. A senator named Tullianus was so powerful in the province of
Lucania et Bruttii that he was able to raise a peasant army against Totila.[57]

Senate and senators—these terms did not entirely overlap in Theoderic's
kingdom. In Italy at the time, there probably lived several thousand people who
bore the title of *vir clarissimus* or *vir spectabilis* and thus were members of the
two lower grades of the senatorial order (*ordo senatorius*). The vast majority of
these senators had made their abode in a municipal community (*civitas*) outside Rome; upon doing so, they ceased to belong to the senate as an assembly,
but they continued to count as members of the senatorial order. These provincial senators usually had acquired their rank with governorships and offices at
court. They made up the highest level of the local elite where they settled; they
outranked the councilmen of provincial cities but shared with them their
municipal field of operations. We thus will come back to discuss them again in
the context of cities.[58]

Senators domiciled in Rome had access to the senate as an assembly even if
they merely held the rank of *vir clarissimus* or *vir spectabilis*. When the son of a
senator registered in Rome reached the required age, he was formally admitted
to the senate; he thereafter was permitted to take part in senate meetings and
probably also was allowed to speak. This right to speak, however, was purely
theoretical for senators of the rank of *vir clarissimus*. The solicitation of opinions
among the senators obeyed a strict hierarchy that left those who held a rank
lower than *illustris* hardly a chance of getting a word in. The highest-ranking
senator, the *caput senatus*, spoke first; after him, the senator who was second on
the official ranking, then the senator who held third place, and so on. *Patricii*,
moreover, outranked other *illustres*; within the group of *patricii*, the year in
which the title had been conferred was decisive. Only then, after all those present had given their opinion (*sententia*), did the senators ranked as *viri spectabiles*

get their turn — if the debate had not already been closed. And it is probable that it normally was cut off simply because some 80–100 *viri illustres* were members of the senate; deliberations would have taken hours even if only every *vir illustris* declared his position. Senators ranked *viri clarissimi* or *viri spectabiles* thus will normally have been limited to the role of spectators. They participated in the decision-making process only by joining in the acclamations with which the late Roman senate typically passed its resolutions.[59]

The senate of the late fifth and sixth centuries thus was dominated by an exclusive group of senators who held the rank of *vir illustris*; these men were senators in the narrower sense of the word. There were only two ways to obtain the rank of *vir illustris*: by holding offices that conferred it or by royal privilege. These offices were awarded by the king, and all of them, with the exception of the urban prefecture, were located at the royal court. Once one had obtained the rank of *vir illustris*, whether by office or by privilege, admission to the senate was a formality, even if the *vir illustris* in question had not previously been a member of the senate at all. Of course, not everyone who had the privilege to call himself *vir illustris* in Theoderic's kingdom took advantage of this custom; the king also distinguished Goths with this rank. Since they declined to apply for admission to the senate, however, the Romans had the senate to themselves as long as Theoderic lived.

Anyone who wanted to climb to the top of the senatorial hierarchy had to serve the king for a certain time as a court official or win his favor some other way. The same is true of *viri spectabiles*. This rank also required one to hold an office that conferred it, such as governor of many provinces. The only alternative was, again, a royal privilege. Anyone who did not hold office in the royal administration and was not raised by the king personally to *vir spectabilis*, or indeed to *vir illustris*, spent his life with the lowest rank, that of *vir clarissimus*, no matter whether he had ancestors who had been *viri illustres*. Membership in the senate could be inherited but not one's position within the order. The hierarchy within the senatorial order was determined by the king. He also had considerable influence on the composition of the senate since he could confer the rank of *vir illustris* on men who had no senatorial ancestors if they had the ambition of joining the senate. Hence the scions of old families who had long lived in Rome and could look back on many senatorial ancestors sat side by side with *homines novi* ("new men"), who were the first members of their families to obtain admission to the senate and often had property in northern Italy. These men owed their rise solely to the king and his court. They often had held office at court for many years before they were admitted to the senate. They thus were well connected at court and had the king's confidence. From the start, they were preferred to *illustris* families as appointees to head the two traditional "finance ministries," and in the latter half of Theoderic's reign they also frequently took a turn as praetorian prefects. Since royal service required one to be present at court, their membership in the senate did not take effect until they left and moved their household to Rome. These social climbers were not pro-Goth in the sense that they would have advocated an alliance between the two peoples. They had been socialized and educated as Romans, were status-conscious, and were anything but bureaucrats. Their loyalty was to the king, not to his people. But they benefited more than any others from cooperating with Theoderic and his successors, although their connection to the city and idea of Rome was still not as strong as that of the members of established illustrious families. It would be misconceived, however, to imagine long-standing members on one side and newcomers on the other as two entrenched camps that pursued diametrically opposed interests. The scions of old families also needed the king if they were to reach the highest rank of the senatorial order. Even a man like Faustus Niger was not too proud to serve Theoderic for several years as praetorian prefect. Vice versa, newcomers who held several offices at court and reached the consulate for the first time in their families, like Cassiodorus, quickly adopted the value system of the men in whose exclusive circle they had been admitted. Since landed property dispersed across several provinces was the economic basis of all senators, their interests did not fragment into regional blocks, even though men who predominantly lived in northern Italy could be present at court more easily by reason of geographical proximity. That, of course, is not to say that peace and harmony always reigned among senators: competition and conflict belonged to every senator's self-conception. Their coalitions were as complex and variable as their causes. Senators fought bitterly over the election of the bishop of Rome and sued one another over land disputes. Even the bearers of prestigious names like Basilius and Praetextatus were not immune to an accusation of availing themselves of "magic arts." Theoderic had a senatorial commission investigate their case.[60]

The Decii were the most important entrenched aristocratic family in Rome. No fewer than three of the ten consuls for the western half of the Roman Empire from 480 to 490 came from the *gens Decia*: all three of them were sons of Caecina Decius Basilius, who himself had attained the consulship in 463. The western consul in the year 480 was named Decius Marius Venantius Basilius, and that of the year 486, Caecina Mavortius Basilius Decius. In the next generation, all four sons of the prematurely deceased Maximus Basilius (cos. 480) reached the consulship: Albinus in 493, Avienus in 501, Theodorus in 505, and finally Inportunus in 509. On top of that, all four of them also received the rank of *patricius* from Theoderic, which elevated them above all other *viri illustres*. But they were not the only members of the *gens Decia* to become consuls in the first two decades of Theoderic's reign. The only known son of Basilius Decius (cos. 486), Basilius Venantius, also reached this office, indeed a year before Inportunus. Basilius Venantius himself, moreover, was able to see two of his own sons become consuls after Theoderic's death: Decius junior in 529 and Paulinus junior in 534. Vettius Agorius Basilius Mavortius, finally, consul in the year 527, was at least closely related to the consul of 486.[61]

The Decii surpassed all other senatorial families of their time in wealth and power, but there were others who also held the highest offices for several generations and so could always be found in the exclusive circle of illustrious senators. Two such families were the Anicii and the Symmachi. The head of the Symmachi family in the age of Odoacer and Theoderic was Aurelius Memmius Symmachus; he was the son of the western consul of the year 446 and became both consul (485) and urban prefect himself. He had three daughters but apparently no son. One of these three daughters, Rusticiana, married Anicius Severinus Manlius Boethius, the orphaned son of the consul of 487, about whom we will have occasion to say more. This marriage produced two sons who held the consulship jointly in the year 522: one was named Boethius after his father, the other Symmachus after his father-in-law. Scholars have frequently overestimated the influence of the *gens Anicia*; be that as it may, the family still produced two senators in our period who were both named Faustus and so were differentiated by the additional epithets Niger ("black") and Albus ("white"). Anicius Acilius Aginantius Faustus iunior Albus, son of the western consul of 438, was urban prefect and consul (483) under Odoacer; he seems to have served as urban prefect a second time under Theoderic. Anicius Probus Faustus iunior Niger was consul in the year 490 and later held high office at Theoderic's court, first as *quaestor sacri palatii* (503–505/6) and then as *magister officiorum* (509–512), which gave him the ranks of *illustris* and *patricius*.[62]

Theoderic first had to work to win over the old families of Rome. Odoacer had followed the same policy and nominated members of these families to the consulship. Theoderic also recognized the principle that the scions of the great families had a kind of birthright to the highest honors. They therefore not only were preferred for appointment as consul and urban prefect—prestigious but also costly offices that were held in Rome itself—but were also often entrusted with the office of praetorian prefect. The king could dispense with the examination of the merits of senators with illustrious ancestors, Cassiodorus declared in Theoderic's name, since their pedigree was certification enough. In a letter to the senate that he wrote on the occasion of the elevation of Inportunus (cos.

509) to *patricius*, Cassiodorus explains the difference between *homines novi* and a member of the *gens Decia* as follows:

> We are pleased to bring new men to the pinnacle of honors. We delight in grafting men of foreign stock to the lap of Liberty so that the chamber of the senate may blossom with sundry virtues. Such a multitude adorns the assembly, and this distinguished company gladdens its public face. It is proven to be far more gratifying to Us, however, when We restore to high rank men who have grown from the very luster of the curia because Our scrutiny of you is not needed since you transfer goods [to the next generation] which have been judged beforehand [*praeiudicata bona*], showing merits at the light of birth. Your very background is glorious: praise is the crib-mate of nobility. The beginning of life, for you, is the beginning of public repute. In you, the most eminent honor of the senate is inborn, to which few attain even in ripe, old years.
>
> Although we deem this truthfully about all of you, such that [Our] favor for senators embraces the spirit of the entire order, the bloodline of the Decii, which has dazzled unchanged with the luster of virtue consistently for so many years, shines forth most in the eyes of Our Serenity: no matter how rare glory may be, it is not found to vary in so long a genealogy. For generations, this vein has produced preeminent men: nothing mediocre can grow from it. As many men of proven worth as have been born and—which hardly occurs—an elite abundance of them. Behold, from one seed sprout fourfold distinction, civil honor, ancestral glory, and a boon to the senate—who, though they dazzle with their shared merits, you still will find one you can praise for his own qualities.

Cassiodorus continues by celebrating Inportunus as the epitome of a Roman aristocrat:

> Look indeed on the young man, who pleases by the grace of his looks and even more so with the beauty of his mind. His face recalls the distinction of his blood; the nature of his spirit is betrayed by his countenance, and the fairness of his body dispels even the clouds of the mind. Truly, he has embellished these natural gifts with the adornment of letters so that refined by the whetstone of the high arts the interior of his mind shines forth even more brightly. He learned in the books of old writers of the ancient Decii and their noble lineage yet living for the distinction of a glorious death. Most fruitful is the labor of study for the man whose good fortune it is to learn the poetry of the old ones through his kinsmen and to educate the beginnings of his tender breast in his ancestral glory.[63]

The young man's nobility, according to Cassiodorus, stems in part from his natural gifts: his appearance is comely, his demeanor dignified and cheerful. He is, moreover, clever and educated. Since he belongs to the family of the Decii, the study of literature feeds his ancestral pride. Livy's history of Rome, *From the Founding of the City* (*Ab urbe condita*), enjoyed the status of a classic in Latin Antiquity and excerpts of it were read in school; hence Cassiodorus had no need to inform the senators that Livy mentions several consuls of the fourth and third centuries BCE whose family name was Decius. In his account, the first of them, Publius Decius Mus (cos. 340 BCE) willingly sacrificed his life to win victory for Rome in a battle against the Latins.[64]

Only a few senatorial families of the sixth century dared to extend their family tree back to the Roman Republic like the Decii. Among them were the senators who traced the ancestry back to the Acilii Glabriones and the Corvini. Normally, however, senatorial genealogies ended much sooner; indeed only a few senators bore names that already appeared in Livy. Nonetheless, the *viri illustres* represented in the senate considered themselves the guardians of Roman tradition. In their eyes, the history of the Roman state, the *res publica Romana*, was a continuum that reached all the way to the present day. This history had begun in the regal period and continued through the Republic to the imperial period, but it had not at all come to an end with the disappearance of the Roman imperial monarchy in Italy, even if power had been transferred to barbarian kings, because in their eyes the Republic continued to exist as long as the senate did. Did not Livy report that the senate had already existed in the regal period? Kings and emperors had come and gone, but the senate remained; its existence guaranteed Rome's persistence through the ages.[65]

The illustrious senators of the early sixth century were still very rich, although they had probably lost the vast majority of their possessions in North Africa, Spain, and Gaul in the course of the fifth century. We cannot give a numerical estimate of the extent of the landholdings of individual senators. A senator like Basilius Decius, for example, could afford to drain a swamp south of Rome at his own expense. His wealth was undoubtedly extraordinary, but all senators had to be able to bear the expense of maintaining a lifestyle appropriate to their rank in Rome. That included a magnificent house (*domus*) and a large number of servants. To the Eastern Roman Olympiodorus, who visited Rome in the early fifth century, the houses of Western Roman senators looked like moderate-sized cities with their own hippodromes, forums, temples, fountains, and baths. Rome no longer seemed quite so imposing at the beginning of the sixth century. The population had shrunken, many areas stood empty, and not a few buildings were crumbling or in ruins. Nonetheless, the senators still lived high on the hog. Cassiodorus celebrates the *patricius* Symmachus for the magnificent houses he had built in Rome. The *patricius* Albinus requested and received permission from Theoderic to build over the Porticus Curva in the Forum of Nerva to extend his private home. In this case, the king privatized a public building in the monumental heart of Rome that was apparently threatening to collapse. But Albinus' building project also reveals that Roman senators still lived in this area. "The Romans," Procopius declared, "love their city more than any other people we know and strive to maintain and preserve all their ancestral heritage so that none of Rome's old glory is lost."[66]

Rome remained the center of senatorial life under Theoderic as well. It was there that the senators had their official residences, there that they spent most of the year. They left the management of their estates to stewards. If a senator wished to leave Rome for a protracted length of time, he required the king's permission—that is, unless the king himself had summoned him to court or entrusted him with a task that could not be completed from Rome. Since the city had ceased to be an imperial residence after barbarian kings ruled Italy instead of Roman emperors, senators no longer had to share the public arena with their ruler. The senate and people of Rome had the theater, the amphitheater, and the circus to themselves, with the addition of the Roman Catholic clergy at mass and processions. The best seats everywhere were reserved for senators; they were passed down in the circus and amphitheater from father to son. At the Colosseum, where men battled against wild animals, senators documented their claims to their stone seats by having their names and titles inscribed on them. The last additions are from the time of Theoderic. The senators and the Roman people interacted without the direct involvement of a monarch as under the Roman Republic. They erected statues to Theoderic and commemorated him in the form of acclamations, but the king was not present when the senators and the people gathered to take in burlesque and pantomime shows, chariot races, and animal hunts.

At these venues, the senators acted as the lords of the city and patrons of the people. They bore a significant part of the expenses for the games and took responsibility for the smooth operation of chariot races as patrons of the rival clubs (*factiones*)—the Blues and the Greens and the Whites and Reds. Chariot races and animal hunts were especially expensive. In the early fifth century, senators paid up to 4,000 pounds of gold for the games they held on the occasion of their appointment to the praetorship. The expense on the occasion of a consulship was even greater. The expectations placed on the munificence of senators were much lower in Theoderic's day; praetorian games no longer took place. But the consular games still gobbled up vast sums of money. Anyone who tried to cut corners was personally admonished by the king not to be stingy with his wealth. Senators who reached the consulship gave their fellow senators folding tablets made of two panels of ivory, so-called consular diptychs, which depict the officeholder hosting games. On the consular diptych of Boethius Sr. (fig. 8), we see the consul of the year 487 and father of the homonymous philosopher holding an eagle scepter in his left hand and a cloth (*mappa*) in his right hand; sacks of money and palm branches lay at his feet. These objects allude to the consul's role at chariot races: by dropping the *mappa*, he started the race, and at the end he distributed palm branches and money to the victors.[67]

When someone obtained the consulship and held games, he won prestige that distinguished him among his peers. But spectacles were also important for the senators' relationship with the lower classes. Enthusiasm for mime and pantomime shows and chariot races remained great. Actors and drivers were idolized by fans from all walks of life. The people honored the financial and personal engagement of senators by conceding them a dominant role in the theater, amphitheater, and circus. The social order was performed and affirmed at spectacles. But that was not their only function. Spectacles also presented an opportunity to express requests and complaints. These could take forms that would have incurred harsh punishment as verbal insults (*iniuria*) in other circumstances. What was denied to the common people elsewhere was tolerated at spectacles. The crowd's expectations were directed first at the senators present, including the urban prefect, and only secondarily at the absent ruler.[68]

The interaction of the senate and people in the context of spectacles was by no means always harmonious. Despite all their ritualization, emotions at the theater and circus could easily explode, especially on account of the fierce rivalry between the two big clubs of the Blues and the Greens. There were brawls, which sometimes escalated to riots. From 506 to 509, the question of whether the pantomime actors Helladius and Theodoron would dance for the Greens or for the Blues split the entire city in two. The king expected the senators to exercise a moderating influence on the fans; he thus commissioned the *patricii* Albinus and Avienus to succeed their deceased father Decius Basilius (cos. 480) as patrons of the Greens and to resolve the dispute. But the Greens refused to be tamed so easily and assailed the *patricius* Theodorus and the consul Inportunus with insults at the circus. They in turn had no intention of tolerating such abuse; they had their servants lure fans of the Greens into a trap and attacked them, killing one. When the Green faction then complained to Theoderic in 509, the king had their accusations investigated by the senators Caelianus and Agapitus. He further instructed the urban prefect Agapitus to keep the peace during spectacles; to avoid strife, the pantomime actor Helladius

Fig. 8. Consular diptych of Boethius, cos. 487. Museo Santa Giulia, Brescia, Italy. akg-images/Album/Oronoz.

would no longer appear for either the Greens or the Blues but rather only for the Whites or the Reds. In a letter to the senate, Theoderic demanded that senators surrender any servants who had been involved in homicides to the urban prefect. He urged the people of Rome by edict not to insult dignity and decency even during spectacles; the urban prefect would harshly punish verbal injuries against senators.[69]

Senators of the sixth century were not only wealthy and class-conscious; they also prided themselves on their education. A senator could ride and fence; Ennodius even derided the "unwarlike right hand" of the philosopher Boethius. But military experience and skill in combat did not factor into the senatorial self-conception. The days in which senators commanded troops lay two centuries in the past. Education in Late Antiquity meant an active command of the language of Latin literature and knowledge of the texts that were considered classical and thus part of the literary canon. A person was considered educated if he could express himself in an artificial idiom far removed from the everyday vernacular. This skill was acquired through years of laborious study of the Latin language and literature. Good character was taken for granted; the students came from "superior" society, after all. Hence the goal of education was defined as *vir bonus dicendi peritus*: "an upright man who knew how to speak." Teachers called "grammarians" taught the first stage of the curriculum; students studied language and the texts of the classics under them. "Rhetors" taught the second stage; their job was to impart the ability to deliver an appropriate speech on any occasion. Using examples normally drawn from mythology, students practiced speeches for every real-life situation: accusation and defense, advice, and entertainment. They learned how to place themselves in given situations and roles, how to find arguments and present them effectively. Such schools existed in Rome and Milan and presumably also in Ravenna. In Rome, there even still were public chairs for rhetoric; the incumbents were selected by the senate and received a salary from the king. A rising senator was sufficiently prepared for his place in society if he had acquired this form of education. Legal expertise was prized but not expected. The study of medicine was regarded as beneath a senator's station. Very few were versed in Greek philosophy and theology and usually only by way of translations.[70]

There were some senators in Theoderic's kingdom whose intellectual horizons extended far beyond the curriculum sketched above. Boethius possessed a profound knowledge of all branches of philosophy. He translated Aristotle's writings on logic into Latin and wrote commentaries on some of them. He composed works on logic, mathematics, and music, theological treatises, speeches, and poems. In the year of his consulship (510), he worked on a commentary on Aristotle's *Categories*. But Boethius was an exception and recognized as such by his contemporaries. His father-in-law, Symmachus, edited Macrobius' commentary on Cicero's "Dream of Scipio" (*Somnium Scipionis*) and composed a *Roman History* in seven books. Cassiodorus also composed more than just his *Variae* and *Gothic History*. While serving as praetorian prefect, he wrote a short book, *On the Soul*, and began working on an extensive commentary on the Psalms. After his conversion, he wrote the *Institutes of the Divine and Secular Learning*, a kind of handbook for monks. This or that senator also dabbled in verse. Faustus Niger, for instance, composed an encomium of Como. Maximianus, who has left behind elegiac poems on love and old age, also appears to have moved in these circles for a while. He later joined the courtly society that gathered around Theoderic's nephew Theodahad in Etruria.[71]

Theoretical philosophy and speculative theology were the preserve of a few initiates. Every senator, however, was expected to be able to give an appropriate speech and compose a polished letter. Anyone who thought highly of himself wanted to be educated in this sense. In 512, two young men from good families, Ambrosius and Beatus, asked Ennodius for advice about studying in Rome. The clergyman cited the virtues of respect (*verecundia*), modesty (*pudicitia*), and right belief (*fides*); moreover, he urged them to study grammar and rhetoric diligently. He recommended as mentors senators who were distinguished equally by their exemplary way of life and by their education. The young men would find the best teachers among them. The nine men he named all had held high office and attained the consulship. In addition to Boethius (cos. 510) and Symmachus (cos. 485), they were Faustus Niger (cos. 490) and Faustus Avienus (cos. 502)—both then at Theoderic's court and thus not in Rome—Festus (cos. 472), Probinus (cos. 489) and his son Cethegus (cos. 504), Agapitus (cos. 517), and Probus (cos. 513). Ennodius also mentioned two women of senatorial rank, Barbara and Stephania, the sisters of Faustus Niger, who combined female virtue with the greatest learning. In the eyes of these senators, the late antique Christian poets were the contemporary heirs of the Augustan poets. The *vir illustris et patricius* Asterius read and corrected a manuscript of Vergil's *Eclogues* in the year of his consulship (494); he also edited the *Easter Poem* (*Carmen paschale*) of the Christian epicist Sedulius. The last known holder of a Roman chair of rhetoric, Felix, edited the *Epodes* of Horace together with the senator Mavortius, consul in the year 527. Ennodius' advice, incidentally, proved good in the end: one of the two ambitious young men, Ambrosius, went on to a successful career at Theoderic's court; he first became the chief minister of the privy purse (*comes rei privatae*) and then quaestor.[72]

Even though the senators of the early sixth century felt like they were the descendants of the men who had once defeated Hannibal and Hellenistic kings, they nevertheless were Catholic Christians. Cassiodorus thus says in a "little book" (*Libellus*) that he dedicated to senatorial authors of his time that his father-in-law, Symmachus, was "a modern imitator of ancient Cato" who, however, "surpassed the virtues of the old [Romans] with [his devotion to] the most holy religion." In a text composed in defense of the so-called Palmary Synod (*synodus palmaris*) convened in 501, Ennodius goes one step further by contrasting the Christian present with the heathen past: the great families of the past, the Curii, Torquati and Camilli, the Fabii and Decii, were burning in hell, despite their services to the *res publica*, because they had sacrificed to idols. Now, however, idolatry had vanished from the senate, the "sanctuary of freedom." Then he has Roma, the personification of the city, say the following:

> Behold the crown of honors, the *genius* of the world, the flower of Rome, full of sanctity, tramples under foot the altars it long worshipped. Behold my curia is summoned to heaven, praised, welcomed. And I cannot say I lost my progeny after the grace of baptism, which indeed a sudden death took away. The supreme ruler embraces many possessors of consular robes and chairs without detriment to their reverence or rank. Now the munificence of earthly triumph virtually purchases divine favor, and it redounds to Christ's grace that you strive to be venerable to the world. I would be lying if indigent throngs did not await the arrival of your consulships to relieve their misery. For your purple, with which you ennoble the name of the year, drives away with generous gifts of clothing the cold that nips at the wretched.

No senator prayed to the gods of the *maiores* or sacrificed animals to them in Theoderic's kingdom. Jupiter, Juno, and Minerva, who had once constituted the Capitoline Triad, had abdicated. But that does not mean that every senator was a good Christian as the Church would have liked. Opinions were split as to how a senator should live if he wanted to be a true Christian. Pope Gelasius accused the senator Andromachus and other senators of worshipping idols because they staged the ancient festival of the Lupercalia on February 15, which was originally in honor of the god Faunus; no baptized Christian could take part in this shameless festival, he argued; only heathens could celebrate it. This accusation was payback for criticism that these senators had voiced against Gelasius for acquitting one of his priests of immoral conduct. In the eyes of these senators, the Lupercalia was not idolatry but rather a folk festival, even if some people might have believed that the rituals could ward off evil. They celebrated the Lupercalia because their ancestors had done so, because the people wanted to, and because it did no harm.[73]

The senators viewed the bishop of Rome as the bishop of their city and naturally wanted to have their say in his appointment. Even though the senators

took pains as a group to protect their interests as laymen and donors, their support was by no means unanimous when the succession of St. Peter was at stake.
From 501 to 504, the assembly was divided into two camps: the majority supported Pope Laurentius; a minority, Pope Symmachus, who ultimately prevailed with Theoderic's help. Obviously, the senatorial patrons of the rival
popes were also fighting to see who would push his candidate through and thus
demonstrate his superiority in this dispute. But the senators' relationship with
the bishop of Rome was not purely instrumental. They viewed him as their
designated dispenser of salvific Christian resources. Of course, most of them
were neither willing nor able to follow the subtle debates of Greek theologians
about the divine and human nature of Jesus Christ. But they took part in heresy
trials and synods and asked the pope for advice in theological matters. The
senators kept the ascetic movement at arm's length. When the *patricius*
Theodorus—the same man who had sicked his clients on the fans of the Greens
in 509—decided years later to lead a life of humility and privation, he attracted
great attention but did not inspire any imitators for a long time. When
Cassiodorus then likewise underwent such a conversion, the Gothic kingdom
in Italy already lay in ruins. Female members of senatorial families, in contrast,
took vows to dedicate their lives to God more often already in Theoderic's day.[74]

The *res publica* was still the central reference point of the lives of senators.
They understood their lives as service to a great tradition and their privileges as
the epitome of liberty (*libertas*). Hence in their eyes, the senate was the seat of
Roman liberty (*Romana libertas*) par excellence. They regarded Theoderic as
the "master of liberty" (*dominus libertatis*), "protector of liberty" (*defensor libertatis*), and "guardian of liberty" (*custos libertatis*) because and as long as he
respected and protected this liberty. Although the senators under Theoderic
were by no means willing to take orders from the emperor in Constantinople,
they regarded themselves as part of an order that encompassed both halves of
the Roman Empire and viewed the senators of the east as peers. On a diptych
made on the occasion of the consulship of Orestes in the year 530, we see the
Western Roman consul between two personifications, old Roma on the Tiber
and new Roma on the Bosporus. Since the idea that the Roman Empire existed
in two parts presumed its factual separation, it in no way diminished loyalty to
the king as long as the emperor did not attempt to put a violent end to the rule
of the Gothic kings in Italy and force the senators to choose sides. This never
happened in Theoderic's lifetime, even if war came precariously close to breaking out between 504 and 508, when Theoderic's generals attacked a Byzantine
army and the emperor sent a fleet to devastate the Adriatic coast of Italy in
retaliation a few years later. Despite that, Western senators' ties to the emperor

in Constantinople remained intact; they could still imagine that they might be drawn closer together again sometime in the future.[75]

4. *UTRAQUE RES PUBLICA:* KINGDOM AND EMPIRE

When Theoderic became sole ruler of Italy, his legal relationship to the emperor was uncertain. Delegations in the years 490 and 492 had not obtained the desired confirmation of Theoderic's position as ruler. His proclamation as king in Italy in early 493 was perceived as usurpation in Constantinople. An agreement was not reached until five years later. In 498, a delegation led by the same Festus who had traveled to Constantinople for Theoderic in 490 hammered out a peace treaty with Emperor Anastasius that explicitly recognized Theoderic as ruler of Italy. The *Anonymus Valesianus* states laconically: "Once Festus had concluded peace with Emperor Anastasius concerning his [Theoderic's] arrogation of royal power, he [Anastasius] returned the insignia of the palace that Odoacer had sent to Constantinople."[76] This passage is also puzzling. By returning the "insignia of the palace" to Theoderic, Anastasius symbolically demonstrated that he recognized Theoderic as the ruler of Italy. That much seems certain. But what were the "insignia of the palace," and what purpose did they serve Theoderic? If they were identical to the insignia of the Western Roman emperor, Anastasius cannot possibly have meant Theoderic to use them as such going forward. Anastasius had no intention of elevating Theoderic to Western Roman emperor, nor had Theoderic even claimed this position. For contemporaries, however, insignia were more than superficial trappings: they were a visual representation of power and status. The return of the insignia of the Western Roman emperor thus would merely have demonstrated that the emperor had no plans to revive the Western Roman imperial monarchy. Most modern scholars, however, favor a different interpretation: if the insignia that Anastasius provided to Theoderic were different from those of the emperor, then—and only then—could he have actually used them. We indeed know that Eastern Roman emperors conferred insignia on foreign rulers who were prepared to accept a formally subordinate position. The act took place in a ceremony, however, that required the presence of the ruler who was to be recognized and so was always performed in Constantinople. Such rulers were regarded as clients of the emperor—that is, as "client kings"—by the Eastern Roman Empire. Thus, for example, Justinian recognized a certain Tzath as king of Lazica in 522, conferring on him regalia that consisted of a thin circlet, a white cloak and tunic, high red boots with pearl trim, a pearl and gold-studded belt, and a purple cloak. This costume resembled that of an emperor;

the most important difference, however, was that the client king did not wear a diadem—a headband decorated with large gemstones—but rather a narrow circlet on his brow. Of course, client kings always exercised their power outside the territory of the Roman Empire, which (as we shall see) was precisely *not* the case with Theoderic, at least from the emperor's perspective, which is what matters here.[77]

We thus can say little with certainty about Theoderic's costume and insignia. The only thing that seems certain is that he wore purple garments on ceremonial occasions. On the medallion of Morro d'Alba, the king appears in the dress of a Roman general; there is no sign of a diadem. Of course, this depiction could be determined by the fact that the medallion was a special issue for the army. Ennodius needles Anastasius with the remark that Theoderic's magnificent hair accomplished what a diadem achieved "for other princes," insinuating that the Eastern Roman emperor wore a diadem to hide his baldness. This polemical jab would have been completely misplaced if the king himself wore one. Of course, we cannot rule out that on certain occasions, the king may have worn a headband that could be interpreted as a diadem. It has been speculated that the mosaic portrait of a ruler wearing a diadem adorned with pearls (located inside the basilica of Sant'Apollinare Nuovo, the erstwhile court church) originally depicted Theoderic and was reworked into a portrait of Justinian only later; the title IVSTINIAN above it was added in the nineteenth century. Even if the identification of the portrait with Theoderic is accurate, however, it remains uncertain whether the diadem was part of the original. There is no doubt, in contrast, that Theoderic took off an ornamental head covering (*ornatus*) when he greeted Bishop Caesarius of Arles at the palace in Ravenna in late 513. What this ornamental head covering looked like, however, remains unknown.[78]

A ruler who wanted to be accepted by Goths and Romans needed insignia that distinguished him from his subjects and symbolized his claim to their obedience. There may have been such insignia of power among the Ostrogoths before Theoderic. It was still better when the emperor conferred such insignia: they simultaneously reflected the emperor's recognition. But Theoderic was not content with that. He wanted to manage his relationship with the emperor in a way that was unambiguous and binding. Since, almost thirty years later (in 526), Cassiodorus asked Emperor Justin to establish peace and friendship with Theoderic's grandson Athalaric on the same conditions that his predecessor had given Theoderic himself, there is no doubt that the treaty struck in 498 established Theoderic's relationship to the emperor in detail. This treaty, however, has not been transmitted to us; hence scholars have long disputed Theoderic's legal position. The *Anonymus Valesianus* repeatedly attaches the title of *patricius*

Fig. 9. Portrait of a ruler inscribed *IVSTINIAN(VS)* in Sant'Apollinare Nuovo,
Ravenna. Reproduced with the kind permission of Carola Jäggi, *Ravenna. Kunst und
Kultur einer spätantiken Residenzstadt* (Regensburg, 2007), fig. 121.

to Theoderic in its account of the war against Odoacer. Theodor Mommsen therefore inferred that Theoderic ruled in Italy as the holder of an office that he had received from the emperor; *de jure*, Theoderic's kingdom in Italy would have meant the reunification of the Western and Eastern Roman Empires. This view still persists among some scholars today. It cannot be correct, however, because Theoderic never bore the title of *patricius* after his Goths declared him king of Goths and Romans in Italy.[79]

Theoderic's official name was Flavius Theodericus rex. The name "Flavius" did not imply any kind of fictive kinship with the family of Constantine the Great, as some have believed. In the fifth and sixth centuries, "Flavius" was not a family name but rather a conventional status indicator in the Roman army; Theoderic had adopted it when he was the emperor's *magister militum*. The name already appears on Egyptian papyri from the year 484, the year of Theoderic's consulship. His position as ruler of Italy was reflected solely by the title *rex*. Theoderic essentially used this title without any qualifiers. Since he viewed his kingdom as one over Goths and Romans, he could not tie it to a specific ethnicity as the Vandal kings had done, for example. "King of Goths and Romans"—this title would not have been acceptable to the senators and definitely not to the Goths. Theoderic's subjects called him *rex, princeps,* or simply *dominus* and also used nontechnical periphrases, but they never called him *patricius*, like one of the Eastern Roman emperor's officials, or used titles that would have put him on par with the emperor in Constantinople. There is only a single exception to this rule: the senator and *patricius* Basilius Decius (who drained a swamp northwest of Terracina, turning it into arable land at Theoderic's behest between 507 and 511) had inscriptions erected to commemorate this feat in which he calls Theoderic not only "most glorious and famous king" (*gloriosissimus adque inclytus rex*) and victor and *triumphator*, but also "perpetual Augustus" (*semper Augustus*). Since the title "Augustus" remained the emperor's prerogative, Basilius Decius here went beyond what Theoderic claimed for himself, but he did so in a remote place in the Pontine Marshes that the king had given him as a reward for his investment.[80]

The view Constantinople took of Theoderic's status is an entirely different question. It goes without saying that the imperial court continued to presume that Italy was still part of the Roman Empire and inferred from that that Theoderic ruled at the emperor's pleasure. Nonetheless, Anastasius still referred to Theoderic simply as "king" in a letter to the senate in the year 516 and stated that he had been entrusted with power over Italy; he thus declined to assert any sort of superiority. Instead, the emperor used a formula in his letter that had been devised by the royal chancellery to link the factual separation of the two

realms with the notion of unity: he spoke of *utraque res publica*, "both republics," thus evoking the idea that the Roman Empire was an overarching conceptual unit made up of two commonwealths that were constituted as *res publicae*.
Various *regna* ("kingdoms") and *gentes* ("peoples") might exist elsewhere, but
no other *res publicae* existed besides these. In a letter to Anastasius that was
composed when relations were fraught, Theoderic's chancellery alluded to this
formula with artful turns of phrase:

> And therefore, most pious of princes, it befits your power and honor that we
> should seek concord with you, from whose love we have benefited up to
> now. For you are the most beautiful ornament of all realms [*regna*], you the
> salvific bullwork of all the earth, to whom all other rulers rightly look up,
> because they recognize that something unique dwells in you — we especially,
> since with the help of God we learned in your republic how we might equi-
> tably command Romans. Our kingdom [*regnum*] is an imitation of yours, a
> representation of a good design [*forma boni propositi*], a model of the only
> empire [*unici exemplar imperii*]: we excel all other peoples only insofar as we
> follow you.
>
> You often urge me to love the senate, to embrace the emperors' laws gra-
> ciously, to set in order every part of Italy. How could you separate from the
> Augustan [i.e., imperial] peace someone you hope will not deviate from your
> ways? Add to that love of the venerable city of Rome, from which those
> things that have been joined in unity of name cannot be sundered. Hence
> we have decided to dispatch so-and-so as envoys to Your Most Serene Piety
> so that the integrity of the peace, which we know was marred by emerging
> circumstances, may be restored to full strength and abide thereafter, when
> all controversies have been wiped away. Because we believe you will not
> permit any discord to remain between the two republics [*inter utrasque res
> publicas*] that notably always constituted one body under the old emperors
> [*antiqui principes*]. They should not only be joined in peaceful love, but
> even join forces to help one another. May the Roman Empire always have
> one will, one counsel. And whatever we can do, let it be attached to the
> praise due you.[81]

Theoderic grants the emperor honorary precedence in this letter and concedes that his kingdom is part of a single Roman Empire. By the same token,
however, he treats its separation into two *res publicae* as given and contends that
his own domain corresponds exactly to the emperor's own: "Our kingdom is an
imitation of yours" (*regnum nostrum imitatio vestra est*). In point of fact, the
treaty that Theoderic made with Anastasius in 498 largely gave the king free
rein in Italy. We can deduce its content with some certainty because Theoderic's

Figs. 10a and 10b. Gold coin (*solidus*), obverse and reverse, with
a portrait of Emperor Anastasius, minted in Ravenna (enlarged).
From Michael A. Metlich, *The Coinage of Ostrogothic Italy*
(London, 2004), pl. II, no. 15.

nephew and successor, Theodahad, offered Justinian to forgo the rights that his uncle had exercised with Anastasius' blessing. Procopius describes them in detail: the treaty did not impose any limitations on the king with respect to foreign policy other than stipulating that peace and friendship should prevail between the two parties. The king likewise could conduct his domestic policy as he pleased with the emperor's blessing and few restrictions. The emperor conceded him the right to appoint high officials and one of the two consuls, thus leaving him in complete control of the state apparatus. His powers as judge were also unlimited. In return, however, Theoderic had to pledge not to violate some of the emperor's prerogatives. He could issue normative regulations, but he could not formulate them as statutes (*leges*); Theoderic's decrees therefore had the status of edicts, which could also be issued by officials of the emperor. Theoderic also gave up the right to mint gold and silver coinage bearing his own name and portrait; the gold and silver coins issued in his kingdom thus bore Anastasius' name and likeness. The emperor was and remained ever-present in this medium even under Theoderic.

Barring that exception, the emperor did not insist on a place in the visual and performative representation of Theoderic's reign: the king was permitted to display his image without that of the Eastern Roman emperor, thus depicting himself (or permitting himself to be depicted) as the independent and sole ruler of Italy. It was also permitted to acclaim the king without mentioning the emperor. Commemoration of the emperor thus was dropped from the ceremonial that surrounded the ruler. The treaty probably also included a stipulation to respect the rights of the senate and the Catholic Church. The duration of the treaty is not attested. It is at any rate inconceivable that it extended beyond

Theoderic's lifetime since waiving his right to rule the west explicitly and permanently was out of the question for the emperor.[82]

With the treaty of 498, Theoderic achieved recognition as the virtually unlimited ruler of Goths and Romans in a kingdom that was still described as part of the Roman Empire in diplomatic relations with the Eastern Roman emperor. He secured his power against the military threat that emanated from Constantinople and made it easier for his senatorial subjects to view him as a legitimate ruler. Of course, Theoderic knew that even sworn treaties did not guarantee peace and friendship between states and rulers. His relationship with Anastasius indeed did not remain free of friction; that is illustrated by the letter cited above, which had been preceded by armed conflict. As the king reached old age, the question of how he might transfer his position to a successor who could win the emperor's approval became acute.

THEODERIC'S DUAL STATE

1. THE COURT: THE CENTER AND THEATER OF POWER

Theoderic's power cannot be traced back to a single source. The reasons that induced his subjects to accept him as their ruler were as diverse as their own social circumstances and cultural backgrounds. Hence the old question—what was the basis of Theoderic's legitimacy?—leads us down a dead end: a search for consensus about norms, symbols, and procedures. The concept of "acceptance" (from German *Akzeptanz*), in contrast, directs our attention to the actors, their interests and motives, and disabuses us of the illusion that every subject would have carried out the king's commands without question. It was precisely the groups whose support Theoderic needed the most who pursued their own interests. Their support hinged on whether the king would and could satisfy their expectations. To some, preserving ancestral tradition was very important; to others, it mattered less or indeed not at all. And, of course, there were varying degrees of willingness to accept a ruler who had come to power in a civil war, cultivated a non-Roman identity, and adhered to what was considered a heretical faith. The spectrum ranged from active cooperation to mere acceptance of the status quo.[1]

In the eyes of his Goths, Theoderic was king not only by virtue of his descent from a king, but also and above all because of his outstanding achievements and triumphs. Roman senators viewed him as the successor of the Western Roman emperors even though his position was irreconcilable with traditional concepts of Roman political thought. Local elites had neither the means nor a reason to oppose Theoderic: he exercised power in the conventional way and recognized their social privilege as soon as his Goths had been successfully settled. The bishops of Italy and later Gaul were glad that the new ruler treated them with respect and made no move to propagate his own heretical confession. To the majority of people in the cities and countryside, the artisans and petty merchants, farmers and peasants with or without land, fishermen and shepherds— to all these people, the change at the top meant very little. To them, Theoderic was simply the man who had defeated Odoacer and now collected taxes, dues, and services just as the Western Roman emperors had done before him. And for beggars and slaves, even that was practically inconsequential.

The court is a key institution for every monarchic government. It constitutes the social space where personal interaction mediates between the ruler's claim to his subjects' obedience and their own expectations. It was at Theoderic's court that the people who approached the king for particular reasons—messengers, petitioners, envoys—met those who constituted his permanent retinue. The court consisted of all the members of the king's household, but it also included the men who held office in immediate proximity to the king or who sat on his council of state, the "consistory" (*consistorium*). This group of people was known as the *palatini* ("palatine officials, courtiers") because they served the king in the *palatium* ("palace"). The *aula* ("court") was another name for this social space: courtiers were also called *aulici* after it. Their most common designation, however, was *comites*, "companions" (singular: *comes*). This term had been coined at a time when the emperors still constantly traveled; the court as a social organism was hence called the *comitatus* ("retinue"). The *comites* of the emperor had been divided into three classes (*ordines*) in the fourth century: a first-class *comes* (*comes primi ordinis*) had the right to kiss the hem of the ruler's purple garment at audiences; this gesture was called *adoratio purpurae* ("adoration of the purple"). The occupants of the highest offices at court belonged to this first class *ex officio*.[2]

This court hierarchy of three classes, however, was overlaid by another one in the fourth century, a hierarchy that was based on the division of the senatorial order into *viri clarissimi*, *spectabiles*, and *illustres* (literally: "most famous," "distinguished," and "illustrious" men). This status system supplanted the old senatorial hierarchy whereby a senator's rank depended on which stage of the standard sequence of magistracies he had reached (the *cursus honorum*): a former praetor outranked a former aedile, but he himself was outranked by a former consul. These magistracies lost all meaning for a senator's status after the fifth century; only the consulship remained as the highest office, elevating its occupants above other *viri illustres*. Originally, the rank of *vir spectabilis* or *vir illustris* could be obtained only by holding an office in the emperor's service. Hence the senatorial hierarchy was determined by the ruler alone. At the same time, the office one held at court also determined which senatorial class a senator joined and so already had established a new court hierarchy by the late fourth century. But holding an office that conferred the rank of *vir spectabilis* or *vir illustris* was by no means the only way to obtain these ranks. The emperors also began to confer them in an honorary capacity at an early date. People who could make a claim to the emperor's favor could thus gain a mark of distinction that translated into social capital without ever having had to weather the rigors of office. The emperors, in turn, were able to multiply the number of favors they could grant without incurring any additional expense. But they soon found themselves forced to make it clear that persons who held the rank of *vir spectabilis* or *vir illustris* without holding office had to yield precedence to those who had in fact served the emperor as officials. Then, over the course of the fifth century, a third group was squeezed in between the first two as the emperors began to award people with titles of rank as hypothetical officeholders. These so-called *vacantes* were, in a way, titular officeholders who did not actually serve. The class of *viri illustres* was thereafter divided into three groups, in ascending order: those who had obtained the title as an honorary rank, titular occupants of an illustrious office (i.e., *vacantes*), and men who actually had held or still held an *illustris* office.[3]

Theoderic had come to know this complicated status system in his youth, when he lived as a hostage in Constantinople. He himself acquired the highest rank at the Eastern Roman court as *magister militum* and consul for the year 484. When he became ruler of Italy, he adopted this rank system unchanged but made it serve his purposes by conferring the ranks of *vir spectabilis* and *vir illustris* on Goths who served him at court or in the provinces. These Goths thus were superficially put on an equal footing with the Romans at Theoderic's court; they thereby also obtained a rank that set them above local elites since the latter seldom rose above the rank of *vir clarissimus*. The old court hierarchy based on division into three classes, meanwhile, continued to exist under Theoderic; the rank of *comes primi ordinis* was still awarded. Cassiodorus' *Variae* includes a whole series of model appointment letters elevating people to titular officeholders or distinguishing them with an honorary rank.[4]

Theoderic's court was quite rightly called the *comitatus* because it was highly mobile. In contrast to the Eastern Roman emperors of the fifth and sixth centuries, who very seldom left Constantinople and only for a short time, if at all, the king traveled regularly. The range of his trips, however, was confined to northern Italy: he maintained and used palaces in Ravenna, Ticinum, Verona, and Modicia (Monza) near Milan, but he came to Rome only once and apparently never visited southern Italy. A fort at Galeata near Forlì may have served him as a kind of hunting lodge for getaways. Although the king traveled around northern Italy year after year, only one city served as his preferred residence and came to be regarded as the *urbs regia* ("royal city") par excellence: Ravenna was the physical and symbolic center of Theoderic's kingdom in Italy. It was there that the king normally spent most of the year and there that the key officials of the civil administration were based. The personnel who worked in the various court ministries and for the praetorian prefecture of Italy, each consisting of hundreds of people, resided in Ravenna, where the central archives must also have been located.[5]

Theoderic systematically developed Ravenna as his primary residence. The king had numerous buildings repaired, repurposed, or built *ex novo*, including a palace, an aqueduct, and a mausoleum constructed in the 520s, where he ultimately was buried. The palace had been used as a domicile by Emperor Honorius, but now it was expanded and surrounded with a colonnade. Construction, admittedly, was still incomplete at Theoderic's death. Next to the palace arose a major new basilica dedicated to Christ the Redeemer. It has been identified as the "Palace Church" on account of its location; today it is known by the name Sant'Apollinare Nuovo. An inscription located in the apse declared that King Theoderic had built it from the ground up in the name of our lord Jesus Christ. The Palace Church, however, was hardly the only cult building constructed under Theoderic for fellow members of his faith. With the king's backing, the episcopal church of the Homoeans—today the Church of Santo Spirito with its so-called "Arian Baptistry"—and half a dozen more churches were built inside and outside the territory of the city, most of which have vanished without a trace today.[6]

Theoderic had material for his buildings brought from neighboring cities, in some cases from as far as Faenza, Rome, and Constantinople. The capitals of the church today known as Sant'Andrea dei Goti bear his monogram. For work on a basilica named after Hercules, the king summoned stonemasons from Rome with experience in working marble. He had a swamp in the vicinity drained and a garden built on it that he personally cultivated.[7]

It was Theoderic's will that Ravenna, as *urbs regia*, should be equal in rank to the *urbs aeterna*, the "eternal city" of Rome, which was home to the senate and still regarded as the symbolic center of the Roman world on account of its unique history, even if its rival, the New Rome on the Bosporus, had surpassed it in size and importance. Ravenna was the seat of power; even senators had to seek out the king there if they wanted to communicate with him personally, no matter whether he had summoned them to appear at his court, whether they were dispatched there on behalf of the senate, or whether they made the journey of their own accord and on their own business. Senators who held an office at court had to move their domicile to the Adriatic at least for their term before they could return to Rome.[8]

Fig. 11. *Invicta Roma*, copper coin worth 40 *nummi*, obverse and
reverse. Classical Numismatic Group, LLC., CNG 102, Lot: 1215,
http://www.cngcoins.com.

Not only the buildings mentioned above unmistakably signaled that
Theoderic regarded Ravenna as the seat of his kingdom; images also proclaimed
this message. In the pediment of the main entrance to the palace, Theoderic
could be seen in armor, with shield and lance, standing between a personification of Rome, with lance and helmet, and a personification of Ravenna, who
had placed her right foot on the sea and her left on the earth and was hastening
to the king. Rome and Ravenna appeared as a pair in this now lost image, but it
was Ravenna who was welcoming the king. Rome and Ravenna also appear as
a pair on copper coins; they were worth little but were minted in large quantities and served as an everyday means of payment. In Rome, the king had copper
coins tariffed at forty *nummi* minted showing a personification of Roma with
the legend *Invicta Roma* ("Invincible Rome") on their obverse and an eagle on
the reverse. Copper coins tariffed at ten *nummi*, in contrast, showed a crowned
female figure on the obverse with the legend *Felix Ravenna* ("Fortunate
Ravenna") and the city's monogram on the reverse. The same obverse also
appears on five-*nummi* issues from the mint of Ravenna, but there it is paired
with a reverse depicting the goddess Victoria between the letters R and V.[9]

Theoderic went far beyond his predecessor Odoacer in elevating Ravenna to
urbs regia. Odoacer had also probably resided predominantly at Ravenna, but
there is no indication that he tried to leave his mark on the city with monumental
buildings like Theoderic; Odoacer left no traces behind in Ravenna's cityscape at
all. Theoderic's decision to take up residence in Ravenna, moreover, continued a
tradition that had been established by the Western Roman emperors of the fifth
century. The city had intermittently been the preferred residence of the imperial
court between 408 and 450 because it was easily defensible, but the transfer of the

Fig. 12. *Felix Ravenna*, copper coin worth 10 *nummi*, obverse and reverse. Classical Numismatic Group, LLC., CNG 75, Lot: 1183, between "LLC.," http://www.cngcoins.com.

imperial residence there was regarded as temporary. With money tight, the emperors only begrudgingly outfitted Ravenna with the monumental buildings that were entirely conventional at other imperial residences. The city was fortified with walls under Valentinian III but did not receive an aqueduct until Theoderic's reign. The mausoleum of the imperial dynasty was built, not in Ravenna, but at Old St. Peter's in Rome. Valentinian III stayed frequently in Rome again from the 440s on, and Emperor Anthemius resided there continuously.[10]

The elevation of Ravenna to the *urbs regia* accordingly was the result of a deliberate decision. Ravenna indeed had several advantages that appealed to a ruler like Theoderic. These advantages were partly strategic in nature: proximity to the main Gothic settlement zones, the Alps, and the Adriatic. But the decision to take up residence in Ravenna also delivered political advantages: by residing far from Rome, Theoderic escaped the constant need to represent his rule in forms that satisfied the expectations of the senate and the urban population of Rome. He did not have to subordinate his actions to Rome's festival and ritual calendar or have his own reign incessantly measured up against the imperial grandeur of Rome, the history of which was present in monuments at every turn. And lastly, Theoderic avoided the impression that he had replaced the Western Roman emperor by leaving Rome to the senators and the pope as their own stage where they could showcase themselves undisturbed.

The decision to reside in Ravenna also opened up possibilities to Theoderic that Rome could not offer him: only in Ravenna could Theoderic convincingly stage the cooperation of Goths and Romans that the king propagated and the biconfessionality it entailed. In a city with an estimated population of 5,000–10,000 inhabitants, Theoderic's court cast a much longer shadow purely in

numbers than would have been the case in Rome, whose population still probably numbered 50,000–100,000 people. In Ravenna, the parity of the two peoples was a lived reality.[11]

Ravenna also lacked the social forces that could have counterbalanced the
court. The municipal council of Ravenna consisted of men who had at most
risen up to the lowest rank in the senatorial order (*vir clarissimus*). They thus
would not have been peers of senators with the rank of *vir illustris*. Since the
council, moreover, had surrendered key tasks to royal officials, it led a shadowy
existence as an assembly. The market was overseen by delegates of the *magister
officiorum*; the praetorian prefect organized the importation of grain from provincial tax revenues. The king himself awarded a monopoly on the sale of sarcophagi to a certain Daniel. The leadership of the municipal administration
was likewise placed in the hands of an official appointed by the king. In the fifth
century, the prefect of the fleet (*praefectus classis*) had performed this task;
under Theoderic, it was probably the *comes Ravennatis*. A "prefect of the city
watch" (*praefectus vigilum*), also installed by the king, kept the peace. And
finally, in contrast to Rome, Ravenna was not a monumental museum of
Roman history, even though the city had some edifices that recalled the reign
of the emperors of the fifth century. Theoderic truly could define the urban
image of Ravenna with his own building projects.[12]

Since Ravenna was the king's preferred residence, the city also served as a
space for royal representation. Ravenna was not only a center of power; it was
also center stage. The king's throne stood in the palace; it was here that he
granted audiences and received ambassadors, convened the consistory, conducted business, heard his officials' reports, and took council with his advisers.
The palace was also where the king lived with his family; it was here that they
dined, celebrated weddings, and lay down to rest. This palace is depicted in a
mosaic at the so-called Palace Church; we thus have a rough idea of how the
main entryway and adjoining colonnades looked, even though the images of
the courtly society that once appeared between the columns on the wings and
a picture of Theoderic on his throne in the center of the palace facade were
removed after Ravenna was captured by Justinian's general Belisarius. Curtains
hung between the columns; Victories dressed in turquois appear in the span-
drels over the arches. We know little about the interior of the palace; its layout
and floor plan can no longer be reconstructed. A kind of court architect with
the title of *cura palatii* was responsible for the maintenance and construction of
palaces.[13]

We are better informed about the administration of the royal household. The
household was known as the *cubiculum* ("bedchamber"); the people employed

Fig. 13. Mosaic on the south wall of Sant'Apollinare Nuovo (Ravenna). In the lower
register Theoderic's palace (inscribed *palatium*); in the foreground, a throne hall
between two-story porticoes; behind, the city of Ravenna; on the right, city gate
inscribed *civitas Ravenn(as)*; center, men with haloes wearing *tunicas* and mantles,
holding either a roll or a codex; in the upper register, biblical scenes. Reproduced
with the kind permission of Carola Jäggi, *Ravenna. Kunst und Kultur einer
spätantiken Residenzstadt* (Regensburg, 2013), fig. 98.

there thus were known as *cubicularii* ("chamberlains"). They provided for the
physical well-being of the ruler and his family and were at their service at all
times. A man who bore the title of *praepositus sacri cubiculi* ("high chamberlain") and held the rank of *vir illustris* oversaw the household. Since he could
speak to the ruler at any time, he wielded great influence. In return, he was a
target for the envy of all who believed they had a better right to the ruler's favor.
In the Later Roman Empire, this "high chamberlain," as well as many or most
of the other chamberlains, had always been a eunuch. They normally came
from lands outside the territory of the empire and so had no ties to the Roman

elite and were incapable of founding a family of their own. We know only two of Theoderic's *cubicularii* by name; both of them were Goths. One was named Seda and was a eunuch; when he died at the age of forty-one in 541, he held the honorary designation of *vir sublimis*. The other was named Tuluin and went on to a brilliant career outside the *cubiculum*, as we shall see below. The fate of the "high chamberlain" was inextricably linked to that of the ruler; because he was a social outsider, if he fell out of favor, nothing could arrest his fall. In the event of regime change, he had to fear for his life. Odoacer's personal servants cannot have expected anything good from Theoderic, even if we have no information about them. At any rate, it appears that the king entrusted the management of his household to Goths because Cassiodorus probably would have included a model appointment letter for this office in the *Variae* if a Roman could have held it.[14]

As a matter of fact, Theoderic's only known high chamberlain bears a Gothic name that is transmitted in the form Triwa or Triggvila, meaning "faithful, loyal." Boethius, who had few kind words for this man, accuses him of exercising a bad influence on Theoderic; the *Anonymus Valesianus* blames him for Theoderic's favorable measures toward the Jews. If he is identical with the "Triggva" to whom Ennodius imputes influence at court in 510, then he must have managed Theoderic's household for at least a decade and a half. He also managed the royal treasury in this capacity. This treasury would have consisted of precious metal, partly in coin, partly in bullion, that was augmented by gifts. After Theoderic extended his domain to the Gothic kingdom in Spain, revenue from this province would also have flown into this treasury, which he could use as he pleased.[15]

The women of the royal family had their own, female, servants, called *cubiculariae*, just like the staff of the former empresses. Theoderic's wife Audefleda, a sister of the Frankish king Clovis, is practically invisible in our sources. Their wedding must have taken place soon after victory over Odoacer because she bore Theoderic a third daughter around 495: Amalasuintha. (Theoderic already had two other daughters from a previous alliance.) Audefleda appears to have adopted her husband's religion. Theoderic's mother, Ereleuva, comes into view because she was Catholic and received letters from Pope Gelasius. According to these, Ereleuva held a highly respected position at court. Gelasius addresses her as queen (*regina*) and asks her for support; he thus presumed that she could get somewhere with her son. Ennodius also hints at a close relationship between mother and son in his *Panegyricus*: he has the king deliver a speech to his "holy mother" (*sancta mater*) and his "venerable sister" (*venerabilis soror*) prior to the Battle of Verona (489).[16]

Theoderic's sisters left the court a few years after the conquest of Italy to marry Germanic kings: Ostrogotho married the Burgundian heir Sigismund between 494 and 496, and Thiudigotho married the Visigothic king Alaric before 500. Amalafrida, who had two children from her first marriage, married the Vandalic king Thrasamund in the year 500. These connections were intended to reinforce political alliances. The royal chancellery explicitly opined that these women would advise their husbands and so foster harmony among the kings. As we shall relate below, these hopes were dashed across the board.[17]

Finally, Theoderic's nephews, nieces, and grandchildren also grew up at court. His niece Amalaberga married the Thuringian king Hermanfrid in 510. The royal chancellery praised the bride on this occasion as the "ornament of the courtly home, the increase of the dynasty, the solace of faithful counsel, the most delightful conjugal sweetness." Of course, this praise was highly conventional: beauty, fertility, prudence, and spousal affection were regarded as the paramount virtues for a young queen. Theoderic's daughter Amalasuintha, who was educated by a Roman noblewoman, learned Latin and Greek at court in addition to her native language and was regarded later by Cassiodorus as highly educated. Theoderic's grandson, Athalaric, in contrast, grew up in the company of young Goths residing at court. Tuluin, one of the most influential Goths at Theoderic's court, had served as one of the king's *cubicularii* as a young man.[18]

Certainly over 1,000 and perhaps more than 2,000 people belonged to Theoderic's court. In a city like Ravenna, the court would thus have comprised a significant portion of the entire population. If the king took a trip, not all of his palatine officials would have followed him, but his retinue still undoubtedly numbered in the hundreds. On such occasions, deliveries that were normally sent to supply Ravenna had to be rerouted to the king's new whereabouts. It was for this reason that the king commissioned the *saio* Wiligis between 507 and 511 to load every barge he could find in Ravenna with the grain collected as tax and to ship it up the Po to Liguria, where the court was residing, so they did not suffer any scarcity: "Let Ravenna give to Liguria the abundance it is used to receiving," Cassiodorus adds in justification. "Since [Liguria] currently sustains Our presence, it ought to find consolation for many people. Our court indeed draws throngs of visitors and, in the rush to obtain favors, necessary supplies are required for the people."

The *comes patrimonii* had to ensure that the necessary provisions were available wherever the king resided. Ravenna received grain by sea not only from Liguria, but also from Calabria and Apulia. It was not only critical that the required amounts were punctually delivered, but the king also wanted to regale his guests with exquisite food and drink. Cassiodorus explicitly mentions that

the king was not least concerned about the impression that a richly laden table
would have on the envoys of foreign rulers:

> When envoys come from almost every corner of the world and take part in
> our feasts, they marvel to find in abundance what they know is extraordi-
> narily rare in their homeland. They also are amazed that the surfeit of a sin-
> gle table can satiate such great throngs of servants, leading them to think that
> the items consumed grow back from where such great amounts evidently
> come. Then they have something to talk about in their homeland, when
> they are eager to tell their kinsmen what they saw.[19]

But feasts obviously did not serve merely to flaunt the king's wealth before
foreign envoys. The king's table was also a place where he could socialize con-
vivially with select persons unencumbered by the strict rules of court ceremonial. Feasts gave him the opportunity to reassure people of his favor and to
distinguish them above their peers. It was an honor to dine with the king. The
atmosphere was jovial but not egalitarian. The seating arrangement, the order in
which the guests were addressed and how often, and the tone and content of the
conversation all indicated where they stood in the king's graces. And Theoderic
naturally could also get an idea of the general mood that prevailed at court from
eating and drinking with its members. We can assume that his Gothic counselors
in particular were often, perhaps even regularly, invited. Procopius calls it an old
custom for many Goths, especially the bodyguards, to stay close to the king at
meals. At the king's feast, Roman aristocrats reclined beside Gothic warriors;
men like Cassiodorus or Boethius, who flaunted their erudition, dined alongside
men like Pitzia or Vitigis, who prided themselves on their feats of valor. The
king valued conversation with Romans like Cassiodorus and Artemidorus. But
the group that gathered around Theoderic was not linked by shared cultural
values, like the guests at a feast thrown by Emperor Majorian for high-ranking
imperial officials in Arles in 461; as one of the participants reports, the dinner
guests vied with one another in wit and eloquence in the emperor's presence;
anyone who could improvise a snappy distich earned thunderous applause.[20]

Since Theoderic's Goths neither could nor presumably wanted at all to compete in this area, this cultural code was problematic at his court. That need not
have spoiled the convivial atmosphere. The guests definitely indulged in wine,
and things could get loud. A jumble of Gothic and Latin was probably spoken.
In Vandalic North Africa, a Roman litterateur derisively wrote, "In the midst of
Gothic cries of 'Health! Let's get us some food and drink!' no man dares recite
respectable verse." The epigram depicts "Barbarian Feasts" (that is its title) as
noisy debauches of gluttony and inebriation where no one knew to appreciate

Latin poetry. That is a polemical depiction and not aimed at Ravenna. But the Goths in Italy were also said to have a predilection for the excessive enjoyment of wine. The epigram, at any rate, shows that the exclusionary *habitus* of Roman aristocrats, based on elite socialization and education, was difficult to reconcile with the social forms common among many Goths.[21]

In Ravenna as elsewhere, guests were entertained with verse and song. The Frankish king Clovis requested a citharode—a singer and player of the *cithara*, a kind of lyre—from Theoderic because the fame of his brother-in-law's banquets had traveled as far as Gaul. Such a bard was expected to sing of the glory of the king while providing musical accompaniment on the *cithara*. Similar performances would have occurred in Ravenna. Boethius was familiar with Gothic tonalities and thought they appealed to wild peoples. Even though we have no direct evidence, it is very plausible that Gothic songs were performed at Theoderic's court: where else could Cassiodorus have become acquainted with the Gothic oral tradition that he elaborated in his *Gothic History*?[22]

The royal court also served as a setting for ceremonial speeches in Latin, for which the speakers drew on the canon of classical literature. Encomia in honor of the king, like the surviving *Panegyricus* of Ennodius, were traditional elements of courtly feasts. Fragments also survive of a speech that Cassiodorus delivered in 536 at the wedding of King Vitigis and Theoderic's granddaughter Matasuintha. The orator describes the palace of the Gothic kings in Ravenna in the style of an ecphrasis. Using every available literary means of visualization, he compares the palace to those of the legendary Babylonian queen Semiramis and the Persian king Cyrus. The royal family also commissioned historiographical works. Cassiodorus composed his *Chronicle* at the behest of Eutharic, Theoderic's son-in-law and presumed heir, for his consulship in the year 519. Sometime probably in the 520s, Theoderic himself commissioned Cassiodorus to compose a *Gothic History*, which he finished after Theoderic's death. The royal court in Ravenna was also interested in geography and medicine. Theoderic had a personal doctor who bore the title *comes archiatrorum* ("count of archdoctors"), enjoyed free access to the court, and was supposed to exercise a kind of superintendency over all doctors in the kingdom. Anthimus, a Greek doctor with the rank of *illustris comes*, who addressed an epistolary treatise on dietetics to the Frankish king Theuderic I (511–533), may have been one of them. In the vicinity of the court, two works of the Greek doctor Oribasius were translated into Latin, a manual for traveling doctors and a medical guide for laymen. A Goth by the name of Athanarid wrote a work about the lands and peoples of western, central, and northern Europe. We regrettably cannot identify who commissioned these works.[23]

Only a select few took part in the king's banquet. The circle of people who were admitted to the court was also exclusive. Anyone who did not hold an office required an invitation from the king; such an invitation was called an *evocatoria*. Now and then, the king himself personally invited people whose presence seemed desirable; such an invitation could not be refused. But it was also possible to request an invitation. Cassiodorus preserves a model text for both contingencies. The senator Artemidorus, who was urban prefect of Rome in the years 509–510, requested such an invitation and received the following answer:

> It is fitting to adorn Our court with noble men so that both their wish may be fulfilled and the merits of individuals may decorate our service. Hence We summon by this oracle Your Greatness to our sight, which We have no doubt is most welcome to you, so that you who have been with Us for so long may be captivated by the sweetness of Our presence. He who can only see his prince be propitious toward him hastens to see him, after all. For he who is permitted to enjoy Our conversation believes it is a gift from heaven. Therefore, We will not postpone the desire of one whose sight We wish for. We believe you will come rejoicing, whom We will welcome gladly.[24]

The king encountered large crowds only on special occasions and in the context of more or less strictly orchestrated ceremonies. Theoderic summoned his Goths to court once a year to assess their battle readiness and to renew his ties to his army. Large quantities of gold were distributed on this occasion. We may assume that the king greeted his warriors and delivered an address, although our sources say nothing about it. When Theoderic came to Rome in the year 500, he solemnly entered the city in an *adventus* ("arrival") ceremony. His arrival will have proceeded similarly elsewhere, such as Verona or Ticinum, when the king paid these cities a visit, or at Ravenna when he returned. But nothing about that survives either. Roman emperors had appeared on certain occasions before the population of the city where they resided within a locally defined ceremonial framework. The emperor's presence was anticipated especially at chariot races, where he sometimes was forced to hear his subjects' vociferous complaints and demands. During his time as a hostage in Constantinople and on later visits, Theoderic had experienced how much pressure the Eastern Roman emperor had to face when he stepped out of his carefully insulated palace and took his seat in the imperial loge for a chariot race.[25]

The prerequisites for such rituals had been lacking while the Gothic kings ruled on the Balkan Peninsula. We may doubt whether Theoderic conducted himself in Ravenna like the Roman emperors in Constantinople. It is anything but certain whether there was a hippodrome in Ravenna at all. Chariot races in

Rome and Milan are attested in Theoderic's reign, but there is no clear and decisive evidence for Ravenna. It thus is quite possible that this tradition did not exist in Ravenna at all. Theoderic's ruling ideology, which was based on the coexistence and cooperation of two peoples, could hardly be demonstrated in the hippodrome, where the spectators were divided into rival fan clubs. We know in contrast, however, that there was a theater in Ravenna where regular performances apparently took place. Bloody battles of man against beast were also held in both Ravenna and Ticinum. Amphitheaters were maintained in both cities for that purpose. The amphitheater in Ticinum had in fact been restored at Theoderic's behest and was still in operation under his successor, Athalaric. An "entertainment officer" (*tribunus voluptatum*; literally "tribune of pleasures") appointed by the king took care of the organization of such "spectacles" (*spectacula*). The spectators came from all walks of life, even from the clergy: in 530 Pope Felix IV (526–532) lamented finding out that clergymen from the Catholic church of Ravenna had attended such spectacles.[26]

2. THE LIMITS OF MONARCHICAL POWER: THEODERIC'S RULING STYLE

When Theoderic decided to rule in place of the emperor in Italy, but over two peoples, the responsibilities he thereby assumed went far beyond what he had tackled previously as the king of a Gothic army. While he was responsible only for his Goths, he had as little need of a bureaucratic apparatus to exercise power as Attila the Hun. He would, however, have had a kind of chancellery at his disposal. He had to correspond with the imperial court and the military offices of the Eastern Roman Empire, after all. Income and expenditure would have been recorded, and perhaps lists of men and supplies were kept. But an administrative and legal system based on writing was inconceivable as long as Theoderic's army was constantly on the move. At that time, the king remained close to his people; he met them in the camp, on the march, and in battle. He conferred with the great men among his followers, mustered his army now and then, and sent messengers to those who were away from the main camp.

After victory over Odoacer, Theoderic's ruling style fundamentally changed. The king was now also responsible for the 4–7 million Romans who lived in his kingdom. The number of his subjects had been multiplied many times over. Moreover, he now stood at the head of a bureaucratic state apparatus that relied on a sophisticated written culture. State officials in the provincial and central administration communicated predominantly by letter, collected and compiled fiscal data, and produced and archived an astonishing plethora of documents for premodern conditions. Trials involving sums in excess of a certain amount could be set in motion before the provincial governor by the filing of written claims. The proceedings were recorded, and the judgments were prepared in writing; it also was possible to appeal to several higher judicial instances. Real estate transactions did not take effect until they were entered into the municipal archive and required state approval when they involved the landed property of curials (who had hereditary tax obligations to the state).[27]

This bureaucratic apparatus had survived the death throes of the Western Roman Empire and the reign of Odoacer largely unscathed. If Theoderic wanted to rule, he could not afford to leave it to its own devices, as had sometimes been the case in the fifth century. He thus had to deal with the myriad problems that were brought to his attention "from below," by officials, corporations, and private subjects. People expected an answer to complaints, petitions, and requests that were presented to Theoderic orally or in writing. Of course, a ruler could—and indeed had to—delegate a large portion of these routine responsibilities. But in doing so, he ran the risk of losing control if his subjects got the impression that he was insulated from them. Theoderic's position was made even more demanding because he simultaneously had to meet the expectations of his Goths, who now were supposed to pay taxes and respect Roman law like all Theoderic's other subjects. The fact that he was ready and able to play this part was key to his success.[28]

After victory over Odoacer, Theoderic was the sole and absolute ruler of Italy. It was undisputed that the king's will was law. Like the Roman emperors before him, Theoderic also insisted that he would always use this unlimited power for the good of his subjects and would respect the norms of Roman law. The royal chancellery justified his actions to his subjects with familiar leitmotifs that had a long-standing tradition: in everything he did, the ruler always had the common good (*utilitas publica*) at heart. He collected taxes and dues not for himself but rather for the commonwealth (*res publica*). "Obeying the commonwealth" (*rei publicae parere*) meant paying one's taxes. The ruler accordingly demanded his subjects' loyalty and devotion (*fides* and *devotio*). *Fides*, the old concept for the reciprocal obligations between a client and his patron, had become synonymous with a subject's loyalty. In the imperial period, *devotio* meant a soldier's willingness to sacrifice his own life for the emperor. Under Theoderic, this virtue was extended to every subject but in such a way that the demands made of Romans and Goths were defined differently. Roman *devotio* was expressed primarily in the merry fulfillment of one's obligations as a taxpayer; Gothic *devotio* consisted in unconditional obedience and unflinching courage in war.[29]

The royal chancellery attributed all the traditional virtues of Roman emperors to Theoderic. It incessantly stressed that he acted out of *pietas*, out of his sense of duty toward God and toward men. He avoided all excess, demonstrating the virtue of moderation (*temperantia, moderatio*). The king's actions still obeyed the principles of justice (*iustitia*) and equity (*aequitas*): the king provided for justice by penalizing violations of the law and obeying them himself. He also, however, mitigated the severity of the laws, whenever it seemed right and reasonable to do so, by reducing punishments or granting pardons. Justice and equity were not antithetical but rather complemented one another. Hence mercy, which we encounter under the names of *clementia* and *mansuetudo*, was a ruler's virtue par excellence. It was invoked incessantly to counteract the fear that one was at the mercy of a capricious, all-powerful despot. A good ruler should be not only just and merciful, but also—and especially—generous. He was expected to share his wealth with his subjects; no one who loyally served him should go without his due reward. The royal chancellery also claimed this quality, called *liberalitas* ("liberality"), *largitas* ("lavishness, giving largesse"), or *munificentia* ("munificence"), for Theoderic and his successors.[30]

Cassiodorus recycled this canon of virtues, which was as old as the Roman monarchy itself, in ever new variations. In the proems of the *Variae*, these motifs occur en masse—for instance, when Cassiodorus has Theoderic declare, "We take no delight in unjust profits, nor do things bereft of the grace of probity enter into the mind of Our Piety [*pietas*]. Indeed, the commonwealth [*res publica*] has always increased by the law of equity [*aequitas*], and when moderation [*temperantia*] is cherished, benefits swiftly ensue." There also, however, were significant neologisms in the political vocabulary. That applied first and foremost to the term *civilitas*, which had a lengthy prehistory but only now came to the forefront of the political discourse with a new meaning. The adjective *civilis* ("civil," from *civis*, "citizen") had been attributed to emperors in the early imperial period who conducted themselves "like a citizen" (*civiliter*) among senators; that is, they hid the real imbalance of power between themselves and the senate. In Late Antiquity, the substantive noun *civilitas*, derived from *civilis*, conveyed the expectation that an emperor would behave affably toward those who came into his presence; it was the opposite of arrogance and hubris. *Civilitas* was thus not a term used by the imperial chancellery; it does not appear in the collections of late antique imperial laws. *Civilitas* designated a manner of behaving that was expected of rulers in encounters with social elites and was deliberately demonstrated by them. That changed radically under Theoderic: his chancellery used *civilitas* to denote a political and social ideal, a state of affairs in which Roman laws and civilized manners were the rule. In Cassiodorus' usage, *civilitas* indicated a legal order antithetical to violence and despotism, civilization as opposed to barbarism. Actions that squared with this norm were qualified as *civilis* or *civiliter*; the opposite, as *incivilis* or *inciviliter*.[31]

The central role played by the concept of *civilitas* in the royal discourse reflects the importance that Theoderic attached to keeping the peace in his conception of governance. Peace (*pax*) abroad and security (*securitas*) at home were the prerequisites of the cooperation of Goths and Romans. The ideal of *civilitas* applied to every subject, Gothic and Roman. Above all, however, it made an appeal to the armed power in the land: the king asked his Goths to recognize Roman law and respect civil judges. Hence it was precisely what Theoderic intended when Cassiodorus urged the Gothic governor (*comes*) of Syracuse not to interfere in matters that fell under the jurisdiction of the "ordinary judge" and pointedly added that "the glory of the Goths is the protection of the civil order [*civilitas*]." For Roman subjects, this *civilitas* discourse was a kind of promise — namely, that the king would defend the law and keep his Goths in check. Men like Ennodius were thus very receptive to this ideal.[32]

The royal chancellery mentioned liberty (*libertas*) especially when it turned its attention to the Roman senate. Cassiodorus apostrophizes it with a variety of phrases as the abode and embodiment of liberty: *gremium libertatis, atrium libertatis, aula libertatis*, and *curia libertatis*. The Gothic king thereby reflected a key element of the senators' self-conception back at them: in their minds, "liberty" was not an empty word but rather the epitome of their privileged status and therefore inseparably linked to the validity of Roman law. This order was felt to be under threat: in Ennodius, we read that the rhetoric teacher Deuterius in Milan prevented the downfall of *libertas* by educating advocates. He has the distinguished young men Severus and Paterius say at their enrollment that it was thanks to their family that *civilitas* still stood firm even in adverse conditions. This feeling of insecurity was another reason why it was so important to invoke *civilitas*. Lastly, the royal chancellery constantly emphasized that Theoderic considered it his duty to preserve or restore public buildings. The chancellery proclaimed a veritable ideology of restoration in this area, which it evoked with the buzzword *reparatio*. Cassiodorus formulated it for Theoderic in the following maxim: "The restoration [*reparatio*] of ancient cities is the glory of Our age." Since preserving the urban fabric of earlier times had become an oppressive burden in late antique Italy, men like Ennodius hailed this program.[33]

Theoderic communicated his rulings in the form of letters, rescripts, and edicts as Roman emperors had done for centuries. Out of respect for the Eastern Roman emperor, however, he avoided calling these pronouncements *constitutiones* ("constitutions") or *leges* ("laws"), although they often formulated legal principles and administrative rules of general validity (*generalitas*). Edicts as such were not a prerogative of the emperor but could also be issued by high Roman magistrates; Cassiodorus, for one, made sure to include his own edicts as praetorian prefect in the *Variae*. The difference between Theoderic's edicts and imperial laws was purely formal, however, because the king's edicts created law that was just as much in force in his kingdom as the statutes of earlier Roman emperors had been, insofar as they had not been rescinded or superseded by later legislation. Theoderic explicitly recognized the laws of Roman emperors who had ruled the Western Empire in their entirety; those of the Eastern Roman emperors, however, only after they had been received in the West. The laws of Emperor Anastasius were not ratified in Theoderic's kingdom.[34]

The Roman Empire had long had nothing like a modern law code. An official collection of the decisions of Roman emperors with precedential character was first compiled under the Eastern Roman emperor Theodosius II and ratified as a kind of law code in the year 438. In sixteen books, this *Theodosian Code* (*Codex Theodosianus*) contains excerpts, organized by topic, from imperial constitutions that the Roman emperors had issued between 312 and 437. Later constitutions were called *novellae* (*leges*)—that is, "new laws." The only collection of such "novels" available in the Western Empire was compiled under Emperor Majorian; it thus did not contain the laws of the last Western Roman emperors. The *Theodosian Code* remained in use in the post-Roman kingdoms, but the post-Roman kings also began to produce their own collections of legal norms. The first to do so was the Visigothic king Euric, who sponsored a law code known as the *Codex Euricianus*. This code, from which substantial fragments survive, simplified Roman law so as to adapt it to changed circumstances, while also supplementing it with norms that break with Roman legal tradition and are thus considered Gothic. At the end of the fifth century, the Burgundian king Gundobad commissioned the codification of his and his predecessors' constitutions; this codification survives and is known as *Liber constitutionum* ("Book of Constitutions") or *Lex Burgundionum* ("Law of the Burgundians"). The *Lex Burgundionum* also combines Roman law with concepts and customs that were introduced by the immigrant warrior confederation. The *Breviarium Alaricianum* ("Breviary of Alaric"), in contrast, was a law code based exclusively on Roman law; Alaric II issued this abridged and commented version of the *Theodosian Code* for the Roman population of the kingdom of the Visigoths in the year 506.[35]

Theoderic also published a collection of legal norms that had been excerpted from the writings of the Roman jurists and the laws of the Roman emperors; it is known as the *Edict of Theoderic* (*Edictum Theoderici*). The *Edict of Theoderic* contains 154 norms derived from the laws (*leges*) of the Western Roman emperors and the writings of the Roman jurists, jurisprudence (*ius*). This collection is framed by a prologue and epilogue. In formal terms, Theoderic's *Edict* corresponds to the edicts that Roman magistrates conventionally issued to publicize the legal principles by which they intended to hold office; like these edicts, Theoderic's is neither systematic nor exhaustive. A table of contents at the beginning served to help users orient themselves. The *Edict* covers a wide variety of legal subjects, including adultery, arson and rioting, land theft, cattle rustling and fugitive slaves, sorcery, the desecration of graves, and wills. The *Edict* takes aim at corruption in the administration of justice and taxation, at violence, self-help, and vigilantism; it protects property, liberty, and marriage. The legislator himself declares in the prologue that he issued the edict because a high number of complaints had reached him: the laws were being trampled underfoot in the provinces. To put a stop to these abuses, justice should henceforth be administered according to the regulations contained in the *Edict*, which applied equally to both Romans and "barbarians," as he calls the Goths in this text. In the epilogue, the legislator again emphasizes that the *Edict* should suffice for the purposes of all barbarians and Romans, and he threatens judges — primarily Roman governors but also Gothic *comites* in the cities and provinces — with "proscription and deportation" if they should violate his measures. If a powerful person, whether Roman or barbarian, prevented the *Edict* from being applied in a case, it was incumbent on the judge either to take action against him or to inform the king.[36]

Unfortunately, we cannot say with certainty when Theoderic published this edict. Byzantine chroniclers associate it with the king's visit to Rome in the year 500. The collection indeed fits this context very well in terms of form and content: Theoderic never presented himself "more Roman" than during these six months. The king solemnly promised the Romans of Rome that he would leave in force all the legislation of previous emperors. The *Edict* served as a medium of communication between Theoderic and his subjects in this situation; the king above all wanted to signal to the Western Roman senators, as well as to the Eastern emperor, that he would exercise power like a Roman magistrate. That translated into a legislative style modeled on the formal legislative power of Roman magistrates, which set Theoderic significantly apart from the Burgundian kings; Gundobad and his successor Sigismund had no compunction about declaring their own measures *leges* that should remain in force forever. By virtue of the sovereignty of their kingdom, they issued norms that were called "constitutions," like the statutes of late Roman emperors, and they collected them in a codification that was arranged chronologically and called *Novels*, like the collections of the late Roman emperors. The *Edict of Theoderic*, in contrast, cites sources of law that could also be issued by imperial magistrates.[37]

It is difficult to say to what extent the *Edict of Theoderic* was actually used in court. The *Edict* was apparently known in Gothic Provence. It was not a summary of existing law and was not intended to replace earlier collections; hence it was not a law code in the modern sense. Theoderic used it primarily to proclaim his intentions and principles: the king wanted to present himself as the defender of the law by insisting that all his subjects must obey the law. He depicted himself as a tireless ruler who was concerned for the common good, one who would defend property, liberty, and marriage. In doing so, he signaled to his Roman subjects that he could restrain his army, and he let his Goths know that they were also subject to Roman law. The communicative function of the *Edict of Theoderic* is reflected by the way in which it was publicized: according to the prologue, it was supposed to be posted publicly. We can assume that it was read aloud at the assemblies of provincial notables and then displayed for thirty days at a place suitable for such proclamations, as is explicitly attested for one of the edicts of Theoderic's successor, Athalaric. According to the *Anonymus Valesianus*, Theoderic was considered a strong—that is, effective—king "on account of his edict."[38]

Edicts, admittedly, constituted only a small proportion of the pronouncements that streamed forth from the royal chancellery. The chancellery issued letters in the king's name to foreign rulers, including the Eastern Roman emperor; to the senate of Rome and Roman senators; to the directors of the central ministries and provincial governors; to Gothic *comites* in the provinces and cities; to Gothic generals; to *comitiaci* and *saiones*; to the population of provinces and cities; to municipal magistrates; to Jewish communities; to bishops of both confessions; and to Romans and Goths who did not hold office—not all of whom were members of the ruling class, although that class is heavily overrepresented. There is also a small number of letters addressed to a Roman synod that survive outside the *Variae* and were not drafted by Cassiodorus. The vast majority of the approximately 400 preserved letters of Gothic kings and queens are addressed to Romans; only 60 are addressed to Goths. The total volume of royal correspondence, of course, was many times greater. Everyone who held an office associated with a senatorial rank received an official letter of appointment; for the occupants of *illustris* offices, these were called *codicilli* and were presented in the form of ivory diptychs. The king informed the senate of the reasons for the appointment in a separate letter and asked the senate to endorse his decision enthusiastically. These letters were always elaborately stylized with their aristocratic addressees in mind. The royal chancellery made no less effort to stylize diplomatic correspondence, even though a letter to the king of the Thuringians contains the remark that the king had instructed the bearers of the letter in the "ancestral language" (*patrius sermo*)—that is, Gothic.[39]

A majority of the business that preoccupied Theoderic day to day consisted of responding to his subjects' complaints, petitions, and requests. He definitely was personally involved in the fate of individuals. When, for instance, the blind Goth Anduit complained that Gudila and Oppane had claimed him as their slave, although he had previously served as a free man in Theoderic's army and his freedom had been confirmed, the king commissioned the high-ranking Goth Neudis to ascertain whether Anduit could indeed prove his freedom; if he could, then Neudis should reject Gudila and Oppane's baseless claims. Since it was often difficult for the king to judge the veracity of such petitions, he normally delegated the responsibility of investigating such cases to others. The investigators could be *saiones* or *comitiaci* or even senators and members of the royal family. Theoderic instructed his nephew Theodahad, for example, to pass judgment over a man who refused to appear before the court of a high-ranking Goth named Suna.[40]

The king also sometimes summoned plaintiffs and defendants to court to investigate a case himself. When a certain Patzen complained that his wife Regina had been violently assaulted three times by Procula, the wife of Brandila, while Patzen was on campaign in Gaul, the king wrote to Brandila that he should punish his wife appropriately or appear with her at the royal court to defend her. It turned out, however, that the king had made his decision with insufficient information. He later learned that the victim had married the defendant's husband in her own husband's absence. The assault had thus been preceded by adultery. The king thereupon instructed the Gothic general Wilitanc to bring both parties to trial at his court; if proof of the adultery should be found, the delinquents were to be punished according to the law—with death.[41]

Family and inheritance disputes were routine for the king. Alongside many individual decisions, model texts also survive. On request, the king confirmed marriages, legitimated children, released minors from guardianship, and granted dispensation from the prohibition on marrying a maternal niece (*consobrina*).[42] Theoderic also undoubtedly reserved the right to decide whether someone received the king's protection or not since his credibility would have been at stake if he left these petitions to others. Even so, demand must have been very high; that is shown not only by surviving model letters, but also by the number of individual cases that are attested. *Saiones* and *comitiaci* were not the only ones instructed to impose the king's protection; other officials were commissioned to do so as well. That could be the *comes* of a province, like

Adila, who was instructed to extend the king's protection to the possessions of the church of Milan on Sicily as requested by the bishop Eustorgius. Theoderic also once commissioned a high-ranking senator to protect the property of another senator (Agnellus) while the latter was away on a diplomatic mission in North Africa.[43]

The king also decided whether to grant subjects' requests to take possession of public buildings. This procedure was used only when a community was incapable of restoring public buildings that were in poor condition or in danger of collapse. In this case, the king was prepared to transfer ownership of the real estate in question to a private individual, provided that the latter pledged to carry out repairs. It was a routine procedure for which Cassiodorus' *Variae* preserve a model letter. The king's policy in this area was likewise highly reactive and always dependent on the information presented to him. When it was reported that a bronze statue in the city of Como had disappeared, he had the *comes* Tancila announce a reward of 100 *solidi* for the person who could identify the thief. If no one came forward, then Tancila was instructed to round up the local craftsmen and interrogate them under torture (*sub terrore*) because, the king argued, no one could have removed the statue without their help.[44]

The king likewise preferred to decide about the remission of taxes personally. When the praetorian prefect presented him with reports from provincial governors to the effect that the stewards of senatorial estates were refusing to pay the tax they owed on them in full, Theoderic wrote a letter chastising the senate of Rome. In his letter, he noted that the city councillors responsible for collecting the tax either passed the deficit on to other taxpayers or were forced to pay it themselves, and he demanded that the senators pay off their tax debt in full. He granted the senators the privilege, however, of delivering their taxes directly to the vicar of the city of Rome, thus sparing them the fees that would have accrued to local tax collectors. In an edict that was simultaneously sent to every province, Theoderic informed the provincials that he had written to the senate on account of these abuses and declared that he was prepared to grant an audience to any landowner or curial who wished to file a claim to the effect that he had been burdened with someone else's tax debt. Theoderic thus not only declined to punish the senators' tax evasion; he even rewarded it by granting them a privileged payment method. Yet he still asserted the fiscus' rights before the senators and propagated the image of a caring king who protected his subjects from unjust demands. When Theoderic discovered that the Goths residing in the provinces of Picenum, Tuscia Annonaria, and Tuscia Suburbicaria refused to pay their taxes, he dispatched the *saio* Gesila with the mission of forcing them to pay. The property of anyone who resisted would be confiscated.

It was far from an enviable mission for Gesila: the king does not outline how he was supposed to secure obedience in these three provinces.[45]

Theoderic also took time for the petitions of individual cities, churches, and taxpayers who asked for temporary tax relief. He confirmed, for example, that the magistrates of the city of Trento did not need to pay the tax known as the *tertia* ("third") on a plot of land (*sors*) that he had given to the Gothic presbyter Butilan. The king was also prepared to provide help when the tax capacity of an estate had been greatly overestimated. Cassiodorus preserves a model letter for this process as well. The precondition for reducing the tax burden on such a piece of land was that the owner possessed only this estate and could prove that the income this land yielded in no way sufficed to cover the payments demanded of him. Whether that was actually the case was carefully scrutinized.[46]

Regular reports were sent to the king from Rome by the urban prefect. For at least a few years, there also was a high-ranking Goth in Rome, named Arigern, who acted in the king's interest and communicated with him directly. Since senators also had privileged access to the king, Roman affairs always had a high profile at court. In this area as well, however, the king normally only reacted to complaints, petitions, and requests submitted by his subjects and officials.[47]

But the king was by no means always passive. Sometimes he took the initiative himself. The royal chancellery also sent instructions and proclamations that the recipients had not solicited. Such letters were frequently prompted by the king's building projects, court journeys, or troop movements. Thus, for example, the king requested stonemasons from Rome to work marble for a basilica in Ravenna named after the Greek demigod Hercules. The city of Ticinum was ordered to prepare a ship and five days' provisions for Heruli who were on their way to Ravenna. After the king decided to admit fleeing Alamanni into his kingdom, he instructed the inhabitants of the province of Noricum Mediterraneum to exchange their cattle with those of the passing Alamanni, whose cattle had been weakened by the long journey but were larger than their own. The same order was given to the inhabitants of the provinces of Venetia et Histria and Liguria when a large number of Gepids were relocated to Gaul between 523 and 526. They were also asked to take consolation in the thought that even though the cattle they received in exchange were exhausted, they were still greater in stature than their own. The king also spontaneously took measures to secure northern Italy. For instance, he ordered the Goths and Romans living in Feltre to expand the fortress (*castellum*) of Verruca, situated on the hill Doss Trento, into a fortified refuge. A similar order was sent to the Romans and Goths in Tortona (Dertona). The landowners of Feltre were, moreover, supposed to help fortify a city being built on the territory of Trento.

This was probably the context in which we should place an order addressed "to all Goths and Romans," but probably intended for a specific city, that calls on the addressees to gather stones that were lying around unused and make them available for the construction of a city wall.[48]

An order to build a fleet of no fewer than 1,000 light warships (*dromones*) also was the result of strategic planning at the court. The praetorian prefect Abundantius was put in charge of this project; he had to find the necessary timber and recruit the crews. The order that sparked this naval project is preserved. The *comes patrimonii* Wiliarit also was involved. Since the timely completion of the objective quickly proved difficult and unanticipated problems emerged, Theoderic took a series of flanking measures. The king sent Abundantius and Wiliarit additional instructions and, at their request, dispatched *saiones* to bring the naval recruits to Ravenna, to press ahead with the acquisition of timber, and to remove obstacles on navigable rivers. Only part of this naval project was completed by Theoderic's death, after which it was quietly dropped.[49]

If the king got the impression from complaints that reached him that serious abuses were being committed in a province, he often gave detailed instructions to the persons he dispatched in response. At the same time, the royal chancellery wrote to the inhabitants of the province, commending the new officeholder to them and declaring that he would blamelessly perform his duty and put an end to the wrongs they had protested. Cassiodorus preserves examples for the provinces of Pannonia, Savia, Dalmatia, and Sicilia. The abuses about which the provincials had complained are listed in detail. To make it clear to the provincials that their complaints to the king had not fallen on deaf ears, these texts were publicly read and posted as edicts.[50]

In order to sustain this workload, the king needed many helpers. Theoderic not only had written requests to answer, but he also granted audiences. He received delegations from foreign powers, provinces, and cities, as well as senators and bishops. To avoid drowning in this deluge of routine business, the decision-making process had to be prepared for him. It was customary and practical for the king to consult persons of trust on matters of political and military significance. The emperors of the Later Roman Empire had an official council of state, the "consistory" (*consistorium*). The men admitted to it were predominantly Romans and were styled *comites consistoriani*. The heads of the palatine ministries belonged to the consistory *ex officio*, as did the *magistri militum* and praetorian prefects when they were at the court. The minutes were kept by a corps (*schola*) of clerks (*notarii*) of senatorial rank. Theoderic did not dissolve this council and continued to confer the rank of *comes primi ordinis*, which gave the recipient access to the consistory. He rarely convened this ponderous advisory board, however, which is why the position of "silentiary" (*silentiarius*), whose job was to ensure that silence was kept at meetings of the *consistorium*, was regarded as a sinecure under Theoderic.[51]

In everyday government, Theoderic preferred to work with individual officials who presented petitions and legal cases to him. For that purpose, there were "referendaries" (*referendarii*); these officials assisted the king at audiences by summarizing the case at hand and explaining the king's verdict to the parties. They gave the king a concise overview of written petitions and a recommendation as to what he should decide. In a letter to the senate on the occasion of the promotion of the long-tenured *referendarius* Cyprianus to *comes sacrarum largitionum*, Cassiodorus has Theoderic say the following:

> Welcome, therefore, as a colleague, a man whom Our palace approved after long scrutiny: a man who served Our royal utterances so fearlessly that he would explain Our orders often while We Ourselves looked on—and praised him. You indeed know what We are talking about: who among you has been sent away from Cyprianus' devotion? Indeed, anyone who sought solace from him soon received benefits from Us. He frequently accomplished on Our excursions what usually was done in consistories [*consistoria*] of old. If, for instance, We wished to relieve Our mind, wearied by care for the commonwealth [*res publica*], We sought out exercise on horseback so that the firmness and vigor of Our body might be refreshed by the variety of activities. Then this entertaining presenter [*relator*] brought Us manifold cases, and his reports were not loathsome for the wearied mind of the judge. Thus, while this kindly artist produced reasons for granting favors, Our mind was refreshed, fired by eagerness to do so.

Cassiodorus writes about the consistory as an institution of the past and makes it clear that Theoderic was glad to escape the pomp and circumstance of court. A referendary like Cyprianus could apparently be summoned at any time. In a letter sent to Cyprianus himself, Cassiodorus celebrates his ability "to set forth the confused complaints of petitioners in an extremely precise and clear report." By doing so, he enabled the king to decide cases presented to him quickly: "A case set forth by you was quickly reviewed: and why should the conclusion of the case be delayed, after you had concluded your proposal with clear concision?" Cassiodorus states.[52]

In addition to the senators who served the king as high officeholders in the civil administration, Theoderic also gathered a group of Goths around him on whom he conferred the titles of *comes* and the rank of *vir illustris*. He thereby set them on par with senators, although none of them appears to have requested admission to the senate. Some also bore the honorary title of *vir sublimis*, which had not yet hardened into a formal predicate of rank and so could still be conferred on both *viri illustres* and *viri spectabiles*. The king himself called these men *maiores domus*. He thus communicated that they held their position not by virtue of an office of the *res publica Romana* but rather on account of their standing in the king's household (*domus*). It was from this group that the king selected his generals, to whom he relinquished command in the field after he came to Italy; he entrusted them with the administration of frontier provinces and the most diverse special missions. We unfortunately know very little about most of these Gothic *comites*. Few of them come distinctly into view in our sources. One was Ibba, who won a victory over the Franks for Theoderic in 508 and then fought successfully in Spain from 511 to 513. Pitzia was another important man. Ennodius describes him as one of the noblest Goths. In 504 and 505, he led the military operations that resulted in the capture of Sirmium. If he is identical with the *comes* Petia, whom Theoderic killed in 514, he must have been rehabilitated posthumously.[53]

Arigern and Tuluin come clearest into view. Arigern was sent to Rome with the *maiores domus* Gudila and Bedewulf to ensure the safety of Pope Symmachus and to negotiate with bishops who had gathered there for a synod. Arigern subsequently spent several years in Rome. During this time, he kept watch over law and order (*disciplina*) on the king's behalf and appears to have sent Theoderic regular reports. Theoderic writes to the senate, for instance, that he had heard about anti-Jewish riots from Arigern and had ordered him to investigate. When the Roman church complained to Theoderic that the Jews had claimed a house to which they were not entitled, he commissioned Arigern to decide the case. For the magic trial against the senators Basilius and Praetextatus, it fell to Arigern to monitor the senatorial court. After the conquest of Provence, Theoderic entrusted Arigern with the task of organizing the provinces that fell within its territory. When Arigern returned to Rome in 510 after accomplishing his mission, the king urged the senate to obey his commands as it had done before. Arigern was apparently the most powerful man in Rome in these years and perhaps Theoderic's closest confidant. He disappears from the sources shortly afterward.[54]

Tuluin is the only one of Theoderic's Gothic advisers about whose career we know any details. He was of noble descent but left his family at an early age to serve Theoderic as a *cubicularius*. He distinguished himself in the war over Sirmium (504–505); on his return, he received a position of trust in the king's household, apparently as *maior domus*. A few years later (508), Tuluin set out on the Gallic campaign as one of several generals and was wounded in battle at the bridge over the Rhône at Arles. When the Franks attacked the kingdom of the Burgundians at the end of Theoderic's reign, Tuluin was again sent to Gaul. This time, he succeeded in winning the Burgundian part of Provence for his king without taking part in the fighting. Theoderic rewarded him with properties when he returned. At Theoderic's death, Tuluin was so influential and so highly respected that he was viewed as a potential successor. After he declined to pursue the throne, he was placed in command of the Gothic army and became the first and only Goth to join the senate. On that occasion, Cassiodorus wrote a letter to the senate for Tuluin, in which the latter boasts that he always used his influence with Theoderic in the senators' interest:

> When offices [*honores*; literally "honors"] were sought from Theoderic of glorious memory, prince among kings, I often joined my wishes in your support so that I appeared to have sent such favors in advance to the men whom it beseemed me gratefully to join. For that which is sped along by gifts conferred is sought all the more confidently. Through my intercession, I often promoted consuls, patricians, and prefects, striving to obtain for you what I could scarcely have wished for myself. Rejoice under my auspices now [i.e., as new king], Conscript Fathers, as I have always favored your honors [*honores*].[55]

3. UNDER THE KING'S WATCHFUL EYES: THE CENTRAL ADMINISTRATION

Ravenna was not only Theoderic's preferred residence, the *urbs regia* par excellence, but it was also the home of the central ministries of his kingdom. These ministries could not accompany the ruler on his journeys; their organization was too complex, their personnel too extensive, and their methods of operating too reliant on written documentation and correspondence. Each of the five "palatine ministries" at the court employed several hundred people, and the praetorian prefecture probably even more. They thus needed a fixed location with offices and archives. Of the heads of these ministries, probably only the *magister officiorum* and the quaestor could always be found close to the king; hence, in contrast to the three "finance ministers," they received appointment certificates but not written instructions addressed to them in the chancellery style.

The competences of these ministries were distinct but still overlapped at several points. They also were not internally consistent but rather performed a wide range of responsibilities. With one exception, all the ministries of the civil administration were headed by Romans who held the rank of *illustris* and so were full members of the Roman senate. The only ministry that was entrusted to a Goth was responsible for the king's personal domains. This ministry was also the only innovation added to the administrative structure that had existed under the last emperors; all the other offices had been created in the early fourth century.

The highest-ranking "minister" appointed by the king bore the title of *magister officiorum*, which indicated that he was the chief of all the administrative offices (*officia*) located at the court. The responsibilities and powers of the *magister officiorum*, however, were much more wide-ranging than his title suggests. He was still the commander of the *scholae palatinae*, the corps that had once served as the palace guard—under Theoderic merely paid sinecures. The *magister*, as he was frequently called for short, also still exercised judicial and disciplinary power over all the subaltern officials employed at court. He introduced high-ranking personages and foreign ambassadors at audiences and meetings of the consistory and thus influenced who had access to the king; at the same time, he also served as master of ceremonies on such occasions. Together with the praetorian prefect, who headed the provincial administration, the *magister officiorum* oversaw the *cursus publicus*, the state courier and transportation service, and distributed the authorization certificates (*evectiones*) required to use it. In Theoderic's kingdom, moreover, the *magister* acquired the job of controlling the prices of food in Ravenna; he appointed officials called *peraequatores* ("regulators") for this purpose.

Above all, however, the *magister officiorum* headed the *officium comitiacum*, a department whose employees' job was to enforce the king's will everywhere he could not personally be present. This department included the agents who delivered the king's commands to Roman officials and subjects and were supposed to ensure that they were carried out. Their most important job was to facilitate the administration of justice by forcing defendants to appear before a judge and then enforcing his ruling. These agents were normally called *comitiaci* but were sometimes also known as *magistriani* (i.e., "men of the *magister*"). Such agents had existed in the past, although they were called *agentes in rebus* before Theoderic. In Theoderic's kingdom, these Roman agents were now joined by counterparts responsible for Gothic affairs who answered directly to the king: *saiones*. This competition diminished the importance of the subordinates of the *magister officiorum* as facilitators of communication and control between the ruler, his officials, and his subjects since the *comitiaci* were responsible only for Roman affairs.[56]

The corps of *comitiaci* still held a central position among civil officials because the chiefs-of-staff of most of the higher officials in the central and

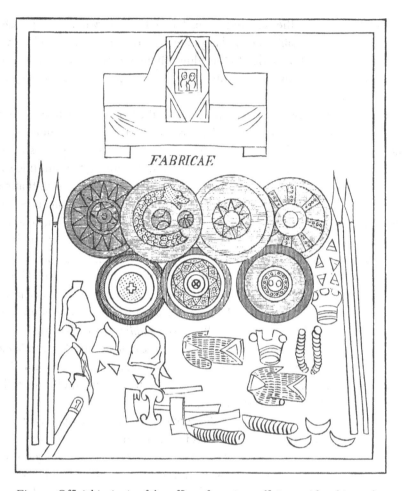

Fig. 14. Official insignia of the office of *magister officiorum* (sketch): on the table in the background, a codicil (letter of appointment) with an image of the emperors. From Otto Seeck, *Die Notitia dignitatum* (Berlin, 1876), 144.

provincial administration were drawn from their ranks. The chief-of-staff of the praetorian prefect was also appointed by the *magister officiorum*. This official, known as the *princeps officii*, thus always came from outside the *officium* he headed. Since he had to sign off on all official business, his position was both influential and lucrative—both for the *magister officiorum* who filled the position and for the man who held it. The former collected a sum of money called a *suffragium* ("support, backing") for the promotion; the latter collected high fees (*sportulae*) for every official act he authorized. It is debated whether the chiefs-of-staff of other bureaus still answered to the *magister officiorum*; even if that was still the case, though, they would have been wary of making an enemy of their new boss by reporting any abuses to their old one, especially since their term lasted only a year.[57]

In contrast to the other high court officials, the quaestor did not have a staff of his own but instead relied on the staffs of other officials. The primary function of the quaestor was to dress the king's will in words. He formulated all texts issued in the king's name, including those addressed to Goths; the royal chancellery used Latin exclusively. His insignia of office thus show scrolls and a kind of cabinet with the inscription *leges salubres* ("salubrious laws"). Cassiodorus, who was quaestor for many years, has left behind a model appointment letter for his own position, in which he has the king say the following:

> If ranks shine only as much as they enjoy Our sight, if frequent presence betrays the ruler's favor, then no judge/governor could be more glorious than the man who has been invited to share Our thoughts. To some, We assign the oversight of state money; others We permit to try cases; and to still others We delegate the rights of Our patrimony. But We embrace the quaestorship with Our whole heart, which We deem to be the voice of Our own tongue. Of necessity, the quaestor is intimately involved in Our thoughts so that he can say in his own words what he knows We think. He lays down the judgment of his own will and takes up the desire of Our mind so that what he says is thought instead to have come from Us Ourselves.[58]

Cassiodorus emphasizes that the quaestor had to serve as the king's mouthpiece. It was for this reason that he prefaced the last two books of the *Variae*, which consist of letters that he wrote as praetorian prefect, with a separate foreword in which he notes that he was speaking in these letters in his own voice. We may in fact presume that the occupants of the quaestorship took care to formulate the king's will in a way that would win his approval. The likely starting point was often enough probably a stenograph of an order that the king had given orally. We are able to compare such a draft and the official version in just a single case, but this sample confirms the suspicion that any revisions were purely formal in nature.[59]

The quaestor had to possess an exceptional command of language and be steeped in Latin literature. The mannered style of the late antique Roman chancellery required a mastery of Latin that realized the ideals of late antique education but was by no means easy to find, even at court. Even after the quaestorship was in other hands, Cassiodorus still occasionally drafted royal pronouncements. The quaestor also needed a solid knowledge of Roman law

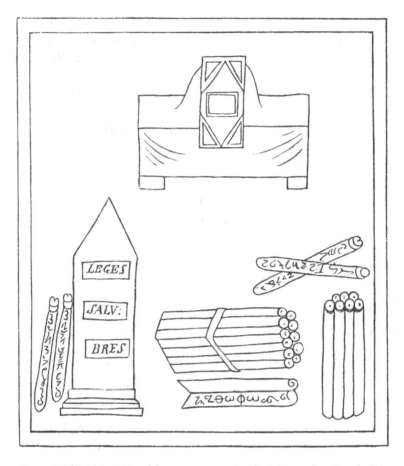

Fig. 15. Official insignia of the *quaestor sacri palatii*. From Otto Seeck, *Die Notitia dignitatum* (Berlin, 1876), 147.

because a large part of royal correspondence concerned legal disputes. His workload thus was heavy: the quaestor composed edicts and answers to the petitions of officials and subjects. He also drafted the appointment documents for officials and the letters in which the king informed the senate of appointments that opened the door to membership in that august body. The fact that the king's entire written correspondence could pass over the desk of a single man shows that its volume was not at all comparable to that of early modern state ministries. The occupants of the quaestorship held a position of trust under the king; without their support, Theoderic could not have communicated his power in forms that were tailored to late Roman conventions. We thus may presume that men like Cassiodorus were privy to the king's thoughts and plans. Their

Fig. 16. Official insignia of the *comes sacrarum largitionum*. From Otto
Seeck, *Die Notitia dignitatum* (Berlin, 1876), 148.

regular dealings with the king also gave them the opportunity to present propos-
als of their own. They competed, however, with many other people close to
the king and so were hardly in a position to influence personnel and policy
decisions over the long term.

The three "finance ministers"—the *comes sacrarum largitionum*, the *comes
rei privatae*, and the *comes patrimonii*—likewise held the status of *illustris* but
ranked behind the *magister officiorum* and the quaestor at the court. The *comes
sacrarum largitionum* got his name from the fact that he had to ensure that the
emperor had the necessary means to lavish gifts (*largitiones*, "largesses") on his
subjects, especially soldiers. These gifts were made in precious metal, whether

in coin or in bullion, and were called "sacred" because everything in the Roman Empire that had something to do with the emperor had long come to be regarded as "sacred." That did not change under Theoderic, although the adjective "sacred" was seldom still used as an attribute of the king. Since the troops in Theoderic's kingdom received a yearly donative of five gold *solidi*, over 100,000 coins were probably used for this purpose alone.[60]

The *comes sacrarum largitionum* oversaw all taxes and dues that did not fall under the authority of the praetorian prefect. That included the tax on the capital assets of merchants and artisans that was collected in gold every five years and hence known as the "five-year gold payment" (*collatio auri lustralis*) or simply the "gold tax" (*auraria*). This tax was still collected in Theoderic's kingdom and under his successors, whereas in the Eastern Empire it was abolished by Anastasius. The *siliquaticum*, a tax introduced in the Western Roman Empire by Emperor Valentinian III, amounting to one-twenty-fourth of the value of merchandise, was also peculiar to the Western Empire. It took its name from the fact that the *solidus* was made up of twenty-four *siliquae* ("carats"). Collecting this tax required the close monitoring of places where commercial activity was concentrated. The job of doing so was leased to investors called *siliquatarii*; these tax farmers stood under the supervision of the *comes siliquatariorum*, an official at the provincial level who in turn answered to the *comes sacrarum largitionum*. The latter was also responsible for collecting a tax in lieu of the former levy on clothing (*vestes*) for the army (*canon vestium*); this tax was called the "collection of two and three per unit" (*exactio binorum et ternorum*). The new name reflects the commutation of a duty collected in kind into a monetary tax, whereby two different rates were used.[61]

The portfolio of the *comes sacrarum largitionum* went far beyond the administration related to these three taxes. He also supervised customs officials, managed the state salt monopoly, and oversaw the mints. Gold and silver coinage was minted in Rome, Ravenna, and Milan under Theoderic, and copper coinage was also minted in Rome and Ravenna. The directors of these mints were appointed by the king himself. The *comes sacrarum largitionum* also supervised the state weaving mills; a *comes vestiarii* subordinate to him secured clothing for the court. Lastly, the *comes sacrarum largitionum* had taken over a job that had once belonged to the *primicerius* of the royal bedchamber (a senior eunuch): he managed the money that was paid to reward chamberlains for backing aspirants to paid positions.[62]

In addition to the money that the king received from the sources mentioned above, he also drew income from his personal domains. Like the Roman emperors before him, Theoderic was also the wealthiest landowner in Italy. The administration of Theoderic's domains was split between two ministries. One was called the *res privata* and was under the authority of the *comes rei privatae*. *Res privata* meant private property, but in reality it consisted of crown land, and the income it generated was used to fund a variety of public functions, not at all exclusively for the king's own budget. The estates that made up the *res privata* were let to major tenants (*conductores*) on hereditary leases. It was the job of the *comes rei privatae* to collect the rent (*canon*) owed on them. He also had to seize the land of owners who had died without legal heirs or had been punished with confiscation. If the state's claim to such ownerless lands (*bona vacantia*) was disputed, the decision lay in the hands of the *comes rei privatae*. Since he was both judge and party to the same case, however, he tended to prioritize the interest of the state over equity. When Ennodius attempted to secure the restitution of confiscated estates for his nephew Lupicinus, the *comes* Tancila informed him that it was very difficult to get something back once the king had claimed it for himself. Theoderic was well aware that a conflict of interest existed in this field but had no intention of eliminating this structural problem. He was no more likely to separate administration and jurisdiction than the Roman emperors before him. Hence it was not at all shocking that the *comes rei privatae* presided as the judge of last resort in cases concerning incest and the desecration of graves.[63]

The other part of the royal domains comprised the *patrimonium* that was under the authority of the *comes patrimonii*. This official stayed in constant contact with the king and could also be a Goth. The office had apparently been created under Odoacer, who appointed a *comes et vicedominus* to administer his domains in the recently recovered provinces of Sicily and Dalmatia; under Theoderic, he also collected the land tax (*annona*) in these provinces. He thus was responsible for the entire tax system insofar as it did not fall within the purview of the *comes sacrarum largitionum*. In Italy, in contrast, the *comes patrimonii* was and remained the sole official responsible for managing the king's domains, both those that were let out like the estates of the *res privata* and those that were worked directly by the king's stewards (*vicedomini*). We know as little about how the *res privata* and the *patrimonium* were divided as we do about the size and location of their respective landholdings. Since the *comes patrimonii* was responsible for the provinces recovered under Odoacer and Theoderic, his area of competence must have expanded dramatically. The income he managed served to pay the salaries of the *comites Gothorum* and other Goths who held office. He could command the people who lived and worked on the land under his direct supervision as he saw fit—for instance, by obligating them to serve as rowers. The *patrimonium* also provided food and drink for the king's

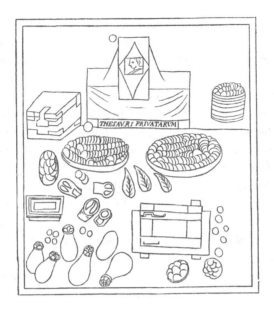

THESAVRI PRIVATARVM

Fig. 17. Official insignia of the *comes rei
privatae*. From Otto Seeck, *Die Notitia
dignitatum* (Berlin, 1876), 154.

table. Like the *comes rei privatae*, the *comes patrimonii* also acted as judge in his
area: he likewise decided lawsuits brought by major and minor tenants.[64]

We have no information about the amount of revenue that flowed into the
coffers of the *comes largitionum*. Since collecting the taxes he supervised
entailed considerable expense, we may presume that maintaining the necessary
collection apparatus was worth it, particularly as Theoderic's government still
collected monetary taxes that had either been abolished in the Eastern Roman
Empire or had never been introduced. We likewise have no quantifiable data
for the *res privata* or *patrimonium*. We thus have to content ourselves with the
conclusion that the income generated sufficed to finance the royal court.

All five of the "ministers" mentioned above sat *ex officio* on the king's council
of state, an advisory committee that Odoacer and Theoderic had inherited from
their imperial predecessors. It was called the "consistory" because members
were required to stand (Latin, *consisto*) in the ruler's presence. Many people
had the right to attend meetings of this committee in addition to the holders of
illustris offices at court because Theoderic conferred the rank and title of *comes*
on a large number of people. The group was traditionally subdivided into three
classes (*primi, secundi, terii ordinis*). Under Theoderic, however, the consistory

was not nearly as important as it had been under the emperors. For one thing, Theoderic preferred to be informed by the quaestor and referendaries than to convene the cumbersome consistory. For another thing, he also gathered a Gothic retinue around him when he needed to make decisions with political repercussions. It did not have an official name, but Theoderic evidently consulted this group often. Before we discuss Theoderic's governing style in greater detail, however, we should introduce the most important civil ministry: the praetorian prefecture.

4. CENTER AND PERIPHERY: THE REGIONAL ADMINISTRATION

The Later Roman Empire was divided into provinces, dioceses, and prefectures. Two of these prefectures lay in the western half of the empire: the prefecture of Gaul, which included Hispania, and the prefecture of Italy, which was also competent for North Africa. As the Western Roman Empire gradually lost control of Hispania, North Africa, and finally Gaul over the course of the fifth century, only one prefecture remained. This prefecture encompassed Italy and Sicily but not Sardinia and Corsica, which had fallen under Vandalic rule. The territory of the prefecture was divided into thirteen provinces: Venetia et Histria, Liguria, Alpes Cottiae, Aemilia, Flaminia, Picenum, Tuscia et Umbria (Tuscany), Valeria, Campania, Samnium, Apulia et Calabria, Lucania et Bruttii, and Sicilia. The provinces Raetia I and Raetia II beyond the Alps also belonged to the prefecture of Italy.[65]

The prefecture of Gaul was reestablished in 510, after Theoderic brought Provence under his control. This revived Gallic prefecture, however, encompassed only parts of three provinces—Viennensis, Narbonensis I, and Alpes Maritimae—and so lagged far behind Italy in terms of its importance. The provinces to the east of Italy, in contrast, which had once belonged to the diocese of Illyricum, were not placed under any prefecture but instead were governed by men who answered directly to the king.[66]

Prefectures were headed by a Roman with the rank of *vir illustris*. He was called the praetorian prefect (*praefectus praetorio*) because his office had evolved from that of the commander of the praetorian guard (*praetorium*) that had once protected the emperor in Rome under the Principate. This originally collegial military office transformed into the most important civil office in Late Antiquity. Cassiodorus, who held the office of praetorian prefect as the last in his long career (533–537), traced it back to Joseph's service for Pharaoh and ascribed it a standing only slightly lower than that of the king himself. In a model text, he has the king say the following:

Map 9. The Provinces of Italy in Late Antiquity.

We and this official indeed share rights. He summons faraway persons without privilege of venue [*sine praescriptione (fori)*]; he imposes great fines on
wrongdoers; he disburses state money at his discretion; he grants passes for
the post [*evectiones*] with similar authority; he confiscates ownerless land; he
punishes the crimes of provincial governors; he pronounces sentences. What
is there that has not been entrusted to him, whose very speech is a judgment?
It is almost as if he can legislate since His Reverence can conclude lawsuits
without appeal. On entering the palace, he is frequently adored as is customary for Us, and such an act of homage violates convention, which would
result in charges against others. No official is his equal in power. He presides
with sacred authority [*vice sacra*—i.e., as the emperor's proxy] in any case.
No officer [*miles*] can object to him on the basis of privilege of venue with
the exception of the staff of the *magister militum*.[67]

The competences of the praetorian prefect were indeed extensive. Like the
king, the praetorian prefect published edicts that contained instructions for subordinate officials and established maximum prices. He supervised provincial
governors and was the supreme judge for the entire provincial administration,
as well as the judge of last resort for all cases in which an appeal was made
against a subordinate's verdict. A litigant could appeal from the court of a provincial governor directly to the praetorian prefect; in contrast, in the provinces
of southern Italy, which were grouped in a diocese called Italia Suburbicaria,
the "vicar of Italy" (*vicarius Italiae*) served as an intermediary instance between
the provinces and the prefect. In principle, the verdicts of the praetorian prefect
were unappealable. The best that a defeated litigant in his court could hope for
was that the king himself might void the judgment and reopen the case. There
were so many important cases to be heard before the praetorian prefect of
Oriens that the number of advocates admitted to this court was repeatedly limited to 150. Even though the prefecture of Italy was much smaller in Theoderic's
day, we still may presume that several dozen lawyers were active at this court.[68]

The prefect's financial responsibilities were even more important than his
judicial duties. The praetorian prefecture managed the *annona*, a tax that
brought in far more revenue than all other taxes and dues because it was levied
on all arable land, no matter in whose possession it happened to be. Romans,
Goths, the king—they all were obligated to pay this land tax into the treasure
"chest" of the praetorian prefect (*arca praefectoria*). The *arca* funded all the
salaries collected by the personnel of the civil administration. On top of that,
the praetorian prefecture was also responsible for maintaining the army and the
court, insofar as the *comes patrimonii* was not obliged to pay. Hence Cassiodorus
declares that the praetorian prefect sustained the palace, maintained the king's

Fig. 18. Official insignia of the *praefectus praetorio*: in the foreground,
his car; in the background, a large inkpot stands next to a table, on which
rests a codicil and four candles. From Otto Seeck, *Die Notitia dignitatum*
(Berlin, 1876), 107.

servants, furnished judges their salaries, and "satisfie(d) the voracious envoys of
foreign peoples with his arrangements."

The state apparatus as a whole could function only if the *arca* of the praetorian prefect was filled year after year with sufficient revenue to cover the sundry
expenses detailed above. To ensure that it was, the requisite amount was calculated and then distributed to the taxpayers. In a very crude procedure, the size,
quality, and use of taxable land were determined, and the number and gender

of the laborers who worked it were also taken into account: a female laborer counted only half as much as a male. On the basis of these data, abstract tax units were generated called *iugum* ("yoke") and *caput* ("head"); the process of tax assessment was thus called *iugatio* or *capitatio*. It was up to the praetorian prefecture to distribute the estimated cost of the budget to the taxpayers in the provinces by calculating how much each should pay per unit. To accomplish this, the prefecture relied on regularly updated cadasters that documented the entire kingdom. The process of updating them took place in a fifteen-year cycle called the "indiction," which was also used for dating. Time was counted not by indiction number but rather by the years within the cycle—that is, the first, second, third year of the indiction, and so on.

As soon as the budget had been calculated for the entire prefecture, a "tax proclamation"—also called an *indictio*—was made to the provincial governors. The governors then, with the help of their official staffs, had to apportion the amount due from their province among its civic communities (*civitates*). They were monitored during this process by officials dispatched from the prefecture, the *canonicarius* and the *cancellarius*. The *canonicarius'* job was to oversee the collection of the regular tax allocated to the province, which was called the *canon*. The *cancellarius* took his name from the barrier (*cancelli*) that separated a judge from litigants; he was originally an aide who served there. The *canonicarii* sent to the provinces were supposed to look over the governors' shoulders and review their bookkeeping. The actual collection of the land tax was left to the curials of the cities, who employed officials of their own, "collectors" (*exactores*) and "receivers" (*susceptores*), to carry it out.[69]

The tax year began on September 1 and was divided into three trimesters since the land tax was paid in three installments. If the municipal tax collectors failed to meet their quotas, the praetorian prefect sent his own officials to reiterate the state's demands. These officials were called *compulsores* because their job was to *compel* the taxpayers to fulfill their duty to the state. The land tax was paid partly in kind but predominantly in gold. Collecting taxes in kind made sense when goods were produced in sufficient quantities where they would be consumed; in that case, transportation costs could be saved. For taxes paid in kind, the goods were stored in depots (*horrea*), for the maintenance of which civic communities were also responsible. It was the taxpayers' obligation to deliver their goods there. Collection in gold was the rule, though, because it simplified the transfer of resources. The gold was received from the taxpayers and transported where payments needed to be made. Rates that were supposed to be based on market prices were issued for converting goods to cash (*adaeratio*). Since the state claimed a right of first refusal, it could always buy locally at a good price; this process was called *coemptio*. Gold was not necessarily required; the state could deduct the price of the goods it bought against the tax that the producers owed. This procedure facilitated the cashless transfer of resources for the state while offering subordinate officials ample opportunity to enrich themselves at the taxpayers' expense because market prices could vary widely by region and season. Hence frequent complaints were made about these forced purchases.[70]

The land tax was assessed according to the state's needs, not the taxpayers' ability to pay it. If it could be anticipated that the state would require more in the coming year than in the preceding one, the tax rate was raised accordingly. It was for this reason that the king praised his prefect Liberius for being able to avoid such a tax hike. If it only emerged in the course of the tax year that the income from the *annona* would not meet the prefecture's expenses, an additional tax was levied from the taxpayers, called a *supraindictio* ("additional levy") or *augmentum* ("increase"). Such additional tax levies also occurred under Theoderic, although we do not know how frequently. The tax burden meanwhile could be raised only within very narrow limits in premodern societies because yields tended to stagnate in the middle term, while they were also subject to inevitable and unpredictable fluctuations caused by natural factors, above all climate. In the event of natural disasters or wartime devastation, the authorities had to forego collecting the tax in full. They were very careful, however, not to forgive the taxpayers more than what was absolutely necessary so as not to destroy their livelihoods. When the province of Campania asked for its tax burden to be eased after an eruption of Mt. Vesuvius, Theoderic instructed the praetorian prefect Faustus Niger to assess how great the damage caused by the eruption really was; Niger was to entrust the task to a reliable man "who would both bring aid to the injured yet leave no place for fraudulent requests."[71]

In Gothic Italy, the praetorian prefecture was also responsible for collecting a tax that is not previously attested, the *tertia*. It was probably levied on properties where no land had been surrendered for the settlement of Goths. The name presumably derives from the fact that a third of the rent on such lands was to be paid to the prefecture.[72]

The praetorian prefect relied on a very large staff for premodern conditions. We know this official better than any other because Cassiodorus published the correspondence he maintained as the occupant of this office as books 11 and 12 of his *Variae*. In addition, John Lydus, a high-ranking officer in the prefecture of Oriens, published a history of the offices of the Roman state two decades later, in which his own plays a major part. We also exceptionally have specific information on the size, organization, and salaries of the staff of the prefecture because a personnel list is preserved for the prefecture that Emperor Justinian established in North Africa in the year 535. Since Justinian wanted to cut costs and the territory of the prefecture of Italy was significantly larger, we may presume that the most important civil official in Theoderic's kingdom had a significantly larger staff. The personnel list for the prefecture of Africa provided for four hundred positions; the prefecture of Italy thus will have employed considerably more people, perhaps even over a thousand.[73]

The praetorian prefecture was split into two divisions; one was responsible for the administration of justice, the other for finance. Both divisions were in turn subdivided into bureaus (*scrinia*). In addition to the officials who worked in these two divisions, the prefecture also employed support personnel for all kinds of other tasks. Since no education was necessary for these jobs, these staff members were labeled *officiales illiterati*. The bureaus in the finance division were headed by *numerarii*. Accountants and bookkeepers (*chartularii*) who had not yet been placed in a bureau were used as needed and constituted the *schola chartulariorum*. In the same way, the legal division had several different specialized bureaus and a corps of shorthand writers (*exceptores*) who did not belong to any bureau but were freely available.

A strict and steep hierarchy was the rule for the prefecture's staff. At its summit stood the prefect's two senior advisers (*consiliarii*); one was always promoted from the office of the *magister officiorum*; the other was appointed at the discretion of the prefect himself. After the *consiliarii*, who were recruited from outside the prefecture, came the rest of the prefecture's personnel; they were called *praefectiani*. All the employees of the prefecture were listed in a register that was kept by an official called the *cancellarius*, like the officials dispatched by the prefecture to monitor provincial governors. He also was chosen at the prefect's discretion. Some of the prefect's staff had the opportunity to rise up the ranks. The requirement to do so was a higher general education that was based, not on professional expertise, but rather on the acquisition of linguistic and cultural competence. Hence these men were called *officiales litterati*.

In the judicial division, the highest-ranking officer was the *cornicularius*, who originally took his name from a military decoration called a *corniculum* ("little horn"). He served as the prefect's secretary, when the latter acted as judge, and redacted and certified records of proceedings. The second-ranking officer was the *primiscrinius*, who prepared judicial decisions. His title marks him out as the first (*primus*) man in his bureau. The *commentariensis*, who took his name from the official logbook called *commentarii*, was the superintendent of jails. Then there was a handful of further senior officials: the *scriniarius actorum* headed the bureau in which records of proceedings (*acta*) were prepared;

the *cura epistolarum*, whose bureau handled correspondence with other officials; and the *regendarius*, who prepared passes for the state transport service.
Officials in the financial division of the prefecture could earn promotion to
head financial official (*numerarius*) or to personal adviser of the prefect (*cancellarius*). Since the top positions in the legal division were held only for a year and
those in the finance division seldom for several years, promotions occurred at
regular intervals. Rising through the ranks, however, took a very long time for
those who did not enjoy special patronage. The support staff was on principle
barred from joining the ranks of the *officiales litterati*.[74]

The personnel of late antique "ministries" like the praetorian prefecture was
animated by a pronounced *esprit de corps*. On ceremonial occasions, the entire
officium accompanied its chief. Collective names like *praefectiani, magistriani,*
and *privatiani* emphasized affiliation with a specific ministry. These officials
saw themselves as the indefatigable servants of the commonwealth and
demanded appropriate remuneration. The men working in each department
paid close attention to whether the hierarchy was respected. Clerks in the legal
division looked askance at their counterparts in the finance division. Every year,
the hierarchy was put on display at Christmas, when the prefect solemnly
announced promotions in the legal division and retiring officials bade farewell;
a similar ceremony took place in the finance division on September 1, when the
official year began.[75]

The prefect himself earned a yearly salary of 7,200 *solidi*; that was ten times
what his two *consiliarii* received. The yearly salary of the *cancellarius* amounted
to 252 *solidi*. Everyone else was left far behind these top earners. Career officers
were divided into six pay grades: their annual salary was 9 *solidi* at the lowest
grade, 11.5 *solidi* at the second, 14 *solidi* at the third, 16 *solidi* at the fourth, 23
solidi at the fifth, and 46 at the sixth and highest grade. Even the highest-ranking career officers thus earned only a tiny fraction of what the *consiliarii* and the
cancellarius made, to say nothing about the prefect himself. Three-fourths of all
career officers were, moreover, at the lowest pay grade. Still, their yearly earnings could rise to more than five times their entry salary by the end of their
careers, although the climb from the lowest to the highest pay grade was long
and laborious and scaled only by a small minority.[76]

Service in the prefecture or in one of the other central ministries would have
had little appeal for members of the civic middle and upper classes if career
officers did not have other sources of income besides their annual salary, especially since they were required to make payments to their superiors for every
promotion. In reality, however, they collected significant fees for every official
act—from filing claims and summonses to producing records of proceedings

and copies of judgments and even for receipts for tax payments. These fees (*sportulae*) dramatically improved subaltern officials' earnings; they indeed might easily have outstripped their yearly salaries several times over. Fees were not unique to the central ministries but rather were collected at every level of the civil administration. Official schedules fixed what amount one had to pay for a specific service. But the directors of the highest ministries still often had cause to admonish their subordinates for failing to abide by these rules. In contrast to modern officials, late antique public servants did not accumulate a pension but rather were discharged at the end of their careers with twice their annual salary but no other benefits. Anyone who wanted to plan for old age had to set aside enough money by then that he could live off it in retirement.[77]

The prefects took up office without previous experience and normally stayed only a few years. The career of a prefectural official, in contrast, probably lasted at least twenty years and often even longer. He joined the bureau as a young man and left it in his old age. During these long years of service, staff officials acquired the specialized knowledge needed for their profession, gaining a significant edge in competence over the actual "ministers." At the same time, despite all the rivalry between the two divisions, they developed a strong sense of comradery. Hence the *officia* of governors and ministers were often threatened with collective punishment in legislation. Vice versa, the *officium* was urged to report abuses committed by the chief. The fact that we do not know of a single case in which an official staff reported its superior, however, also illustrates that the effort to play staffs off against their chiefs was by and large unsuccessful.[78]

Since Cassiodorus published his official correspondence as praetorian prefect, we know far more about how he administered his office than any other occupant. Of course, Cassiodorus is an exceptional case in more than just that regard. He headed the praetorian prefecture during a period of crisis, when rulers succeeded one another in rapid succession and the war against Justinian broke out. The support of the senate, the Catholic bishops of Italy, and the pope was thus crucial to him. When Cassiodorus published the *Variae*, he strove to depict himself as an exemplary servant of the Roman state who had fulfilled his duty no matter who the ruler was. At the same time, he made sure that his star shone especially brightly against the foil provided by his predecessor, Faustus Niger, who is repeatedly criticized in texts that Cassiodorus wrote in the name of Theoderic. In the edict that Cassiodorus had posted publicly in every province at the beginning of his term, he solemnly pledged to conduct himself justly and incorruptibly, and he urged taxpayers to satisfy their obligations to the state without hesitation. He instructed the governors under his authority about their official duties and reminded them that they should strive for justice and scorn unjust profits:

> Act so that when proven justice is sought after, your year should seem too brief. Let honors be offered to you: for you will lose the need to court them if you win for yourself the provincials' good will. We appoint no guards to watch over your conduct nor place a judge's mind under private assessment: instead, do everything to ensure that what we now deem the utmost disgrace should not prove necessary. You [will] hold a dignity [also: rank] like our own if you act with purity of conscience. Confront the evil, while comforting the innocent no less. If though anyone should dare rise up against your fasces with brazen daring and you cannot carry out what is just, either dispatch the plaintiff [to us] right away with a report of your own or, if he is bereft of the means of coming, let the case be detailed in a report addressed [to us] since you have received passes for the public post [*evectiones*] and we delight in hearing about such things. And so every grounds for excuse has been taken from you since you can either do right by virtue of your position or at the least convey to us what needs to be done.[79]

As prefect, Cassiodorus constantly proclaimed these principles in a variety of forms again and again; he demanded probity, incorruptibility, and diligence. Crimes must be punished inflexibly, the innocent spared, the weak protected from the whims of the strong. In Cassiodorus' mind, the state was absolutely entitled to collect taxes for its objectives, despite the fact that its subjects were not involved in setting them, because the Roman state, in his view, was part of a cosmic order that followed divine will. Paying taxes was a moral duty in his view; resisting the authorities, a crime. The social hierarchy itself was part of this divinely ordained world order. He looked down on people who earned a meager living on the land as free or dependent peasants with a mixture of contempt and compassion; they could not be left to starve, but they also need not be taken seriously. A man of senatorial rank had no dealings with them unless perhaps as their landlord.[80]

Provincial governors had different titles and ranks but in essence the same job. A governor with the title of *praeses* (plural: *praesides*) ranked as *vir clarissimus*; a governor with the title of *consularis* or *corrector* (plural: *consulares, correctores*) held the rank of *vir spectabilis*. The history of the province, not any functional differences, determined a provincial governor's title and rank. The provinces of northern Italy were normally governed by a *consularis*; the border provinces of Alpes Cottiae, Raetia I, and Raetia II were the exception: their governors were called *praesides*. The provinces of southern Italy were also governed primarily by *consulares*, though the governors of Apulia et Calabria and Lucania et Bruttii bore the title of *corrector*. A *consularis* served in the province of Dalmatia, but probably a *corrector* in the province of Savia.[81]

Provincial governors basically had two jobs: they were supposed to adjudicate legal disputes between Romans and to organize and oversee the collection of taxes and duties. Since the dispensation of justice took up a large amount of their time and attention, they were often addressed as *iudices* ("judges"). As at the praetorian prefecture, the governor admitted a certain number of professional lawyers (*advocati*) to his court who offered their services to litigating parties for an honorarium.[82]

Since governors traveled through their provinces, even subjects who did not live where the governor's headquarters (the *praetorium*) was located had the opportunity, once a year, to bring their claims before him without having to travel. The governor stopped at every city as he made his circuit, just as his predecessors in the late imperial period had done. He normally followed a traditional itinerary; that enabled provincial cities to prepare for this important visit. Once the governor reached the territory of a city, he was solemnly escorted in. He greeted local notables, including the bishop, and then administered justice in a public square or building. Anyone who wanted could present a claim on this occasion—that is, provided he was willing and able to pay the requisite fees. Country dwellers had to come to the city; the provincial governor's route passed only from one city to another. Of course, the host cities were glad if the governor's visit, with all his retinue, did not drag on too long: as hosts, they had to pay for their food and lodgings. In the final years of his reign, Theoderic therefore renewed the decree of Emperor Majorian that a city did not have to provide hospitality to a governor for more than three days a year after the landowners of the province of Savia complained that they were inordinately burdened by the governor's stay. Cassiodorus found himself obliged to reiterate this rule during his own tenure as prefect, reminding the governors that they were forbidden to collect a duty called "dust money" (*pulveraticum*) from the cities they visited on their tour.[83]

The governor's other main job was to make sure that taxes and duties were collected punctually and in full. For this, the governor was assisted by an *officium* of approximately 50–100 employees. That, at least, is the rough size of the provincial staffs found in the provinces of the Eastern Empire in Justinian's legislation. The internal organization of the governor's office corresponded to that of the central ministries, headed by a *princeps* and *corniculus*. There were two chief accounting officials called *tabularii*, one for the taxes that went into the *arca* of the praetorian prefect and another who monitored the collection of taxes allocated for the "finance ministry," the *sacrae largitiones*. The *tabularii* were required to present a detailed report about outstanding taxes to their superiors every four months. They in turn were monitored by the *canonicarius* dispatched to the governor's office by the praetorian prefect. There also was an official in every governor's office who supervised the jail, the *commentariensis*. The governor's *officium* was based in the largest and most important city of the province, the *caput provinciae*, where its archives were also located, containing records of proceedings, cadasters, and incoming and outgoing correspondence. The governor probably spent only the part of the year there in which he was not traveling through his province.[84]

Late antique governors' terms in office were brief. Cassiodorus considered it exceptional when a governor remained in office longer than a year. He reasoned that a longer term in office would lead to abuses and would reduce the number of positions to which people could be promoted. The extension of one's term beyond a year thus would be regarded as a special distinction. The idea that such brief terms discouraged innovation would never have occurred to Cassiodorus; in his view what was long established was tried and true. Provincial governors in Theoderic's kingdom predominantly held the rank of *vir spectabilis*. They thus outranked curials, who were *viri clarissimi* at most, but did not necessarily outrank former officials who lived in their province (*honorati*). *Viri spectabiles*, however, were nothing compared to the illustrious members of the Roman senate. The authority of governors thus was limited. The value of their patronage to cities and curials was diminished by their short terms in office. When the council and people of Venafrum resolved to erect a bronze statue, a very rare distinction at the end of the fifth century, in honor of Flavius Pius Maximus, the governor of the province of Samnium and patron of the city, they must have had a very special reason to do so. Maximus presumably had ties to the city of Venafrum before his governorship.[85]

We know very little about the social profile of governors under Theoderic and his successors. That is primarily because the custom of immortalizing someone's career with an honorific inscription of his career had vanished in Italy already by the late fifth century. Hence the governors of Gothic Italy remain shadowy figures for us in contrast to their predecessors under the Principate and High Empire, whose origins and doings are known to us from thousands of inscriptions documenting their careers. In most cases, we cannot say where a governor came from, what office he previously held, or whether he held another one afterward. It seems quite doubtful that there was a regular succession of offices (*cursus honorum*) at all. There is no evidence to suggest that one first had to govern a province before assuming an *illustris* office at court. Members of illustrious families seem to have held governorships now and then but normally only where they had extensive landholdings. In this way, they could protect their economic interests, cultivate regional networks, and fulfill the obligations they had accepted as the patrons of cities or whole provinces. Cassiodorus' father served as governor of Lucania et Bruttii, where a large number of his properties were located, after he ensured that the province took Theoderic's side in the war against Odoacer. Cassiodorus himself wielded great influence in the province, although it is not at all certain whether he also held the office of governor there. Venantius, the *corrector Lucaniae et Bruttiorum*, may also have come from the province he governed, because Procopius mentions a wealthy landowner named Tullianus, son of the Venantius who mobilized the peasants of the province in 546 to fight against the Goths.[86]

It also is clear that the old rule that a governor could not come from the province he was governing—still observed in Justinian's empire—was no longer in force in Theoderic's kingdom. In a text that Cassiodorus wrote as praetorian prefect to a certain Valerianus, who was probably governor of Lucania et Bruttii, he emphasizes that officials had a special responsibility for those they were close to: colleagues deserved moderation, fathers respect, fellow citizens general goodwill, and children special affection:

> The power of family ties is so great that no one feels as if he has been disrespected if he sees that another person's children have been preferred to himself. And so it is not something unjust to be more concerned for one's homeland [*patria*], especially at the present time, when we seem to be rushing to its aid. For we are thought to love those more whom we hasten to rescue.[87]

Governors received a salary like all officials in the civil administration. Again, we do not have precise numbers for Theoderic's kingdom. If we take the figures in Justinian's legislation as a starting point, a governor at the rank of *vir spectabilis* may have earned approximately 700–800 *solidi* annually—that is, about a tenth of what a praetorian prefect made. If we take into consideration that such an office was practically unattainable without paying considerable sums to people who could influence the appointment, this yearly salary was not very high. Since a governor's term in office often lasted only a year, it made financial sense to hold office only if the governor had additional sources of income during his year on top of his salary. The fees that were due for all official acts, especially trials, were one legal means of improving one's income. There also were other means that were punishable by law but quite difficult to suppress. The spectrum ranged from using defective weights and measures to assess payments in kind to manipulating the prices for commuting payments in kind into cash, to embezzlement and extortion. All these abuses of gubernatorial power were exploited in Theoderic's kingdom and so were frequently the subject of texts that Cassiodorus composed in Theoderic's or his successors' names. Corruption was a punishable crime, but it was not at all shocking. It was in fact expected and, to a certain extent, accepted that an influential person's support for others would not go unrewarded. Hence, it was difficult to draw a clear line between lawful patronage and illegal corruption. A corrupt person was some-one who asked for more than was just and reasonable, someone who failed to keep his promises, or someone who supported a bad cause for his personal advantage. In other words: corruption was what other people did.[88]

Be that as it may, the governors in Theoderic's day had a limited scope of action because they were monitored by supervisory officials dispatched to their headquarters from the praetorian prefecture. These men, the *canonicarius* and the *cancellarius*, maintained close communications with the prefect and were supposed to ensure that no irregularities occurred in the collection of taxes and duties. Vice versa, the governors could request assistance from the prefecture if municipal tax collectors were unable to enforce the state's demands. Then *compulsores* took action and threatened offenders with high penalties. If members of the Gothic army or Roman senators offered resistance, however, the gover-nors' clout soon reached its limits: the former were essentially exempt from their jurisdiction, and the latter were vastly superior in rank and influence.[89]

A different situation presented itself in the border provinces, where military governors with additional civil powers held office. In the two provinces of Raetia, the military governor bore the title of *dux*. The only known occupant of this post, one Servatus, had a Latin name but need not have been a Roman; the command of troops was fundamentally reserved for Goths, and not every Goth actually had a Gothic name. In the provinces of Dalmatia, Savia, and Pannonia Sirmiensis, which was added after 504, the military governors bore the title of *comes*, which identified them as members of the royal court. Cassiodorus' model text for appointing such a *comes provinciae* emphasizes that their office defied the strict separation between the civil and military administration, and he urges the incumbents to make moderate use of the death penalty. Since *comites provinciae* also supervised the collection of taxes, the responsibilities of the Roman governors, who also served at least in the provinces of Dalmatia and Savia—which were fused together toward the end of Theoderic's reign—may have been reduced to the administration of justice between Romans. These governors were not subordinate to a praetorian prefect like the others because Theoderic had declined to revive the prefecture of Illyricum to which they had once belonged.[90]

5. GOOD GOVERNMENT? THE REALITY OF THE ADMINISTRATION OF THEODERIC'S KINGDOM

Measured by the standards of a modern welfare state based on the rule of law, the government of Theoderic's kingdom was inefficient, corrupt, and brutal. A significant portion of all taxes and duties disappeared into the pockets of the people responsible for collecting them. Provincial justice was expensive and difficult to obtain. The governor's court heard capital crimes and cases involving high amounts in dispute. Very few indeed could afford to appeal to the court of the praetorian prefect. The ministers of the privy purse (*res privata*) and the king's *patrimonium* presided over cases that directly involved them. Judgments rendered always took the identity of the person affected into consideration; people with rank and influence were openly favored.

If we want to understand this system in its historical context, however, we must take into account that state action in Late Antiquity had far more limited objectives and obeyed different rules than it does today. Late antique Roman emperors had never conceived of providing a kind of welfare state for the entire population. Helping the poor was thought of as the Church's job, according to the philosophy that each community should care for its own widows, orphans, and beggars. It was in accordance with this division of labor that Theoderic chastised a bishop who stood accused of enriching himself at the expense of an orphan, reminding him that he and his fellow bishops taught that one should not ignore the "voices of the poor" (*voces pauperum*).[91]

Collecting taxes and duties in Theoderic's kingdom served primarily to finance the civil and military apparatus, including the royal court, just as it did in the Eastern Roman Empire. The king distributed whatever was left over at his discretion to persons to whom he wanted to show favor. He disbursed the income from Hispania to the Visigoths and Ostrogoths as a kind of annual pension. Surpluses were not invested but stored; a few years after Theoderic's death, the royal treasury in Ravenna contained at least 40,000 pounds of gold, which was still only an eighth of what Emperor Anastasius allegedly left his successor, Justin, in 518. The royal administration gave support to taxpayers in the event of natural disasters if a decrease of economic capacity could be demonstrated. In such exceptional situations, taxes and duties were temporarily reduced or remitted entirely.[92]

Be that as it may, Theoderic still claimed to protect his subjects from external threats and to keep the peace and the rule of law domestically. Italy really was largely, albeit not completely, safe from external threats under Theoderic. It is an open question, however, whether the provincial or central administration was capable of imposing the king's will and maintaining law and order. Ennodius' panegyric to Theoderic and the *Anonymus Valesianus* paint a picture of a wise ruler who takes care that his subjects in the city and countryside can enjoy their prosperity in complete security. Ennodius praises the king by declaring, "The resources of the commonwealth [*res publica*] have increased with the advancement of private citizens. There is never any illicit office-seeking at your court while there is an outpouring of wealth everywhere. No one departs empty-handed and no one groans over the evils of proscription." The *Anonymus Valesianus* claims that the city gates never needed to be closed under Theoderic; gold and silver were as safe in the countryside as in a city. The price of wheat was allegedly only a third of the amount that Emperor Valentinian III had set for sales to soldiers fifty years before: 60 instead of 40 bushels (*modii*) per *solidus*. All these are obviously panegyrical topoi that presume an ideal as the reality. The *Variae* contain a model text for gatekeepers, so they were needed after all: their job was to keep the city gates closed overnight. Cassiodorus also reveals that the royal administration sold wheat at a rate of 25 bushels per *solidus*, while a *solidus* purchased only 10 bushels on the open market. It is thus astonishing that such panegyrical verdicts can still be found in modern scholarship.[93]

If we read Cassiodorus' *Variae* or the *Edict of Theoderic* against the grain, so to speak, we may come away with the opposite impression—that the civil administration of Theoderic's kingdom was unable to enforce the legal norms then in force, that indeed the administration itself was largely out of control, as these texts constantly address violence and coercion, tax evasion, abuse of office, and other disciplinary offenses. But this reading would also be one-sided and superficial. The royal administration intervened only when complaints were brought to its attention; if things functioned as usual, there was no reason to intercede. Local authorities were primarily responsible for solving local problems; that meant civic notables, including the bishop. Contemporaries did not at all take the discourse of the royal administration as pure ideology; if Cassiodorus could have anticipated that his readers would consider Theoderic's dual state inefficient, corrupt, and brutal, he would not have published a collection of the texts he composed in the name of the Gothic kings at all. Cassiodorus was undeniably a Roman aristocrat steeped in the prejudices of his class—but he was no cynic, publicly advocating what he secretly despised.[94]

Cassiodorus' collection also reveals, however, that the ideal of *civilitas* touted by Theoderic, the peaceful coexistence of Gothic warriors and Roman civilians under Roman law, was definitely under threat. Since his Gothic subjects enjoyed a privileged judicial status, conflict was inevitable. The combination of military and judicial power in the hands of Gothic *comites* invited inroads on the competences of the Roman governors. The king's correspondence indeed records serious abuses rampant in the administration of Hispania, Dalmatia, and Sicily at the end of Theoderic's reign. After the conquest of Provence, the royal chancellery declared that its inhabitants had to relearn how to resolve disputes in court; according to its depiction, Pannonia Sirmiensis was governed by the law of the jungle. These provinces, obviously, lay outside the Italian peninsula, but the structural problems were similar; the provincial governors there also had less power than in earlier centuries on account of their short terms in office and relatively low rank. Theoderic's nephew Theodahad was able to seize control of large parts of Tuscany, not only harming local landholders, but also damaging the reputation of the royal family. That did not, however, prevent Theoderic from entrusting his nephew with the duties of a judge. The central administration often had to send out agents to bring cases to trial and to enforce verdicts. The weakness of the ordinary territorial administration is also reflected in the great importance of the king's personal protection for his subjects. It is not a good sign when the *patricius* Agnellus asks the king to protect his properties from attacks before leaving for North Africa as an ambassador and then the king gives this job to the *patricius* Festus, who had no office at the time. If a man from the highest echelons was afraid for his property as soon as he could no longer take care of it personally, what must ordinary curials or simple peasants have feared?[95]

8

RELUCTANT EXPANSION?
THEODERIC'S FOREIGN POLICY

1. A "FAMILY OF KINGS"? DIPLOMACY AND CRISIS
MANAGEMENT IN 506–507

When the Frankish king Clovis conquered the kingdom of Syagrius in northwestern France in 486–487, he became the immediate neighbor of the Visigothic king Alaric II. Relations between them did not stay peaceful for long. Armed conflict broke out repeatedly in the 490s; then in the latter half of 506, Clovis and Alaric became involved in a dispute yet again. An effort to settle their differences through negotiation failed. Clovis, who had just won a major victory over the Alamanni, was unwilling to make any concessions. Now the two sides armed for war.[1]

The court in Ravenna watched these developments with concern. To prevent the impending war, Theoderic sent envoys first to see Alaric, then to the Burgundian king Gundobad and a series of other kings, and finally to Clovis. One of the envoys was Senarius, a Roman who had undertaken several diplomatic missions for Theoderic. Cassiodorus preserves the letters that were given to the envoys to deliver. Theoderic urged the Visigothic king to think sensibly: Alaric should not needlessly risk a military conflict, especially since his people, who had not waged war in a long time, were no longer ready for battle. Victory over Attila at the Catalaunian Plains (451) was a long time ago. Theoderic, moreover, did not want to see his kinsmen wage war against one another. Alaric should not let third parties, "who malevolently delight in others' strife," goad him on but rather should maintain the truce and let the dispute be settled by a court of arbitration consisting of Theoderic's friends. His envoys would make

Map 10. Western Europe in the Year 506.

the same proposal to Clovis; when Clovis sees that he has Theoderic and his sworn allies against him, he will be ready to submit to arbitration.[2]

After Alaric, the envoys traveled on to Gundobad. They asked the Burgundian king to join forces with Theoderic and the peoples allied with him "so that the dispute contested between you can be resolved in a reasonable way by friendly mediators." The letter to Gundobad justifies that argument as follows:

> It is a great evil to see clashing wills between dear and royal personages and to watch idly as if they were not, so that something regrettable might come of one of them. It will proceed not without enmity toward Us, if We suffer our kin [*affines*] to fight to their destruction. All of you have pledges of great favor from me; none of you is separated from another; if you do wrong to one another, you sin gravely to my grief. It falls to Us to guide royal youths [*iuvenes*] by citing reason because if they truly realize that what they inadvisably want displeases Us, they will not be able to retain the audacity of their will. Let them respect their elders, though they be burning with the flower of youth. Let them know that We are opposed to their dissension and wish to ensure that neither side does anything excessive. For it behooves Us to use harsh language to prevent our kin from resorting to extremes.[3]

From Gundobad, Theoderic's envoys proceeded to unknown kings of the Heruli, Warni, and Thuringians, whose names Cassiodorus suppressed when he published the *Variae*. All three kings received the same letter, with the exception of the address. The envoys' itinerary is also unknown. We know of a Rudolf as king of the Heruli at this time; his kingdom lay on the middle Danube. These Heruli, however, lived far away from the Franks and Visigoths. Some scholars place Theoderic's addressees on the lower Rhine, although no Herulian king is known there. Warni living under a king are attested on the eastern bank of the lower Rhine in the sixth century. The third stop was apparently the court of a Thuringian king located somewhere between the middle Elbe and the Saale. Theoderic impressed on these three kings that Clovis would threaten them, too, as soon as he had defeated Alaric; someone willing to take on so large a kingdom would not hesitate to attack a smaller one. Hence they should send envoys to Clovis together with Theoderic and Gundobad to deter him from attacking Alaric.[4]

At last, the envoys sought out Clovis himself, whose primary residence was at Soissons at the time. Cassiodorus also preserves this letter. Theoderic explicitly warns Clovis not to start a war against Alaric; "the malevolence of others" (*malignitas aliena*) must not be permitted to sow discord between them. Theoderic then invokes the "divine laws of kinship": Alaric and Clovis were brothers and Theoderic their father. He continues:

I will say what I think openly; I will say it with affection: it is an impatient mind that takes up arms in response to the first embassy. Let what your kinsmen [*parentes*] request be sought from chosen judges. For those whom you wish to make mediators between such great men will be eager to give. What would you yourself think of Us if you should learn that We had forsaken your objectives? May this conflict, in which one of you will suffer in defeat, never come! Cast away the sword, you whose desire to fight brings me into disrepute. I threaten you by a father's and lover's right; he who believes that such advice should be scorned—which we think unlikely—will have both Ourselves and Our friends against him.[5]

These letters present Theoderic as the central figure in a web of political relationships that extended to every major king in western continental Europe: Clovis, Alaric, and Gundobad, as well as the kings of the Heruli, Warni, and Thuringians. These rulers were linked to Theoderic in various ways: the kings of the Heruli, Warni, and Thuringians, as well as the king of the Burgundians, had sworn treaties with Theoderic. In the case of Alaric and Clovis, Theoderic cited rights and duties stemming from kinship: Alaric was Theoderic's son-in-law because he had married Thiudigotho, one of Theoderic's daughters. Clovis was Theoderic's brother-in-law because Theoderic had married his sister Audefleda. These marriage alliances had thus translated into family ties.

Theoderic interpreted these family ties in terms of a political hierarchy: he claimed for himself the part of the loving father who could and should chastise his sons to protect them from making mistakes. He further posed as a mentor who outstripped the hotheaded young kings in age and experience. Theoderic wanted to appear as the head of a family of kings. Obviously, this is a self-characterization, particularly since Theoderic was in fact not much older than Alaric or Clovis. But there is something else that is striking: the royal chancellery is arguing with personal categories; it describes political relations as familial relationships. This way of thinking is unique to Theoderic's dealings with Germanic kings. In his diplomatic relations with Constantinople, he invoked abstract political concepts like the *res publica* or *imperium*, the meaning of which was determined by Roman tradition. These concepts had ceased to apply to the new, multistate world that had come into being in the western Mediterranean of the fifth century. Now there were many rival kings who rejected the Roman political framework, even if they sometimes held Roman titles.

Theoderic's attempt to prevent a military conflict by mediation is equally striking. Theoderic mobilized his allies to pressure the two principal adversaries to forego armed conflict and instead allow a third party to resolve their dispute. He neither wanted to stand idly by while Clovis and Alaric fought it out, nor did he want to take sides: his goal was to maintain the political status quo. This policy was certainly not altruistic. The status quo that Theoderic hoped to maintain was a political order in which he himself held the leading position among Germanic kings. In advocating for the status quo, he was also protecting his own hegemony. But his policy was not geared toward expansion at this time. Theoderic accepted the coexistence of several kingdoms in western Europe, independent of the Byzantine emperor, as a given and immutable fact; to that extent he broke radically with past Roman emperors' pretentions to universal rule (*imperium sine fine*). Theoderic used marriages and treaties to protect this order against the ambitions of individual rulers. At the same time, he claimed for himself a dominant position over the other kings, a position that he derived not from his rule over Italy or from any Roman office but rather from factors inseparably linked to his own person.

The attempt to avert impending war between Clovis and Alaric, documented in Cassiodorus' *Variae* (and only there), presents Theoderic as both author and guarantor of the peace among the Germanic kings of western Europe that was threatened by Clovis' expansionism. That is precisely why Cassiodorus included these letters in his collection. At a time when the Byzantine Empire was no longer willing to tolerate the rule of Gothic kings in Italy, Cassiodorus wanted to depict Theoderic as a king who, while indeed very powerful, was not interested in expansion but on the contrary was trying to keep the peace among the kings. Many modern treatments of Theoderic's foreign policy convey the same impression. Contemporary readers of the *Variae*, however, knew that Theoderic's mediation attempt had failed: Clovis refused to abandon his plans. The Frankish king led his army to Bordeaux and inflicted a devastating defeat on Alaric near Poitiers in the late summer of 507. The site of the battle was a place called the *campus Vogladensis*, which probably lay in the vicinity of Vouillé (fifteen kilometers north of Poitiers). The Visigothic king himself fell in battle. Theoderic's system of political alliances based on family ties and sworn treaties had proven incapable of neutralizing the potential for conflict between rival kings. His warnings fell on deaf ears. How can we explain this failure? Before we can answer this question, we have to look back in time to before the crisis because only then can we understand how this system of alliances had come about in the first place.[6]

2. *PRIMUS INTER PARES*: THEODERIC'S FOREIGN POLICY PRIOR TO THE CRISIS OF 506–507

When Theoderic set out for Italy in 488, he was penetrating into a territory in which the Eastern Roman emperor could exert influence only by diplomatic means. The Western Roman emperor had been succeeded by multiple kings.

Odoacer had reigned in Italy since 476. His most powerful neighbors in the west were the Visigothic king Alaric II, whose kingdom in Gaul extended to the Loire and the Cottian Alps, and the Burgundian king Gundobad, who ruled a kingdom stretching from the Loire to western Switzerland. The settlement territory of the Alamanni began along the shores of Lake Constance and extended to the Main and a little beyond it to the north. The Frankish king Clovis had attracted attention a few years earlier by defeating Syagrius, the son of a Roman *magister militum* who had ruled the territory between the Loire and the Somme from his residence at Soissons. Clovis' territory thereafter extended over Belgium and northern France (with the exception of Brittany). But his kingdom at the time was still far away from Italy.[7]

The kingdom of the Vandals in western North Africa was the only maritime power outside the Eastern Roman Empire. Gaiseric's fleet was also dreaded in Odoacer's kingdom: it had repeatedly devastated the coasts of Italy and the outlying islands. Shortly before his death (476), Gaiseric ceded Sicily to Odoacer in exchange for tribute, but he retained possession of Lilybaeum (modern Marsala) as a naval base. When war broke out between Theoderic and Odoacer, Gaiseric's successor, Gunthamund (484–496), sensed an opportunity to reclaim Sicily as his own. He appears to have achieved some initial success but soon found himself obliged to sue Theoderic for peace. A treaty was struck in 491 under which Gunthamund renounced his right to tribute and probably all claims to sovereignty over Sicily. It was perhaps then that he surrendered Lilybaeum, which appears in Gothic hands in the year 500. This treaty was an important victory for Theoderic because it guaranteed him control of an island that was critical to the grain supply of Rome and relieved him of the need to protect southern Italy from raids. Why Gunthamund was so obliging, despite the fact that Theoderic's victory over Odoacer was by no means certain, remains a mystery.[8]

Theoderic apparently established ties with Alaric soon after the beginning of the war against Odoacer. At the Battle of the Adda River, on August 11, 490, a Visigothic army fought on Theoderic's side. Unfortunately, we know practically nothing more beyond that fact. How had this coalition come about? Theoderic's cousin Vidimir and his people had joined the Visigoths in 475, but that was a long time ago. Alaric's marriage to Thiudigotho, one of Theoderic's daughters, did not take place until years after the Battle of the Adda River, probably in 494, when Theoderic was already the undisputed master of Italy. Prior to that, Theoderic could not have rivaled the power and honor of the ruler of Hispania and southern Gaul. Only his victory over Odoacer made him a peer in the eyes of the Visigothic king.[9]

We also can only guess at the circumstances in which Theoderic courted and married Audefleda, Clovis' sister. They presumably made first contact in the initial phase of the war against Odoacer: Clovis had attacked Gundobad from behind while he was away raiding and plundering northern Italy; Gundobad then hastened home and made peace with Clovis at the River Cure between Autun and Auxerre. Common enemies make for common interests; Clovis and Theoderic may also have recognized that fact. Clovis allegedly was delighted when envoys from Theoderic appeared at his court soon after the victory over Odoacer to ask for Audefleda's hand. To him, this marriage alliance with the new master of Italy meant a significant boost in prestige. What Theoderic hoped to gain from the connection is less obvious: Clovis had not yet brought all the Franks under his control, he was only one of several Frankish kings, he was still a heathen, and he ruled a part of Gaul that lay far away from Theoderic's kingdom. The marriage did not do anything directly to help secure Italy. Perhaps Theoderic hoped to strengthen his position with the Burgundians. At roughly the same time, Clovis married Clotilde (Chrodechilde), the niece of the Burgundian king Gundobad. Clotilde, in contrast to her uncle, was Catholic, and she ensured that the sons she bore Clovis were baptized in this faith.[10]

Gundobad was being courted on several sides at this time because Theoderic also established a marital relationship with the Burgundian royal family in 494. This alliance was very important to him, not only by reason of geographic proximity. After the conclusion of the war against Odoacer, probably over 10,000 refugees or prisoners from northern Italy were in the kingdom of the Burgundians. Theoderic was expected to bring them home. As we saw, two Catholic bishops traveled to Gundobad on this mission, and the king permitted the refugees to return home and the prisoners to be ransomed. That was possible because Gundobad and Theoderic had forged an alliance that was sealed by the betrothal of Ostrogotho, one of Theoderic's daughters, to Sigismund, Gundobad's adult son. The wedding was celebrated soon afterward, probably in 494. In his *Vita* of bishop Epiphanius, Ennodius indicates that Theoderic made this alliance palatable to the Burgundian king by promising to recognize a son from this marriage as his heir in the event that he had none of his own. If that was the case, one wonders why this promise is never mentioned subsequently. Was it formulated so vaguely? In his *Panegyricus* of 507 to Theoderic, Ennodius interprets the alliance forged in 494 as Gundobad's subjugation to Theoderic's will. This interpretation reflects the changed perspective of the Gothic court, which had come to see itself as superior to its allies. When Gundobad assented to the alliance, however, he had good reason to see himself as equal in rank.[11]

Lastly, Theoderic's sister Amalafrida married the Vandalic king Thrasamund in the year 500. This marriage looked like the crowning achievement of a policy of marriage alliances that united all the significant rulers of the western Mediterranean into a "family of kings." After the Frank Clovis, the Visigoth Alaric, and the Burgundian Gundobad, now the Vandal Thrasamund became Theoderic's kinsman. The political situation by then, however, had dramatically changed, especially after Theoderic was officially recognized by the Eastern Roman Empire in 498. When Thrasamund asked Theoderic for his sister's hand in marriage, he was clearly the Goth's inferior, even if Amalafrida brought her groom the naval base of Lilybaeum as her dowry. On her arrival in Carthage, the Amal princess was accompanied by no fewer than 1,000 bodyguards and 5,000 armed squires. That was a real private army; Thrasamund himself had hardly twice that number of warriors at his command. Theoderic provided his sister with such formidable resources because he intended for her to play an independent part at the Vandalic court. Ennodius unabashedly voiced this expectation when he said in his *Panegyricus* that the Vandals "have deserved to be kin because they do not refuse to obey."[12]

Ennodius' *Panegyricus* makes it seem as if Theoderic's policy of marriage alliances had stifled the rivalry of the Germanic kings. But this picture is deceptive. Alaric and Clovis clashed several times after the Frankish king expanded his territory into Brittany between 486 and 494. After defeat at Clovis' hands, Syagrius took refuge with Alaric and was extradited only after negotiations. Frankish advances reached Saintes by 496 and Bordeaux by 498. Two years later, Clovis made common cause with the Burgundian king Godegisel, who had hitherto ruled jointly with his brother Gundobad but now wanted sole rule for himself. The three armies met at Dijon. With Clovis' help, Godegisel seized control of almost the entire Burgundian kingdom, while Gundobad retreated to Avignon. After Clovis led his army home, Gundobad mustered his forces again and besieged Godegisel in Vienne. After taking the city by treachery, he killed his brother, together with his wife and children. He sent the Frankish warriors who had been in Godegisel's service to Alaric, who had supported him in his hour of need; he thus left Alaric the profit that could be made from ransoming or selling them into slavery. Gundobad may also have ceded the city of Avignon to Alaric. The conflict between Alaric and Clovis formally ended two years later, when the two kings made peace on an island in the Loire near Amboise.[13]

Clovis not only plagued the territory of the Visigothic and Burgundian kings at this time. The Frankish king's victories also unleashed a martial dynamic that he neither could nor would arrest. Since every warrior was entitled to a share in the booty, warfare was profitable for everyone, especially — but not exclusively — when the entire army was victorious. Proving oneself in combat, moreover, raised a man's profile as a warrior, his "honor," and opened the door to an exalted place in the king's retinue. This prospect was so enticing because the social hierarchies of warrior societies were comparatively flat and permeable. Clovis' warriors, who were mustered on the "March field" (a Frankish *campus Martius*, as it were) every spring, expected the king to continue to give them opportunities to win booty and glory. Reasons for campaigns were quickly found because there was great willingness to resolve conflicts with violence on all sides. Several Frankish kings often banded together to wage war.[14]

The settlement area of the Franks under Clovis' control now abutted that of the Alamanni to the southeast, whose land lay between the upper Rhine and the Main. Several "petty" kings of Alamannic bands—as many as seven at a time—had ruled this territory in the fourth century. These kings had occasionally banded together on joint campaigns, but they otherwise went their separate ways. Some scholars assume that this was still the case in the late fifth century. Others, however, believe that a "large" Alamannic kingdom had coalesced in the intervening period, of which no explicit evidence has survived, and that the Alamanni that confronted Clovis were under the rule of a single king. In this view, something like an Alamannic kingdom was a major power between the territories of Clovis, Gundobad, and Theoderic. The *rex Alamannorum* Gibuld, whom Severinus persuaded to release his prisoners near Passau in 470, would have been the first and only known "great" king of the Alamanni.[15]

In point of fact, Gregory of Tours reports in his history that Clovis waged war *contra Alamannos* in the fifteenth year of his reign—that is, 496–497. His army supposedly fell into dire straits in a battle. The Frankish king thereupon called on the god whom his wife Clotilde worshipped and swore to be baptized in His name if He would come to the king's aid against the enemy's onslaught. The Alamanni then miraculously turned to flee and finally surrendered when they saw that "their" king had been killed.[16]

The Frankish bishop Gregory tells this story almost a century after the events (taking it, obviously, from earlier sources) because he wanted to explain how and why Clovis was the first Frankish king to convert to Christianity and why he adopted it in the form that the narrator considered to be Catholic and hence orthodox. Gregory was uninterested in the actual circumstances of Clovis' victory over the Alamanni. He thus mentions neither the site of the battle nor the name of the fallen king. The battlefield is often placed near Zülpich (west of Cologne and Euskirchen) because Gregory mentions in passing elsewhere that another Frankish king had been wounded in a battle against the Alamanni there. It is by no means certain, however, that both passages concern the same battle. We thus cannot rule out the possibility that the Alamannic king whom Clovis defeated after vowing to receive baptism was only one of several. Ten years later, we again hear of a battle in which the Alamanni lose "their king"; the kingdom of the Alamanni thereafter vanishes. After this second victory over the Alamanni, Clovis extended his domain to the southern edge of the Alps, where he came into direct contact with Theoderic's kingdom for the first time.[17]

The Frankish victory over the Alamanni in 496–497 not only affected the balance of power among the kings. As we saw in Gregory's account, the battle was also the reason behind Clovis' vow to receive baptism, a vow that he kept. Clovis was baptized in Reims by the bishop Remigius. Gregory does not name the year of his baptism, which scholars dispute. Some consider Gregory's chronology to be a pseudo-historical construction and separate Clovis' baptism from the victory over the Alamanni; they then date his baptism to the year 508. If, however, we accept Gregory's chronology — and there are good reasons for doing so — and there is a causal relationship between the victory and baptism, then it must have taken place in 498 or 499 since the ritual presumes lengthy preparations. Hence not only did Clovis' political and military actions from an early date undermine the peaceful hegemonic order that his brother-in-law sought to realize, but he also moved away from Theoderic with the choice of his confession. Clovis adopted Christianity in a form that set him apart from Theoderic, as well as from Gundobad, Alaric, and Thrasamund, while aligning himself with Theoderic's Roman subjects and, at least potentially, with the distant Byzantine emperor. In contrast to the kings of the Visigoths, Ostrogoths, Burgundians, and Vandals, Clovis now belonged to the same religious community as the Roman population of his kingdom. Since his Franks soon also adopted Christianity in the form that was obligatory for the Roman population, he commanded a confederation of subjects that was not divided along religious lines.[18]

Scholars sometimes doubt the received account — namely, that Clovis resolved to be baptized in the Catholic Church because he had sought (and evidently received) divine aid in battle, but it is in fact quite credible. For one, the decision by no means came out of the blue: Clotilde and others had pushed for Clovis' conversion for a long time. Moreover, the idea that the power and truth of a god manifested themselves in whether he could deliver aid in one's hour of need was self-evident to contemporaries. Germanic kings and Roman emperors prayed to God to help them defeat their enemies. This notion does not, however, explain why Clovis decided in favor of Catholic and against Homoean Christianity. He must have seen potential advantages in this decision that extended beyond the day of the battle. Some of them are obvious: first and foremost, he would achieve religious harmony within his own family. He then may have hoped to tie Gallo-Roman elites to his person in this way. It is also possible that he interpreted baptism as a kind of alliance with the Catholic bishops that would facilitate more effective cooperation and control. If he belonged to the same church, it would be much easier to influence the appointment of clerics, to convene synods, and to set their agenda. Then the king would be the defender and master of the Catholic bishops of his kingdom without any qualification or reservation. Clovis' baptism, moreover, raised hopes outside his kingdom—namely, in places where Catholic bishops owed their allegiance to a Homoean king. His conversion to Catholicism opened up new perspectives, even though the political loyalties of Gallo-Roman elites under Burgundian and Visigothic kings were by no means solely dependent on matters of faith.[19]

Bishop Avitus of Vienne, which belonged to the kingdom of the Burgundians at the time, congratulated Clovis on his baptism in an artfully stylized letter that highlighted the implications of his decision:

> The adherents of various schisms have endeavored with their opinions, being of varying purport, sundry in number, and bereft of truth, to shroud the acumen of Your Brilliance in a shadow of Christian pretense. But while we entrust our fate to the Eternal, while we leave what each and every one rightly thinks to the coming judgment, a dazzling ray of truth has shown through even now in the present. Divine providence has indeed found a judge for our times: in choosing for yourself, you judge for all. Your faith is our victory.

Avitus emphasizes that Clovis had broken with his ancestors by receiving baptism but also had laid down a binding rule for his descendants. His decision was of immense importance not only for his subjects, but also for all orthodox Christians, insofar as they lived outside the territory of the Eastern Roman emperor; now the true faith also had a pillar in the Occident. With respect to the Eastern Roman Empire, the bishop states, "Let Greece rejoice that it has a prince who obeys our law, but not as if Greece alone deserves to be distinguished by so great a gift, since its radiance may also be found in the rest of the world. For a light of new radiance flashes forth from a long-standing king in western parts." Avitus describes the act of baptism as a ritual that guarantees that the king will be victorious: "Whatsoever fortune has granted thus far, sanctity will now increase it." He then reminds Clovis that it was only thanks to the bishops that he could participate in this grace. Lastly, he admonishes Clovis that as a Christian king, it is his duty to propagate the true faith among the heathen: "Since God will make your people [*gens*] entirely His own through you, extend seeds from the good store of your heart to further peoples, who, still living in natural ignorance, have not yet been corrupted by the fruits of twisted dogmas."[20] This appeal is explicitly limited to the heathen. The worldly bishop is wary of asking Clovis to proselytize to Homoean Christians; he did not want to give the impression that he was inviting the Frankish king to interfere in the affairs of his Burgundian or Gothic counterparts. Avitus' letter nonetheless shows that Clovis' baptism had made him the focus of expectations that Homoean Christian kings could not fulfill for their Catholic subjects.

The system of alliances that was intended to secure Theoderic's kingdom in Italy from outside threats was thus by no means completely intact when the king successfully integrated the Vandals in to the "family of kings" in the year 500. Clovis and his Franks had no interest in preserving the status quo; their thirst for feats of arms could not be quenched by marriages and treaties. Gundobad had hardly been able to fight off his brother Godegisel and his Frankish allies, and only then with Visigothic support. These tensions only intensified in the following years.

As we have seen, Theoderic clearly recognized that the order he had hoped to establish among the kings was under threat and took measures to stabilize it. He himself, however, was not least to blame that such measures were necessary. The king was not content to rule forever over the territory where Odoacer had once reigned. In 504, he sent an army under his "generals" Pitzia and Herduic to the vicinity of Sirmium. The Gepids, with whom Theoderic had clashed on his way to Italy, still lived there, but their king, Thraustila, had been succeeded by his son, Thrasaric. Theoderic's army routed Thrasaric and captured his mother. Thrasaric took refuge in Constantinople, where the emperor made him an honorary *comes domesticorum*; this title appears before that of "King of the Gepids" on his recently discovered tombstone. The territory Thrasaric had ruled was incorporated into Theoderic's kingdom as the province of Pannonia Sirmiensis; this province was placed under an official with the title of *comes* who had both military and civil powers and was probably a Goth, even though his name, Colosseus, derives from the Greek word *kolossos*.[21]

At Theoderic's court, the annexation of Sirmium, a former imperial residence, was celebrated as the reconquest of a territory that was legally part of *Italia* but had been lost on account of the negligence of the last Western Roman emperors. Hence Cassiodorus remarks in his *Chronicle* for the year 504 that "Italy reconquered Sirmium after defeating the Bulgars, thanks to the valor of our lord and king Theoderic." Ennodius uses similar language in his *Panegyricus*. *Italia* here stands for the western half of the Roman Empire; "Greece" (*Graecia*) serves as its counterpart. *Italia* and *Graecia* are the names of the two parts of the one Roman Empire that Theoderic's chancellery also called *utraeque res publicae*. Like this formula, talk of the recapture of Sirmium for Italy was tailored to

Map 11. Theoderic's Conquests, 489–524.

a Roman audience. In a letter sent by Cassiodorus to the military commander responsible for the new province, however, another viewpoint suddenly flashes before our eyes: there he describes the territory of Sirmium as the "erstwhile home of the Goths." This statement refers to the time before 473, when Theoderic's father and uncle had ruled in Pannonia. From a Gothic perspective, this past possession apparently legitimated present claims.[22]

From the perspective of Constantinople, Theoderic's war of conquest against Thrasaric's Gepids overstepped the authority they had conceded to him; that would have been provocation enough. But the annexation of a former imperial residence was not all. In the course of operations, Theoderic's generals also clashed with the troops of the imperial general Sabinianus, who was leading Bulgarian *foederati* against a certain Mundo. Mundo was the nephew of the Gepid king Thraustila, who had opposed Theoderic in 488. After Thraustila's death, however, he had made way for Thrasaric and so had gathered men around him who lived from raiding and plundering. With their help, he built himself a small domain centered around a tower called Herta at the mouth of the Morava. From a Roman perspective, Mundo was little more than a successful bandit chief. When one of the emperor's armies marched against him, Mundo turned to Theoderic's generals in the vicinity for help, and they did not hesitate to lend him their support against Sabinianus. The fact that Mundo had been in contact with Theoderic previously may have played a part. A battle took place at Horreum Margi in the Morava valley: with 2,000 infantry and 500 cavalry, Theoderic's general Pitzia routed the emperor's Bulgarian *foederati*. It was an undisputed victory, even though no one counted the bodies, which were left unburied on the battlefield. Mundo subsequently pledged allegiance to Theoderic and remained loyal to him as long as the king lived.[23]

Theoderic may have had many reasons to mobilize an army against Thrasaric. Ennodius accuses Thrasaric of unspecified "daily provocations" and indicates that he cultivated a confidential relationship with Gunderith, the king of "other Gepids" whose territory lay on the Tisza. Theoderic apparently wanted to prevent these two Gepid groups from building a joint military power that could pose a threat to him. The area around Sirmium also was strategically important to Theoderic because whoever controlled this region controlled access to Italy. Pitzia and Herduic were allegedly under orders not to attack Thrasaric until he refused to submit. Theoderic obviously presumed that Thrasaric would reject this ultimatum because his generals spared Thrasaric's territory from plundering; they evidently planned to seize Sirmium for Theoderic all along. The conclusion that Theoderic had intended to capture Sirmium from the start, despite the fact that he was thereby advancing into a region claimed by the Eastern Roman emperor, is practically inescapable. Theoderic himself may have viewed the assault as a defensive maneuver to protect Italy from attack—as preventive expansion. Of course, acting in the interest of one's own security at the expense of others is normally perceived by the others as aggression. Anyone who decides in favor of such actions is accordingly taking a significant risk.

Direct military confrontation with imperial troops was, of course, far riskier, whether they were *foederati* or not. It is certainly conceivable that the decision to support Mundo against Sabinianus was made without consulting Theoderic. It was a long way to Ravenna, and time was of the essence when Mundo's request for help arrived. But even if Pitzia acted on his own initiative, Theoderic retroactively condoned his actions: Pitzia's victory, Ennodius emphasizes, was Theoderic's victory. The king had no intention of shifting blame to others; on the contrary, he claimed all the glory for himself. The campaign against the Gepids was an experiment in this respect too. Never before had Theoderic's Goths won a significant victory under the command of another general. The experiment was a success: Pitzia was victorious for his king as if he were serving a Roman emperor. Theoderic could count on his men.

When Theoderic gave the order to march against Thrasaric, he may have speculated that the Byzantine emperor's hands would be tied by his fight against the Persians. Anastasius could not sustain a second front in the west as long as he was under pressure in the east. Indeed, the emperor did not initially launch a retaliatory strike in response to Theoderic's attacks. But he mobilized diplomatic resources to check Theoderic's power. What move made more sense than to forge an alliance with Clovis? The Frankish king was willing and able to oppose Theoderic's hegemonic ambitions, and his domain, moreover, lay so far away from the empire that the emperor need not fear any serious conflict of interest.[24]

Clovis' warriors duly undertook a campaign in the early summer of 506 that brought them dangerously close to the borders of Italy. Cassiodorus congratulated the Frankish king in Theoderic's name on a major victory over the Alamanni, but he also urged him to show moderation toward the vanquished. In this letter, Theoderic distinguishes between the leaders of the Alamanni, who had deserved their punishment as the "authors of perfidy," and those who had fled to Theoderic's territory. The latter deserved mercy:

> It is a memorable triumph to have terrified the boldest Alamannus so utterly that you force him to beg for his life. Let it suffice that that king has fallen together with his people's pride! Let it suffice to have subjugated an innumerable people, some by the sword, and some by enslavement! For if you battle with the survivors, no one will believe you have conquered all of them.[25]

Like Gregory, Cassiodorus also neglects to mention the name of the vanquished king and the site of the battle. The Alamanni vanquished ten years before had apparently risen up against Frankish rule; hence Cassiodorus speaks of the "perfidy" of the leaders, which warranted punishment. The king who led this uprising must have commanded a large band of warriors because Ennodius states in his *Panegyricus* that Theoderic had settled "the general population of Alamannia within Italy's borders without any loss to Roman property." The Alamanni thereby became the guardians of the kingdom that they had previously devastated with their plundering raids. This statement makes sense only if Theoderic had granted refuge to a band of several thousand Alamanni by settling them in the northern foothills of the Alps, in the provinces of Raetia I and Raetia II. There, they were under the command of a military governor with the title of *dux Raetiarum*. We cannot say anything more concrete about the location of their settlements. Between 523 and 526, some of these Alamanni marched through Noricum with Theoderic's blessing. Since they were on their way east, they probably settled in a border region of the kingdom, in Pannonia. King Vitigis formally surrendered sovereignty over the Alamanni to the Franks in 536 or 537.[26]

Citing humanitarian reasons for admitting Alamannic refugees was the last thing Theoderic's chancellery wanted to do; it was asking for mercy for the vanquished. There also was no reason to disclose Theoderic's political calculation: by granting the Alamanni refuge in the northern foothills of the Alps, the king could create a buffer zone between Italy and Clovis' territory. Cassiodorus instead casts moderation in victory as a maxim of foreign policy that governed all of Theoderic's actions: "Heed one who has extensive experience in such cases: those wars turned out well for me, because they concluded with a moderate ending. He who knows to treat all things with moderation is constantly victorious because pleasant prosperity prefers to flatter those who are not rigid with excessive severity."[27] At first glance, it might seem that Theoderic's warnings had the desired effect: Clovis did not take military action against the Alamanni who had placed themselves under Theoderic's protection. But any joy over averting this crisis was short-lived because by late summer of the same year, 506, the conflict between Clovis and Alaric that we discussed at the beginning of this chapter broke out. As we saw, Theoderic tried to force the two adversaries to submit to arbitration before friendly kings; whoever opposed this proposal would have to deal with Theoderic and his allies. But this initiative was a complete and utter failure. Clovis' army crossed the Loire in the summer of 507 and joined forces with a Burgundian army led by Gundobad's sons Godomar and Sigismund near Poitiers. This Frankish-Burgundian army encountered Alaric's army at Vouillé. The battle ended in complete victory for Clovis, who allegedly slew his royal rival Alaric with his own hands. The defeated Visigoths fled to Narbonne and elevated Gesalec, an illegitimate son of Alaric's, as their king. Gesalec was unable to hold the city against Gundobad, though, and retreated across the Pyrenees to Barcelona. Amalaric, Alaric's underaged son by Theoderic's daughter Thiudigotho, was brought to safety in Hispania. Clovis and his allies proceeded to Bordeaux, where they spent the winter. In the following year (508), they took Toulouse, the residence of the Visigothic kings, and looted the part of the royal treasure that was located there. Clovis then returned to his kingdom via Angoulême and entered Tours in triumph, which we will have occasion to discuss below. His son Theuderic took charge of the Frankish army and proceeded to capture Albi, Rodez, and Clermont-Ferrand. In the meantime, a Burgundian army led by Gundobad drove Gesalec out of Narbonne and laid siege to the old imperial residence of Arles. An Ostrogothic army under the command of Ibba arrived on the scene in the summer of 508.[28]

3. THE POWER GRAB IN THE WEST: THEODERIC AND THE KINGDOM OF THE VISIGOTHS

The war between a Frankish-Burgundian coalition and Alaric's Visigoths shattered Theoderic's foreign policy conception. The "family of kings" fragmented in armed strife. Theoderic's allies were not prepared to act under his leadership to maintain the peace. Theoderic was especially disappointed in Gundobad's conduct: the Burgundian king not only had not lifted a finger to prevent the impending war, but had, on the contrary, personally participated in the assault on the Visigothic kingdom. Why, however, did Theoderic not intervene until Alaric had already lost the battle and his life? Already contemporaries were evidently asking this question; the Visigothic king had supposedly held out hope for support from Theoderic until the very end and had joined battle only at his warriors' insistence.[29]

Mobilizing the Goths in Italy undoubtedly required several months of preparation; the deployment had to be planned, quarters and provisions had to be procured. But pointing to a lack of preparation merely shifts the problem elsewhere. Clovis' attack did not come out of the blue, after all; Theoderic himself had threatened military intervention. His hesitation makes sense only if we assume that he was unsure how the Byzantine emperor would react. Since Constantinople's war with Persia had ended by treaty in late 506, Theoderic must have believed that the emperor would again have the resources for military operations in the west the following year; he thus had to anticipate an attack. It was an obvious assumption that Anastasius would meddle in the conflict between Clovis and Alaric; that was why Theoderic had warned Clovis not to be pushed into war by "the malevolence of others" (*aliena malignitas*). Anastasius, for his part, did not openly take sides until the Frankish-Burgundian victory had already been secured; when Clovis arrived in Tours in late 508 to visit the tomb of St. Martin, an imperial delegation awaited him, delivering him a letter of appointment as honorary consul and probably also declaring him *patricius*. The ceremonies surrounding his arrival can hardly have been coordinated with Constantinople, though, because they combined gestures and insignia that ran counter to their original purport; clad in a purple tunic and a military cloak, the king rode from the church of St. Martin to the cathedral of Tours wearing a diadem, the imperial emblem par excellence. The much-debated question of whether Anastasius had appointed Clovis a kind of client king in Tours is therefore misconceived: it was Clovis who wanted to present himself as a victorious, pious, and generous king before the representatives of his newly conquered territories.[30]

When Theoderic was forced to recognize that his allies in western Europe had left him in the lurch, he initially sought the support of the Vandalic fleet. He accordingly sent a delegation to the court of Thrasamund in Carthage. At approximately the same time, he appears to have adopted the Herulian king Rudolf as his son-in-arms. If this interpretation is correct, Theoderic would have gained an ally on the middle Danube. Of course, Rudolf ultimately proved to be little help to Theoderic because he himself soon succumbed to the Lombards, who had hitherto been subjects of the Heruli.[31]

Theoderic's fears were by no means unfounded. While war raged in Gaul, a Byzantine fleet of 200 ships carrying 8,000 soldiers devastated the Adriatic coast of Italy as far as Tarentum. Apulia was hit especially hard. The operation was retaliatory in nature, its goal to inflict as much damage as possible on the enemy; it was not preceded by an official declaration of war. Theoderic could do little in response to these surprise attacks by sea; since he had no fleet of his own at his disposal, his troops always arrived too late to defend the coastline. Thrasamund, meanwhile, was wary of sending his fleet into battle against the emperor's; his good relations with Anastasius were more important to him than his obligations as Theoderic's ally. It would not be the last time that Theoderic was disappointed by the husband of his sister Amalafrida.[32]

Preparations for military intervention in Gaul were under way at roughly the same time. An expeditionary force was ordered to assemble on June 24, 508. All the units involved were to gather at the point of departure by that date. Theoderic stayed in Italy this time as well and again entrusted supreme command to someone else: the army would set out under Ibba's command. The Ostrogothic army marched along the Riviera on the Via Iulia Augusta, crossed the Cottian Alps, and reached Marseille via Fréjus. It broke the siege of Arles and, after fierce fighting, forced the Burgundian-Frankish army to retreat.

The details of the hostilities remain unclear. No coherent account survives, and sporadic notices paint a contradictory picture. As it appears, military operations lasted several years, from 508 to 511. The battle at Arles falls in the year 508. Two Ostrogothic armies were apparently active in Gaul in the following year: Ibba led his warriors south and drove the Franks out of Aquitania. A large battle took place at an unknown location in which no fewer than 30,000 Frankish warriors allegedly perished. This victory gave occasion to a major celebration in Ravenna. In his *Chronicle*, which Cassiodorus composed at the court's request in 519, we read that Theoderic had "won for his kingdom Gaul, which had been devastated by the Franks." That was a gross exaggeration because the Franks kept the greater part of their conquests, but it was the picture that Theoderic wanted to propagate. While Ibba won Septimania, the region west of the Rhône, a certain Mammo led an Ostrogothic army into the kingdom of the Burgundians; a local chronicle laconically remarks that the "Gothic general" (*dux Gothorum*) Mammo "devastated part of Gaul."[33]

Who was responsible for the devastation of Gaul depended on one's perspective. To the civilian population, the difference between Franks, Burgundians, and Goths was slight. Confessional differences were also secondary in this war. Clovis may have tried to win over Alaric's Catholic subjects, but he enjoyed little success: the Gallo-Roman senators of Auvergne fought on the Visigoths' side. The population of Arles suffered especially horribly: the city was contested for a long time, seemingly for several months. A convent outside the city walls was reduced to rubble, the city walls and towers were damaged, and the countryside devastated. Since it was impossible to work the fields, the urban population, which had swollen with refugees, suffered famine not only during the siege itself, but also in the following year; plague followed.[34]

Bishop Caesarius of Arles depicts the horrors of the war in a sermon delivered soon after the end of the siege to illustrate the vanity of earthly values to his congregation:

> The truth speaks to you, lovers of the world: "Where is what you loved, where is what you considered great, where is what you refused to let go? Where are so many regions, where are such great and magnificent cities? Have these not been punished all the more severely because they refused to accept the lesson provided from the chastisement of other provinces?"
>
> These things are said in grief rather than in mockery: the mind touched inwardly by this feeling of compassion cannot remain unmoved by those disasters. Merely hearing of them would evoke heavy feelings. But when a dire calamity had struck our eyes at the time of the siege and now afflicts them in this time of plague, and those who remain are scarcely enough to

bury the bodies of the dead; and we reflect on the evils that we endured by the just judgment of God, when whole provinces have been led away into captivity: matrons abducted, pregnant women cut open, infants torn from the hands of their nurses and thrown half dead in the streets, and the women were allowed neither to keep their living children nor to bury their dead children. . . .[35]

Arles was not an isolated case. The damage from the war was so extensive that Theoderic declined to levy the land tax from his new subjects, and it could hardly have been collected at all. The harvest had largely been destroyed, and sowing for the coming year was possible only to a limited extent. The Franks and Burgundians had abducted thousands of people, free and unfree, who could return home only if a ransom was paid for them. Only some will thus have been able to return, despite the fact that the administration Theoderic installed in Provence made money available to Avitus, the bishop of Vienne, to purchase their freedom. Theoderic's victorious Goths, meanwhile, secured booty that was at least equally rich. A large number of prisoners came to Arles, where Caesarius bought the freedom of some with his church's funds. For the rest, Arles was probably only a stopover on a longer journey. Many prisoners unwillingly accompanied the Gothic army back to Italy. Caesarius encountered such "displaced persons" years later in Ravenna. Avitus asked the bishops of Milan and Ticinum to help ransom prisoners. A priest from Avitus' diocese traveled personally to Italy in search of a certain Avulus, the son of a relative of his, who had been taken hostage years before by a Gothic *comes* named Betanc.[36]

Theoderic did not hesitate to annex Provence to his kingdom. The king issued an order not to treat the conquered lands like enemy territory. The Gothic commander of Avignon was instructed not to permit acts of violence against the population; the Gothic army should treat the Romans like citizens (*civiliter*). Ibba himself was instructed to ensure personally that the church of Narbonne recovered properties that had illegally fallen into the wrong hands. To avoid requisitions, the king had grain for the army shipped to Marseille; it was still the provincials' responsibility to transport it to Durance, where the Gothic fortresses were located. Theoderic provided money to repair the fortifications of the city of Arles. The collection of the *siliquaticum*, a kind of sales tax, was suspended for grain, wine, and oil to make importing food in Gaul more attractive to seagoing merchants. The royal chancellery was especially concerned about the rights of landowners: the "swordman" (*spatharius*) Unigis was dispatched to make sure that fugitive slaves were returned to their masters as required by Roman law; a "defender of liberty" could not abet "lowly slaves."

Unigis reinstated a rich landowner who had taken refuge among the Franks during the hostilities in his full rights along with all his property—lands, rural and urban slaves—as the Roman law of return (*postliminium*) stipulated.[37]

Probably at some point before the end of 508, Theoderic commissioned a Roman named Gemellus to organize the civil administration of the Gallic provinces. Gemellus received the office of vicar (*vicarius praefecturae*) to do so. The royal chancellery depicted the beginning of Theoderic's rule as liberation from barbarism and a return to Roman ways. In a text addressed to all the provincials of Gaul, the transition is described in the following words: "We dispatched the vicar of the prefecture to you so that We might be seen to establish civil order with so high an office. You will enjoy what you hitherto have only heard of. Realize that men are preferred for reason rather than physical force and that those who can do justice to others deservedly prosper."[38]

The speed with which Theoderic seized Provence for himself leads us to ask what his real objectives in intervening in Gaul were. When his army arrived on the scene, the Visigoths already had a new king, the Gesalec mentioned above. Gesalec was the offspring of a relationship between Alaric and a concubine; he was preferred over Amalaric, Alaric's son by Theoderic's daughter Thiudigotho, because, in contrast to the latter, he was old enough to lead an army. Gesalec was elevated in Narbonne but then fled to Barcelona after suffering a defeat at the hands of Gundobad's Burgundians. Theoderic appears to have recognized Gesalec at first. He thus apparently presumed that there would still be two Gothic kingdoms after the war. The goal of his intervention in Gaul then, logically, cannot have been the unification of all Goths under his rule. But he also did not lend Gesalec his support out of the kindness of his heart. On the contrary, Theoderic claimed possession of the rich and profitable provinces of the French Mediterranean coast. Whether the border would have subsequently been drawn along the Rhône, where it ran after 526, remains unknown, but the question is moot regardless because Theoderic soon found himself obliged to change plans. Gesalec survived as king for only a few years because he proved unable to turn the tide of the war. His failure to deliver victory made him vulnerable. In 510, he had the *vir illustris* Goiaric murdered in the palace of Barcelona; Goiaric was the man who had produced a law code at Alaric's behest for his Roman subjects a few years before. His execution points to opposition at court, as does the elimination of an otherwise unknown *comes* named Veila the following year.[39]

In these circumstances, Theoderic turned his back on Gesalec. Ibba led an Ostrogothic army across the Pyrenees in 510 and routed Gesalec. What happened next reads like an adventure novel: Gesalec fled to the Vandalic court in

Carthage, was given money by King Thrasamund, and returned to his king-dom. He assembled an army in Aquitania, met Ibba in battle again in 511, twelve miles from Barcelona, and was defeated a second time. The hapless king now sought refuge in the kingdom of the Burgundians. He was caught fleeing there near Durance, just shy of the border, and killed.[40]

The attack on Gesalec presumes that Theoderic had changed his plans for the Visigothic kingdom. Who, though, should take Gesalec's place? Theoderic's grandson Amalaric was still too young to rule; his turn would not come until after Theoderic's death. We find claims in a series of sources that Theoderic reigned in Hispania as Amalaric's guardian after defeating Gesalec. Theoderic himself had perhaps propagated this claim at the beginning of his rule in Hispania to spare the Visigoths' pride. He must have claimed full rights of king of the Visigoths very soon, however, because the list of Visigothic kings and the *Gothic History* of Isidore of Seville attribute fifteen regnal years to Theoderic as king of the Visigoths. They thus counted from Gesalec's death in the year 511 to Theoderic's death in the year 526. Only afterward does Amalaric appear as king of the Visigoths. Contemporary synodal proceedings are dated according to Theoderic's regnal years. Theoderic thus extended his domain to the Iberian Peninsula in 511, thereby becoming by far the richest and most powerful king in the entire Mediterranean world.[41]

Gesalec's demise had diplomatic repercussions. For Theoderic, the support that Thrasamund had given Gesalec was a clear breach of the treaty that had established peace between the Vandals and Ostrogoths. He therefore voiced serious reservations toward his brother-in-law Thrasamund in a letter:

> Although, to reinforce concord [*concordia*] with sundry kings, We joined to them, at their request, either nieces or daughters as God inspired Us, still We think We conferred on no one anything comparable to making Our sister, the singular glory of the Amal line, your spouse: a woman your equal in wisdom [*prudentia*], a woman who can be admired for her council even more than she should be revered by your kingdom.
>
> But I am stunned that, despite the fact that you were obligated by these favors, Gesalec, who joined our enemies while favored by Ourselves, was received into your protection in such a way that, although he came to you abandoned by his forces and bereft of means, yet he was outfitted with a sudden abundance of money and sent over [the Mediterranean] to foreign peoples [*gentes exteras*]; and though he proved utterly harmless, thanks be to God, he still unveiled the nature of your mind.
>
> What can the rights of foreigners expect, if kinship by marriage [*affinitas*] deserves such treatment? If he was received in your kingdom out of pity, then

he should have been held there; if he was expelled for Our sake, then he should not have been sent with riches over to the kingdoms of others, which Our struggles absolutely prevented from becoming hostile to yourself.[42]

By the time Thrasamund received this letter, Theoderic had not only put Clovis and Gundobad in their place, but had also risen to become the master of the Iberian Peninsula. The Vandalic king hastened to appease his brother-in-law. He showed due remorse and asked Theoderic for forgiveness. His envoys delivered precious gifts of gold. Theoderic responded graciously: he accepted Thrasamund's apologies but returned the gold. In a letter his envoys brought back to Carthage, Theoderic showcased his magnanimity and superiority: he was glad that Thrasamund had corrected the error of his ways so swiftly, for humility was as glorious among princes as arrogance was hated among commoners. He also urged the Vandalic king to learn from his mistake and to be more careful in the future, and he affirmed their mutual bond. Until his death in 523, Thrasamund never again dared to provoke Theoderic; the treaty struck in the year 500 still stood. It would be his successor, Hilderic, who broke with this policy by recalling Catholic bishops from exile and seeking an alliance with the Byzantine emperor.[43]

4. AT THE PINNACLE OF POWER: THEODERIC AFTER CLOVIS' DEATH

It is not recorded whether the war that Theoderic's generals waged against the Frankish and Burgundian armies was formally concluded. It is at least certain that hostilities gradually came to a halt, although the border with the Franks remained volatile and unstable. The attack on the Visigothic kingdom ended in stinging embarrassment for Gundobad and Sigismund: they were forced to give up all the territory they had conquered. The booty that they and their warriors brought home seemed small recompense for the devastation that Theoderic's army had inflicted on their lands. Gundobad, now in his seventies, utterly lost his thirst for raids. His prestige was tarnished; his power tottered.

Clovis, in contrast, could celebrate the outcome of the war as victory. He not only had won booty for himself and his men, but had also significantly expanded his territory. He could not hold on to Septimania, with Narbonne and Rodez, nor probably Albi and Javols, but he kept wide swaths of Aquitania, including Toulouse, which had been the Visigothic kings' most important residence. In the fall of 508, the king returned to his territory beyond the Loire, leaving his oldest son, Theuderic, to prosecute the war. The following years were full of feverish activity. If we can trust Gregory of Tours, Clovis eliminated all three kings of the Rhenish Franks one by one by murder and assassination, thus becoming king of all the Franks. He transferred his residence to Paris, moved into a palace on the Île de la Cité, and had the Church of the Apostles Peter and Paul built; it was later renamed Sainte-Genevieve because it harbored the relics of St. Genoveva. Following the example of Kings Euric, Alaric II, and Gundobad, Clovis published a codification of legal norms, the so-called Salic Law (*Lex Salica*), based in part on Frankish customary law and in part on royal statute. And just as Alaric II had gathered the Catholic bishops in the Gallic portion of his kingdom at Agde in 506 shortly before the outbreak of war, so now Clovis assembled all the bishops whom he regarded as his subjects to a kind of royal synod at Orléans in July 511. Clovis exercised powers at this synod, however, that went far beyond what Alaric had claimed: Clovis set the agenda and had the bishops' resolutions presented to him for approval. The bishops acceded to the church governance of their Catholic king and explicitly decreed that the entry of laymen into the clergy required royal approval; within a generation, that evolved into a general veto on episcopal elections. Clovis died at the age of forty-five, just a few months after the council's conclusion, on November 27, 511.[44]

Clovis' death rid Theoderic of a rival who had proven to be impossible to control. In his thirty-year reign, Clovis had risen up from a petty Frankish king in the province of Belgica II to king of all the Franks, ruling over much of Gaul. He had challenged the king of the Visigoths to a military test of strength and emerged victorious, keeping a significant part of his conquests from Theoderic. Theoderic could breathe easy once again when he learned of the death of his Frankish brother-in-law. And the news that Clovis' empire had been divided among his four sons would have been especially welcome because it spelled the end to the recently unified political and military leadership of the Franks. Now there were four kings of the Franks, each with his own court and army. The details of the partitioning are obscure, but the basic outline is clear enough. The lion's share went to Theuderic, the oldest son: he received the former provinces of Belgica I (capital: Trier), Germania I (capital: Mainz), and Germania II (capital: Cologne); Reims and Châlons; and eastern Aquitania; he resided in Reims. Childebert, who made Paris his residence, received the coast from the Somme to Brittany; Chlodomer, the territory on both sides of the Loire, including Tours, Poitiers, and Bourges; his residence, however, was in Orléans. Lastly, Chlothar's share encompassed Soissons, where he resided, and the adjoining northern territories between the Somme and the Silva Carbonaria. However we explain this curious partitioning, it played right into Theoderic's hands: the threat that the resources Clovis controlled at the end of his life would be used

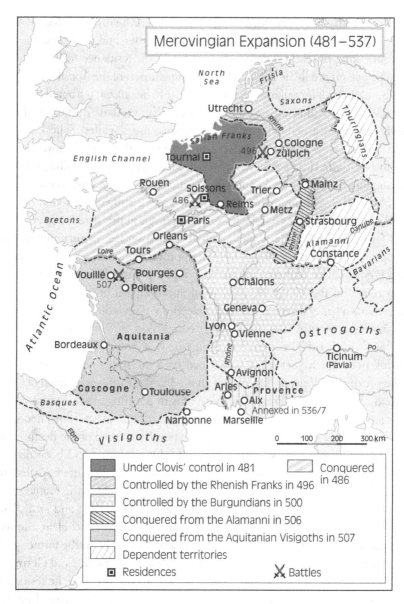

Merovingian Expansion (481–537)

North Sea

Frisia

Saxons

Thuringians

Utrecht O

Rhine

Salian Franks

O Cologne

496 X O Zülpich

English Channel

Tournai ▣

Rouen O

Soissons

O Mainz

486 X ▣

Trier O

Bretons

O Reims

O Metz

▣ Paris

O Strasbourg

Danube

Orléans

Alamanni

Loire

Tours O

Rhine

Constance

Bavarians

Vouillé O X

Bourges O

507

O Poitiers

O Châlons

Geneva O

Lyon O

O s t r o g o t h s

Vienne

Aquitania

Atlantic Ocean

Bordeaux O

Rhône

Ticinum

(Pavia)

Po

O Avignon

Gascogne

O Toulouse

Arles

Provence

O

O Aix

Basques

O Annexed in 536/7

Narbonne

Marseille

Ebro

V i s i g o t h s

0   100   200   300 km

	Under Clovis' control in 481			Conquered in 486
	Controlled by the Rhenish Franks in 496			
	Controlled by the Burgundians in 500			
	Conquered from the Alamanni in 506			
	Conquered from the Aquitanian Visigoths in 507			
	Dependent territories			
▣	Residences	X	Battles	

Map 12. Merovingian Expansion under Clovis and His Sons, 481–537.

by a unified Frankish leadership after his death seemed to have been averted. The four brothers indeed seem to have largely dispensed with military campaigns for the next ten years.[45]

At Theoderic's court, the conquest of southern Provence was stylized as the recovery of land that had belonged to the Roman Empire since time immemorial. Cassiodorus praised Theoderic in the following terms: "Hail thee, o indefatigable *triumphator*, by whose fighting the tired limbs of the Republic are being restored and the blessedness of old is returning to our times. We used to read that Gaul was Roman only in annals." The implication of this statement— that Gaul was Roman again—was bold in several respects. After all, the conquered territory covered only three provinces, and not even all of them. According to Theoderic's plan, a "praetorian prefect of Gaul" would again oversee this area, as had been the case before 476. In 511, Theoderic appointed a senator to the consulship who lived in Rome but had Gallic ancestors and had also been born there: Arcadius Placidus Magnus Felix, whose father, Magnus Felix, had headed the Gallic prefecture in 469, four decades before. Theoderic notified Emperor Anastasius of the appointment by letter, reminding him of the long tradition of Gallic senators in the Roman senate and asking him to assent to the appointment. This request, however, was merely a formality because Theoderic simultaneously notified Felix of his appointment as consul without mentioning the emperor. The king recommended Felix to the senate as a senator who thoroughly deserved the consulship by reason of his distinguished birth, learnedness, and dignified conduct, as well as the title of *patricius*:

> Rejoice, senators, that provinces, having ceased to do so for such a long time, are delivering men of consular rank to you, and predict even greater things from this sign. Beginnings usually portend better things; they start out small and subsequently reach sublime heights to great amazement. Noble origin lay idle under Gallic suspension and sojourned, deprived of its honors, as a stranger in its homeland. At last the divine released the oppressed: they regained Rome and glory and gathered their grandfathers' ancient laurels from the distinguished forest of the curia.[46]

From 511 on, Theoderic was officially the ruler of Italy, Gaul, and Hispania and simultaneously king of all Goths because the beginning of his reign in Hispania was celebrated as the reunification of the Gothic people after long separation. Cassiodorus later claimed in his *Gothic History* that this occurred in the two thousandth year of Gothic history. That was court propaganda, which lionized Theoderic as an "indefatigable *triumphator*," but it still rang true for many contemporaries because Theoderic's accomplishments were really undeniable.

No other ruler seemed to have deserved the epithet *invictus*, "unconquered" and therefore "invincible," as much as Theoderic: he had not only put Clovis, Gundobad, and Thrasamund in their place, but he had also brought the northern coast of the western Mediterranean completely under his control. By integrating Provence into his empire and subjugating the Iberian Peninsula, he gained access to additional resources that he could redistribute to serve his purposes. The wars he fought from 505 to 511 gave Theoderic enormous prestige as a general and made him the wealthiest king of the post-Roman West. In this way, he earned the respect of foreign rulers and, in particular, secured the support of Roman elites in Italy and the devotion of his Goths.

The war against the Franks and Burgundians had a major impact on Theoderic's foreign policy. His attempt to create a peaceful hegemonic order through marriages and treaties had failed. At the conclusion of the war, Theoderic's great kingdom, which stretched from the Atlantic to the Adriatic, faced a multitude of smaller, but largely independent, powers in the interior of western and central Europe. The geopolitical landscape had also changed since 506 because the ethnic and political conditions in the thinly settled regions east of the Rhine and on the Balkan Peninsula were in constant motion. Warrior bands grew and shrank with success and failure or disintegrated entirely; they undertook campaigns, migrated, or were driven out. Even when settlement areas stabilized, their spheres of action extended far beyond, and it was well-nigh impossible to draw borders. They competed for scarce resources; imperial subsidies and tribute were much sought after. Leaders who failed to prove themselves quickly lost support, were run off, or killed. Transferring power to one's son was always precarious; struggle for power was always on the agenda and was waged with all possible means. Power was not institutionalized at all and so depended on the personal qualities and accomplishments of each ruler in the extreme.

Anyone who wanted to pursue a broad policy in this territory had to adapt to rapidly changing circumstances while also keeping a vigilant eye on the superpower on the Bosporus. As we have seen, Theoderic had allied himself in 506 with a Thuringian king. That may have been Hermanfrid, one of three brothers who ruled over the Thuringians until Hermanfrid first killed Bertachar and then, with Frankish help, Baderic. At least Baderic was still alive, though, when Hermanfrid courted Theoderic's niece Amalaberga in 510. This marriage raised great expectations in Ravenna. It was hoped that Hermanfrid would permit his bride to share in his power, a hope that was voiced aloud.[47]

Conditions on the middle Danube, the gateway to both Theoderic's kingdom and the Byzantine Empire, were especially complex. After the kingdom of the Rugi in Lower Austria had been shattered, the Lombards advanced into the territory and soon advanced to the Morava Field (Marchfeld) east of Vienna; they had their own king but were dependents of the Heruli who lived farther to the east in northern Pannonia. Across the Danube, between the Maros/Mureş and the sources of the Körös/Criş, lived the Gepids. After Theoderic's victory over Thrasaric, these peoples no longer posed a threat to him, even if they still had kings and still functioned as independent warrior bands. Mundo was a loyal ally on the frontier with Gothic Pannonia, keeping the Gepids in check. In 523, Theoderic was even able to station Gepid warriors in Gaul to guard the border; that might indicate internal conflict and dissension among the Gepids or alternatively suggest an arrangement or alliance. The old enmity between the Goths and Gepids first flared up again after Theoderic's death, when Mundo changed sides in favor of the emperor. The Gepids tried to reconquer Sirmium for the first time in 530 but were beaten back. They were successful only after Justinian attacked the Gothic kingdom in Italy.[48]

The Heruli were neighbors of the Gepids and had brought several peoples under their dominion, including the Lombards. They thus could be useful to Theoderic to play off against the Gepids. His adoption of the Herulian king Rudolf served precisely that purpose. But the Heruli were unable to hold on to their strong position. Theoderic's son-in-arms Rudolf suffered a devastating defeat at the hands of a Lombard army led by their king Tato; Rudolf himself was killed in battle. The survivors split into several groups: some of them joined the victorious Lombards; others supposedly returned to Scandinavia. The largest share fled first to the Gepids but then asked Emperor Anastasius for admittance into the Byzantine Empire and settled in the vicinity of Belgrade in 512. These Heruli henceforth lived outside Theoderic's sphere of influence but did not pose an immediate threat since they proved to be unreliable allies of the emperor. Only a small number of Heruli sought refuge in Theoderic's kingdom. The king had the city of Ticinum furnish a ship and provisions for five days to one group that wished to come to his court shortly after 510.[49]

With their victory over Rudolf's army, the Lombards cast off the Herulian yoke; the battle was regarded ever after as the beginning of Lombardic greatness. King Tato, however, did not enjoy his glory for long; he was killed by his nephew Wacho not long afterward. Wacho was a confident ruler who did not let himself become ensnared in Theoderic's designs. That is shown already by his choice of a wife: he first married Ranigunda, the daughter of a Thuringian king, then the Gepid princess Austrigusa, and finally Salinga, the daughter of a Herulian king. The king defeated the Suebi on the Danube and extended his domain into northern Hungary; he had a palace in Bohemia. After Theoderic's death, Wacho married one of his two daughters to the Frankish king Theudebert, Theuderic's son, and the other daughter to Theudebert's son Theodebald, and he forged an alliance with the Byzantine emperor before 539.[50]

Theoderic navigated the crisis-ridden years of 506–511 without leaving Italy. That was possible because he had reliable helpers who undertook diplomatic missions and conducted military operations on his behalf. These men and their deeds are usually elusive in the sources. That is particularly true of the Gothic generals, Pitzia and Mammo, Ibba and Tuluin. The envoys who conducted negotiations for Theoderic are normally better known since they often were senators whom we know from the *Variae*. One of these envoys, however, over-shadows all others—at least for us: Senarius, who tried in vain to prevent the outbreak of war between Clovis and Alaric. Theoderic was nonetheless very satisfied with Senarius. He appointed him *comes patrimonii* for the year 509–510. On this occasion, Cassiodorus composed a veritable paean to Senarius in the king's name: "Having long lent double obedience to Our decrees, you both shared Our counsel and carried out Our orders with laudable enthusiasm. You have often endured arduous diplomatic duties: you opposed kings, proving to be their equal in disputes, forced to demonstrate Our righteousness to men who could scarcely grasp reason in their crude obstinacy. Incensed royal authority did not frighten you in quarrels; on the contrary, you subjugated audacity to truth and, in following Our decrees, you drove barbarians back onto their own guilty consciences." Senarius apparently was among the Romans who enjoyed Theoderic's confidence at the time: Cassiodorus praises him for always keeping secrets and never acting arrogantly despite being privy to many affairs. Senarius had begun his career as a secretary (*exceptor*) at the royal court and was a prac-ticing Catholic; he had a deacon of the Roman church explain to him why the Roman baptismal liturgy was so different from that of the Eastern churches. He apparently lived in Ravenna, where he still wielded influence in 516, but he died before Theoderic. Senarius had served Theoderic for many years as a kind of counselor until he took over the management of the king's landholdings as *comes patrimonii*. He was also regularly dispatched on diplomatic missions. According to his funerary inscription, Senarius set out on such missions no fewer than twenty-five times; he traveled to the Byzantine Empire, into the far north, to the Iberian Peninsula, and to Africa; in one year, he even made the journey from the Atlantic to Pontus twice, back to back.[51]

Not every journey that Senarius undertook as Theoderic's envoy need have taken him outside of Italy; in some cases, he may have been dispatched to the senate or to the pope. Be that as it may, Senarius' career illustrates how Theoderic's diplomatic contacts spanned the entire Mediterranean world and even extended into northern Europe, to the Baltic, and perhaps even beyond. The geographical horizon of the court at Ravenna stretched from Scandinavia to the Black Sea. We do not know whether the princely chiefs who lived in great halls in central locations in modern Denmark ever paid visits to Theoderic, whether in person or through envoys. A visit by Goths from the Crimea is also feasible but impossible to prove. It is explicitly attested, however, that delegates from the Esti, who inhabited the Baltic coast east of the Vistula, brought Theoderic a gift of amber between 523 and 526 and took a courtly letter of thanks home with them. The Neo-Persian Empire, in contrast, which Theoderic would have known from his youth in Constantinople, apparently lay beyond the lands traversed by the king's envoys. The Byzantine emperor probably claimed exclusive diplomatic rights with Persia that Theoderic respected. Only much later, when Justinian's war to reconquer Italy was in full swing, did a Gothic king (Vitigis) attempt to forge an alliance against the emperor with the Persian Great King.[52]

5. EXPANSION AND INTEGRATION 1: PROVENCE IN THEODERIC'S KINGDOM

In an edict sent to the inhabitants of the conquered territories of Provence, the royal chancellery equated the beginning of Theoderic's rule with the return of Roman order after a period of barbaric chaos. Henceforth, the addressees would be governed in Roman fashion, thereby regaining their freedom (*libertas*): "You must gladly obey the Roman custom, to which you have been restored after a long time, because a welcome return lies where your ancestors are known to have prospered. And therefore, having been summoned to your ancient freedom by grace of God, dress yourselves in the ways of the toga, shed barbarism, cast off cruel minds, because it is unbecoming that you should live according to foreign ways under the equality of Our age."[53] This proclamation was addressed to "the inhabitants of the provinces of Gaul" (*provinciales Galliarum*), which were placed under the authority of a "praetorian prefect of the Gallic provinces" in 511. In reality, this prefecture contained only parts of three late Roman provinces—Viennensis, Narbonensis II, and Alpes Maritimae. Theoderic's Gallic prefecture extended in the west to the Rhône; beyond the river lay Narbonensis I. The border with the kingdom of the Burgundians, which was fortified with castles, ran along the Durance. The prefecture of Gaul was thus in no way comparable in size to the prefecture of Italy; it even fell far short of the former diocese of Septem Provinciae. Its name reflected an imperial pretense that was completely at odds with reality.[54]

Despite that, it was not only the illusion that Theoderic had reconquered all Gaul for the empire that made this territory a valuable commodity: Provence in 500 was a prosperous region with many cities and a sophisticated commercial economy. The *Notitia Galliarum*, a provincial index from the middle of the fifth century, lists a total of twenty-nine civic communities (*civitates*) for the provinces of Viennensis, Narbonensis II, and Alpes Maritimae. These cities normally had given up some of the public buildings that had defined their appearance in the High Empire; besides the temples of pagan gods, these included the theaters and amphitheaters, which had long ceased to host regular spectacles, and in some cases also the Roman fora, which had previously been the heart of civic life. Since the cities continued to function as central locations, however, numerous churches were built both inside and outside their walls. The region was connected to the interior by the Rhône and to the western coast of Spain, North Africa, and the Levant by the ports of Fos and Marseille. Terracotta eating and drinking vessels (known as "red slip ware") and oil were imported from North Africa. Papyrus, still the most important writing material, came from Egypt. A large portion of maritime trade between Gaul, the western Mediterranean, and the Levant passed through Marseille in Late Antiquity. The city harbor was therefore repeatedly improved and even expanded over the fifth century. Its fortifications were reinforced by the construction of a forewall in 475. Monumental churches were built both inside and outside the city walls; the baptistry of the cathedral of Marseille was by far the largest and grandest in all Gaul, outshining even the baptistries of the imperial residences in Milan and Rome. Whereas the population and prosperity of many cities in the interior had declined since the third century, late antique Marseille grew in size and significance.[55]

The possession of Arles was hardly less lucrative and even more prestigious. The city extended onto both banks of the Rhône, thus dominating the most important water route into the interior. When Arles became an imperial residence in the early fourth century, a new period of prosperity commenced. The baths were expanded and a palace was constructed. A basilica approximately 58 meters long and 20 meters wide, resembling the Aula Palatina of Trier but probably dating from the fifth century, served as a throne room and audience chamber. The circuit of city walls was reduced in the fifth century to make the city more easily defensible. The theater, amphitheater, and hippodrome were still standing in Theoderic's day, but they were no longer maintained and only seldom used for spectacles. Chariot races and animal hunts had become a rarity. Private dwellings were built in the arcades of the hippodrome. Craftsmen went about their work in the stands of the theater. The civic elite invested continuously in Christian cult buildings from the fourth century on. Arles received monumental churches earlier than any other city of Gaul and presented itself to visitors in the age of Theoderic as a Christian city. In the early sixth century, a massive basilica at least 55 meters long was built in the southeastern section of the city; it should presumably be identified as the cathedral, which was dedicated to St. Stephen.[56]

Arles possessed an exceptionally large territory and controlled shipping on the Rhône. When the headquarters of the prefecture of Gaul was moved from Trier to Arles around the year 400, the city also became the seat of a major imperial official. Emperor Honorius elevated Arles to a metropolis in 418 and decreed that delegates from the seven provinces of southern Gaul, comprising the diocese of Septem Provinciae, should meet there annually. The Gallic senator Avitus was declared emperor in Arles in 455; Emperor Majorian resided there from 459 to 461. The Visigothic kings repeatedly tried to capture the city. They had always been beaten back until Euric finally seized the city permanently in 476; Arles was under Visigothic rule for the next thirty years. The prefecture of Gaul was dissolved, the mint closed. The city still retained considerable political importance since it served its new masters as an additional residence alongside Toulouse and Bordeaux. Euric died at Arles in 484.[57]

Wealthy landholders whose ancestors had held high office in the emperor's service resided in Arles and Marseille. They cultivated the late Roman aristocratic lifestyle, owned magnificent houses in the city and country villas on their estates, studied secular and Christian literature, and exchanged elegantly mannered letters. Proud, learned clerics like Sidonius Apollinaris and Ennodius found like-minded peers in this milieu. Of course, this education was no longer taught in public schools in the year 500 but rather at home, by relatives or tutors. The families these men came from had not had a chance to renew their status by holding imperial office in a generation because Provence had been under Visigothic rule since 476. That did not mean, however, that they no longer regarded themselves as members of the senatorial order, especially since they had relatives across the Alps, in Liguria, who were senators in the traditional sense. For Gallo-Roman aristocrats of the early sixth century, ancestry alone determined whether one was a senator. Not a few of them had come to view the office of bishop as appropriate to their rank, although it limited its occupant to the narrow sphere of action of a civic community.[58]

When Theoderic appointed Felix, a senator with Gallic roots, consul for 511, he declared that other senators from Gaul would soon follow him. In reality, though, Felix remained the only senator from Gaul to hold an *illustris* office under Theoderic. The senators of Gaul, who left their homeland only seldom, and even then usually for only a short time in the fifth century, evidently had little enthusiasm for making their status dependent on a king who lived in Italy, as their Italian peers did.[59]

Theoderic probably did not take the decision to incorporate the former Visigothic territories along the Gallic Mediterranean coast in a separate prefecture until he felt secure in his possession. Gemellus, whom he put in charge of the civil administration in 508, was thus initially subordinate to the praetorian prefect of Italy, Faustus Niger, as his *vicarius*. Gemellus was not the only person responsible for organizing the new province. Theoderic also dispatched his trusted adviser Arigern to Gaul with extensive powers, despite the fact that he did not hold an office at the time. After he recalled Arigern in 510 to send him to Rome, he appointed a prefect specifically for the Gallic provinces, the same Liberius whom he had charged to carry out the land distribution a decade earlier. Liberius took up residence in Arles, where he used the basilica mentioned above as his official headquarters. Gemellus served thereafter as his subordinate and seems to have remained in office concurrently with him at least for a while.

In the Later Roman Empire, provincial governors (and vicars) stood between the praetorian prefects and the cities as the lowest level of the provincial administration; Gothic Italy was no different. There is no evidence, however, of provincial governors in Ostrogothic Gaul. Since the territory of the Gallic prefecture was hardly larger than a province of the High Empire, the administration could do without this level, which had already disappeared under the Visigoths. In this regard, the prefect of Gaul was like that of Italy only in name. Military command in Gaul lay in Gothic hands, just as in Italy. In addition to the generals Ibba and Mammo, Arigern also seems to have commanded troops as long as he was in Gaul. During the war, military commanders with the title of *comes* are attested in Marseille and Avignon and in Arles too after its conclusion. These men commanded the troops quartered in the cities; they corresponded to the *comites civitatis* in Italy and were probably called such, as well.[60]

Our information about the administration of Ostrogothic Gaul pertains almost exclusively to the exceptional situation of the war and its immediate aftermath. The royal administration tried to keep the payments in kind needed to maintain the army within limits by importing grain, but it still relied on its new subjects to transport it. It remitted taxes for regions that had been especially hard hit and provided money to repair the city walls of Arles. The king apparently also shared in the expense of ransoming prisoners. Liberius sent money for that purpose to Bishop Avitus of Vienne, and his *vicarius* Gemellus appears to have done the same. All these measures were limited in terms of space or time. Afterward, routine tax collection could commence, but our sources say nothing about that. Few people will have enjoyed a permanent exemption from payments and dues. Seemingly little confidence was placed in the public courts; the royal administration explicitly urged its new subjects to reacquaint themselves with settling disputes in court. Gemellus and Liberius were instructed to administer justice according to Roman law, deciding cases in fair and incorruptible fashion. As a matter of fact, a collection of legal norms with supplements to the *Codex Euricianus* was made in Province around the year 520, known as the *Fragmenta Gaudenziana* after their discoverer. There thus still were jurists who knew Roman law in Provence.[61]

The separation of civil and military jurisdiction was by no means strict, and the coexistence of Gothic soldiers and the Gallo-Roman civilian population definitely led to conflict. When the *illustris femina* Archotamia of Marseille accused her former daughter-in-law Aetheria of depriving her children from her first marriage of property, Theoderic instructed Gemellus and Marabad to investigate the dispute jointly with the assistance of three Roman jurists and to decide it according to the law. These instructions violated the principle that Gothic judges were competent only when at least one party was Gothic, although they at least attempted to ensure that Roman law was applied correctly. Marabad, however, then decided the case alone. When Aetheria's second husband protested his decision, the king ordered Marabad to reach a settlement that was satisfactory to all parties; if that proved impossible, the parties should send authorized representatives to the royal court so that the dispute could be resolved there. There thus was no more talk of involving civil judges or applying Roman law. Abuses committed by soldiers against the civilian population were also a problem in Ostrogothic Gaul; hence the king urged the commander of the Gothic troops in Avignon to maintain strict discipline. But what could anyone do when the commander himself made common cause with his men? Tenant farmers of the church of Arles, who were regularly beaten by the Gothic *comites* and their men, turned to the bishop for help. Even the Catholic clergy was not immune to interference: an archdeacon of the church of Nîmes was brought to Arles in chains on the orders of the Gothic *dux* Ara. Ara released him because it turned out to be a case of mistaken identity and later commended him to the community of Nîmes as bishop. It is not attested whether this recommendation corresponded to the wishes of the community itself.[62]

The Goths' relationship with the Catholic Church in Provence emerges somewhat more distinctly from our sources. During the war, Theoderic ordered his general Ibba, in accordance with the decrees of Alaric II, to restore to the church of Narbonne all the property that had been taken from it illegally. Of course, it remained to be seen whether the decision would have precedential character. Other churches had also received privileges from Alaric, such as the church of Arles, and now were worried about their possessions and status under their new lord. To dispel such concerns, Ennodius wrote a brief panegyric to Theoderic in letter form to a Catholic bishop of the recently reconquered territories, presumably Caesarius of Arles. Ennodius assured his addressee that the king would not touch the Catholic faith but in fact would increase the property of Catholics; they could only hope that Jesus Christ would grant Theoderic a successor from his own family so that his acts of kindness would survive him.[63]

One man towered over all the other Catholic bishops of Ostrogothic Gaul: Caesarius of Arles. Having grown up in Chalons-sur-Saône in the kingdom of the Burgundians, he entered the monastery of Lérins (near Cannes) in 486–487 at the age of eighteen. He moved to Arles shortly thereafter, where he was made abbot of a monastery in 499 and consecrated bishop in 502. Caesarius saw himself as a preacher and church reformer; he called on the clergy to cultivate the same ascetic lifestyle that he himself practiced and paid little heed to diocesan boundaries. If he deemed it necessary, he had no scruples about using church property for charitable and monastic purposes. He was accordingly controversial among his clergy and his fellow bishops. Denounced by a notary from his own church, he was accused before Alaric of supporting the Burgundian king, in whose kingdom his family lived. He was banished to Bordeaux and not allowed to return to his see for some time. But he ultimately was rehabilitated; he presided over the first and last synod of Catholic bishops in Visigothic Gaul, which took place with the king's permission in September 506 in Agde, and he presumably would have played the same part at the regional synod that was supposed to meet in Toulouse the following year but was cancelled on account of the war. During the siege of Arles by the Franks and Burgundians, Caesarius was placed under arrest on suspicion of intending to deliver the city to its besiegers. When captive Burgundians were subsequently brought to Arles and confined in the churches, Caesarius violated the decrees that had just been passed in Agde by selling church property to ransom them. That won him the gratitude of the Burgundian king but exposed him to accusations of damaging the church in Arles. When Caesarius transferred revenue from church property to a convent he had personally founded, his enemies had had enough. We do not know how their denunciation reached Ravenna; we merely know that Theoderic took up the case.[64]

Caesarius was placed in custody in late 512 and brought to the royal court. In the biography that Caesarius' students dedicated to their master shortly after his death, we read that Theoderic rose to his feet when Caesarius entered the throne room, took off his ornamental head covering, and cordially greeted the bishop. The king then inquired about the rigors of his journey, his Goths (*de Gothis suis*), and the population of Arles; after dismissing Caesarius, he openly and explicitly acknowledged the sanctity of the man before his courtiers and described him as equal to the apostles. He later allegedly had a 60-pound silver bowl and 300 gold pieces brought to Caesarius' lodgings and did not hold it against the bishop when he used this royal gift to ransom prisoners. This depiction obviously serves to illustrate the dead bishop's sanctity while certifying it with the testimony of a famous king; it should not be taken as unadulterated truth. Since Caesarius traveled on from Ravenna to Rome and was received there by senators and the bishop of Rome, we may presume that Theoderic certainly had his own interests at heart when he showed Caesarius favor and dismissed him. The king must have had the impression that the controversial bishop of Arles was an equally reliable and effective partisan in whose hands he could confidently place leadership of the Catholic Church in Ostrogothic Gaul. That does not mean that he had Caesarius brought to Ravenna for that purpose and that purpose alone. The king wanted to get to know the man before he made his decision. Ennodius, who had good connections at court, was relieved when he learned that Caesarius had passed the test.[65]

Caesarius' involuntary trip to Italy ushered in a new phase of cooperation between the bishop of Arles, the bishop of Rome, and the Gothic monarchy that lasted beyond Theoderic's death. In order to understand this convergence of interests, we must backtrack somewhat. In the latter half of the fourth century, it was the rule in Gaul and elsewhere that the bishop of the city where the governor had his residence—the so-called *metropolis*—held the rank of metropolitan bishop, thereby wielding disciplinary power over all bishops in his province. This hierarchical administrative structure was based on the division of the Roman Empire into provinces. In the province of Viennensis, however, the governor's headquarters in Vienne competed with the imperial residence in Arles. Hence after the fourth century, disputes repeatedly broke out over how the jurisdictions of the bishops of Arles and Vienne should be separated from one another. Bishops of Arles also laid claim to parts of neighboring provinces, and for a while it looked as if their claim would be recognized. Pope Leo the Great (440–461), meanwhile, firmly rejected these efforts in 445 with imperial backing: every province of Gaul should now have its own metropolitan. Five years later, the pope divided the province of Viennensis into two ecclesiastical districts, each with its own metropolis; the north, with Valence, Tarentaise, Geneva, and Grenoble, would fall under the jurisdiction of the bishop of Vienne; the other cities "of the same province" (*eiusdem provinciae*) would be subordinate to Arles. The purport of this decision was fiercely contested. In

Arles, the bishop interpreted it as indicating not only the southern part of Viennensis, but also the two neighboring provinces. When the area across the Durance became part of the kingdom of the Burgundians, the bishop of Arles was dealt a heavy setback: his area of jurisdiction shrank to the part of Viennensis on the near side of the Durance, which initially remained under the control of the Western Roman emperor and after 476 became subject to the Visigothic king. It did little good when Pope Symmachus again explicitly limited the juris-diction of the bishop of Vienne to the cities named by Leo because his ruling was unenforceable in the kingdom of the Burgundians. For a bishop like Caesarius, who wanted to reform the church in Gaul and knew that he had to overcome resistance, it was an intolerable state of affairs.[66]

Caesarius needed Theoderic's support if he wanted to realize his reform pro-gram outside the few sees that recognized him as metropolitan. Otherwise, any attempt to bring the bishops of the two neighboring provinces under his control was doomed to fail. The king's favor alone was not enough, however: Caesarius also needed the support of the bishop of Rome, who had great authority in southern Gaul. Therefore, after visiting Ravenna, Caesarius traveled to Rome to meet with Pope Symmachus, who had recognized Arles' claim to the greater part of Viennensis thirteen years before. Symmachus was eager to support a Gallic metropolitan who enjoyed Theoderic's favor and unconditionally recog-nized Roman primacy. Since Germanic kings ruled Gaul and Hispania, these lands lay largely outside the immediate sphere of influence of the see of Rome. Symmachus therefore granted Caesarius' wish that he should confirm the spe-cial status of the bishop of Arles: Symmachus affirmed that episcopal sees beyond the Durance in the kingdom of the Burgundians were also supposed to be under Caesarius' authority as metropolitan. Moreover, he conferred on Caesarius the symbolic vestment of the *pallium*, a white woolen sash adorned with small crosses that was draped from the shoulders down the chest and back.[67]

Caesarius interpreted Symmachus' decision as a mandate to bring all the Catholic bishops under Ostrogothic rule under his jurisdiction. When the bishop of Aix-en-Provence, the capital of Narbonensis II, refused to recognize Caesarius' seniority, Symmachus not only confirmed his previous decision of 514, but also instructed Caesarius to oversee ecclesiastical affairs "in Gaul and Hispania." To do so, Caesarius should convene councils and investigate disputes; and vice versa, no one "from Gaul or Hispania" should travel to the Apostolic See without notify-ing Caesarius first. It is often alleged that the papal chancellery did not intend the Iberian Peninsula with the term "Hispania" but rather only Septimania, the remnant of the Visigothic kingdom in Gaul. That is unlikely: such a deviation from the normal use of the term would demand an explanation. At any rate,

Symmachus' decision resulted in a massive expansion of the powers of the bishop of Arles. As apostolic vicar, he was now charged with overseeing the Catholic bishops of faraway provinces, regardless of whether they lived under the rule of Frankish, Burgundian, or Gothic kings.[68]

Whether Caesarius really believed he could enforce this claim can stay an open question. He must have quickly recognized, however, that his power did not extend beyond Ostrogothic Gaul. He therefore did not convene a synod for an entire decade. When he then invited participants to a synod in Arles in 524 to issue rules for the election of church officials, a mere fourteen bishops accepted the invitation, although Ostrogothic Gaul now extended to the Isère. Caesarius was able to gather his suffragans more often in the following years—at Arles (527), Carpentras (527), Vaison (529), Orange (529), and Marseille (533)—but no more than fifteen participants ever attended any of these synods. Caesarius was and remained the apostolic vicar for the bishops of Ostrogothic Gaul.[69]

Just as Caesarius stood at the top of the hierarchy of Catholic bishops in Ostrogothic Italy, so Liberius stood atop the civil administration. Both men had their headquarters in Arles and worked closely together. This collaboration was founded on personal trust and was also put on public display: when Bishop Apollinaris of Valence, the brother of Avitus of Vienne, once visited Arles to pay reverence to the remains of the local martyr Genesius, Caesarius and Liberius harmoniously came forth to meet him, the bishop accompanied by his congregation, the prefect surrounded by his official staff. To the anonymous biographer of Apollinaris describing the scene, Caesarius and Liberius jointly represented the city of Arles itself. The Gothic garrison only marred this image of concord, not least because it consisted entirely or primarily of heterodox Christians.[70]

This account of the reception of Apollinaris is nonetheless more than a hagiographical ideal. That is shown by the proceedings of a synod that met under Caesarius' presidency in Orange in 529, three years after Theoderic's death. Caesarius had assembled his suffragans there to consecrate a basilica that Liberius had sponsored. The deliberations centered on the question of whether human nature contained an undefiled remnant that enabled it to receive divine grace or whether instead the grace of God worked alone without any human agency, as Augustine of Hippo had taught. Critics of the latter view objected, asking what was the point of striving for perfection if salvation depended solely on God's free and unfathomable election of grace. This doctrine was thus received with reservation, especially in monastic communities. Vice versa, Augustine's defenders accused their opponents of propagating the long-since condemned errors of Pelagius. Caesarius broached the issue yet again in 529 because a council over which Bishop Julianus of Vienne presided in Valence, on Burgundian soil, had recently cast doubt on his orthodoxy. The best way to clear himself of this accusation was a council that adopted Caesarius' position as its own and condemned that of his adversaries as heresy. That is precisely what Caesarius' thirteen suffragans then did. The canons of the council, however, were signed not only by the bishops present, but also by Liberius and seven other laymen, all of whom held the rank of *vir illustris*. Their signatures, moreover, were accompanied by a declaration that they agreed with the decrees. The proceedings demonstrate, on the one hand, the interest that Liberius and other prominent members of the lay elite took in complicated theological questions. On the other hand, they also make clear how important it was to Caesarius to rally the ecclesiastical and secular elite to support his theological position.[71]

Liberius was the most powerful Roman in Ostrogothic Gaul. He stayed in office a full twenty-four years, longer than any other prefect of Late Antiquity. Theoderic's praetorian prefects in Italy always served for only a few years, just as had been late antique practice. On Theoderic's death, Liberius was given the task of ensuring that his grandson and successor, Athalaric, was recognized in Ostrogothic Gaul, and he carried this mission out successfully. Under his direction, Gallo-Roman civilians and Gothic warriors jointly swore an oath of allegiance to the new king. Liberius was not recalled until 533 in the final, crisis-ridden phase of Athalaric's rule, when he was appointed supreme commander in Ravenna (*patricius praesentalis*) and then sent to Constantinople as an envoy a year later. His exceptionally long tenure in Gaul leads one to ask why he was not replaced sooner. What made him virtually untouchable in this office? And why was this post in particular, far from the center of power, so attractive to Liberius? One explanation might be that Liberius had roots in the region, yet he seems instead to have owned lands near Rimini, where he was buried. Hence it is plausible to assume that his wife Agretia came from Provence. Liberius then would have been able to exploit economic resources and social contacts that Agretia had brought into the marriage.[72]

6. EXPANSION AND INTEGRATION
2: HISPANIA UNDER THEODERIC

After 511, Theoderic was not only king of the Goths in Italy, but also king of the Goths in Hispania. He thus succeeded his brother-in-law Alaric, who had fallen in the Battle of Vouillé in 507. He had achieved this goal not without a fight: he first drove Alaric's son Gesalec, who had been made king after his father's death, out of his kingdom and then had him eliminated when he returned with an army to claim his throne. It was not easy for Gesalec's defeated followers to accept a king completely unknown to them. Theoderic also had trounced the rights of Amalaric, Alaric's other son by his marriage to Theoderic's daughter Thiudigotho. After 511, Theoderic was the only king of the Goths in Hispania and remained so as long as he lived. What role could and should Amalaric then play? Theoderic claimed a kind of guardianship over Amalaric but did not have the youth brought to Ravenna. Amalaric remained in Hispania, perhaps in Narbonne. This arrangement was a recipe for conflict. By its very nature, guardianship is of limited duration: as soon as Alaric's son was old enough to bear arms, he could also conceivably become king, both in the eyes of those around him and in his own.[73]

Theoderic had fused the conquered territory on the Iberian Peninsula to his Italian kingdom, including Provence, by a kind of personal union. The year 511 was thus considered the first year of Theoderic's reign in Hispania. Whether the two kingdoms might be separated again remained an open question. Hispania was also not placed under the newly appointed praetorian prefect of Gaul; Septimania was already outside Liberius' jurisdiction. It is hard to determine the full extent of Theoderic's Visigothic kingdom. It stretched at least as far as southwestern France, to Aquitania and Septimania. Where exactly the border with the Frankish kings ran shifted and can scarcely be determined now. The borders of Gothic rule in Hispania are even hazier. That is partly a consequence of the scarcity of our sources but also a reflection of the fact that the Visigothic conquest of the Iberian Peninsula—not to mention the organization of its administration—was by no means complete when Theoderic's general Ibba crossed the Pyrenees. From the surviving accounts, which amount to a handful of lines, earlier scholars constructed a consolidated Visigothic kingdom in Hispania that covered the entire peninsula. In reality, the conquest of the Iberian Peninsula had only just begun under Alaric's predecessor, Euric. The Visigothic king Theoderic II (453–466) had confined the kingdom of the Suebi in the northwest of the peninsula and forced them to recognize his suzerainty: King Rechimund agreed to be adopted as Theoderic's son-in-arms in 465, but the Suebi still had their own king until 585. Euric's generals had conquered the cities in the northeast and had penetrated southwest as far as Mérida, where a military commander was installed. Large parts of the country, however, still lay outside his control. The area south of the Guadalquivir (Baetis) had lacked a central authority for a long time. The conquered territory first began to be consolidated under Alaric II. The process was centered around the province of Tarraconensis and suffered several setbacks. The *Chronicle of Zaragoza* laconically lists rebellions that probably took place in this territory. The same chronicle reports for the year 494 that the Goths seized possession of the province of

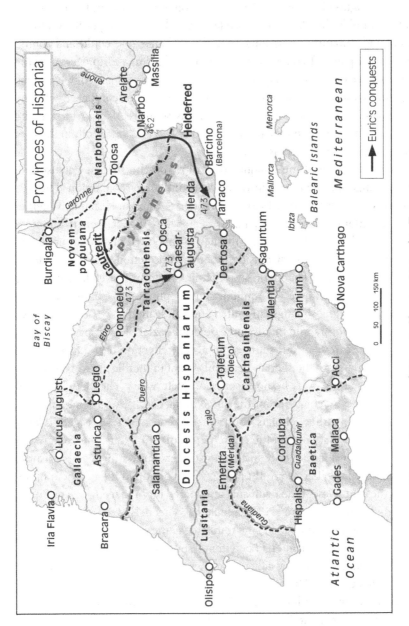

Map 13. Provinces of Hispania Showing Visigothic Expansion.

Hispania and for the year 497 that they received dwellings there. These meager remarks are the basis of the widespread assumption that a wave of Visigothic immigration commenced in northeastern Hispania in the wake of Euric's campaigns of conquest. The form and scale of this immigration, however, are entirely unknown. The mass exodus of population groups presumably began after the defeat to Clovis and lasted for decades. Procopius reports that many Goths migrated from Aquitania to Hispania after 531.[74]

Hispania in 500 was plagued by violence and lacked an organizational center. The institutions of the late Roman regional and provincial administration had vanished in the wars and civil wars of the last quarter of the fifth century. The peninsula was divided into five provinces at the beginning of the fifth century: Tarraconensis in the northeast, with its capital of Tarraco (Tarragona); Carthaginiensis in the southwest, with its capital of Carthago Nova (Cartagena); Baetica in the south, with its capital of Corduba; Lusitania in the southwest, with its capital of Augusta Emerita (Mérida); and Gallaecia in the northwest, with its capital of Bracara (Braga). Together with the province of Tingitana in western Morocco, these five provinces comprised the diocese of Hispaniae, which was in turn part of the late antique praetorian prefecture of Gaul. The Spanish diocese was headed by a *vicarius Hispaniarum* whose headquarters was located in Mérida, like that of the governor of Lusitania. These complex offices with their specialized personnel disintegrated as the Roman central administration lost control of the Iberian Peninsula; there is no evidence of any Roman civil official in Hispania after 420. The Suebian king Rechila resided at Mérida after 439. After that, the late Roman provincial organization was of interest only to the Catholic Church. The official districts of Visigothic "governors" were much smaller and, insofar as they were defined in spatial terms at all, probably coincided with the territory of cities; these officials were called *comites civitatis*. Alaric's law code was intended for their use.[75]

As the Roman imperial superstructure collapsed, cities became autonomous centers of power. Whoever wanted to rule the land had to control them. But cities were also worth possessing because in them local elites still accumulated and invested considerable wealth, generated primarily by agriculture. As in Italy, their estates were worked predominantly by small tenant farmers who were subject to legal limitations on their personal freedom but were not chattel slaves. Economic activity was not uniformly high in every part of the country. The range and volume of commerce declined in the interior. Urban elites there grew poor; not a few places lost their urban character or were abandoned entirely. Coastal regions facing the Mediterranean, in contrast, remained linked to transregional trade; cities like Barcelona and Cartagena continued to function as economic centers. The same is largely true of cities in major river valleys, like Tarragona on the Ebro and Mérida on the Guadiana. In Tarragona, the theater, circus, and forum were abandoned in the fifth century, but city walls and several churches were built in return. At Mérida, the damaged bridge over the Anas (Guadiana) was repaired and the fortifications reinforced; churches also were built inside and outside the walls. It is not clear when the much smaller city of Toledo, located at the intersection of important commercial routes, fell under Gothic rule; the city is not attested as a royal residence until decades after Theoderic's death.[76]

Theoderic adapted the civil administration of Hispania only superficially to the structure he had found in Italy. That is reflected not least by the fact that the royal chancellery called Theoderic's entire Iberian domain the "province of Hispania" (*provincia Hispaniae*). That would have hardly been possible if the term "province" still designated a subordinate administrative unit. We can detect only three officials who held prominent administrative posts for Theoderic in Hispania: Theudis, the *vir spectabilis* Liwirit, and the *vir illustris* Ampelius. Theudis was an Ostrogoth who commanded Theoderic's army on the Iberian Peninsula; when he replaced Ibba in this function is unknown. He also retained a kind of private army, 2,000 men strong. According to Jordanes, Theoderic made him Amalaric's "guardian" (*tutor*).

Ampelius and Liwirit jointly received two letters from Theoderic that permit inferences about their responsibilities. Ampelius presided over trials as judge and oversaw the collection of taxes. He thus performed duties that had previously fallen to the *vicarius Hispaniarum*, but he did not serve as an intermediary official between provincial governors and the praetorian prefect. Ampelius, who was a Roman on the evidence of his name, apparently held a position in Hispania similar to that of Liberius in Provence. Like the latter, he answered only to the king and, also like Liberius, he intervened directly in civic affairs with the help of his subordinates. Ampelius had a staff of officials at his disposal (*compulsores*) who collected outstanding tax debts when the civic tax collectors (*exactores*) fell short. He could also utilize the state courier service (*cursus publicus*), for which subjects had to provide horses. Whether Ampelius held the title of *praefectus praetorio* like Liberius, however, is uncertain. A prefect for the province of Hispania is attested for the first and only time a few years after Theoderic's death. It thus is quite conceivable that Theoderic conferred on Ampelius the traditional title of *vicarius*. Liwirit has a Gothic name and was responsible for the administration of the royal domains in Hispania, which were let out to major leaseholders. He appears to have directed the Hispanic division of the *patrimonium* and may have held the title of *vicedominus*.[77]

The tax administration seems to have functioned more or less successfully in the heartland of the province of Hispania. Cadasters and tax registers (*polypticha publica*) were maintained. The most important tax was levied on arable land, but transit and export duties were also collected. Revenue flowed into a special treasury of the king, called the *cubiculum*, part of which was transferred to Italy. The Spanish possessions were thus profitable over the long term.

Things of course looked different from the perspective of tax-paying subjects. In a letter that Theoderic sent to Ampelius and Liwirit in the last years of his reign, we find a veritable litany of abuses that stemmed from victims' complaints. The king explains he had been informed that many people in the province of Hispania had lost their lives over trivial disputes, and he orders the addressees to travel across the entire province (*per universam Hispaniam*) and severely punish murderers and thieves. They likewise should force major leaseholders to pay their rent in full, stop mint workers (*monetarii*) from enriching themselves, and prevent estate stewards (*vilici*) from making people their dependent clients against their will. Goths stationed in the cities, who had been sent to Hispania "to fight for freedom," were to stop demanding that free people perform menial labor. Above all, however, the king lists a multitude of crimes that harmed his tax-paying subjects: the use of defective weights and measures, the unauthorized requisition of courier horses, excessive demands for duties and taxes. According to his information, more was being taken from the provincials than what was paid into the exchequer of the royal bedchamber (*cubiculum*). Theoderic ordered them to carefully review tax obligations and to reduce them to the amount that had been collected in the reigns of Alaric and Euric. Cassiodorus included this letter in the *Variae* because he wanted to show how far Theoderic's power reached and especially because he wanted to paint a picture of a king who cared for all his subjects, no matter how far away they were from his residence. Indeed, late Roman emperors regularly found themselves obliged to take action against abuses just like those that Theoderic attests for Hispania. The number, variety, and countrywide pervasiveness of the crimes, however, are unusual—particularly in light of the fact that the letter was not addressed to some public audience but rather was intended as an official communication. If Ampelius and Liwirit took the king's instructions seriously, the thought of how they should carry them out must have filled them with dismay and concern.[78]

Theoderic gave the Catholic Church in Hispania the same freedom of action that Alaric had granted it. Ecclesiastical jurisdiction (*episcopalis audientia*) was also not curtailed. In contrast to Alaric, however, Theoderic had no intention of organizing the Catholic bishops in Hispania and Gaul into a kind of national church. Only provincial synods still took place under Theoderic. The bishops of the province of Tarraconensis met for synods in 516 and 517, over which the bishop of Tarragona presided. The first council met in Tarragona itself, the second one in Gerona. The participating bishops discussed questions of church discipline and liturgy. The proceedings are dated according to the Western Roman consuls and Theoderic's regnal years in Hispania but otherwise make no explicit reference to the distant king. That need not mean that the bishops neglected to include the homoean king in their prayers: the proceedings of a provincial synod that took place in Toledo in 531 end with a prayer for divine mercy for "our glorious lord, King Amalaric, asking that in the innumerable years of his reign, he may grant us the freedom to do everything concerning the practice of the faith."[79]

The political union of Hispania and Italy prevented the church of Hispania from splitting off as a separate regional church and paved the way for its orientation toward Rome. Theoderic would have been well aware of that as well. In early 517, a bishop named John from the province of Carthaginiensis informed Pope Hormisdas by letter that he would soon visit and asked him for his support. Hormisdas answered on April 2, 517, with a letter to John himself and two more addressed "to all bishops of Hispania." He appointed John his vicar for Hispania and instructed him to monitor whether ecclesiastical rules (*canones*) were being observed and to report back to the Apostolic See. Hormisdas' decision, however, was in no way received with unanimous agreement by the bishops of Hispania. Sallustius of Seville, the metropolitan of the province of Baetica, informed the pope that one of his predecessors, Pope Simplicius (468–483), had already conferred the apostolic vicariate in Hispania on the metropolitan of Seville. Hormisdas, who had overlooked this, corrected his mistake in 519 by dividing the vicariate between the two bishops: Sallustius would be responsible for the provinces of Baetica and Lusitania; John, for Carthaginiensis. The curia does not seem to have troubled itself as to how that squared with the vicariate of Caesarius of Arles. When Theoderic's Mediterranean kingdom fell apart at his death, the question lost its practical significance. Hormisdas informed his colleagues in Hispania about the resolution of the schism between Rome and Constantinople in 521. After that, correspondence breaks off for two generations.[80]

It is remarkable that Theoderic's rule in Hispania was never openly contested before his death. Since the king never visited the Iberian Peninsula, personal ties between him and his Visigothic subjects existed only in exceptional cases. The Goths in Hispania obeyed a king whom they knew only by hearsay. They had not taken part in his victories; on the contrary, at least some of them had been defeated by one of Theoderic's generals. The Visigothic warriors thus felt hardly the same allegiance to Theoderic as did the Goths in Italy. To the Visigothic nobility, the geographical distance from the king meant that they had little chance of enjoying the king's generosity and patronage, and they were almost completely excluded from the contests for power at court. Confident noblemen could hardly stay satisfied with this state of affairs forever. They had had their own king and their own royal court until then. The Visigothic nobility, however, also had much more autonomy than its Ostrogothic counterpart. Armed retinues were commonplace. The fact that Theudis kept 2,000 men in his service was remarkable only for their great number. This institution was explicitly recognized in the Code of Euric around 475.[81]

What bound the Goths in Hispania to their king in Ravenna? Obviously, Theoderic had an army stationed in Hispania. Some of the warriors whom Ibba led across the Pyrenees presumably never returned to Italy. Some had their families follow them; others married Visigothic women. But the military presence is not a sufficient explanation, especially since we can presume that the Ostrogoths who settled permanently in Hispania developed local identities and interests over the years; that, at any rate, is precisely what one contemporary, Procopius, claims. Theudis married a rich Roman woman from a senatorial family and acquired extensive landholdings in Hispania. It is also attested that Theoderic distributed a portion of the tax revenue that he received from Hispania among the Visigothic warriors. The Goths in Hispania, like the Goths in Italy, were thus the beneficiaries of the organized redistribution of resources. But they received only part of the taxes collected on the Iberian Peninsula. The rest went to the Goths in Italy. Things were different when the Visigoths had a king of their own: under Alaric, only the Goths who lived in Hispania and Gaul had benefited from the king's generosity. Perhaps some of them took the disappearance of their own monarchy better after Theoderic had a Visigoth living in Hispania, Eutharic, brought to his court and systematically began to build him up as his designated heir. Eutharic married Theoderic's daughter Amalasuintha in 515 and held the consulship of 519 jointly with the Byzantine emperor Justin. That seemed to guarantee that the ties between the two Gothic kingdoms would outlive Theoderic, but Eutharic died before him.[82]

Even after his plan for the succession fell apart, Theoderic maintained his claim to Hispania until his own death. That is proved not only by the two letters to Ampelius and Liwirit, which date to the last years of his reign; the fact that it was Theoderic's successor who returned the royal treasure of the Visigoths, which had been brought to Ravenna, speaks for itself. For Theoderic, keeping the Visigothic treasure (at least what had not fallen into the hands of the Franks) was a kind of protection against usurpations: anyone who wanted to be recognized as king needed a "treasure," an impressive collection of gold, silver, and gems. But ambition and reality stood even further apart in Hispania than in any other part of Theoderic's kingdom. The collection of taxes and duties seems to have functioned well at least in the northeast of the kingdom, and that also appears to be true of the administration of the royal domains. But Theoderic's officials were apparently unable to keep the peace. In particular, the longer Theudis held on to his command in Hispania, the more he acted like his own master. Procopius reports that Theoderic did not dare to depose Theudis because he feared that the Visigoths would rise up against him. It was for that reason that the noblest Ostrogoths wrote to Theudis on Theoderic's behalf, asking him to come to Ravenna. Theudis continued to pay tribute to Theoderic but refused to leave Hispania. In fact, Theudis—unlike Liberius—never saw Italy again. After Theoderic's death, Theudis served Amalaric, who received the kingdom in Hispania while Athalaric succeeded their common grandfather in Italy. When Amalaric was killed by his own men in 531 after a defeat against Childebert's Franks, Theudis seized the crown himself; he ruled until 548 as the third and final king of the Visigoths of Ostrogothic background.[83]

9

A "GOLDEN AGE"? ITALY UNDER GOTHIC RULE

1. RURAL SOCIETIES: ECOLOGY AND DEMOGRAPHY

The Roman elites of Gothic Italy lived in cities, even though they might have spent part of the year on their rural estates. Their economic power, however, stemmed from landed property holdings: they owned the land and collected rent. The economic relationship between city and country was thus close but unequal: the wealth that was consumed in the city derived overwhelmingly from agricultural production. The vast majority of the population, however, lived on the land and was engaged in food production. City and country were also linked by virtue of the fact that the land was always assigned to a city as its territory and governed from there. Municipal officials collected the taxes that the rural population was obligated to pay. The people who lived in the countryside and whose labor made ancient culture possible, however, are elusive in our sources. The peasants of late antique Italy, no matter whether free men or slaves, landowners or tenants, did not leave behind written testimony of their own. What once existed, primarily letters and lease agreements, has been completely lost. Archeology can fill this gap only to a limited extent because the rural settlements of Late Antiquity have been researched only for about the past thirty years. This research has produced information about settlement forms and land use, but it gives scant insight into social relations. Insofar as we can glimpse life in the countryside at all, we see it from the perspective of the landowners, who lived off the rent that their free and unfree tenants paid, or from the perspective of the state, which looked after the rural population because it could tax the land only if it was being worked.

Be that as it may, written sources for the agrarian history of late antique Italy are still richer than those for many other parts of the Roman and post-Roman

West. Since the land tax was also the most important source of income for Theoderic (in addition to revenue from his royal domains), the royal administration regularly addressed agricultural and rural social problems. Theoderic's *Edict* also contains a series of measures concerning rural society. The last ancient handbook about agriculture written in Latin is the fifth-century work of the *illustris* senator Palladius, who probably came from Gaul but owned several estates in Italy and presumably also lived there. Palladius composed a kind of "farmer's almanac" that follows the months of the year; in it, he gives a detailed description of the components of an estate and instructions for working the fields in every season. The most information about the management of large estates, however, comes from the papal chancellery. There also are legal documents (usually donations or sales and wills) that have survived in the original or in copies.[1]

On account of the small number and narrow perspective of the sources, key aspects of rural life are virtually invisible in the written sources. These gaps can be closed in part by applying data collected in other contexts to late antique Italy. This approach presumes, of course, that there are good reasons for believing that similar conditions prevailed in the two societies being compared. This assumption seems justified, for instance, if we inquire about life expectancy. For premodern societies, we generally can assume high child mortality. Life expectancy at birth was between twenty and thirty years; it may have been somewhat higher for men than for women. Thirty percent of newborns died within the first year of life; almost half did not survive past the age of ten. Anyone who survived childhood sicknesses had a good chance of living to the age of fifty or older. Average life expectancy for a twenty-year-old adult was approximately fifty years.

These shocking numbers can easily be explained: diets were usually unbalanced—people mostly ate bread and other dishes prepared from cereals—and food was often insufficient. There was no protection against bacteria and viruses and no way to cure infectious diseases. Other pathogens such as insects, worms, and parasites had free rein. Hence epidemics constantly broke out, and many people in cities and the countryside suffered from chronic diseases. Malaria seems to have been endemic in some parts of Italy: in the Pontine Marshes, Tuscany, the Roman Campagna, and the city of Rome itself. Late antique estate owners took this fact of life into account. Palladius advised his peers to scrutinize the health of the inhabitants of an estate before buying it: if they had a healthy skin tone, clear eyes, undiminished hearing, and a clear voice, then the air was good. If they had lung ailments or bladder problems or if they were tormented by pain and swelling in the stomach, intestines, sides, and kidneys, then the water was bad. A shrewd agronomist refrained from a purchase under such circumstances. In societies in which death occurred so frequently and so soon, family planning was attended by great risks; because of the high mortality rate, many births were necessary to ensure the survival of a family (and with it, care for the parents in old age). A large number of children, however, became a burden when food was scarce, as normally was the case for peasant families.[2]

Late antique Italy was also a premodern agrarian society insofar as yields depended primarily on natural factors: the quality of the soil, the water supply, the climate, and the weather. Palladius explains that one had to take four factors into account in choosing a field and then profitably cultivating it: "air, water, soil, and diligence. Three of these are determined by nature; one is a matter of ability and will." Without artificial fertilizers, crop yields could be increased only with intensive labor and within narrow limits; it was extremely difficult to protect crops effectively against pests without pesticides. Natural conditions also were extremely varied. The well-watered Po Valley, for example, is unsuitable for cultivating olives but ideal for grain and wine. In light of the many rivers and lakes, fresh-water fishing was also important. The foothills of the Alps provide rich summer pastures for sheep, goats, and cattle. The chain of the Apennines, however, impedes commerce between east and west and creates many small settlement pockets. Almost every settlement lay within sight of the mountains, which were used as summer pastures. In mid-fall, large flocks were driven down from the hilly regions to winter in the coastal plains of Apulia. The climate is subtropical in the north, with cool winters and hot, damp summers; it is Mediterranean in the south, with mild winters and hot, dry summers. This difference, however, tells us little about specific local conditions. The ecological range of the peasant economy was narrow: people lived and labored in a micro-region with a distinct climate, water resources, soil type, and accessibility to people and animals. Then within this framework, a field's location, water supply, soil quality, and utilization were also all major factors. This variety translated into a wide range of ecological risks; crop failure on account of drought or hail, livestock epidemics, and pest infestations constantly occurred but seldom affected an entire province uniformly.[3]

All work was performed by the muscle of man or beast. There were few significant exceptions to this rule: sailboats used favorable winds; water mills used the current of flowing water. Palladius is the first agricultural author to recommend installing water mills: with their help, it was possible to grind grain without human or animal labor. The fastest method of traveling overland from one place to another was riding on horse, mule, or donkey. Pope Gregory chided the ecclesiastical estate manager on Sicily: "You gave us one bad horse and five good donkeys: I cannot ride the horse because it is bad; I cannot ride those good donkeys, though, because they are donkeys!"[4]

Whatever could not be carried was loaded onto oxcarts or pack animals. Transporting goods by land was thus slow and expensive. It has been calculated that a load of grain doubled in price if transported by cart over 300 miles. Thus transporting goods like grain, wine, and oil by land from one province to the next was not economically feasible. Even the paved roads that were still kept more or less passible at least in central Italy in Theoderic's day did not change this fact. Special care was taken of the Via Flaminia, which linked Rome to Ariminum (Rimini), and the Via Appia, which ran from Rome to Brundisium (Brindisi). Theoderic had the urban prefect Caecina Mavortius Basilius Decius repair the Decemnovium, a nineteen-mile-long (hence the name) stretch of road along a canal that ran from Tripontium to Terracina. A generation later, Procopius expressed his admiration for the paving of the Via Appia, which was still completely intact. Paved roads made it possible to travel in bad weather and to use wagons. Despite these advantages, however, travel by land was slow; only a small proportion of cities were, moreover, connected to the road network.[5] Waterways were the most important commercial arteries for that very reason. Long-distance trade thus targeted cities that lay by the sea or on navigable rivers. Cassiodorus emphasizes that the cities of Calabria were regularly supplied with goods because of their proximity to the coast: "[Bruttium] thus overflows with an abundance of its own fruits and is also filled with foreign wares on account of its proximity to the shores." In northern Italy, the Po and its tributaries were the most important transport routes. The Po Valley constituted the axis of a northern Italian trade network. The Tiber and Arno performed a similar function in Etruria and Latium. Wherever the sea or navigable rivers were far away, the transport of goods was limited to a local or, at best, regional range.[6]

2. AN EPOCHAL DEBATE: THE END OF THE SLAVE ECONOMY AND THE TRANSITION FROM ANTIQUITY TO THE MIDDLE AGES

For over a century, the development of the rural society of Italy has been at the center of debate as scholars have sought to explain the transition from the ancient slave economy to the medieval manorial system. Every discussion of the end of antiquity or the rise of feudalism as problems of social history begins with Italy because all the ancient handbooks on running an estate with slave labor — the works of Cato, Varro, and Columella — concern Italy. An economic system thrived in the early imperial period, at least south of Rome, that relied on slaves housed in barracks (*ergastula*) to mass-produce goods for the market. It was a kind of plantation economy like that of early modern Brazil, the Caribbean, and the American South. Such an estate that relied on slave labor and special-ized in wine was excavated at Settefinestre near Cosa in Etruria in the 1970s, and the findings were presented in an exemplary publication.[7]

A totally different picture emerges in the early Middle Ages. In the Carolingian period, we find large, interconnected estate complexes. A small part of them was worked by the landlord personally, while the majority were let out to peasants who worked the fields independently. These peasants were obli-gated to pay dues and perform regular services, known as corvée, several days a week on the lord's manor; hence the term "manorial system." Since the sources also use the multivalent word *villa* for such manors, scholars also call the phe-nomenon "villication" and the "villication system."

For a long time, it was thought that the manors of the Carolingian age had evolved directly from the slave plantations of the Roman Empire, a view that can still be found today. A theory formulated in 1896 by the sociologist Max Weber (1864–1920) was very influential. When Rome stopped waging wars that led to territorial gains, the supply of slaves dried up. Roman slave plantations, however, needed a constant supply of slaves from outside because labor condi-tions there left little room or opportunity for raising children. Since the money economy and long-distance trade declined to the point of insignificance over the course of the imperial period, however, a different method of production ultimately won out that met the needs of the landlords while also ensuring the reproduction of their laborers: the early medieval manorial system. An autar-chic natural economy established itself on the manors.[8]

In a posthumous essay published in 1947, the medieval historian Marc Bloch (1886–1944), the founder of the French "Annales" historical school, also inter-preted the manors of the Carolingian age as the direct descendants of the slave plantations of the Roman imperial period. Like Weber, Bloch believed that the decline of the supply of slaves was a factor that led to the abandonment of the plantation system. Bloch, however, emphasized the economic rationalism of the peasant economy. Above all, he reversed the historical perspective: whereas Weber had inquired about the "social reasons for the end of ancient culture," the medievalist Bloch was interested primarily in explaining the rise of a class of peasants who were obligated to pay dues and perform corvée yet were still considered free men. In his view, these peasants were predominantly former slaves who had been manumitted on the condition that they owed their masters these dues and services.[9]

The Anglo-American ancient historian Moses Finley (1912–1986) joined this interpretive tradition in 1980. He was searching for the answer to the question of how and why the typical form of organized labor in classical Greece and early imperial Italy (normally, chattel slavery) vanished. Finley also dated the proliferation of dependent peasants to the Later Roman Empire and attributed it to the decline of the supply of prisoners of war. He stressed, however, that the demand for chattel slaves had also declined as petty farmers slipped into initially economic dependence on and then into legally sanctioned subservience to large landowners. In Late Antiquity, therefore, unfree peasants who were bound to the soil, whom Finely designated with the ambiguous word *coloni*, took over the role once played by chattel slaves. The "colonate" thus replaced the plantation economy as the dominant form of production (see below). Starting from Marxist premises, the English ancient historian Geoffrey de Ste.-Croix (1910–2000) arrived almost simultaneously at similar conclusions to Finley's: as the supply of prisoners of war dried up, they were replaced by dependent peasants who had once worked the land as free tenants. De Ste.-Croix viewed this phenomenon as a medium-term consequence of poor citizens' loss of the right of political participation.[10]

In the last thirty years, however, scholarly debate has shown that this model is based on false premises, even though part of the scholarly community still stubbornly defends it. For one thing, there is no evidence that the number of slaves dramatically declined in Late Antiquity, at least not in proportion to the total population, which was probably smaller overall than it had been in the early imperial period. At best, for want of statistical evidence, we can only roughly estimate the number of slaves in late antique Italy, just like the size of the total population itself, which amounted perhaps to one million people. But the sources also reveal that agricultural work was frequently performed by slaves in Late Antiquity; the sources, moreover, show that this legal status, which was typical of the rural economy of central and southern Italy in the early imperial period, had spread evenly across late antique Italy. Slavery thus was not only ubiquitous in Italy in Theoderic's day, but it also was a significant factor in the rural economy insofar as many farmers were legally slaves. For another thing, there is no evidence that free or unfree tenants were obligated to perform labor on their landlords' estates regularly to any notable degree. The only known example concerns estates owned by the church of Ravenna; these, as far as we can tell, were located on the territory off Padua. This case from the mid-sixth century, however, cannot be generalized. In other words, the rural economy of late antique Italy was not characterized by manorialism.[11]

Agrarian conditions in late antique Italy exhibit a distinct form that differs from both the production system based on chattel slavery of the early and high imperial period and from the early medieval manorial system. It is characterized, on the one hand, by a concentration of landed property in the hands of the

upper classes, even though small, independent peasant farmers had not completely disappeared. This concentration of landed property, however, which
was probably higher than that of the earlier imperial period, was accompanied
by the decentralization of production: large landholdings now normally did not
constitute a single operation under central management but rather were dispersed and divided into many small farmsteads that were worked autonomously
by free and unfree tenants. The basic unit of production thus was the peasant
family, which leased the land and paid the landlord a portion of the yield, drawing on the support of day laborers or permanent servants according to need and
resources. From an economic perspective, a tenant differed from a peasant
owner merely by virtue of the fact that he was obligated to pay rent (and both
statuses could also obviously be combined). It thus was a type of peasant economy like the system first analyzed in the 1920s by the Russian economist
Alexander Chayanov (Tschajanow).[12]

3. "SLAVES OF THE SOIL": THE LEGAL STATUS, MODE OF PRODUCTION, AND SOCIAL STANDING OF PEASANTS

To give this abstract model visible contours, we must differentiate three fac-
ets of the peasant economy: first, the organization of labor and the economic
framework; second, social conditions, which were determined by multiple factors and thus subject to subtle nuances; and third, legal status, which the state
defined by normative acts. We will begin with the legal status of peasant farmers.

Roman law drew a strict distinction between freedom and slavery. A slave
(*servus*) was equivalent to an object; he was not a person who could claim public or private rights. Cassiodorus thus poses the rhetorical question, "What
should public law have had to do with slaves, who did not even have legal per-
sonhood [*persona*]?" Slaves were subject to the virtually unlimited power of
their masters, who could sell, rent, or punish their slaves as they pleased. This
power extended to the offspring of slaves: the children of a slave mother were
slaves themselves. Although the cohabitation of slaves (*contubernium*) was tolerated, it was not recognized as marriage (*matrimonium*) and did not produce
any legal claims under family law. The children of slaves were treated as if they
were not related to their parents. What a slave acquired as his own "special
property" (*peculium*) with his master's blessing remained the latter's property in
the event of the slave's death. The church also recognized the legal barrier
between free persons and slaves: a slave could not join the clergy unless his
master first manumitted him.[13]

These principles remained in force in Theoderic's kingdom and were reiterated in his *Edict*. The enslavement of a free person was a serious crime. Anyone who held a free person in bondage but could not prove that he was indeed legally a slave could be prosecuted for slander (*calumnia*) and injury (*iniuria*). Anyone who kidnapped someone (*plagium*) to sell into slavery or to use as one's own slave faced the death penalty. If a relationship between a free person and a slave produced children, the mother's legal status was decisive: as noted, the children of a slave woman were slaves, no matter what the legal status of the father was. Since a slave was equivalent to an object under Roman law, it was up to the slave owner whether the killing of one of his slaves would be prosecuted under criminal law or not. Theoderic's *Edict* gave him the choice between a criminal trial and a civil suit for damages: "If another person's slave or peasant is killed by someone, his master has the option either to proceed with criminal charges over the death of his dependent and accuse the murderer of a capital crime or to file a civil suit for damages from the lost slave such that he should receive two such slaves in return for the one slain."[14] The fundamental distinction between freedom and slavery by no means meant that every legally free Roman was recognized as entitled to freedom of movement and freedom of profession. Soldiers, municipal council members (decurions, curials), and craftsmen were obligated to perform specific duties (*munera*) for the state; to prevent these men from evading these obligations, the late antique state declared membership in these classes of people hereditary. Similar considerations played a crucial part in the creation of an institution known as the "colonate" among modern scholars. (This term is derived from the Latin word *colonus*, which could mean any farmer or peasant and did not indicate a specific legal status.) As the Roman state began to levy a land tax that took into account the number of people who cultivated a unit of land in addition to its size and yield, the rural population came to be recorded in tax registers. Tenants who owned no land of their own were registered under the name of the owner of the land together with his estates; tenants who also owned land of their own, in contrast, were registered under their own names with their own land.

To maintain this taxation system, the state had to prevent the people registered for a specific property from escaping their tax liability by moving elsewhere. Beginning with Constantine the Great, the Roman emperors issued a series of laws that were predicated on the rule that peasants (*coloni*) were not permitted to leave their farmsteads: "Although they may appear freeborn [*ingenui*] according to their legal status, they nonetheless should be categorized as slaves of the soil [*servi terrae*] on which they were born," reads one law from the year 393. This legislation gradually produced the hereditary legal status of peasants "bound to the soil," which was first juridically systematized under Emperor Justinian. People with this status were legally free yet simultaneously tied to the land that they had leased. Such peasants were called (*coloni*) *adscripticii*, because their names had been "added in writing" (*adscripti*) to the tax registers, or (*coloni*) *originarii*, because they were forbidden to leave the place where they were registered, their *origo*. As noted above, this legislation was motivated by fiscal considerations: the state restricted the freedom of movement of free tenants so that it could tax them. But the emperors were merely ratifying in law what was already an existing practice in certain regions of the empire. Binding tenants to the soil was in the interest of large landholders because it prevented tenants from leaving their leaseholdings when better conditions presented themselves elsewhere. Such alternatives always appeared when labor was in short supply. Vice versa, this legislation also limited the power of landlords and protected tenants from being chased off their land after the expiration of their lease contract.[15]

Over time, the legal status of *coloni* approached that of slaves, as late Roman legislation inclined to subject peasants bound to the soil (*originarii*) to the same punishments established for slaves. That of course was true of the lower classes generally since the status of citizen had become virtually meaningless after it was extended to (nearly) every free inhabitant of the Roman Empire in the early third century. Merely being a Roman citizen no longer sufficed to justify equal treatment before the law. In criminal law, a distinction was drawn between upper-class citizens (*honestiores*, "more respectable ones") and lower-class citizens (*humiliores*, "humbler ones") according to their social prestige.

Theoderic's *Edict* mentions peasants bound to the soil in the same breath as slaves; after all, both groups of people were in a hereditary relationship of subjugation to a master, whom they could escape only by running away. The editors of the *Edict*, for example, inserted the word *colonus*, meaning a peasant bound to the soil, next to *servus* in a law of Constantine the Great that was dedicated to the crime of harboring fugitive slaves:

> Whosoever knowingly harbors or hides a fugitive slave [*servus*] or *colonus* belonging to someone else, he shall return the fugitive to his master with his wares and personal property [*peculium*], as well as a second [slave or *colonus*] of the same value. But if the person who had harbored the fugitive decides to do so a second or third time, he shall hand over three others to his master in addition to the fugitive himself. So that the chattel slave [*mancipium*] was not cunningly and treacherously sent by his master to the house of the person who harbored him so as to make a profit, the slave himself must be tortured during the investigation: if the interrogation of the presiding

investigator reveals that he was fraudulently sent to another's house by his master, he shall immediately be confiscated to the benefit of the fiscus.[16]

Knowingly harboring a fugitive *colonus* was accordingly penalized in the same way as for a fugitive slave: if someone harbored such a person in his third attempt to flee, the guilty party had to surrender three people of the same status to the fugitive's master. Theoderic did not resolve the conceptual tension between personal freedom and one's being bound to the soil by formally declaring *coloni* to be slaves. Instead, this fundamental distinction lived on in Theoderic's kingdom. In his *Edict*, Theoderic explicitly recognized the legal capacity of soil-bound peasants in a critical area to them: in the event of crop theft, both the landowner and his tenant could initiate a trial.[17]

In economic terms, the rural economy of late antique Italy is marked by a high concentration of landed property in few hands, decentralized production, a market orientation, and monetarization. Of course, all these statements merely indicate basic tendencies and as such are in need of qualification. Even though the greater, more valuable part of the land undoubtedly lay in the hands of the elite, peasant land ownership never disappeared. We cannot quantify the extent and importance of peasant land ownership or determine its regional distribution, but the sources give the impression that small and middling peasant farmers with their own land still held their own in late antique Italy. Peasant farmers may be mentioned only occasionally in the sixth century, but it is significant that Cassiodorus preserves a *formula* for remitting the taxes owed by the owner of a single homestead (*casa*) if he can prove that it produced less than his personal tax liability.[18]

The richest man in Gothic Italy was the king: his property stretched across the entire peninsula and Sicily. After him came senators with the rank of *illustris*, who also owned estates in many provinces. Quintus Aurelius Symmachus, consul in 391, owned estates and villas in central and southern Italy, Sicily, and North Africa. When the senatorial matron Melania the Younger decided to adopt an ascetic lifestyle together with her husband Pinianus, she sold landed estates in Italy, Sicily, North Africa, and Britain. When the Western Roman Empire shrank to Italy, Italian senators lost properties that were now located in the territory of Germanic kings. But Italian senators still possessed very extensive landed property in Theoderic's day, normally extending over several provinces. Important episcopal sees like Rome and Milan were also major landowners.[19]

Our information about the administration of private landholdings almost exclusively pertains to senators, court officials, high-ranking military commanders, and the Roman Church. We rarely catch a glimpse of landowners from among the municipal elite. Large landholdings consisted of units called *fundi*. The size, composition, and yield of a single *fundus* varied widely; attested annual revenues range from 20 to 400 *solidi*. A *fundus* normally comprised several homesteads (*casae*) that usually did not make up a self-contained complex. A *fundus* thus was not an economic unit but rather an administrative one. In some cases, a manor may have served primarily as the administrative center of a *fundus* and of course could also be used as a country residence when the owner visited. Palladius describes such a manor, which should have granaries and a wine cellar, a wine and oil press, stables for horses and cattle, apiaries and aviaries, a threshing floor, and, if possible, a water mill. A manor should also have baths for the owner's convenience. Above all, though, a manor such as the one Palladius describes provided a place for storing dues paid in kind, although some limited home industry was also anticipated.[20]

The largest part of a *fundus* consisted of farmsteads that were let out to tenants. Such farmsteads were called *casae*. If the tenants sold their produce at market, they paid their rent in gold coins. Otherwise—and this may have been the norm—they delivered a certain portion of their crops, which were stored at the manor and sold later. The manager of the *fundus* was required to pay a fixed sum of gold coins to the landlord. For this reason, the value of a *fundus* was indicated by its yearly revenue in gold coins. The greatest landowners grouped their *fundi* in an overarching unit called a *massa* (plural: *massae*). Such *massae fundorum* placed widely scattered and disconnected properties under a single administration. One *massa* of the church of Rome located on the territory of Signia (Segni) in Latium comprised no fewer than thirty-one *fundi*; another on the Via Appia comprised only ten. Before her spectacular conversion, Melania owned no fewer than forty villages (*villae*) in Campania, all of which were part of one and the same estate complex. Four hundred slaves to work the fields (*servi agricultures*) lived in each of these villages, her biographer claims.[21]

The management of such extensive properties was very complex. Lauricius, who was once the high chamberlain of Emperor Honorius, living in semi-retirement in Ravenna after the emperor's death, owned three *massae fundorum* on Sicily, the yearly revenue of which was assessed at 756, 500, and 445 gold coins, and he also owned three more individual *fundi*; all together, the annual rent owed him amounted to 2,175 *solidi*. Lauricius let these complexes of estates out to large-scale leaseholders or contractors (*conductores*): the *massa Fadilliana* to just one, the *massa Emporitana* to two, and the *massa Cassiana* to three, one of whom was also involved in the general lease for the *massa Emporitana*. Lauricius also had agents oversee his possessions on Sicily. Lauricius put a court official, the (*notarius et*) *tribunus* Pyrrhus, in charge of these agents to act as a kind of business manager (*procurator*) responsible for all his Sicilian estates. Pyrrhus, however, proved unable to meet expectations; he returned to Ravenna and reported to Lauricius that he had been unable to collect the rent for the years 444–445 and 445–446 in full; instead of 6,150 *solidi* (including arrears from earlier years), he delivered only 4,216 *solidi* to his master. Thereupon, the contractor Sisinnius, who had also come to Ravenna, was given the task of collecting the outstanding rent. We do not know whether Sisinnius proved equal to his task.[22]

Another far-flung, albeit less lucrative, complex of properties emerges from a donation that was also drafted in Ravenna in 489: King Odoacer had promised Pierius, the commander of his bodyguard, land valued at 690 *solidi*, and he initially awarded him the island of Melite (Mljet) in Dalmatia, which brought a revenue of 200 *solidi*, and land from the *massa Pyramitana* in the territory of Syracuse, valued at 450 *solidi* annually. Since that was still 40 *solidi* shy of the full 690, Pierius again approached Odoacer, who finally gave him the *fundus Aemilianus* from the same *massa Pyramitana*, the outstanding part of the *fundus Dubli*, and part of the *fundus Putaxiae*.[23]

The landed property of Theodahad, Theoderic's nephew, was concentrated in Etruria. He allegedly had seized most of the estates there, leading to numerous lawsuits against him. After the death of his mother, Amalafrida, he even received part of the *massae* that had made up her *patrimonium*. Theodahad's agents were charged with executing this bequest. A certain Theodosius served as the head of the entire household (*maior domus*?). We can measure the profitability of these estates from the fact that Theodahad asked Justinian for an annual pension of 1,200 pounds of gold to resettle in Constantinople; that amounted to 86,400 *solidi*. In the early fifth century, the Greek historian Olympiodorus had cited the same amount as the income of a moderately wealthy Roman senator.[24]

Senators and other major landowners normally let out such estate complexes to major leaseholders for a fixed payment. These contractors then collected the rent from the small tenants on individual farmsteads. For the owners, this process had the advantage of freeing them from personal involvement in the operations of their estates while guaranteeing them a fixed income; by the same token, it had the disadvantage that they could not profit from price increases on produce that occurred, for instance, because of crop failures. For that reason, landowners secured themselves a right of first purchase, so they could sell produce from the estates locally through agents (*actores* or *procuratores*), if it was advantageous to do so.[25]

Major leaseholders were influential personalities who might possess considerable wealth. At the same time, however, they were not always free men: some were slaves. Pope Gelasius declared void the will of a slave of the church of

Rome who was also a large leaseholder on the grounds that, first, as a slave he was incapable of making a will and, second, he moreover owed significant sums to the church; if he died, his property should go to his sons, who would take over his lease and become liable for their father's debts. Agents came predominantly from the ranks of slaves, although Palladius warns masters against entrusting such tasks to a favorite because one ran the risk of letting such a slave get away with too much. This juxtaposition of free and unfree in the management of large operations is an especially vivid reflection of the fact that one's legal and social statuses might vastly differ.[26]

Farmsteads were integrated into the market both vertically and horizontally. On the one hand, part of the yield had to be paid as rent. Peasants normally delivered this portion to the leaseholders. The latter in turn sold the crops to obtain the money that they owed the landowners as general rent. They sold the crops either at local or regional markets or to specialized large-scale traders (*negotiatores*). That was why the major leaseholders of royal estates in Apulia requested that their rent be reduced after the Byzantine fleet attacked the Adriatic coast: the profits they might have made from trade had shrunken because the grain had been burned in enemy raids. The royal administration commissioned large-scale traders to buy provisions for the army and court; when those in Apulia and Calabria complained that they were being forced to pay an additional commission in cash (*interpretium*) even though they had delivered the agreed amount of grain to the praetorian prefecture, Theoderic brusquely chastised the praetorian prefect Faustus Niger: if the grain delivered by the traders was insufficient, his officials should sell it themselves and make the money that way. During the war in Gaul, the king ordered the ship owners (*navicularii*) of Campania, Lucania, and Etruria to transport food to Gaul and sell it there at market prices.[27]

Not a few of these ship owners may have also controlled extensive landholdings. Landowners also traded high-volume products like grain, wine, and oil while they had administrators manage their local businesses. Since major estate leaseholders maintained their own granaries, they could take advantage of lucrative market opportunities. If prices rose in centers of consumption after poor harvests, they could sell grain at a profit that greatly exceeded the income they drew from fixed rents. The aforementioned high chamberlain Lauricius, for example, owned his own granary in Rome, as did many senators, and this enabled him to bring some of the produce of his Sicilian estates on the market in Rome.[28]

Agricultural products were bought and sold at markets that were held at widely differing intervals: daily, weekly, monthly, or yearly. Market days on which the products of an entire region were for sale usually took place only once a month. But there also were annual markets that attracted merchants from farther afield; Cassiodorus describes one such market that was held every year at a place called Marcellianum in the territory of the city of Consilinum in Lucania. On September 16, the Feast of St. Cyprian, products from all Lucania and the surrounding provinces were set out for sale there in booths and tents:

> This gathering is both celebrated with exceedingly great crowds and highly beneficial to the surrounding provinces. For everything special that either industrious Campania exports or the rich Bruttians or the well-moneyed Calabrians or wealthy Apulians or even the province [of Lucania] itself possess is put on display there to adorn that beautiful market so that you would rightly consider it a vast collection assembled from many regions. You would see the widest fields sparkling with the most beautiful stands and suddenly temporary houses thatched with charming leaves, and a throng of people singing and enjoying themselves.[29]

The peasant economy, however, was linked to markets not only vertically. Peasants also may have sold their wares personally. It made perfect sense for them to do so since they had to pay their rent in cash. Fluctuations in market prices had a direct impact on such peasants. If a harvest was very good, there was plenty to eat, but the surplus brought in marginal profit. If the harvest was very bad, prices rose, but the yield scarcely sufficed for oneself. Between these two extremes, a decent living was possible. Sharecroppers, who paid a certain portion of the harvest instead of a fixed sum of gold, were better protected from price fluctuations because the landlord was also involved in the risk: if less was harvested, less was paid or delivered. But sharecroppers were by no means completely cut off from the market. The size of the share of the harvest that they could sell depended on several factors over which they had little to no control: the land tax, which was determined by the needs of the state; their rent; the quality of the harvest; and the size of the family they had to feed. We may presume, though, that in middling and good years, a portion was left over that was sold at local markets, probably at the nearest city in ordinary circumstances.[30]

Bad years, of course, came time and again. The peasant economy was not a subsistence economy in which a family produced food only for its own use. As we have seen, the opposite was the case, but securing sufficient food remained the family's most urgent objective. Since crop yields were subject to wide fluctuations, peasants could never predict whether they would meet this objective in the coming year. Hunger was a constant companion. Little could be done against heat and cold, drought and floods, hail and pests. But ancient peasants had learned how to distribute the inherent risks of agriculture and avoid disaster. A series of measures was taken to save the soil from rapid exhaustion in late antique Italy: the two-field system, whereby half of a field was always left fallow; mixed farming, whereby several plants were cultivated simultaneously on the same field; and crop sequencing, whereby different plants were sown one after another several times on the same field. Palladius recommended planting barley (*hordeum*) in January, millet (*panicum, milium*) in March, and wheat (*triticum*) and emmer (*adoreum*) in September. Vegetables and legumes, which required different growing conditions than varieties of grain did, were also important for peasants' personal needs. Wine and oil were produced primarily for export. Anyone who could afford an ox could use its feces as manure.[31]

The fragmentation of landed property is also a tried and tested means of distributing the risk of crop failure. We know too little, however, about peasant landholding in Italy to estimate whether it was a factor there. Since tenants had to generate both taxes and rent, they could not concentrate their production solely on meeting their own needs. The state reduced its demands only when dramatic crop failures were evident. The sharecropping system distributed risk equally between tenants and landlords, but since small peasants found themselves at the bottom of the social pyramid, they could do little to resist the fiscal demands of the state and the economic pressure applied by large leaseholders, estate managers, and landowners. This arrangement could give rise to the paradoxical situation (from a modern perspective) in which the producers of foodstuffs themselves suffered famine.[32]

The mechanisms that took effect in such circumstances are illustrated vividly in a circular letter that Cassiodorus sent to the bishops and notables (*honorati*) of an unknown province on behalf of King Athalaric soon after Theoderic's death:

> We have learned from the complaint of the landholders [*possessores*] of your territory that, in addition to the duress of the season, they are also weathering the detestable savagery of some of their own fellow citizens, who bought up an amount of millet early in the year and stored it in their own reserves, anticipating a steep rise in prices for those of middling means [*mediocres*], so that they could inflict abominable nakedness [i.e., helplessness] on those who set aside more sparingly, since those who are in danger of famine make pleading bids to those they know have the power to despoil them. For there is no fighting over prices in a hunger crisis, as people let themselves be cheated so as not to be struck down because of hesitation.[33]

In the unknown province, the name of which Cassiodorus omitted when he redacted the *Variae*, large landowners had bought up the entire millet harvest and stored it in their granaries, speculating that prices would soon dramatically rise.

This conduct, however, was condemned by "people of middling means," who turned to the king for help. The royal chancellery then wrote a letter to the local bishops and secular powerbrokers to inform them that in this crisis each landlord could keep only as much as he needed for himself and his household (*familia*). Any excess he had he was obliged to offer for sale at a "fair price" that was higher than the normal price but less than the going market price. The addressees were admonished to carry out this command gladly "because you ought to look out for yourselves in this regard, so you do not—Heaven forbid—wish for something criminal while seeking excessively high prices." At the same time, the recipients were informed that the bearers of the letter had been instructed to oversee the execution of the king's command. In this case, the royal administration intervened to protect landholders of modest means from falling into economic dependence on large landowners. These farmers were apparently in debt because they otherwise would not have sold all their millet immediately after harvest (in September). The mandatory reduction in prices was in the interest of everyone who bought millet on the market, and probably above all the urban population. Whether it benefited small tenants, however, is doubtful. When harvests disappointed, such tenants did not have enough buying power to obtain food on the market.[34]

Nothing illustrates the scale of the distress in which free peasants might fall on account of crop failure or debt more vividly than the fact that, again and again, parents sold their children into slavery. It was technically prohibited yet still widespread. Augustine reports that slave traders in North Africa purchased their wares under the eyes of the imperial authorities. Imperial legislation took only halfhearted action against the enslavement of children. The emperors endlessly repeated that liberty was a boon that could not be sold at any price; this principle is also repeated in Theoderic's *Edict*: "Parents who are compelled by emergency to sell their children for food do not prejudice their freeborn status. For a free man cannot be assessed at any price."[35] But no one seriously intended to punish the buyers. On the contrary: when the heads of households sold their children and relatives into slavery, to save themselves from starvation during a famine that struck all Italy in the year 450, Emperor Valentinian III indeed condemned it at length. Such a contract violated the law and so did not cause one to lose his freedom, he argued. At the same time, however, he determined that the purchase contract could be voided only if the purchase price was restored to the buyer with an additional 20 percent for the latter's expenses. The emperor says nothing about how people who had sold their children and relatives under duress were supposed to find this money.

Only the act of selling a free person into slavery to barbarians or overseas was explicitly penalized. Cassiodorus also regarded the sale of children into slavery as something normal that could even prove beneficial to the children in question. It emerges from his depiction of the Marcellianum mentioned above that boys and girls could also be purchased there. Cassiodorus believed that parents sold their children with good reason because the children would profit from the transition to a master's service: "For there is no doubt that slaves who transfer from working the fields to serving in the city can fare better." This comment may sound like sheer cynicism to our ears, but it again illustrates the fact that free status was by no means always and in all circumstances preferable to slavery: slaves who served in their master's house did not fear starvation in the event of crop failure. This guarantee presumably also benefited slaves who worked the land as tenants, albeit probably to a lesser extent.[36]

Our sources for late antique Italy give us virtually no insight into the inner workings of the peasant economy. The individual farmstead that was worked by the peasant and his family thus largely eludes our power of imagination. In his *Dialogues*, Gregory the Great (590–604) paints a scene in which an anonymous tenant (*colonus*) on an estate in the mountains of Samnium invites his neighbors to a feast. The tenant is not a poor man because he owns a slave and can serve meat to his neighbors. When his son decides to become a monk, however, he must obtain permission from the landowner, a senator named Venantius of the family of the Decii. This anecdote squares perfectly with the model of the peasant economy that was developed from data taken from prerevolutionary Russia. The word "family," incidentally, should not be taken too literally. Not everyone who worked on a farmstead was related to everyone else. If the farmstead permitted it, farmhands were also employed; these workers did not belong to the peasant's nuclear family but were still considered part of the owner's *familia*. Whoever could afford to do so would hire day laborers for the harvest. Property and wealth were by no means evenly distributed. Gregory the Great distinguishes between "poor" and "rich" peasants (*rustici*) on the Sicilian estates of the Roman Church. Although the life of a peasant family was hard and uncertain, it did not consist solely of work. On the contrary, the workload fluctuated with the rhythm of the seasons. Months with a very high workload were followed by months in which there was not much to do. Since rent was normally fixed by custom and thus stable, the intensity of labor was influenced above all by the family cycle; the decisive factor was the ratio of those who lent a hand to mouths to feed. If it was necessary to feed small children or old, sick, or disabled people, peasants had to work harder than if the ratio between the generations was balanced. Severinus of Noricum is said to have healed a woman suffering a long, severe illness by praying for her at the request of her nearest kin (*proximi*). Three days later, his biographer claims, the woman resumed working in the fields with her own hands "according to the custom of the country" (*iuxta morem provinciae*).[37]

We also know little about the settlement patterns of peasants in late antique Italy. Scholars formerly often assumed that peasants lived scattered on individual farms. Growing archeological evidence, however, has emerged for rural settlements consisting of several farmsteads that recall the structure of hamlets or small villages. Such settlements have now been identified in Piedmont, Apulia, and Sicily. Still, there is good reason to believe that villages were at most a marginal form of social organization in late antique Italy. It cannot be coincidence that we never encounter villages in the written sources as protagonists negotiating with landlords or state actors or disputing with one another, as so frequently is the case in Egypt, Syria, and Asia Minor. In late antique Italy, rural property was registered by estate, not by village. In contrast to the Byzantine Empire, it was not what village one belonged to that was essential for personal identification but rather to which estate, a private administrative unit, one was attached. This suggests that villages were fairly insignificant as reference points for local identity.[38]

Under the late antique peasant economy, free peasants bound to the soil worked the land in the same way as slaves who cultivated an estate for their master; these two categories of people thus frequently worked in spatial proximity to one another, and their living conditions were also fundamentally similar. Regardless of whether they were *coloni* or slaves, they all worked the land autonomously with the help of their family members, while at the same time they paid dues to a master or landlord who was vastly superior, indeed who towered over them, in power and prestige.[39]

A letter of Gregory the Great illustrates this convergence of slaves and free peasants especially vividly. Gregory had learned that Jewish landlords in the territory of Luni employed Christian slaves on their estates. He thereupon instructed the local bishop to see to it that these slaves were manumitted as required by law because it was prohibited for Jews to own Christian slaves. Gregory hastened to add, however, that these slaves should still work their former masters' land after manumission; they should "pay rent and do everything that the law prescribes with respect to *coloni* and *originarii*." Their masters now would be breaking the law if they sent their tenants to another location as they pleased, which they were allowed to do as long as the latter had the status of slaves.[40]

The social status of a peasant did not depend primarily on his legal status but rather on social and economic factors: the size and fertility of the land he worked, the amount of rent that he had to pay his landlord, the amount of taxes that the state levied on his land, and the size of the family that supported him and that he had to feed, to name only the most important factors. Slaves who managed estates on their masters' behalf were wealthier and more influential than tenants who enjoyed free status but cultivated small farms. Since one's social status need not correspond to one's legal status, the barriers that Roman law placed between free and slave were not insurmountable in reality. One reflection of this boundary blurring is the fact that the cohabitation of free persons and slaves was apparently common. Late Roman legislation repeatedly prohibited it, but such laws were of no avail if the master gave his blessing: no complaint, no crime. The *Edict of Theoderic*, incidentally, confirmed the old rule that the children of a female slave would be slaves regardless of whether the father was a slave, a *colonus* bound to the soil, or a free man. But if the mother was a *colona* bound to the soil (an *originaria*), her legal status also passed down to her children.[41]

All these measures were difficult to enforce. No one batted an eye when slaves ran away from their masters because they could not stand living with them anymore or because they hoped for a better life somewhere else. Aristocrats took it for granted that they would help one another track down runaway slaves. Ennodius happily reported to the praetorian prefect Faustus Niger that he believed he had recognized a slave that had run away from Niger three years earlier and sent him a description of the individual for identification. The Catholic clergyman gave a man who was traveling to the kingdom of the Burgundians in search of runaway slaves a letter of recommendation addressed to the courtier Laconius.[42]

A change of scenery was appealing to unfree peasants, especially when they had no land of their own and knew that other landlords were looking for new tenants. Otherwise, fugitive *coloni* and slaves faced the prospect of living as day laborers or beggars, not to mention the danger of being caught and punished. Despite repeated prohibitions, not a few large landowners were apparently willing to engage unknown peasants of any legal status to gain additional manpower. Theoderic continued the policy of late Roman emperors in this regard too; as we have seen, the *Edict of Theoderic* explicitly took action against people who knowingly harbored runaway slaves or *coloni*. The old master's claims did not lapse until thirty years had passed. Another loophole was the clergy. Pope Gelasius chastised bishops several times because they had ordained slaves or bound tenants against their master's will. In these cases, Gelasius took up the cause of the highest senatorial class. Even in cases of abuse, the church granted slaves asylum only to a very limited extent. The *Edict of Theoderic* formulated a rule whereby slaves who sought asylum in a church would be immediately surrendered to their masters if the latter promised clemency—that is, to forego punishing the slaves for running away. Ennodius had to defend himself against an accusation that he had harbored someone's slaves in his own church, and he in turn demanded the return of a slave who had taken refuge with a bishop named Senator.[43]

Only in wartime did runaway slaves and *coloni* become a threat to the social order. After the conquest of Provence, Theoderic issued an order that runaway slaves be returned to their owners. Large numbers of unfree persons also fled from their masters during Justinian's Gothic War, whether it was to join Totila's army or to seek safety. Justinian therefore decreed in a "pragmatic sanction" for reconquered Italy that slaves and *coloni* must be returned to their masters, although he reluctantly recognized the validity of marriages contracted between free persons and slaves during the war. Vice versa, the campaigns that Theoderic conducted in Gaul and Hispania brought numerous captives back to Italy.[44]

The countryside was also not free of violence in peacetime. The removal of boundary markers, cattle rustling, armed assaults, and arson figure as typical crimes in the *Edict of Theoderic*. Cassiodorus wrote the letter about the annual market at Marcellianum that was cited above because he had been approached by traders who had been the victims of robberies that they blamed on the peasants. Cassiodorus instructed the governor of the province of Lucania et Bruttii in the king's name to take preventative measures together with the landowners and leaseholders of the surrounding estate complexes: peasants or dependents (*homines*) who were suspected should be apprehended, flogged, and paraded about in a kind of shaming procession. In another case, the royal administration ordered the same governor to search for horse thieves in the neighborhood of Squillace (in Calabria) at the request of the *vir spectabilis* Nymphadius. These suspects were also sought among the peasants. Nymphadius had thus turned to the court in Ravenna to get back horses that had been stolen from him in Calabria. These examples reveal a structural dilemma and a pattern of social behavior. Since governors had only a small staff that could be employed for policing, it was virtually impossible to fight banditry without the support of local elites. This cooperation reinforced the social hierarchy by involving influential private citizens in the repression of criminality, but it served to keep the peace only as long as local elites themselves did not participate in criminal activities, which, of course, was not always the case. In several passages, the *Edict of Theoderic* anticipates that dependent persons might commit crimes at the behest or with the connivance of landlords, estate managers, and large leaseholders.[45]

Peasants had little leverage over landlords and managers, large leaseholders, tax collectors, officials, and soldiers. Hence the protection that influential persons might provide them was very valuable. Such a patron could put tax collectors in their place, bring his influence to bear on officials, or resolve disputes with neighbors or fellow villagers. His protection served as a deterrent and as such promised safety from extortion, theft, and attacks. Peasants also hoped that their patron might grant them a loan in times of need or defer due payments. The more powerful the patron, the more respected his client. In Cassiodorus' opinion, the way that tenants on royal land behaved bordered on the outrageous. Of course, such a patron was not easy to get for simple peasants. Even as a landlord, the king was out of their reach. Senatorial landowners visited their estates only seldom, and their peasants may have hardly known them. Local elites, in contrast, were somewhat closer to their tenants both spatially and socially. The Goths settled on municipal territory also came into consideration as patrons: Theoderic's *Edict* presumes that not only Romans, but also "barbarians" were asked to defend clients in court, to support them as advocates, or to press charges on their behalf.[46]

Despite the distance, the rural population's ties to their landlords and their local representatives still appear to have been strong. At the outbreak of Justinian's Gothic War, major landowners and leaseholders in Bruttium mobilized their peasants against marauding Gothic troops. During the war, not a few unfree persons joined Totila's army, but a social revolution failed to materialize. The senator Tullianus was even able to muster his tenants against Totila's army. In ordinary circumstances, peasants without land of their own had to deal largely with leaseholders and managers. Much depended on the personality and administrative style of the latter. They could make life difficult for the tenants, bully and exploit them. But they also could make sure that the landowner's sheep were not shorn too close to the skin. There was little room for collective protest or social utopias under such circumstances. Peasants' hopes and fears always centered on specific people: social relations were personalized to a very high degree.[47]

Roman elites in Late Antiquity lived in cities but were intimately familiar with agriculture; metaphors from this field came quickly to their lips. Cassiodorus gives a technical description of the quality and use of the dry soil of Reggio di Calabria. But he sees the landscape with the eyes of a landlord, surveying his estates from the city; around his hometown of Squillace, one can see the "pretty spectacle of the laborers" and recognize rich vineyards, fruitful threshing floors, and verdant olive trees. Men like Cassiodorus looked down on the country people. He advised the monks of his monastery in Vivarium to instill good manners in their peasants and not burden them with additional dues. It was well known, he went on, that stealing was as common among them as worshiping at shrines; at Vivarium, though, they should live a life of innocence and simplicity. Similar statements appear not only in the *Variae*, but also in the works of clergymen like Ennodius and Caesarius; "rusticity" (*rusticitas*) was regarded by men of the civic elite as the epitome of boorishness and superstition. According to the Gallic senator Sidonius, "the educated are no less superior to unlettered rustics [*rustici*] than men are to beasts."[48]

In point of fact, Christianity was an urban religion in Late Antiquity; every city had its own bishop, and bishops lived in cities. The target audience for sermons and pastoral care was the urban population. Christianity spread in the countryside only after long delay. The network of rural parishes only gradually became denser over the course of the fifth century. It was often large landowners who built churches on their properties and furnished them with income. Thus the former urban prefect Trygetius built a church dedicated to the Archangel Michael and St. Marcus on the *fundus Sextilianus* near Potenza under Pope Gelasius. The praetorian prefect Faustus Albinus (cos. 493) came forward under Pope Symmachus as the sponsor of a basilica for St. Peter, which he had built on his land along the Via Tiberina twenty-seven miles outside Rome. Such oratories built on estates far from a city have been identified from archeological remains at San Vincenzo al Volturno in Samnium and San Giusto in Apulia. It was inevitable that the sponsors of these churches claimed special rights, as had been routine in the profane realm since time immemorial. Pope Gelasius opposed these efforts; he stressed that sponsors should not claim any such rights over congregation members and insisted that the approval of the Apostolic See was necessary for the consecration of such churches.[49]

It is difficult to estimate how deeply Christianity had penetrated the life of peasants around the year 500. The *Vita* of Severinus of Noricum composed in Gothic Italy gives the impression that the peasants in this outpost of the Roman Empire put all their hopes in Christ: during a plague of locusts, the community of farmers from the town of Cucullis gathered together inside the church; when blight threatened to wipe out the harvest, they began to fast and pray. But since the hagiographer sought to illustrate the power of St. Severinus with these examples, we may doubt whether he painted a realistic picture of peasant religion in Noricum. In Italy, some rural shrines apparently continued to function well into the sixth century. People were still seeking healing at a sanctuary of Pan at a place named Pantalla, somewhere near Perugia, in the 540s, when the presbyter Floridus persuaded the local population to destroy the god's temple. Benedict of Nursia is credited with smashing a temple and razing a sacred grove on the hill Montecassino in Campania, where in the late 530s he founded a monastery that became famous much later as the first house of the Benedictine order.[50]

On Sardinia, which of course was never under Gothic rule, the peasants still stubbornly clung to their traditional rituals at the end of the sixth century; they paid off imperial officials to be allowed to practice them undisturbed. At the same time, the bishop of Tyndaris on Sicily requested help converting the pagans, who were being protected by powerful patrons and their remote locations.[51]

We can get a relatively concrete idea of what peasant religion was like in the early sixth century only for Provence, where Caesarius as metropolitan of Arles waged an uncompromising campaign against all practices that he regarded as pagan and thus reprehensible. He depicts the hinterland of Arles as a refuge of pagan customs: the peasants of his diocese held feasts in groves, at trees, and at fountains that were considered holy. Men and women did not rest from work on Sunday, the Lord's Day (*dies dominicus*), but rather on Thursday, the day of the god Juppiter (*dies Iovis*). Some made noise with horns, bells, and shouting at lunar eclipses to shoo away the darkness. Peasants wore amulets and magic spells on their persons to ward off evil. If they fell sick or their wish for children went unfulfilled, they consulted healers who dispensed herbs and potions and knew magic spells. They observed omens to avoid evil and asked diviners to learn the future. If they had to make difficult decisions, they hoped to obtain advice from oracles or by opening the Bible to a random verse (bibliomancy). They celebrated the new year by exchanging gifts with their friends (instead of giving alms to the poor), holding feasts, and organizing relaxed processions at which men wore stag or cow masks or dressed as prostitutes.[52]

The vast majority of the people whom Caesarius accused of pagan practices viewed themselves as Christians. To the peasants in the hinterland of Arles, Diana, the Roman goddess of the hunt, the moon, and childbirth, was an evil spirit that invaded people and made them sick. In a sermon, Caesarius mentions people who not only refused to destroy pagan sanctuaries, but even rebuilt those that had already been destroyed or beat good Christians who tried to burn sacred trees or topple altars. The people he was talking about evidently did not want to be Christians, but they also obviously were not present when Caesarius railed against them. His sermon was intended for members of the congregation who came to his church but did not want to foreswear traditional rituals: "And although we are glad, dearest brothers, to see you faithfully run to church, we still are saddened and aggrieved because we know that some of you regularly go to the old worship of idols, just as pagans without God and without the grace of baptism do. We have heard that some of you make wishes at trees, pray at fountains, consult diabolical omens."[53] In another sermon, Caesarius cites objections he had to anticipate: "What should we do if omens and sorcerers or diviners predict the truth?" Or: "Sometimes, if not for enchanters, many people fall into mortal danger because of a snakebite or some other sickness." Not even Caesarius dared to claim that such practices were nothing more than hocus-pocus: God permitted the devil to use them to test Christians. A true Christian, though, would have nothing to do with them.[54]

The peasants of Provence stubbornly clung to their traditional practices and rituals because they had been sanctified by age and proven effective. In a world that was full of unpredictable risks, it seemed unwise to drop time-honored means of passively avoiding and actively warding off evil. But that was not the only reason why they disobeyed the words of their pastor. A priest's blessing and a healer's spell, prayer and an amulet, a church and a holy grove were not incompatible antitheses in their eyes. On the contrary, they were convinced that there was no need to reject the ways of their ancestors to be Christians. And, moreover, if it made people happy, what could be so wrong? On the night of June 23, which preceded the feast of John the Baptist on June 24 in the middle of the harvest, they bathed in rivers or lakes that had seemed to be holy places to their ancestors. What Caesarius perceived as idolatry was, to them, merely one way among many of guaranteeing the support of supernatural powers.[55]

We can only guess what Christianity meant to the rural population of sixth-century Italy. The same Cassiodorus who attributes to peasants a predilection for worshiping groves reports that an annual market that was celebrated in his day on the feast of St. Cyprian had once been associated with a festival in honor of the sea goddess Leucothea. This festival had taken place in a cave that contained a pool filled with fish. This cult site had then been repurposed: when Cassiodorus wrote his letter, the fish pond served as a baptismal font. We know that trees in the vicinity of Terracina still received cultic worship in the late sixth century because Pope Gregory accused the local bishop of not responding to the practice with the necessary strictness.[56]

Further age-old customs intended to increase fertility and ward off harm also survived in Italy, as in many agrarian societies. The "farmer's almanac" of Palladius lists a plethora of natural and supernatural compounds and practices that were supposed to protect one's fruits and crops and people and animals from evil. To ward off hail, one covered a millstone with a blood-red cloth or threateningly raised bloody axes to the sky. Peasants lined their gardens with white briony, nailed an owl with outspread wings to a post or wall, and smeared iron tools with bear's fat. The range of remedies to fight pests and ward off caterpillars and snails, ants and mosquitos, mice and locusts was even wider. Here, too, the boundary with magic was hazy: "All garden and field seeds are said to be protected from all evils and pests if they are first soaked in the ground roots of wild cucumber. Moreover, the skull of a mare, but one that has already foaled, should be put inside the garden, or even better a she-ass. They are believed to fertilize what they see by their presence." Magic was also indispensable to animal medicine. If horses or other animals came down with worms, Palladius recommended the following: squat down before sunrise and throw dust or feces over one's shoulder, first with the left hand, then with the right, and then once more with the left, and say each time, "As I throw this, so should the worms be thrown out of so-and-so's horse," always making sure to indicate the color of the animal. "This heals a cow, horse, or any other animal," Palladius insists.[57]

4. REBORN FROM RUINS? CITIES IN THEODERIC'S KINGDOM

When Ennodius composed his panegyric to Theoderic in the year 507, he praised the king not only as an invincible warrior, but also as a ruler who provided for the welfare of his people in peacetime. Under his reign, Italy was enjoying a "golden age" (*aureum saeculum*), he claimed. Among its blessings, the clergyman included the revival of cities: "I see the glory of cities has emerged unexpected from ashes and the roofs of palaces glow red in the fullness of the civil order [*civilitas*]. I see buildings finished before I can even learn they were commissioned. The mother of cities itself, Rome, is rejuvenated, cutting away the drooping limbs of old age. Forgive me, you sacred beginnings of the spirit of the Lupercal: it means more to drive away decline than to make the start."[58] Ennodius contrasts Theoderic here with the mythical founders of Rome: Romulus and Remus had allegedly been suckled by the she-wolf in the Lupercal, a cave on the Palatine. Just as Romulus and Remus had once founded Rome, now the Gothic king reversed its decline: cities that had lain in rubble now shone with new radiance under Theoderic's reign; new buildings rose everywhere. This depiction corresponds exactly to the way the king wanted to be perceived. The *Variae* are full of sentences that elevate the preservation of the urban fabric to a royal mission. Hence, for example, "We want to preserve most what seems to adorn the appearance of the city"; "The restoration of old cities gives grounds to praise our times"; and "It is indeed our intention to build new buildings, but even more so to preserve the old." Cassiodorus also praises Theoderic's reign as an age of royal building activity and urban renewal in his *Chronicle* of 519: "Under his felicitous reign many cities are renewed; redoubtable fortresses are constructed; astonishing palaces rise up; the ancient marvels are surpassed by his great works."[59] The propaganda of the royal court is also reflected in the work of the *Anonymus Valesianus*, who celebrates Theoderic as a "lover of buildings and restorer of cities" (*amator fabricarum et restaurator civitatum*), citing building projects in the northern Italian residences of Ravenna, Verona, and Ticinum as evidence:

He restored the aqueduct in Ravenna that Emperor Trajan had built and brought water again into the city after a very long time. He completed construction of a palace but did not dedicate it. He completed colonnades around the palace. In Verona, he built baths and a palace and added a colonnade from the gate to the palace. He restored an aqueduct that had long been destroyed and had water flow through it again. He ringed the city with new walls. At Ticinum, he built baths, an amphitheater, and new city walls. And he also did many good deeds for other cities.[60]

These sources celebrate Theoderic as a builder and restorer of cities. They thus place the king in a tradition that extended back to the beginnings of the Roman imperial monarchy: Augustus himself had adorned Rome with magnificent buildings, and Constantine the Great still emulated his example by constructing baths and churches in the Eternal City. Imperial engagement in Italy and elsewhere, however, had shifted in the fourth century to the preservation of existing buildings and had come to an almost complete standstill in the fifth century. That also emerges clearly from the way that Theoderic is celebrated as a builder: new construction is overshadowed by repairs. The type of building projects that are attributed to Theoderic is also striking: besides palaces, aqueducts, and baths, an amphitheater, city walls, and fortresses are mentioned. Royal building activity thus concentrated on the water supply and bathing facilities, on venues for games, and on fortifications. Missing from the texts cited above is the forum, which had constituted the heart of Roman cities and been decorated with monumental buildings, basilicas, colonnades, and temples in earlier centuries. It is notable that only cities appear as the beneficiaries of building projects, although the vast majority of the population lived in the countryside. Of course, the way that this praise of Theoderic is formulated also makes it obvious that not every city received such benefits to the same extent. New buildings are mentioned explicitly only for royal residences in northern Italy: Ravenna, Ticinum, and Verona. Ennodius emphasizes Rome but does not mention any royal building projects.[61]

Cassiodorus and Ennodius describe Theoderic's building activity as restoration, presumably of a state that had already been lost or that was at least threatened with destruction. A program of restoration (*renovatio*) presumes decline: "It means more to drive away decline than to make the start." The royal chancellery in fact often mentions the decay of public buildings. In a letter to the notables of a city that should probably be identified as Sestino, the king explains that he has learned that "columns and stones toppled by the malignancy of age lie unused" around their city and orders that they be transported to Ravenna.

The *domus Pinciana*, a royal villa in Rome, was also used as a stone quarry to beautify Ravenna at Theoderic's request. More examples could be cited.[62]

Among modern scholars, it was long the dominant view that the decline of the ancient city in Italy had been halted once more under Theoderic. The early sixth century was interpreted as a phase of regeneration after the invasions and disasters of the fifth century, an "Indian summer," the effects of which were wiped away by Justinian's Gothic War and the ensuing invasions of the Franks and Lombards. Even scholars who viewed Theoderic and his Goths as infiltrators in the heartland of ancient culture credited him with a final blossoming of cities under his rule, although estimations of how much of that development should be attributed to Theoderic varied widely. Against the background of humanistic ideals, Theoderic seemed to be a figure who delayed the demise of ancient culture in Italy until the barbarian migrations swept it away with the arrival of the Lombards.[63]

This model was never uncontested and has increasingly lost its plausibility in the past decades, as scholars have learned to read the *Variae* critically and archeological research has brought to light clear evidence of impoverishment. Late antique Italy is no longer viewed in isolation but rather is placed in the context of the evolution of the city in the Later Roman Empire and its successor states. These debates are often put under the rubric of "Decline or Change?" That reflects a relativization of "classical" Antiquity, but also postmodern reservations toward any kind of value judgment. Although this discussion has sometimes lost itself in unproductive polemics—the meaning and justification of value judgments with respect to the remote past are excellent subjects for controversy—it has also spurred research and led to important results. Now there is a broad consensus that the institutional and urbanistic development of the cities of Italy and North Africa was characterized by a high degree of continuity during the fourth century, indeed even by deliberate conservatism. Obvious change does not begin until the early fifth century and accelerates toward its end. It thus is necessary to differentiate within the period known as Late Antiquity. The sixth century can be adequately assessed only when it is viewed in the light of long-term developments. This perspective also means qualifying the impact of Justinian's Gothic War on the development of cities. Already by the year 500, the cities of Italy had ceased to be what they once had been in the fourth century.[64]

The debate over the transformation of the late antique city has made it very clear that it is important to distinguish the dimensions of this secular process with care. The Roman city was an extremely complex phenomenon: a political and administrative center that controlled its own territory; a commune with rights of self-governance and yet also a bastion of imperial rule; an economic base and a center of consumption but also an architecturally defined space in which a specific way of life was cultivated—to name only the most important aspects. A great deal depends on whether one views the evolution of the city as a political institution, as an architecturally defined space, or as a way of life. Since these different aspects are never equally prominent in every place and also did not develop synchronously, differentiation in both spatial and chronological terms is imperative. There were major differences in the size and built environment, in population and wealth, in economic basis and social structure. Especially in the south, there were dozens of small towns that never met the urbanistic standards of the high imperial period. The inhabitants of Osimo and Urbino fetched their drinking water from a single fountain. Milan and Aquileia, in contrast, were major cities for premodern conditions. The hierarchy of cities depended not least on their political and administrative function: provincial capitals were favored in several respects, residences especially so, and Rome was a special case regardless. The development of cities could also be heavily influenced by external events. In places that emerged virtually unscathed (as in North Africa) or at most only lightly damaged (as in Italy) from the wars and civil wars of the third century, the development of cities extended uninterrupted until well into the fourth century. Hence it is the fifth century that marks a caesura for many cities in these regions.[65]

Anyone who attempts to paint a picture of the cities of Italy in Theoderic's day thus must take many factors into account and also resist the temptation to reduce the unruly diversity of phenomena to a tidy simplification. Already under the high imperial period, Italy was a land of many cities; the exact number is unknown, but 400 may be approximately correct. Of course, these cities did not meet the modern criterion of having at least 100,000 inhabitants. At best, only Rome would have satisfied this criterion in the year 500, and even that is not certain. Many cities had only a few thousand inhabitants; some, even fewer. What was decisive was a city's status as an autonomous territorial corporation, even though the fine distinctions in the legal status of cities disappeared in the fourth century. This network of cities proved to be astonishingly stable: some 70 percent of the cities of northern Italy survived until the High Middle Ages; as the seats of secular powerbrokers or bishops, they remained central places for their territories. In the province of Venetia et Histria, for example, almost every one of twenty-six urban communities that can be identified for the early fourth century still existed at the end of the sixth. The number of urban communities shrank more significantly in the south because there were many more small cities and towns there that rested on a very tenuous economic basis. In the province of Tuscia et Umbria, roughly one-fifth of the approximately seventy cities appears to have disappeared over the course of Late Antiquity. In the vast majority of cases, no details are known about the process itself, but some of these failed cities have been studied closely—for example, Veleia in Emilia, Luna in Liguria, Rusellae in Etruria, and Herdonia in Apulia.[66]

Theoderic thus conquered a land that was heavily urbanized for premodern conditions. It was also still very much part of superregional networks of exchange. Especially the cities that had harbors or were connected to water routes by navigable rivers imported and exported goods from overseas prior to Justinian's Gothic War. Grain, wine, oil, salted pork, and timber are mentioned as exports; slaves were also sold across borders. Trade ships sailed back and forth to Italy, Gaul, Hispania, and North Africa under Theoderic and his successors. Our sources, of course, do not permit us to say how frequently they did so. Since the destinations were usually chosen on a short-term basis, we probably should not presume regularly traveled routes. Merchants from Italy, however, do appear to have often made for the Bosporus. In the year 530, Emperor Justinian abolished a one-year limitation on lawsuits over contracts that were struck in Italy because the application of this limit had given rise to an "enormous mass" of disputes; such contracts therefore must have been numerous and important.[67]

Vice versa, all kinds of luxury goods from the Byzantine Empire were imported to Italy. The indispensable writing material for official documents, papyrus, came from Egypt. The royal court ordered valuable architectural elements like capitals from the stonemasons of Constantinople. Large quantities of goods for daily use were still imported from North Africa around the year 500, especially valuable eating and drinking vessels (African red slip ware), as well as oil. The volume of these imports had significantly declined since North Africa had come under Vandalic rule because it was no longer possible to collect oil and grain in the form of a tax there. The fiscal motor driving the exchange of goods between North Africa and Italy was thus cut off, but trade relations were not severed entirely. Between the years 500 and 515, a warehouse in Classe, the port of Ravenna, burned down and was subsequently abandoned. During excavations, a large number of amphorae, tableware, and lamps were found—all of them imported from North Africa.[68]

The volume of this long-distance trade in bulk products is impossible to quantify. It was certainly lucrative to lease the right to collect the duties and taxes that applied to it. Tax farmers (*siliquatarii*) bought the contract at auction for a given amount and pocketed whatever they could collect that exceeded it. Collecting the tax entailed considerable effort, since buyers and sellers naturally both tried to evade paying it. We do not know, however, how high the bids were or how great the actual revenue was.[69]

The fact that bulk commodities were imported from overseas does not at all mean that the entire peninsula was involved in this commerce. This notion is simply irreconcilable with the conditions of commerce and also entirely unsupported by the literary and documentary sources. For a long time, scholars had to content themselves with this negative conclusion because there were no data that permitted more precise insights into economic processes. This radically changed, however, once it became possible in the 1970s to determine the date and location of the production of late Roman ceramics with sufficient accuracy. Ceramics thereby became the index fossil of late antique economic history. Their analysis has shown that people in the interior of the Italian peninsula largely used vessels that were produced in each respective region. From the Po Valley to Basilicata, locally produced unpainted pottery predominated (*acroma deputata*), as well as "red painted ware." In northern Italy, fine "Roman glazed ware" is also found. The dissemination of these ceramic types is a barometer for the economic integration of the peninsula: bulk commodities circulated within regions, not across the entire peninsula. At the same time, it emerges that the Po Valley constituted a region unto itself. The south, in contrast, remained heavily focused on Rome, even though Lucanian pigs were no longer driven from their breeders' farmsteads to Rome year after year; in 452, Emperor Valentinian III commuted this duty into a monetary payment, the amount of which had dropped from 6,400 to 1,200 *solidi* by 535. The king also had extensive lands in Apulia. Under Theoderic, grain from Calabria was shipped to Ravenna.[70]

Not only was the network of cities basically stable in Late Antiquity, but the idea that one could lead a cultivated lifestyle only in a city lived on as well. Elite forms of communication and representation were and remained focused on immediate and reciprocal interaction; they presumed spatial proximity and publicity. Only a city provided the appropriate framework for this "face-to-face society" of the rich and powerful. That did not preclude regular retreats to one's country estates: "What could be more fortunate than to work the fields and dazzle in the city?" the *formula* for titular officeholders (*vacantes*) declares. The country homes of senators and municipal notables were often built as magnificent summer residences. Cassiodorus praises the spectacular villas that encircled the banks of Lake Como; Ennodius describes the expense of maintaining them as ruinous. But such villas were by no means the primary residences of the elite, whose lives were centered on cities. By the early sixth century, many had even lost their function as elite residences, were abandoned, or were split into smaller, less imposing units.[71]

Urbanity remained an ideal way of life for elites. That is attested by many sources far into the sixth century. Cassiodorus eloquently expressed this ideal in a

letter that he composed for Theoderic's grandson Athalaric. He issued the following admonishment to the municipal notables of Bruttium (Calabria) in the king's
name:

> May the cities therefore return to their former magnificence! Let no man set
> the beauty of the countryside above the walls of the ancients! How can one
> flee the very thing for which one must undertake war to prevent its devasta-
> tion? To whom does a meeting with nobles seem less welcome? Who does
> not love to exchange words with his peers, to visit the forum, to inspect the
> honest crafts, resolve one's disputes by the laws, even occasionally indulge in
> the game tokens of Palamedes, go to the baths with one's fellows, host lun-
> cheons with shared furnishings? A man who wants to spend all his life with
> his slaves misses all these things.[72]

Cassiodorus describes the city as a space where one interacts with one's peers
in public, cultivates cultural interests, visits the baths, and gives banquets. He
contrasts this urban conviviality with the isolated existence of people who live
in the countryside surrounded by their servants. One hundred fifty years earlier,
the Antiochene rhetor Libanius had praised life in the Syrian metropolis of
Antioch in similar tones. Cassiodorus would not have written this paean to
urban life, however, if this ideal had been attractive to everyone equally. His
letter concludes with a request that in the future the notables spend most of the
year in the city again. The notables of Calabria evidently preferred country living to the city. This case, however, cannot be generalized. The cities of Calabria
were small and insignificant; they had few amenities. In other parts of Italy,
elites kept their chief residence in the cities, although their facilities and appearance changed dramatically over the fifth and sixth centuries. We can better
understand the transformation of cityscapes, however, if we imagine the late
antique city first as a political institution and social organism.[73]

5. NOTABLES, CURIALS, PLEBEIANS: THE MAKEUP OF LATE ANTIQUE CITIES IN ITALY

Anyone seeking to understand the social and political structure of late
antique Italy has to begin with the elite. They held the reins, and they alone left
traces behind that produce a clear picture. The urban elite consisted of people
who differed significantly from one another in terms of rank and prestige, property and power, lifestyle and self-conception. In many Italian cities over the
course of the fifth century, the bishop became a powerful figure who played a
major part in local politics. He controlled the personnel and income of his

church, distributed alms to the poor, and exercised free arbitrational jurisdiction, known as *audientia episcopalis*. We shall discuss him further below.

Secular elites were recruited from people who owned land within a city's territory. There were considerable differences between them in terms of social status. The royal chancellery distinguished three groups: *honorati*, *possessores*, and *curiales*. *Curiales* were the members of the *curia*, the municipal council. Curials had to perform duties for the state; they organized the collection of taxes on the local level and registered the transfer of real estate. Membership in this group of people was hereditary; their names were recorded in an official register (*album*). *Possessores* were all those who owned land within the territory of a city. Residents of a city who had served the ruler and thereby acquired senatorial rank were called *honorati*; the title refers to their office in the emperor's service, which was regarded as an honor (*honos*).[74]

In the early and high imperial period, civic elites were largely identical with curials because only a relatively small number of people, such as members of the equestrian order and senators were exempt from obligations to a provincial city. Beginning in the early fourth century, however, the number of people who acquired senatorial rank in the service of the emperor grew exponentially. These men, who received the rank of *vir clarissimus* or *vir spectabilis* from the latter half of the fifth century on, settled down in their home cities after leaving office; there they made up the highest echelon of the local elite but did not belong to the local curia. The chancellery of Theoderic and his successors took this change in the local power structure into account by addressing letters to cities not solely to the councilmen, but rather to the *honorati*, *possessores*, and *curiales*. It always put the *honorati* first because they were the most influential and prestigious local group. The *possessores* also usually take precedence before the curials, who normally appear last, in third place, in this address.[75]

The curials of Late Antiquity had lost much of their prestige since the early and high imperial period. Membership in the *ordo decurionum*, the order of municipal councilors, had long since ceased to be the highest goal to which social climbers aspired. On account of the obligations that curials had to meet, membership in this order could become an oppressive burden. There was no shortage of attempts to cast off this burden by seeking a position that gave one immunity from curial obligations: service as a clergyman or as an imperial official. Both avenues were prohibited by law but difficult to suppress. Late Roman emperors found themselves constantly obliged to reiterate the rule that a curial could leave the order only if he transferred his property to someone else who could take his place. This legislation was intended to ensure the functionality of municipal curiae as the lowest level of the administration and tax collection.

Since the imperial administration itself neither could nor would assume these tasks, the involvement of curials was indispensable. Emperor Majorian therefore openly declared that curials were the "sinews of the commonwealth" (*nervi rei publicae*) and the "inner organs of the cities" (*viscera civitatum*).[76]

Theoderic and his successors continued this policy. When the curials of the city of Sarsina complained that some peers had fled to the clergy of Bishop Gudila, Theoderic ruled just as his imperial predecessors would have done: if the complaint proved correct, the persons in question would have to return to the curia of their home city. The rule that a curial could sell his land only if he proved that he could not meet his financial obligations in any other way likewise remained in force. Only the king could grant permission to sell; Cassiodorus preserves a model letter for doing so. Soon after Theoderic's death, an edict was issued in the name of his grandson Athalaric to protect curials from abuse at the hands of royal agents (*saiones*) and other functionaries: everyone who demanded more from a curial than he was obliged to perform would have to pay ten pounds of gold as a punishment. The curials are addressed in the edict as follows: "Raise your heads, you who are oppressed! Lift up your spirits, you who have been loaded down by a burden of evils! Strive to recover what you see you have wretchedly lost! To every citizen, his city is the commonwealth [*res publica*]. May your orders [*ordines*] live equitably with one another. Do not oppress those of middling wealth [*mediocres*] so that the more powerful [*potiores*] may not justly oppress you! The punishment for that sin is that each one receives what he brazenly inflicts on another."[77] Athalaric's edict depicts curials as a class that relies on the king's protection. But the rhetorical pathos of the royal proclamation should not mislead us to conclude that curials stood near the bottom of the social hierarchy of a late antique city. As the royal chancellery perceived them, they indeed ranked below "the more powerful," but above "those of middling wealth" who did not belong to the municipal council. In another letter, the royal chancellery represents leaving the curial class as outright social decline, because *possessores* were vulnerable to harassment by municipal tax collectors. Even though this depiction may have applied only to small landholders, curials were far superior to the lower classes of cities in prestige, power, and wealth. On account of their involvement in tax collection, curials were persons that common folk had to beware. The clergyman Salvian in Provence viewed them as a scourge to their fellow citizens; he argued that in many places "there are as many tyrants as there are curials" (*quot curiales, tot tyranni*). Curials were also in constant competition for power and property with one another and with the *possessores* in their city.

Caesarius of Arles describes the mechanisms of such competition very vividly in a sermon: if you had a rich and powerful neighbor, then you did not covet his land. If he was poor (*pauper*), though, or found himself in financial difficulties, then you forced him to sell his little homestead (*casella*) by sending the municipal tax collectors after him or by making sure that he had to perform an expensive duty (*munus*) for the city. If the neighbor asked for a loan, you claimed you did not have the liquid capital; if he was ready to sell, however, you jumped at the chance. The poor neighbor Caesarius is describing here may have been a small farmer, but he may also have been a curial. The royal chancellery thus had every reason to urge the curials to show harmonious goodwill to one another.[78]

Circa 500, almost every city in Italy still seems to have had a curia. Theoderic's *Edict* requires that property transfers be registered in the city archive in the presence of three curials and the municipal magistrates. If municipal magistrates were unavailable, then the registration should take place in the neighboring city. The legislator thus presumed that there were curials in every city, even if some cities did not or did not regularly appoint magistrates. Such magistrates are attested by papyri in Ravenna and Faenza during and after Gothic rule. We can trace them across three generations of the families of the Melminii and Flavii of Ravenna. These officeholders were still called *duumviri* or *quinquennales*, as under the high imperial period.[79]

These traditional offices, however, lagged far behind two other offices of far more recent date. The one was the *curator civitatis*; the other, the *defensor civitatis* ("defender of the city"). The office of *curator civitatis* had been created at the beginning of the second century; originally, such a curator was appointed *ad hoc* by the emperor to oversee the administration of the curials of a specific city. Over time, however, the curator developed into a regular municipal executive office whose incumbent was elected by the curia and confirmed by the ruler. It was still the same in Theoderic's Italy. The *Variae* preserve a model letter for this procedure in which the curator is given the task of guiding the municipal curia and regulating prices. Curators also occasionally still appear in inscriptions. In Tarquinia in the province of Tuscia et Umbria in 504, the curator Gloriosus restored at his own expense a bath that was reserved for the city's curials; his father Proiecticius, a *vir clarissimus*, was in charge of the construction. A funerary inscription from the year 522 preserves the memory of a certain Mamercius Marcellinus, who held the same office in Beneventum (in Campania).[80]

In the early fourth century, the curator represented the top of the municipal government. Yet he swiftly lost his leading position when Emperors Valentinian and Valens introduced the office of the *defensor civitatis* across the empire. The defender was supposed to serve as judge for all cases up to a value of 50 *solidi*; in other words, he provided inexpensive and accessible adjudication in everyday affairs. At the same time, the defender acted as a kind of "ombudsman" for the ordinary population: he had received a mandate in the emperor's name to take action as the *defensor plebis* ("defender of the common people," the "plebs") against abuses committed in the collection of taxes and administration of justice. His term in office originally ran for five years. Like the curator, the defender was also supposed to be nominated by municipal councils, but in contrast to him, the defender himself could not be a curial. The office of defender was thus reserved for men who had served the emperor and settled down in their hometowns after leaving office—that is, someone from the group of people known as *honorati*. The right to nominate the defender was also no longer held exclusively by the local curia but rather, after the late fourth century, by the *honorati*, *possessores*, and *curiales* of the city. Thus these officials were elected by an assembly that included every person of rank and influence living within a city's territory. Modern scholars conventionally call these people "notables."[81]

By virtue of his imperial mandate and high rank, the defender held an influential position in his city. He quickly became a sought-after patron. Whoever needed protection against a member of the municipal elite was well advised to turn to him. Hence the defenders soon acquired additional responsibilities with imperial support: they took part in the administration of municipal landholdings, in building projects, and in the documentation of legal transactions; they oversaw the curia and corporations, and they assumed all kinds of police duties. Emperor Majorian granted defenders a kind of general authority in 458: they were to protect the people of the cities, the emperor declared, and either take on their own initiative what measures they deemed appropriate for the public welfare or suggest them to himself. Moreover, they should enjoy free access to all the emperor's functionaries and report directly to him about conditions in the provinces about which he did not know "because [the emperor] was burdened by greater cares."[82]

We must read Cassiodorus' model letter for the appointment of a *defensor* against the background of this development because his responsibilities are only described allusively there:

> Our authority, moved by the supplication of your citizens, permits you to be the defender of such-and-such city for such-and-such indiction. May you seek to do nothing corrupt, nothing immoral, you who are called by such a title. Regulate the transactions of the citizens with equitable moderation in keeping with the times. Keep firm what you have decreed because the difficulty of selling is not collecting money but rather religiously observing the statutory prices. You will truly fulfill the duty of a good defender if you permit your citizens neither to be oppressed by the laws nor devoured by scarcity.[83]

The model letter emphasizes price controls and adjudication as a defender's two chief tasks. This portfolio overlaps in part with that of the curator. The defender, however, was the real head of the municipal government. Letters sent to cities by the royal chancellery were only ever addressed to the defender, never to the curator, and indeed he always appears before the curials, albeit after *honorati* and *possessores*. In documents from Ravenna, the defender leads the series of municipal magistrates. Cassiodorus' model letter, moreover, shows that the defender's term in Gothic Italy had been reduced to a year. This reduction can be explained by the defender's outstanding status: since no other office was as desirable as this one, the ruler did not want to limit opportunities to hold it with long terms in office. At the same time, the short term also strengthened the position of the men who elected the defender.[84]

Among modern scholars, the formal recognition of a municipal leadership that acted alongside the traditional organs of municipal government was viewed as a symptom of the decline of the ancient city, understood as an autonomous civic community; in this view, by putting people in charge who were not subject to the rules of the curial municipal administration, the imperial government contributed to the disintegration of the city as a community of citizens with certain rights and duties. The willingness of local elites to intercede on behalf of the city in which they lived would have declined. Against this interpretation, however, it has been objected that the rise of the defender to the elected supreme magistrate of the late antique city integrated the old and new elites; his limited term prevented the dominance of individual *honorati*; at the same time, the electoral nature of the office ensured that the curials would have a significant influence on the appointment. This new form of municipal government was also not completely unregulated; the notables of a city met, after all, to deliberate and reach joint decisions. It remains true, however, that tasks were distributed very unevenly among the leading classes of late antique cities; only members of the curia were liable to the central administration for the payment of taxes.[85]

Wherever troops were stationed in Gothic Italy, local notables were joined by a Gothic officer who had judicial powers. In conflicts between the Gothic immigrants and the Roman population, it was this *comes* and not the defender who was the competent judge. It seems plausible to presume that the municipal elites perceived this officer as an infiltrator and so closed ranks against him. When a bronze statue vanished without a trace in Como, Theoderic ordered the *comes* to locate it without involving the municipal authorities in any way whatsoever. That does not suggest smooth collaboration between the civil administration and military authority in this city. After Theoderic's death, the notables and the defender of Syracuse complained about the *comes* responsible for their city. The notables of Catania, apparently unanimously, also requested permission to use stone from the theater to build a defensive wall. But the non-curial notables of a city did not always work so harmoniously together with the curials. In some cases, the curials of a city approached the king on their own, without the obvious involvement of local notables. When conflicts within the elite of a city escalated, they sometimes were brought to the attention of the royal administration. Hence, Theoderic once instructed the *comes patrimonii* Senarius to investigate and resolve a legal dispute between the curials and the *possessores* of the city of Velia in Campania.[86]

If the royal administration had something to communicate to a city, it normally addressed itself to all the notables who resided there. The model letter in which a city is informed of the appointment of a *comes civitatis* is addressed to *honorati, possessores,* and *curiales*; likewise, the letter for the *comes* of Syracuse. The *honorati, possessores,* and curials of Forlì should see to it that wood is transported to a nearby river; those of Parma, that drainage canals are dredged. The *possessores* of Feltre were ordered to help construct a fortified settlement in the territory of Trento, some eighty kilometers away. A command to clear plants from the aqueduct of Ravenna was likewise addressed to the *possessores* of the city. Of course, the royal administration did not follow a rigorous system: an order to procure and outfit a ship for Heruli en route to the royal court was sent to the Gothic *comes*, the Roman defender, and the curials of the city of Ticinum.[87]

We know little about the urban lower classes. What is clear is that they belonged to very different groups. The service staff in the houses of the municipal elite probably consisted predominantly of unfree men and women who had no personal rights as slaves but belonged to their master's household as servants. In addition to the servants of local elites, craftsmen and petty traders who owned a shop or workshop also lived in the cities with their own households. This class consisted of people who largely had the status of free men. But they were not at all equal before the law to the elites. On the contrary, it had long been conventional in criminal law to distinguish between people of lower status and people of higher status. The former were normally punished more severely than the latter and were not protected from corporal punishment. Some craftsmen and tradesmen joined together in corporations (*collegia*) that were obligated to perform services for the city and thus came under its supervision. Membership presumed landholdings and passed from father to son. The membership list of a professional corporation from Ravenna in the time of Diocletian (284–305) lists fifty-five "masters" (*magistri*), thirteen patrons from the municipal elite, and twelve "sponsors" (*amatores*). Such corporations still existed under Gothic rule, but we have no evidence about the origins and status of their patrons.[88]

The central administration of the king took interest in municipal tradesmen and petty merchants above all because a tax on their assets was collected every five years. It was called the *auraria* because it had to be paid in gold (*aurum*). Moreover, half of the sales tax that was due when goods were sold had to be paid by the seller. Members of these professional groups never appear as individuals in the royal correspondence. Theoderic's court dealt with the smiths and potters, carpenters and masons, cobblers and tanners, butchers and bakers, bartenders and shopkeepers who went about their business in the provincial cities of Italy only in fiscal terms.[89]

At places that served as entrepôts for trade goods, the exchange of goods was overseen by the tax farmers who had purchased the right to collect the sales tax. Beyond that, however, market supervision was the preserve of the municipal authorities. Rome and Ravenna were exceptions in this respect. A certain Florentius, who died in 548 at the age of seventy-two, was hailed by his successors decades later with palpable pride as the "father of the bakers of King Theoderic." The *praefectus annonae*, who was appointed by the king, was responsible for the bakers of Rome. Rome's lime burners answered to a royal functionary with the title of *praepositus calcis*, and some of the brickyards were state-owned. The state arms factories (*fabricae*) were distributed across several cities. A series of industries were treated as state monopolies: the production of purple dye, mining, and salt extraction. In Ravenna, the production of sarcophagi was also a monopoly. The owner, a certain Daniel, was instructed by Theoderic to observer moderation in setting prices. This measure was in the interest of the wealthy inhabitants of the city because only they could conceive of having themselves interred in such an expensive way.[90]

The task of providing food for the army and the royal court was given to contractors; the contracts ran for five years. The suppliers for the army received a fixed sum of gold from the royal administration and in return had to deliver goods to the Gothic troops stationed in northern Italy, as well as to Ravenna and Rome: wheat, wine, cheese, and meat and hay for the horses. This job was apparently lucrative or at least could be if the procurement and delivery costs were kept below the sum paid to the contractors. During the initial phase of Justinian's Gothic War, conflict broke out over the awarding of these contracts. With the help of influential patrons at court, certain persons who had not yet received a turn managed to have the previous contracts dissolved or not extended and then won new contracts on better terms. In the process, these people had circumvented Cassiodorus, who as praetorian prefect was officially responsible. Cassiodorus made sure that the decision was quickly rescinded. At the same time, he enabled the contractors to buy provisions at reduced prices. Since prices had dramatically risen because of crop failures, they would have suffered a loss otherwise: the contractors had calculated with lower prices when they had bid for the contracts. The people selling the goods were thus forced to make up the difference.[91]

Long-distance merchants who often came from the East—from Egypt, Syria, and Greece—lived in some coastal cities. There also were Jews among them, although they were by no means in the majority. In Naples, a merchant named Antiochus who had emigrated from Syria won wealth and prestige; he apparently belonged to a group of Jews who did business there. The silk trader Georgius, the son of one Julianus from Syrian Antioch, was a *vir clarissimus* and hence a member of the municipal elite of Ravenna. In the first quarter of the sixth century, a banker there named Julius acquired sufficient wealth to finance the church of San Vitale; construction began in 521 and reportedly cost 26,000 *solidi*. After the end of Gothic rule in Ravenna, Julius founded two more churches: Sant'Apollinare in Classe and San Michele in Africisco. We do not know, however, for what purpose Julius lent money; the loans may have been for state contracts, private trading ventures, or expenditure on a status-appropriate lifestyle and consumption. Trading carried a stigma in the eyes of the landholding elite. Merchants had a reputation for immoral conduct and living. Cassiodorus argues that all merchants (*negotiatores*) should be condemned because they all strove to buy low and sell high. That obviously was true of all craftsmen, he continued. Hence those who chased excessive profits and broke oaths to do so deserved one's utter disgust.[92]

6. LOSS OF URBANITY: CHANGING CITYSCAPES

For all their differences, the Italian cities during the heyday of the imperial period exhibited a high degree of uniformity in their institutions and in the fundamental structural elements of their central places; even small cities frequently had a central square, the forum, that was ringed by public buildings like curias, basilicas, and sanctuaries. These buildings constituted a privileged space for political communication and representation; statues and inscriptions commemorated local benefactors of the city and documented their relationships with imperial elites and the emperors. The cityscape was characterized by paved thoroughfares that were diligently kept clear. Public baths and venues for spectacles were maintained; there was almost always a theater, not uncommonly also an amphitheater for battles of man against man or man against beast, and in some isolated cases even a hippodrome. The realms of the living and the dead were strictly separated: necropolises were always located outside the inhabited area. In the imperial period, a city that fell short of this urbanistic standard was regarded as a primitive relic.[93]

The built urban environment that had accumulated by the third century remained largely intact in most Italian cities in the fourth century. New buildings of a secular nature had become rare, though, as the effort to maintain what already existed consumed the strength of many places. If resources were limited, utilitarian structures took precedence: baths, aqueducts, and city walls. In cities that already possessed city walls, they were renovated or reinforced; other cities now received a ring wall for the first time. The rise of Christianity to prominence resulted in the closing of the temples of the old gods within cities by the early fifth century; they were left to decay or repurposed. Christian communities initially erected churches on peripheral sites, but beginning in the late fourth century they increasingly built them in the heart of cities.

The previously gradual transformation of the cityscape accelerated dramatically over the fifth century. By the end of the sixth century, the amenities and appearance of Italian cities had radically changed. Although this development proceeded differently from city to city, we can still identify basic trends. Spolia—parts of older buildings such as columns, architraves, capitals, and blocks—were used almost exclusively as building materials for stone structures. Their reuse could serve an ideological purpose, as, for instance, when one prominently integrated spolia from a defunct temple into a newly built church; but there was also the very pragmatic reason that it was easier and cheaper to use spolia than to produce new architectural elements. Public squares were given up and built up with small structures; the monumental buildings on their periphery were put to private use or fell into disrepair. This trend was possible because the forum had lost its meaning as a representational space: the practice of honoring deserving citizens, patrons of the city, and members of the imperial household with statues came to a halt in northern Italy by the middle of the fourth century. In the south, it persisted until the early fifth century, but only in Rome down to the century's end. With statues, there also vanished the honorary inscriptions that previously would have been carved on their bases. As the forums were surrendered to private use, the strict separation of areas used for public purposes and those in which people lived, traded goods, or practiced an industry also lapsed. Cities thus gave up their old political centers. The functions of these spaces passed only in part to others, often coalescing around bishops' churches. And last but not least, the formerly strict separation of the realms of the living and the dead disappeared as corpses began to be buried ever more often within the city walls from the fifth century on.[94]

The venues for spectacles and amusements were also now abandoned in many places as people no longer had any use for them. In Theoderic's kingdom, plays were staged regularly only in Rome and a handful of other cities. Most amphitheaters also lost their function. Battles between gladiators had been suspended over a century before. In few cities could patrons still afford to put on animal hunts (*venationes*)—Rome, Ravenna, and Milan. In many places, however, people still worked to maintain structures connected to the water supply. This was a necessary condition for keeping the public baths operational.[95]

Most new buildings of the fifth and sixth centuries were churches. In addition to those sponsored by Theoderic, which we shall discuss below, private individuals financed the construction of several major churches for the Catholic community of Ravenna. In Rome, Pope Felix IV converted a building on the Forum Pacis into the church of Santi Cosma e Damiano. Churches were also built in many provincial cities: in Aosta (Augusta Praetoria), Padua, Trento (Tridentum), Vicenza (Vicetia), Trieste (Tergeste), Pula (Pola), and Parenzo/Poreč(Parentium). Members of *illustris* families, but also municipal notables and clergymen, appear as sponsors. At St. Peter im Holz (ancient Teurnia) in the province of Noricum Mediterraneum (in modern Carinthia), the *vir spectabilis* Ursus and his wife Ursa sponsored the mosaic floor of a basilica.[96]

For the period from 450 to 600, we thus can identify a broad trend of material impoverishment accompanied by population decline in the cities of Italy. The vast majority of cities, however, retained their economic, social, and administrative function as the central place of a given territory. At the end of this period, the outward appearance of cities had dramatically changed. Many features that were considered typically urban in the fourth century had disappeared. The technological sophistication of construction had also declined: new private dwellings were now built of wood, not stone, and luxurious urban houses were subdivided into numerous small apartments. If we measure the cities of Italy circa 600 against the standards of previous centuries, we must conclude that although the cities endured, a specific form of urban life and its associated urban framework had disappeared; ancient *urbanitas* had been lost.[97]

Since the processes outlined here can be dated only within a span of approximately fifty years, it is impossible to determine how advanced the transformation was at a given place in Italy when Theoderic came to power. We can clearly identify only the state that had been reached around the year 600, after Justinian's Gothic War had devastated broad swaths of Italy. It thus remains difficult to give a precise description of the structural condition of Italian cities in Theoderic's day. Only in exceptional cases are excavations possible in cities that are still inhabited today. We have already discussed Ravenna: there Theoderic enlarged the palace and surrounded it with a colonnade; he also built the adjoining "Palace Church" (Sant'Apollinare Nuovo today) and the now lost

Basilica Herculis. The king furthermore had Ravenna's aqueduct restored. The city continued to enjoy royal patronage under Theoderic's successors. Theodahad reinforced its fortifications by digging a ditch in front of its walls.

Ticinum also served as one of Theoderic's residences, and the king seems to have invested considerable funds in building projects there, too, although their archeological remains have not yet been identified: a palace, baths, an amphitheater, and two "new" city walls. The amphitheater was apparently completed after Theoderic's death because his grandson Athalaric had seats constructed in it. Ticinum was located at a bridge across the Po, was heavily fortified, and was the base of a Gothic *comes*. During the second phase of Justinian's Gothic War, it was one of the Goths' most important strongholds, along with Verona; Totila had the royal treasure kept safe in Ticinum.[98]

We have no way of knowing whether Theoderic used the old imperial palace in Milan as a dwelling; the fact that he had a residence built in nearby Monza would appear to suggest that he did not. The transformation of the cityscape sketched above was also in full swing in Milan during Theoderic's reign. The city had served as an imperial residence until the year 402 and boasted a hippodrome in addition to a theater and amphitheater. After the amphitheater was torn down in the early fifth century, however, its demise was followed by the demolition of the major colonnaded street in the southeastern part of the city (the Via Porticata). The monumental heart of the city, however, remained partly intact into the sixth century, as did its churches. Milan was, moreover, the only city in Italy other than Rome where chariot races were still held now and then in Theoderic's time. Milan defected from the Goths in the year 537, was recaptured by them a year later after a protracted siege, and was heavily damaged.[99]

Verona was significantly smaller than Milan, although its amphitheater from the high imperial period, still intact today, could hold 30,000 spectators. Theoderic had seized Verona in 490, and the city remained a Gothic stronghold in Italy until the end. His palace on the Colle di S. Pietro was later demolished, but it is depicted on a view of the city from the tenth century, the so-called Iconographia Rateriana. Founded as a Roman colony in 89 BCE, Verona was surrounded by a ring wall that was renovated in the third century CE. Theoderic had these walls reinforced and extended to the far bank of the Adige so that they encircled his palace. Excavations within the urban area, which are sporadically possible in Verona, show that its public spaces and buildings had also lost their old functions. The forum was partly abandoned in the fifth century; the capitolium was torn down in the early sixth century. The amphitheater was used as a quarry. Smaller dwelling spaces were built into a series of luxurious townhouses. The *Anonymus Valesianus* accuses Theoderic of destroying the altar of the basilica of Santo Stefano, which is still standing today. Since the basilica was located outside the city walls but in immediate proximity to the palace, it has been conjectured that a rededication of the church for the Homoean cult may lie behind this accusation; in light of its location, Santo Stefano would have been ideal as a kind of court church.[100]

Brescia, like Verona, is one of the few cities of northern Italy the late antique development of which has been well studied by archeologists. Like Verona, Brescia also remained under Gothic rule until the fall of the kingdom. Founded as a Roman colony under Emperor Augustus, Brescia had possessed a monumental urban core with a capitolium and basilica since the Flavian dynasty (69–96); a theater and baths stood nearby. This area lost its representative character and political function in the early fifth century. Wooden structures were built on the forum. Parts of the unwalled area were abandoned; luxurious houses in the south crumbled. The aqueduct, however, remained operational under Gothic rule, and although the circuit of the city walls was shortened, it was also reinforced. An expansive cathedral complex was built in the western part of the city that served as a new center.[101]

While the Po Valley made up the heartland of Gothic rule in Italy, Aquileia found itself on the periphery. The city was founded in 181 BCE as a Roman colony on a navigable river a few kilometers from the lagoon of Grado. When Diocletian divided Italy into provinces, Aquileia became the seat of the governor of the province of Venetia et Histria. The city was home to several emperors in the late third and fourth centuries, and for this purpose it received a palace and a circus. The cathedral of Aquileia is one of the earliest in all Italy. Aquileia was besieged and captured, however, by Attila's army in 452. The city never recovered from the destruction, not least because trade in the Danube region probably declined steeply during the restless decades that followed. The forum and adjoining market buildings were abandoned, and the ring wall was significantly shortened by the construction of a transverse wall. The old monumental center of the city thereafter lay outside the city walls. The cathedral complex, in contrast, was restored and developed into the new center of the city. Aquileia apparently received additional city walls under Gothic rule. During the war against Justinian, wine and wheat were requisitioned for the Gothic army on the territory of Aquileia. No trace has been found, however, of a Gothic garrison; Aquileia did not play a part in Justinian's Gothic War. Soon after the conclusion of the war, its former harbor, Grado, rose up to become the "new Aquileia."[102]

These examples attest to the king's care for the cities that served him personally as residences. What measures did the central administration take to maintain the urban infrastructure of ordinary provincial cities? The list of examples that can be compiled from the *Variae* and other texts is short. Theoderic restored the aqueduct of Parma; after his death, the notables of the city were ordered in the name of his grandson Athalaric to clean its clogged sewers. Theoderic instructed the *architectus* Aloiosus to restore the thermal baths at Abano near Parma. Theoderic awarded the city of Spoleto additional resources to support its baths. He transferred ownership of a public colonnade that was no longer being used in the same city to his personal physician Helpidius on the condition that he restore it. Finally, he told Aemilianus, the bishop of Vercelli, to bring construction work on the city's aqueduct to a conclusion. We learn nothing about the finances of the project on this occasion.[103]

Every one of these cases concerns measures intended to maintain the water supply of cities. They are limited to a small number of cities in northern Italy and very seldom entailed financial investments. The second area in which the royal administration took an active part was the construction or reinforcement of fortifications. After Arles was conquered, its walls and towers were to be repaired with resources that the king had made available. In Syracuse, the *comes* Gildila levied dues to repair the city walls, although these funds were ultimately diverted to another purpose. In Catania, in contrast, the municipal notables asked the king for permission to use stone from the city's dilapidated theater to repair the walls; they were granted permission, but the project apparently was never carried out.[104]

The northern Alps had been secured by a line of *castella* ("fortresses") since the fifth century. In part, these fortifications consisted of outposts for only thirty to fifty soldiers at strategic points; others, however, were major fortresses that covered up to fifty hectares and could hold many men in the event of war. This defensive line was maintained and reinforced under Gothic rule. In this sense we can understand the order issued to the Goths and Romans living in Tortona, an unfortified city, to reconstruct a nearby *castellum* into a kind of fortified refuge and the analogous order issued to the Goths and Romans of Feltre. In the latter case, it is explicitly stated that a Gothic commissary (*saio*) would oversee the work. The construction of a fortified settlement near Trento, which is described as a city but the name of which Cassiodorus regrettably leaves out, probably also served military purposes. The surrounding cities were obliged to carry out the work, for which they were supposed to receive appropriate compensation. As for what might lurk behind the name of a place called Theodericopolis in the anonymous *Cosmography of Ravenna* from approximately the year 700, we are in the dark; this place has been identified with the city of Chur (Curia) in the province of Raetia II (in modern Graubünden), which was subsequently renamed after the king, but it has also been placed in the neighborhood of Lake Constance. We thus cannot say who took the initiative in this case.[105]

It remains for us to cast a glance at Rome. In the year 500, Rome was still the largest and most populous city in the western Mediterranean. It was the official residence of the wealthiest senators and the seat of the bishopric with the greatest resources. The city had lost some of its old luster, however. Cassiodorus describes Rome in a nostalgic tone:

> It is obvious how great the population of the city of Rome was, such that provisions obtained from faraway regions satiated it while the surrounding provinces sufficed to feed foreign visitors since that imported abundance was kept for the city itself. For how could the city that possessed the governance of the world be small in number? The vast expanses of the walls; the wide embrace for spectacles; the astonishing size of baths; and that multitude of mills, which served specifically to provide food, attest to the throngs of its citizens. For if this equipment had not become conventional, it would not have been needed since it neither serves as decoration nor suits any other purpose. And finally these things, like precious garments for bodies, are traces of cities, for no one agrees to make superfluous things that he knows can be realized only at great expense.[106]

Cassiodorus compares Rome of the early sixth century to a person whose old clothes have become too big. The city walls were too extensive, the baths and venues for games too large, the mills too numerous for the present population. The population of Rome indeed fell to a fraction of its former size over the fifth century: between 50,000 and 100,000 instead of at least 500,000. Within the massive circuit of walls that Emperor Aurelian built and Emperor Honorius had reinforced, there must have been quarters that had only a few inhabitants left. Here, houses stood empty, roofs caved in, and trash heaps piled up in open spaces.[107]

The decay was undoubtedly worse in outer districts, but it did not spare quarters that had formerly been the favorite haunts of senators. The *mons Caelius*, where the palace of Melania the Younger had been just one of many aristocratic houses in the year 410, was almost completely abandoned by its inhabitants in the latter half of the fifth century. On the *mons Oppius*, a cemetery buried the Porticus Liviae, a large colonnade that had been financed by the wife of Emperor Augustus. Preserving the monumental buildings in the heart of the city had become too great a burden. After a fire in the early fifth century, only the facade of the Basilica Aemilia next to the Curia was restored. The urban prefect Quadratianus deemed it appropriate to note in an inscription that he had restored the dilapidated baths of Emperor Constantine, which had suffered from neglect and the consequences of civil war, as best he could "with a small budget," as far as "the limited resources of the commonwealth" allowed. Emperor Majorian introduced draconian punishments for demolishing public buildings to obtain building materials for private projects. He decreed in a law that in the future public buildings could be torn down only with his permission and even then only if the senate came to the conclusion, after careful study, that restoration was no longer possible.[108]

Rome clearly looked like it had seen better days in the year 500. Even so, its collection of monumental buildings was still impressive. The houses of senatorial families in the heart of the city still resembled palaces. Considerable effort was made to preserve the architectural legacy of the past. A whole series of officials was engaged in monitoring public buildings. The *comes formarum* watched over the water conduits of the city (*formae*). An official with the title of *comes Romanus* was supposed to prevent Rome's countless statues from being damaged or stolen. A "building official" (*architectus*) was responsible for the cityscape as a whole. These officials were obviously overwhelmed. In 510, Theoderic had to send the *vir spectabilis* John to Rome as a special commissary because it had been reported that bronze and lead had been stolen from public monuments and water had been diverted from the aqueducts for private mills and gardens. There was still a kind of fire department under the authority of the *praefectus vigilum*. The king also appointed a *comes* responsible for Portus and Ostia, the two harbors of Rome. The office of *curator riparum et alvei Tiberis et cloacarum*, who was responsible for protecting the often-flooded banks of the Tiber and keeping the sewers clean, seems to have lapsed under Gothic rule. This job was presumably let out to contractors. Since there were complaints, though, the special commissary just mentioned was also instructed to look into them.[109]

The king cared about the preservation of the public buildings of Rome and used his own resources to preserve them. "Care for the city of Rome is always alive in Our thoughts. For what might be worthier of Our attention than to carry out the restoration of the city that adorns Our commonwealth?" Cassiodorus wrote in the king's name to the urban prefect Argolicus. When Theoderic came to Rome personally in the year 500, he gave the city 120,000 bushels of grain to help the poor and made available 200 pounds of gold annually for repairs to the palace and city walls. This sum, however, was supposed to come out of the wine treasury of the urban prefect. When complaints of irregularities in the management of this building fund reached his ears, Theoderic had the allegations investigated. He instructed the *patricius* Symmachus to restore the Theater of Pompeii, which threatened to collapse, and provided him with money from his own "chamber" (*cubiculum*) to do so. Moreover, Theoderic reopened a depot for roof tiles in the city of Rome, the *portus Licini*, which was supposed to deliver 25,000 tiles annually to repair roofs in the city. Adjoining depots that had been occupied by private citizens were supposed to be made usable again for the same purpose. The tiles themselves were produced by entrepreneurs who had leased the royal clay supply and tile manufactures (*figlinae*). Numerous roof tiles stamped in Theoderic's name have in fact been found in Rome, in especially high concentration near the churches of San Martino ai Monti (on the Esquiline) and Santi Cosma e Damiano (at the Forum Pacis), which were repaired or renovated under Popes Symmachus and Felix IV. Theoderic apparently shared the expense by providing roof tiles.[110]

Fundamentally, of course, Theoderic viewed the maintenance of the public buildings of Rome as the senators' job. He was happy to create incentives for them by authorizing the privatization of dilapidated buildings if the recipients promised to repair these structures. The *patricius* Albinus received the Porticus Curva for private use; the *patricius* Paulinus (cos. 498) acquired some state granaries that were no longer needed and had become dilapidated. The king had to realize, however, that the recipients did not always keep their promises: temples and other buildings were not repaired but rather simply torn down after they passed into private ownership. Theoderic himself did not hesitate to use the *domus Pinciana*, a palace owned by the crown, as a quarry to decorate his own residence in Ravenna.[111]

The will to conserve is most conspicuous in the heart of Rome. Not a few monuments were repaired for the last time in their history under Odoacer and Theoderic. The urban prefect Venantius repaired the podium and the arena of the Colosseum after an earthquake in 484. The site was still used for animal hunts under Theoderic, but corpses were already being buried in the vicinity, although the king had explicitly reiterated the prohibition on burials inside the city walls of Rome in his *Edict*. The Circus Maximus was also still operating in the middle of the sixth century; the last known restoration was undertaken by an unknown urban prefect in the late fifth century. The urban prefect Valerius Florianus had repairs made to the Curia; an inscription dates the measure to the reign of "our lords" (*domini nostri*), the "perpetual emperor" (*perpetuus Augustus*) Anastasius, and the "most glorious and triumphant man" (*gloriosissimus ac triumfalis vir*) Theoderic. Repairs were also made under Theoderic to the Crypta Balbi, a complex enclosed on three sides on the Campus Martius that began to decay in the fifth century and was already used as a dump. In all these cases, inscriptions ensured that the restorations were documented publicly and permanently.[112]

Rome was exceptional in every way in Theoderic's kingdom. The king not only invested in preserving its monumental buildings; he also provided large sums to purchase food for its common population. Since the third century, the people of Rome received not only bread and wine, but also pork at no expense. The *praefectus annonae*, who was appointed by the king, was still responsible for organizing this service. There also still existed publicly funded chairs for the "liberal arts" (*artes liberales*), grammar and rhetoric. Admittedly, just a single rhetor can be identified with certainty as the occupant of such a chair; two other rhetors may have been private citizens. A public chair for law is also attested for the first time under Theoderic, although it can hardly have been created by him. After Theoderic's death, the royal administration wanted to reduce this chair's stipend on the occasion of appointing a new occupant but withdrew the proposed reduction after the senate protested. These institutions were unique; even in Milan and Ravenna, higher education in the sixth century was available only in private schools.[113]

7. THE KING AND HIS LAND: DID THEODERIC HAVE AN ECONOMIC POLICY?

With respect to the rural population, Theoderic's government by and large continued the policy of the late Roman emperors. Like them, Theoderic attempted to conserve the social order as he had found it. The taxation system depended on agricultural production, after all. He still, however, indulged large landholders more than the late Roman emperors had done, allowing landlords to transfer slaves that had leased land and soil-bound tenants to other owners while keeping the land itself. In Theoderic's *Edict*, Theoderic states,

> May every master be permitted to transfer rural slaves of either sex, even if they are bound to the soil [*originaria*], from estates that he possesses physically and by legitimate title to other places he controls, or to assign them to urban duties, such that they become attached to the estates to which they have migrated according to their master's will or are rightly considered members of the urban house-servants; nor may any investigation be launched into such actions and orders, as, for example, on the grounds of their origin [*origo*]. Masters shall be permitted to alienate persons of the aforementioned condition without any portion of land with written documentation—or to cede, sell, or donate them to whomever they please.[114]

The vast majority of the rural population did not have any direct connection to the king and his court. For slaves and soil-bound *coloni*, the royal administration could be reached only by way of patrons—through major leaseholders, estate managers, and landlords. The royal administration took pains, however, to protect small landowners from abuse at the hands of their more powerful neighbors. When a certain Castorius complained that the praetorian prefect Faustus Niger had illegally seized his estate, the king ordered the *saio* Triwila and the aide (*apparitor*) Ferrocinctus to make sure that the *illustris* senator surrendered the estate and added a second one of equal value. Some letters addressed to the owners of small and middling estates have also survived. On these occasions, the royal chancellery emphasized that protecting people of humble status (*humiles*) was especially close to the king's heart. A complaint by two Romans that a Goth named Tancan had illegally seized their small plot (*agellus*) and robbed them of their freedom moved Athalaric's government to dispatch the high-ranking Cunigast to investigate the matter. In three further cases, the royal chancellery wrote to bishops accused of illegally seizing private land. Not a single letter addressed to a peasant, however, survives. Instead, excepting the administration of royal estates, we encounter only the managers of large estates who worked on behalf of senators of *spectabilis* or *illustris* rank as the addressees of letters in rural contexts.[115]

The late Roman state was a major economic factor. That is also true of Gothic Italy. A considerable portion of all the arable land belonged to the king, who leased it out to contractors. The royal administration collected taxes in gold and used it to finance the court and the army. By paying the salaries of civil officials and awarding donatives to soldiers and by buying large quantities of food to provide for the troops, the city of Rome, and the royal residence, the royal administration not only drove the distribution of resources, affecting the standard of living of broad sections of society—positively for some, negatively for others—but also influenced the specialization of regional production. It created demand and buying power according to its needs. The administration, moreover, awarded lucrative contracts to entrepreneurs who delivered goods to the army and court or collected taxes for the king. The late Roman state also provided an institutional framework for economic activity and encouraged the exchange of goods by inspiring confidence in the smooth conducting of business. It did so above all by providing a stable currency, sophisticated legal institutions, judicial dispute resolution, and (admittedly, quite imperfect) protection from violence.[116]

The fact that the late Roman state itself was an economic actor and provided an institutional framework to reduce transaction costs does not mean that it pursued anything like an economic policy, understood as a deliberate effort to regulate and promote the overall functioning of the economy. Neither Theoderic nor the late Roman emperors had the will or means to do so. The royal administration closely monitored trends in market prices because it collected taxes primarily in gold, but it spent the lion's share of these funds to buy food. If one wanted to prevent price fluctuations to the detriment of the state, one had to know the prices that were paid on the market. In that regard, the late Roman administration thought in highly economic terms. But it had no interest in calculating the kingdom's total economic performance—its gross national product—nor would it have been capable of doing so.

The royal administration naturally presumed that it could collect more taxes when harvests were especially abundant. Experience had also shown that the absence of war stimulated agricultural production. Cassiodorus justifies a tax hike for Sicily (which he was rescinding in Athalaric's name!) with the argument that a long period of peace had made it possible to work the fields undisturbed and caused the population to grow. But the authorities were always aware that agricultural yields would not rise continuously because an increase in productivity was possible only to a limited extent. Growth was thus pursued by enlarging the area of cultivable land, not through technological innovation or by improving the institutional framework. It was not considered the ruler's job to ensure that the economy as a whole steadily grew. No one asked for government loans to found businesses; no one regarded an individual's level of education as a decisive factor in his economic situation. The idea that the government should bolster weak regions by transferring tax revenues there was also irrelevant; there was no structural economic policy in this sense.[117]

The late antique state nonetheless presented an incentive for investment insofar as it was prepared to surrender untilled land to private individuals who accepted the obligation to pay taxes on it, as in the case of the marshes between Tripontum and Terracina known as the Decemnovium. In another example, two *viri spectabiles* pledged to drain a swamp in the territory of Spoleto; when one of them failed to fulfill his part of the bargain, the other one claimed the entire land for himself. The procedure for public buildings that could no longer be maintained was similar. Direct engagement by the king, in contrast, was viewed as something exceptional: the fact that Theoderic had a swamp drained and a fruit garden planted on it at his residence in Ravenna was celebrated in an inscription and gave Ennodius material for a panegyrical poem.[118]

While acting as the guardian of the legal order, the king strove to maintain the conditions that facilitated the exchange of goods. He also ensured that there was a generally accepted currency. Like the Roman emperors, Theoderic and his first two successors issued coins in all three metals—that is, in gold, silver, and copper—that were supposed to be accepted and exchanged at their nominal value. The kings of the Burgundians, in contrast, minted only gold; those of the

Vandals, only silver and bronze. The coin production of the Gothic kings was centralized at a handful of places in Italy and under the supervision of the *comes largitionum*; the personnel of each mint was under the authority of officials appointed by the king. Counterfeiting and debasing coins were subject to severe punishments. The most important gold coin was the *solidus*, weighing approximately 4.5 grams; seventy-two *solidi* were struck from a single Roman pound. Smaller gold denominations corresponded in weight and value to one-half (*semissis*) and one-third (*tremissis*) of a *solidus*. Theoderic also issued silver coinage, which, in contrast to his gold coinage, featured monograms on the reverse that marked them as minted by the king. The nominal value of gold coins was high and guaranteed by their weight and purity; they thus were used to accrue wealth; to pay taxes, fees, and rents; and to purchase real estate and luxury goods. For everyday business, one needed bronze or copper coins, indeed in great numbers. Around the middle of the fifth century, a wide gap had opened between the smallest gold denomination, the *tremissis*, and the only bronze coin that was still minted at the time, the *minimus* or *nummus*: one *tremissis* was worth no less than 2,400 *nummi*. Beginning around the year 490, copper coins worth forty *nummi* began to be minted in Italy and later also coins worth twenty, ten, and five *nummi*. This coinage reform undoubtedly simplified buying and selling on the market. But Theoderic hardly had these coins minted merely to reduce transaction costs: the king provided his warriors with small change because he wanted them to pay for what they needed to live rather than simply take it. It was for similar reasons that Theoderic's nephew and successor Theodahad had large quantities of copper coins minted when he moved the royal court from Ravenna to Rome in the winter of 535–536. Like that of the Roman emperors, the coinage of the Gothic kings served primarily to finance state needs and political objectives; economic considerations were secondary at best.[119]

It was definitely possible to borrow money in Theoderic's kingdom; moneychangers and moneylenders are attested in Ravenna and Rome. The banker Julius of Ravenna made a fortune from this profession. But there was no royal central bank, and the notion of regulating the amount of money in circulation by imposing an official interest rate was unknown. The royal administration intervened in market developments only in exceptional cases, when crop failures or war threatened to cause or had already caused food to become scarce. In such cases, the government decreed price reductions, which were justified not in economic but in ethical terms: a good king did not let his subjects go hungry. Strict price controls were observed at the imperial residence of Ravenna because here the king had to show himself as a caring ruler in everyday interactions. Otherwise, it was the rule that "the selling of foodstuffs ought to be subject to the exigencies of the time so that neither excessively high prices are demanded in times of plenty nor excessively low prices in times of dearth," as Cassiodorus once declared: just as sellers should not overprice foodstuffs after a good harvest, so buyers should not demand discounts when food is scarce.[120]

The royal administration taxed imports and exports but restricted them only in exceptional cases. During the war in Provence, it prohibited the export of pork (*laridum*), which was evidently needed for the army. The task of enforcing this ban was placed on the contractors for the sales tax—that is, on private citizens, who maintained offices in the port cities. Theoderic reminded the praetorian prefect Faustus Niger on this occasion that grain could not be exported from a province until the needs of the state had been completely satisfied. That was the extent of direct state intervention in the market.[121]

Theoderic did not pursue an economic or social policy; he did not seek to make the social order or economic system of Italy conform to a given model. On the contrary: as soon as he had secured his Goths with a guaranteed livelihood on Italian soil, all his thoughts and actions served to maintain the status quo he had created. The development of Roman law was also regarded as complete in Theoderic's kingdom. Cassiodorus explains that it was customary among the ancients to decree new laws to close loopholes; in the present day, however, it sufficed to preserve the ancients' decrees. Although prizing the way of the ancestors (*mos maiorum*) was in keeping with Roman tradition, this attitude was not inevitable in the sixth century. Emperor Justinian pursued a policy of legal and social reform until the 540s; he incessantly proclaimed that he wanted to eliminate all ambiguities and contradictions in the legal system and close loopholes by systematizing and codifying the law; he would replace norms that had become obsolete with better ones. This determination to bring change garnered the emperor the reputation of a revolutionary in conservative circles. Theoderic and his successors, in contrast, totally lacked the ambition to shape law, state, and society; the Gothic king was no "reformer," nor did he aspire to be one.[122]

10

A HERETIC KING: RELIGIOUS DIVERSITY AND THE IMPERATIVE OF ORTHODOXY

1. THE "CHURCH OF GOTHIC LAW"

The core of the army with which Theoderic conquered Italy consisted of warriors who viewed themselves as Goths. These warriors differed from the population of Italy not only by virtue of their military function, which defined their lifestyle and outward appearance, but also in language and religion. Like Theoderic himself, his warriors normally spoke Gothic, and also like Theoderic they belonged to a religious community whose professed faith had been regarded in Italy as heretical for over a century. The majority of the population of Italy viewed members of this religious community as "Arians"—that is, followers of the Alexandrian presbyter Areios (Latin: Arius), whose teachings had been condemned in 325 at the Council of Nicaea and had been considered the epitome of heresy ever after.[1]

In reality, the creed of the church to which Theoderic and the vast majority of his warriors belonged bore little resemblance to the teachings of Arius: it was based more on the decrees of the Council of Constantinople of the year 360. The relationship between God the Father and God the Son had been defined as "similar" (Greek: *homoios*), but the council made no attempt to define this similarity more specifically, instead describing it as "similar according to Holy Scripture." For this reason, modern scholars call this the "Homoean" creed and its adherents "Homoeans." The Gothic theologian Wulfila interpreted this compromise formula as the unity of God the Father with the subordinate God the Son. His creed is transmitted to us in Latin by his student Auxentius:

I, Wulfila, bishop and confessor, have always thus believed and cross over to my Lord in this faith alone. I believe [*credo*] that there is only one God the

Father, unbegotten and invisible, and [I believe] in his only begotten Son, our
Lord and God, creator and maker of all creation, having no one like himself—
and hence the one God of all things, the Father, is the God of our God—and
[I believe] in the Holy Spirit, illuminating and sanctifying virtue, as Christ said
to his apostles after his resurrection: "Behold I send among you the one promised by my Father, but you sit in the city of Jerusalem until you are clothed in
virtue from on high" [Luke 24:29]; and, moreover, "You will receive the virtue
that comes over you from the Holy Spirit"—neither god nor master but the
faithful servant of Christ, not equal but subordinate and obeying the Son in all
things, and the Son subordinate and obeying his God the Father in all things.[2]

In the Roman Empire, the Homoean Creed was condemned at the Council
of Constantinople in 381 and replaced in almost every Christian confession by
the Nicene-Constantinopolitan Creed, which is still recognized today. Homoean
bishops were expelled from their churches by order of Emperor Theodosius I,
and their communities were driven underground. Shortly before the Homoean
Creed was declared heretical in the Roman Empire, however, it had been
adopted by Fritigern's Goths. These Goths did not go along with the reversal of
imperial religious policy and continued to adhere to Homoean Christianity after
the Council of Constantinople of 381. Gothic missionaries quickly disseminated
it to other peoples who spoke a form of Germanic, making use of a Gothic translation of the Bible that could be readily understood in the broader Germanic
language community. The Vandals had adopted Homoean Christianity before
they crossed to North Africa. When this confession reached the Goths living in
Pannonia in the middle of the fifth century is not transmitted. It is certain,
though, that Theoderic grew up as a Christian and that his army was accompanied by Christian priests.[3]

By approximately the year 500, Visigoths and Ostrogoths, as well as Gepids,
Suebi, Burgundians, and Vandals all adhered to the Homoean Creed. The followers of this confession viewed themselves as members of the one universal
and orthodox church of Christ. Hence in their own minds, Homoean communities were "orthodox" and "universal" (*catholicus*) because these same terms
that are used to designate certain Christian confessions today meant the same
thing to contemporaries then. Since both Homoean clerics and their opponents were convinced that orthodoxy was the non-negotiable precondition of
membership in the one true church of Christ, they regarded all Christians who
rejected their creed as heretics. That included the vast majority of Christians
both inside and outside the Roman Empire in the year 500, including those
who made common cause with the bishop of Rome and have been called
Roman Catholic in retrospect.[4]

Salvian, a presbyter from Marseille who composed a text in 440 to show that the Romans' defeats at the hands of the Goths and Vandals were the deserved punishment of God, describes the relationship between the Homoean barbarians and the Catholic Romans in the following terms: "They therefore are heretics, but not knowingly. In a word, they are heretics among us; they are not among themselves. They deem themselves to be so Catholic that they dishonor us ourselves with the label of 'heretics.' Therefore, what they are to us, we are to them. We are convinced that they insult divine generation because they say the Son is less than the Father. They consider us disrespectful toward the Father because we believe [Father and Son] are equals."[5] Auxentius, one of Wulfila's students, reports that his teacher claimed in his sermons and teachings that "all heretics are not Christians but rather antichrists, not pious but rather impious, not religious but irreligious, not full of the fear of God but rather shameless, not hopeful but hopeless, not worshippers of God, but rather godless, not teachers but rather seducers, not preachers but prevaricators." In another passage, he explains that Wulfila taught that there was only one church of Christ and only one community of Christians; all other communities were "not churches of God, but rather synagogues of Satan."[6]

Ecclesiastical communion with Christians of other confessions was unthinkable under these conditions. Homoean clerics viewed baptism as valid and effective only if it had been performed by a clergyman from their own ranks, and they insisted on repeating baptism if a Christian wanted to convert to their faith.[7]

The everyday ecclesiastical life of Homoean communities also distinguished them from their surroundings in the Gothic and Vandalic kingdoms because mass was normally celebrated in the Gothic language. Since only recently we also now know of an example of this practice: a few years ago, the remains of a sermon written in Gothic were discovered in Bologna; a text of Augustine had been copied over it. Yet even when Homoean clerics preached in Latin, they cited the Gothic Bible. Gothic-Latin editions of biblical texts were produced for this purpose. The Gothic formula for *kyrie eleison* ("Lord, have pity") is transmitted from Vandalic North Africa: *froja arme*. In the fragments of Wulfila's translation of the Bible, we can read the Lord's Prayer in Gothic; it begins with the following words (in modern transcription, in which *ei* should be pronounced as a long *e* as in "bee," *ai* as a short *a* as in "hay," and *þ* as *th* as in "then"):

atta unsar þu in himinam | weihnai namo þein, qimai þiudinassus þeins,
    wairþai wilja þeins | swe in himina jah ana airþai.
    (Thou our father in heaven | holy be thy name, thy kingdom come, thy will be done | as in heaven so also on earth.)[8]

Homoean communities also followed their own calendar of feast days. As emerges from a fragmentary list of martyrs, the Gothic Homoeans of the early fifth century celebrated Gothic martyrs on certain days of the year, in addition to the apostles and Emperor Constantius II, who had wanted to impose the Homoean creed on the entire empire. Finally, the Homoean liturgy differed from the usual practice of adherents of the Nicene Creed in an essential point: whereas the latter praised God with the words "Honor be to the Father and to the Son and to the Holy Spirit," among the Homoeans this prayer was worded, "Honor be to the Father through the Son in the Holy Spirit.[9] Homoean theologians refused to take theological positions that were not directly supported by passages from the Bible; they thus opposed efforts to formulate Christian doctrine with concepts drawn from ancient philosophy. Theological literature in Gothic and Latin was composed in the territories of the Gothic and Vandal kings; as might be expected in light of the fundamental biblicism of Homoean theology, it consisted of exegetical rather than systematic works. The problem of translating biblical texts into other languages received particular attention. In the view of the Homoean church, the development of Christian doctrine had reached its conclusion. Homoean theologians, as far as we can tell, did not participate in the debates in the East over the divine and human nature of Jesus Christ or in the discussions about human free will and divine grace that were triggered in the West by Pelagius and Augustine.[10]

The structure of the Homoean churches in the Germanic kingdoms differed significantly from those that had emerged in the Roman Empire. They had ecclesiastical offices just like the imperial church, ranging from lectors (young men responsible for reading Holy Scripture aloud) to deacons and presbyters to bishops at the head of congregations; in contrast to the imperial church, however, under which theoretically every city had its own bishop, the bishops whose congregations consisted of Germanic warriors of the Homoean confession were not indissolubly tied to individual cities. It was neither sensible nor feasible to assign bishops to a single local community as long as the faithful they served were frequently on the move. The ties between priests and Homoean congregations thus were personal rather than territorial; the clergy was part of a broader mobile group. In contrast to the emperor's Catholic soldiers, who could normally expect to find religious infrastructure at their place of deployment within the Roman Empire and thus required special military clergymen only in exceptional cases, Homoean warrior bands brought their clergy with them. During such phases of migration, just a single bishop might have sufficed for the entire band if there was a sufficient number of presbyters on hand to hold mass for smaller groups.[11]

Because Germanic warriors did not settle en bloc in the post-Roman kingdoms, the need for priests and bishops rose dramatically after they dispersed to their sundry settlement areas. But even in the Germanic kingdoms, there were not enough Homoean bishops to create a dense network across an entire territory. A Homoean bishop naturally held office where the king made his residence, thereby becoming a kind of court bishop by virtue of this physical proximity. Homoean bishops probably also served in some other cities where a Homoean congregation could be found. We incidentally learn of a Homoean priest or bishop (*sacerdos*) named Wicthar who owned land in the territory of the city of Agen (in Aquitania) in the reign of Alaric II. Many cities, however, probably had neither a Homoean clergy nor a Homoean bishop because there was no congregation that they might have served.[12]

Under these conditions, it was unnecessary to hold annual provincial synods as the imperial church typically did. Homoean bishops appear to have met one another more or less regularly at the royal court. On account of their small number and weak ties to the majority population, Homoean bishops were much more dependent on the king's favor in the Germanic kingdoms than their Catholic counterparts were. They thus did not constitute an independent ecclesiastical power that might have opposed the secular authority. It is no coincidence that our sources never show Homoean bishops in opposition to the king. Homoean congregations may have viewed themselves as part of a worldwide church of Christ, but in practice they existed as territorial churches, each of which was focused on its respective ruler. Contacts among Homoean bishops scarcely extended beyond the territory of the king who protected them and who expected unconditional loyalty in return. They had no official connection to the Catholic bishops of the imperial church or to the bishop of Rome. Moreover, there is no trace of links to fellow bishops of the same confession in other kingdoms. Homoean bishops' sphere of action and communication was limited to the territory of individual kings; political and ecclesiastical borders thus broadly coincided. Hence Homoean kings did not need to bring the bishops of their faith together at general councils. Such territorial synods took place in the sixth century only where Germanic kings endeavored to assemble the Catholic bishops of their kingdom into an organizational unit: at Agde in the Visigothic kingdom under Alaric II in 506; at Orléans in France under Clovis in 511; and at Epao in the Burgundian kingdom under Sigismund in 516. The political fragmentation of the post-Roman West also resulted in ecclesiastical fragmentation in Catholic territory, but it was only just emerging in Theoderic's day and had not yet culminated in complete isolation from the outside.[13]

The Homoean faith had been prohibited in the Roman Empire since 381 and gradually disappeared from its cities; it stubbornly persisted, however, in the imperial army until well into the sixth century. Since the emperors recruited some of their soldiers from Germanic peoples outside the empire, they were forced to tolerate in the army a confession that was prohibited for civilians. In the kingdoms that were founded on the territory of the Western Roman Empire over the fifth century, in contrast, the Homoean confession stood under royal protection and could flourish freely, but it was actively propagated only in exceptional circumstances for reasons of political expediency. That was because even in the Germanic kingdoms, the privileged warriors of the Homoean faith who helped their kings exercise power remained no more than a small minority in comparison to the great majority of native-born Catholics. The confessional antithesis created by this arrangement highlighted the ethnic identity of these two populations since the ethnic and religious boundaries between them largely coincided. This fact cannot have escaped contemporaries, particularly since all the Germanic groups that adopted Christianity in the fifth century did so deliberately in opposition to the prevailing confession of the empire, thus choosing a form of Christianity that was independent of the imperial church.[14]

Over the course of the fifth century, Homoeans were excluded from social life in Italy no differently than they were in the rest of the Roman Empire. Even in Italy, however, Homoean Christianity stayed alive and well in the army. The last Western Roman emperors were far too dependent on their Germanic soldiers and officers to dare to deny them their own churches as some earlier emperors had done—namely, Valentinian II in 387 at the instigation of Ambrose of Milan, and Arcadius under pressure from Bishop John (known as "Chrysostom") of Constantinople. The *magister militum* Ricimer sponsored a church for Homoean services in the 460s on the Viminal in the middle of Rome; it still exists today as Sant'Agata dei Goti (St. Agatha of the Goths). A second Homoean church, which Pope Gregory the Great seized for the Catholic Church at a much later date, may also have been built at this time in the fifth century. It is possible but cannot be proved that the Homoeans also had a church in Ravenna at this time, where the imperial court had resided since 425.[15]

When Odoacer deposed Emperor Romulus in 476, power passed into the hands of a man who was a heretic in the eyes of the Catholic Church. For the first time in the history of late antique Italy, the lord of the land stood outside the community of faith to which the vast majority of the population belonged. It was a potentially explosive situation. Pope Gelasius I called Odoacer a heretical barbarian after the latter's death and prided himself on disobeying unspecified commands that, in his view, undermined the Catholic faith. Gelasius did not, however, go so far as to call the king a persecutor. Ennodius also declined to level this accusation against Odoacer in his panegyric to Theoderic, although he otherwise tore him to shreds. Odoacer in fact appears to have treated the Catholic clergy with respect; as one and the same Ennodius reports in a different context, the king was willing to receive Catholic bishops as ambassadors, and he showed favor to Epiphanius, bishop of Pavia.[16]

After the death of Pope Simplicius, Odoacer intervened through his praetorian prefect Basilius in controversies then raging in Rome over the succession. In an assembly dominated by laymen, the praetorian prefect proclaimed that Simplicius had decreed that no decision could be made about his successor without consulting Basilius; on his own authority, Basilius furthermore prohibited the sale of ecclesiastical real estate and ordered the restoration of lands that had been owned by the Roman church two generations ago but had been sold since that time. This intervention may have seemed illegitimate to the Roman clergy, but it accorded with the wishes of lay sponsors in Rome, who wanted to limit the discretionary power of the bishop of Rome over church property. We thus have no way to decide whether the deacon Felix, who ultimately succeeded Simplicius, was the candidate favored by Basilius, Odoacer, or both. At any rate, he was the first pope whose forebears had held senatorial office.[17]

We have no reliable information about Odoacer's relationship with the Homoean communities of Italy; the *Anonymus Valesianus* claims long after Odoacer's death that the king favored them, but this claim is vague and, moreover, polemically motivated. We also do not know whether the king stepped forward as a church builder. It has been conjectured that Odoacer sponsored the construction of the monastery of St. Severinus in Ravenna, although it is first attested at a much later date. The king even is said to have granted Severinus' request per letter that he pardon a certain Ambrosius. But it is unlikely that a church was dedicated to Severinus under Odoacer since his remains were not brought to Italy until much later, under Theoderic.[18]

All his life Theoderic himself professed allegiance to the church that observed the Homoean creed. Ennodius praises the king for the fact that he had been instructed in the Christian faith since childhood. It is an open question as to who gave him this instruction and what it consisted of. It is difficult to assess the role played by his mother, Ereleuva, who converted to Catholicism, because the date of her conversion is unknown. There was a Homoean community in Constantinople to which Aspar and his sons belonged when Theoderic lived there as a hostage. The Gothic prince might have joined it, but we find no such report in our sources. Be that as it may, Theoderic could quote passages of the

Bible when he was king. He had no discernable interest, however, in theological controversies. In that respect, Theoderic differed from contemporaries like the king of the Vandals, Thrasamund, who challenged the Catholic bishop and theologian Fulgentius to debate the nature of God, or the king of the Burgundians, Gundobad, who corresponded with the Catholic bishop Avitus of Vienne about dogmatic, exegetical, and ethical questions.

We would love to know whether Theoderic viewed correct belief as a precondition for successful action. It is reported that the Visigothic king Euric believed that his plans would be crowned with success because he adhered to the true faith. Theoderic may have privately shared the conviction that God supported those who believed the "true" faith; as king of Goths and Romans, however, he declined to make this connection explicit publicly. His personal beliefs largely remain a mystery to us. According to Cassiodorus, he frequently prayed, perhaps even daily like the Visigothic king Theoderic II; in what manner he did so—whether alone or with others, aloud or silently, on his knees or standing, at what times, at what places, and with what words—all that is unknown. We also do not know whether he publicly showed contrition and did penance like the Christian emperors of his day.[19]

It is beyond doubt that Theoderic energetically promoted the Homoean church in his kingdom. The evidence unsurprisingly focuses on Ravenna, which the king systematically built up into his *urbs regia*. Ravenna was not, however, the only city where a Homoean bishop held office during Theoderic's reign. The congregation in Rome probably also had its own bishop under Theoderic, as had already been the case under Odoacer. As tiles bearing Theoderic's monogram demonstrate, the roof of the Homoean church on the Viminal (Sant'Agata dei Goti today) was repaired during his reign. Moreover, we encounter bishops with Gothic names in Cassiodorus' *Variae* who were evidently Homoeans but cannot be identified with a specific city.[20]

In Ravenna, and apparently only there, Theoderic profiled himself as a builder of magnificent churches dedicated to the cult of the Homoean community. He had a church dedicated to Christ the Redeemer built next to his palace and adorned it with glorious mosaics; it survives today under the name Sant'Apollinare Nuovo. In light of its physical proximity to the palace, we may speculate that Theoderic's court visited this church especially often; in that sense, we can call it a court church. It is unknown whether all members of the court or only those who practiced the Homoean faith followed the king into this church. It is not impossible that the Catholics stayed for mass until after the sermon since the creed was not yet a regular feature of the liturgy. Vice versa, Theoderic visited St. Peters in Rome in the year 500.

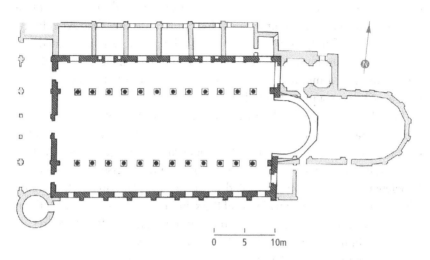

Fig. 19. Floor plan of the basilica of Sant'Apollinare Nuovo (Ravenna). Reproduced
with the kind permission of Carola Jäggi, *Ravenna. Kunst und Kultur einer
spätantiken Residenzstadt* (Regensburg, 2013), fig. 103.

Unfortunately, the original iconographic program of this "court church" can
no longer be completely reconstructed because some of the mosaics were
reworked after the end of Gothic rule and the apse was destroyed by an earthquake in the seventh or eighth century. Three tiers of mosaics were installed on
the lateral walls of the church. The highest tier showed scenes from the life of
Jesus, arranged as a continuous narrative: his miracles appear on the north wall,
his Passion and Resurrection on the south. The middle tier showed thirty-two
apostles and prophets between the windows of the church. The lowest tier today
shows twenty-six male saints proceeding toward Jesus on the north wall and
twenty-two female saints, led by the Three Magi, moving toward the Mother of
God with Baby Jesus on the south wall. These two processions date from the
560s, however, when Bishop Agnellus (557–570) had some of the original decorations removed because they were found offensive after the end of Gothic rule.
Only the views of the cities of Ravenna and Classe, the starting points of the two
processions, are original. The people depicted standing outside the walls of
Classe and between the columns of the palace facade in Ravenna were removed
when the mosaics were reworked. In all probability, they were members of the
Gothic court and the Amal family (or the Amal family exclusively); a depiction
of Theoderic himself may have appeared in the middle of the palace facade. It
seems as if this series of mosaics originally depicted a procession of the royal

court divided by sex as it made its way to Jesus Christ and the Mother of God. The original iconographic program of the church was thus focused entirely on Theoderic, his family, and his retinue. The king, who was celebrated as the builder of the church in a monumental inscription on the cornice of the apse, wanted to erect a monument to himself and his court that could survive the ravages of time in a prominent place.[21]

The Homoean episcopal church in Ravenna, which still exists today under the name Santo Spirito, may also have been among Theoderic's building projects. In Gothic times, it was probably under the patronage of Saint Anastasia, who had been martyred in Sirmium during the Great Persecution of Emperor Diocletian; a church was dedicated to her at this place in the fifth century. Theoderic's people probably knew of the saint from Pannonia; Theoderic himself, however, may have encountered her in Constantinople, where her relics were brought in the year 457. The Homoean episcopal church in Ravenna had a baptistry known as the "Arian Baptistry" today. In its dome, the baptism of Jesus Christ is depicted: a naked young man appears in the center of the image; John the Baptist stands to his right; a gray-haired old man, a personification of the Jordan, sits on his left; a dove, the symbol of the Holy Spirit, hovers over Jesus' head. The image depicts Jesus as a corporeal human being, but this representation is by no means unique to the Homoean conception of Christ, although it is very rare in Late Antiquity. A similar image is found at an even earlier date in the baptistry of the Catholic episcopal church of Ravenna.[22]

By the fall of the Gothic kingdom, far more churches of the Homoean community existed in and around Ravenna that have since vanished but are mentioned in the *Liber pontificalis* of Agnellus of Ravenna. Unfortunately, information about how these buildings were financed is almost always lacking; in only one case is a Bishop Hunimund mentioned as the sponsor. Even he would hardly have been able to muster the necessary resources, though, if Theoderic had not at least lent a hand. It was thanks to royal munificence that Ravenna was the only city in Gothic Italy in which the monumental presence of the Homoean community was hardly inferior to that of the Catholic Church.[23]

The church of Ravenna is also the only Homoean community on the organization of which the sources shed some light. This is thanks primarily to a document drawn up in the year 551. In it, the "entire clergy" of a church, which calls itself the "Gothic church of Saint Anastasia" (*ecclesia gotica sanctae Anastasiae*) or the "church of the law of the Goths of Saint Anastasia" (*ecclesia legis Gothorum sanctae Anastasiae*) cedes ownership of a pond or pool valued at 180 *solidi* to a man named Peter, who had leased it from the church for 120 *solidi* sixteen years earlier, when the city was still the residence of the Gothic kings; the difference is paid to the church. The church in question was the episcopal church of the Homoean community of Ravenna, but the see was vacant in 551, when the contract was drawn up. On top of that, the church had fallen on financial hardship; it was for that reason that it had to sell property. Since the document includes a list of signatories, we can reconstruct the size and composition of the personnel of this church; hence in addition to the bishop himself, one of the most important Homoean churches of Ravenna had two presbyters, a deacon and subdeacon, and five more people who are called *clerici* in the strict sense; at least some of them were lectors. Thus, counting the bishop, ten ordained clergymen served in this church. Then there were ten more people who are included as members of the *clerus* although they had not been ordained: five porters (*ustiarii*), an "administrative lawyer" (*defensor*), and four members of a kind of lay confraternity who are designated by the Greek loan word *spodei* (from *spoudaîos*, "zealous"). Two of these *spodei* are also called "book writers" in Gothic (*bokareis*); the church thus housed a scriptorium that produced manuscripts for ecclesiastical use. It may have been in this scriptorium where a magnificent Gothic evangelion was written, of which 188 of an original 336 pages survive today. It is called the *Codex argenteus* ("the silver codex") because it was written in silver ink on purple-dyed vellum.[24]

The document not only gives us information about ecclesiastical offices and their hierarchy; it also permits us to draw inferences about the clergy's self-conception and level of education. The twenty signatories predominantly bear Gothic names. A certain Ufitahari signs first; he calls himself *papa*, a synonym for presbyter in this context. The other names are almost all biblical, such as Peter, Paul, and Daniel. We cannot infer from the preponderance of Gothic names, however, that the clergy could not speak Latin, although one presbyter, one deacon, and the two scribes signed their names with a Gothic sentence. Six others signed in Latin. Eight used marks, either because they were visually impaired, like the second presbyter, for instance, or because they could not write at all, like the five porters. The community that belonged to the church of the Homoean bishop of Ravenna was thus made up of people with widely varying levels of education, from professional scribes to illiterates. With just ten clergymen and ten laymen, the size of the personnel of this church lagged far behind that of the Catholic bishop of Ravenna, as we shall see.

Like the "court church," the church of the Homoean bishop controlled an unknown number of properties for which it presumably had royal munificence to thank. These landholdings, like all property owned by the Goths of Ravenna, were transferred to the Catholic Church by an edict of Emperor Justinian in 561. At least the educated portion of the Homoean clergy of Ravenna was bilingual, but it attached great importance to its Gothic identity, which it emphasized with Gothic signatures. Conversion from Homoean to Catholic Christianity undoubtedly occurred in Theoderic's kingdom. As long as Gothic rule endured, however, it remained the exception; only two examples are known, and both cases concern women. One of the two women suffered significant property losses in consequence of her change of faith. When Procopius has Gothic ambassadors claim that Goths who converted to Catholicism were not punished for doing so, we should by no means infer that they did not suffer any disadvantages.[25]

The full name of the church of Saint Anastasia in Ravenna illustrates more vividly than anything else that the Homoean faith had become an inextricable aspect of Gothic identity to the Goths in Italy; it was for this reason that the church of Saint Anastasia was called not only the "Gothic church," but also the "church of the law of the Goths." "Law" (*lex*) was a conventional designation for Christian doctrine, which was viewed as a rule for one's life and belief. The expression "law of the Goths" thus designates Homoean Christianity as the obligatory confession of Goths.[26]

2. A TOLERATED MAJORITY: THE CATHOLIC CHURCH

The vast majority of Theoderic's approximately six million Italian subjects belonged to a community of faith that not only regarded itself as "catholic" (as in "universal"), but also is called such ("Catholic") by modern scholars. The institutional basis of this community was a dense network of bishoprics that covered the entire country. By the year 500, virtually every one of the 200 civic communities (*civitates*) of Italy was also the seat of a Catholic bishop, albeit vacancies also constantly occurred. About two-thirds of these sees were located in southern Italy (Italia Suburbicaria), where there were many more cities, although these were usually very small; only a third was located in northern Italy (*Italia annonaria*). In some cities, especially Rome and Ravenna, a Homoean bishop held office in addition to a Catholic bishop, but in normal circumstances the Catholic bishop was the only local community leader.[27]

Everywhere, the bishop was the spiritual head of the community; he preached and held mass. At the same time, he was the leader of an ecclesiastical organization that maintained salaried personnel and controlled its own resources. Even though sharp boundaries between clergy and laity had not yet been drawn, the ranks of presbyter, deacon, subdeacon, and lector were regarded as steps on an ecclesiastical career ladder (*cursus ecclesiasticus*) that one began ascending with the office of lector in one's youth and that might culminate in the office of bishop. The local bishop controlled one's progress up to the rank of presbyter, but he was obliged to promote candidates according to years of service unless there were reasons against it. While presbyters were responsible for celebrating mass and providing pastoral care, deacons managed church property and organized alms for the poor. Lectors read from scripture. The clergy in the strict sense was complemented by the rest of the church personnel, which frequently consisted of laymen: mass attendants (*acoluthi*) and porters, "administrative lawyers" (*defensores*) and singers.[28]

Differences between bishoprics were nonetheless great. In the small cities of southern Italy, the office of bishop may have guaranteed only a modest livelihood for its incumbent. Presbyters, deacons, and lectors earned proportionally less. A clergyman's income, of course, depended less on the rank he held in the ecclesiastical hierarchy than on the size of the resources of the church to which he belonged. The latter varied from several thousand to fewer than ten *solidi* per year. A fixed ratio was applied to the allocation of church income: one-quarter went to the bishop, one-quarter to the clergy, one-quarter toward the maintenance of church buildings, and one-quarter to the poor. Only churches that were independent of a bishop were structured differently because they possessed their own clergy and income, as was often the case in the countryside. Gelasius I pushed to consecrate only churches that had sufficient resources for their endowment; at the same time, he tried to prevent laymen who sponsored the construction of new churches from claiming special privileges.[29]

The property of episcopal churches consisted of real estate, especially landed estates that had accrued to them from donations and bequests since the reign of Constantine the Great, and liturgical instruments like silver candelabras and bowls. Ecclesiastical estates were normally leased like those of secular landowners and worked with the help of more or less unfree laborers, including slaves. The financial clout of individual bishoprics varied greatly. Where the local elite was small and not especially wealthy, the church normally received only small donations and had to make do with modest means. In large cities, where rich donors dwelt, a bishop's church commanded extensive properties and vast income. The richest of all was the church of Rome; its landholdings had been scattered across the entire Roman Empire in the fourth century but were concentrated in central and southern Italy and Sicily around the year 500. The churches of Milan and Ravenna were also amply endowed; they likewise owned landholdings in Sicily. A specific number, however, is transmitted only for the Catholic Church of Ravenna: under Pope Felix IV (526–532), its annual income amounted to 12,000 *solidi*, roughly 166 pounds of gold. In addition to this, it also collected dues in kind; around the middle of the sixth century, these consisted of 888 hens, 266 chicks, 8,800 eggs, 3,760 pounds of pork, and 3,450 pounds of honey per year.[30]

The Catholic bishop of Ravenna received an annual salary of 3,000 *solidi*; another 3,000 *solidi* were paid to his clergy. This sum was distributed among a group of people that was several times larger than the personnel of the Homoean episcopal church in Ravenna. We know about its size and composition because of a dispute that broke out shortly after Theoderic's death between Bishop Ecclesius and members of his staff over the management of church property, a dispute that Pope Felix IV was compelled to arbitrate. The settlement agreement, which is stylized as a letter from the pope, lists the names of sixty-one people who traveled to Rome for arbitration. Among them, we find eleven presbyters; eleven deacons; five subdeacons; twelve mass attendants; twelve lectors; four singers; three administrative lawyers, one of whom also acted as secretary (*notarius*); two cemetery wardens (*decani*); and a storeroom attendant ([o]*rrearius*).

We can be quite certain that this list is incomplete because hardly the entire personnel of the church can have undertaken the journey to Rome. Porters, for instance, are missing from the list because the churches of Ravenna could not be left unguarded. Hence even though we cannot make an exact comparison, the numbers are eloquently clear: the settlement agreement alone lists twenty-seven presbyters, deacons, and subdeacons. The Homoean episcopal church of Ravenna, in contrast, had only two presbyters, a deacon, and a subdeacon; it had no need for a storeroom attendant and had no mass attendants, singers, or cemetery wardens. An onomastic comparison is also instructive: not a single Gothic name appears in the settlement agreement of the Catholic Church.

Just as the property of the Catholic Church of Rome surpassed that of all other Italian congregations, its clergy was also the most numerous by a wide margin. Already by the middle of the third century, the church of Rome employed 46 presbyters; 7 deacons; 7 subdeacons; 42 mass attendants; and 52 exorcists, lectors, and porters—a total of 154 people. That number may have at least doubled by the year 500; the number of presbyters had risen to some 80. There were 19 deacons at the end of the sixth century. The presbyters and deacons constituted colleges with a hierarchical organization; an *archipresbyter* stood atop the college of presbyters and an *archidiaconus* atop that of deacons. Since the presbyters had to ensure that mass was celebrated in all the churches of Rome under the pope's authority (known as *tituli*, "titular churches"), they were scattered across the city and gathered together only at major ecclesiastical feasts. Deacons, in contrast, who were responsible for administering church property and organizing alms for the poor, went about their business in immediate proximity to the pope and were in constant contact with influential laymen;

they also were well acquainted with one another. It was for this reason that a deacon had much better odds than a presbyter of becoming pope someday. Of the fifteen people elected pope between 440 and 535, twelve had previously been archdeacons or deacons, and only two had been an archpresbyter or presbyter.

A large number of laymen were also personnel of the Roman church. Their number in Rome was especially high because the Roman church owned more property, employed more people, and supported more poor people than any other church. For this reason, only the royal administration itself surpassed the size and complexity of the papal administration headquartered at the basilica of St. John Lateran. The curia employed numerous clerks (*notarii*) responsible for the its bookkeeping and correspondence; they constituted a college (*schola*) under the direction of a chief officer (*primicerius*). For typical procedures and transactions, they used standard forms that were compiled in the so-called *Liber diurnus* in the seventh century. The administrative lawyers of the Roman Curia locally supervised the leasing and cultivation of the church's far-flung estates. In the first half of the sixth century, these estates were integrated into regional economic units called *patrimonia* under the supervision of *rectores* ("directors, managers"). The latter leased the *patrimonia* to contractors (*conductores*) who either sublet the land or concluded lease agreements directly with the peasants themselves. The curia issued receipts in the name of the pope for rent payments.[31]

Bishops were appointed in a procedure that the clergy and people called elections. Exactly who, however, was eligible to vote in these elections was an open question. Probably all of the relatively small number of clergymen normally participated. Whether broader segments of the population also were a factor depended on the circumstances; the demand for popular participation was regarded as satisfied if the civic notables gave their assent. There was also no consensus over whether votes should be counted or weighed. Unanimity was the ideal to which the church aspired; hence an election and proclamation of its outcome ideally converged in the act of acclamation. If agreement could not be reached, the group of voters split, resulting in schism.[32]

The bishops of late antique Italy normally came from the upper levels of urban society; they were often related to the families that sat on the local municipal councils. Bishops thus possessed the education that was needed to exercise their office, and they were sufficiently acquainted with the etiquette of high society to be able to represent the interests of the church before members of the local elite. Of course, more than half of all bishops did not come from the city in which they had been raised; since they had to assert themselves in a new environment, new bishops could not immediately take advantage of the social connections that they had acquired from their backgrounds. Bishops were not expected to live ascetic lives; monks were seldom elected bishop in Italy prior to the late sixth century, and not a few bishops were married. The ideal of celibacy, however, was powerful enough that clerical dynasties remained a rare exception; the son of a bishop almost never became bishop himself. It accordingly created a stir when, in the year 536, ten years after Theoderic's death, Silverius, the son of Pope Hormisdas, ascended the *cathedra Petri* at the behest of King Theodahad.

The office of bishop in the provinces had little appeal to members of the senatorial order because there the bishop's sphere of influence was limited to the territory of a single, often remote, city; the office demanded lifelong engagement in mostly petty affairs for a relatively small income. In the major cities, in contrast, the office of bishop began to become attractive to senators around the year 500. Considerable sums were spent in bishoprics like Milan, Aquileia, and Ravenna, to say nothing of Rome, to buy votes for episcopal elections. Consecration as a priest in return for money was, admittedly, illegitimate in the eyes of the church and repeatedly prohibited as "simony": had not Simon Magus been severely reprimanded when he tried to buy the gift of the Holy Spirit from Peter (Acts 8:5–244)? In Late Antiquity, however, it was customary to pay supporters and voters, notwithstanding all such ecclesiastical bans. Anyone who brought his influence to bear in a personnel decision expected material compensation for his efforts. The word *suffragium*, which had denoted a citizen's right to vote in the Roman Republic, came to indicate a supporter's intercession in the ecclesiastical world exactly as it did in the secular world.[33]

Bishops from senatorial families were nonetheless a rarity in late antique Italy. The division between the ecclesiastical and secular elite was especially strict in Rome because the local elite there was identical with the civilian imperial elite. The popes of the fifth and sixth centuries were normally men who came from insignificant families and had risen up through the ranks in the service of the church. In 483, a pope with senatorial forebears was elected for the first time—Felix III—but he remained an exception until Gregory the Great. Bishops derived their power from several sources in their cities. They represented the one, universal church locally by administering the sacraments, which were considered a necessary precondition of admission to the kingdom of heaven, and they interpreted the word of God in a way that was binding for their congregation. They preached, baptized, and excommunicated. Bishops also provided free arbitrational jurisdiction in civil disputes, known as *episcopalis audientia*. As long as a bishop more or less met the expectations of his community, his office conferred a certain authority on him. Since the bishop appeared publicly on many occasions, he also held a position of prominence

that guaranteed him a place alongside the secular elite. He already had authority to issue commands to the local clergy.[34]

Care for the poor could also give a bishop power. As the patron of beggars,
he acquired a clientele personally devoted to himself among those who lived off
of alms from the church. If a church had a large endowment, the bishop also
had considerable leeway in sponsoring the construction of new churches and
monasteries. Last but not least, bishops were very well connected with one
another; they met in Rome or at synods elsewhere every year and stayed in
touch with one another by letter. Some bishoprics, especially but not exclusively that of Rome, even maintained ties extending beyond the borders of
Theoderic's kingdom.[35]

Catholic bishops in late antique Italy may have belonged to the urban elite,
but they were by no means the dominant force in local politics. The bishop was
only one political player among many, and he only occasionally concerned
himself with routine municipal business; municipal officials were still responsible for such things. Only in exceptional situations did bishops act as spokes-
men for their communities, let alone provinces. Bishop Epiphanius of Pavia,
for instance, represented the province of Liguria before both Odoacer and
Theoderic. Bishops were sometimes also entrusted with diplomatic missions.
Epiphanius mediated between Emperor Anthemius and his *magister militum*
Ricimer; he traveled to Toulouse to meet with Euric, king of the Visigoths, on
behalf of Emperor Julius Nepos, and to Lyon (together with Bishop Victor of
Turin) on behalf of Theoderic to meet with Gundobad, king of the Burgundians.
But these missions were exceptional. Most Italian bishops steered clear of the
doings at the political center. It thus would be misconceived to imagine the
bishops of Italy as the "masters" of their cities; not even the bishop of Rome
exercised anything resembling such authority over his city in the year 500.
Previous scholars also greatly overestimated the convergence of the ecclesiastical and secular elite in Gaul. The office of bishop there was in no way the
exclusive preserve of families that could claim senatorial ancestors. In Italy,
Catholic bishops were an independent social power that was linked to the secular elite in a variety of ways, but they had not merged with it.[36]

One bishop towered over all others in Italy: the bishop of Rome, who viewed
himself as the successor of the apostle Peter and, since Pope Leo the Great,
claimed primacy over all other Christian bishops as Peter's early representative.
In a series of sermons that he held on the anniversary of his consecration, Leo
elaborated the idea that he should preside over all Christendom because Peter,
to whom Jesus Christ had given the keys to the kingdom of heaven, was at work
within him. In one of these sermons, Leo said, "And yet from the whole world

Peter alone was chosen to be put in charge of the vocation of all peoples and of all apostles and of all the fathers of the church; thus, although the people of God have many priests and many shepherds, Peter governs all of them, strictly speaking, whom Christ himself governs in the first instance."[37] Leo claimed for himself no less than the role of supreme arbiter of ecclesiastical and doctrinal questions. His claim extended to the entire church and thus the entire Roman Empire, including the Germanic kingdoms in the west. Under Felix III, this claim was translated into practical policy toward the imperial church when the pope excommunicated all bishops who accepted the Henotikon ("formula of unity") issued as an edict by Emperor Zeno in 482. The purpose of the Henotikon had been to reconcile the numerous adversaries of the Council of Chalcedon (451) with the bishops of the imperial church who recognized it. The doctrine decreed at the Council of Chalcedon and supported by Leo (namely, that a distinct human and a distinct divine nature coexisted simultaneously and inseparably within Jesus Christ) had met with fierce resistance in Egypt, Palestine, and Syria. The opponents of Chalcedon were by no means in agreement with one another either, but many of them believed that such talk of two natures split Christ into a human and a divine part. Hence they argued that the Redeemer had only one, human-divine nature (*physis*), which is why modern scholars have called them "Monophysites" or "Miaphysites." This controversy resonated with people from all walks of life and provoked violent unrest; whole provinces threatened to slip from the Eastern Roman emperor's grasp. Zeno sought to restore the unity of the imperial church by having Acacius, the patriarch of Constantinople, draft a formula that omitted the source of the controversy—the Council of Chalcedon and its decrees. The emperor hoped that this compromise formula would be acceptable to a broad majority of Christian authorities, especially bishops but also monks.[38]

Felix III resolutely opposed this policy of reconciliation through compromise. The confrontation stemmed from a dispute over the succession to the patriarchate of Alexandria, where in 482 the emperor installed Peter Mongus, who had previously been condemned as an opponent of the Council of Chalcedon. Acacius assented to his appointment after Mongus recognized the Henotikon. The bishop of Rome, however, turned himself into the champion of John Talaia, who had sought refuge in Rome after he was defeated by Peter in Alexandria. Felix denied the patriarch of Constantinople the right to receive a condemned heretic back into communion with the church without the assent of the successor to St. Peter. By communing with bishops who were regarded in Rome as heretics, Acacius, moreover, placed himself outside the orthodox church. When Acacius in turn ordered Felix not to interfere, Felix had him excommunicated by a synod in Rome. The same ban applied to all bishops in the imperial church who refused to split with Acacius. In this way, Felix brought about a schism between the bishops of the west and the imperial church in the east that would last until the year 519; it is called the Acacian Schism after Acacius, who had formulated the Henotikon. The pope used the leeway that Italy's new position outside the emperor's territory gave him to oppose Zeno and a majority of the bishops in the Eastern Roman Empire; Zeno had no means of imposing his policy on Odoacer's kingdom by force.[39]

As archdeacon under Felix III, Gelasius I played a leading part in formulating this position and emphatically defended it in his own pontificate. He even strengthened the bishop of Rome's assertion of primacy by claiming that bishops and emperors represented two powers created by God, of which the former was competent for religious affairs, the latter for state affairs. In a letter he sent to Emperor Anastasius shortly after the beginning of Theoderic's rule, he formulated this "Two-Swords Theory" in the following terms:

> There are two things, August Emperor, by which this world is ruled: the sanctified authority of pontiffs [*auctoritas sacrata pontificum*] and royal power [*regalis potestas*]. Of the two, the burden of bishops is heavier to the extent that they must also render an account before the divine judgment for the kings of men. For you know, most merciful son, that although you preside over the human race by virtue of your rank, yet you bow your neck with devotion to the overseers of divine affairs and expect from them the sources of your salvation. And you recognize that in properly receiving and administering the heavenly sacraments you must submit to the order of religion [*ordo religionis*] rather than oversee it, and that you thus depend on their judgment in these matters, rather than seek to place them under your will. For if the ministers of religion obey your laws, insofar as the public order is concerned, recognizing that imperial power [*imperium*] has been conferred on you by divine ordination, so they should not appear to oppose a judgment rendered in secular affairs; with what volition, I beseech you, should you obey the men who have been charged with disbursing the venerable mysteries?[40]

These carefully weighted sentences make clear that Gelasius, who viewed himself as the earthly representative of Peter, had the last word concerning the Christian faith, and indeed everywhere, even in the Eastern Roman Empire. Of course, a chasm yawned between the pretention and reality of papal primacy. Gelasius was able to convince only a few bishops in the Eastern emperor's territory to change sides; their sees were located in Latin-speaking border provinces. The bishops in Greek-speaking provinces yielded the bishop of Rome honorary precedence since his church had been founded by the apostles Peter and Paul, but they were unwilling to recognize him as the final authority in dogmatic or disciplinary questions. They considered the bishops of Constantinople, Antioch, Alexandria, and Jerusalem equal in rank to the bishop of Rome. Questions of faith, in their view, could be decided only by synods. The North African church had already gone its own way in the days of Augustine (354–431); since 484, the Catholic bishops of the kingdom of the Vandals had been subjected to state-sponsored reprisals and been largely cut off from Italy. *De facto* autonomous regional churches emerged in the Germanic kingdoms of Gaul. Pope Symmachus tried in vain to counteract this development by appointing Caesarius, bishop of Arles, his vicar. But not even in Italy could the bishop of Rome enforce his claim to govern the entire church everywhere.

Only in southern Italy, with its numerous small cities, was papal supremacy generally recognized. The pope regulated the ordination of clerics and the election of bishops in this region and intervened when rules were broken. Moreover, he invited the bishops in his diocese to Rome every year for the feast of the apostles Peter and Paul on June 29, but he also held synods for special reasons. Forty-five bishops from southern Italy came together at one such synod on March 13, 495. The bishop of Rome intervened in an astonishing variety of everyday problems in southern Italy. He preoccupied himself with the administration of ecclesiastical estates and the consecration of churches. He was especially in demand as a judge whenever charges were raised against clergymen. If the case could not be heard in Rome, the pope delegated the investigation of the facts to bishops who enjoyed his trust.[41]

In many places in northern Italy, in contrast, the bishop of Rome was denied the right to intercede. Around the year 300, there were three sees whose occupants exercised the power of a metropolitan; the oldest and most important of these bishoprics was Milan (in the province of Liguria), which was joined by Aquileia (in the province of Venetia et Histria) and Ravenna (in the province of Aemilia) around the middle of the fifth century. The metropolitans of Milan, Aquileia, and Ravenna consecrated bishops within their dioceses and thus were in a position to exert a decisive influence on the election of bishops. The metropolitans of Milan and Aquileia were appointed to their offices without Rome's involvement because they consecrated one another. The church of Ravenna, in contrast, had close ties to Rome; the popes took action against the local bishop several times in the last quarter of the fifth century. As we have seen, the clergy of Ravenna subsequently appealed to Pope Felix IV to arbitrate a dispute over the use of church property.[42]

The bishop of Rome also viewed himself as the champion of orthodoxy in Italy, and he kept vigilant watch to ensure his sheep did not stray from the correct faith. Of course, after 476, the popes could no longer ask for the emperor's help to force Christians who disagreed with the Catholic Church to abandon their error. When Pope Gelasius received news that the teachings of the theologian Pelagius, who had been condemned by Pope Innocent in 417, were being spread in Dalmatia and in the province of Picenum, he immediately wrote to Honorius, the bishop of Salona, and ordered him to take action with the other bishops of Dalmatia against this dangerous heresy. Honorius bristled at this rebuke, however, declared that Gelasius had received false information, and demanded that the pope name the slanderers. Gelasius rebuked the bishops of the province of Picenum for permitting a priest to spread Pelagian heresies there and go unpunished; the offender supposedly claimed that man was born without sin and could achieve salvation on his own, without divine aid; he was also accused of disparaging the memory of Augustine, who had advocated the anti-Pelagian doctrine that every person was implicated in Original Sin from birth and therefore could be saved only by the grace of God. How the bishops reacted is not transmitted.[43]

Homoean Christians who were soldiers had been permitted to practice their religion under the emperors; they were even granted their own church in Rome under Emperor Anthemius at the latest. Pope Hilary (461–468) was not at all pleased, but he could do nothing to prevent it, even though in 467 he reportedly wrested from Anthemius a promise not to grant a request for separate churches for Christians of other confessions made by an otherwise unknown bishop, Filotheus. After the imperial monarchy disappeared in Italy, the popes had to be even more vigilant. Now it was no longer possible to fight the "Arian heresy" openly because it was also the confession of the ruler of Italy. The Catholic Church had to be content to be left in peace.[44]

A glance at the kingdoms of the Visigoths and Vandals reveals why the Catholic bishops in Italy had good reason to be concerned: in southwestern Gaul, no fewer than nine cities no longer had a bishop by 474 because King Euric had prevented the vacant sees from being filled. Sidonius Apollinaris, bishop of Clermont-Ferrand since 471, compared the situation to the Babylonian Captivity of the people of Israel. Euric's successor, Alaric II, initially continued this containment policy. The situation in North Africa was even more disquieting: violent attacks on Catholic churches and clerics had already broken out in the heartland of the Vandalic kingdom, the province of Africa Proconsularis (Tunisia) under King Gaiseric. Bishops were driven away and not permitted to be replaced. The king later ordered the surrender of liturgical instruments and sacred scriptures; even a general ban on assemblies was issued. This persecution temporarily flagged only to peak under King Huneric (479–484). In an edict dated February 24, 484, the king threatened those of his subjects who refused to convert to the Homoean creed with the same punishments that had been established for heretics in the Eastern Roman Empire. Thousands of clerics were deported or exiled; many fled North Africa for Gaul or Italy. King Gunthamund, who succeeded his uncle Huneric in late 484 and reigned until 496, rescinded Huneric's edict but left his predecessor's anti-Catholic measures broadly in force for a full ten years (until 494).[45]

The refugees from North Africa were not exactly welcomed with open arms in Italy. The Curia suspected them of striking a deal with their persecutors before fleeing, if indeed they were not secretly Manichaeans—followers of the Iranian religious founder Mani, who had been persecuted in Rome and Italy with exceptional fervor at the insistence of Leo the Great. In 487, Pope Felix III convened a synod in Rome to establish rules for readmitting refugees who had allowed an "Arian" clergyman to baptize them a second time. The rules were extremely strict: laymen, low-ranking clergymen, and monks who had received second baptism while not under duress had to do penance for twelve years; those who had acted under duress, three years; only immature children were exempt from penance. The synod condemned bishops, presbyters, and deacons to lifelong penance; only on their deathbeds could they receive communion again, and even then only as laymen. The forty-three bishops who assembled around Felix III were unanimous that conversion to Homoean Christianity was a grave sin. Even associating with Homoean clergymen was viewed as polluting. When Bishop Epiphanius of Ticinum visited the Visigothic court in Toulouse as an ambassador in 474, he invented an excuse so he could disregard King Euric's invitation to a feast because, in Ennodius' words, Euric's table was "tainted by his priests."[46]

The civil war that pitted Odoacer and Theoderic against one another confronted the Catholic bishops of Italy with difficult decisions. Laurentius, bishop of Milan, took Theoderic's side early and paid dearly for it when Odoacer reconquered the city. Epiphanius of Ticinum proceeded more carefully; he is said to have successfully maintained friendly terms with both warlords, although Theoderic first quartered his warriors' families and later the allied tribe of the Rugi in Ticinum.[47]

When, after the war, Theoderic deprived everyone who had supported Odoacer in any way of the right to make a will, Epiphanius and Laurentius undertook a mission on behalf of the province of Liguria to ask the king to rescind this decree. As mentioned above, Theoderic largely acceded to the delegation's wishes by merely banishing those followers of Odoacer who were accused of crimes and letting the rest go scot free. The king was not just willing to receive Catholic bishops as envoys from his new subjects; he even entrusted Epiphanius in turn with an important mission of state. The king instructed Epiphanius to go with Victor, bishop of Turin, to the court of King Gundobad to negotiate the ransom of captives who had been abducted and brought to the kingdom of the Burgundians during the war against Odoacer. The two bishops then duly traveled to Lyon to meet Gundobad in early 494. They obtained his pledge to allow those who had fled before the war to return home without ransom; ransom would have to be paid for those who were taken captive during hostilities. The ambassadors then traveled through the territory of Gundobad and his brother Godegisel and ransomed captives with the money with which Theoderic had entrusted them. More than 6,000 refugees and an unspecified number of captives reportedly accompanied them back to Italy. After returning home, Epiphanius then traveled yet again to Ravenna to obtain a tax remission for the province of Liguria, and once again he was successful: the king reduced the land tax for the current year by two-thirds.[48]

Epiphanius' example illustrates how influential representatives of the episcopy of northern Italy did not wait long to treat Theoderic as the legitimate lord of the land. He had come to Italy, after all, with an imperial mandate from the Eastern Roman emperor. The bishops thus not only addressed themselves to the king as petitioners, but also offered their services as envoys. Pope Gelasius also did not hesitate to recognize Theoderic as the new ruler of Italy. He repeatedly wrote letters of recommendation to Theoderic and asked the king's Catholic mother, Ereleuva, to urge her son to give to the poor. Gelasius addressed Theoderic not only as "King Theoderic," but also as "my lord" or "our lord" (dominus).[49]

How confident Gelasius was of his influence with Theoderic emerges from an incident when he threatened a Gothic courtier that he would complain to the king if he did not desist from making life difficult for an "administrative lawyer" of the Roman church (defensor ecclesiae Romanae). He wrote:

> We urge Your Nobility ever more and more that it deign to abstain from ecclesiastical matters and affairs and that you desist from all your agitation and permit the rule of religion to be observed, especially since it is beyond doubt that you belong to another community of faith [communio]. And you should not interpose your person in matters that have nothing to do with you, or you will force us, as we said above, to send a report and bring all these things to the attention of the lord and king, my son. For since he himself, in his wisdom, in no way wants to stand in the way of ecclesiastical affairs, it is

only fair that anyone who lives under his rule should imitate what the magnificent king himself does so as not to appear to transgress his wishes.[50]

A sentence is quoted from a lost letter of Gelasius to Theoderic to the effect
that if the king had decreed that the laws of the Roman emperors would be
observed in transactions between men, then he most certainly will have wanted
them to be observed in their reverential relationship with the blessed Peter.
Theoderic indeed preserved all the tax and legal privileges that the Roman
emperors had granted the Catholic Church. Churches retained their property
and incomes; bishops remained exempt from special duties toward their home
cities and continued to enjoy privileged jurisdiction. When two clergymen of the
church of Nola appealed against their bishop to the king, he sent them back to
the bishop of Rome as soon as he learned that they were not laymen. In contrast
to the kingdom of the Vandalic kings Gunthamund and Thrasamund, Catholic
clergymen had no reason to fear for themselves or their congregations in
Theoderic's kingdom; they were even treated with deference. Obviously, they
could not expect an "Arian" king to sponsor the construction of Catholic
churches, nor could they hope to avail themselves of his aid in the fight for orthodoxy, but both the status of the church and the freedom to celebrate mass were
guaranteed. If they objectively assessed what was in their own interest, there was
no alternative to cooperating with the heretical king Theoderic.[51] The clergyman
Ennodius of Milan explicitly detailed the basis of this cooperation in a letter he
wrote shortly after the annexation of Provence to Theoderic's kingdom:

> And these things are being prepared with heavenly aid as recompense for
> this: that our faith [*fides nostra*] has safe harbor with him, although he him-
> self follows something else. His tolerance [*patientia*] is striking since
> although he clings to his own conception [*propositum*], he does not dim the
> brilliance of others'; for even when the landholdings of our churches return
> [to us], he groans if they have not been enhanced. So it has come about that
> the rich property of paupers keeps its status, and middling property robustly
> grows to extreme opulence. In priests, he both cultivates innate virtues and
> inspires those he does not find already there.[52]

Ennodius praises Theoderic as a ruler who gives Catholics the freedom to
practice their own religion, who protects the property of their churches, and
who shows respect to their priests. At the same time, he suggests that this conduct was in no way self-evident because Theoderic himself professed a different
faith. Many, if not most, of the bishops of Italy may have thought so as well.
Gelasius knew, however, that he could stand up to Emperor Anastasius only
because Italy lay beyond his reach. Hence a heretical yet very tolerant king

represented the lesser evil in comparison to an emperor who forcibly supported a heresy in his empire. This position could also be justified in theological terms: since, in contrast to Anastasius, Theoderic did not claim to belong to the church of which Gelasius considered himself the head, the pope could take the position that he had no jurisdiction over the king; he was not responsible before God or mankind for a declared heretic. Gelasius also considered it essentially commendable that Theoderic was willing to lend an ear to Catholic bishops. This virtue, however, was also a source of some concern for the vicar of St. Peter because it opened the way for his fellow bishops to gain influence that might weaken his own authority. He thus took pains to control direct communication between Catholic bishops and the new ruler of Italy. When Bishop Elpidius of Volterra went to Ravenna without first obtaining permission from the representative of St. Peter, Gelasius issued him a sharp rebuke: no bishop was allowed to approach Theoderic's court without the pope's permission.[53]

Theoderic worked to win the support of the Catholic bishops of Italy from the beginning of his reign and apparently even during the civil war against Odoacer. Confrontation was not in his interest since the overwhelming majority of his new subjects belonged to the Catholic Church. To consolidate his power in Italy, he needed the cooperation of its ecclesiastical elites. Since the king himself belonged to the Homoean church, he could not achieve this objective simply by adopting the role of defender of the Catholic Church, as the Eastern Roman emperors claimed to be. Instead, Theoderic proclaimed the maxim that he would not interfere in church affairs unless they affected the public order. The king had announced to a synod of Italian bishops meeting in Rome—which we shall discuss at greater length below—that he did not regard it as his responsibility to make decisions in ecclesiastical affairs. Dogmatic controversies and disciplinary conflicts should be resolved without his involvement. The king wanted to intervene only if he was summoned to uphold the law or if the public order was in jeopardy. In that event, the king would proceed with strict impartiality within the framework of the law laid down by the Roman emperors.

Theoderic remained faithful to this maxim for a long time. The letters to bishops and clergymen prepared in his name and on his behalf by the royal chancellery always use the same respectful tone regardless of their recipients' confession. Each of them is addressed as *vir venerabilis* ("venerable man"). In the case of a presbyter named Laurentius, who was accused of grave robbing, Theoderic declined to punish the offender at all "on account of the honor accorded to priests" (*pro sacerdotali honore*). If Laurentius was convicted, then he should lose his ill-gotten loot; otherwise, though, he could go unpunished.

If the king was called on as judge in matters concerning the Catholic Church, he gladly left the decision to bishops. When a certain Germanus accused Bishop Peter of illegally appropriating part of the property his father had left him, Theoderic remanded the case to the court of the accused bishop. He did likewise when a certain Julianus complained that men working for Bishop Aurigena had unjustly seized his wife and his property. Theoderic appealed to the clergymen's self-image as men living by especially strict rules. He also made this appeal, however, when he decided a case himself: Theoderic ordered Januarius, the bishop of Salona, to immediately pay an outstanding bill for sixty casks of lamp oil. When a certain Stephanus accused Bishop Antonius of Pola of sending people to seize property that rightfully belonged to him, Theoderic decided that the bishop either had to surrender the property or send a proxy to defend himself before the king's court.[54]

There is clear evidence that Theoderic also applied existing laws to his own Homoean church: he instructed the praetorian prefect Faustus Niger that the church of Bishop Unscila was exempt from paying an additional tax (*supraindictio*) only for the part of its property for which the king had granted a privilege; the church was just as liable as all other landowners for the tax on the rest of the property that had been transferred to it. When Bishop Gudila of Sarsina was accused of harboring persons in his clergy who were obligated to serve their communities of origin as curials, the king warned him either to dismiss these clerics from the clergy or to dispatch an attorney to the king's court to undertake their defense. Theoderic banished the priest or bishop Wicthar from Hispania to Italy at the request of Visigothic nobles; the grounds for this action are, however, unknown.[55]

Theoderic considered himself obligated to protect Catholic clergymen and churches from abuses and was even willing to confer additional privileges on particular communities. The king extended the Catholic Church of Milan protection from oppression by people "of whatsoever ethnicity" (*cuiuslibet nationis*) on its Sicilian properties and exempted one of its merchants from taxes on trade. The king even entrusted special missions of state to Catholic bishops now and then. He urged Bishop Aemilianus, who had undertaken the repair of an aqueduct, to bring it swiftly to conclusion. He gave a certain Severus, whose bishopric is unknown, the job of distributing 1,500 *solidi* to people in his province who had suffered damage when royal troops had marched by. When the bishop of Turin was accused of betraying his city, Theoderic commissioned the bishop of Milan, Eustorgius, to investigate the case and confirmed his decision to acquit the accused. Theoderic did not, however, refuse in principle to haul Catholic bishops before his court: when Caesarius of Arles was accused of embezzling church property, Theoderic summoned the bishop to Ravenna before ultimately acquitting him.[56]

Theoderic treated Homoean and Catholic bishops as representatives of two Christian religious communities, of "confessions" in the modern sense of the word, who were entitled to his protection. In this sense, Theoderic spoke of "bishops of our and your *religio.*" A state of *de facto* biconfessionality thus prevailed in Theoderic's kingdom. This situation was based not on an accord between the two confessions but rather on the toleration of the stronger confession by a ruler who belonged to the weaker of the two. Since the religious tolerance of Theoderic and his successors ran contrary to the expectations of both these "confessions," it could not officially be proclaimed or propagated. Instead, in Late Antiquity, the decision not to take action against people of a different faith called for justification. Hence Theoderic's only explicit acknowledgment of his toleration of a divergent faith appears in a letter in which he explains why he approved the repair of a synagogue despite his disapproval of Judaism: "We cannot command religion [*religio*] because no one can be forced to believe against his will."[57]

This maxim should not be confused with the modern concept of toleration that is predicated on acknowledging religious freedom as an inalienable right. That is out of the question for Theoderic. The king declared religious coercion unfeasible, not illegitimate; he cited not legal or ethical reasons but rather the factual limits of his power. Belief could not be compelled, not even by the ruler himself. Theoderic, moreover, had no intention of applying the principle of toleration to all religious communities. Pagan cults were and remained prohibited; Manichaeans continued to be persecuted just as under the Roman emperors. Many people were brought to court in Rome during Theoderic's reign to answer charges of Manichaeism. Anyone found guilty was punished with banishment. Manichaean texts were confiscated and publicly burned. Even though the initiative was always taken by the popes—Gelasius, Symmachus, and Hormisdas— these trials could be held only before the senate and the urban prefect. The persecution of the Manichaeans was predicated on the king's consent.[58]

In light of the numerical inferiority of the Homoean church in Italy, Theoderic's religious policy was based on an objective assessment of his interests. Toleration was nonetheless anything but self-evident. The confessional situation of the North African kingdom of the Vandals was not much different, but there Kings Huneric and Gunthamund pursued a contemporary policy of confrontation and indeed, at times, of open persecution. Theoderic may have had personal reasons for choosing a different path. His mother, Ereleuva, was a Catholic, and his personal physician, Helpidius, was a Catholic clergyman.

Theoderic thus was capable of respecting people who adhered to a different confession, although he also expected them to acknowledge the right of his own confession to exist.[59]

Toleration of heterodox Christians connects Theoderic to the Burgundian king Gundobad, who was likewise a Homoean ruling over a Catholic majority, and differentiates him from a whole series of other contemporary rulers, especially from the first Byzantine emperors of his time (such as Zeno, Anastasius, Justin, and Justinian), and from some Vandalic kings (such as Huneric, Gunthamund, and Thrasamund). Most strikingly, though, Theoderic's policy contradicted the theological teachings of every Christian confession. A theological basis for the coexistence of two Christian religious communities was as inconceivable to the Homoeans as it was to the Catholics. In the eyes of the latter, it was merely a compromise that unfavorable circumstances had made necessary. The coexistence of two confessions in Theoderic's kingdom was thus not guaranteed by a theoretically supported consensus about the principle of toleration.

Cassiodorus first formulated ideas that come close a theological basis for religious toleration years after Theoderic's death, writing in the name and on the behalf of King Theodahad. The occasion for doing so was the case of a woman named Ranilda, who had apparently converted from Homoean to Catholic Christianity under Theoderic and had suffered material disadvantages in consequence. Years later, Emperor Justinian befriended her and asked Theodahad to indemnify her. Theodahad was willing to do so and declared that he did not want to arrogate to himself any power to decide questions of faith. As his justification, he explained that the diversity of Christian confessions was the will of God and hence was removed from human intervention. Even though these ideas reflect the attitude of a Gothic king who was versed in Platonic philosophy rather than represent an official ecclesiastical position, they deserve to be quoted in full:

> Concerning Ranilda's case, about which Your Serenity deigned to admonish me, although it happened a long time ago under our parents' reign, it was nonetheless necessary for us to settle it from our own munificence, so that, having done so, she should not regret her change of religion [mutata religio]. We do not presume to adjudicate these matters, for which we have no special mandate. Since the deity permits there to be different religions, we do not dare to impose one. We recall reading that we should willingly sacrifice to the Lord [Ps 53:8], not by the command of someone forcing us. If anyone attempts to do otherwise, he obviously is contravening heavenly commands. Your Piety justly invites us to do what divine instructions prescribe.[60]

The idea that the diversity of confessions is the will of God is a notion that stands in isolation at this date; it transcended the framework of Christian theology. Contemporaries accordingly had to make a great effort just to put the coexistence of two Christian religious communities in words. The royal chancellery used the word *religio* as an overarching term for Catholics and Homoeans, thus investing it with the meaning "confession." The Catholics were not prepared to take this step. Of course, they avoided angering the king by not publicly calling his brand of Christianity into question. Pope Gelasius spoke to Theoderic of the "piety of your Christian mind" (*Christianae mentis vestrae pietas*); Ennodius called him a "worshipper of the supreme god" (*summi dei cultor*). But they could not bring themselves to call the king's faith *religio*. Gelasius called the Homoean church the "other community" (*altera communio*), and Ennodius described Theoderic as following "the notion of other people" (*propositum alienum*). The coexistence of two confessions demanded great restraint on both sides. The king expected loyalty and abstention from confessional polemics and agitation. The Homoean church depended on his protection. The Catholic Church, in turn, could accept a heretic as king only if he guaranteed its rights in full. This explosive situation could be managed only if every party involved acted with due diplomacy and tact. The willingness to do so began to wane only toward the end of Theoderic's reign.[61]

3. TWO POPES IN ROME: THE LAURENTIAN SCHISM

Since Italy had been ruled by kings who did not belong to the Catholic Church since 476, the bishop of Rome could openly oppose the religious policy of Emperors Zeno and Anastasius. Felix III and Gelasius I did so from the safe cover that Odoacer and then Theoderic gave them. Of course, for the same reason, their claim to be the head of the entire church was also purely theoretical. Papal primacy was not even undisputed in Italy. Moreover, the disappearance of the imperial monarchy in Italy enabled the senators of Rome to gain greater influence over their own bishopric. Despite his claim to universal leadership, the pope was first and foremost the bishop of the city of Rome. It was here that he held office and here that he was elected like every other bishop — and indeed without the involvement of representatives of other communities. Senators living in Rome had a massive interest in the election of the occupant of the see because as donors and sponsors they played a key part in augmenting church property. They wanted to ensure that their name was permanently associated with their donation; hence they fundamentally rejected the sale (or any form of alienation) of church property. Meanwhile, the popes, who wanted to erect buildings in their own name or improve care for the poor, which would redound to their glory and expand their clientele, had to use church property to raise additional funds. They thus were interested in relaxing the prohibition on the sale of church property.

The conflict of interests between senatorial donors and the Curia first came to light when Odoacer's praetorian prefect Basilius proclaimed a strict prohibition on the sale of church property; the rule was contested over the following decades. But that was not the only fault line. The uncompromising position that Felix III and Gelasius I took toward the imperial church and the Eastern Roman emperor also split opinions, and indeed both within the senate and within the clergy. Gelasius' successor, the Roman deacon Anastasius II (496–498), struck a more conciliatory tone with Emperor Anastasius, although he still maintained that the emperor should prevent the names of bishops condemned by Rome, especially Acacius, from being read at mass. Anastasius II may have instructed an embassy that traveled to Constantinople with the highest-ranking Roman senator, Festus, in 497 to hint at the possibility of an arrangement; at any rate, he welcomed in Rome a deacon of the bishop of Thessalonica who belonged to the imperial church—or rather had split from the true church from the Roman perspective. If Anastasius really was mulling ending the schism with the imperial church, though, he was unable to carry out his plan: he died on November 19, 498, after barely two years in office. Three days later, on November 22, two successors were simultaneously declared at different places in Rome only a few hundred meters apart. While the majority of the Roman clergy in the *basilica Constantiniana* (St. John Lateran) elevated the deacon Symmachus to successor of St. Peter, the archpresbyter Laurentius was elected in the *basilica sanctae Mariae* (Santa Maria Maggiore). A smaller number of clergymen was among Laurentius' supporters, but he was backed by a majority of the senators, led by the former consuls Festus (cos. 472) and Probinus (cos. 489). We can still infer their motives to some extent: Laurentius' supporters hoped to reach an agreement with the Eastern emperor and the imperial church; at the same time, they wanted to protect the influence of laymen on the Roman church. Symmachus, in contrast, called for repressing the influence of laymen and was unwilling to make even the slightest concession to the emperor and imperial church.[62]

It was by no means unheard of for a dispute to break out after a bishop's death because the clergy and people could not agree on a successor. A double election had happened once before even in the see of Rome: after the death of Pope Zosimus on December 26, 418, the archdeacon Eulalius and the presbyter Boniface were simultaneously elected pope. The urban prefect Symmachus, a pagan, then sent a report to Honorius, who first decided in favor of Eulalius but then retracted his decision and, after further hemming and hawing, finally recognized Boniface as bishop of Rome. Eighty years later, the parties again agreed to appeal to the ruler to settle the dispute. In doing so, they followed a pattern of behavior that had been used inside and outside Rome often in the past.[63]

In contrast to the double election of 418, however, the ruler now stood outside the community of faith whose dispute he was asked to resolve. A heretic now would determine who was St. Peter's legitimate successor and representative. The decision to turn to Theoderic was feasible at all only because the senators and clergy believed that he would resolve the question impartially. As a matter of fact, the king substantiated his decision with formal arguments: in early 499, he confirmed Symmachus on the grounds that he had been elected first and had a majority on his side. Theoderic's reasoning was hard to dispute, even if Laurentius' supporters subsequently and rightly emphasized that Symmachus had spent considerable sums of money to win the goodwill of the court for his case.[64]

Symmachus thereupon returned from Ravenna to Rome while Laurentius was consecrated bishop of Nuceria (Alfaterna) in Campania. The looming schism thereby seemed to have been averted. On March 1, 499, Symmachus was solemnly feted in Old St. Peter's by seventy-two bishops, who in well-rehearsed acclamations wished him and Theoderic a long life. The synod then passed guidelines for papal elections, punishing with deposition any presbyter or deacon who committed himself to vote for a new pope in any way during the lifetime of the incumbent. When Theoderic traveled to Rome for the first (and only) time to celebrate his thirty-year jubilee as king, Symmachus went forth to welcome him at the head of the Catholic community.[65]

This peace, however, was deceptive. Symmachus remained controversial in the city even after Theoderic confirmed him; influential senators and many clergymen rejected him. The pope was accused of immoral conduct and the embezzlement of church property. The fact that Symmachus celebrated Easter in the year 501 on March 25, while it would have been celebrated on April 22 according to the Alexandrian calculation customary in the imperial church, raised tempers even higher: many contemporaries found it outrageous that the Roman church would not celebrate the feast of the crucifixion and resurrection of the Redeemer together with the rest of Christendom. The senate and clergy appealed to the king again and brought charges against Symmachus. Theoderic summoned the pope to Ravenna to defend his divergent calculation of Easter. This set in motion a series of events that led to the outbreak of a schism in Rome that was not resolved permanently until 514. The episode is known as the Laurentian Schism because Symmachus ultimately prevailed, whereas Laurentius was remembered as an "antipope" whose obstinacy had caused the break.

There are two conflicting accounts of the course of events. One was composed by one or more followers of Symmachus and is included in a collection of papal biographies titled the *Liber pontificalis* ("Book of Pontiffs"); it begins with Peter and ends with Symmachus. The other account describes the events with clear sympathy for Laurentius and was originally included in a collection of papal biographies from which only that of Laurentius survives intact. This source is known as the "Laurentian Fragment."

According to the Laurentian Fragment, Symmachus set out for Ravenna and waited in Ariminum for the order to appear at court. During a walk on the beach there, Symmachus is said to have encountered women whom Theoderic had summoned to Ravenna to testify against him. This assertion may or may not be malicious slander. It is a fact, however, that Symmachus returned from Ariminum to Rome and barricaded himself in Old St. Peter's. Presbyters, deacons, and other members of the Roman clergy traveled on to Ravenna and raised serious accusations against their bishop, who had supposedly sold church estates in violation of the ban pronounced in 483. Members of the senate and clergy asked the king to convene a synod to investigate these accusations, and he granted their request by inviting the bishops of Italy to Rome to try Symmachus in the year 502. At the same time, Theoderic suspended Symmachus for the duration of the investigation and appointed Peter of Altinum *visitator* of the Roman church to carry out the bishop's duties in his stead. The king thus did not intend to try the case himself but rather saw it as his responsibility to convene a synod to investigate the case and deliver a ruling.[66]

In the early summer of 502, over one hundred Italian bishops gathered in the *basilica Iulia* (Santa Maria in Trastevere). A faction from northern Italy had previously gone to the royal court and expressed doubts about the legitimacy of the trial; these bishops claimed that there was no precedent that the successor of St. Peter had ever been subject to the judgment of other bishops. Theoderic, however, dispelled these reservations by noting that Symmachus himself had assented to the trial by letter. Symmachus indeed appeared before the synod, over which Laurentius of Milan, Marcellianus of Aquileia, and Peter of Ravenna presided. The pope declared his willingness to submit to the bishops' judgment. He set two conditions, however: the *visitator* Peter had to leave Rome, while Symmachus himself recovered control over his churches. The bishop forwarded his demands to Theoderic, who rejected them. Despite that, Symmachus stated he was willing to come to the second session of the synod at the basilica of Santa Croce in Gerusalemme. On the route there, which led from the Vatican across the entire city, he and his followers were attacked by partisans of Laurentius; people were killed in the ensuing melee. Symmachus fled back to Old St. Peter's and refused to appear before the synod again.[67]

The synod thereafter met without the defendant. The accusation was read and entered in to the records, but the bishops did not dare to pronounce on the charges without interrogating Symmachus himself. Vice versa, many senators and many members of the Roman church were unwilling to welcome Symmachus back unless he first cleared himself of all accusations. As negotiations between the bishops, senators, and Roman clergy stalled and a significant number of the bishops departed, the participants in the synod turned again to Theoderic. They asked the king to convene a synod in Ravenna and requested that he personally attend. The king, however, declined this request in a letter dated August 8, 502, and instructed Laurentius, Marcellianus, and Peter, along with the rest of the bishops left in Rome, to promptly decide the case; he convened a third session on September 1 for that purpose. At the same time, Theoderic indicated that he might personally return to Rome if they again failed to reach a decision.[68]

Two weeks later, on August 27, the king urgently told the bishops to bring the trial finally to a conclusion, if necessary even without investigating the charges brought against Symmachus:

> If, however, you want the case that has been brought to proceed without discussion, may you and God know what you ordain, so long as peace is restored to the clergy, senate, and people of Rome under your ordination. Behold, We have cleared our conscience before God and men by entrusting everything to your discretion, as was fitting: only let you show that under your ordination the matter is at last at an end and unity has been returned to the dissidents. For it is neither tolerable nor does the love for the royal city by which We are bound permit it that, while the world has been pacified by God's dispensation, Rome alone should not have the peace from external enemies that we enjoy while heavenly favor fights on our side. It is indeed a disgraceful and astonishing contrast that the affairs of Rome [*Romanus status*] are governed peacefully on the frontier with foreign peoples and thrown into chaos in the midst of the City, with the result that the civil order [*civilitas*] should be missed in the citadel of Latium, yet untroubled in proximity to the enemy.[69]

Since Symmachus claimed he would have to fear for his life if he appeared again before the synod, Theoderic informed it in the same letter that he had sent three high-ranking Goths—Gudila, Bedewulf, and Arigern—to Rome to vouch under oath for Symmachus' personal safety. This assurance, Theoderic believed, would give Symmachus no choice but to face the synod and answer the charges against him.

But the king's hope was misplaced. As the bishops informed him in a detailed letter, Symmachus remained unwilling to submit to a trial before other bishops even after the arrival of Theoderic's envoys. A majority of the bishops, however, could not bring themselves to investigate the charges brought against Symmachus in his absence; they also rejected the idea of condemning him for contempt of court. Faced with this impasse, the bishops resorted to proposing to the king that he himself should "provide for the reunification of the church, God willing, and for the peace of the Roman civil order and of the provinces." Since they could not reach a decision, they sought leave to return to their churches.[70]

Theoderic sternly replied to the bishops' request on October 1 with orders to end the dispute promptly by delivering a verdict. He rebuked the bishops for consulting him yet again and reminded them that he himself had the power to pass judgment but had declined to do so for reasons of principle:

> We are surprised to be consulted again because, if We had wanted to decide the present case, after discussion with Our foremost men [*proceres*], We could have found a path to justice with God's guidance that would have displeased neither the present age nor indeed future times. But because We did not deem it Our task to decide anything concerning ecclesiastical affairs, We therefore had you summoned from sundry provinces so that the source of the entire controversy should pass under your dispensation in fear of divine judgment, and the harmony We long for might be restored to Our city through you by grace of God.[71]

In the instructions to the envoys who delivered this order from Ravenna to Rome, the king reiterated that the bishops did not need to take him into consideration and should not let anyone intimidate them. The envoys were instructed to tell the bishops on the king's behalf that giving a decision without investigating the case would set a bad precedent:

> Do not dread My person, you who shall give account in the sight of God: what matters is that you dismiss the senate, clergy, and people in peace and write what you have judged. . . . Therefore, do not have anyone's person before your eyes, although, if someone should wish to impose on you something unjust by force, you ought to relinquish your property to protect justice. For many bishops of both your and Our religion have been cast out of their churches and their property and yet still live. I do not solely impose [My will on you] but also ask you to do what God has commanded and what you

read in the Gospel and Apostle. If however, you discuss the case, even in a somewhat heated fashion, you will judge the case better. If, though, you dismiss it without discussion, you will give priests/bishops an utterly terrible example of conduct.[72]

Since Theoderic was unwilling to release the synod from its duty, negotiations started all over again. The senate maintained its position, however, that Symmachus could be reinstated only if he could refute the allegations raised against him. This was acceptable only to a minority of the bishops at the synod. The majority continued to refuse to investigate the charges against Symmachus in his absence. Only after Symmachus' adversaries withdrew from the synod could a consensus be reached. The remaining bishops agreed to reinstate Symmachus in office but not to deliver a verdict about the specific allegations brought against him. "Insofar as it concerns men," they concluded, Symmachus had been acquitted since men could not pass judgment on the occupant of the Apostolic See; it thus would be left to God himself to judge the legitimacy of the allegations.[73]

Symmachus capitalized on the presence of so many supporters in Rome to convene a synod at Old St. Peter's hardly a week later, on November 2, 502; seventy-nine bishops took part. The synod invalidated the decree of 483 about the inalienability of the property of the Roman church on the grounds that laymen had no authority to pronounce such decrees without consulting bishops. At Symmachus' behest, the synod issued an ordinance (*constitutum*) that applied exclusively to Rome, limiting the prohibition on selling church property to landholdings while explicitly permitting the sale of urban properties once again.

Symmachus' acquittal was not at all, however, received with unanimous approval. The concluding protocol, dated October 23, was signed by seventy-six bishops and thirty-seven Roman presbyters. Since it is reported that one hundred fifteen bishops had originally taken part in this Palmary Synod we can calculate how many bishops had departed before Symmachus' acquittal was decreed. One of them was Marcellianus of Aquileia, while Laurentius of Milan and Peter of Ravenna stayed by Symmachus' side until the end. Opposition among the Roman clergy was even stronger: the thirty-seven presbyters who signed were barely half of the total. Influential senators also continued to reject Symmachus. Together with the clergymen hostile to him, they addressed a petition to Theoderic in which they asked the king to grant Laurentius, then residing in Ravenna, permission to return to Rome. Theoderic granted their request and enabled Laurentius to return, whereupon he seized control of every important church in the city (with exception of the Lateran).[74]

There thus were two popes in Rome for the following four years (502–506): Symmachus, who had been reinstated by the Palmary Synod but now was recognized only by the clergy of churches outside the city walls and of the Lateran, and Laurentius, who controlled all the churches within the city walls with the help of his senatorial patrons, Festus and Probinus. The two camps fought violent street battles during these four years in which people lost their lives. The "Book of Pontiffs," written by Symmachus' partisans, reports the following:

> At the same time, the Head of the Senate [*caput senatus*], the ex-consul Festus, and the ex-consul Probinus began to fight with other senators and especially with the ex-consul Faustus within the city of Rome. And there was slaughter and murder within the clergy out of hatred. Those, however, who could be found within the city who righteously communed with the blessed Symmachus were slain by the sword; and casting out women and virgins who had taken holy vows from their convents or dwellings, exposing their feminine sex, they injured them by striking them with blows; and every day they fought battles against the church in the middle of the city. He [they?] also killed many priests, including Dignissimus and Gordianus, presbyters of St. Peter *ad vincula* [San Pietro in Vincoli] and Sts. John and Paul, whom they killed with cudgels and sword. For [they killed] many Christians, so that it was not safe for anyone from the clergy to walk about the city day or night. Only Faustus, the ex-consul, fought for the church.[75]

Even though this account is one-sided, blaming Laurentius' supporters for all the violence, it nonetheless gives a lively impression of the bitterness of the dispute between the respective allies of Laurentius and Symmachus. Both sides repeatedly tried to persuade the king to intervene during this period, but years passed before they had success. Theoderic finally agreed to intercede in the fall of 506. At the request of a delegation from Symmachus led by the deacon Dioscorus of Alexandria, he instructed the ex-consul Festus, Laurentius' most fervent supporter, to depose Laurentius and to see to it that the titular churches of Rome were transferred to Symmachus' control. Laurentius obeyed the king's orders without protest and withdrew to an estate owned by his patron Festus, where he lived for several years until his death.

Now there was only one pope in Rome, but he still was not universally recognized. Many clergymen—as well as many senators like Cassiodorus—refused to commune with Symmachus even after Laurentius' deposition. For them, the schism did not end until Symmachus' death in 514. The clergy of the basilica of St. Paul Outside the Walls (San Paolo fuori le Mura) was among these opponents; during the schism, they had biblical depictions of all the successors of

Fig. 20. Portrait of Pope Laurentius in the basilica of San Paolo fuori le Mura (Rome), preserved in *Codex Vaticanus Barberinus latinus* 4407, fol. 53 (recto). © Biblioteca Apostolica Vaticana, Rome.

St. Peter who had held the Apostolic See legitimately painted on the nave and transepts. Laurentius' image appeared in this gallery until the year 1823, when the church was almost totally destroyed by fire. We know of the portrait from a seventeenth-century copy.[76]

The reception of the Palmary Synod's decision was mixed outside Rome as well. Symmachus' acquittal had been unanimous, after all, only because the bishops who opposed it had already left. Symmachus' lay adversaries—probably members of the senatorial elite—published a pamphlet, "Against the synod of improper absolution" (*Adversus synodum incongruae absolutionis*). The original has been lost, but its content can be reconstructed in outline because the Milanese deacon Ennodius, who took Symmachus' side like his bishop Laurentius, wrote a riposte, "Against those who dared to write against the synod" (*Libellus adversus eos qui contra Synodum scribere praesumpserunt*), which has survived. Opponents of the synod had taken the view that an acquittal without an investigation of the grounds of the accusations ran contrary to every principle of secular and ecclesiastical law; even the bishop of Rome had to stand before his peers in judgment if serious accusations were made against him; otherwise, the privileges of the Apostolic See included the freedom to sin.

Ennodius set out to refute this position. The Milanese deacon emphasized Symmachus' innocence while avoiding going into the specific accusations that had been brought against him. Ennodius elevated the dispute to a matter of principle. He argued that the bishop of Rome could not be judged by any man; he was accountable only to God. Since the pope was the successor of St. Peter, whom God had made the head of the entire church, he could not be judged by men, not even by a synod. Contemporaries distilled this position into a brief formula: *Prima sedes a nemine iudicatur* ("The first see is judged by no one"). Centuries later, this principle became a permanent feature of canon law; Pope Gregory VII (1073–1085) cited it during the Investiture Controversy.

Ennodius wrote his treatise, which was organized according to the rules of late antique rhetoric, primarily for a senatorial readership. Other supporters of Symmachus sought to reach a wider audience by inventing past trials of earlier popes and circulating fake records of proceedings from these spurious trials. Texts composed as trial records were popular literature at the time, combining drama with an illusion of authenticity. The forgers' goal was to justify the principle that no man could judge the pope, thereby lending it venerable antiquity. Since the forgers came from Symmachus' circle of supporters, these texts are called "Symmachian forgeries."

In one such text set during the Diocletianic Persecution, a synod convened at Sinuessa (on the border of Latium and Campania) summons Pope

Marcellinus, who is accused of having offered incense to the pagan gods; but it repeatedly states that only the pope could render judgment over himself. Marcellinus confesses his guilt and is accordingly condemned. His successor, Miltiades, then remarks, "He has justly been condemned by his own mouth. . . . For no one has ever judged the pontifex nor a bishop [*praesul*] the supreme priest because the first see shall not be judged by anyone." In the records of a trial that was allegedly heard against Pope Xystus III under Emperor Valentinian III, senators accuse Xystus of seducing a nun. The emperor convenes a tribunal composed of senators and clergymen but then recognizes the principle that it is not allowed to pass judgment over the pope, whereupon his accusers repent and implore the pope in vain to forgive their sins. The "Book of Pontiffs" mentioned above, the earliest version of which ended with a biography of Symmachus, takes similar liberties with the historical record. Since almost nothing was known about the bishops of Rome in the first and second centuries, the authors filled these gaps with freely invented details to present Symmachus as the last link in a chain of legitimate successors to St. Peter. In the Laurentian Fragment, in contrast, the history of the popes culminates in Laurentius, a view that was also reflected in the gallery of paintings in the basilica of St. Paul, also mentioned above.[77]

The majority of senators, gathered around Postumius Festus (cos. 472) and Petronius Probinus (cos. 489), sponsored Laurentius for a long time. Only Faustus Niger (cos. 490) appears to have supported Pope Symmachus from the beginning. When the *patricius* Symmachus (cos. 485) first became his papal namesake's patron is unknown; he is not attested in this role until 502. Several years later, the *patricius* Liberius also appears in the Symmachians' camp: after the death of Marcellianus of Aquileia, who refused to associate with Symmachus to the end, Ennodius congratulated Liberius on his choice concerning the succession. Liberius had thus campaigned for a man (whose name is not known to us) who was palatable to the Symmachians. It is especially unfortunate that we do not know when Festus and Probinus buried the hatchet with Faustus and Symmachus. It is merely clear that they did so before the year 512 because that is when all four appear together in a text by Ennodius. This change of heart might have taken place several years earlier because Theoderic's decision in favor of Symmachus had robbed Laurentius' cause of any prospect of success.[78]

The sources do not reveal how it came about that these senators finally dropped Laurentius. Scholars have not infrequently pointed to the new international situation: an undeclared state of war had prevailed between King Theoderic and Emperor Anastasius since 505. In these circumstances, Theoderic drew a clear line by deciding in favor of a pope who was guaranteed

not to make any concessions to the Eastern Roman emperor. This interpretation is uncertain, however, because it presumes that Laurentius had already lost
his senatorial support; otherwise, his deposition would have only entrenched
the opposing fronts. There is no doubt, in contrast, that after Laurentius' deposition the senators were concerned to protect their influence as the donors of
church property. At their insistence, Theoderic confirmed the prohibition on
the sale of church property in such a way that permitted no exception. The letter in which he conveyed this decision to the senate survives:

> King Flavius Theoderic to the Senate of the City of Rome, the conqueror of
> the world, guardian and restorer of liberty.
>   A report that was sent for the good of the church has reached Us, con-
> script fathers, and the welcome ordination of your sacred assembly has struck
> the heart of Our Mildness. And though after the venerable synod the ordina-
> tion of your judgment would suffice for such decrees, still We gave answer
> to your consultation in the present oracle so that no priest [i.e., bishop] of
> any church may legitimately conclude a contract for the alienation of any
> property. They will instead grant their usufruct to anyone they wish while
> observing equity. For property that is owed to all outsiders [*peregrinis omni-
> bus*] or delivered to the church should not be negated solely by the wish of
> the pontiff or clergy. For what is so profane as that the intention of the donor
> should be violated in this regard, while private persons claim for themselves
> under contract [of purchase/conveyance], instead of usufruct, the property
> that each intended to belong to the church. Therefore, if anyone should
> presume with criminal daring to undertake forbidden transactions and
> desires to keep a thing given by a bishop or clergy beyond usufruct, the alien-
> ated property shall be claimed with its fruits immediately by the venerable
> governor. Etc.[79]

Theoderic's role in this complicated series of events is difficult to discern.
The king intervened four times in this dispute: the first time, after the double
election of 498 at the request of both parties; the second time, in 501, when he
convened a synod in Rome at the request of Symmachus' opponents but with
his consent; the third time, in 502, at the request of Laurentius' supporters,
when he allowed Laurentius to retake possession of Peter's throne; and the
fourth time, in 506, at the request of Symmachus' supporters, when he executed
the judgment handed down four years earlier by the Palmary Synod. Theoderic
thus never intervened in the affairs of the Catholic Church unless he was asked.
The king also refused to investigate the accusations against Symmachus personally and insisted that judgment be rendered by bishops. Theoderic's actions
thus accorded with his declared principle of not interfering in church affairs.

Of course, this statement must not be misinterpreted as a commitment to the modern principle of the separation of church and state, which was inconceivable to contemporaries. Theoderic made his decision in favor of Symmachus after the double election of 498; four years later, he informed the synod then meeting in Rome that he voluntarily declined to arrogate the judgment in Symmachus' case to himself. Since Symmachus was unwilling to make any concessions to Emperor Anastasius, one might think that the king favored him from the start. In reality, though, Theoderic did not press the synod in Rome to acquit Symmachus in any way. On the contrary: if Theoderic had had his way, the charges against Symmachus would have been investigated. Symmachus' opponents even claimed that the king was on their side. Moreover, for four long years, Theoderic made no move to enforce the decision of the Palmary Synod and permitted Laurentius to return to Rome. However welcome Symmachus' intransigence toward the Eastern Roman emperor might have been, the king's actions in the Laurentian Schism were not dictated exclusively by considerations of foreign policy.

Emperor Anastasius disapproved of Symmachus' acquittal; in a letter to the pope that is known only from the latter's reply, Anastasius seems to have insultingly called Symmachus a Manichaean. Symmachus responded no less brusquely, denying the emperor the right to meddle in ecclesiastical affairs with reference to the "Two-Swords Theory." At the same time, he flung the insult of Manichaeism back at the emperor: it was the emperor who was persecuting Catholics as patron of the Manichaeans. That all but killed any chance of subsequent compromise; the emperor and pope had declared each other heretics.[80]

Symmachus' profile in the post-Roman West, in contrast, rose after the Palmary Synod. Bishop Avitus of Vienne wrote to the senators Faustus Niger and Symmachus, Pope Symmachus' patrons, on behalf of the Catholic bishops of the kingdom of the Burgundians to express his joy at the outcome of the dispute. Symmachus' acquittal was, in his view, a victory for the entire church because the bishop of Rome was the first among all Catholic bishops: "In the case of other bishops, if something should perhaps call for it, it can be fixed; but if the pope of the City is called into question, the episcopacy itself, not just a bishop, will seem to totter."[81]

To Symmachus, the requirement that any bishop who had failed to break with Acacius and all his followers could not be in communion with the Roman church was non-negotiable. The question of whether a bishop acknowledged the formula of Chalcedon, in contrast, was secondary. One bishop from the northeastern Balkans asked Symmachus to take a more lenient stance toward bishops of the Eastern church who embraced Chalcedon but could not

renounce communion with the Acacians because they then would be driven
out of their bishoprics. To this request, the pope replied that a Catholic must be
prepared to suffer martyrdom for the true faith. Symmachus also had no interest
in a theological compromise. To deflect criticism of the doctrine that Christ
was one person "in two natures"—which was widely attacked in the East for
allegedly splitting the unity of the Redeemer—the anonymous spokesman of
these eastern supporters of Chalcedon suggested that the church might allow
one to use the formula "of two natures" as a complementary and fully legitimate formulation of the same doctrine. This proposal set Boethius thinking, but
Symmachus did not even dignify it with a refutation; the idea remained taboo
in Rome for many years to come. Pope John II first declared the formula "of two
natures" orthodox in 534.[82]

Symmachus died on July 19, 514, and was buried in St. Peter's. The deacon
Hormisdas was consecrated as his successor the next day. During his pontificate, negotiations to end the schism with the imperial church were again set in
motion. The initiative was taken by Vitalianus, a general (*comes foederatorum*)
of Emperor Anastasius who was a strict adherent of the Chalcedonian Creed.
Vitalianus, who had a strong following in Thrace, marched on Constantinople
and forced Anastasius to invite Hormisdas to a synod on July 1, 515, that would
take place in the city of Heraclea in the province of Europa, deep in the emper-
or's territory. The pope would act there as a mediator to settle the disputes over
the correct belief that had arisen in the Scythian provinces. Hormisdas
announced his readiness to make peace per letter and requested more information about the agenda of the planned synod.[83]

The pope sought to cover his bases on all sides before he took the next step.
First, he secured the assent of a Roman synod. Then he traveled to Ravenna.
Only after the king had given his approval did Hormisdas send an embassy to
Constantinople. In addition to Ennodius, who had now climbed to bishop of
Ticinum, the embassy included Bishop Fortunatus of Catania and three mem-
bers of the Roman clergy. In a letter to Caesarius of Arles, Hormisdas also
informed the Gallic bishops of the mission. The papal envoys took precise
instructions with them on their journey. The key points were recognition of the
Council of Chalcedon and the Christological letter of Leo the Great (the *tomus
Leonis*) read there and the condemnation of Acacius and all those who maintained communion with him. The bishops of the imperial church should both
proclaim their assent publicly before their communities and confirm it by signing
a declaration prepared in Rome, which is known as the "formula of Hormisdas."
Anyone who signed it declared his intention to distance himself in no way from
the belief that the successors of St. Peter had always kept pure and condemned

all those whom the bishop of Rome had excommunicated. In an attached letter to the emperor, Hormisdas declined the emperor's request that he come to Heraclea personally, but he indicated that he might be willing to leave his bishopric in the future if it helped advance the restoration of the faith.[84]

The outcome of the talks was awaited in Italy and Gaul with bated breath. Avitus of Vienne tried to come by information from Ravenna and Rome. The demand that bishops of the imperial church unconditionally submit to the will of the bishop of Rome, however, was decisively rejected in Constantinople. Anastasius did not, however, abandon the plan to reconcile with the Apostolic See for that reason. The emperor explained to the pope by letter that the Henotikon observed in his empire was not an attack on the Council of Chalcedon, and he indicated that he could not erase all memory of Acacius, who was dead, without provoking bloodshed among those who were living. In July 516, another embassy came from the Byzantine emperor to Italy. In addition to a letter from the emperor to the pope, it also brought a letter addressed to the senate of Rome. Anastasius appealed to the senators to urge Theoderic to help the two halves of the empire (*utraeque res publicae*) to heal and thrive — that is, to end the schism. We do not know how the senators received this proposal. Might they have hoped to serve as mediators among the pope, the king, and the emperor? If they did, then this hope was dashed by Theoderic's opposition because in their reply to Anastasius the senators indicate that the king had ordered them to carry out the pope's instructions. Perhaps, however, the senators were relieved that they could hide behind the king, who protected both themselves and the pope from Anastasius' reach. East and West nonetheless did not move a single step closer together because Hormisdas still demanded that the emperor disown those whom the Apostolic See had condemned.[85]

In April 517, yet another papal embassy set out for Constantinople. Its mission had also been coordinated with Theoderic. This time, however, reconciliation was only ostensibly the purpose: Hormisdas' envoys were instructed to seek support for the pope's position among the clergy, monks, and laity of Constantinople and the eastern provinces of the empire. To that end, in addition to a letter to the emperor, they brought along no fewer than nineteen promotional letters that they were supposed to disseminate among the opposition. When word of this leaked out, the emperor immediately broke off negotiations; he had the papal envoys expelled and promptly brought by ship back to Rome. Anastasius followed up with a letter dated July 11, 517, in which he declared that the negotiations were over; he reminded the pope of Christ's humility and concluded with the words, "But from now on, We bury our requests in silence, deeming it senseless to address the goodness of prayers to those who scornfully reject being asked. For We can endure being insulted and frustrated; We cannot be commanded."[86]

With this letter, the restoration of church unity between East and West seemed to retreat to an insurmountable distance. Theoderic had done his part to bring this about since the popes' diplomatic maneuvers had received his blessing in advance. He could only be pleased when the gulf between his Catholic subjects and the Eastern Roman emperor widened even more. The schism guaranteed him the loyalty of senators and bishops because a "Manichaean" emperor must have seemed far more dangerous than an "Arian" but tolerant king. How long this state of affairs would persist, of course, was impossible to divine: Anastasius was already over eighty years old at the time. Who might succeed him was anyone's guess.

4. UNDER THE KING'S PROTECTION: THE JEWS

There were supposed to be only two peoples in Theoderic's Italy: Goths and Romans. The population of the country was split into two groups according to ethnicity, even though the dividing line largely, albeit not completely, coincided with that between Catholics and Homoeans. The Jews made up the largest and most influential group that did not conform to this binary concept. The Jews defined themselves primarily as members of the people of Israel, even if they also had obtained Roman citizenship. There were numerous adherents of the Jewish religion throughout the Roman Empire, especially in its cities. Even though educated Romans regarded Judaism as superstition (*superstitio*) and segments of pagan society fiercely rejected it, the practice of Judaism was protected by imperial privileges. That changed little in Late Antiquity, although Christian preachers warned their congregations of the pernicious effect of associating with Jews. The emperors initially upheld the Jews' old privileges. Relations did not dramatically deteriorate until the early fifth century, when Jews were prohibited from joining the imperial civil service and military (*militia*) in the eastern and western halves of the empire. The construction of new synagogues or the expansion of existing synagogues was also no longer allowed. Jews were, however, still allowed and obligated to serve as decurions; the emperors still reiterated that the Jews stood under their protection and permitted Jewish communities to manage their own internal affairs. Judaism was the only non-Christian religion that was officially permitted in the Christian empire of Late Antiquity.[87]

The history of Jewish communities in Italy extends back to the first century BCE. Jewish communities can be identified in many Italian cities around the year 500 CE: in large cities like Rome, Naples, Ravenna, Milan, and Genua, but also in Venusia (Venosa) on the border between Lucania and Apulia and in Bova Marina, a small town on the southern tip of the peninsula. These communities were integrated linguistically and culturally into local society; most of their members wrote in Latin, and many bore Latin names. In a Latin epitaph (with a blessing in Hebrew) for a Jewish woman named Augusta, who was buried in the catacombs of Venusia in 521, her husband Bonus claimed the title *vir laudabilis*, which was used by members of municipal councils. Both Augusta's father and (maternal?) grandfather, however, not only had biblical names, but also bore the honorary title *pater* ("father") that indicated a leading position within a Jewish community—the former in Lypiae (Lecce) in Apulia, the latter in Anchiasmus (Saranda) in Epirus (Albania).[88]

Jewish communities were also capable of articulating and advocating their collective interests, but they had no institutional ties to one another. There also was no single religious authority to which all Jews might turn after the end of the Jewish Patriarchate (the Sanhedrin) sometime before the year 429. Jewish communities were distinguished from their social context by their cultic practice and religious customs; they also had their own cemeteries. There is no evidence, however, for specifically Jewish professions. The synagogue stood at the center of Jewish communal life; it was far more than a house of prayer. In addition to being a hall for reading scripture, it included dining halls, storerooms, and living quarters. Hebraic was widely used for reading the Torah but was not yet obligatory; shortly before the demise of the Gothic kingdom (553), Justinian ordered that Latin and Greek translations must be permitted for this purpose in addition to the original. Besides rabbis, who were recognized as teachers on account of their knowledge of the Torah and the collection of religious texts known as the Mishnah, men known as "elders" (*presbyteroi*) or "fathers" (*patres*) and by various other titles played a leading part in Jewish communities.[89]

With respect to the Jews, Theoderic continued the policy of the late antique emperors who had reigned before him. In his *Edict* (§ 143), it is stated, "Concerning the Jews, the privileges conferred by the laws shall be maintained; those quarreling among themselves and living under their laws must have as judges those whom they have as the teachers of their cult." It was wholly in keeping with this policy when the king explicitly confirmed for the Jews living in Genua that he would uphold all statutory privileges that "antiquity" (*antiquitas*) had granted Jewish institutions. This declaration also included the Samaritans, who like the Jews viewed themselves as descendants of the people of Israel and referred to the five books of Moses but had constituted their own communities for centuries. When lawyers of the Roman church complained that a Samaritan was claiming for a synagogue a building that Pope Simplicius had lawfully acquired, Theoderic instructed Arigern, who was residing as his envoy in Rome at the time, to investigate the matter thoroughly and decide the case.[90]

The legal situation created by the laws of the Western Roman emperors delineated a boundary that Theoderic did not want to cross: when the Jews of Genua asked for his permission to renovate a synagogue, he gave them permission to repair the roof of the building but explicitly forbade them to enlarge or beautify it, citing the "divine constitutions" (*constituta divalia*) of the emperors. Moreover, he was conspicuously at pains to anticipate the accusation that he was acting out of sympathy for the Jews, explaining, "Why do you seek what you ought to flee? We grant you permission, but We laudably condemn the wish of those in error: We cannot impose religion by fiat because no one can be forced to believe against his will."[91]

The same effort to distance himself can also be detected in a letter that the king sent toward the end of his reign to the Jews of Milan after they had asked for his protection from attacks by clergymen. Cassiodorus states in the king's name that even those who err in their belief must not be denied justice. He then gives the king's decision in the following words:

> Since you allege you have been maltreated by the boldness of certain persons and report that the rights that belong to your synagogues are being violated, the requested protection of Our Mildness will come to your aid, so that no associate of the church [*ecclesiasticus*] may violently seize what belongs to your synagogue under the law or interfere with untoward bitterness in your affairs, but just as they are distinct with respect to their religious practice [*religionis cultus*], so too shall they be in their involvement in transactions. We grant you this privilege of princely aid, however, on this condition: that you too do not unlawfully [*inciviliter*] attempt to appropriate what indisputably belongs to the rights of the aforesaid church or indeed by law to religious persons.[92]

The king's protection was so important to Jewish communities because, as a heterodox and exclusive minority in a society that viewed itself as Christian, they often were targets of collective violence. In the event of theft, arson, assault, and murder, the victims still clung to the hope that the king would give them satisfaction and punish the perpetrators. The king in fact took up such a complaint after a synagogue in Rome was set on fire between 507 and 511. Even if the motive behind the fire is unclear—apparently some Christian slaves had been executed for murdering their Jewish masters—it is obvious that the king had no intention of tolerating this course of action. Informed of the incident by the *comes* Arigern, Theoderic instructed the senate to investigate the case and severely punish the perpetrators. At the same time, he told the senators to check whether the Jews themselves might also have been partly at fault.[93]

Italy's Jews appreciated the fact that Theoderic gave them protection. His successors also observed this policy. Justinian, in contrast, enacted a series of repressive measures against the Jews in his territory beginning in 527. After the Byzantine general Belisarius had destroyed the kingdom of the Vandals (535), synagogues located there were converted into churches. It thus is not surprising that the Jewish community of Naples stayed on the Goths' side to the bitter end when Belisarius besieged the city the following year.[94]

Conflict between Jews and Christians put Christian rulers in a difficult position. Even the emperors were pressured to justify themselves when they extended protection to Jews, because bishops and clergymen expected them to show open partiality toward the "true faith." The dispute between Theodosius the Great and Ambrose of Milan over whether the synagogue of Callinicum on the Euphrates, which had been destroyed by Christians, should be rebuilt is only the most famous example. On that occasion (388), the emperor had yielded, declined to punish the perpetrators, and gave no restitution to the victims.[95]

For a ruler like Theoderic, who himself belonged to a Christian minority, conflicts between Jews and Catholics were especially delicate because the Homoeans were already suspected of siding with the Jews. That sounded plausible to many Catholics because both Jews and Homoeans were accused of denying that Jesus Christ was divine like God the Father. Even if the Homoeans did not call Jesus a mere mortal man as the Jews did, it was argued, they still denied his full divinity. In Catholic polemics, both positions were deemed a hostile act directed at Jesus Christ. Hence Theoderic had to fear that Catholics might interpret measures taken to protect the Jews as favoring the enemies of Christ and proof of a secret accord. To Catholics, it was a fact that "not only all pagans, but also all Jews and all heretics and schismatics, who end their present life outside the Catholic church, will go into the eternal fire that has been prepared for the devil and his angels," as the Catholic theologian Fulgentius, who was banished for several years from North Africa to Sardinia and was well connected with Roman senators, formulated the doctrine of his church.[96]

As a matter of fact, the king found himself in the crossfire at the end of his reign, when serious riots broke out against the Jewish community in Ravenna in his absence. If we are to believe the *Anonymus Valesianus*, some Jews had mocked Christians by throwing wafers in water at a procession. Then "the people" formed a mob and set the synagogues on fire. The Jews then hastened to Verona, where Theoderic was residing at the time and incited him against the

Christians with the support of the high chamberlain Triwa. Theoderic finally decided that the Roman people of Ravenna had to rebuild the synagogues at their own expense. Anyone who could not contribute money would be beaten and paraded in public, while a herald called out his name. Theoderic instructed his son-in-law and presumptive heir Eutharic and Peter, the Catholic bishop of Ravenna, to carry out his decision. When the *Anonymus Valesianus* attributes this action, which was in complete conformity with the law, to a secret alliance between "Arians" and Jews, he likely was expressing views that were widespread in ecclesiastical circles. Later, it was even alleged that the king had decreed three days before his death that the "Arians" should occupy all the Catholic churches. Again, it was claimed that a Jew had put him up to it.[97]

FROM COOPERATION TO CONFLICT: THEODERIC'S FINAL YEARS

1. EUTHARIC AND THE FAILURE OF THE SUCCESSION

Ennodius concluded his panegyric to Theoderic in the year 507 with the wish that an heir and successor might be granted to the king: "May a purple-clad offspring of yours increase the boons of this golden age! May an heir to your kingdom play in your lap, so that a sacred little one may ask us for these libations of words that we offer you, as we bear witness to similar joys."[1] In this passage Ennodius expressed a hope that many of Theoderic's subjects undoubtedly shared. The king was over fifty years old at the time, but he had no son to succeed him. Since there was no binding rule as to how one should proceed in such circumstances, what would happen after Theoderic's death was an open question. The absence of an heir to the throne was a source of concern to those who were in Theoderic's debt and fired the imagination of those who were dissatisfied with their standing. The surest way to banish this uncertainty was always to found a dynasty. Succession from father to son guaranteed a smooth transfer of power; it promised continuity and stability. For Theoderic's Roman subjects, dynastic rule was above all the alternative to civil war for supremacy. Among the Goths, dependence on Theoderic's person was also a factor because it was widely believed that individual traits were heritable; a son was considered his father's likeness. This warrior population had already witnessed the successful transfer of power from father to son once: Theoderic himself had succeeded his father as ruler of the "Pannonian" Goths in 474. Hopes that Theoderic's marriage to Audefleda, the sister of the Frankish king Clovis, would produce a son, however, were ultimately dashed. Amalasuintha, born in the year 495, remained the only offspring of this union, the youngest of Theoderic's three daughters (including two from a previous marriage). Twenty years later, when there was no longer any hope for the birth of a son, Theoderic set about to regulate the succession by other means: he married Amalasuintha to a Visigoth named Eutharic, whom he fetched from Spain to Italy expressly for this purpose. Theoderic then systematically groomed this Eutharic, who had been practically unknown in Italy beforehand, as his successor. The wedding was celebrated in the year 515. The following year, Amalasuintha bore her husband a son who was named Athalaric ("noble king"); a daughter—Matasuintha—came into the world next.[2]

Many Goths and Romans were probably surprised by Theoderic's choice of Eutharic, not simply because they did not know who he was in Italy. There had been another candidate in Theoderic's own family, the son of his sister Amalafrida, who was already of an age fit to reign. This nephew of Theoderic was named Theodahad, and he was as well educated as he was unwarlike. Instead of training in mounted combat, he pursued philosophical and theological studies. He thus was the perfect antithesis of Theoderic's ideal successor. Theodahad had long had to content himself with only the second-highest rank at court and had been publicly reprimanded by his uncle. Hence rather than reside at his uncle's court, he preferred life in Tuscany, where he owned extensive landholdings that he continually expanded at his neighbors' expense. In Tuscany, Theodahad was his own master, owned several residences—some of them fortified—and gathered a circle of devotees around himself that included Roman senators.[3]

Eutharic was a blank page to Theoderic's Italian subjects. To Theoderic, though, Eutharic's origin in Hispania was an advantage because it opened up the possibility that he might succeed Theoderic as king over both the Ostrogoths and the Visigoths. Eutharic's dynastic claim to the throne, however, was tenuous because it was his marriage to Amalasuintha that had introduced him to the royal family. To amend this defect, a genealogy was quickly fabricated that made Eutharic into a distant relative of Theoderic and a member of the Amal clan.

Theoderic was aware, however, that Eutharic's succession would not be secure unless he was also accepted by the Byzantine emperor. Theoderic actually achieved this goal after Emperor Anastasius died in July 518 and was replaced by Justin. Justin declared that he was willing to confer the consulship of the year 519 on Eutharic, who would be his own colleague in office; moreover, he accepted the Goth as his son-in-arms by solemnly conferring military equipment on him. That Eutharic could hold the consulship as the emperor's colleague was an unheard of honor at this time, especially since he was not even a Roman citizen. Even if the two consuls never met or even acted jointly, the fact that both their names were used to date the year in East and West signified the harmony between the two halves of the Roman Empire.⁴

Eutharic's inauguration was celebrated with great pomp and circumstance in Theoderic's kingdom; the celebrations marked the second high point of Theoderic's reign after his visit to Rome in the year 500, even though Theoderic stayed behind in Ravenna this time and let his son-in-law travel to Rome alone. The senate and people gave Eutharic a magnificent welcome. Cassiodorus played a prominent part in it, delivering a panegyric to the heir apparent in the senate, fragments of which have survived on papyrus.⁵

Before the senators, the orator first praised the blessings of the reign of the absent king Theoderic: "This sanctuary"—meaning the senate—"he fills with your honors, he feeds the people with fixed expenses, he pacifies the provinces with the serenity of justice, he restrains the proud peoples [*gentes*] with his command. And whatsoever is found to be alien to his kingdom appears to be confounded down to the ground. Hail, tireless triumphator! Through your battles, the tired limbs of the Republic are restored and ancient felicity returns to our times." Later, Cassiodorus evoked the devotion of Theoderic's subjects to Eutharic and the latter's influence on the Gothic king. He addressed Eutharic as the lord (*dominus*) of Roman senators while simultaneously describing him as the counselor of the prince (*princeps*):

> That is why, most merciful lord [*dominus*—meaning Eutharic], the populace of the cities will not permit you to depart but rather all want you to come to them. Bitter is the life that fails to merit your glance; and it is wearisome to linger in one's own abode when you have been forced to abandon it by the exigency of affairs. Justly, therefore, the longing of all is kindled for your presence, and you make your subjects sad because you are known to be loved too much. But you, lord, give Your Majesty's [*maiestas*] counsel to our most prudent prince [*princeps*]: mortal wishes cannot foresee what they should choose. Ensure that he always does what you know to be generally beneficial to all.⁶

Cassiodorus' purpose was not merely to sing the praises of the king and his presumptive successor before the senate. He additionally composed a "chronicle" on this occasion at Eutharic's behest, beginning with the creation of the world and then proceeding past the kings of the four world empires and the Roman consuls down to Eutharic's own consulship. In this way, the present day was represented as the triumphant consummation of the history of Rome.

Theoderic made sure that his son-in-law's appearance met the expectations of a ruler's visit to Rome. Joined by an envoy from the Byzantine emperor, who did not leave Constantinople, Eutharic held chariot races in the Circus Maximus and animal hunts in the Colosseum; for the latter, wild animals were imported from North Africa at great expense. Perhaps Eutharic also paid his respects to the bishop of Rome during his visit by donating two silver candelabra (weighing seventy pounds each) to St. Peter's in Theoderic's name. At any rate, Eutharic conferred ranks (*dignitates*) on senators and lavished gifts on both Goths and Romans. Then, breaking with all tradition, this elaborate program was repeated soon afterward in Ravenna—excepting the chariot races since Ravenna did not have a hippodrome—and at this second celebration of Eutharic's consulship Theoderic appeared personally with his son-in-law and presumptive heir before the Goths and Romans.

The consular games of the year 519 impressively showcased the fundamental principles of Theoderic's reign: harmony between Goths and Romans and harmony between king and emperor. Theoderic courted the senate and people of Rome as much as he did the populace of Ravenna, dominated by Goths. The old metropolis, "invincible Rome" (*invicta Roma*), received the same attention as the new one, "happy Ravenna" (*felix Ravenna*). The concluding joint appearance of Theoderic and Eutharic seemed to guarantee that the Gothic kingdom in Italy would continue under the next generation. But Eutharic ultimately could not play the part devised for him: he died before Theoderic, certainly after 520 and probably before 523. We know neither Eutharic's precise date of death nor how old he actually was when he died.[7] The only thing that seems certain is that he was somewhat younger than his father-in-law. According to Jordanes (Jord. *Get.* 298), drawing on Cassiodorus, Eutharic was prudent, valorous, and hardy. The *Anonymus Valesianus* (Anon. Val. 80) describes him, in contrast, as a harsh man and an enemy of the Catholic faith. The only specific action for which Eutharic is blamed in the sources may illuminate what Anonymus meant: while Theoderic was far from Ravenna, Catholic Christians burned down the local synagogue in the year 519–520. As mentioned above, the king instructed Eutharic to see to it that the congregation of the Catholic bishop Peter rebuilt the synagogue, which is what then happened. From the perspective of the *Anonymus Valesianus*, the rebuilding of the synagogue was a hostile act directed against Catholic Christians. It was, however, completely in keeping with the official policy of Theoderic and his imperial predecessors, who had pledged to protect the Jews from wanton violence. By carrying out the king's instructions, Eutharic exposed himself to the accusation of being an enemy of the Catholic faith.[8]

Eutharic's death was a disaster for Theoderic: all his efforts to ensure the succession were undone at a stroke. The problem presented itself now with even greater urgency: Theoderic was now in his seventh decade, and a mausoleum that would serve as the king's final resting place had begun to rise before the walls of Ravenna. It was inevitable that people started to wonder what would happen after his death, both among the Gothic aristocracy and among the Roman senators. Both parties had much at stake: every change of ruler carried hidden dangers for those who enjoyed the old ruler's favor and opened up new opportunities for those more distant to him. It also was by no means a foregone conclusion that Theoderic's policy of separation and cooperation between Goths and Romans would be continued after his death. In fact, there were signs that some Roman senators had their own ideas about Theoderic's succession and that the king was monitoring such ideas with mistrust.

2. HIGH TREASON IN THE SENATE? THE TRIALS OF ALBINUS, BOETHIUS, AND SYMMACHUS

Anicius Manlius Severinus Boethius was not merely the greatest scholar of his time but also belonged to an old senatorial family that commanded great wealth and prestige. His father, Flavius Marius Manlius Boethius, had held the highest offices in the Western Roman Empire several times and attained the rank of *patricius*; he had been consul in the year 487. While his father may have died prematurely, Boethius nonetheless was welcomed into the house of Quintus Aurelius Memmius Symmachus, consul of the year 485. This connection was reinforced by Boethius' marriage to Rusticiana, Symmachus' daughter. Like his father and father-in-law, Boethius also reached the highest offices that were open to a senator; he held the consulship in the year 510 and obtained the rank of *patricius*, despite the fact that he had not held a single office before that, on account of his preference for leisurely scholarly study to a high position at the royal court. Twelve years later, Boethius was honored by Theoderic again in downright spectacular fashion: at the beginning of 522, his two sons, tellingly named Symmachus and Boethius, jointly entered upon the office of consul in Rome. Boethius lived to see the two youths be escorted by senators from his home to the senate house on the Forum Romanum to the acclaim of a throng of people. After they took their places in the consuls' seats of office, Boethius personally delivered the obligatory panegyric to the reigning ruler. Then he opened the chariot races in the Circus Maximus together with his sons and distributed a generous donative to the people of Rome.[9]

A moment like this must have seemed like the pinnacle of earthly felicity by senatorial standards, and every observer knew that Boethius had the king's favor to thank for it. Boethius in fact soon took over the key position of *magister officiorum*, whose chief area of responsibilities was oversight of the court chancelleries. In the fall of 523, however, Boethius was accused of treason, condemned to death, and executed after a long incarceration. His property was confiscated by the king. Soon thereafter, Boethius' father-in-law, Symmachus, who stood at the peak of the senatorial hierarchy as "head of the senate," suffered the same fate; he too was condemned and executed.[10]

How did this abrupt fall from the lonely pinnacle of senatorial bliss come about? The *Anonymus Valesianus* reports the following:

> Cyprianus, who was a referendary [*referendarius*] at the time and later *comes sacrarum* [*largitionum*] and *magister* [*officiorum*], was driven by greed to allege that Albinus the *patricius* had sent a letter to Emperor Justin against his [Theoderic's] rule. When he [Albinus] was summoned and denied he had done so, then Boethius the *patricius*, who was *magister officiorum*, said in sight of the king, "Cyprianus' accusation is false; but if Albinus did that, then I and the entire senate did it with one mind. It is false, my lord king." Then, after some hesitation, Cyprianus produced false witnesses not only against Albinus, but also against his defender, Boethius. But the king was laying a trap for the Romans and looking for a way to kill them; he believed false witnesses more than senators. Then Albinus and Boethius were put into custody in the baptistry of the church. The king, however, summoned Eusebius, the urban prefect, to Ticinum and delivered a sentence against Boethius without hearing him.[11]

According to this account, the accusation that led to Boethius' condemnation was not originally against him but rather against another high-ranking member of the senate, Albinus, a *patricius* who had been the first consul of the Western Roman Empire appointed by Theoderic thirty years earlier (in 493). This Albinus was accused by Cyprianus, one of the king's referendaries, of composing a letter addressed to Emperor Justin, the content of which was deemed to be treasonous. Boethius defended Albinus against this accusation before Theoderic and thereupon was also accused of treason. The king, however, believed false witnesses and refused to hear Boethius' defense because he was only looking for an opportunity to harm the Romans.[12]

In this case, we exceptionally are able to hear from the accused himself because while Boethius was awaiting execution in prison, he composed a text titled *The Consolation of Philosophy* (*De consolatione philosophiae*), in which he discussed fundamental questions of human existence while also defending himself against the allegations against him. In its essentials, this self-portrayal by the accused is in complete agreement with the version of events in the *Anonymus Valesianus*. Boethius likewise draws attention to Cyprianus, the accuser of the two senators. The philosopher also, however, mentions the names of the people who testified against him—Basilius, Gaudentius, and Opilio (Cyprianus' brother)—and a series of courtiers of Theoderic hostile to him. Above all, though, over the course of his defense Boethius provides additional information about the charges brought against him. He mentions three. First, Boethius allegedly attempted to prevent the surrender of texts with which the senate could have been accused of violating the king's majesty (*maiestas*). Second, he allegedly expressed the hope in a letter that "Roman liberty" (*Romana libertas*) would be restored, thereby committing high treason (*perduellio*). And third, he committed sacrilege by resorting to magic to increase his rank (*dignitas*). Boethius indignantly disputes all three charges and bitterly laments that his senatorial peers condemned him on account of such baseless allegations. His death sentence was thus not pronounced by Theoderic but rather by senators. It is only uncertain whether the court that condemned Boethius consisted of five senators under the presidency of the urban prefect of Rome—the so-called five-man court (*iudicium qinquevirale*)—or rather of the senate as a body.[13]

Modern scholars normally have believed Boethius' protestations of innocence, particularly since they are confirmed by the *Anonymus Valesianus*. Members of the senate were by no means exempt from accusations of practicing magic in this period—a senator named Basilius had been burned alive in the middle of Rome for this reason in the year 511—but that Boethius of all people, who had long steered clear of the court, should have attempted to win rank and influence in this way seems implausible and fabricated. Boethius, moreover, firmly denies the accusation that he had made treasonous statements about Theoderic and does so indeed at a point in time when he no longer had any hope of reprieve. Otherwise, he would not have branded the king a tyrant in his *Consolation*. His condemnation thus probably was unjust, and Boethius had good reason to rail against his fate.[14]

There is less scholarly consensus as to how the trial got under way and what part the king played in it. The *Anonymus Valesianus* suggests that Cyprianus brought charges against Albinus out of greed; Boethius himself describes his opponents as corrupt and unscrupulous. We can neither confirm nor refute accusations of this kind with the resources at our disposal. Experience teaches us that courtiers strive for power and wealth, but that does not permit us to conclude that they really would use any means necessary. Historical analysis shows us, instead, that a social distinction separated the two men accused and their adversaries: whereas Albinus and Boethius descended from established families in Rome who had belonged to the senate for generations, Cyprianus and Opilio had risen through the ranks in Theoderic's service; both of them had even learned Gothic, which was extremely rare among senators. Gaudentius also definitely did not belong to the old Roman aristocracy. Boethius also had enemies among influential Goths at Theoderic's court; the high chamberlain, Triwa, in particular frequently clashed with the philosopher. Against this background, we can better understand why the accusation of high treason, which had originally been brought only against Albinus, was broadened to include Boethius when he stood up in his peer's defense. There were powerful men in the king's inner circle who had no reason to intercede for someone like Boethius and may have even welcomed his fall. But this explanation is obviously insufficient because the decision to hold a trial was taken by the king. What compelled Theoderic to believe the witnesses and evidence produced by Cyprianus?

For the *Anonymus Valesianus*, the matter was simple: Theoderic was looking for and found an opportunity to harm the Romans because he had been possessed by the devil. If we leave Satan out of the picture, though, the argument must proceed on the basis of evidence: it is beyond doubt that both Albinus and Boethius were accused of high treason. Boethius' father-in-law was also charged with this crime. In Albinus' case, the allegation was proven by a letter that he had written to Emperor Justin; its authenticity was not disputed but rather its interpretation. An incriminating letter was also produced against Boethius; the content of this letter was manifestly treasonous, but the defendant insisted it was a forgery. Theoderic, however, accepted the allegations without giving Boethius the chance to respond, despite the fact that he had little respect for the men who testified against Boethius. It is thus hard to escape the conclusion that Theoderic mistrusted the accused senator. Why did the thought that senators were corresponding with the emperor unsettle the king? Officially, perfect harmony reigned between Theoderic and Justin. We can find a clue, however, in the report that in the letter attributed to Boethius, the philosopher supposedly hoped for the restoration of Roman liberty. Since Theoderic claimed to safeguard precisely this liberty for the Romans, this expression could be—indeed had to be—seen as an attack on his rule. Theoderic's concern would be especially plausible if the letters touched on a subject where he was especially vulnerable: the question of who should eventually succeed the king. The death of the presumptive heir, Eutharic, had dashed Theoderic's plans and made the future uncertain. Theoderic's life's work was threatened with failure. It would be understandable if the aged king was indignant when he was confronted with letters that seemed to show that high-ranking senators, whom he had especially decorated, were corresponding with the emperor about the succession behind his back.

The fact that Theoderic transferred the trial of Boethius to a senatorial tribunal shows that he was very much aware of how sensitive the affair was. Treason trials against former consuls of the rank of *patricius* jeopardized the compromise on which the cooperation between the Gothic king and the Roman aristocracy had been based. Albinus and Boethius may indeed have had enemies outside Theoderic's court among their peers in Rome. The Roman aristocracy itself was not a homogeneous group but was split into various camps. Struggle with and against one's peers was part of the senatorial way of life. But when the privileges of the order itself were threatened, senators closed ranks; they were extremely sensitive to death sentences and confiscation. Theoderic believed he could shift responsibility for the executions by not presiding as judge himself. Hence he made sure that the verdict was reached without his involvement. Whether the court that found Boethius guilty consisted of five senators or the entire body is a secondary question. This maneuver fell flat, though, because it was obvious to contemporaries that the final verdict could not defy the king's will. Some senators may have hoped that the king would pardon Boethius. This hope was not entirely baseless. By pardoning Boethius, Theoderic would have been able to demonstrate the virtue of clemency expected of a ruler after he had sent a clear signal against any sort of conspiracy. Theoderic made no use of this opportunity, not even by granting the children of the philosopher their father's property. For this reason, he himself had to bear responsibility for Boethius' death: after he let the death sentence be carried out, there could no longer be any doubt that it was what he wanted. The fact that Theoderic also had Boethius' father-in-law, Symmachus, executed a year later can only have reinforced this impression.

Our sources are silent about how the trial and execution of Albinus, Boethius, and Symmachus affected the relationship between the king and the senate. Superficially, little seems to have changed. But the senators' confidence in the Gothic king had been sorely tested. The executions went into the collective memory of the senatorial order as Theoderic's original sin. That is how it appeared to the Byzantine historian and senator Procopius, and that is also how it appeared later to Pope Gregory the Great, who came from an old senatorial family and had been urban prefect of Rome before his ordination as priest. There is also some indication that Theoderic himself viewed the execution of Boethius and Symmachus in hindsight as a political blunder. It was said, at any rate, that the king regretted it. After his death, Amalasuintha reduced the punishment that Theoderic had imposed on Boethius' descendants by causing his confiscated property to be restored to his children.[15]

3. TESTS OF STRENGTH: THEODERIC AND POPES JOHN I AND FELIX IV

After senators, Catholic bishops numbered among the pillars of Theoderic's rule over Italy. They accepted the king as a secular authority; they even called on him to arbitrate internal church disputes. Vice versa, Theoderic recognized the Catholic Church of Italy with all its privileges and treated its representatives with respect. This cooperative relationship had begun during the pontificate of Gelasius and continued under Hormisdas. Theoderic had monitored but not impeded Hormisdas' efforts to heal the schism between Rome and Constantinople. Reconciliation did not become feasible until Anastasius died on July 10, 518, and his successor, Justin, immediately set out on a completely different course in his religious policy. The patriarch of Constantinople, John II, submitted to all the conditions of the Roman see at the emperor's behest on March 28, 519, and condemned Acacius and all others who had not explicitly renounced him. Theoderic openly hailed the restoration of church unity between Rome and Constantinople. A donation by the king in St. Peter's symbolized the good relations that prevailed between the "Arian" king and the spiritual head of the Catholic majority of his subjects. When Hormisdas died on August 6, 523, there was no sign that anything would soon change. His successor was consecrated just a week later; he was called John, the first pope to bear this name. As for his origins, the *Liber pontificalis* (55, 1) merely reports that he came from Tuscany and that his father's name was Constantius. There is reason to suspect, however, that he is identical with the deacon John attested in the service of the Roman church since the year 512, who was regarded as a theological authority. He composed a long letter to explain the Catholic rite of baptism to the *vir illustris* Senarius and regularly corresponded with Boethius concerning Christological questions. If this identification is correct, Pope John was a theologically astute man who had good connections to the senatorial elite.[16]

Only a single event is transmitted from the thirty-two-month pontificate of John I: an embassy to Constantinople that he undertook at Theoderic's behest in fall 525 or early 526. This mission was already notable because never before had the bishop of Rome left his city to travel to the imperial court on the Bosporus. Still more unusual was the purpose for which the pope was traveling: the successor of St. Peter intended to intercede before Emperor Justin for the rescission of measures that had been enacted against "Arian" heretics in the

Eastern Roman Empire. This mission stood in complete contradiction to the self-conception of the bishop of Rome, who considered the fight against heresy his highest priority. Even more remarkable is the treatment John received when he returned to Italy in May 526 and reported to the king in Ravenna. The *Anonymus Valesianus* (93) reports that Theoderic "treacherously" (*cum dolo*) received John and proclaimed that the pope had fallen into disfavor (*in offensa sua*); a few days later, the pope died. The *Liber pontificalis* (55, 6) even reports that John had been imprisoned by Theoderic and died as a martyr in captivity.

These events raise many questions. What exactly was the purpose of Theoderic's embassy to Emperor Justin? Why did Theoderic force the pope to intercede for a cause that contradicted his self-conception as guardian of the true faith and damaged his reputation, and why did John himself agree to it? And finally: why was Theoderic dissatisfied with his papal ambassador? Every attempt to interpret these events begins with the account of the *Anonymus Valesianus*:

> Returning to Ravenna, the king acted not like a friend of God but like an enemy of his law, forgetful of all the benefits and grace that God had given him, and instead trusting in his arms and believing that Emperor Justin was afraid of him, he sent for and summoned John, the overseer of the Apostolic See, to Ravenna, and said to him: "Go to Constantinople to Emperor Justin and tell him, among other things, to restore those who have been reconciled in the Catholic faith." Pope John responded to him as follows: "What you intend to do, king, do swiftly; behold, I stand before you in your sight. I will not promise you that I will do this, nor will I say that to him. For in other matters, with the help of God, I will be able to obtain from him what you have commanded."[17]

The *Anonymus Valesianus* depicts Theoderic as the enemy of God who used the pope to lead subjects of the emperor, who had already been won for the true faith, back into the perdition of heresy. This account is carefully stylized: the use of direct speech lends it vividness and gives the impression that the author had firsthand information. By putting the words that Jesus says to Judas in the Gospel of John (13:27) in the pope's mouth, the *Anonymus* underscores the message that Theoderic had fallen from God and was persecuting orthodox Catholics. The factual core of this tendentious episode appears to be that Theoderic ordered the pope, "among other things," to ask the emperor to nullify forced conversions from the "Arian" to the Catholic faith. The pope steadfastly refused to carry out this request but declared he was willing to do the rest.

The earliest version of the *Liber pontificalis* may provide an answer as to what that may have been. This passage reports that Theoderic had demanded the restoration of churches that had been taken from "Arian" heretics and that the emperor actually granted the pope's request. If we take both reports together, we come to the conclusion that John was not willing to intercede for the return of people who had already converted back to their old faith, but he was prepared to demand the restoration of churches to "Arian" communities.[18]

This involvement was downright alarming from a Catholic perspective, which is why we can scarcely imagine that the pope would have put himself at Theoderic's disposal unless he was under massive pressure. As a matter of fact, several sources state that Theoderic had threatened John with executions. The composition of the embassy also reinforces the impression that the mission was a matter of great urgency to Theoderic. In addition to the pope, four more bishops were involved, including Ecclesius, the Catholic bishop of Ravenna. But by no means did the embassy consist exclusively of clergymen: it also included four high-ranking senators. Three of them were former consuls of the rank of *patricius*: Theodorus (cos. 505), Inportunus (cos. 509), and Agapitus (cos. 517); the fourth was also called Agapitus and is difficult to differentiate from his namesake. Theodorus and Inportunus belonged to the family of the Decii; they were brothers of the same Albinus who had been accused of high treason two years earlier.[19]

Since Theoderic sent prestigious and influential members of the senate to Constantinople in addition to the pope and the bishop of his primary residence, Ravenna, it is difficult to dismiss speculation as to whether the treatment of Theoderic's coreligionists in the emperor's territory was really the only point that the envoys were supposed to negotiate with Justin. It is conceivable that Theoderic also tried to obtain the emperor's approval for his handling of the succession, as it was announced after his death, but this remains speculation in light of the silence of our sources. Even if the instructions given to the embassy to Emperor Justin were presumably more extensive than what our sources reveal, we still must recognize that Theoderic flouted the rules of political prudence by having it intercede on behalf of the "Arians" in the emperor's territory because Theoderic thereby humiliated the pope and jeopardized the compromise on which his good relations with the Catholic episcopacy of his kingdom had hitherto been based. Since Roman senators viewed the bishop of Rome as their spiritual shepherd, it was foreseeable that there would be political repercussions. Theoderic, moreover, antagonized the Byzantine emperor, who viewed and presented himself as the protector of the true faith, by meddling in the latter's affairs. This conduct was certainly unwise, especially if Theoderic was also working to secure the emperor's recognition of his grandson Athalaric as heir to the throne.

It is difficult to explain the embassy in which John took part as a political calculation. Was it a demonstration of power intended for the senators and bishops of Italy? If so, then the king deliberately chose the pope and leading senators to force them to prove their loyalty. Or did the king see himself as the patron of all Homoeans, no matter where they lived? The fact that the emperor had decreed compulsory measures against those who shared the king's religion, while, vice versa, the Catholics were allowed to practice their own faith in Theoderic's kingdom unimpeded, may have offended Theoderic's sense of justice. But was he ready to provoke the pope, the senate, and the emperor for that reason? About a decade earlier, the Catholic bishop Avitus of Vienne had voiced his expectation that Theoderic would not sit idly by if the Homoeans in the kingdom of the Burgundians were oppressed. Now, however, much more was at stake. If Theoderic really acted for reasons of conscience in 526, then he was taking a great political risk.[20]

Similar problems emerge if we try to understand why Theoderic received the pope with displeasure on the latter's return. John had put on a happy face in this unpleasant game, asking Emperor Justin to return churches that had previously belonged to "Arian" communities, as Theoderic had requested. The emperor granted his request and let the "Arians" in his territory have their churches back. Thus Theoderic's coreligionists in the Byzantine Empire could again practice their religion freely until their churches were again, this time permanently, confiscated in the year 538, after the reconquest of North Africa from the Vandals.[21] Was this success not reason enough to be satisfied with John and the other ambassadors? Since this was evidently not the case, Theoderic's annoyance must be explained some other way. The reason seems to lie in the way that John had conducted himself during his stay in Constantinople. From our sources, we learn that the pope received a magnificent welcome in the imperial city on the Bosporus. The successor of St. Peter was met twelve miles outside the city; the emperor himself paid him respect with self-abasing gestures—a kiss and bow? On Easter, John was allowed not only to take the seat of honor on the emperor's right in the Hagia Sophia (while the patriarch of Constantinople had to content himself with the left), but even to celebrate the resurrection of the crucified Son of God with the Sacrifice of the Mass—and indeed according to the Roman rite. During this service, the bishop of Rome received the prerogative of placing the emperor's crown on his head after the latter took it off to demonstrate his humility. This may not have been the "first papal coronation of the emperor," as some have argued, but it certainly was an impressive demonstration of harmony between emperor and pope, the two powers that claimed a universal position of leadership that was not limited to a specific territory.[22]

We can well imagine that Theoderic interpreted this situation as a threat and viewed John's behavior as disloyal. We certainly may presume that word of it reached the king. Of course, even if Theoderic had good reason to assume that the pope, as Theoderic's subject, had crossed a line in Constantinople, we again must ask whether the king sanctioned this behavior in a way that served to stabilize his power or ultimately effected the very opposite.

Our assessment of this question is complicated by the fact that we do not exactly know how the king expressed his displeasure. According to the *Liber pontificalis*, Theoderic imprisoned not only John, but also all members of the delegation, including the three senators who had returned, allegedly intending to execute all of them. The incarceration of the envoys on their return, as well as the claim that Theoderic was plotting to kill them, may be no more than a malicious invention, although none of the three senators is ever mentioned again. The *Anonymus Valesianus* merely states that the king had withdrawn his favor from the pope in Ravenna. In doing so, Theoderic may have basically declared John an outlaw, but he did not treat him like a prisoner. Instead, the declaration that the pope was no longer under the king's protection invited John's opponents to pursue their goals with violence, if necessary.[23]

We finally set foot on solid ground again when we turn to the aftermath of the pope's death. His body was immediately brought to Rome and buried in St. Peter's only a week later on May 27, 526. The *Anonymus Valesianus* gives the following account of the events that took place during his funeral procession: "Therefore, as the populace went before his corpse, suddenly someone in the crowd was taken by a demon and fell down. When the people carrying the bier on which he was laid reached this man, he suddenly stood up healthy and marched in the procession. When the people and senate saw this, they began to take relics from his [John's] clothing. Thus the body was brought outside the city to the great jubilation of the people."[24] This account reveals that "the people and senate" of Rome transformed John's funeral into a demonstration of solidarity with their dead bishop. A modest miracle that took place during the funeral procession fed the belief that John had been no ordinary bishop. A hunt for objects that had been endowed with miraculous power through contact with his body allegedly started during the funeral. When Theoderic died of an illness three months after John, the chain of evidence seemed complete: God had sent the persecutor of Christians his due punishment. In this way, John, who had been humiliated by the king, was transformed shortly after his death into a martyr who had perished for his faith. The martyrdom of John entered into the collective memory of the church of Rome and spread from there. His funerary inscription calls him a bishop of God who had perished as a sacrificial lamb of Christ. In a biography of John that was composed close to the Curia and integrated into the *Liber pontificalis*, John figures as a martyr who is persecuted for his belief and ultimately killed by the heretic Theoderic. The account of the *Anonymus Valesianus*, written after the fall of Gothic rule in Italy, is not much different. Toward the end of the sixth century, Pope Gregory the Great told of how Pope John and the *patricius* Symmachus had punished Theoderic by stripping him of his belt and shoes and binding his hands before throwing him into the crater of the volcano on the island of Lipari, which was thought to be the entrance to Hell. In Gaul around the same time, Gregory of Tours reported that Theoderic had imprisoned John because he had opposed the bloody persecution of Christians in Italy; the pope was tortured in prison and died of his injuries.[25]

An unusually long vacancy followed the death of John; the throne of St. Peter remained unoccupied for almost two months. There must have been disputes over the election of the next occupant of the Roman see during this time. John's successor, consecrated on July 12, 526, was named Felix and came from Samnium, a territory in the southern Apennines; he had been deacon of the Roman church and in 519 had traveled to Constantinople at the behest of Pope Hormisdas. Felix was the first and only pope who was consecrated on Theoderic's explicit orders. From a letter to the senate that Cassiodorus composed shortly after Theoderic's death for his successor Athalaric, it emerges that with Theoderic's help, Felix had defeated another candidate who was backed by at least some members of the senate. In this letter, Athalaric declares that he is glad that the senate respected Theoderic's judgment; even though Theoderic belonged to a different confession (*religio*), he had chosen a pontifex to whom no one could object. With Felix, the senate had received a man who had been decorously educated by grace of God and passed the king's test with commendation. Hence the faithful had lost nothing, even though "a person had been removed" (*summota persona*), because they still possessed the priestly office they had desired.[26]

It is not known who had to be "removed" so that Felix could win general recognition, nor can we now reconstruct how it came about that Theoderic intervened. After his clash with John, the king may have insisted that the potential candidates for his successor be presented to him before the election. It is also conceivable, though, that a double election had happened, as had been the case in 498; in this instance, Theoderic's intervention might even have been requested by the disputing parties or by the senate. The only thing that is certain is that Theoderic's decision in favor of Felix met with resistance in the senate and that Felix was considered Theoderic's man by the clergy. Theoderic's relationship with the senate became strained yet again, even if the king was potentially asked to intervene. As the aforementioned letter to the senate shows, not every senator had come to terms with Felix as pontifex at the time of Theoderic's death.

4. SPLENDID ISOLATION? THEODERIC AND HIS ALLIES

Theoderic had won Provence and the Iberian Peninsula for himself in his wars against Clovis and Gundobad, thereby keeping the Frankish and Burgundian kings far from the Mediterranean; he controlled the ports and collected taxes on imported goods. The kingdom of the Burgundians still functioned as a buffer zone between the Frankish kingdoms and Theoderic's own. After Gundobad murdered his brother Godegisel in 501, he made his son Sigismund co-regent, although he retained a superior position as long as he lived. Sigismund, like his father, originally adhered to the Homoean creed, but he converted to Catholicism at some point prior to the war against Alaric II, as Avitus reported to Pope Symmachus in a jubilant letter. Thereafter, a Catholic king in Geneva ruled the kingdom of the Burgundians alongside the Homoean king in Vienne. Sigismund also publicized his conversion with symbolic gestures outside his territory: he was the first in a long line of Germanic kings to travel to Rome as a pilgrim. There, Sigismund paid his respects to Pope Symmachus, who gave him precious relics in turn. After returning to Geneva, Sigismund sponsored the construction of a church dedicated to the apostle Peter. He intended to be buried in it and requested additional relics for it from Rome. Gundobad did not offer his son any resistance; he himself corresponded with Avitus about controversial questions of faith and hosted discussions between representatives of both confessions at his court. He remained true to the Homoean creed, however, and insisted that his son celebrate Easter with him jointly.[27]

Then Gundobad died in 516. Sigismund was his sole successor, as planned, while his brother Godomar was excluded from power. Sigismund withdrew the kingdom's support for the Homoean church. The Catholic bishops of his kingdom soon met to discuss the new situation at Epao, which should probably be identified with Saint-Romain-d'Albon, south of Vienne. Avitus of Vienne and Viventiolus of Lyon had convened this synod and presided over it jointly. Since they could not anticipate that the king would ban the Homoean church and drive it underground, the bishops prepared themselves for a long transitional phase; they avoided any indication of triumphalism and instead behaved prag-matically and with moderation. Clergymen who accepted an invitation to a banquet from a "heretical" clergyman would be excommunicated for a year, if they were older; younger clergymen would receive a beating. Anyone who had accepted the Homoean creed and thus broken with the true faith could not be welcomed back into the bosom of the church until he had performed a two-year penance. That was significantly less harsh than the typical rules at this time, which called for seven, ten, or twelve years of penance for this crime. The churches of the "heretics" would remain untouched with the exception of those that had been taken from Catholics by force. These buildings were impure, the bishops declared; but that did not mean that political motives did not also play a part. Avitus discloses in no uncertain terms in a letter to Bishop Victor of Grenoble that it was impossible to know whether Sigismund's son and heir would practice the same confession as his father. On the one hand, Avitus thus feared that Sigeric, Sigismund's son from his marriage with Ostrogotho, Theoderic's daughter, might rescind his father's decision. On the other, it was important to recall that a "neighboring king, who lived under a different law," might take revenge on the Catholics in his kingdom if he saw his coreligionists in the kingdom of the Burgundians treated in a way that he disapproved of. This neighboring king was none other than Theoderic. Avitus thus viewed Theoderic as a kind of patron of the Homoeans; the bishop thought he was capable of inflicting reprisals on the Catholics of Italy if the Homoeans in the kingdom of the Burgundians were oppressed. Avitus' advice thus was not to imitate the bad example of the heretics, who had no compunction about robbing the Catholics of their churches; instead, it was best to avoid their places of worship "like the workhouses of slaves."[28]

Religious policy was not the only reason, however, why Theoderic might have been dissatisfied with his Burgundian son-in-law. Sigismund had received the title of *patricius* from the Byzantine emperor even before 515. After his father's death, he was able to dictate foreign policy in his kingdom entirely by himself. He immediately dispatched an embassy to Constantinople to inform the emperor. In a letter that Avitus composed for Sigismund, the king stressed his devotion (*devotio*) to Anastasius and noted the honorary military titles (*militiae tituli*) that he and his ancestors had received from the emperor; he considered himself the emperor's soldier (*miles*) while he ruled his people; he was governing distant regions for the emperor, who could not be present personally. We should not take this claim at face value: the king knew, after all, that the emperor had no business issuing commands in the kingdom of the Burgundians. The letter shows, however, that Sigismund was aspiring to cooperate closely with the Byzantine Empire. The emperor appreciated this attitude because he depended on his allies in the West, and he assured the king of his favor. He did not, however, make Sigismund his *magister militum*, as scholars continue to claim even today; this office would not have conferred any additional powers or resources on the king and ranked below that of *patricius*.[29]

Theoderic may have viewed the alliance between Sigismund and Anastasius as a latent threat. We do not know whether or how he became aware of the content of Sigismund's letter, but it is a fact that the embassy that was supposed to bring it to Constantinople was detained in Italy and returned to Sigismund's court without accomplishing anything. The envoys had presumably stopped over at Ravenna, intending to travel by sea from there. When an imperial embassy visited Sigismund soon afterward to congratulate him on the beginning of his sole rule, the king seized the occasion to complain to Anastasius about Theoderic: Theoderic bore sole responsibility for the fact that the emperor had not already received a letter from Sigismund because he had blocked the way of Sigismund's envoys. This conduct, however, Avitus proceeded to explain on behalf of the Burgundian king, went to show how loyal Theoderic really was toward Anastasius. Sigismund had in fact dispatched the ambassadors, he wrote,

> . . . after taking confidence from the fact that the ruler of Italy was publicly applauding peace with you [*pax vestra*] and spreading a rumor to the effect that he had regained the favor of the East [*Oriens*]. Therefore, the route we took to dispatch our reports was cut off and prohibited. Certainly, he himself will see what the course of the truth shall hold for him before [Your] August Happiness. It is a paltry token of friendship to refuse to allow the man whom you claim you cultivate to be honored by others; for all of us who look up to you with due reverence should want everyone to do so. For he shows too little devotion of his own who curtails the freedom of movement and strives to make others *un*devoted [*indevoti*].[30]

Avitus insinuates with biting irony that in contrast to Sigismund, Theoderic was merely feigning loyalty to the emperor. Such insinuations were attentively registered at the imperial court. But the emperor also knew that Theoderic did not need to grovel before him like Sigismund, and he had no intention of disputing Theoderic's right to rule Italy. At approximately the same time, Anastasius himself sent a letter with Theoderic's blessing to the senate of Rome to ask for its support in ending the schism between the bishops of Rome and Constantinople; in this letter, he explicitly and openly recognized Theoderic's rule over Italy, not only by calling Theoderic "most glorious king" (*gloriosissimus rex*) and "exalted king" (*excelsus rex*), but also by stating that Theoderic had received the power and responsibility (*potestas vel sollicitudo*) of ruling the senate. Anastasius also spoke of the "parts of the two republics" (*utriusque rei publicae membra*), thus adopting the official language that Theoderic's chancellery used to describe its relationship with the Eastern Roman Empire. Anastasius' successor, Justin, accepted Eutharic as Theoderic's successor, as we have seen.[31]

Relations between Theoderic and his son-in-law Sigismund were already tense when the latter's wife, Ostrogotho, died. Sigismund married one of his deceased wife's servants soon afterward. A few years later, Sigismund had Sigeric, his son from his marriage with Ostrogotho, killed. Sigeric's stepmother allegedly drove her husband to this misdeed by telling him his stepson wanted to rule as king in his place. The story obviously plays on the motif of the wicked stepmother; perhaps it was completely invented. Or perhaps not: conflicts between father and son in ruling families not uncommonly took on murderous dimensions. The only thing certain is that Sigismund publicly regretted his action: the king did penance in the monastery of Saint-Maurice d'Agaune, which he had founded not long beforehand (515). This penance was later associated with the introduction of continual singing of the psalms (*laus perennis*) in this monastery.[32]

Theoderic received the murder of his grandson as a provocation. The king may have abandoned hope of his son-in-law's political loyalty long before; now, though, his honor as a warrior was at stake. Attacks on close relations and wards called for retaliation; anyone who failed to avenge such bloody deeds exposed himself to accusations of cowardice and dishonor. Theoderic could not accept that and made ready for war. He was beaten to the punch, however, by the Frankish king Chlodomer, whose kingdom bordered directly on that of the Burgundians. Gregory of Tours, our only source, imputed this war to blood vengeance as well: Clotilde, Clovis' widow, allegedly asked her sons to avenge Gundobad's murder of her parents. That, of course, is not very convincing: the murder in question had happened twenty years before. It is more plausible that Chlodomer gathered his army because he had learned of Theoderic's impending attack, whether the Frankish king acted on his own initiative or had arranged it with Theoderic in advance. Be that as it may, Chlodomer's warriors defeated the Burgundian army. Sigismund fled to the monastery of Saint-Maurice in Agaune; there, he donned a monk's habit, hoping to save his life and that of his family, but to no avail: he was found out by some of his former subjects, turned over to the Franks, and brought to Chlodomer's residence in Orléans. The Frankish king had Sigismund, his wife, and his children thrown in a well shortly thereafter.[33]

After the Franks returned home with numerous captives, the vanquished Burgundians regathered their strength. They now elevated Sigismund's brother Godomar to king. It was at this point, at the latest, that Theoderic entered into a military alliance with Chlodomer. According to Procopius, the two kings agreed that they would each send an army to fight the Burgundians. If, however, one of them defeated the Burgundians without the other's help, then the party that did not participate in the battle would pay the other a sum of money; the conquered territory would be divided equally. Theoderic thus instructed his generals to await the outcome of the battle and seized half of Burgundy after the Franks' victory. Gregory of Tours tells a different story. The Frankish bishop and historian relates that Chlodomer's brother Theuderic joined the second campaign against the kingdom of the Burgundians; the two armies joined forces at Vézéronce near Vienne, defeated Godomar's warriors, and subsequently seized all Burgundy. Both authors agree that that was a Frankish victory. Other sources, however, reveal that Procopius and Gregory were perpetuating a Frankish fabrication. In reality, Chlodomer fell in battle. Godomar stood his ground; the Frankish army returned home in defeat. Procopius' account of Theoderic's behavior, however, is accurate. As Cassiodorus emphasized a few years later, Tuluin secured a "bloodless victory" over the Burgundians in this war on Theoderic's behalf. The king was able to expand his territory from the Durance to the Isère; ten urban communities (*civitates*), including Vaison, Orange, and Avignon, thereby became part of the Gallic prefecture.[34]

Theoderic declared war on Sigismund because he both wanted and had to avenge his grandson's death. He continued the war, however, even after he had achieved this goal. The purpose of his alliance with Chlodomer was to expand his territory. Theoderic also achieved this goal, indeed without even having to send his warriors into battle. Nonetheless, it is worth asking whether he was or even could be completely satisfied with the outcome of the conflict. By annexing part of Burgundy, he weakened a power whose strength was desirable if he wanted it to stand up to the Merovingians; at the same time, Theoderic threw away any credibility he might have had as an enemy of the Merovingians. An anti-Frankish alliance with the kingdom of the Burgundians was out of the question now, although Godomer had to anticipate further Frankish attacks and therefore set out to increase his kingdom's military potential. The Merovingians, meanwhile, could not be trusted. They may have laid low while Theoderic still lived, but in 532 Chlothar and Childebert launched a new war that ended a few years later with Godomar's expulsion and the collapse of his kingdom.[35]

Developments in the kingdom of the Vandals also gave Theoderic growing cause for concern in these years. After Thrasamund's attempt to gain influence in Spain with Gesalec's support had failed, he gave up an independent foreign policy and played the part of the dependent ally that Theoderic had intended for him. Thrasamund had his hands full fighting Mauri tribes that challenged

him for control of the border regions of his kingdom. He continued his predecessors' repressive religious policy; Catholics waited in vain for an amnesty for
their banished bishops, for the restoration of their confiscated property and
voided privileges, and for permission to hold councils again. It thus appeared as
if Theoderic had no need to fear any changes in North Africa. But this seeming
stability was a mirage. The kingdom of the Vandals observed a fixed order of
succession; according to a decree of Gaiseric, power passed to the oldest male
relative of the king. Theoderic thus had to presume that eventually Hilderic,
the son of King Huneric and the emperor's daughter Eudocia, would succeed
Thrasamund. Hilderic, however, was known to oppose his uncle's political policy; he set no store by the separation of Romans and Vandals but rather advocated assimilation; Hilderic rejected repression as an instrument of religious
policy and wanted to free himself of Theoderic's influence through an alliance
with the Byzantine emperor. For this reason, Hilderic was forced to swear an
oath that he would not return to the Catholics either their churches or privileges once he was king. Of course, Hilderic found a way out of this oath when
Thrasamund at last died in the summer of 523. The banished bishops returned;
the Catholic churches that had been closed were reopened. Hilderic sent rich
gifts to Constantinople and emphasized his friendship and devotion. Theoderic's
sister Amalafrida fled to the Mauri after her husband's death. She had known
Hilderic, who was already an old man, for many years and had every reason to
fear for her place at court and probably also for her life. If she had still controlled an armed retinue of several thousand men, as she did on her arrival in
the year 500, she would have been able to stand up to the new king. But her
retinue by now had either returned to Italy or broken up; she had only a few
loyal companions left at her side. Hence she sought refuge in the Mauri kingdom of Capsa, presumably in hope of overthrowing Hilderic with Mauri help.
This plan went awry: a battle was fought, Amalafrida was captured, and her
Gothic retinue was killed. Thereafter the queen was a captive and evidently
died in the course of the year 526.[36]

Amalafrida's demise signaled the end of the alliance between Theoderic
and the kingdom of the Vandals; it made it painfully clear that the king had lost
his last significant ally. The fall and death of his sister, moreover, did massive
damage to Theoderic's honor. Already contemporaries must have asked themselves, "Why did Theoderic not come to his sister's aid in her hour of need?"
According to Procopius, Theoderic did not take revenge because he felt unable
to sail to Africa with a strong fleet. Theoderic indeed lacked the requisite number of seaworthy ships, even counting the small number of ships he maintained
on the Po.[37]

But the lack of a fleet was hardly the only reason why Theoderic could not bring himself to commit to military intervention. As we have seen, news of Amalafrida's flight may have reached Theoderic at approximately the same time that he was mobilizing his army for the campaign against Sigismund. The old king did not want to wage war on two fronts. Even after these events, Theoderic was still the most powerful ruler in the western Mediterranean, but he was largely isolated in international politics, even though Hilderic probably did not formally renege on the treaty that Thrasamund had struck with Theoderic twenty years earlier. Clovis' sons were out for booty and conquest; the kings of the Burgundians and Thuringians were too weak to stand up to them. Theoderic's relationship with the Byzantine emperor seemed secure since Justin had accepted Eutharic as Theoderic's successor, but then Eutharic died and the question of what would happen after Theoderic's own death was thrown wide open again. It was probably this ominous situation that prompted the king in 525 to mobilize on an unprecedented scale. Theoderic gave the order to construct and man a large fleet, and the praetorian prefect Abundantius was instructed to carry it out. The letter that was sent to him on this occasion survives. There we read, "Since Our mind has often been struck by the concern that Italy has no ships, where so great a supply of timber abounds that it exports it to other provinces that request it, God has inspired Us to decree that We shall undertake to build one thousand *dromones* to ship public grain and, if necessary, sail against enemy ships. And We believe that the execution of this great undertaking that We desire shall be performed under the responsibility of Your Greatness."[38] Theoderic's fleet was to consist of no fewer than one thousand units that are called *dromones*. This type of ship was new at the time. *Dromones* had a flat keel, a single bank of oars, a mast, and a crew of twenty to thirty men, who were protected from enemy fire by a covering. *Dromones* were thus much smaller than the warships with which the fleets of Hellenistic kings and the Roman Republic had once fought naval battles. *Dromones* sailed up rivers and along the seacoast. The logistical effort to construct and man one thousand *dromones* was nonetheless massive. Some twenty to thirty thousand men were needed to man them; that corresponded roughly to the size of the Gothic army. Timber for the ships had to be cut and transported to the site where they could be built. Abundantius received precise instructions regarding that as well:

> Therefore, direct craftsmen to seek timber suitable for the work throughout
> all Italy, and wherever you find cypresses or pines near the shore, see to it
> that the owners receive appropriate compensation. For only the value of
> these trees shall be assessed; the rest do not require an assessment on account

Fig. 21. *Dromones* in the *Vergilius Romanus*, fol. 77 (recto). From
D. H. Wright, *Der Vergilius Romanus und die Entstehung der
mittelalterlichen Buchmalerei* (Stuttgart, 2000), 25.

of their low value. But so that Our decree is not left to languish half-finished,
We already order you now, by this decree, to secure an appropriate number
of sailors with the help of God. And if a person deemed necessary to Us is
someone's slave, either rent him to serve on the fleet or, if [the owner] himself should prefer, let him accept the price [for the slave] and cede ownership to the public finances. If the person chosen enjoys his liberty, however,
let him know that he shall receive a donative of five *solidi* and appropriate
pay [*annona*].[39]

This naval initiative demanded steep investments. Financing it must have
strained the king's finances in the extreme. The timber was supposed to be
bought at appropriate prices. The rowers were supposed to be hired, rented, or
purchased for cash, and then they would receive wages on top of that. Recruiting

the crews was as laborious as it was expensive, particularly since the fleet was
not supposed to recruit fishermen because of their importance to the food supply. It is probably not a coincidence that at precisely this moment (525),
Theoderic decreed to raise the rate for the land tax (*tributum*) in Sicily. Since
the province had produced large surpluses of grain, he presumably hoped
that he could cover his heightened financial needs in this way. Although the
additional income was not expected until the following year (526)—and in
point of fact it never materialized—the ambitious naval initiative was realized
at least in part. At least, Theoderic paid glowing tribute to Abundantius sometime later:

> You have suddenly brought before Our eyes a forest of ships, waterborne
> houses, feet for an army that shall not fail under any labor but will bring men
> unscathed to their destinations, a trireme-like vehicle that shows a great
> number of oars while carefully hiding the faces of the rowers. We read that
> the Argonauts were the first to devise this [ship], which has proven to be both
> suitable for armed men and appropriate to trade. Thus We who wished to
> gaze on foreign fleets now send both terror and glory to other provinces. You
> have adorned the commonwealth [*res publica*], which has been restored by
> your efforts to outfit it. The Greek has nothing to chastise and the African
> nothing to mock. They enviously see blossom among us that by which they
> fulfilled their wishes at great expense.[40]

Abundantius thus really had delivered a considerable number of *dromones*. It
admittedly came nowhere near the target of one thousand. The forced purchase of such vast quantities of wood met with resistance; the number of available shipwrights also was insufficient. Therefore, wood was to be cut in the
royal forests and shipwrights sought on the royal domains. But crews and equipment, especially rigging, were in short supply. Abundantius was told to see to it
that the fleet could be presented ready for action at Classe on June 13, 526. That
presentation never took place; when the Gothic War began ten years later,
Theoderic's successors still did not have a fleet.[41]

What had prompted Theoderic to resort to such an expensive and laborious
measure? The letters to Abundantius reveal that the fleet was to serve a dual
function. One declared purpose was to transport public grain—that is, grain
collected as tax by the administration. Navigable rivers, especially the Po, but
also the Tiber and Arno, were to serve as transportation routes. For this reason,
an order was issued to clear the rivers of weirs that blocked the way of ships.
Theoderic wanted to move goods and people from one place to another by
water more easily and more quickly. That would increase both the flexibility of

the tax administration and the mobility of the army. The other declared purpose was to ward off enemy attacks. The royal chancellery unmistakably alludes to the potential threats: the Greek—which is to say the Byzantine emperor, as so often—and the African—meaning the Vandalic king Hilderic. Wherever Theoderic looked, he saw only threats.[42]

5. MOUNTING PROBLEMS AND A CRISIS OF CONFIDENCE: THEODERIC AT THE END OF HIS LIFE

Problems mounted in various areas in Theoderic's final years, exacerbating one another and proving impossible for the king to solve. Theoderic was largely isolated on the international political stage after the kingdom of the Vandals adopted a pro-Byzantine stance after Thrasamund's death. Even though Theoderic himself had benefited repeatedly from Frankish expansion, after 523 there no longer was any power in the western Mediterranean that he could depend on for support. The king now feared aggression from the Byzantine emperor as well; he wanted a navy so that he could ward off attacks by sea. Theoderic may still have regarded Hispania as a province of his kingdom and tried to impose his will there, but his regional administrator Theudis was unwilling to submit to the king's judgment by coming personally to Ravenna.

Inside the kingdom, the compromise with indigenous elites had not been renounced at Theoderic's death, but it had come under significant pressure. Undoubtedly, a wide majority of senators were still willing to cooperate with the Gothic king; there was no feasible alternative since the military might of Italy stood resolutely behind Theoderic. But trouble was brewing beneath the surface. The naval initiative was expensive and was supposed to be financed with tax hikes in Sicily. Senators who held land there cannot have been pleased. The treason trials against Albinus, Boethius, and Symmachus did serious damage to the reputation of the king, who had aspired to be regarded as the defender of Roman liberty. To senators, liberty meant the complete and completely safe enjoyment of their privileges. The humiliation of Pope John not only turned members of the Roman Curia against Theoderic, but also inflicted a crisis of conscience on some senators. The decision to appoint the deacon Felix as John's successor was also unlikely to win broad support in the senate, whatever Theoderic's motive may have been. After the double election of 498, Theoderic had been sought out as arbitrator to decide who was the legitimate successor of St. Peter. At the end of his reign, a rumor made the rounds that the king was planning to persecute Catholics: the "Arians" would seize all the Catholics'

churches. Had not the king already "toppled" the altar of the church of Santo
Stefano near his palace in Verona?[43]

These internal tensions were connected to Theoderic's failure to designate a
successor in his lifetime. The death of the presumptive heir created uncertainty
and awakened ambitions; conjecture and rumors about the future of the Gothic
kingdom in Italy fostered a climate of mistrust that placed a heavy strain on the
relationship between the king and his Roman subjects. Theoderic was no longer sure whether he could count on the unconditional support of the senators
and bishops of Italy. Vice versa, his conduct fed doubts as to whether he really
would always respect the privileges of the Catholic Church and the Roman
senate. We certainly must acknowledge that there was very little Theoderic
could do to mitigate the international political developments that beset him at
the end of his life. Domestically, he had more room to maneuver. But insofar
as the trust of a ruler's subjects, which must be constantly renewed, is indispensable to the stability of a monarchy, then we must conclude that Theoderic
himself was partly to blame for the problems that plagued him in his final years.

THE GOTHIC KINGDOM IN ITALY
AFTER THEODERIC

1. A HEAVY LEGACY: ATHALARIC, AMALASUINTHA, AND THEODAHAD (526–535)

Theoderic the Great died on August 30, 526, in the same place where his reign as king of Goths and Romans had begun thirty-three years before, in Ravenna. He was buried in the mausoleum that he had commissioned in a cemetery to the northeast of the city. The two-story monument is 15.41 meters high and made entirely of limestone; it has a massive, stout appearance. The lower level is decagonal; a frieze decorated with pincer-like ornaments—the *Zangenfries* in German—encircles the top of the outer wall of the narrower, upper level. The structure is surmounted by a dome consisting of a single stone measuring 10.36 meters in diameter and weighing roughly 230 tons. Twelve "handles" bearing the names of the twelve apostles rest on the outer rim. No sculptural decoration has survived and was perhaps never present.

Theoderic's mausoleum was situated outside the city walls and protected by a high metal screen. The choice of location is significant. The mausoleums of the Christian emperors had always been linked to a church. In Constantinople, the emperors were buried in close proximity to the Church of the Apostles; the mausoleum of the Theodosian dynasty abutted St. Peter's in Rome. Theoderic's mausoleum, in contrast, was a freestanding structure. The king wished to be close to the apostles but also sought to assert his independence from ecclesiastical powers. If a grave cult existed at all at the mausoleum, it was probably located on the lower level. Previous scholars have tried in vain to detect elements in the features of the mausoleum that reflect its occupant's Gothic

Fig. 22. Mausoleum of Theoderic (Ravenna). Reproduced with the kind permission
of Carola Jäggi, *Ravenna. Kunst und Kultur einer spätantiken Residenzstadt*
(Regensburg, 2013), fig. 134.

identity; although there are no known Roman antecedents of the *Zangenfries*, it
also has no connection to Gothic traditions. For his sepulchral monument,
Theoderic thus chose a hybrid form that defies ethnic categorization. If his
tomb was intended to send a message to posterity, it was the preeminence of its
occupant, who claimed a unique status for himself and probably also for his
descendants.[1]

Theoderic erected his imposing funeral monument in his own lifetime, but
he constantly put off a decision about a successor after his son-in-law Eutharic
unexpectedly died. If Pope John was also supposed to negotiate Theoderic's
succession in Constantinople, the talks were inconclusive. The king seemed to
be in good health on John's return to Ravenna in May 526. In July, he was still
well enough to oversee the appointment of a new occupant of St. Peter's throne.
Theoderic's health appears to have deteriorated suddenly, perhaps only a few
weeks or days before his death on August 30. The sources report that Theoderic
was near death when he summoned the Goths and Romans in his retinue and
told them that he had appointed his grandson Athalaric, Amalasuintha's son,
his successor. Those present immediately swore an oath of allegiance to the
new king.[2]

We have no means of determining whether this account corresponds to the facts. Since the surviving reports all derive more or less directly from the official version that was disseminated after Theoderic's death, it is not impossible that the court legitimated a decision that Theoderic was no longer able to make by attributing it to him posthumously. Even if it was Theoderic's last will that Athalaric should succeed him, the decision must have surprised many contemporaries. Athalaric was probably only ten years old at the time and thus incapable of reigning alone. It had happened now and then in the relatively recent past that a child reigned nominally as emperor. Roman senators had not forgotten that Valentinian III ascended the throne as a six-year-old in 425 and remained under the guardianship of his mother Galla Placidia until 437. A child-king was a novelty for Theoderic's Goths, however, because hitherto proven valor in battle had been the indispensable criterion to be recognized as king by this warrior confederation. It was virtually unheard of to them, however, that Athalaric's reign would entail his mother's regency; real power would rest in the hands of Amalasuintha, who did not remarry after her husband's death.[3]

It was also difficult to argue that a child should succeed Theoderic because there were other candidates who were passed over. Theodahad, Theoderic's nephew, was left empty-handed yet again; Theoderic evidently regarded him as unfit to be king. But Theoderic's grandson Amalaric, the son of the Visigothic king Alaric (d. 507) and Thiudigotho, was also overlooked, despite the fact that by 526 his age qualified him to assume power in the eyes of contemporaries. He was presumably in Hispania at Theoderic's death, far from the center of events. The circle of people under discussion as potential successors to Theoderic was by no means limited to the Amals, notwithstanding Theoderic's efforts to propagate his family's exclusive right to the monarchy. Goths in particular declared in favor of making Tuluin, Theoderic's proven and successful general, their new king.

The fact that these parties in Ravenna finally agreed on Athalaric was the result of an alliance between Amalasuintha and a group of Goths and senators at court who took action before others who were farther away could intervene. This alliance was possible because Tuluin declined to test his strength and instead paid homage to the new king. Of course, he was richly rewarded for doing so: he received supreme command of the Gothic army, which came with the title of *patricius praesentalis*. This position had remained vacant during Theoderic's life because the king himself had held supreme command; now the position had to be filled because neither Athalaric nor Amalasuintha could hold it. We know the names of some senators who strongly supported Amalasuintha's regency. Cassiodorus, then *magister officiorum*, and Abundantius, the praetorian prefect of Italy, played a key part. Ambrosius and Opilio also belonged to the inner circle: Ambrosius, the head of the administration of the royal domains, brought the happy news to Rome and subsequently was promoted to *quaestor palatii*; Opilio—the same man who had accused Boethius—spread the word in Liguria and was made head of the finance ministry. Arator, who was assigned to Tuluin as an adviser, and Reparatus, who took over the urban prefecture, may also have been involved.⁴

Since Theoderic's successor had been determined without consulting the senate in Rome, the Goths in Italy, or the emperor in Constantinople, Amalasuintha and her supporters must have anticipated that Athalaric's recognition would not be a foregone conclusion. They anticipated military intervention from the Byzantine Empire; hence troops were stationed on the Adriatic coast. Cassiodorus assumed responsibility for organizing their provisions. At the same time, however, he wrote a letter to Emperor Justin on Athalaric's behalf, in which he sought peace for the king and the renewal of friendship (*amicitia*) on the same terms on which it had been granted to Theoderic; hate and wrath, he wrote, should be buried with the dead. The new regime thus clung to the view that the Gothic kingdom was inseparably tied to the Roman Empire, as one of the two *res publicae*, but was otherwise independent.

Even more urgent than obtaining the approval of the emperor and the renewal of friendship with the Byzantine Empire was the need to secure for Theoderic's grandson the acceptance of his subjects on as broad and firm a basis as possible. At the same time that the embassy to the emperor set out for Constantinople, the news spread across Theoderic's kingdom: the king is dead; long live his grandson and successor Athalaric! Cassiodorus wrote a series of carefully crafted letters for this purpose, addressed to people and groups whose support the new king needed; the extant letters include those sent to the senate and people of Rome; to the Romans in Italy and Dalmatia; to the Goths in Italy; to Liberius, the praetorian prefect of Gaul; to the Goths and Romans in the Gallic provinces; and to the Catholic bishops of the kingdom. The content and wording of each letter were tailored to the respective addressees, but all of them had the same drift: in Athalaric's name, Cassiodorus invoked the consensus of the two peoples, the Goths and Romans, and promised to remain faithful to Theoderic's principles of government.⁵ In the letter to the people of Rome, for example, we read, "We have instructed the bearers of these letters to promise you, with God as their witness, that, with the help of God, We will maintain justice [*iustitia*] and equitable mercy [*aequabilis clementia*], which nourish the peoples [*populi*], and that the law shall be shared [*ius esse commune*] among us between Goths and Romans, and nothing will be separate between you except that the former shall undertake the labors of war for the common good, whereas you shall multiply from a peaceful life in the city of Rome."[6] In every letter, the order that the subjects should swear loyalty to the king was accompanied by an oath by the king to his subjects, which the messengers took in his name. This reciprocal swearing of oaths served to create a powerful moral bond between the various people and groups whose loyalty was needed for the success of Athalaric's reign and the king himself by means of a public ritual. It was unprecedented and thus shows especially clearly that power definitely did not pass from Theoderic to Athalaric without any friction. The effort to impose Theoderic's last will indeed was not successful everywhere.

Athalaric was accepted as Theoderic's successor by the Goths and Romans of Italy, Dalmatia, and Provence, but the intensity of their approval varied quite widely. While some Roman senators viewed this dynastic succession primarily as a guarantor of stability, the Goths in Italy were swayed by their dependence on Theoderic and his family, as well as by Tuluin's assent. The Catholic bishops did not have a strong preference as to who became the Gothic king of Italy as long as they need not fear any measures to their detriment, let alone persecution. On the Iberian Peninsula, however, the Visigoths were not prepared to accept Theoderic's decision in favor of Athalaric after the fact. Instead, they broke with the Gothic kingdom in Italy and proclaimed Theoderic's grandson Amalaric king. We know very little about this event and its background. The breakaway proceeded peacefully, however, and was ratified by treaty. The Rhône was declared the boundary between the two kingdoms, and the Visigothic royal treasure, which Theoderic had shipped to Italy, was returned to Spain. Every Ostrogoth, moreover, who had taken a Visigothic woman to wife, was given the choice to stay in Amalaric's kingdom, and Procopius reports that many exercised this option. Since Athalaric thus lost the taxes and dues that Theoderic had collected from his Iberian subjects, the Gothic kingdom in Italy was painfully weakened by the separation of the two kingdoms.[7]

The foreign policy that Amalasuintha pursued in her son's name was marked by the effort to avoid military conflict. Even the murder of Theoderic's sister Amalafrida by the Vandal king Hilderic elicited nothing more than powerless protest from Ravenna. Theoderic's fleet-building initiative was canceled after intervention from the Byzantine Empire failed to materialize. Amalasuintha pinned her hopes on cooperation with Constantinople; good relations with the emperor were her highest priority. The Byzantine government indeed seemed genuinely interested; her request to renew the pact of friendship that Anastasius had once struck with Theoderic was granted.[8]

Since Theoderic's daughter was looking for support against Gothic nobles who wanted to influence the juvenile king, she was willing to go out of her way to accommodate the wishes of Justinian, who officially became co-ruler as Augustus in April 527 and then sole ruler after his uncle's death on August 1 of the same year. In 530, Gothic troops clashed with the soldiers of Mundo, who had stayed loyal during Theoderic's lifetime but had now changed sides and joined Justinian. Amalasuintha did everything to prevent an open dispute with the emperor from erupting. When Justinian dispatched his general Belisarius with a fleet in June 533 to conquer the kingdom of the Vandals, Theoderic's daughter provided friendly support by permitting the fleet to obtain provisions on Sicily. She refused to receive an embassy from the Vandal king Gelimer at all. If Amalasuintha had hoped that the emperor might thank her, however, she was disappointed: after the fall of the kingdom of the Vandals, when Amalasuintha claimed the city of Lilybaeum, which had been integrated as part of Amalafrida's dowry, Justinian had his ambassador Alexander submit a complaint.[9]

Amalasuintha's international compliance was a consequence of domestic weakness. Her role as regent was not formalized at all; although she ruled *de facto, de jure* she was merely the king's mother. Every decision that she made was proclaimed in Athalaric's name. In contrast to Galla Placidia, she did not even take a title befitting a queen. A depiction of Amalasuintha and Athalaric on a consular diptych from the year 530 discreetly suggests this arrangement: in the two round portraits in the top field, Athalaric appears to the left of a cross, wearing a tunic and coat but no royal insignia; his mother, Amalasuintha, appears on the right, also without explicit royal insignia. She wears a mantle with a jeweled collar, pearl necklaces, and a pearl-lined head covering the meaning of which is uncertain; proposed interpretations range from a diadem to a Phrygian cap to a bonnet or special hairstyle.[10]

Amalasuintha's standing with the Gothic aristocracy was already complicated because she was a woman. Roman senators could live with the *de facto* rule of a woman for a while because their concept of a ruler was not defined primarily by martial abilities. From the Gothic perspective, however, this state of affairs was totally unacceptable. The men who had served Theoderic wanted to be ruled by a king who was formidable in battle; some of them believed they themselves could claim the succession if Theoderic's descendants failed.

The conflict between Amalasuintha and the Gothic aristocracy manifested itself in a dispute about the education of the young king. Amalasuintha wanted to give Athalaric a literary education as she herself had received, following the Roman model. The Gothic aristocracy feared, however, that Athalaric would become alienated from them if he was educated in the Roman way, and they cited the example set by Theoderic himself, who had always rejected—or so they claimed—the idea of Goths going to school. Amalasuintha was forced to

Fig. 23. Consular diptych of Orestes, cos. 530. Photo by Marie-Lan Nguyen, https://commons.wikimedia.org/wiki/File:Diptych_Rufus_Gennadius_ Probus_Orestes_VandA_139-1866.jpg.

yield: the young king broke off his study of Latin literature to spend his time with his Gothic peers.[11]

Within the kingdom, Amalasuintha revived the policy of cooperating with the senatorial elite that her father had pursued until shortly before his death. She distanced herself with symbolic gestures from measures with which Theoderic had deviated from his own basic policy. She restored the family property of Boethius and Symmachus to their children and indicated that the execution of senators would not be repeated under her son's reign. She adhered to the principle of the functional separation of Goths and Romans and regarded the monarchy as the institution that bound the two peoples together. In an edict that was issued in Athalaric's name soon after Theoderic's death, she committed herself to the good of the commonwealth (*res publica*) and promised the municipal councilors of the urban communities of Italy her protection from extortion and arbitrary abuse at the hands of royal officials.[12]

In Ravenna, Amalasuintha permitted the Catholic community to build monumental churches. Santa Maria Maggiore and San Vitale were begun under Bishop Ecclesius between 526 and 532; Sant'Apollinare in Classe, under Bishop Ursicinus, who held office from 532 to 536.[13] In Rome, Pope Felix IV appears to have fully met the expectations that Theoderic had placed in him. The new administration exempted his clergy from the jurisdiction of other courts and permitted Felix to decide a dispute between the bishop of the royal city and his clergy in Ravenna. The pope consecrated the church of Santi Cosma e Damiano at the Forum Pacis, in the monumental heart of Rome; its roof was covered with tiles that bore Theoderic's name.[14]

Felix proved unable, however, to designate his successor within his own lifetime, in violation of the ecclesiastical custom. He successfully won over a senate majority in favor of his designated choice, the archdeacon Boniface, a wealthy man. The senators decreed that negotiations or deals prior to a papal election would henceforth be penalized with high fines. Yet a schism still occurred after Felix's death: only a minority of the clergy ordained Boniface on September 22, 532. The majority simultaneously elected the deacon Dioscorus, an Alexandrian who had played a major part in the Roman church for decades. The schism was short-lived, however, because Dioscorus died just three weeks later; there thus was no need for the queen regent to intervene. Boniface humiliated his opponents by making the sixty priests who had opposed him sign a confession of guilt. He went too far, however, when he then also tried to designate the deacon Vigilius as his own successor. Boniface was compelled to retract this nomination at a synod in which senators also participated and declare himself guilty of violating the voting rights of the senate and people of Rome.[15]

Two and a half months of *sede vacante* ensued after Boniface's death. Several candidates vied for the voters' favor. In the event of their election, they promised gratuities far in excess of their personal wealth. A concerned administrative lawyer of the Roman church hastened to Ravenna and alleged that church property that actually belonged to the poor had been pawned for electoral purposes; even sacred vessels had supposedly been sold. Amalasuintha thereupon confirmed the prohibition on the buying of votes for episcopal elections that the senate had decreed during Boniface's pontificate. The queen regent also established an upper limit for sums that could be paid after the election to needy persons (*pauperes*) who had backed the victorious candidate; no more than 3,000 *solidi* in Rome and 2,000 *solidi* elsewhere could be disbursed for this purpose. The urban prefect Salventius was instructed to erect an inscription with "his [i.e., the king's] command and the decree of the senate" in marble in the atrium of Old St. Peter's. On January 2, 533, the presbyter Mercurius of San Clemente at last became the successor of St. Peter, serving until May 8, 535. The fact that he took the name of the "martyr pope" John sent a signal: the new pope did not intend to be an obedient instrument of Gothic policy. Shortly after his election, he confirmed the orthodoxy of an edict concerning the faith that Justinian had issued in his empire on March 26, 533, despite the fact that it contained the so-called Theopaschite formula ("one of the Trinity suffered in the flesh"), which had hitherto always been rejected by the Roman church. The pope celebrated the emperor, who had recognized the supremacy of the successor of St. Peter over all other bishops of the East, as the most Christian of princes who ensured the unity of the church in the true faith. John attempted to placate high-ranking senators at the Gothic court, including Cassiodorus and Liberius, who were indignant because they had not been informed, in an open letter.[16]

In the early 530s, Amalasuintha's situation rapidly became critical. The Gothic aristocracy now loudly called for the queen regent to withdraw from the palace. Her opponents pointed to the unimpeded progress of Frankish expansion: in 531, Childebert, one of Clovis' four sons, defeated Amalaric, Theoderic's grandson and king of the Visigothic kingdom, who was killed soon afterward. At approximately the same time, his half-brother Theuderic destroyed the kingdom of the Thuringians; King Herminafrid was captured; his wife, Theoderic's niece Amalaberga, fled with her son Amalafridas to Italy. The king of the Burgundians, Godomar, was defeated in battle at Autun in 532, and his kingdom was divided among the three Frankish kings, Chlothar I, Childebert I, and Theudebert I.[17]

This external threat intensified the domestic pressure on the queen regent. She defended her position by any means necessary. First, she removed three influential Gothic nobles from the court by assigning them military commands that took them to the borders of Italy. When that failed to weaken the opposition as she had hoped, she secretly gave the order to kill all three of them. The names of these three Goths are not transmitted, but it is very probable that one of them was Tuluin, who held supreme military command, because he vanishes from the sources without a trace after his promotion to *patricius praesentalis*. Since the queen regent could not be sure, however, that the assassinations would succeed, she simultaneously contacted Justinian and asked to be admitted to his empire; she sent a ship loaded with 40,000 pounds of gold ahead of her. It was to wait for her in the harbor of Dyrrachium (modern Durrës on the Albanian coast). Only after Amalasuintha received news that her most dangerous adversaries had really been eliminated did she order the ship to return to Ravenna.[18]

The assassination of the three Goths, who presumably had been members of Theoderic's "old guard," appears to have initially weakened opposition to Amalasuintha, but it also made bitter enemies of the victims' kin. Now the queen regent redoubled her efforts to win the support of the senate and the Catholic episcopacy; in 533, she appointed Cassiodorus, who had withdrawn from court in 527, to the office of praetorian prefect of Italy, despite strong opposition. At the same time, she entrusted Liberius, who was serving far from court as praetorian prefect of Gaul, with supreme command of the military as *patricius praesentalis*, the office that Tuluin had held. In a long edict, Athalaric's second, that was published in every province, Amalasuintha promised her subjects on her son's behalf that she would take decisive action against the abuse of office and corruption to ensure that the laws were obeyed.[19]

On taking office, Cassiodorus sent letters to Pope John II and to certain Catholic bishops to encourage them to support the government in an advisory capacity. At the same time, he composed a long letter to the senate that contained what amounts to a panegyric to Amalasuintha. In this text, Cassiodorus breaks with every convention that had previously applied to the representation of a ruler: he praised a woman who did not even hold the title of queen as a well-educated ruler who held supreme power in her hands; as an idealized depiction of a woman who was not merely a supporting figure in the representation of a ruling dynasty, but rather was the ruler herself, the text is one of a kind. At least some excerpts warrant being quoted verbatim:

> O blessed fortune of this age! The affection of a mother reigns under an unoccupied prince [*sub principe feriato*]. Everything is done through her, so that we feel her general love protect us. He whom all things serve pays glorious heed to her and with the astonishing temperance of concord already commands by

virtue of his character before he can rule over peoples. . . . But let us attribute this marvel to both their characters: for so great is his mother's genius that even an unrelated prince would rightly have to serve her. All kingdoms most deservedly revere her, whom merely to see is reverence itself; to hear speak is marvelous. In what language is she not a proven expert? She is versed in the clarity of Attic eloquence; she glows in the pomp of Roman grandiloquence; she glories in the richness of her native speech; she excels all others in their own languages, as she is equally remarkable in all of them. If it behooves a clever person to know one's native language well, what shall we think of such wisdom that observes so many forms of eloquence with flawless practice?

Cassiodorus then praises Amalasuintha's governance: she knew how to defend the kingdom from outside threats; she had put both Justinian and the kings of the Franks in their place; the king of the Burgundians had surrendered to her without a fight. As important as her deeds in war may have been, far more important were her deeds in peace. Amalasuintha personally embodied all the virtues that her ancestors had possessed:

> If that royal cohort of her forebears should look on her, it would instantly see its own praises as if in a crystal-clear mirror: Hamalus dazzled with luck [*felicitas*], Ostrogotha with forbearance [*patientia*], Athala with mildness [*mansuetudo*], Winitarius with fairness [*aequitas*], Unimundus with comeliness [*forma*], Thorismuth with chastity [*castitas*], Walamer with loyalty [*fides*], Theudimer with piety [*pietas*], and with wisdom [*sapientia*], as you yourselves have seen, her famous father. All of them would individually recognize their own virtues but would also gladly confess they had been surpassed because the praise of only one virtue rightly cannot equal that of a throng.[20]

It is unlikely that the senators were impressed by this paean. They knew all too well that the international situation was anything but rosy; a year later, the kingdom of the Burgundians became the Merovingians' prize. Above all, though, Amalasuintha's position as queen regent could not last forever. When Cassiodorus wrote the lines above about an "unoccupied prince" who let his mother act on his behalf, Athalaric was already seventeen years old. Just how long, then, should the grandson of Theoderic remain under his mother's guardianship? Moreover, there was reason to worry that Athalaric might not be equal to his responsibilities as king at all. According to Procopius, he ran riot with his drinking companions and prostitutes and ruined his health. There must be more to this description than malicious gossip, even though the cause—bad company, frustration, diabetes?—can no longer be identified; it is telling that Cassiodorus refrains from explicitly praising the young king's lifestyle.

Athalaric indeed died on October 2, 534, at the age of eighteen. To the Gothic aristocracy, the question of who should become king was again wide open. Amalasuintha, however, was not ready to lay down the power that she had wielded since 526 and submit to the whims of a successor chosen by someone else. Theoderic's daughter instead stormed ahead and had herself proclaimed queen in Ravenna. She subsequently appointed Theodahad her co-ruler, without marrying him, after first making him swear that he would not tell her how to rule. This shocking turn of events must have provoked disapproval and even indignation outside the royal court. Neither the senate in Rome nor the emperor in Constantinople had been consulted. Justinian and the senate instead were informed after the fact by letters that Cassiodorus composed on Amalasuintha's and Theodahad's behalf. There is also no indication that the Gothic aristocracy had been initiated into the plot.[21]

The dual monarchy of a woman and a man who were not bound by marriage was an unprecedented experiment, and the choice of Theodahad as co-ruler was hard for many to understand. It is not surprising that Amalasuintha shied away from ruling as queen alone; both Goths and Romans expected their ruler to be a man. Why, however, her choice for co-ruler fell on Theodahad, who had already been passed over for the succession twice, was probably a mystery to many contemporaries, even though he was not entirely without supporters. From Amalasuintha's perspective, it may have been in Theodahad's favor that his way of life and education met senatorial standards, while as an Amal he also could make a legitimate claim to the throne in the eyes of the Goths. Moreover, in contrast to Amalasuintha, he had a son—named Theudegisel— who could guarantee dynastic continuity. Amalasuintha may also have viewed the unwarlike disposition of her co-ruler as an advantage because Theodahad could not win acclaim among the Goths as a general and gain prestige that was denied to her as a woman. This dual monarchy under Amalasuintha's leadership, however, could only function if Theodahad permanently was resigned to standing in the shadow of Theoderic's daughter. It would soon become evident that this condition was illusory.[22]

2. THE EMPIRE STRIKES BACK: JUSTINIAN'S GOTHIC WAR TO THE CAPITULATION OF VITIGIS (535–540)

On August 1, 527, Justinian became sole ruler of the Byzantine Empire, after the death of his uncle, Justin. Justinian promptly launched a variety of initiatives, at first primarily of a domestic nature. He commissioned a major codification of Roman law, which was brought to a conclusion in 534; issued laws against heretics, Samaritans, and pagans; and tried to bring about a rapprochement between the supporters and opponents of the Council of Chalcedon and its Christological formula that had been rejected especially in Egypt and Syria. In January 532, Justinian put down an uprising in Constantinople in which tens of thousands of people perished and wide swaths of the city were reduced to soot and ash. Since on this occasion he was able to settle the score with senatorial opposition to his rule, he sat even more firmly in the saddle thereafter.

In his foreign policy, the emperor was initially preoccupied with the Persians. Great King Kavad I invaded the empire in 530 but was defeated by Justinian's general Belisarius at Dara (in northern Mesopotamia). The Byzantines, admittedly, suffered defeat at Callinicum (Ar-Raqqa) on the Euphrates the following year. The tide soon turned, though, because Kavad died and his son and successor, Chosroes, had his hands full asserting himself against his domestic enemies. A peace treaty that restored the status quo ante thus was concluded between the two empires in the summer of 532; since it was supposed to last forever, it is called the "Perpetual Peace."[23]

Earlier scholars often assumed that Justinian had planned to restore the Roman Empire to its full extent from the very beginning of his sole rule. They accordingly interpreted the measures that Justinian took in the first years of his reign as preparations for the later offensive against the barbarian kingdoms in the West. Indeed, Constantinople had probably never accepted the fact that the Western Roman Empire had fallen into the hands of barbarian rulers who effectively stood outside the emperor's control. That does not, however, mean that the imperial court believed the reconquest of the West was a goal within reach, let alone that it had devised concrete plans to achieve it. The last attempt to reconquer North Africa had ended in catastrophic failure in 468; the Eastern Roman Empire had had other priorities since then. The sequence of events itself also militates against the assumption that Justinian systematically worked toward destroying first the Vandal kingdom and then the Ostrogothic kingdom starting in 527. The opportunity for military intervention in North Africa arose from a conflict within the Hasding dynasty that culminated in the deposition of King Hilderic by Gelimer in the summer of 530. Gelimer had himself proclaimed king shortly thereafter. Justinian, who had been on friendly terms with Hilderic, rejected Gelimer's request for recognition and demanded Hilderic's reinstatement. It took the emperor two years before he finally decided to enforce this demand with an armed expedition.[24]

Contrary to expectations, this expedition, which commenced in June 533 under Belisarius' command, brought about the destruction of the Vandalic kingdom within a few months. Carthage fell into Roman hands as early as

September 533, after Belisarius won a glorious victory at Ad Decimum; Hilderic had been executed not long beforehand. Gelimer surrendered in January 534 after suffering a second defeat at Tricamarum. A few months later, he was paraded before the people of Constantinople at victory celebrations in the hippodrome, where he cast himself in the dust before Justinian. The ordinary Vandal warriors were deported from Africa and integrated into the Byzantine army. Their families stayed behind in North Africa; the women were forced to marry soldiers of the emperor. The history of the kingdom of the Vandals in North Africa was over.

The almost effortless reconquest of North Africa made Justinian and his counselors ponder how they might also bring the kingdom of the Goths in Italy back under Byzantine control. There was no lack of indications that an upheaval might also erupt there; the queen regent Amalasuintha herself had briefly deliberated fleeing from her kingdom to the emperor, after all. In the summer of 533, Justinian had ambassadors deliver a complaint about incidents in the border regions between the Byzantine Empire and the Gothic kingdom. He particularly stressed the solidarity of the two halves of the empire by issuing a law on June 1, 534, that was addressed both to the senate of Constantinople and to the senate of Rome.[25]

In the case of Italy as well, developments that were not the emperor's doing provided the occasion for military intervention: the death of Athalaric in October and the ensuing dual monarchy of Amalasuintha and Theodahad. Amalasuintha had believed, or at least had hoped, that Theodahad would content himself with his royal sinecure, but Theodahad soon had the queen taken into custody and then confined on an island in Lake Bolsena (in Tuscany), far from the center of power. An embassy was instructed to inform the emperor about her deposition but not to mention her imprisonment. Theodahad chose two senators whose loyalty seemed beyond question to carry out this delicate mission: Liberius, who had served the Gothic kings for more than forty years, had administered the praetorian prefecture of Gaul for almost twenty-five years, and had been supreme commander since 533; and Opilio, who first obtained *illustris* office after Theoderic's death. Opilio did as instructed. Liberius, however, informed Justinian of what had really occurred and then prudently declined to return to Italy; he remained in Constantinople and later was entrusted with several important offices and tasks despite his advanced age. After the emperor learned that Amalasuintha was in captivity, he had his ambassador Peter ("the Patrician"), who was already in Italy, declare that the queen was under Justinian's protection. This promise of protection probably accelerated rather than prevented Amalasuintha's demise. The queen was killed on April 30, 535. Relatives of the three Gothic nobles who had been killed on Amalasuintha's orders forced their way into her prison, either on Theodahad's behalf or with his permission, and exacted brutal revenge. Peter was apparently prepared for this contingency because he did not hesitate to declare to Theodahad that with this murder, he and the emperor were now at war. Justinian gave the order to attack soon afterward. Thus began Justinian's war against the Gothic kingdom in Italy in June 535, which led to its destruction seventeen years later.[26]

The Byzantine war plan was to attack the Gothic kingdom from two sides: while the *magister militum* Mundo was instructed to invade Dalmatia, Belisarius' mission was to conquer Sicily with a fleet. At the same time, an embassy traveled to Gaul to persuade the Frankish kings to invade Italy, which they agreed to do. The operations of the imperial armies initially proceeded according to plan; Mundo captured Salona, and Belisarius took possession of Sicily almost without a fight. In Syracuse, on December 31, 535, he solemnly laid down the consulship that he had taken up in Constantinople at the beginning of the year.[27]

Theodahad had become king only because Theoderic's daughter did not believe she could rule over the Goths in her own name without any male support. As soon as Theodahad had rid himself of her, however, it became obvious that his supporters' goals were utterly irreconcilable. On the one hand, there was a small group of Roman senators who saw Theodahad as a Romanized Goth; on the other, there were the Gothic noblemen who had rebelled against the rule of a woman because they wanted a warrior king. Theodahad tried to broaden his power base by having a woman from the Amal family marry Maximus, the consul of 523, whom he rewarded with extensive landholdings. At the senate's request, Theodahad swore an oath that he would protect the security of Rome and stationed Gothic troops outside the city walls. When the senate complained about the burden their presence created, he assured them that food for the troops would be purchased at market prices and dispatched his *maior domus* Wacces to suppress abuses by the soldiers. Diplomatic exchange with the emperor continued in the meantime.[28]

In the months after Amalasuintha's murder, further embassies from Theodahad traveled to Constantinople, for which Cassiodorus composed cover letters. When these also failed to bear fruit, the king threatened the senators and the bishop of Rome in the late fall of 535 that he would have them and their families all executed if they did not appeal to the emperor to end the war. Cassiodorus thereupon wrote a letter to Emperor Justinian in the senate's name to persuade him to cease hostilities. Pope Agapetus, who succeeded John II on May 13, 535, undertook the mission of presenting the king's wishes to the emperor personally. Agapetus was a wealthy and educated man and a friend of

Map 14. The Gothic War, 535–540.

Cassiodorus; they had wanted to found a kind of Christian university together in Rome. The war thwarted their plan. Like John I ten years earlier, Agapetus now traveled to Constantinople on orders from a Gothic king, and like his predecessor, he too was unable to fulfill his mission. Agapetus died on April 22, 536, without persuading Justinian to cease hostilities. By that time, Theodahad was already in Rome; the king had moved his court along the Via Flaminia in the middle of winter to the Tiber, which he crossed on a ship bridge erected for that purpose. Theodahad moved into the imperial palace on the Palatine in January 536, where Theoderic had lived thirty-five years before him; he would reside there until shortly before his death.[29]

At this juncture, Justinian was not yet committed to destroying the Gothic kingdom by military means. He thus sent Peter back to Italy around the turn of the year 535–536 to offer Theodahad terms of a peace treaty. Peace had its price, though: the king was to surrender Sicily to the emperor and pay an annual tribute of 300 pounds of gold. Theodahad would, moreover, be obligated to provide the emperor with 3,000 Gothic warriors on request and give up the power to condemn senators to death and to confer high ranks. Two more conditions further underscored the supremacy of the emperor: he would always receive acclamations first, and no statue could be erected for the king unless a second statue was erected on its right for the emperor. Although these conditions entailed the loss of an economically prosperous province that was critical to the food supply of Rome, as well as public recognition of a subordinate position, Theodahad accepted Justinian's offer.[30]

Peter had hardly left Rome to inform the emperor when Theodahad was stricken with doubt over whether the emperor was really willing to make peace on these terms. He apparently feared that the war would soon be decided in the emperor's favor and wanted to ensure that he would not suffer any personal harm from defeat. He therefore recalled Peter and asked him whether he believed that the emperor would ratify the draft treaty. When Peter indicated that there was no guarantee, Theodahad instructed him first to present the draft treaty to the emperor; if he rejected it—but only then—he should declare that Theodahad was ready to abdicate if in exchange he received the rank of *patricius* and an annual pension of 1,200 pounds of gold. Peter would not have been the emperor's faithful servant if he had not immediately informed him of these details. Justinian thus commanded Peter to return to Italy with a certain Athanasius to finalize Theodahad's abdication.[31]

When the two envoys appeared before Theodahad in April 536, the king had changed his mind yet again; now he no longer was willing to give up the throne. Theodahad had taken new courage because the Byzantine offensive had

ground to a halt: the emperor's troops vacated Dalmatia after their leader
Mundo fell in battle at Salona. A revolt that broke out in North Africa forced
Belisarius to intervene, thus keeping him from crossing over to Italy. Theodahad
therefore brusquely refused to step down; he even had the emperor's envoys
imprisoned. Soon afterward, he extracted a promise from the kings of the Franks
to provide military support against the emperor if he paid them 1,000 pounds of
gold and surrendered the Gothic part of Provence. Theodahad now felt strong
again. When news of the death of Pope Agapetus reached him, he rammed
through the subdeacon Silverius as his successor against the will of the Roman
clergy. Silverius, consecrated on June 8, 536, would be the last pope to ascend
St. Peter's throne with the help of a Gothic king.[32]

Theodahad's optimism soon proved to be unwarranted. When an imperial
army attacked Salona by sea in June 536, the Gothic commander Gripas hastily
vacated Dalmatia and returned to Ravenna; the Goths living in Dalmatia joined
forces with the Byzantine general Constantinianus. In the south, Belisarius went
on the offensive again after the revolt in North Africa had quickly collapsed. The
general crossed the strait of Messina and seized the province of Lucania et
Bruttii (modern Calabria) largely unopposed, after the Gothic commander
Ebrimud, Theodahad's son-in-law, defected to the emperor with his men, for
which Justinian richly rewarded him. Belisarius' army continued its northward
march along the coast without encountering resistance. Only Naples refused to
surrender; the Gothic garrison, supported by the local Jewish community,
grimly resisted the besieging army for twenty days. When the city was taken by
cunning in November 536, the population was massacred.[33]

Theodahad had idly watched Belisarius' advance, which cost him the support of the Gothic warriors. The fall of Naples was the last straw. An army stationed near Rome that considered itself the armed part of the Gothic people
declared Theodahad deposed in November 536 at Regata (near Terracina) and
proclaimed Vitigis in his place, a man who was not related to the Amals but
who had made a name for himself as a brave warrior. Vitigis was already sixty
years old; he had distinguished himself in the war for Sirmium (504). He had
been called to serve on the king's guard as a *spatharius* during Amalasuintha's
regency and held this position after Athalaric's death; he thus was one of the
closest allies of Theodahad, who had appointed him general. When Theodahad
received the news of Vitigis' betrayal, he tried to flee from Rome to Ravenna,
but the king never reached his destination: a certain Optaris, who wanted
revenge for an insult, hastened after Theodahad on Vitigis' orders, caught him
fifteen miles from Ravenna, threw him on his back, and cut his throat. Thus
died the last king of the Amal dynasty.[34]

Figs. 24a and 24b. Copper coin of Theodahad worth 40 *nummi*,
obverse and reverse (enlarged). From Michael A. Metlich, *The
Coinage of Ostrogothic Italy* (London, 2004), pl. XI, no. 89a.

Vitigis felt that he was inadequately equipped to fight the imperial army; he
thus wanted to reach Ravenna as quickly as possible so that he could raise reinforcements; the greater part of Gothic troops was stationed in northern Italy,
after all. He stopped at Rome on the way to Ravenna. There he received news
of Theodahad's death and had his son Theudegisel taken into custody;
Theudegisel did not survive his father for long, but he at least received a proper
burial from his sister Theodenanda. Vitigis stayed only a short time in Rome;
when he departed from the city, he left behind a garrison of over 4,000 Goths
under the command of Leuderis to defend it. He made Pope Silverius and the
senate and people of Rome swear loyalty to him beforehand. The king did not,
however, want to rely only on this oath; he also forced a large number of senators to accompany him to Ravenna, where they could serve as hostages to guarantee the good behavior of their peers.[35]

Vitigis took a series of measures to protect his power from domestic and foreign threats. In a circular letter to all the Goths—composed by Cassiodorus yet
again—Vitigis courted their support by declaring that he had not become king
"in closed bedchambers," like Theodahad, but rather had been raised on a
shield "according to the way of the ancestors" (*more maiorum*) in an open field:
"Let you know that I was chosen not in the confines of a bedchamber but on
wide-open fields; I was sought after not amid the dainty talk of flatterers but in
the midst of blaring trumpets so that, roused by such clamor and desirous of
their native valor, the Gothic people should find a warlike king for itself. For
how long could brave men raised on raging battles tolerate an unproven prince
so that they suffered on account of his reputation, although they were confident
in their own valor?"[36]

Figs. 25a and 25b. Silver coin of Vitigis (half-*siliqua*)
with portrait of Justinian, obverse and reverse (enlarged).
From Michael A. Metlich, *The Coinage of Ostrogothic Italy*
(London, 2004), pl. VII, no. 63.

Vitigis legitimated his rule with reference to the will of the Gothic army and
to his own martial prowess; at the same time, he promised to rule as Theoderic
had done because, he continued, every ruler was rightly considered outstanding to the extent that he appreciated Theoderic's decisions. To produce a familial relationship with Theoderic and his daughter, Vitigis divorced his wife and
married Amalasuintha's daughter Matasuintha—against her will, it appears.
Their wedding, at which Cassiodorus delivered a speech, was the last major
celebration that a Gothic king would stage in Ravenna. Vitigis benefited from
this connection with Theoderic's granddaughter not merely because she was
someone who could win him more Gothic supporters; he also tried to use it to
placate the emperor. In a letter to Justinian, the king argued that war was superfluous because he had avenged Amalasuintha's murder and wed her daughter.
He had copper coins minted in Ravenna that displayed the portrait and name
of Emperor Justinian on the obverse and Vitigis' own name in a wreath with the
title of king on the reverse.[37]

Vitigis certainly did not count on the possibility that Justinian might be willing to cease hostilities. Instead, he prepared for further warfare by raising a large
army that he outfitted with horses and weapons. Of course, many Goths were
still stationed in the Cottian Alps to guard the border against the Franks. To
secure his rear for the war against the emperor, Vitigis was really prepared to
make good Theodahad's offer to cede Provence to the Franks. After the king
obtained the consent of the Gothic aristocracy for these concessions at a council of war, he dispatched envoys to effect the cession and deliver the promised
gold. Moreover, the king formally renounced the Gothic protectorate over the

Alamanni, who were already under Frankish rule anyway. In return, the three Merovingian kings, Childebert (511–558), Chlothar (511–561), and Theudebert (533–547), promised to support the Goths against the emperor. They could not do so publicly, however, because they had already bound themselves to him by treaty. They thus could not send Vitigis any Franks, but they could send members of other peoples who were their subjects. The Alamannic chiefs Butilin and Leuthari immediately declared themselves ready to take the lead. Since Vitigis was in complete agreement, he could withdraw the Gothic troops from the Alpine border; they received the order to make way to the king under their commander Marcias.[38]

More bad news reached Ravenna while Vitigis was busy mustering this large army. Not only the province of Calabria et Apulia, where no Goths lived, had surrendered to Belisarius, but around the turn of the year 536–537, the Goths stationed in the province of Samnium also defected. Hardly had Vitigis left Rome when imperial troops entered the city on December 9, 536. Since the Romans feared they would suffer a similar fate to that of the Neapolitans in the event of a siege, the senator Fidelis offered to surrender the city to Belisarius without a fight. The Gothic garrison thought it was pointless to resist and quickly vacated the city; thus while Belisarius' soldiers entered Rome through the Porta Asinaria, the Goths left through the Porta Flaminia. Belisarius rewarded Fidelis by appointing him praetorian prefect of Italy and ordered the fortifications of Rome to be repaired without delay and supplies of food to be stockpiled—to the horror of the inhabitants, who had wanted precisely to avoid a siege. Although his army at this point consisted of scarcely more than 5,000 men, Belisarius sent troops to the province of Tuscia et Umbria, and they successfully captured the cities of Narni, Spoleto, and Perugia.[39]

Belisarius' successes forced Vitigis to act. Even before Marcias had led the border army out of the Alps, Vitigis sent ground troops and a fleet to Dalmatia with orders to drive out the imperial soldiers. Soon afterward—Marcias had arrived in the meantime—Vitigis himself led an army to the walls of Rome, the surrender of which he now regretted. Procopius speaks of 150,000 mounted warriors, most of whom were just as well armored as their horses. Without a doubt, this number is greatly exaggerated. The king's army was not large enough to invest Rome completely; modern estimates put its size at 25,000–30,000 men. At any rate, Vitigis' army was numerically far superior to Belisarius', although the latter had received reinforcements in the meantime. The siege began in February 537 and lasted until March 538; no fewer than sixty-nine armed skirmishes took place between the besiegers and besieged during these twelve months. Since the population of Rome had to endure great hardship during this time, the mood soon turned against the supposed liberators. Should they not have held out with the Goths? Belisarius, who was residing in a palace on the Pincio, accused Pope Silverius of conspiring with the enemy and deposed him. Silverius was replaced by the deacon Vigilius, who had almost become the successor of St. Peter in 530.

For all his efforts, Vitigis still could not take the city; his army endured heavy losses from the enemy and epidemics; it also suffered from famine because it could not be adequately supplied. In December 537, the king therefore offered to Belisarius to cede Sicily and Campania and pay annual tribute, but he obtained only a three-month cease-fire that was soon broken anyway. Since food and fresh troops had reached the city by sea in the meantime, Belisarius' army was so much stronger by early 538 that he sent troops to attack Picenum, where numerous Gothic families lived who were helpless to defend themselves. The Byzantine general John—Vitalianus' nephew—advanced as far as Rimini, the Gothic garrison of which retreated to Ravenna, which lay only a day's journey away. Since this advance threatened a key Gothic settlement area and, moreover, the center of royal power, Vitigis lifted the siege of Rome in March 538 and led his army across the Apennines back to Ravenna, where he henceforth stayed.[40]

Vitigis' failure at Rome severely damaged his reputation among the Goths. They had made him king because they needed a capable general, but now they found that despite all his mobilization efforts he was no more successful than his predecessor Theodahad, whom they had deposed as a failure. Most of the senators defected to the emperor when Belisarius marched on the city; those who followed Vitigis to Ravenna were executed on the king's orders a few weeks after the beginning of the siege of Rome if they had not already fled to safety. This massacre amounted to a declaration of war on the entire senatorial order and erased any hope of a future reconciliation. Cassiodorus, who had served Theoderic's daughter Amalasuintha after Theoderic's death and then her murderer Theodahad, held out longer than most senators from distinguished families. He was still in office when Vitigis became king and had Theodahad killed. Soon after the murder of the hostages, however, probably in early 538, he laid down his office as praetorian prefect of Italy.[41]

Vitigis' hold on power was further strained by the fact that crop failures caused by the war led to a famine in early 538, which hit Roman civilians in cities and the countryside especially hard. Milan, the second-largest city of Italy, defected from the Goths in June 538 and was then invested by a Gothic army led by Uraias, who was soon joined by roughly 10,000 Burgundians sent by the Merovingian king Theudebert. Milan was besieged for nine months; after several relief efforts failed, the city fell in March 539. Probably the worst excess of violence during the war took place on the storming of the city: embittered by the duration and ferocity of the resistance, the besiegers slaughtered the majority of the male population and enslaved the women and children.[42]

The victory tour of Byzantine troops slowed after 538 since the commanders could not agree on a joint course of action. It was a war of attrition without open battles; each side fought for individual cities and strongholds with varying success. A Gothic counteroffensive failed to materialize; indeed, Vitigis could not even drive the imperial troops out of Rimini or relieve the Goths under siege at Osimo and Fiesole. In early 539, a Frankish army led by King Theudebert appeared in the Po Valley, but it treated the Goths as the enemy as much as the emperor's troops did and returned to Gaul laden with booty several months later. When the Gothic garrisons of Osimo and Fiesole surrendered in the fall of 539, all central Italy was in imperial hands. Belisarius could now begin to besiege Ravenna, which was invested from both sides.[43]

The siege of Ravenna had already begun when an embassy from the kings of the Franks reached Vitigis, offering to send a large army to Italy to drive out the emperor's forces. Vitigis' fear of the Franks, however, was greater than his fear of the emperor.[44] He rejected the offer with the approval of the Gothic aristocracy and instead entered into negotiations with Belisarius. The king was now running a race against time because the besiegers had cut Ravenna off from the outside world; since a fire in the city's granaries also had destroyed a significant amount of its stockpiled provisions, the people were hungry. In early 540, two senators arrived before Ravenna as envoys of the emperor and first called on Belisarius. What ensued is one of the most perplexing episodes of the history of the Gothic kingdom in Italy, rich as it is in mysteries already.

Procopius, who was in Belisarius' headquarters at the time, reports that the imperial envoys presented Belisarius with a draft treaty that would have permitted Vitigis to remain king north of the Po if he ceded all Italy south of the river and half of the Ostrogothic royal treasure. The envoys then proceeded to Ravenna, and both the Goths and Vitigis himself were supposedly overjoyed to accept peace on these terms. Belisarius, however, thought that the conquest of all Italy was within his grasp and therefore refused to sign the draft treaty. Thereupon the most distinguished Goths had envoys deliver him a proposal to have him proclaimed sole ruler—the word in Greek is *basileus*, which can mean both a barbarian king and a Roman emperor. When Belisarius accepted—not in earnest, Procopius assures us—Vitigis also agreed to the solution. The Goths dropped all resistance, and Belisarius entered Ravenna at the head of his troops.[45]

Procopius, who witnessed the Roman army's entrance into the city, could account for the Goths' behavior only as the interference of a supernatural power (*daimonion*):

> The Goths greatly surpassed their adversaries in number and strength and had not been tested in battle since they had been in Ravenna, and they did not have a servile disposition in any other way. Yet they were captured by fewer men and did not consider the name of "slave" degrading at all. Their wives, though—who had heard from their husbands that the enemy soldiers had powerful physiques and superior numbers—all spit in their husbands' faces when they saw them all sitting around the city; and they pointed to the defeated men with their fingers and accused them of cowardice.[46]

Thus ended the reign of Vitigis in May 540. He, his wife Matasuintha, and a series of Gothic noblemen were brought to Constantinople soon afterward; the deposed king was received with honor and died two years later as a Roman *patricius*. His widow later married Germanus, Justinian's nephew.[47]

Procopius' account raises many questions. Why did Vitigis' reign collapse without so much as a whimper? And with what did the Gothic aristocracy intend to replace him? In other words, did they want to proclaim Belisarius emperor of the Western Roman Empire or king of the Goths? The reason why modern scholars have not been able to reach a consensus on this question derives from the peculiarity of our only account of these events. On the one hand, Procopius is at pains to exculpate the unauthorized actions of his superior, who could not have let himself be proclaimed king of a barbarian people and absolutely not emperor without Justinian's blessing. On the other hand, Procopius uses the Greek word *basileus* to designate the position that the Goths intended for Belisarius, a term that could mean a Roman emperor or a ruler of a barbarian people. The fact that Procopius describes the position that Theoderic and Vitigis held in similar terms militates in favor of the latter interpretation; the unauthorized proclamation of an emperor in the west would, moreover, have been highly unlikely to end the war with the Byzantine Empire. There is no way to be certain, however, particularly since the Goths had never before proclaimed someone their king who was not a recognized member of their community.

The fact that the Goths trapped in Ravenna urgently wanted to end the siege can be explained by the dire situation in which they found themselves. But there must have been further reasons to account for their willingness to depose Vitigis and submit to Belisarius in his place. When it is possible to depose a king, the subject people treat the monarchy itself like an institution they can control. That fact illustrates how intimately the general acceptance of Gothic kings depended on their success. Loyalty to Theoderic's family was never so entrenched that mere kinship with the Amal family sufficed for a smooth succession. Amalasuintha had to deal with an opposition that refused to come to terms with the reign of a woman. Theodahad was deposed because he failed in the fight against the emperor's armies, and Vitigis fared no better. The behavior of the Gothic warriors was dictated above all by their effort to retain their status as privileged landowners in Italy. The fate of the Vandal warriors who were deported to the East to serve as mere mercenaries against the Persians flashed before their eyes as a warning. The Goths in Italy wanted to avoid losing their families and possessions at all costs; for that purpose, they were sometimes forced to replace their king.

3. THE HORRIFIC END: TOTILA AND TEIA (541–552)

In the year 540, it seemed as if the Gothic kingdom in Italy was at an end. Belisarius took Vitigis and Matasuintha and a number of Gothic noblemen captive and dismissed the rest of the Goths, as long as they lived south of the Po, to return to their estates since he had guaranteed their property by treaty prior to entering Rome. The Gothic garrisons in Venetia soon also surrendered to the imperial commander. But not all the Goths north of the Po were ready to submit. There were still Gothic garrisons in Verona and Ticinum whose commanders were waiting to see how events would unfold. As word got around that Belisarius did not intend to wield the power that had been offered to him, but instead was preparing to depart for Constantinople, the mood among the Goths soured because on Belisarius' return to the emperor it seemed as if what the Goths feared most might come to pass—namely, that they would be forced to leave Italy. Preeminent Goths who refused to allow that to happen thus gathered together and traveled to Ticinum to offer the throne to Uraias, Vitigis' nephew. Uraias declined, however, and instead suggested that they proclaim Hildebad, the commander of the garrison at Verona, king. Hildebad was the nephew of Theudis, who had become Amalaric's successor as king of the Visigoths in 531. This proposal received general approval; the Goths thus quickly fetched Hildebad, dressed him in a purple garment, and paid homage to him as their new king. Hildebad accepted, however, only on the condition that they should first ask Belisarius again to become the ruler of the Goths and Romans in Italy. The Goths thus sent envoys to Ravenna, but they returned without accomplishing anything: the general reiterated his refusal and soon left Ravenna for Constantinople. While imperial officials went about organizing the collection of taxes and dues as profitably as possible according to the Byzantine model—which quickly made the new rulers unpopular—those who were unwilling to submit to the faraway emperor flocked to Hildebad. Initially, only about 1,000 warriors joined Hildebad, but his following rapidly grew after he won his first victory at Treviso (over the imperial general Vitalius).[48]

Hildebad's reign, however, lasted barely a year. The king was murdered at a banquet in May 541; the perpetrator was a Gepid named Velas who wanted to avenge a personal insult Hildebad had inflicted on him. The Goths yet again had no political or military leadership. The Rugi were the quickest to act; they had come to Italy with Theoderic and were officially considered Goths yet had retained their own distinct identity. The Rugi proclaimed one of their own, a man named Eraric, king. He, however, met with considerable resistance among the rest of the Goths, particularly because he did not try to continue the war against the Byzantine Empire but instead sent ambassadors to Justinian whose official mission was to conclude peace on the basis of the draft treaty of 540. If that could not be done, Eraric sought an appropriate pension for himself and the rank of *patricius*.[49]

While this embassy negotiated with Justinian, the Gothic noblemen who were dissatisfied with Eraric agreed at the beginning of 542 to offer the title of king to Totila, a nephew of Hildebad who was in command of the garrison of Treviso. Totila had offered to surrender the garrison to the emperor's troops shortly beforehand if they would spare him, but he was willing to become king if the Goths first killed Eraric. They accepted this condition: Eraric was treacherously killed. Thus ended the reign of Eraric of the Rugi only five months after it began.[50]

With the proclamation of Totila, whose official name was Baduila, the second phase of the Gothic War began, lasting until 552. Although Totila initially had only 5,000 warriors at his disposal, he soon won significant victories against Justinian's generals. Within a short time, he recovered large parts of Italy for the Goths, although Ravenna remained firmly in imperial hands. He took Naples (543) and captured numerous cities in Tuscany and Picenum (545). In December 546, he even successfully retook Rome after besieging the city for an entire year. These victories gave Totila immense appeal: soon some 20,000–25,000 men were following him, including many defectors from the emperor's army, as well as unfree Romans. The core of his army, though, consisted of Goths, battle-tested warriors who proved equal to, and in some situations even superior to, the elite soldiers of the emperor, who were recruited from all over the world. Totila's generals and closest confidants were named Bleda (like the brother of Attila the Hun), Ruderic, and Viliarid; Procopius calls them "the most valiant men among the Goths."[51]

Totila was a young king who had earned respect from both friend and foe for his valor as a warrior; he charged into battle at the head of his troops without regard for his personal safety. At the same time, he was a skilled tactician and organizer. We thus may credit him for fully unleashing the fighting power of the Goths, who had long lacked a capable leader, after 542. Yet Totila's victories would scarcely have been possible if Justinian had not dramatically cut the wage payments for his Italian army after Vitigis' capitulation because he had had to go to war against the Persians yet again after 540. Moreover, plague raged across wide swaths of the empire, claiming hundreds of thousands of victims. Famines broke out on account of the plague, lasting until 546. That meant the emperor had to make do with dramatically less tax revenue. In this difficult situation, Justinian decided to concentrate his resources on the east. When the soldiers' wages went unpaid, morale in Justinian's Italian army plummeted. The Byzantine war effort was also crippled because Justinian refused to place the entire Italian army under centralized command. Thus the emperor's various generals constantly quarreled and could not agree on a common strategy. Belisarius could do little to change that after he returned to Italy in 544. He indeed recaptured Rome for the emperor in 547, but then he was recalled yet again in 548 because he had not secured any breakthroughs or lasting successes.[52]

Totila, meanwhile, was unable to turn his adversary's military weakness into political capital. His policy was simply too contradictory and inconsistent. The king tried to win back lost trust by showing clemency to the inhabitants of conquered cities. At the same time, however, he had their city walls torn down because he did not want to rely on the loyalty of Romans. His actions toward the city of Rome were similarly contradictory. In 544, he sent several letters to the senate and people of Rome to persuade them to defect to the Goths' side. When he captured Rome in 547, however, he had the senators he found there taken into custody and brought to Campania. The king made ostentatious displays of clemency but then proceeded with great cruelty again, not even sparing clergymen. He paid a visit to St. Peter's, but he could not prevent the plundering of the catacombs and churches.[53]

Hope of reconciliation with the senate died the moment that Totila claimed for himself rents paid by tenants, in addition to the taxes paid by Roman landowners to the state. This measure amounted to expropriation and inevitably was rejected by the senators, whose wealth was based on land ownership. Obviously, it was not the product of a revolutionary social agenda; it was intended rather to finance the war at a time when the complex tax system of Italy began to collapse from its consequences. Since Totila could no longer rely on a functioning

Figs. 26a and 26b. Copper coin of Totila worth 10 *nummi*,
obverse and reverse (enlarged). From Michael A. Metlich, *The
Coinage of Ostrogothic Italy* (London, 2004), pl. XI, no. 93.

government apparatus to collect taxes and dues, his army gradually reverted to
what it had been before Theoderic turned his warriors into a standing army: a
community of violence that secured its material existence with requisitions and
plundering. On the march across Italy, Totila's Goths lived predominantly on
what they found locally or seized by force. His generalship thus was heavily
influenced by the exigencies and ideas of the moment, particularly since conquests were often rapidly lost. After a few weeks, Rome fell back into the hands
of imperial troops; Ravenna could not be retaken; Otranto, the most important
imperial foothold in Apulia, remained out of reach.[54]

   Totila's diplomacy also exhibits no clear, consistent policy. He ceded the
Cottian Alps and Venetia to the Merovingian king Theudebert to create a buffer zone to protect himself from attacks from Dalmatia by imperial troops.
Above all, however, Totila constantly tried to persuade Justinian to end the war.
At the beginning of his reign, Totila had coins minted that bore Justinian's portrait. In 543, he replaced Justinian's portrait with that of Anastasius, who had
once recognized Theoderic's position by treaty; even if Totila was no longer
loyal to the reigning emperor, he was still loyal to the empire itself. After the
recapture of Rome in 547, Totila sent the Roman deacon Pelagius as an envoy
to Justinian to sue for peace but also to threaten the emperor with the destruction of Rome, the massacre of senators, and the invasion of Illyricum should he
refuse. In 550, after Totila captured Rome for the second time, he again turned
to Justinian, this time offering to cede Sicily and Dalmatia, pay an annual tribute, and send troops to fight any opponents the emperor pleased. Only after the
emperor also rejected this offer did Totila commit himself to the final break by
having coins minted with his own portrait, both in silver and in copper.[55]

When Totila first recaptured Rome (547), he had long sections of the city walls torn down. When he took the city a second time on January 16, 550, he treated it as if he were returning to his residence. He called on the senators now in his power to repair dilapidated or damaged buildings, and he staged chariot races in the Circus Maximus, perhaps the last that were ever held there. A few months later, the king marched to southern Italy and crossed to Sicily, which he plundered as if it were enemy territory. He left the island before the end of the year.[56]

In Constantinople, Roman senators had long advocated a new offensive in Italy. They were supported by Pope Vigilius, who had resided on the Bosporus against his will since the beginning of 547. The Gothic invasion of Sicily gave their pleading additional weight. In the summer of 550, Justinian sent the aged general Liberius—the same man who had served Theoderic as praetorian prefect of Gaul for more than twenty years—to Syracuse. Since the city was then being besieged by the Goths, Liberius sailed on to Palermo, where a second fleet under the command of Artabanes arrived several months later. While Liberius reached Sicily by sea, Germanus raised a large army on the emperor's behalf in Thrace and Illyricum, with which he intended to attack the Gothic kingdom by land. Since Germanus had married Matasuintha, Vitigis' widow, he carried the hopes of those who wanted to see the compromise between the Goths and Romans in Italy continue. Before Germanus could set out for Italy, though, he died of disease in the fall of 550.[57]

After Germanus' death, it was Narses' time to shine. He was a eunuch of Armenian descent who had long been one of the emperor's confidants. He had already held military command in Italy from 538 to 539, and now he received supreme command. Narses knew the risk he was taking in accepting this mission, so he insisted on receiving sufficient monetary resources to raise a potent army. Since Justinian granted his request, he was able to engage numerous Lombards, Heruli, and Huns in addition to the Byzantine troops that Germanus had already mustered.[58]

Narses left Constantinople in April 551, but he took almost a year to plan his offensive. During this time, the Goths conducted operations at sea with varying success. A Gothic fleet of 300 ships attacked the island of Corcyra (Corfu) and sank a large number of Byzantine ships in early 551. They plundered both the island and the facing mainland, especially Nicopolis, the capital of the province of Epirus.

In Italy, in contrast, a Gothic fleet that had been dispatched to cut off besieged Ancona by sea suffered a heavy defeat at nearby Sena Gallica. Although it was only slightly outnumbered by the imperial fleet, it could not hold its

The Gothic War (551–552)

FRANKISH KINGDOM

OSTROGOTHIC KINGDOM

Milan

Lake Garda

Narses 552

Po

Genua

Ligurian Sea

Arno

Faesulae

Ravenna

Ariminum

Tiber

Tadinae 552

Salona

Adriatic

Corsica

Rome

Naples

Mons Lactarius

552

Bari

Tarentum

Hydruntum

Sardinia

Tyrrhenian Sea

Mediterranean

Palermo

Rhegium

Sicily

Ionian Sea

Carthage

EASTERN ROMAN EMPIRE

0   50   100   150 km

→ Easter Roman campaign (Second Gothic War)

✗ Major battle

Map 15. The Gothic War, 551–552.

formation in battle and turned to flee; thirty-six ships with their crews were lost; another eleven that escaped were subsequently destroyed by order of the Gothic commander Indulf. The Battle of Sena Gallica was the last major naval battle in the Mediterranean for a century, but it hardly decided the outcome of the war, as Procopius claimed. Totila conquered Sardinia and Corsica in the fall of 551 with a new fleet.[59]

After Narses had completed his preparations, he set out from Salona in April 552 and marched for Venetia. Since the Franks in the vicinity refused to grant him passage and the route via Verona was blocked by the Gothic commander Teia, Narses had his army advance along the coast, using ship bridges to cross the river mouths. He reached Ravenna on June 6 and Rimini soon afterward. Since the Goths had broken down the stone bridge over the Ariminus, he had a wooden bridge thrown over the river, unimpeded by the Gothic garrison, and turned down the Via Flaminia, which leads over the Apennines to Rome.[60]

When Totila saw that his attempt to block Narses' way had failed, he sought a decision in direct confrontation. After taking 300 children as hostages from the notables of Italian cities, he marched from Rome to meet the imperial general and pitched camp at Tadinae in Umbria. The two armies clashed at a place here called Busta Gallorum ("Graves of the Gauls") in late June 552. Totila, whose army was outnumbered, ordered his cavalry to charge the enemy ranks only with their lances; he apparently hoped they could run right over the imperial army. Narses, in contrast, had his own cavalry dismount because he was counting on his archers. The Gothic assault collapsed in their hale of arrows: some 6,000 Goths lay dead on the battlefield; Totila himself was also killed. The king managed to escape the battle, but he died at a place called Caprae while fleeing. Two versions of his death circulated. According to one, he was wounded by an arrow in the battle and died several days later; according to the other, he was overtaken while fleeing by the Gepid Asbad and killed with a lance. The only thing certain is that Totila was hastily buried by a handful of loyal followers, and then Narses' men reopened the grave to verify that the Gothic king had really been killed. Once they were convinced, they sent a helmet adored with precious gems and the king's bloodstained garment to Constantinople as trophies. After his victory, Narses immediately proceeded to Rome. He captured the city after a short siege; the last defenders took shelter in the Mausoleum of Hadrian, which had been converted into a fortress (the Castel Sant'Angelo), but surrendered after receiving a guarantee that their lives would be spared. Rome thus fell to the emperor for the third time. It would remain in Byzantine hands for the next two hundred years.[61]

Figs. 27a and 27b. Silver coin of Teia (half-*siliqua*), obverse and
reverse (enlarged). From Michael A. Metlich, *The Coinage of
Ostrogothic Italy* (London, 2004), pl. VII, no. 74a.

Even after the devastating defeat at Tadinae, by no means every Goth was
prepared to submit to the emperor. A few weeks later, a man named Teia was
proclaimed king by a group of Goths in Ticinum, where a portion of Totila's
treasure was kept. We do not know why they chose him for their king, and all
we know about his family is that he had a brother named Aligern whose job was
to guard the greater part of the Gothic royal treasure. There also were some
places in southern Italy that were still under Gothic control at this time; the
part of the royal treasure guarded by Aligern was located at Cumae on the Gulf
of Naples. Teia wanted to combine his troops with his brother's and so marched
to Campania. On the way, he executed not only the 300 hostages he had taken,
but also any senators who fell into his hands because they had thought they
could return to Rome after Totila's death. Teia was forced to make many detours
on his way south since Narses' troops constantly blocked his way. At last, he took
up position south of Vesuvius, apparently intending to take Cumae by sea.
Teia's and Narses' armies encamped on opposite banks of a river for two months.
Teia's position became untenable, however, after the commander of the Gothic
fleet defected to Narses; the king then retreated with his people back to the
nearby *Mons Lactarius* ("Milk Mountain").[62]

The decisive battle was fought in this hilly terrain in late October 552. Little
is known with certainty about the course of events. The account of the battle by
Procopius, who knew of it only from hearsay, is detailed but one-sided and
implausible in its particulars. The historian stylizes Teia as the antithesis of the
unwarlike Justinian by presenting the Gothic king as a hero of Homeric dimensions: protected by his shield, Teia stood with only a few followers on the front
line and endured the barrage of Roman lances for several hours. Only when he
was forced to replace his shield, which had been struck by twelve enemy lances,

and thus let down his guard for an instant, was he finally overcome. At that very moment, an enemy lance struck and killed him on the spot. Since his corpse fell into enemy hands, the imperial troops cut off his head and stuck it on a lance. They carried this trophy back and forth between the two hostile armies to demoralize the Goths and inspire the Romans. But the Goths refused to give up even after their king's death; they fought on until dark and lined up for battle the next day. At the end of the second day, however, Gothic noblemen came into the Roman camp and offered to surrender. According to Procopius, Narses assured the survivors by treaty that they would be permitted to leave Italy to settle outside the empire. Agathias' account is more credible on this point. According to him, the defeated Goths received permission to return to their estates.[63]

The defeat at Mons Lactarius spelled the end of the Gothic kingdom but not the end of the Goths in Italy. When an Alamannic-Frankish army, lured by the prospect of booty, crossed the Alps in early 553, the Goths rebelled against the Byzantine emperor yet again and put themselves under the leadership of Butilin and Leuthari. This band of warriors plundered and pillaged as it marched down to the southern coast of Italy and split up on the way back. One part was decimated by epidemics; the other offered battle to Narses near Capua in the fall of 554 and was utterly defeated. This defeat robbed the surviving Goths of the courage to proclaim yet another king from their ranks, especially since Teia's brother Aligern had entered the emperor's service around the turn of the year 553–554. From the walls of Cesena, Aligern supposedly shouted to passing Franks that any attempt to revive the Gothic kingdom was pointless because the royal treasure with all the insignia of power was already in Byzantine hands. In early 555, some of the Goths who had taken part in Butilin and Leuthari's raids surrendered to Narses and then entered the emperor's service. Isolated pockets of resistance held out for several years; the *comes Gothorum* Widin in Verona did not capitulate until 562 and was brought to Constantinople as a prisoner. But people who viewed themselves as Goths nonetheless continued to live in Italy. The last traces of them finally vanish in the High Middle Ages.[64]

13

THEODERIC THE GREAT: METAMORPHOSES OF A FIGURE

1. FROM RAVENNA TO VIVARIUM: CASSIODORUS AFTER HIS CONVERSION

In the year 580, in his ninety-third year on this earth, Cassiodorus wrote the preface to his last book, *On Orthography* (*De Orthographia*). He says the following about his inspiration: During a discussion of his "explanations" (*Complexiones*) of the acts and epistles of the Apostles, *his* monks had cried out, "What good is it for us to learn what the ancients did or to know in detail what Your Prudence endeavored to add if we are utterly ignorant of how we should write those things down? We also cannot transmit with our voice what we are unable to understand in writing." Cassiodorus replied that the study of the ancient authors was absolutely indispensable so that contemporaries did not mistakenly believe they were the originators of things they had inherited from others. He therefore compiled what twelve earlier authors could teach about orthography so that future correctors and copyists would no longer get mixed up. The man who, over half a century earlier, had held high office at Theoderic's court, presents himself in this text as the spiritual head of a monastic community dedicated to studying and copying biblical and theological texts. This community lived in a monastery called Vivarium, founded by Cassiodorus himself. It was located in Squillace, where Cassiodorus' family had lived for generations. Vivarium was under the authority of an abbot and had close ties to a second monastery, where eremites lived under an abbot of their own in strict isolation from one another.[1]

It is not recorded when Cassiodorus founded this double monastery. Perhaps he did so while he was still serving the Gothic kings. Cassiodorus laid down the

office of *magister officiorum* soon after Theoderic's death; he took over as praetorian prefect at Amalasuintha's request in 533. He served no fewer than four
rulers while holding this office (two of whom were murdered): first Athalaric,
then Amalasuintha and Theodahad jointly, then Theodahad alone, and finally
Vitigis. Cassiodorus did not retire from serving the Gothic court for good until
the year 538, after Vitigis ordered the senatorial hostages in his power to be
murdered. He never again held political office.

The Gothic kingdom in Italy was already a distant memory when Cassiodorus
wrote his book about orthography. Narses, Justinian's general, had triumphed
over the last Gothic king, Teia, in 552. Two years later, the emperor issued a
package of measures at the request of Pope Vigilius that were intended to restore
the status quo before Totila's reign, the so-called Pragmatic Sanction. All of
Totila's acts were voided; slaves and *coloni* who had come into the possession of
different masters were to be returned to their former owners or landlords.
Justinian also confirmed the privileges of Rome: henceforth, the emperor himself would pay for the distribution of food; the maintenance of public buildings;
and the salaries of the professors of grammar, rhetoric, medicine, and law. In a
departure from Theoderic's time, Justinian again limited the jurisdiction of
military courts, which had been competent for all cases involving soldiers under
Gothic rule, to trials that were brought against soldiers. The emperor, moreover, gave civic notables and bishops the right to elect their provincial governors, and he promised senators free access to the imperial court. These orders
and promises, of course, were a dead letter from the start. Long after Justinian's
death in 565, the entire administration of Italy was *de facto* under the control of
Narses. After seventeen years of war, large swaths of Italy had been devastated;
Rome and Milan were in ruins.[2]

Senators who had hoped that Justinian would treat Italy as the Byzantines'
equal, as the Western Roman Empire, were quickly disillusioned. Justinian had
no intention of reviving the court offices of the Western Empire and appointing
senators from Italy to them. He had Italy managed by a praetorian prefect sent
to Ravenna from Constantinople; from 584, if not earlier, a high-ranking military commander with the title of *exarchus* stood by the prefect's side. By this
time, the emperor's governors did not even rule over the entire Italian peninsula. Only a few years after Justinian's death, the Lombards, led by their king,
Alboin, crossed the Alps and brought northern Italy under their control. Verona
and Milan fell to them in 569; Ticinum, in 572. Alboin himself, however, was
killed in 572, and his successor, Cleph, was murdered two years later. Ten years
without a king ensued until Cleph's son, Authari, was elected king in 584. In
this period, Lombard groups advanced into central Italy and founded duchies

centered around Spoletum and Beneventum. On one of their raids, they destroyed the monastery that Benedict of Nursia had founded on Monte Cassino while Italy was still under Gothic rule; the surviving monks fled to Rome. Large parts of the old Gothic kingdom thus lay outside the territory controlled by the emperor.[3]

The inferior status of Italy did not remain the only disappointment that Justinian's policy had in store for senators. In his effort to reconcile the hopelessly divided Christians of the East, the emperor issued an edict in 544 that condemned the doctrines ("chapters") of three deceased theologians who were especially offensive to opponents of the Council of Chalcedon—the so-called Three Chapters—and he asked all the patriarchs, including the pope, to support his decision. Pope Vigilius initially refused. After he was forcibly brought to Constantinople, however, he declared in 548 that he too was willing to condemn the Three Chapters. This about-face was received as the betrayal of the true faith by the vast majority of the bishops in North Africa and Italy; an African synod excommunicated Vigilius in 550. The major council that was held in Constantinople in 553, which today is counted as the Fifth Ecumenical Council, only exacerbated the division. Vigilius died in 555, before he could return to Rome; his successor, Pelagius (556–561), fought in vain to be recognized by the bishops of northern Italy. In 573, the bishop of Milan again resumed ecclesiastical communion with Rome, but the bishops of Aquileia long persisted in their alienation. Italy in 580 was fragmented not only politically, but also ecclesiastically.[4]

How had Cassiodorus experienced these events? It is hard to say because there is very little evidence about his life after he withdrew from politics. When he compiled the *Variae*, he still seems to have believed that the cooperation of Roman senators and Gothic kings had a future. Soon afterward, at the behest of his friends, as he says, he wrote a small treatise, *On the Soul*, which he added to the twelve books of the *Variae* as the thirteenth. While still in Ravenna, however, he conceived the idea of commentating on Psalms, a project that would occupy him for an entire decade, at least until 547. None of the secular offices and ranks that are mentioned in the title of the *Variae* appear in the title of this voluminous work. The author of the commentary on Psalms calls himself an "insignificant servant of God" (*exiguus servus dei*) who had converted (*conversus*) with the help of the Lord. In the preface to his book about orthography, Cassiodorus describes this commentary as the first work that he had undertaken at the time of his conversion. He then lists six more titles, his *Institutions of Divine and Secular Learning* in two books and a series of exegetical and grammatical works. He makes absolutely no mention, in contrast, of the numerous works he composed before his conversion, neither the *Variae* nor his *Gothic History*. At the end of his long life, Cassiodorus no longer attached any importance to these works.

We should be wary of the assumption that Cassiodorus renounced the world completely at a stroke in the year 538, even if that is how it may have seemed to the ninety-two-year-old in hindsight. Cassiodorus did not burn all his bridges to the world he had lived in after his conversion. Instead, he relocated to the imperial city on the Bosporus, probably after Vitigis' capitulation, where he maintained close ties to other senators who had sought refuge with Justinian and urged the emperor to prosecute the war vigorously. In addition to Liberius, the long-serving praetorian prefect of Gaul, these senators included Cethegus, who had held the consulship under Theoderic as a young man in 504 and had been the highest-ranking Western Roman senator in 545; Cassiodorus dedicated a brief account of his own family to him. The surviving excerpt, entitled *Ordo generis Cassiodororum*, covers Cassiodorus himself as well as Symmachus and his son-in-law Boethius. At that time, Cassiodorus still possessed a copy of his *Gothic History* for Jordanes to borrow.[5]

Cassiodorus was not impartial in the acrimonious dispute over the Three Chapters. With the help of his learned friend Epiphanius, he published a narrative church history that covered the period from Constantine the Great to Theodosius II (324–439). As he explains in the preface, it was a collection of excerpts culled from the three ecclesiastical histories written in Greek that Epiphanius had translated for him into Latin. For this reason, the compilation was called the *Historia tripartita*. This narrative form allowed Cassiodorus to incorporate hidden criticism of the emperor's religious policy. He celebrated Theodore of Mopsuestia, whom Justinian had condemned as one of the original authors of the Three Chapters, as a "teacher of the entire church" and a tireless adversary of heresies without taking full responsibility for these statements as author. In his commentary on Psalms, Cassiodorus praises Facundus of Hermiane, who had just composed a treatise in defense of the Three Chapters in Constantinople. Despite these reservations toward condemnation of the Three Chapters, Cassiodorus remained loyal to Pope Vigilius, to whom he dedicated his commentary on Psalms. Between Easter 549 and March 550, he and others, including Cethegus, attempted to convince two deacons of the Roman church, who had rejected the condemnation of the Three Chapters and renounced their allegiance to Vigilius, to submit to their supreme pastor—which they proved unable to do. Vigilius, in turn, describes Cassiodorus as *religiosus vir*—that is, as a layman who led an exemplarily Christian life.[6]

Cassiodorus was still firmly convinced of the value of a traditional education; of course, now he viewed it only as an indispensable aid for biblical exegesis. In his commentary on Psalms, Cassiodorus systematically applies the methods of ancient rhetoric, psalm by psalm, to the biblical text. Christian doctrine and ancient education appear in perfect harmony. Cassiodorus also potentially composed his *Institutions of Secular Learning* in Constantinople, which he later combined in revised form with his *Institutions of Divine Learning*.[7]

It is not transmitted when Cassiodorus returned to Italy. Perhaps he was still in Constantinople when Justinian exposed Vigilius in his absence at the council of 553, where he arranged to have texts read that proved the pope had promised to condemn the Three Chapters before the council had even begun. Although two abbots were in charge of his double monastery in Calabria, Cassiodorus enjoyed great authority, both as founder and on account of his learning. Cassiodorus devised a curriculum for his monks that encompassed both spiritual and secular "learning" (*litterae*) and set it down in a new version of his *Institutions*. In the preface, Cassiodorus looks back at the failed project of founding a kind of Christian university in Rome that he had conceived with Pope Agapetus (535–536). "Since my wish was impossible to fulfill on account of the raging wars and chaotic battles in the kingdom of Italy," he writes, Cassiodorus found himself forced to compose the *Institutions*, with the help of God, as a teacher (*magister*) to familiarize readers with a series of sacred texts and to impart a basic understanding of secular learning. In the first book, he gives reading recommendations in the form of a commented bibliography for each book of the Bible along with the available commentaries at the time, supplemented by some works of Christian historiography and contemporary theology, geography, medicine, and agronomy. Cassiodorus recommended that his monks read Palladius' treatise on agriculture, as well as the "chronicle" of Marcellinus, an author close to Justinian who depicts Theoderic as a cruel and faithless barbarian. The second book gives a brief introduction to the seven "liberal" arts: grammar, rhetoric, dialectic, arithmetic, music, geometry, and astronomy. These seven arts seemed indispensable to Cassiodorus for a full understanding of biblical texts. In this book, he refers several times to texts on mathematics and logic that the "*patricius* Boethius" had translated into Latin. He says not a word, however, about the *Consolation of Philosophy* either here or in his *Ordo*. Had it become too embarrassing for him that he had taken Boethius' place as *magister officiorum* after the latter had fallen out of favor?[8]

The ideal way of life for the aged Cassiodorus is that of a scholar who is both a reader and a scribe of holy texts. Such a scholar can comprehend their meaning in its entirety because he possesses the philological expertise to recognize false readings. By determining and writing down the correct wording, he helps spread the word of God; the scribe thus converges with the priest:

I confess my preference: of all the endeavors that can be accomplished by you with bodily labor, those of copyists, so long as they write accurately, not undeservedly please me perhaps the most because they [copyists] salvifically edify their minds by rereading the divine scriptures and disseminate the precepts of the Lord far and wide by copying them. A happy purpose, a laudable diligence to preach to men with one's hand, to open tongues with one's fingers, to grant salvation to mortals in silence, and to fight the illicit tricks of the devil with pen and ink![9]

The monastery Vivarium seems to have dissolved soon after Cassiodorus' death; Gregory the Great is the last author to mention it. Cassiodorus' library apparently was brought to Rome, where the generosity of the popes scattered it to the four winds. Only about half a dozen surviving manuscripts today can be connected more or less certainly to Vivarium. The so-called Codex Amiatinus is normally considered one of these; one of the oldest comprehensive texts of the Bible, it was written at St. Paul's monastery in Jarrow near Newcastle upon Tyne around the year 700. One of its magnificent illuminations depicts the Jewish priest Ezra reading and writing before an opened bookcase in which the books of the Bible, bound in nine codices, can be seen. It has been conjectured that the picture was inspired by Cassiodorus. That must remain speculation. What is certain is that the image reflects what mattered most to the elderly man who had once been Theoderic's "chancellor": study of the Christian Bible and its dissemination in unadulterated form.[10]

2. NO HEROES TO BE FOUND: THEODERIC IN THE TWENTY-FIRST CENTURY

All consideration of history presumes a point of view rooted in the present, and this "point of observation" can change over the course of someone's life. The perception and assessment of events changes as interests, norms, and orientations shift, as new experiences compel one to rethink events both witnessed personally and transmitted by others. This rule is true not only for Cassiodorus, but for ourselves, too, because every image of the past is influenced by one's perspective. The greater the distance from the persons and events of the past, the easier it becomes to recognize perspectivity. Modern historians, however, still took a very long time before they could escape the suggestive power of the letters that Cassiodorus composed in the service and largely also in the name of the Gothic kings; until well into the twentieth century, the depiction the royal central administration painted of itself was often taken at face value. As we look back at Theoderic and the Gothic kingdom in Italy from the twenty-first century, however, we should take advantage of the chance to free ourselves of this perspective. The goals that men like Theoderic and Cassiodorus considered worthwhile and the standards of their time are no longer our own. The questions that we ask ourselves are different from those that the royal chancellery sought to answer.

If we consider Theoderic from his origins, he first comes into view as the leader of a community of violence that had crisscrossed Western Europe in Attila's army before the Goths successfully freed themselves of Hunnic domination. Theoderic had proven himself as a warrior in his youth and, after his father's death in 474, assumed command of this warrior confederation, which depended on plunder, subsidies, and tribute to survive. Theoderic labored for almost a decade and a half in vain to win formal recognition from the emperor as leader of an allied warrior people. During this time, he led his people back and forth across the Balkans, and the number of his followers sometimes shrank dramatically. The death of his rival Theoderic Strabo enabled him to unite the vast majority of the Goths on the Balkan Peninsula under his leadership, but his Goths' material existence still remained precarious. Only after the conquest of Italy did Theoderic gain access to resources that enabled him to transform his vagabond warrior confederation into a standing army whose members could live off the rents they collected as landlords. He successfully persuaded the power brokers of this conquered land to cooperate by recognizing their privileges and conferring important tasks and offices on them. He made the state apparatus serve his purposes and, in this way, created a dual state in which the civil administration was run by Romans while the military was the Goths' business. He won over the bishops of the Catholic church by giving them the freedom that they needed to pursue their activities. Nonetheless, Theoderic always remained a Gothic king as ruler of Italy: the support of the men with whom he had defeated Odoacer in a four-year-long war was and always remained the fundamental basis of his power. Theoderic never completely cast off the warlord of his early years.

Theoderic's ruling concept must be understood as an answer to the urgent problems that he had to solve after the conquest of Italy. The king was confronted by the need to reward the army to which he owed his victory. He therefore furnished his warriors with landed estates so that they could live comfortably off the rent they collected. Since Theoderic defined this army as the Gothic people in arms, his warriors stood opposite the Romans as a military elite who cultivated a specific lifestyle and who were supposed to maintain their cultural distinctness. This policy amounted to integration through separation. At the same time, Theoderic recognized that he needed the support of the Roman elites if he hoped to take advantage of the resources that ruling a land like Italy offered. He therefore left the civil administration that he inherited essentially unchanged. This state apparatus brought him so great a steady income that he could pay his soldiers, finance the civil administration, adorn his residences with buildings, hold court magnificently, and generously reward his faithful servants.[11]

Theoderic's ruling concept was by its very nature conservative. Since Theoderic defined his army as the Gothic people in arms, he set in stone a division of labor between immigrants and natives that presumed that Goths and Romans would go separate ways. The cultural assimilation of the Goths to their Roman environment was not at all desirable, even if it was impossible to prevent in everyday life. The social fusion of Goths and Romans was simply incompatible with Theoderic's ruling concept. Theoderic did not at all intend to change, let alone "reform," the social conditions that he found in Italy; he wanted to make permanent the state of affairs he himself had created when he settled the Goths on the land.

In the first phase of his reign in Italy, Theoderic tried to protect his kingdom by entering into treaties and marriage alliances with other Germanic rulers. After he had consolidated power, he enlarged his kingdom by military means as opportunities arose. He sought to prevent war between the Visigoth Alaric and the Frank Clovis. When that failed, he seized the opportunity to annex Provence to his Italian kingdom. He soon also extended his rule to the Gothic kingdom in Hispania. Theoderic was at the peak of his power in the second decade of the sixth century. The succession also seemed to be secure when Emperor Justin held the consulship of the year 519 together with Theoderic's son-in-law Eutharic.

No other barbarian ruler of his time could point to successes comparable to Theoderic's. The Vandal Thrasamund tried in vain to halt the decline of royal power in his kingdom until his death in 523. The Frank Clovis waged war incessantly since 482 and ultimately brought most of Gaul under his control, but his kingdom was cut off from the Mediterranean and was divided among his four sons after his death in 511. The kings of the Burgundians, Thuringians, Heruli, and Lombards were no competition for Theoderic at all.

This success story is only one side of the coin. On the other side, there is the fact that the Gothic kingdom founded by Theoderic lasted only two generations. Theoderic was isolated internationally at the end of his life. After Eutharic's early death, the question of the succession was put off until a lethal sickness suddenly forced Theoderic's (or his court's) hand. Athalaric's reign was a temporary measure that met with resistance from the Gothic aristocracy. The double monarchy of Amalasuintha and Theodahad swiftly collapsed. Amalasuintha's murder gave Justinian the opportunity and justification to launch a war against the Gothic kingdom that ended seventeen years later (552) with the dissolution of the warrior confederation that Theoderic had brought to

Italy. This devastating war made a profound impact on Italy. The Roman senate lost the last of its significance; all trace of it vanishes in the early seventh century. Now there was no body that might have represented the political unity of Italy. When the Roman senate disappeared, so too did the idea that there might be a second political center of the Roman Empire besides Constantinople.[12]

Anyone who would hope to do justice to Theoderic must weigh his achievements against his aspirations and goals. The expansion and duration of his reign come into view first. In this regard, the elementary interest of every ruler to hold on to power coincided with the elementary interest of his subjects to live in peace. Theoderic's reign really gave the inhabitants of Italy a thirty-three-year span of largely uninterrupted peace. Until the beginning of the Gothic War, the people in the cities and countryside were, with rare exceptions, safe from enemy attack, siege, and plundering raids. There also were no rebellions or usurpations. This peaceful state of affairs was good for all inhabitants of Italy, as unequal as their opportunities, property, power, and prestige may have been. Those who experienced the horrors of the Gothic War may well have longed for Theoderic's reign in hindsight. It was in this light that Machiavelli saw Theoderic: to him, Theoderic was "an excellent man in war and peace" (*uomo nella guerra e nella pace eccellentissimo*) because, in an age of often violent upheaval, Theoderic had given Italy three decades of peace.[13]

This does not mean that Theoderic pursued a "policy of peace"; this would be true only if his actions had consistently been geared toward the creation and preservation of a stable, peaceful order in the western Mediterranean. But that applies at most only to the first half of his reign in Italy. The king indeed initially used peaceful means to protect his kingdom against external threats. During this phase, he established familial relationships with the Germanic kings of the post-Roman West through marriages. These alliances were supposed to prevent the emergence of powers that might turn on Theoderic's kingdom. Theoderic did not hesitate, however, to resort to military means when Clovis threatened to obtain access to Provence with his victory over Alaric (507). Theoderic's foreign policy was subsequently dictated by the effort to contain Frankish expansion in Gaul and to increase his own strength; that definitely included territorial expansion. Theoderic guaranteed his access to the Gothic kingdom in Hispania and then annexed it to his own. He later participated in the partitioning of the kingdom of the Burgundians. That notwithstanding, war ceased to be Theoderic's preferred means of maintaining and strengthening his power after he controlled the resources of Italy. Since his Goths received rent and donatives, he no longer needed to take the field with them at short intervals to seize plunder—that distinguished Theoderic from his brother-in-law Clovis, whom he urged to show moderation in victory, a political maxim that he had found valid from firsthand experience. Theoderic's ambitions and goals were not infinite; he did not aspire to universal dominance but rather recognized a plurality of equally legitimate powers. In this respect, his foreign policy was thus diametrically opposed to the ideology of *imperium sine fine* under the Roman Empire.[14]

In the nineteenth century, it was customary to ask whether a ruler was a "statesman." A "statesman" was something better than a mere "politician"; a "statesman" did not seek to preserve his personal power at all cost but rather served the common good by pursuing long-term goals. A scholar's assessment of someone to whom such goals were attributed depended on that scholar's opinion of those goals; if they were considered desirable, it remained to be determined whether they were also at least theoretically feasible, particularly if they had been achieved either not at all or only in part. If great value was attached to the goals, although they were never realized, nineteenth-century scholars typically called this failure "tragic." In Theoderic's case, the key question since the early nineteenth century was always how he intended to shape the relationship between the Goths and Romans. Did he strive to fuse the two peoples into one? Or did he plan to keep the Goths and Romans separate? Anyone who believed in German nationalism, in the superiority of the German *Volk*, or indeed of the Aryan race inevitably rejected such a fusion of peoples since it entailed that the Germanic minority would be subsumed in the Roman majority and so lose its distinctive identity.

From this vantage point, a policy that aimed for the assimilation of Goths and Romans inevitably seemed misconceived or, at best, no more than "romantic idealism" (as noted by Felix Dahn). Of course, it had been disputed for ages whether the king really hoped to bring about such a fusion. Ever since Edward Gibbon, scholars had repeatedly taken the view that Theoderic actually aspired to prevent any such fusion. Anyone who accepted this then had to wonder whether the separation of Goths and Romans was ever sustainable. Was it inevitable that the conquerors and conquered would ultimately grow together as one?

With that question in mind, scholars often compared (and still compare) Theoderic with Clovis; by converting to Catholicism, Clovis tore down the religious barrier between Franks and Romans, thereby enabling their social fusion. Theoderic, in contrast, always prevented this from happening in his own kingdom, or at least made it more difficult, by clinging to the Homoean faith. He thus pitted himself against the inevitable, against the "march of history." It then often is said that Clovis' decision was "forward thinking" because a modern observer knows, after all, that by the end of the sixth century the Catholic faith ultimately prevailed in every Christian kingdom of the western Mediterranean.

Of course, this development still lay far beyond Theoderic's horizon. Theoderic's brother-in-law Clovis undeniably sent a signal with his baptism at Reims. Religious discussions were held at the court of the Burgundian king Gundobad, and the presumptive heir to the throne, Sigismund, Theoderic's son-in-law, accepted the Catholic creed at an early date, but because the Visigoths and Vandals still adhered to the Homoean faith, they long remained exceptions.

To Theoderic, it was an imperative of political prudence not to propagate the Homoean faith of the Gothic minority among the Roman majority. The choice to keep the Homoean faith for himself and his Goths, however, was a feature of his ruling concept, which assigned different responsibilities and lifestyles to Goths and Romans. The ecclesiastical separation of Homoean Goths and Catholic Romans served to prevent the Goths in Italy from being subsumed by their Roman environment, while it simultaneously shielded them from the influence of Catholic bishops.

Theoderic treated the two Christian confessions as equal. A *de facto* state of affairs that can be called biconfessionality prevailed in Gothic Italy. The fact that the king admitted Christians who did not share his confession into his service and protected Jews from Christian persecution has gained him the appreciation of enlightened minds in every age; to both Jean Bodin and Voltaire, Theoderic was a king who permitted religious freedom and thus kept the peace between rival Christian confessions. In this respect Theoderic stands apart from Emperors Anastasius, Justin, and Justinian, who wore themselves out in the futile attempt to achieve unity among all Christians. Religious toleration is needed today more than ever. But that should not prevent us from asking whether Theoderic's tolerance was also potentially a sign of weakness. Christians of all confessions expected their ruler to defend the "true" faith. A policy that aimed to align society at large with one's own concept of Christianity, such as the policy pursued by Emperor Justinian, however, was beyond Theoderic's capabilities. Since he belonged to a religious minority, he lacked the resources to bend the largest and most influential religious community in his kingdom to his will.[15]

The social and cultural separation of Gothic warriors and Roman civilians could not survive forever; that is self-evident. The Gothic immigrants made up a fragment of the total population of Italy and were, moreover, scattered far and wide. Their linguistic and cultural isolation was hard to maintain in these conditions. Military and civil elites, notwithstanding all their differences in lifestyle and values, also tend in the long run to combine their stores of prestige, power, and wealth. The first steps toward this fusion had already been taken under Theoderic himself. How long Theoderic's ruling concept could have functioned if, for example, the Gothic kingdom had not been destroyed by war, is a much more difficult question to answer. In the Visigothic kingdom in Hispania, King Reccared converted in 587; the transition to Catholicism of king and nobility became official two years later at the third synod of Toledo. No fewer than six generations had passed since the Visigoths had settled in Aquitania in 418. After the synod of Toledo, the sacralization of the monarchy commenced, which in the seventh century would transform the Visigothic king into the earthly representative of Jesus Christ. At the same time, Reccared's conversion enabled him to give orders to the Catholic bishops in his kingdom. The king presided over the synod and set its agenda. Vice versa, he issued anti-Jewish laws that the assembled bishops had promoted. Such close cooperation between the monarchy and the Catholic episcopacy was unthinkable in Theoderic's kingdom.[16]

The question of whether the policy of separating Goths and Romans diluted the military strength of the Gothic kingdom in Italy and to that extent contributed to its early demise, as has been claimed again and again, is an entirely different matter. Undeniably, the fight against Justinian's soldiers was spearheaded by Gothic warriors, even though Totila accepted Roman volunteers in his army after 542, whereas many senators took the emperor's side if circumstances permitted. The separation of civilians and soldiers, however, was no less strict in the Byzantine Empire than in Italy. Anastasius and Justinian likewise did not recruit civilians but instead hired military specialists from outside the empire. The duration and ferocity of the Gothic resistance, incidentally, also militates against the assumption that the Gothic cause was lost from the outset. At times, Totila pushed the emperor's soldiers to the brink of defeat. The Gothic kingdom in Italy apparently stood on a far firmer foundation than the Vandal kingdom in North Africa, which Belisarius was able to capture for the emperor after only two years of warfare.

Theoderic's kingdom was not invincible, though. The Gothic-Roman compromise had not been agreed for eternity but rather required constant renewal. By its very nature, the relationship between the Gothic warriors and Roman civilians was tense. The Gothic aristocracy craved honor and glory. The senators watched jealously over their privileges. The religious equality of the Homoeans was a thorn in the eye of the Catholic bishops. At the end of his life, Theoderic himself helped undermine the trust the senate and Catholic clergy had placed in him. The execution of Boethius and Symmachus was a warning shot; the death of the humiliated Pope John gave the king a reputation as a persecutor. But the reasons for the rapid fall of his kingdom must be sought in places that were largely beyond his influence. The premature death of Eutharic undid at a stroke all Theoderic's plans for the succession. It is easy to accuse

Theoderic of allowing the uncertainty that this caused to linger until his own death, but who among us knows when our final hour has come?

The regency of Amalasuintha weakened the monarchy and thus crippled the foreign policy of the kingdom. It proved fatal to the Goths in Italy that this weakness coincided with the very moment when Justinian was looking for opportunities to subjugate the Germanic kingdoms that had emerged on the former territory of the Western Roman Empire. After the Goths in Hispania split away (526), the remnants of the kingdom of the Burgundians were vanquished by the Franks (532), and the Vandal kingdom was conquered by Belisarius (535), the only allies the Goths in Italy could turn to against Justinian were the Franks. But the Merovingians were resolved not to tie their hands for anyone's sake. The Goths were thus forced to rely on no one but themselves in the fight against Justinian.

The Gothic kingdom in Italy was demographically, economically, and militarily outmatched by the Byzantine Empire. We thus can certainly point to structural reasons for its defeat. But we should be wary of regarding defeat as inevitable for those reasons. Military success in the sixth century was determined to a much higher extent by contingent factors, by the "fortune of battle" and other imponderables, than in the age of mechanized warfare and weapons of mass destruction. The Battle of Tadinae (552) could have ended differently, and no one can say whether Justinian would have sent another army of so great a size to Italy.

For a long time, Theoderic was viewed as a heroic, restrained, and just king. History and myth converged in this image. Even Wilhelm Ensslin still believed he could perceive a "spiritual kinship between the historical Theoderic and the Dietrich envisioned by the poets." Such heroic romanticization is a thing of the past today. It is hard to feel sympathetic toward a ruler who was celebrated for slaying his enemies with his own hand. This is exacerbated by the fact that Theoderic the man, the son and brother, the husband and father, is elusive. Only as a ruler did he leave clear traces behind.[17]

The best starting point for assessing Theoderic's historical significance is the question of what effect he had, whether directly or indirectly, intentionally or unintentionally, in his lifetime or after his death. Theoderic held on to power for half a century. His actions influenced large parts of Europe; in this respect, he towered over the other kings of the post-Roman West, although he fell short of the late antique Roman emperors. Until 488, the king operated in southeastern Europe between Lake Balaton and the Bosporus. Later, he resided virtually exclusively in northern Italy, but his generals and governors acted in an area that stretched from the Iberian Peninsula to Serbia. His diplomatic contacts extended far beyond this area, to the coasts of the Baltic Sea and Scandinavia in the north, to Tunisia in the south, and to the Bosporus and possibly even to the Crimea in the east. Byzantine authors and Syrian chroniclers in the Roman East told of the Goth Theoderic, whom they considered to be a son of Valamir. The Iranian empire of the Sassanids and the Christian kingdom of Ethiopia, in contrast, lay outside Theoderic's world.[18]

Theoderic had a major impact on the development of the post-Roman West for two generations; therein lies his historical significance. He does not, however, belong among the ranks of those whose actions reverberated for whole centuries. His kingdom in Italy was short-lived. He also did not found a political tradition that might have long survived his death. His family quickly died out; Gothic identity did not survive in Italy but rather in the Hispanic kingdom of the Visigoths. Theoderic thus does not measure up to Constantine the Great, the first Christian emperor, or Charlemagne, who revived the Christian imperial monarchy in the West. He also did not go down in history as a legislator like Emperor Justinian, whose *Corpus iuris civilis*, the great codification of Roman law, remained influential until well into the early modern period. The civilian elites of Theoderic's kingdom cultivated the literary legacy of Rome; they wrote letters, speeches, and poems in classical style, the biographies of holy men, theological treatises, and historical chronicles. Cassiodorus composed a *Gothic History*; Symmachus, a *Roman History*. Only the *Consolation of Philosophy* by Boethius attained the status of a classic in the Latin Middle Ages and holds it still today—a book by a man whom Theoderic put to death. Theoderic's afterlife was nonetheless impressive. Until well into the sixteenth century, everywhere where Germanic languages were spoken, tales were told of a king named Dietrich who had once ruled in Italy; this figure of legend, however, had almost nothing in common with the Gothic king beyond his name. In the nineteenth century, Dietrich enjoyed a revival: in addition to ephemeral ballads, epics, and dramas based on the Dietrich saga, historical novels were also dedicated to Theoderic in Italy. It is through this literary medium that Theoderic remains internationally present even today. In 1993, the American author Gary Jennings (1928–1999) put the amoral protagonist of his novel *Raptor* in the world of the Gothic king; a new English translation of Felix Dahn's novel about the demise of the Gothic kingdom in Italy (*Ein Kampf um Rom*; *A Struggle for Rome*) from the year 1876 appeared in 2005.[19]

To an observer in the twenty-first century, the Gothic kingdom in Italy seems at first remote and alien. It undoubtedly is part of the transitional period that modern scholars call Late Antiquity or the transformation of the Roman world; for Italy, the Gothic War marked the beginning of the period that has been called the Middle Ages since the Renaissance. On closer inspection, though, many of the problems that Theoderic and his successors faced prove to be disturbingly relevant. The society of late Roman Italy was neither archaic and backward nor simple and static; instead, it was characterized by a high degree of social inequality and great cultural, religious, and ethnic diversity. This sophisticated society had a high potential for conflict, which was exacerbated by the privileging of a minority of non-native warriors. Old truths—like the Western Roman imperial monarchy—had been shattered. Christian communities that claimed to be the only true orthodox church of Christ were forced to coexist on equal terms with other Christians. The senatorial elite felt as if the political order and cultural tradition with which it identified was threatened and was always aware of the distance that separated the crisis-ridden present from the glorious past. It is no coincidence that the pair of opposites "ancient" and "modern" appeared at precisely this time.[20]

In this way, the Gothic kingdom in Italy takes on exemplary significance. How could the leader of an armed minority establish stable rule over the vast majority of the population for more than three decades? Integration through separation and biconfessionality are no longer acceptable political concepts for us, but they represent responses to phenomena and problems that have not disappeared—to mobility and migration, social inequality and cultural diversity. From a contemporary global perspective, the question of how the ability and willingness to use force promotes the formation and cohesion of social groups remains highly relevant today, much as we may regret it.

3. DESCENT INTO HELL AND *DIE RABENSCHLACHT*: THEODERIC IN THE MIDDLE AGES

Theoderic and the Gothic kingdom in Italy were never completely forgotten in Western Europe. The tradition soon split into two branches, though. One was based on texts in Latin and was preserved by people who were proficient in this language—normally clergymen. Boethius' *Consolation of Philosophy* and the *Dialogues* of Gregory the Great enjoyed the greatest popularity. Boethius had depicted the Gothic king as a tyrant. In Gregory, one could read how he had suffered due punishment for the outrages he had perpetrated: his innocent victims, Pope John and the patrician Symmachus, threw him into a volcano. This "descent into hell" was received by almost every historiographical account of the Middle Ages and shaped the image of the "heretic king" Theoderic. We only sporadically can detect a lay reception independent of the ecclesiastical version. Charlemagne seems to have had a different picture of Theoderic because he had a statue of the king brought from Ravenna to Aachen. This statue prompted the learned monk Walahfrid Strabo to compose a polemic against Theoderic, titled *De imagine Tetrici* (On the image of Tetricus), under Charlemagne's successor Louis the Pious (814–840). According to him, Theoderic was a vain, greedy ruler, a blasphemer, and a persecutor.[21]

Memory of Theoderic survived in some places of Italy out of local interest. In 830, Agnellus, a priest in Ravenna, included some accounts about Theoderic that may derive from local tradition in his book about the bishops of the city. In the early twelfth century, a historical compilation, the so-called *Chronica Theodericiana*, was pieced together at the monastery of Mons Olivetus (Mount of Olives) near Verona from the *Anonymus Valesianus* and the *Gothic History* of Jordanes. The manuscript includes an illustration of single combat between Theoderic and Odoacer, who are depicted in contemporary arms. In the early fourteenth century, Giovanni de Matociis, a Veronese cleric and humanist, included Theoderic in his *Historiae imperiales*, a series of imperial biographies beginning with Augustus; he embroidered the account of the *Anonymus Valesianus* with local tradition.[22]

Parallel to the Latin tradition in literate circles, an oral tradition developed in the Germanic linguistic area, the so-called Dietrich Saga, which told the tale of a homeless king named Dietrich. This Dietrich, who lived in the distant past, sought refuge at the court of the king of the Huns, "Etzel" (Attila), after he was driven out of his kingdom in northern Italy. Dietrich's kingdom was centered on the city of "Bern"—a phonetic variant of Verona. This "Dietrich von Bern" attempts to win back his kingdom with Etzel's help. In the process, he fights a battle that was placed at "Raben" (that is, Ravenna), the *Rabenschlacht* ("Battle of Raben/Ravenna"). But that detail already exhausts the shared feature of all these tales. Not even Dietrich's adversary always bears the same name: while he is still called "Otraches" (Odoacer) at an early stage of the tradition, like the king whom the historical Theoderic defeated and killed, he bears the name "Ermenrich" or "Ermrich" (i.e., Ermanaric) in later stages, like the Gothic king whose death Jordanes placed around the year 375. The Dietrich Saga thus transformed Theoderic, the conqueror of Italy, into a king who was driven out of his kingdom in Italy and connects this king with historical figures who had long been dead when Theoderic defeated Odoacer.

How the historical Theoderic transformed into the Dietrich of legend is an unsolved and probably unsolvable mystery. We first find the Dietrich Saga in a coherent form in texts of the thirteenth century. Only a Norwegian prose text of the mid-thirteenth century, the *Thridrekssaga*, which was based on Low German sources, contains a complete biography of Dietrich. This book recounts the life of Dietrich (called "Thridrek" in this work) from his youth until his death, and in this book he actually returns to his kingdom after several tries. There are, of course, indications that there were tales of an exiled King Dietrich much, much earlier than that. The Old High German *Hildebrandslied* from circa 830, of which only sixty-eight alliterative verses survive, seems to presume such tales, as also does the contemporary Old English poem *The Lament of Deor*. Theoderic also appears to have been known in Scandinavia at this time because the famous Rök runestone (in southern Sweden), which also dates to the early ninth century, also mentions a Theoderic, who sits on a "Gothic steed" and is called the "hero of the Märinge." But even these relatively early witnesses were created a full three hundred years after Theoderic's death in Ravenna.[23]

Several epics in Middle High German transmitted from the thirteenth century are collectively known among modern scholars as the "historical Dietrich epics" because their material is taken from the Dietrich Saga sketched above. The longest epic is *Dietrichs Flucht* ("Dietrich's flight") in over ten thousand lines of rhyming couplets. Its theme is ill-fated victory, which takes various shapes in different versions: again and again, Dietrich must go into exile among the Huns despite the fact that he always defeats Ermenrich because the latter never fails to draw some strategic advantage from military defeat with a trick. The subject of the *Rabenschlacht* (in over 1,100 six-verse strophes) likewise is an unsuccessful attempt at reconquest; in this case, Dietrich cannot take advantage of his victory because the sons of Etzel and his own brother Diether are killed by the traitor Witege. Whereas these epics were soon forgotten, the *Nibelungenlied*, as adapted by the poet and Germanist Karl Simrock (1802–1876), became part of the literary canon of the German bourgeoisie in the early nineteenth century. Even today, the *Nibelungenlied* is still well known outside narrower scholarly circles. The exile situation is also presumed in the *Nibelungenlied*: Dietrich is at Etzel's court, warns the Burgundians in vain of Kriemhild's wrath, but does not intervene in the gory battle with the Huns until Hildebrand informs him of the death of all his retainers. Dietrich then defeats the Burgundians Gunter and Hagen, surrenders them to Kriemhild, and begs for their life. When Kriemhild has Gunter executed and personally beheads Hagen, Dietrich is left behind, stunned and weeping, with a handful of survivors.

In addition to these "historical" Dietrich epics, another narrative tradition blossomed in the late Middle Ages in which Dietrich is made to undertake all kinds of adventures (*Aventiuren*) against the most diverse opponents, who are usually endowed with supernatural powers. Modern scholars usually label these poems "adventuresome Dietrich epics" (*aventiurhafte Dietrichepik*). This hero has nothing but his name in common with the historical Theoderic.[24]

The Dietrich of the vernacular tradition is a wandering, fighting, and patient hero who commands respect and deserves sympathy. In this tradition, the king has cast off all ethnic and family ties and thus is also never called a Goth. Dietrich von Bern was perceived as a figure of the distant past whom no one either could or would assign to a specific people. In the Middle Ages, Dietrich von Bern was everywhere stories were told in a Germanic language; he was an exemplary figure, but he also was no longer a Goth.[25]

The fame of Dietrich von Bern began to wane by the late sixteenth century. He was still very well known during the Reformation; Martin Luther mentions him repeatedly. Emperor Maximilian I (1483–1519) included Theoderic in the gallery of bronze statues that were erected by his tomb in the court church of Innsbruck three decades after his death.[26] Designed by Albrecht Dürer and cast in Nuremberg by Peter Vischer the Elder in 1513, the statue depicts Theoderic as a bearded knight in mail and helmet with an open visor; the inscription on the base calls him "Teodorick König der Goott" (Theoderic, king of the Goths). Surrounded by twenty-seven other statues, it is part of a dynastic representational program that paints the Habsburg Maximilian as the descendant and heir of Christian princes and kings from across Europe.

4. THE KING AND HIS "CHANCELLOR": THEODERIC BETWEEN HUMANISM AND THE ENLIGHTENMENT

The first printed edition of Cassiodorus' *Variae* appeared in Rome in 1529; it contained only excerpts arranged by subject, a kind of prince's mirror intended for Henry VIII of England (1509–1547), to whom the book is dedicated. The humanist and theologian Johannes Cochlaeus, one of Martin Luther's bitterest adversaries, assumed responsibility as editor. Fifteen years later, Cochlaeus, now a canon at Breslau (Wrocław) cathedral, published the first modern biography of Theoderic under the title *Vita Theoderici*. In nineteen chapters, citing Cassiodorus, Cochlaeus paints a highly flattering picture of the king, whose deserved fame was tarnished only by his conduct toward Pope John I and the patricians Boethius and Symmachus. This *Vita Theoderici* was not widely circulated and remained the only book dedicated to Theoderic for one and a half centuries. Swedish scholars explained their ethnic superiority with reference to Gothic ancestors who had conquered half of Europe after setting out from Scandinavia, and Gustavus Adolphus of Sweden (1611–1632) entered into the Thirty Years' War with the intention of renewing the glory of the old Goths, but this "Gothicism" generated little interest in Theoderic, who had been born in Hungary and died in Italy. Still, in 1699, the Swedish scholar Johannes

Peringskiöld (1654–1720) published a second edition of Cochlaeus' *Vita Theoderici* with additional material.[27]

The Counter-Reformation gave the first impetus for critical engagement with the sources for the Gothic kingdom in Italy. The Maurists, learned Benedictines from the Congregation of St. Maur, wanted to separate what was authentic from what was spurious in order to defend the authority of the Catholic tradition against Protestant criticism. They turned to the life and work of Cassiodorus and so inevitably were led to Theoderic. In Rouen in 1679, the Maurist Jean Garet (1627–1694) published an edition of all known works of Cassiodorus at the time and included a brief *Vita Cassiodori*. Garet dedicated this edition, which remained in use until the end of the nineteenth century, to the then chancellor of Louis XIV, Michel Le Tellier, whom he compared to Cassiodorus. Some fifteen years later, the Maurist Denis de Sainte-Marthe (1650–1725), librarian of the abbey of Saint-Germain-des-Prés in Paris, published a detailed biography of Cassiodorus in French (*La vie de Cassiodore, chancelier et premier ministre de Théodoric le Grand*). Sainte-Marthe dedicated this book to Louis Boucherat, who had succeeded Le Tellier as chancellor. Sainte-Marthe made the parallel between Cassiodorus and the dedicatee complete by conferring on Theoderic the epithet "le Grand," which the French king had long borne in his kingdom: Théodoric le Grand thus took his place alongside Louis le Grand. Sainte-Marthe covered far more than merely Cassiodorus' activity as Theoderic's chancellor, however; he gave the first continuous narrative of the Gothic kingdom in Italy, laying a foundation on which later treatments could build.[28]

Edward Gibbon would not have been able to write his *History of the Decline and Fall of the Roman Empire* if the Maurists (and Jansenists) had not provided him the resources to write his grand narrative. Theoderic's particular merit in Gibbon's view was that he gave Italy three decades of peace: "the rare and meritorious example of a Barbarian, who sheathed the sword in the pride of victory and the vigour of his age" (538). Gibbon also applauded Theoderic's religious attitude: without abandoning the faith of his forefathers, the king viewed himself as the "guardian of the public worship" and "nourished in his mind the salutary indifference of a statesman or philosopher" (546). Nonetheless, Gibbon conceded, the king was neither a legislator nor a reformer; he instead had merely copied the seriously defective political system that Constantine and his successors had created. Theoderic's policy in Gibbon's mind was based on the principle of separation. The king had reserved different tasks for Goths and Romans: the arts of war for the one, those of peace for the other. The alliance of two peoples based on this division of responsibilities was rife with conflict and could not last because the Roman majority never accepted the ancestry and heterodoxy of the Gothic conquerors. Precisely Theoderic's tolerance roused the ire of the Catholic Romans, Gibbon continued. At the end of his life, the king was on the verge of persecuting Catholics, and he had, moreover, condemned men to death unjustly.[29]

Gibbon's assessment of Theoderic is oriented according to the political maxims of the Enlightenment; Theoderic's supposed Germanic ethnicity, in contrast, hardly figures at all. Gibbon likewise did not conceive of Theoderic's kingdom as a foreshadowing of an Italian nation-state. To Gibbon, Theoderic was a barbarian king who deserved recognition for ensuring peace and granting his subjects religious freedom. Theoderic had nonetheless neglected to reform the late Roman state, and he could not overcome the resistance of his conquered subjects. Gibbon therefore did not think to confer on Theoderic the predicate "the Great."

5. THEODERIC IN ITALY: EUROPEAN HISTORIOGRAPHY OF THE NINETEENTH CENTURY

In the year 1808, the Institut de France in Paris offered a prize to anyone who could answer the following questions: "What was the civil and political status of the peoples of Italy under Gothic rule? What were the fundamental principles of the legislation of Theoderic and his successors? And, in particular, what distinctions did it establish between the victors and the vanquished?" The immediate relevance of the subject was obvious to contemporaries. In the year 1808, Napoleon's stepson, Eugène de Beauharnais, was viceroy of Italy. At that time, Napoleon's law code, the *Code civil*, was being introduced in the kingdom of Italy and many other European states. What relationship one should establish between conquerors and the conquered was thus a practical political question across Europe. No fewer than six works were submitted in response; two of them were ultimately distinguished in 1810. First prize was awarded to the study by the professor of history at Göttingen Georg Sartorius (1765–1828), *Essai sur l'état civil et politique des peuples d'Italie, sous le gouvernement des Goths* ("Essay on the civil and political state of the peoples of Italy under the government of the Goths"), which appeared in German translation a year later (*Versuch über die Regierung der Ostgothen*). Second prize went to Joseph Naudet (1786–1878), then a teacher at the Lycée Napoléon in Paris; he would later become professor of Latin poetry at the Collège de France and serve from 1830 to 1840 as inspector general of the public education system. Naudet's study, *Histoire de l'établissement, des progrès et de la décadence de la monarchie des Goths en Italie* ("History of the founding, progress, and decline of the monarchy of the Goths in Italy"), was also published in 1811.[30]

Sartorius delivered a very favorable verdict on Gothic rule in Italy, which in no way changed the public or private legal status of the "peoples of Italy." The "difference between the victors and vanquished," in his view, consisted "primarily in that the Goths alone were entrusted with the defense of the country and military service, of which the Romans appeared to be utterly incapable" (240). Theoderic had guaranteed peace abroad and let law and justice prevail at home. Sartorius attributed the failure of the Gothic kingdom to the "pride" of the Romans in Italy: "Had the Romans united with the Goths, had they fused together and a new people, as happened for example in Gaul, grown out of this union, had they wished to become Italians rather than always Romans, how many tears they might have spared their descendants!" (242, German edition).

Naudet judged Theoderic much more harshly than Sartorius did. He conceded that the king had restored law and order to Italy and protected the country against "the other barbarians"; he also had promoted the arts and sciences. Naudet criticized Theoderic, however, for failing to fuse the Goths and Romans into one people. He should have sent the Goths to Roman schools and allowed Romans to perform military service; above all, though, he should have eliminated the religions antagonism between Goths and Romans and converted to Catholicism. On account of these failures, only Theoderic's own person had held the two peoples together. By the time of his death, Gothic rule had become so hated that the Romans took the side of the first conqueror to come their way.[31]

The *Geschichte des Ost-Gothischen Reichs in Italien* (*History of the Ostrogothic Kingdom in Italy*) by Johann Kaspar Friedrich Manso (1759–1826), published in 1824, also belongs in this series. Manso, the long-serving rector of the Protestant Maria-Magdalenen-Gymnasium in Breslau (Wrocław) had already come to prominence with a variety of studies, chiefly on ancient history. His work is superior to Sartorius' treatment in terms of its philological rigor but is intellectually less penetrating. Right at the outset of his book, Manso concedes that the Ostrogoths did not make a lasting impact. He calls them "a transplant people that, having been sent out or having emigrated, settles in foreign soil in isolation, limits the movements of the native-born as need dictates or advantage advises, and, without ever becoming native itself, vanishes again without a trace" (1). Nonetheless, this "fleetingly ephemeral phenomenon" was worthy of study because it "was lacking neither in appealing diversity nor instructive significance" (1–2). In Manso's view, the exemplary significance of the subject derived from the lesson that "in governing states, some things may depend on luck and other things obey the tendency of the masses, but the most always falls to the personality of the individual, the man who directs the whole" (2–3). Theoderic, Manso argued, surpassed all other conquerors of his day in insight and mildness.

As long as he lived, Ostrogothic rule in Italy had rested on a strong foundation; under his weak successors, however, the kingdom quickly collapsed. Although Manso emphasized Theoderic's decisive energy and calls him "the Great" for that reason, he was not uncritical of the king's policies. Indeed, he reproaches the king for his contentment to "provide his people, whom one may rightly view as an immigrant colony of warriors, secure dwellings and a comfortable life" (170–171). The king had failed "to employ an expedient constitution to bring the Goths closer to the Romans and the Romans closer to the Goths, to ennoble the former and to strengthen the latter, above all, however, to effect that both should come to love Italy as their common Fatherland and the Goths should not view themselves as commanding guardians, the Romans as pardoned wards" (171).

Manso had no compunction about calling the Goths German. His book is nonetheless free of nationalistic emphasis. Manso's ideal was a Gothic-Roman symbiosis in Italy. This attitude would slowly but profoundly change in German-speaking lands in the aftermath of Napoleonic rule. The Valhalla monument in Donaustauf near Regensburg marks the turning of the tide. The Bavarian crown prince Ludwig had conceived of this "temple of honor of the Fatherland for gloriously distinguished Germans" already in 1807, when Napoleon's power in Europe seemed unshakable. Construction did not begin until 1827, however, after Ludwig became king of Bavaria in 1825. When it was opened on October 18, 1844, Valhalla housed ninety-six busts and sixty-four plaques bearing inscriptions for those whose likenesses were not known. The royal sponsor personally explained the selected heroes in an accompanying book titled *Walhalla's Genossen* (*Valhalla's Fellows*, 1842). The series begins with Arminius of the Cherusci, also known as Hermann, whom Ludwig calls "the vanquisher of the Romans," and extends down to Johann Wolfgang Goethe, thus very close to Ludwig's own time. A frieze encircling the interior below the ceiling portrays primitive Germanic history in pre-Christian times. In this series of German forebears, "Theoderic the Great, King of the Ostrogoths" follows immediately after "Clovis, King of the Franks." Theoderic is distinguished with the epithet "the Great," in contrast to Clovis, and is thereby elevated above him and all the other rulers of "German prehistory." Whereas Clovis is said to have been "distinguished gloriously as a general, but otherwise far more for ill than for good," Theoderic is described as "a great and, with few exceptions, mild ruler." "The Great" became Theoderic's conventional epithet in German-speaking lands in the latter half of the nineteenth century. When the Prussian historian Otto Hintze (1860–1940) surveyed the known bearers of this epithet in a confidential memorandum for the planned conferral of the epithet "the Great" ("der Große") on Kaiser Wilhelm I, he presumed without question that Theoderic, as "head of the Germanic tribes alongside the Roman emperor," belonged in this series. Theoderic's greatness was also beyond question for the Catholic church historian Georg Pfeilschifter (1870–1936), who published a biography of Theoderic in 1910, *Theoderich der Große*. The king deliberately isolated the Goths from the Romans, he argued, because miscegenation would have led to the demise of the Goths as a people. Theoderic could not have wanted that "because he had a strong Gothic identity and thought in terms of Gothic nationalism" (37). Realizing the weakness that resulted from this policy, he tried "to assemble the fraternal Germanic tribes into a powerful system of alliances" (97). He deserved the epithet "the Great" even more so, however, because he "understood how to create lasting cultural values" (98). With sporadic exceptions, however, Theoderic's epithet "the Great" did not catch on outside Germany. In Anglo-American countries and in Italy and France, people spoke and still normally speak of Theoderic the (Ostro-)Goth when they want to differentiate him from his Visigothic and Frankish namesakes.[32]

The rising importance of national considerations in the study of the past was not a German but a pan-European phenomenon. In northern Italy, the liberal bourgeoisie yearned for independence from Austria, the dissolution of the Papal State, and the unification of all Italians in one state. The search for historical precursors of a unified Italy showed the age of Theoderic and his successors, which had hitherto been regarded as a dark period of foreign rule, in a new light. The fall of the Gothic kingdom, after all, marked the beginning of the division that they aspired to overcome in the present day. Shortly before the failed revolution of 1848, the librarian Paolo Pavirani (1804–1855) of Ravenna defended Theoderic and his successors against the accusation that they were responsible for the demise of ancient culture in a two-volume *Storia del regno dei Goti in Italia* (*History of the Kingdom of the Goths in Italy*). Two years earlier in France, the Marquis Du Roure (1783–1858), then a delegate of the French National Assembly, had published a two-volume *Histoire de Théodoric le Grand, roi d'Italie* (*History of Theoderic the Great, King of Italy*, 1846) to show that the fall of the Gothic kingdom was not a necessary consequence of the king's political conception. He had worked toward the fusion of Goths and Romans, Du Roure argued, but could not overcome the short-sighted resistance of the Catholic bishops and part of the senate. Men like Cassiodorus, in Du Roure's eyes, were pioneers of Italian political independence.[33]

The works of Du Roure and Pavirani fell far short of the standards that began to be expected of scholarly historiographical studies in this period and were quickly forgotten. The light in which they put the Gothic kingdom in Italy, however, is definitely representative. Sympathy for the ideas of the Risorgimento also influenced two of the most significant historical works that were produced in the nineteenth century: the *Geschichte der Stadt Rom im Mittelalter* (*History of the City of Rome in the Middle Ages*), by the liberal East Prussian Ferdinand Gregorovius (1821–1891), which was written in Rome and immediately translated into Italian, and the likewise eight-volume history of late antique and early medieval Italy that the English banker and Quaker Thomas Hodgkin (1831–1913) published from 1880 to 1899 under the title *Italy and Her Invaders*. Both Gregorovius and Hodgkin were independent scholars who never held an academic position.

Gregorovius viewed Theoderic and his kingdom from the perspective of their contribution to the rise of European culture. Gregorovius interpreted this culture as a synthesis of Germanic and Romance elements: "In the heroic figure of Theoderic appears the first attempt of the Germani [Germanen] to erect on the rubble of the [Roman] Empire that new world order that gradually had to emerge from the acquaintance of Nordic barbarians with Roman culture and nationality" (324–325). Gregorovius attributed to Theoderic the plan "to unify all Germanic and Latin peoples in a feudal kingdom like an emperor." This "bold plan," however, ultimately failed because it lacked the support of the Catholic Church on account of confessional animosities; "the West [Abendland]," moreover, could not yet free itself of "Byzantine imperial power" (325). In Gregorovius' view, Italy's transition from Antiquity to the Middle Ages fell in the period of Gothic rule: "The Goths stand on the border of both ages; their undying glory in history is this: that they were defenders of the ancient culture of Europe in the final hours of the Roman world" (455–456). Gregorovius also stressed, however, that the fall of the Gothic kingdom had destroyed the "national unity" of Italy. He cited the small number of Goths and the conflict with the "nationality and religion of the Latins" as reasons for its failure.

Gregorovius called the Goths an "unadulterated primitive people" that was "teachable, mild, and manly" (456), but his assessment of Theoderic and his kingdom derived from a liberal commitment to the idea of Europe (albeit excluding the Slavs). To Gregorovius, Theoderic was above all the precursor of Charlemagne; Theoderic's greatness consisted in his preservation of ancient culture and his alleged plan to unify the Germanic and Romance peoples. This perspective resembles the view that Leopold von Ranke (1795–1886) took more than twenty years later in his unfinished *Weltgeschichte* (*World History*), with the difference, however, that Ranke rated Theoderic's contribution to the rise of Europe much lower than that of Charlemagne. Ranke thus belongs to the very rare historians of the German Empire who declined to confer the epithet "the Great" on Theoderic.[34]

Like Gregorovius, Hodgkin's magnum opus was also inspired by the experience of Italy prior to unification in the year 1870. A few years after he discussed the Gothic kingdom in Italy in the third volume of *Italy and Her Invaders* (1885), he published a stand-alone biography of Theoderic under the title *Theodoric the Goth: The Barbarian Champion of Civilisation* (1891). In the preface, he reports that the thought of the Italy unified under Theoderic's rule had kept alive the hope that the country could again achieve national unity, strength, and prosperity in the present after the failed revolution of 1848. The Gothic kingdom in Italy was thus, in Hodgkin's view, a missed opportunity, "one of the great 'Might-have-beens' of History" (vii). Theoderic recognized, he wrote, what Europe and especially Italy needed at that time: the preservation of an order based on law and justice in an age of social revolution. This plan deserved respect, even though the time was not yet ripe to execute it. Had Theoderic's efforts been crowned with success, Hodgkin argued, Europe would have been spared three centuries of barbarism and misery. Hodgkin praised Theoderic as a "Teutonic warrior" who had transformed into a wise and statesmanlike ruler of Italy who made "the welfare of every class of his subjects the end of all his endeavours" (127); such a "marvellous transformation" was very rare in history, the only exceptions being Augustus and Bismarck. Theoderic ruled Italy justly, strove for the welfare of every class, and labored with almost religious devotion and love on behalf of "civilisation," order, good morals, and education. He encouraged trade and manufacturing, promoted agriculture, and rebuilt cities. The execution of Boethius and Symmachus were the only blemishes Hodgkin found in a glorious reign. No one since Ennodius had praised Theoderic's reign in Italy as enthusiastically as Hodgkin. In his view, the fall of Theoderic's kingdom could be explained only as a contingent result of an outside event, the Byzantine invasion.[35]

6. FROM "KING OF THE GERMANIC PEOPLE" TO "TRAILBLAZER OF THE WEST": THEODERIC IN GERMANY FROM THE EMPIRE TO THE AFTERMATH OF THE THIRD REICH

The turn toward a racialized study of the Goths in German-speaking lands is inseparably tied to the name Felix Dahn (1834–1912). His novel, *Ein Kampf um Rom* (*A Struggle for Rome*), which appeared in 1876, a few years after the founding of the German Empire in 1871, was reprinted no fewer than 180 times by 1924, leaving a lasting mark on the image of Gothic history in German-speaking lands. *Ein Kampf um Rom* was also translated into English and in 1968 appeared first in German and then in American cinemas in a film adaptation directed by

Robert Siodmak. The book is still available in the German book trade today; a new English translation appeared in 2005. Dahn composed numerous other novels, dramas, and poems in addition to *Ein Kampf um Rom*, most of which are set in the age of the barbarian migrations. Dahn's primary occupation, however, was as professor of law, first in Würzburg, then in Königsberg (Kaliningrad), and last in Breslau (Wrocław). He had specialized in the legal and constitutional history of the Germanic kingdoms already as a young scholar. In 1909, three years before his death, he published the eleventh and final volume of his scholarly magnum opus, *Die Könige der Germanen* (*The Kings of the Germani*), on which he had labored for half a century; the first two volumes had appeared in 1861. Although the title might give one the impression that the work revolved around personalities, that is not true; Dahn had in fact written a history of political and legal institutions.

Dahn covered the Ostrogoths in the second and third volumes, which appeared in 1861 and 1866. He had already published a distillation of his basic views in 1859, in an essay titled "Dietrich von Berne." In Dahn's opinion, Theoderic's life's work was "an ingenious, idealistic error" (262). This error resulted from the "great admiration of his lofty soul for ancient education." The king had underestimated the "incurable rot of the ancient world" and failed to believe in the "vocation" of the Germani "to inject healthy, new, more precious material from the as yet untapped treasures of their national character into world history" (262). Theoderic, Dahn argued, wanted to assimilate the Goths to the "Italians" and tried in vain to win over the "Italians" with his exemplary government. His life's work was doomed to failure on account of the small numbers of the Goths and the "national resistance of the Italians to Germanic rule" (269). The Merovingians, in contrast, had prevailed because they always received "constant reinforcements of fresh natural vigor" ("steten Nachschub frischer Naturkraft") from Germania. Dahn also touted the blessings of Theoderic's reign, among which he explicitly included Theoderic's "tolerance" and "mildness" toward heterodox Christians and Jews. In academically watered-down form, this view also pervades Dahn's magnum opus. Dahn introduced an essentialized concept of a people—*ein Volk*—and biological metaphors to research on the ancient Germanic peoples. He thus paved the way for racialized historiography, even though he personally believed that the course of history obeyed inexorable laws and thus inclined to apolitical fatalism himself.[36]

The novel *Ein Kampf um Rom* also reflected a worldview that Dahn regarded as tragic and heroic. He portrayed the fall of the Gothic kingdom in Italy as "the final act of a magnificent historical tragedy" (VII, 5). Fate and race—*Volk*—are the decisive factors. Right at the beginning of the novel, Dahn has the Gothic

protagonists swear, "My people [*Volk*] is the supreme good to me, and everything, everything else is nothing; I want to sacrifice to it everything that I am
and have" (I, 1). Theoderic is tortured on his deathbed by the thought that he
had shown the Romans too much magnanimity (I, 6). His daughter Amalasuintha
values Roman education and even strikes a deal with the enemy; later, however,
she laments this "blindness," blames herself, and hopes to save the Goths from
danger through her own death (IV, 4). The idealist Totila, in turn, chases the
mirage of reconciliation between Goths and Romans. Teia, in contrast, is willing to sacrifice his life and happiness for his people, even though he foresees his
own failure. Only two imperatives operate in this grim world: to resist fate and
subordinate oneself to the *Volk*.[37]

The most significant contributions to the history of the Gothic kingdom in
Italy were made by German-speaking scholars who were political outsiders in
their time. The liberal jurist and ancient historian Theodor Mommsen (1817–
1903) published Jordanes' *Romana* and *Getica* in 1882; his edition, which
remains fundamental today, is based on the premise that the author himself was
responsible for the grammatically incorrect forms that we find in the surviving
manuscripts. Twelve years later (1894), Mommsen published his unsurpassed
and exemplary edition of Cassiodorus' *Variae*, which he produced with the vig-
orous aid of the Latinist Ludwig Traube. Parallel to these editions, Mommsen
concisely analyzed the structure of the Gothic kingdom in Italy in a study titled
Ostgothische Studien (*Ostrogothic Studies*, 1889). This work exercised a decisive
influence on subsequent research, whether in agreement or rejection, for a
century and may be considered a model of scholarly prose even today for its
terse and precise formulation.

Mommsen interpreted Theoderic's rule in Italy as an uninterrupted continuation of the position that Odoacer had occupied before him. Both men had
been, "on the one hand, Roman officials; on the other, tribal leaders of barbarians who had settled in the Roman Empire yet lacked Roman citizenship" (477).
The Goths with whom Theoderic had conquered Italy were, in Mommsen's
opinion, a political rather than an ethnic entity: a "confederation of Germanic
districts [*Gaue*] with no king of their own, unified and bound to him by a collective oath" (479). In this sense, he was a "leader of his people" (*Volksfürst*), but his
people did not comprise all Goths. Mommsen equated Theoderic's twofold
position vis-à-vis the Goths as defined in this way, on the one hand, and the
Romans, on the other, with that of the Arabic tribal rulers who received open-
ended military commands in the province of Arabia from the emperor. This
comparison was insulting blasphemy to those who saw Theoderic and his Goths
as Germans, as Mommsen was undoubtedly aware. His purpose, however, was

to determine the place of Theoderic's rule in the history of the collapse of the Roman Empire, and he had no time for Germanophile sensibilities.[38]

In addition to Mommsen, we must also mention Ludo Moritz Hartmann (1865–1924), who completed his doctorate in Berlin in 1887 and his *Habilitation* soon afterward in Vienna. Because Hartmann was Jewish and, moreover, an advocate of social democracy, he never attained more than the position of a *Privatdozent* for Roman and medieval history until the fall of the Habsburg monarchy. During this period, he wrote his *Geschichte Italiens im Mittelalter* (*History of Italy in the Middle Ages*), which he never finished; the fourth volume appeared in 1915 and ended with the coronation of Henry II in 1004. The first volume, which appeared in 1897, covered *Das italienische Königreich* (*The Italian Kingdom*). To Hartmann, Theoderic and his Goths were and remained barbarians, although he credited the king for granting Italy thirty years of peace: "The population had him to thank for greater protection than they had enjoyed in a long time, for legal certainty and for an administration that was surely better on account of its strict surveillance than in earlier times" (228). According to Hartmann, however, Theoderic's policy was doomed to failure because he could not think beyond the present moment. He had known only "the organization of the Roman state and the desire to adapt the unorganized barbarian masses to it" (227). In so doing, he failed to see the internal weakness of the late Roman state, which kept the broad masses of the rural population dependent on large landowners and thus in political indifference and apathy. Since the idea of "fusing the different classes or the Goths and Romans or creating a completely new state on a new basis" (125) lay beyond his field of vision, the kingdom he founded could not withstand the Byzantine invasion.[39]

After World War I, leading German nationalists regularly cited Theoderic. The popular author and critic Willy Pastor portrayed Theoderic in 1920 as a great German who had "made history" like Frederick the Great and Bismarck and who could serve as a model for a German renaissance. But it was not easy to press Theoderic into service for German nationalistic ends because his dual state in no way conformed to the ideal of a Germanic/German *Reich*. For anti-Semites, it was problematic that the king had protected the Jews in his kingdom. Moreover, he had treacherously slain Odoacer, a Germanic king who had ruled over Italy like himself. Theoderic was thus an awkward figure for the Nazis. Hence the Nazi politician and author Alexander von Wangenheim deliberately made Odoacer, not Theoderic, the hero of a novel titled *Das Ende West-Roms* (*The End of West Rome*) in 1925. In this account, Odoacer fails because he makes too many concessions to the faithless Romans; Theoderic has no compunctions because he had unlearned "Germanic fidelity" (*germanische Treue*) in Constantinople and was influenced by Roman advisers, "first and foremost the Jew Symmachus" (341). After 1933, the image of a Germanic king who had headed a wise government under the Italian sun was propagated in pamphlets and papers. The painter Franz Jung-Ilsenheim designed a mural for schools that depicted Theoderic as an old man from behind against a Mediterranean backdrop. There was no trace of "Nordic heroism" to see here. The author Wilhelm Schäfer (1868–1952) went the furthest in accommodating Nazi ideology. He was included in the "List of the Divinely Blessed" (Gottbegnadeten-Liste) of the Reichsministerium für Volksaufklärung und Propaganda (Imperial Ministry for Popular Education and Propaganda) in 1944. In his novel *Theoderic. König des Abendlandes* (*Theoderic: King of the West*, 1939), Schäfer imputed to the Gothic king a "race-appropriate"—that is, anti-Semitic—Christianity (*artgerechtes Christentum*) that rejected Jewish tradition. When Theoderic reviews designs for the wall decorations of his court church, which featured scenes from the Old Testament, he erupts in rage: "Did Jews or did Goths build this temple?" (162).[40]

The academy, meanwhile, balked at such heavy-handed falsification of history. In his dissertation on "Theoderich und die Ostgoten" ("Theoderic and the Ostrogoths"), submitted in Berlin in 1936 and published in a prestigious series two years later, Gerhard Vetter took great pains to prove that Theoderic had possessed "healthy race consciousness" (*gesundes Rassebewußtsein*) but conceded that the king had strayed too far from the "sources of the power of Nordic humanity" (63) when he founded his Italian kingdom; he did not discuss Theoderic's relationship with the Jews at all. Vetter's historiographical approach—termed "racial" (*rassisch*) at the time—did not go uncontested. Ludwig Schmidt (1862–1944), a kind of Nestor of Germanic studies at the time, fearlessly called Vetter's book a "tendentious pamphlet" (*Tendenzschrift*), which was academic jargon for "unscholarly." The ancient historians Alexander Graf Schenk von Stauffenberg and Wilhelm Ensslin also kept their distance from the "new vision" of history that Nazi functionaries propagated; they emphasized Theoderic's "Roman mission" (*römische Sendung*): the king's devotion to Rome as a political idea predicated on the rule of law and a cultural tradition superior to that of his own Germanic people. At the Seventeenth Biennial Meeting of German Historians, held in Erfurt in 1937, Stauffenberg called Theoderic "the last Roman ruler, the first and only Germanic ruler of the Roman west."[41]

Ensslin's biography of Theoderic, *Theoderich der Große*, the first edition of which appeared in 1947, was written during this period. Ensslin was a conservative historian with German nationalist sympathies. As such, he wrote against

Nazi ideology by emphasizing Theoderic's "Roman character" (*römische Prägung*) in addition to his "Germanic nature" (*germanisches Wesen*), which to Ensslin was beyond question. Ensslin saw Theoderic as "the last of the Germani, who, moved by the spirit of Rome, deployed the strength of the Germanic people and himself for the old Roman world" (344). The king did this so successfully, Ensslin argued, that Italy experienced a "golden age" during his reign. He did not, however, want his Gothic army to merge with Roman society; it rather "should acclimatize to and integrate with the higher civilization, but keep its innate strength undiluted" (188). In his foreign policy, Theoderic always exercised wise self-restraint and sought to establish "a balanced system with the objective of general pacification" (342). Ensslin saw the Frank Clovis as the main culprit for the failure of this policy; Clovis pursued "the expansion of his power, unencumbered by the tradition of Rome, despite the fact that he had become Catholic" (343). Ensslin's book was based on rigorous study of late Roman administrative history and exhibits comprehensive knowledge of the sources. It was hailed on all sides as a standard on its publication and was reprinted unaltered in 1959. A generation that had experienced the horrors of World War II found in it a figure who both seemed familiar and also embodied much of what was missed after the political and ethical disaster of the Nazi era: a Germanic hero who had sought to preserve ancient culture, who remained connected to his people as king of Italy, yet promoted the prosperity of all his subjects and worked for peace and mutual understanding among the rulers of Western Europe. In this respect, Ensslin's biography of Theoderic was typical of many works that appeared in postwar Germany; scholars tried to pave the way for Germany's readmission into the company of West European nations by recalling traditions that had their roots in the nineteenth century but had been suppressed under the Third Reich; now they would serve as the foundation of a Europe united by a common history and shared values—the so-called *Abendland*—and potentially of the entire western world. Anyone in search of pioneers of this vision of Europe could draw inspiration from Ensslin's Theoderic.

APPENDIX

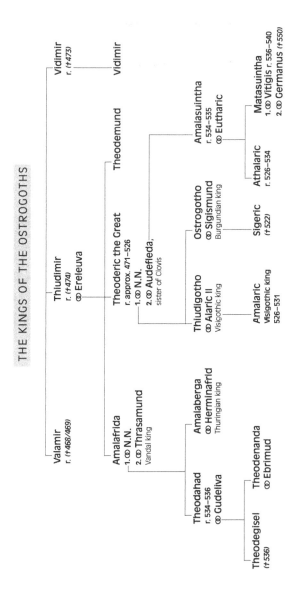

Fig. 28. The Kings of the Ostrogoths.

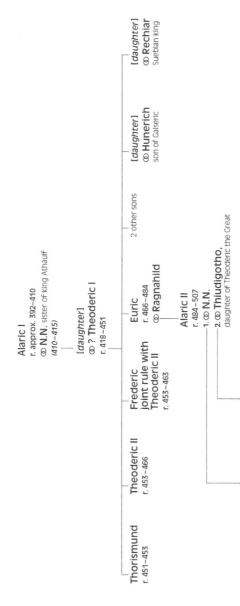

THE KINGS OF THE VISIGOTHS

Alaric I
r. approx. 392–410
⚭ N.N. sister of King Athaulf
(410–415)

[*daughter*]
⚭ ? Theoderic I
r. 418–451

Thorismund
r. 451–453

Theoderic II
r. 453–466

Frederic
joint rule with
Theoderic II
r. 453–463

Euric
r. 466–484
⚭ Ragnahild

Alaric II
r. 484–507
1. ⚭ N.N.
2. ⚭ Thiudigotho,
daughter of Theoderic the Great

2 other sons

[*daughter*]
⚭ Hunerich
son of Gaiseric

[*daughter*]
⚭ Rechiar
Suebian king

Gesalec
r. 507–511

Amalaric
r. 526–531

Fig. 29. The Kings of the *Visigoths*.

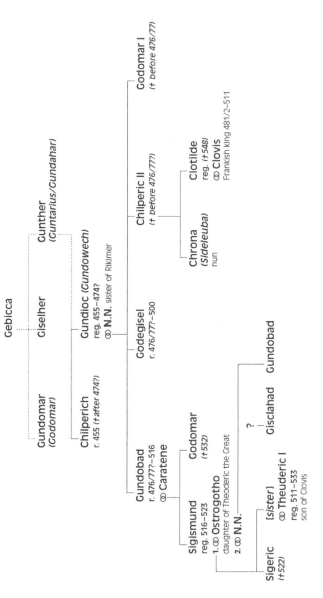

Fig. 30. The Kings of the Burgundians.

THE KINGS OF THE BURGUNDIANS

Gebicca

Gundomar *(Godomar)*

Giselher

Gunther *(Guntarius/Gundahar)*

Chilperich r. 455 (†after 474?)

Gundioc *(Gundowech)* reg. 455–474? ∞ **N.N.** sister of Rikimer

Gundobad r. 476/77?–516 ∞ Caratene

Godegisel r. 476/77?–500

Chilperic II († before 476/77?)

Godomar I († before 476/77)

Sigismund reg. 516–523 1. ∞ **Ostrogotho** daughter of Theoderic the Great 2. ∞ **N.N.**

Godomar († 532)

?

Gisclahad

Gundobad

Chrona *(Sideleuba)* nun

Chilperic II († before 476/77?)

Clotilde reg. († 548) ∞ **Clovis** Frankish King 481/2–511

Sigeric († 522)

[sister] ∞ **Theuderic I** reg. 511–533 son of Clovis

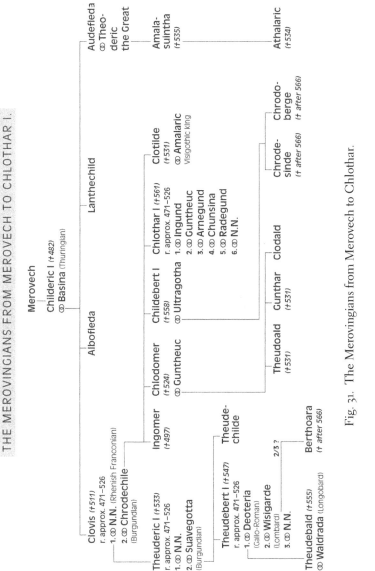

THE MEROVINGIANS FROM MEROVECH TO CHLOTHAR I.

Merovech

Childeric I (†482)
∞ Basina (Thuringian)

Albofleda

Lanthechild

Audefleda
∞ Theo-
deric
the Great

Clovis (†511)
r. approx. 471–526
1. ∞ **N.N.** (Rhenish Franconian)
2. ∞ **Chrodechile**
(Burgundian)

Clotilde
(†531)
∞ **Amalaric**
Visigothic king

**Amala-
suintha**
(†535)

Athalaric
(†534)

Theuderic I (†533)
r. approx. 471–526
1. ∞ **N.N.**
2. ∞ **Suavegotta**
(Burgundian)

Ingomer
(†497)

Chlodomer
(†524)
∞ **Guntheuc**

Childebert I
(†558)
∞ **Ultragotha**

Chlothar I (†561)
r. approx. 471–526
1. ∞ **Ingund**
2. ∞ **Guntheuc**
3. ∞ **Arnegund**
4. ∞ **Chunsina**
5. ∞ **Radegund**
6. ∞ **N.N.**

**Theude-
childe**

Theudoald
(†531)

Gunthar
(†531)

Clodald

**Chrode-
sinde**
(† after 566)

**Chrodo-
berge**
(† after 566)

Theudebert I (†547)
r. approx. 471–526
1. ∞ **Deoteria**
(Gallo-Roman)
2. ∞ **Wisigarde**
(Lombard)
3. ∞ **N.N.**

2/3 ?

Theudebald (†555)
∞ **Waldrada** (Longobard)

Berthoara
(† after 566)

Fig. 31. The Merovingians from Merovech to Chlothar.

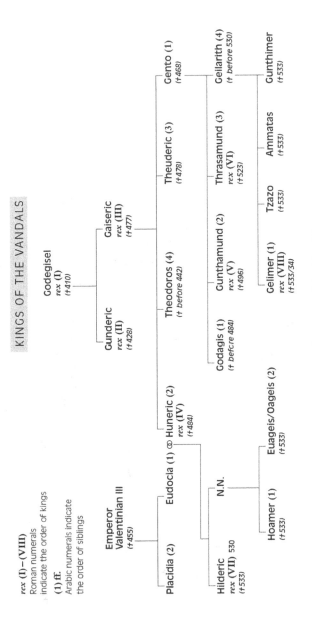

KINGS OF THE VANDALS

rex (I) – (VIII)
Roman numerals
indicate the order of kings

(1) ff.
Arabic numerals indicate
the order of siblings

Godegisel
rex (I)
(† 410)

Gunderic
rex (II)
(† 428)

Gaiseric
rex (III)
(† 477)

Emperor
Valentinian III
(† 455)

Eudocia (1) ⚭ Huneric (2)
rex (IV)
(† 484)

Theodoros (4)
(† before 442)

Theuderic (3)
(† 478)

Gento (1)
(† 468)

Placidia (2)

Hilderic
rex (VII) 530
(† 533)

N.N.

Euageis/Oageis (2)
(† 533)

Godagis (1)
(† befcre 484)

Gunthamund (2)
rex (V)
(† 496)

Thrasamund (3)
rex (VI)
(† 523)

Geilarith (4)
(† before 530)

Hoamer (1)
(† 533)

Gelimer (1)
rex (VIII)
(† 533/34)

Tzazo
(† 533)

Ammatas
(† 533)

Gunthimer
(† 533)

Fig. 32. The Kings of the Vandals.

NOTES

CHAPTER 1. APPROACHING THEODERIC THE GREAT

1. Siege of Ravenna: Proc. *Bell.* 5, 1, 13–25; *Anon. Val.* 51–54; *Fasti Vind. pr.* a. 490–493, no. 639–648; *Auct. Haun.* a. 490–493. Cass. *Chron.* a. 491, no. 1326, records a night-time sally by Odoacer and Theoderic's subsequent victory *ad pontem Candidiani*. *Dromones* at Porte Lione: *Fasti Vind. pr.* a. 493, no. 644; *Auct. Haun.* a. 493, § 1; Agn. 39; on this type of ship, cf. chap. 11, section 4, below. The harbor Porte Lione is mentioned only twice (Agn. 39; cf. 144); according to Agnellus (39), Theoderic built a small palace (*palatium modicum*) nearby after the siege (*postea*); on its remains, see Bermond Montanari 1972; Deichmann 1989, 267; Deliyannis 2010, 122.

2. Negotiations between Theoderic and Odoacer: *Fasti Vind. pr.* a. 493, no. 646–648; *Auct. Haun.* a. 493, § 3; *Anon. Val.* 54; Agn. 39.

3. Perjury and murder: Joh. Ant. *Frag.* 214a Müller = *Frag.* 307 Roberto.

4. Odoacer's death: *Fasti Vind. pr.* a. 493, no. 649; *Auct. Haun.* a. 493, § 6; Cass. *Chron.* a. 493, no. 1331; Jord. *Rom.* 349; Jord. *Get.* 295; *Anon. Val.* 55f.; Agn. 39. On revenge as a duty: Joh. Ant. *Frag.* 214, 3 Müller = *Frag.* 306 Roberto, l. 21f.; Proc. *Bell.* 5, 4, 25; 5, 11, 8; 7, 1, 42f.

5. Babai: Jord. *Get.* 282. Rekitach: Joh. Ant. *Frag.* 214, 3 Müller = *Frag.* 306 Roberto.

6. Theoderic as a personal name: Francovich Onesti 2007, 94, no. 290. Spellings vary widely in the Latin and Greek sources. On Theoderic Strabo, see chap. 4, section 3, below.

7. Sparing of the Bulgarian king: Ennod. *Pan.* 19. According to Paul. Diac. *Rom.* 15, 15, however, Theoderic killed a Bulgarian king named Busan. Revenge as motive for war against Odoacer: Ennod. *Pan.* 25.

8. In Theoderic's day, the idea that the Roman Empire consisted of two parts, one western and one eastern, the *pars Occidentis* and the *pars Orientis*, was still alive, although the last emperor in the West, Julius Nepos, had been murdered in 480. Both halves used the term "Roman" to designate themselves (*Romani* in Latin and Ῥωμαῖοι in Greek). "Byzantium" and "Byzantine," in contrast, are modern terms to denote the

empire that evolved from the Eastern Roman Empire and survived its western counterpart for more than 900 years (until 1453). In this book, "Byzantine" refers to the Romans (as they understood themselves) of the surviving Eastern Roman Empire to avoid confusion with Romans of the city of Rome and the Roman senate in Italy.

9. Odoacer and Bracila: *Auct. Haun.* a. 477; *Fasti Vind. pr.* a. 476, no. 622; Marc. Com. a. 477; Jord. *Get.* 243 (*ut terrorem suum Romanis iniceret*). Gundobad and Anthemius: *Chron. Gall.* a. 511, no. 650; Malal. 14, 45; Joh. Ant. *Frag.* 209 Müller = *Frag.* 301 Roberto. Cass. *Chron.* a. 472, no. 1293, criticizes the deed: Gundobad killed Anthemius in Rome, he argues, *contra reverentiam principis et ius adfinitatis* (in violation of the reverence due to the emperor and the law of kinship); cf. Cass. *Var.* 1, 46, 2. Gundobad and Chilperic: Greg. Tur. *Hist.* 2, 28. Gundobad and Godegisel: Mar. Avent. a. 500; Greg. Tur. *Hist.* 2, 32f. Clovis: Greg. Tur. *Hist.* 2, 27; 2, 40–42 (Sigebert, Chararich, Ragnachar).

10. For analysis of Theoderic's visit to Rome in 500, see Vitiello 2004; Wiemer 2015a, 167–177; Arnold 2017. Cass. *Var.* 12, 18; 12, 19 (written in late 535 in anticipation of Theodahad's move from Ravenna to Rome), gives an idea of the nature and extent of the preparations; see Vitiello 2014b, 111–119; Wiemer 2021b, 61–63 (on coinage). On the Laurentian Schism, see chap. 10, section 3, below. Modern scholars now often, correctly, label Theoderic's creed "Homoean"; on this, see chap. 10, section 1, below. Acclamations for Theoderic at the Roman synod of 499: MGH.AA XII, p. 405.

11. Fulgentius in Rome: Ferr. *V. Fulg.* 9. His biographer calls the location Palma Aurea.

12. Palace on the Palatine in Late Antiquity: Wulf-Rheidt 2017. Circus program: *Anon. Val.* 67 mentions only chariot races; in § 60, however, Theoderic is said to have given games in the circus and amphitheater. Theoderic's dislike of animal hunts: Cass. *Var.* 5, 42. On games in Rome, cf. chap. 6, section 3, below.

13. Theoderic and the Romans: Cass. *Chron.* a. 500, no. 1185; *Anon. Val.* 67. Liberius: *PLRE* II Liberius 3. Theodorus: *PLRE* II Theodorus 62. Building budget: Cass. *Var.* 1, 21; 1, 25; 2, 34; 3, 29–31; *Nov. Just.* Appendix 7, 25. 120,000 *modii* ("bushels") from the *arca vinaria*: *Anon. Val.* 67. 3,000 *medimnoi* ("bushels") for the beggars: Proc. *Hist. Arc.* 26, 27. Donations of grain: Cass. *Or.* 1 (MGH.AA XII, p. 463); Cass. *Var.* 8, 3, 2; *Nov. Just.* Appendix 7, 22. Trajan and Valentinian as models: *Anon. Val.* 60; cf. Cass. *Var.* 7, 6, 1; 8, 3, 5.

14. Quotation: Cass. *Chron.* a. 500, no. 1185. Gilt statue of Theoderic: Isid. *Hist. Goth.* 39.

15. *Tricennalia*: *Anon. Val.* 67 (*per tricennalem triumphans*). Marriage of Amalafrida: *Anon. Val.* 68; Proc. *Bell.* 3, 8, 11–13; Jord. *Get.* 299; Ennod. *Pan.* 70; Cass. *Var.* 5, 43; 9, 1, 1. Audefleda, Ostrogotho, Thiudigotho, Amalaberga (Theoderic's niece), Amalafrida: cf. chap. 7, section 1, below. Memory of Alaric's sack of Rome in 410: Leo *Serm.* 74 Dolle = 84 Chavasse; Gelas. *Tract.* 4, 10 = *Avell.* 100, 25a (*JK* 762 = *HJ* 1321); Cass. *Chron.* a. 410, no. 1185; Cass. *Var.* 12, 20, 4; *Lib. pont.* 45, 1 (*post Geticum ignem*); Meier and Patzold 2014.

16. *Ecclesia Gothorum* in Rome: *Lib. pont.* 66, 5. Sant'Agata dei Goti: Krautheimer 1937, 2–12; Mathisen 2009; Brandenburg 2013, 237f. Execution of Odoin: *Anon. Val.* 68f.; Mar. Avent. a. 500.

17. Medallion of Morro d'Alba: Kraus 1928, 78f., 82, no. 1; Schramm 1954, 227–229 with pl. 15; Bierbrauer 1975, 292f., no. 19; R.-Alföldi 1978 and 1988; Metlich 2004, 83, no. 3. R.-Alföldi 1978 and 1988 makes a good case for dating the medallion to 500. Grierson 1985 argues for 511, while Metlich 2004, 15f., opts for 493. *Barba Gothica*: Ennod. *Carm.* 2, 57 with Ward-Perkins 2005, 72–77; Rummel 2007, 192–196 (criticized by Liebeschuetz 2013, 158f.); Arnold 2013 is unconvincing.
18. Mommsen 1889; Ensslin 1959 (repeated from the 1st ed., 1947), esp. 242f.; 342–344 (cf. also Ensslin 1956b); Wolfram 2009 (1st ed. 1979), esp. 288–290, 331f. (cf. also Wolfram 1979). Multicultural society: C. Schäfer 2001; Spielvogel 2002. Theoderic as Western Roman emperor: Arnold 2014 (see the criticism of Wiemer 2015b; Costambeys 2016). See the recent contributions to *A Companion to Ostrogothic Italy*, edited by Arnold, Bjornlie, and Sessa 2016, and Wiemer 2020a. For a more detailed overview of research in the period 1544–2018, see Wiemer 2020c.

CHAPTER 2. THEODERIC IN THE EYES OF CONTEMPORARIES

1. For editions of the panegyric to Theoderic with commentary, see Rohr 1995; Rota 2002. There is no concrete evidence in support of the assumption that the speech was delivered to the king in Ravenna before he set off for Rome. See Schröder 2005. Theoderic as champion of freedom (*vindex libertatis*): Ennod. *Pan.* 42; cf. § 1. *Civilitas*: Ennod. *Pan.* § 56; 87. *Aureum saeculum*: Ennod. *Pan.* § 93.
2. Life of Ennodius: PCBE II Ennodius. His epitaph: CIL V 2, 6464 = ILCV 1046. Ennodius as an author: Fontaine 1962; Kennell 2000. On the letters, see Schröder 2007 (outstanding); on the epigrams: Di Rienzo 2005 (with Italian translation).
3. Ennod. *Ep.* 9, 31; Ennod. *Opusc.* 5, 20. Theoderic as *dominus libertatis*: Ennod. *Ep.* 4, 26.
4. On the *Anonymus Valesianus*, see Adams 1976 (transmission and language); Barnish 1983 (on its bias); König 1997 (German translation and commentary); Festy and Vitiello 2020 (French translation and commentary). Mommsen already, rightly, rejected the hypothesis that the text was an excerpt from a lost "chronicle" by Maximianus, the bishop of Ravenna (for which see van Hoof 2016). Its language, style, and contents clash with what we know about this work.
5. *Anon. Val.* 59f. The translation follows the text of the recent edition by Festy and Vitiello 2020, which is closer to the transmitted text than that established by their predecessors Mommsen, Moreau, and König. The participle *pergentibus* in § 59 means "travelers," not "followers": Adams 1976, 111f. In § 60 I read *secundum edictum suum, quem ei{u}s constituit*, as suggested by Henri Valois and defended by Adams 1976, 39, 91. Mommsen, Moreau, and König prefer *<quo> {e}ius constituit*: "by which he established the law."
6. Plan to seize all Catholic churches: *Anon. Val.* 94
7. *Nov. Just.* Appendix 7, 8; 7, 22. Cf. chap. 13, section 1, below.
8. Life and works of Procopius: Av. Cameron 1985 (fundamental). For his career, see also *PLRE* III Procopius 2. The revisionist interpretation of Kaldellis 2004 is unconvincing in my view. Outstanding research reports: Greatrex 2003 and 2014. More recent studies appear in the conference proceedings edited by Lillington-Martin and Turquois 2017

and by Greatrex and Janniard 2018; see also *Companion to Procopius*, edited by Meier and Montinaro 2022. Procopius' image of Theoderic: Goltz 2008, 210–266; his image of the barbarians: Greatrex 2018; Wiemer 2021a. Informants: Brodka 2016.

9. Gothic peoples: Proc. *Bell.* 3, 2, 2–7.

10. Overall assessment of Theoderic's reign: Proc. *Bell.* 5, 1, 26–39.

11. Speech of the Gothic ambassadors: Proc. *Bell.* 6, 6, 14–22. Belisarius' reply: Proc. *Bell.* 6, 6, 22–25.

12. Inferiority of the Goths on the battlefield: Proc. *Bell.* 5, 27; in siege warfare: Proc. *Bell.* 5, 21f.; at sea: Proc. *Bell.* 8, 23. Totila's humanity: Proc. *Bell.* 7, 8, 1–3; Totila's justice: Proc. *Bell.* 7, 8, 12–35. Totila's death: Proc. *Bell.* 8, 32, 28–30. Teia's heroism: Proc. *Bell.* 8, 35, 20–29.

13. For the career of Cassiodorus' father, see *PLRE* II Cassiodorus 3.

14. Cassiodorus' life and works: Löwe 1948; Momigliano 1955 and 1978; O'Donnell 1979 (for criticism, see Av. Cameron 1981); Prinz 1992; Giardina 2006; Bjornlie 2013 (for criticism, see Wiemer 2013e; Heather 2016). Cassiodorus after his conversion: Barnish 1987a; Amici 2005; van Hoof and van Nuffelen 2017. Cf. chap. 13, section 1, below.

15. The *Variae*: Krautschick 1983 (chronology); Vidén 1984 (language and style); Gillett 1998 (purpose); Barnish 2001b; Kakridi 2005 (outstanding); Giardina 2006, 1–46. On Boßhammer 2021, see Wiemer 2022b. The commentary on the entire collection edited by Giovanni Cecconi, Andrea Giardina, and Ignazio Tantillo is now fundamental on every aspect of this corpus. As yet, four volumes, covering books 3–12, have appeared. The English translation by Bjornlie (2013) is also useful.

CHAPTER 3. WHO WERE THE OSTROGOTHS?

1. Germanic ideology: See 1970 and 1994c; Wiwjorra 2006. On the equation Germanic = German, see Beck, Geuenich, Steuer, and Hakelberg 2004. On the "German conception of history" in the nineteenth and early twentieth centuries, see the classic study of Iggers 1984.

2. Tacitus' *Germania*: Jankuhn and Timpe 1989; Neumann and Seemann 1992; Timpe 1995 (fundamental).

3. On the modern reception of the *Germania*, see Muhlack 1989; Lund 1995; Krebs 2012. On "German antiquity in Renaissance myth," as constructed by fifteenth-century humanists, see Borchardt 1971.

4. *Germanische Altertumskunde* in the nineteenth century: J. Grimm 1828 and 1835; W. Grimm 1829; Zeuß 1837; Müllenhoff 1870–1908. Jacob Grimm summarized his methodological premises in the preface to his *Deutsche Rechtsalterthümer* (1828, ix) as follows: "Passages from Tacitus, from old laws, from medieval documents, and from *Weisthümer* [traditional oral law] that were not written down until one hundred years ago, are cited in a single breath." On his scholarly agenda, Wyss 1983 is outstanding. For a modern biography of the Grimm brothers, see Martus 2009.

5. German prehistory: Kossina 1912 with the critical remarks of Grünert 2002; Steuer 2001. Criticism of the "ethnic interpretation" was voiced already by Wahle 1941; see now Brather 2004; Brather et al. 2021.

6. Germanic research under the Third Reich: Höfler 1934 and 1938; Vetter 1938; Giesecke 1939; Reinerth 1940; Neckel 1944; see the critical remarks by Lund 1995; See and Zernack 2004; Wiwjorra 2006; Focke-Museum Bremen 2013; and chap. 13, section 6, below. On the Amt Rosenberg and the Reichsinstitut für deutsche Vorgeschichte, see Bollmus 2006, esp 83–235. The fundamental study of Heinrich Himmler's Ahnenerbe is Kater 2006. The authors of the volume *Germanische Altertumskunde*, edited in 1938 by the Germanist Hermann Schneider, in contrast, tried to keep their distance from Nazi-inspired Germanic ideology; see See and Zernack 2004, 17–30.

7. Theory of ethnogenesis: Wenskus 1977 (see the critical remarks of Graus 1963); Wolfram 1979 (5th ed., 2009). Criticism of the continuity theory: Graus 1959 (with the rejoinder of Schlesinger 1963); Graus 1986; Kroeschell 1986. On Wolfram's *History of the Goths*, see Wiemer 2020b, 420–423.

8. Gothic identity: Heather 2007; Kulikowski 2007, 43–70; Liebeschuetz 2011a; Swain 2016 (a useful introduction); Pohl 2020. Ethnicity as social construct: H. M. Chadwick 1907; Weber 1976, 234–244; Barth 1969. Debate over ethnogenesis: Gillett 2002a; Wolfram 2005, 207–224; Liebeschuetz 2007; Pohl 2013 and 2020. Ethnicity as "situational construct": Geary 1983; Amory 1997; Halsall 1999.

9. The Gothic language: Proc. *Bell.* 7, 2, 5; Prisc. *Frag.* 8, 94 Carolla = *Frag.* 11, 2, l. 407–415 Blockley; *Anth. Lat.* 285 Riese = 279 Shackleton-Bailey; *Lib. gen.* 618 (MGH.AA IX, p. 195); Seebold 1986; Haubrichs 2011 and 2012; Kragl 2020.

10. Image and concept of "Germanic" peoples in the sources: Wagner 1986; Timpe 1995; Pohl 2010, 1–44; Wiemer 2021a. Significantly, the Constantinopolitan bureaucrat and scholar John the Lydian describes the Vandals but not the Goths as a Germanic people (*ethnos Germanikon*) that immigrated from the far north: Joh. Lyd. *Mag.* 3, 43; 3, 55.

11. The concept of "Germanic" in the scholarly literature: Wenskus 1986; Jarnut 2004; Pohl 2010, 45–64. Balanced overview from a Roman perspective: Bleckmann 2009.

12. History of the Visigoths: Claude 1970 and 1971a; Heather 1996, 181–215, 276–321; Wolfram 2009, 125–248; Delaplace 2015.

13. *Wisigothae*: Cass. *Var.* 3, 1 tit.; 3, 3, 2. Separation of Visigoths and Ostrogoths: Proc. *Bell.* 3, 2, 1–7.

14. Scandinavian origin: Jord. *Get.* 25–26. Ostrogothae and Vesegothae: Jord. *Get.* 82, 130. Balts and Amals: Jord. *Get.* 42; cf. § 146.

15. Pessimism of Jordanes: Jord. *Rom.* 1–5, 376–388. Depiction of the present: Croke 2005a. Tragedy: Jord. *Rom.* 388. Jordanes' origin: Jord. *Get.* 316: *nec me quis in favorem gentis praedictae, quasi ex ipsa trahenti originem, aliqua addidisse credat.* Jordanes' life: Jord. *Get.* 266; Wagner 1967, 3–59; Christensen 2002, 84–103; Liebeschuetz 2011b; van Hoof and van Nuffelen 2017 and 2020, 1–106. The exact date of writing is disputed; Jordanes himself (Jord. *Rom.* 3; 364) says he wrote in the twenty-fourth year of Justinian, which has been taken to mean either before April 1, 551 (regnal year), or before December 31, 551 (calendar year). Still others have argued for additions made in 552 to a text basically finished in 551.

16. Citation: Jord. *Get.* 1–3. The verb *relegere* here has its usual meaning, "to reread."

17. Purpose of Jordanes' *Getica*: Liebeschuetz 2011b; contra Momigliano 1955; Goffart 1988, 20–111. *Historia Gothica* of Cassiodorus: Cass. *Lib.*; Cass. *Var.* praef.; Cass. *Var.* 9,

25, 4–6; 11, 1, 19; Jord. *Get.* 1; now available with English translation and commentary in *FHistLat* 17. For discussion, see Barnish 1984; Heather 1993, 342–353; Vitiello 2014a.

18. Genealogy of the Amals: Cass. *Var.* 9, 25, 4–6; 11, 1, 19; Jord. *Get.* 78–82; Heather 1989; Christensen 2002, 124–158. The name Ostrogotha, which appears sixth in the Amal genealogy, is now securely attested for a third-century Gothic king (cf. n. 34 below). On the kings of Latium: Cass. *Chron.* nos. 45–73.

19. Two thousand years of Gothic history: Heather 1993, 345f.; Vitiello 2014a.

20. Ancient ethnography: K. E. Müller 1968–1980; Wiemer 2021a. Proof of antiquity: Pilhofer 1990.

21. *Gothi = Getae*: SHA *Caracalla* 10, 6; *Probus* 12, 4; Jer. *Quaest. hebr. in Gen.* 10, 2; Aug. *Civ.* 20, 21; Oros. *Hist.* 1, 16, 2; Philost. 2, 5.

22. Dicineus: Jord. *Get.* 39; 67–72; cf. Cass. *Var.* 9, 24, 8 (Theoderic and Cassiodorus). The geographer Strabo reports that the kings of the Getae were advised of old by a sage who was revered like a god; in the days of Augustus, when Burebista was king, this position was held by a certain Dekaineos: Strab. 7, 3, 5; 7, 3, 11; 16, 2, 39.

23. Jordanes' literary sources: Mommsen 1882, xxx–xliv; Christensen 2002 (discussed by Wood 2003); van Hoof and Nuffelen 2020, 65–99. Symmachus: Jord. *Get.* 83–88. Ablabius: Jord. *Get.* 28; 82; 117; cf. Cass. *Var.* 10, 22, 2: *Ablabi vestry historica monimenta*, where *Ablabi*, however, is Mommsen's conjecture for the reading *abavi* in the manuscripts).

24. Catalogue of peoples: Jord. *Get.* 24 (Scandia) and 116 (*regnum Ermanarici*); Svennung 1967. Isolated kings' names: Jord. *Get.* 43, cf. § 178 (Vidigoia). Non-Amal genealogy: Jord. *Get.* 113 (Geberic).

25. Pre-ethnographic material: *Oium*: Jord. *Get.* 27, *belagines*: Jord. *Get.* 69; *capillati:* Jord. *Get.* 71f.; *anses*: Jord. *Get.* 78; *Gepidoios*: Jord. *Get.* 96; *Gepidae*: Jord. *Get.* 95; *haliurunnae*: Jord. *Get.* 121; *Baltha*: Jord. *Get.* 146. On Jordanes' *capillati*, cf. *Ed. Theod.* 145; Cass. *Var.* 4, 49, tit. and the Gothic verb *kapillôn*; see Green 1998, 203, 233; Rummel 2007, 213–231. Löwe 1991 argues unconvincingly that Jordanes was referring not to the Goths of his own time but to "Daco-Getans."

26. Gothic victories: Jord. *Get.* 26 (*Ulmerugi et Vandali*); Jord. *Get.* 28 (*Spali*); Jord. *Get.* 94–100 (*Gepidae cum Fastida*); Jord. *Get.* 113f. (*Vandali cum Visimar*); Jord. *Get.* 117 (*Heruli cum Halarico*); Jord. *Get.* 247 (*Anti cum Boz*); Jord. *Get.* 250 (*Suavi et Gepidae*). Ermanaric: Amm. 31, 3, 1f.; Jord. *Get.* 116–120; 129–130.

27. Gothic songs: Jord. *Get.* 28; 38; 43; 72; 214; Amm. 31, 7, 11; see also the new Dexippus fragment (f. 194 recto), first edited by Grusková and Martin 2014b. Cf. the proceedings of the Dexippus Conference held in Vienna 2017: Mitthoff, Martin, and Grusková 2020 (with a new edition, 546–564). Tacitus (Tac. *Germ.* 2, 2) also called "old songs" (*carmina antiqua*) the only form of historical memory among the Germani. Heroic poetry: Bowra 1952; See 1978; Millet 2008. On their subject matter, which was transmitted orally (*Heldensage*), see the concise study of See 1981.

28. Vandalarius: Jord. *Get.* 80, 251f. Vinitharius: Jord. *Get.* 79; 246; 248–250; see Heather 1989 and 1991, 19–28; 34–67; Liebeschuetz 2011a.

29. Oral history: Vansina 1985; Ungern-Sternberg and Reinau 1988. As there is a tendency in recent scholarship to regard the Goths as a sort of "people without history"—not

altogether unlike the way Europeans viewed African societies in the nineteenth century—it needs to be stressed that historical consciousness does not presuppose the use
of writing or the practice of historiography.

30. Goths and Scandinavia: Hachmann 1970; Kazanski 1991, 9–28; Bierbrauer 1994, 52–105;
Heather 1996, 11–50; Goffart 2006, 56–72. It should be noted that leading nineteenth-
century scholars rejected the Scandinavian origin of the Goths. See, e.g., Zeuß 1837,
402f. Goths near the Vistula: Strab. 7, 1, 3 (*Gutones*); Tac. *Germ.* 44, 1 (*Gotones*); Tac.
Ann. 2, 62, 2 (*Got[h]ones*); cf. Ptol. *Geogr.* 2, 11, 35 (*Goutai* on the island of Skandia);
Ptol. *Geogr.* 3, 5, 20 (*Gythones* in Sarmatia). Wielbark culture: Mączyńska 2007.

31. Gothic ethnogenesis in the third century: Kulikowski 2007, 43–70; for criticism, see
Liebeschuetz 2011a. Halsall 2007, 132–136, speculates that elite Gothic warriors traveled via the Amber Road into the area of the lower Danube and shaped other ethnic
groups there in their own image.

32. Source problems: Bleckmann 1992 (fundamental); Brecht 1999 (collection of sources).
Histria: SHA *Maximus et Balbinus* 16, 3 = Dex. *Frag.* 20 Jacoby. Argaith and Guntheric:
SHA *Gordianus* 31, 1; Jord. *Get.* 91. Dexippus of Athens: G. Martin 2006; Mecella 2013.

33. Siege of Marcianopolis: Dex. *Frag.* 25 Jacoby (undated); Jord. *Get.* 92 (dated 249).
Sack of Philippopolis: Amm. 31, 5, 17; Jord. *Get.* 103.

34. Cniva and Ostrogotha: Grusková and Martin 2014a, 2014b, 2015, and in Mitthoff,
Martin, and Grusková 2020, 543–548 (most recent edition of the fragments of Dexippus'
Skythika). Jord. *Get.* 101 has Ostrogotha die prior to the war of 250–251; see Vitiello
2020. Further on Cniva, see Dex. *Frag.* 22 Jacoby; Dex. *Frag.* 26–27 Jacoby; Zos. 1, 23;
Jord. *Get.* 101–103; Zon. 12, 20. The battle of Abrittus is also recorded in Cass. *Chron.*
a. 252, no. 956.

35. Gothic raids by sea: Brecht 1999, 237, 250f.; Berndt 2013, 10–23. Gregory Thaumaturgus
discusses the consequences as a Christian pastor in his *Epistula canonica* (Greg.
Thaum. *Ep. can.*). Naval raids in the years 255–257: Zos. 1, 31–35; Jord. *Get.* 107f. with
Paschoud's edition, 154–156, notes 59–63; Goltz and U. Hartmann 2008, 235f., 247f.
Naval raid of 268–269: Dex. *Frag.* 29 Jacoby; Zos. 1, 42f.; 45f. with Paschoud's edition,
162f., notes 70f.; 164f., notes 73f. Naval raid of 276: Zos. 1, 63, 1; Zon. 12, 28 with
Paschoud's edition, 180. Gothic invasion of 262: Cass. *Chron.* a. 262, no. 972; Jord. *Get.*
107–108; Goltz and Hartmann 2008, 275–277 (with all sources). *Gothicus maximus* as
a victory epithet: Peachin 1990, 86f. *Germanicus* (*maximus*): Kneissl 1969.

36. The Gothic wars of Claudius and Aurelian: Amm. 31, 5, 17; U. Hartmann 2008, 297–
323. *Ripa Gothica*: Anon. *Val.* 35

37. Burgundians: Zos. 1, 27, 1; 1, 31, 1 with Kaiser 2004a, 16f.; cf. *Pan. Lat.* 11 (3), 17, 3; Jord. *Get.*
97; Agath. *Hist.* 5, 11, 2. Third-century Gothic leaders: Ostrogotha (Dexippus); Argaith,
Cniva, Guntheric, Respa, Thurwarus, Veduco (Jordanes following Dexippus); Cannabas/
Cannabaudes (SHA *Aurelianus* 22, 2, following Dexippus). Early fourth-century Gothic
leaders: Alica, Aoric, Araric, Geberic. The references may be found in *PLRE* I.

38. "Germani" and "Goths" in the *Res Gestae* of Shapur I (abbreviated ŠKZ, edited by
Huyse 1999): ŠKZ § 6 of the Greek version. Borrowed military terms: *militare* → *mil-
itôn* (military service); *annona* → *anno* (pay); **capillare* → *kapillôn* (soldier's haircut):
Green 1998, 202f., 233.

39. Greutungi, Tervingi, Vesi, and Ostrogothae/Austrogothae: Sitzmann and Grünzweig 2008, 45, 159f., 268f., 307–310. Since Theoderic named a daughter born before 488 Ostrogotho, this group must have used the name Ostrogothae as a self-designation.
40. Earliest mention of the Tervingi: *Pan. Lat.* 11 (3), 17, 1.
41. Goths in Galerius' army: Jord. *Get.* 110. Rausimod: *Anon. Val.* 21; Zos. 2, 21, 3; Theoph. a. m. 5818; Zon. 13, 2, 11. Licinius and the Goths: Eus. *V. Const.* 2, 15; *Anon. Val.* 27; vice versa Jord. *Get.* 111. The Gothic policy of Constantine the Great: Kulikowski 2006b; Bleckmann 2009, 195–209. Gothic treaty of 332: Eus. *V. Const.* 4, 4; *Anon. Val.* 32; Eutr. 10, 7; Jord. *Get.* 112 (anachronistic); Brokmeier 1987.
42. Gothic war of Constantius II: Lib. *Or.* 59, 89–93; Cyr. *Cat.* 10, 19; Amm. 20, 8, 1. Slave trade: Amm. 22, 7, 8; cf. Aug. *Ep.* 10* Divjak. Julian: Amm. 23, 2, 7; Zos. 3, 25, 6.
43. Theophilos: Gelzer, Hilgenfeld, and Cuntz 1898, lxiv. The reference should not be associated with the Goths on the Crimea: Schäferdiek 2007, 292f. On Wulfila, cf. n. 57 below.
44. Valens' Gothic war: Amm. 27, 5; Eun. *Frag.* 37 Müller and Blockley; Zos. 4, 10f.; Lenski 2002, 127–137. Peace treaty with Athanaric: Them. *Or.* 10; Zos. 4, 11, 4. Procopius: Amm. 26, 10, 3; 27, 5, 1; 31, 3, 4; Eun. *Frag.* 37 Müller and Blockley; Zos. 4, 7, 2.
45. Gothic civil war: Socr. 4, 33f. Onslaught of the Huns: Amm. 31, 3; Eun. *Frag.* 41 Müller and Blockley; Zos. 4, 20, 3f.; cf. chap. 4, section 1, below.
46. Crossing of the Danube by the Tervingi: Amm. 31, 3; Eun. *Frag.* 42 Müller and Blockley; Zos. 4, 20, 5–22, 3; Jord. *Get.* 131f.
47. Saphrax and Alatheus: Amm. 31, 4, 12; 31, 5, 3. Suerid and Colias: Amm. 31, 6, 1–3. Gothic slaves: Amm. 31, 6, 5.
48. Battle at Ad Salices: Amm. 31, 7, 6–16. Huns and Alans: Amm. 31, 8, 4. Farnobius' end: Amm. 31, 9, 1–5.
49. Ammianus Marcellinus: Rosen 1982 (research report); Matthews 1989; Barnes 1998; G. Kelly 2008. Battle of Adrianople: Amm. 31, 12–13; Cass. *Chron.* a. 378, no. 1129; Jord. *Get.* 138 with Lenski 2002, 320–367; Brodka 2009. Comparison to Cannae: Amm. 31, 13, 19. Remembering old Roman virtues: Amm. 31, 5, 10–17. Contemporary responses to Adrianople: Straub 1943; Lenski 1997. Massacre of Goths in Asia Minor: Amm. 31, 16, 8; Zos. 4, 26, 2–9.
50. Athanaric in Constantinople: *Cons. Const.* a. 381; Cass. *Chron.* a. 382, no. 1138; see *PLRE* I Athanarichus for further references.
51. Theodosius' Gothic policy: Errington 1996; Heather 2010; Leppin 2010. *Foedus* of 382: Them. *Or.* 16; Heather 1991, 122–128.
52. Athanaric as *iudex* (*dikastēs*): Amm. 27, 5, 6; 31, 3, 4; Ambr. *Spir.*, prol. 17; Aux. *Ep.* 36; Them. *Or.* 10, 134c–135a (misinterpreted by Heather and Matthews 1991, 42f., n. 91); Wolfram 1975a.
53. Archeology of the Tervingi: Kazanski 1991, 39–59; Heather and Matthews 1991, 51–101; Bierbrauer 1994, 105–134; Heather 1996, 63–93; Harhoiu 1997; Gomolka-Fuchs 1999; Ioniță 2004. For Latin *cubitus* → Gothic *kubitus*, cf. Gothic *ankumbjan*, "to lie down": Green 1998, 207–208, 227–229. Treasure of Pietroasa: Harhoiu 1977. Runes: Düwel 2008, 31f. A spindle whorl found in a fourth-century woman's grave in the necropolis of Lețcani near Jassy in northeastern Romania bears a runic inscription, but its meaning is uncertain.

54. *Martyrium of Sabas* (Greek text): Delehaye 1912, 216–221; Knopf 1929, 119–124, no. 33; English translation: Heather and Matthews 1991, 103–132; penetrating analysis by Thompson 1966, 64–77; Schäferdiek 1993.
55. Warlords and followers (*Gefolgschaft*): Schlesinger 1956; Thompson 1965, 48–60; Bazelmans 1991, Heather 1996, 66–75; Timpe 1998.
56. Gothic polytheism: Thompson 1966, 55–63; Wolfram 2005, 96–111; Faber 2014, 69–76. Burial customs: Kazanski 1991, 55f.; Kulikowski 2007, 94–97.
57. Wulfila: *Aux. Ep.*; Philost. 2, 5. Spread of Christianity among the Goths: Socr. 2, 41, 23; 4, 33; Soz. 6, 37; Thdt. *Hist.* 4, 33; Jord. *Get.* 132f.; 267; Schäferdiek 1979b; Heather and Matthews 1991, 133–154; Faber 2014, 69–128.
58. Standard edition of the Gothic translation of the Bible: Streitberg 2000; on the background, transmission and character of the Gothic version of the gospels and the Pauline epistles, see Falluomini 2015.
59. Conversion of the Tervingi to Christianity: Schäferdiek 1979a; Lenski 1995; Faber 2014, 164–176. Thompson 1966, 103–110, and Heather 1986 date the conversion to the years after the Goths had been received into the empire. On the Homoeans, cf. chap. 10, section 1, below.
60. Germanic Arianism (*germanischer Arianismus*): see Giesecke 1939; K. D. Schmidt 1939; for critical analysis, see Brennecke 2002 and 2014a. The "Deutsche Christen" (German Christians) were a movement within German Protestantism in the 1930s and 1940s that unsuccessfully sought to create a "German church" based on Nazi ideas of "racial purity"; on this, see Heschel 2008.

CHAPTER 4. FROM ATTILA TO THEODERIC

1. Battle of the Utus (Vit): Jord. *Rom.* 331; Marc. Com. a. 447. Peace of 448: Prisc. *Frag.* 5, 1–4 Carolla = *Frag.* 9, 3 Blockley; Theoph. a. m. 5942.
2. Valamir and Attila: Damasc. *V. Isid.* 64; Jord. *Get.* 199. For the reading *fortissimus et famosissimus* ("most courageous and renowned"), see Francesco Giunta's note in his edition of the *Getica*, p. 256, note 57.
3. Battle of the Catalaunian Plains: Jord. *Get.* 192–218; Prosp. *Chron.* a. 451; *Chron. Gall.* a. 511, no. 615; Greg. Tur. *Hist.* 2, 7; Demougeot 1958 (fundamental). Visigothic victory over Attila: Cass. *Chron.* a. 451, no. 1253; Cass. *Var.* 3, 1, 1; cf. Isid. *Hist. Goth.* 25. The precise location of the battlefield is unknown. Allies of the emperor: Jord. *Get.* 191; 198. Attila's order of battle: Jord. *Get.* 198f. Death of Theoderic I: Jord. *Get.* 209; Isid. *Hist. Goth.* 25. Andag was probably the father of the *magister militum* whom Jordanes served as secretary before his *conversio*: Jord. *Get.* 265.
4. Prisc. *Frag.* 8, 83–85 Carolla = *Frag.* 11, 2 Blockley, l. 356–372. Graves of the Hunnic royal family: Prisc. *Frag.* 2 Carolla = *Frag.* 6, 1 Blockley. Attila's camp: Thompson 1945; Pohl 2001c, 442–446. Localization in Muntenia: Browning 1953.
5. Attila's empire: Maenchen-Helfen 1978, 93–97. Campaign against the Persians: Prisc. *Frag.* 8, 137–146 Carolla = *Frag.* 11, 2 Blockley, l. 586–636. Frankish petty king: Prisc. *Frag.* 16 Carolla = *Frag.* 20, 3 Blockley.

6. Ammianus' excursus on the Huns: Amm. 31, 2; Matthews 1989, 332–342. Scythians: Hdt. 4, 5–82; Bichler 2000, 69–73. Goths are explicitly called Scythians by Epiphanius of Salamis in *Avell.* 244, 36, and by Oros. *Hist.* 7, 34, 5 (*Scythicae gentes*). Nomad ideology: Shaw 1982–1983.

7. Ermanaric and Vithimir: Amm. 31, 3, 1–3. Jord. *Get.* 129f. gives a different account (calling him Vinitharius).

8. Huns: Thompson 1996; Altheim 1951; Maenchen-Helfen 1978 (groundbreaking but fragmentary); Bona 1991 (archeological evidence); Stickler 2002, 85–154, and 2007; C. Kelly 2008; Kim 2013 (see Meier 2017 for criticism); Rosen 2016 (conventional). Octar/Optar: Jord. *Get.* 180; Socr. 7, 30, 6. Ru(g)a: *PLRE* II Rua. Chronology: Zuckerman 1994.

9. *Haliarunnae*: Jord. *Get.* 121–122. The second part of the word is derived from *runa*, "secret, decree," or **runna*, "way." Huns and Goths: Prisc. *Frag.* 39 Carolla = *Frag.* 49 Blockley; Carolla 2010. Gepids: Pohl 1980.

10. Division of booty: Prisc. *Frag.* 8, 98f. Carolla = *Frag.* 11, 2 Blockley, l. 425–430.

11. *Logades*: Maenchen-Helfen 1978, 147–149 (with all references). Attila's secretaries and interpreters: *PLRE* II Constantius 6; *PLRE* II Constantius 7; *PLRE* II Rusticius 2; *PLRE* II Orestes 2; cf. Wiotte-Franz 2001, 126–129. Languages used by Attila's followers: Prisc. *Frag.* 8, 94 Carolla = *Frag.* 11, 2 Blockley, l. 407–415.

12. Struggles after Attila's death: Jord. *Get.* 259–263; Prosp. *Chron.* a. 453; Eug. *V. Sev.* 1, 1; Paul. Diac. *Rom.* 15, 11. Battle of Nedao: Jord. *Get.* 261f.

13. Pannonia in Late Antiquity: Mócsy 1974, 339–358; for a starkly different picture, see Várady 1969 (but see contra Harmatta 1970; Nagy 1971). Military installations: Soproni 1985; Borhy 2011.

14. Treaty of alliance (*foedus*) with Marcian: Jord. *Get.* 264; Prisc. *Frag.* 28 Carolla = *Frag.* 37 Blockley.

15. *Gothi minores*: Jord. *Get.* 267. Bigelis: Jord. *Rom.* 336. Ullibus: Joh. Ant. *Frag.* 205 Müller = *Frag.* 297 Roberto. Anagast: *PLRE* II Anagastes. Ostrys: *PLRE* II Ostrys. Strabo and the "Thracian" Goths: *PLRE* II Theodericus 5; Heather 1991, 251–263. According to Jord. *Get.* 270, Strabo was already the leader of the "Thracian" Goths when the "Pannonian" Goths struck their treaty with Marcian, but this account may anachronistically reflect later conditions.

16. Malchus of Philadelphia: Wiemer 2009 and 2013a. The reordering of the fragments proposed by Errington 1983 creates more problems than it solves. The standard edition of Malchus, *Frag.*, is Cresci 1982 (see editions of ancient authors). Greek text and English translation available in Blockley 1983.

17. Settlement locations of the Goths: Jord. *Get.* 268; Eug. *V. Sev.* 5, 1; Cass. *Var.* 3, 23; Gračanin and Škrgulja 2014. The precise localization is uncertain: see Ensslin 1928 against Alföldi 1926, 97–104. Archeological investigation: Kiss 1979 and 1996; Bierbrauer 1994, 134–140, and 2011. Cities in Pannonia: Šašel Kos and Scherrer 2003a and 2003b. Sirmium: Mirković, Milošević, and Popović 1971; Mirković 2007; Popović 2007. Fenékpuszta: Heinrich-Tamáska 2011 and 2013.

18. Valamir's victory over the Huns: Jord. *Get.* 268f.

19. Theoderic's birthdate can be inferred from the fact that he celebrated his *tricennalia* in the year 500; that must refer to his victory over King Babai, which he accomplished at the age of seventeen (Jord. *Get.* 282); that victory, accordingly, falls in the year 471. Since Theoderic was surrendered as a hostage at the age of seven (Jord. *Get.* 271) and lived in Constantinople for ten years, this points to the year 453 or 454 as that of his birth. Theodemund: Malch. *Frag.* 18 Cresci, l. 134; 270–285 = *Frag.* 20 Blockley, l. 113; 230–242. Ereleuva/Erelieva: *Anon. Val.* 58; Jord. *Get.* 269; for the name, see Francovich-Onesti 2007, 45, no. 90; Haubrichs 2017, 309, no. 8.

20. Prisc. *Frag.* 28 Carolla = *Frag.* 37 Blockley; Sid. *Carm.* 2, 223–234; Jord. *Get.* 270f. Valamir potentially took Dyrrachium in 459, but this report is poorly attested: *Auct. Prosp. Vat.* a. 459 (MGH.AA IX, p. 492, no. 11).

21. Theoderic as hostage: Jord. *Get.* 271; Malal. 15, 9; Theoph. a. m. 5977. The *Anon. Val.* (61; 79) calls Theoderic *illiteratus*—that is, "uneducated" in the late Roman sense (similarly, Proc. *Bell.* 5, 2, 16); see Ensslin 1940b; Stein 1949, 108, 791f. Malalas and Theophanes claim, in contrast, that Theoderic had received the usual literary education; cf. also Ennod. *Pan.* 11.

22. Aspar and Ardabur: Croke 2005b; Stickler 2015; McEvoy 2016. "Revered like emperors": *V. Symeonis. syr.* 133 Lietzmann = 125 Doran (the word *malkē* appears in the Syrian text, equivalent to the Greek word *basileus*). Hermineric: *PLRE* II Herminericus. The name appears in different spellings, one of them being Ermanaric. Patricius: *PLRE* II Iulius Patricius 15. Only Cand. *Frag.* 1 = Phot. *Cod.* 79 claims that Patricius survived the massacre.

23. Theoderic quoted Aspar's declaration many years later in a letter to a synod of bishops, refusing to pass judgment on Pope Symmachus: *Anagnosticum regis*, MGH.AA XII, p. 425; cf. Siebigs 2010, 670–678.

24. Valamir's death: Jord. *Get.* 276; Jord. *Rom.* 347.

25. Battle at the Bolia: Jord. *Get.* 277–279. Imperial support for the Sciri: Prisc. *Frag.* 35 Carolla = *Frag.* 45 Blockley. Enmity with the Rugi: Eug. *V. Sev.* 5.

26. Victory over Babai: Jord. *Get.* 282.

27. Quotation: Jord. *Get.* 283; cf. Jord. *Rom.* 347: *alter Italiam, alter Illyricum suscepit populandum.*

28. Vidimir: Jord. *Get.* 283f.; Jord. *Rom.* 347. PCBE IV Vittamerus identifies Vidimir with a high-ranking correspondent of Bishop Ruricius of Limoges named Vittamer (Rur. *Ep.* 2, 60; 2, 62). The first part of his name, *vitta-*, however, very probably derives from the Germanic root *wīti-*, "battle," whereas the first part of Vidimir's name, *vidi-*, derives from *widu-*, "forest." (I thank Wolfgang Haubrich for this information.)

29. Booty, protection money, and subsidies: Liebeschuetz 1993, 80–85; Berndt 2011. Teurnia: Eug. *V. Sev.* 17, 4.

30. Lances: Jord. *Get.* 261; see Wiemer and Berndt 2016, 152–157. "Riderization" (*Verreiterung*) of the Goths: Wolfram 2009, 173–175. Agriculture: Prisc. *Frag.* 39 Carolla = *Frag.* 49 Blockley. Herds: Jord. *Get.* 274; Malch. *Frag.* 15 Cresci = *Frag.* 18, 2 Blockley; *Frag.* 17 Cresci = *Frag.* 18, 4 Blockley. *Exercitus pedestris*: Jord. *Get.* 280. Priests in Theoderic's army: Malch. *Frag.* 18 Cresci, l. 163f. = *Frag.* 20 Blockley, l. 136f.

31. Settlement in Eordaia (West Macedonia): Jord. *Rom.* 347; Jord. *Get.* 288. Panic in Thessalonica: Malch. *Frag.* 18 Cresci, l. 6–23 = *Frag.* 20 Blockley, l. 6–19.

32. Jord. *Get.* 285–287; *Anon. Val.* 42.

33. Triarius: *PLRE* II Triarius. Strabo: *PLRE* II Theodericus 5. Not an Amal: Jord. *Get.* 270; *pace* Wolfram 2009, 43. Strabo's kinship with Aspar's wife: Theoph. a. m. 5964 (sister); a. m. 5970 (aunt); Malch. *Frag.* 2. Hermineric: *PLRE* II Herminericus. Aspar's Gothic followers: Damasc. *V. Isid.* 69; Malal. 14, 40; *Chron. Pasch.* 596f.; Laniado 2015. Treaty between Leo and Strabo: Malch. *Frag.* 2.

34. Zeno: Stein: 1949, 7–76, and 1959, 360–400; Lippold 1973; Kosiński 2010 (on his religious policy).

35. Strabo and Basiliscus: Malch. *Frag.* 11 Cresci = *Frag.* 15 Blockley; *Frag.* 17 Cresci = *Frag.* 18, 4 Blockley; Theoph. a. m. 5970.

36. Meeting of the two Theoderics: Malch. *Frag.* 15 Cresci = *Frag.* 18, 2 Blockley; *Frag.* 16 Cresci = *Frag.* 18, 3 Blockley.

37. Zeno's offer: Malch. *Frag.* 17 Cresci = *Frag.* 18, 4 Blockley. Anicia Juliana was the daughter of the Eastern Roman senator Olybrius, who became the Western Roman emperor in 472, but she continued to live in Constantinople: *PLRE* II Anicia Iuliana 3.

38. Panic in Dyrrachium: Malch. *Frag.* 18 Cresci, l. 125–132 = *Frag.* 20 Blockley, l. 105–109.

39. Pautalia: Malch. *Frag.* 18 Cresci, l. 55–73 = *Frag.* 20 Blockley, l. 46–58. Pautalia (Kjustendil, near the border between Bulgaria and the Republic of North Macedonia) was a fortified city in Late Antiquity; its walls enclosed an area of approximately 30 hectares: Katsarova 2012. Proc. *Aed.* 4, 11, mentions five forts located on its territory. Theoderic and Julius Nepos: Malch. *Frag.* 18 Cresci, l. 249–260 = *Frag.* 20 Blockley, l. 212–221. Adamantius: *PLRE* II Adamantius 2.

40. Quotation: Malch. *Frag.* 18 Cresci, l. 268–292 = *Frag.* 20 Blockley, l. 228–248. Sabinianus: *PLRE* II Sabinianus 4.

41. Strabo and Marcian: Malch. *Frag.* 19 Cresci = 22 Blockley; Joh. Ant. *Frag.* 211, 3 Müller = *Frag.* 303 Roberto, l. 38–75.

42. Theoderic's rebellion: Marc. Com. a. 479, § 2; a. 481, § 2; a. 482, § 2; Joh. Ant. *Frag.* 213 Müller = *Frag.* 305 Roberto. Strabo's death: Marc. Com. a. 481; Jord. *Rom.* 346; Evagr. *Hist.* 3, 25; Joh. Ant. *Frag.* 211 Müller = *Frag.* 303 Roberto, l. 6–89; Theoph. a. m. 5970. To judge from *L. Burg.* 18, 2, the risk of accidentally impaling oneself was not entirely negligible. Killing of Strabo's brothers: Joh. Ant. *Frag.* 211, 5 Müller = *Frag.* 303 Roberto, l. 89–91

43. Theoderic appointed *magister militum*: Marc. Com. a. 483; Jord. *Rom.* 348; Malal. 15, 9. Equestrian statue: Jord. *Get.* 289. Dacia Ripensis and Moesia Inferior: Marc. Com. a. 483.

44. Murder of Rekitach: Joh. Ant. *Frag.* 214, 3 Müller = *Frag.* 306 Roberto, l. 19–24.

45. Theoderic versus Illus: Joh. Ant. *Frag.* 214, 6 Müller = *Frag.* 306 Roberto, l. 25f.; Theoph. a. m. 5977; Evagr. *Hist.* 3, 27. Theoderic in Novae: *Anon. Val.* 42 (476); 49 (488); Marc. Com. a. 487; Joh. Ant. *Frag.* 214, 7 Müller = *Frag.* 306, l. 65 Roberto (487); Eug. *V. Sev.* 44, 4 (488); Prostko-Prostyński 2008. Archeological findings: Ivanov 1997, 556–574; Biernacki 2005; Sarnowski 2012. *Primipilarii:* AE 2005, no. 1328–1330;

Smith and Ward-Perkins 2016, 85f. Emperor Justinian reinforced the fortifications: Proc. *Aed.* 4, 6, 1–3.

46. Campaign in Thrace 486: Joh. Ant. *Frag.* 214, 7 Müller = *Frag.* 306 Roberto, l. 54f.; Zach. *Hist. eccl.* 6, 6. Campaign of 487: Marc. Com. a. 487; Joh. Ant. *Frag.* 214, 7 Müller – *Frag.* 306 Roberto, l. 65f.; Theoph. a. m. 5977; Malal. 15, 9; Evagr. *Hist.* 3, 27; Proc. *Bell.* 5, 1, 9–11. Theoderic's sister in Constantinople might have been Ostrogotho, who was also called Areagni (after the empress Ariadne, who was married to Zeno and subsequently to Anastasius): *PLRE* II Aelia Ariadne.

47. Theoderic's mission according to *Anon. Val.* 49: *cui* [sc. *Zenoni*] *Theodericus pactuatus est, ut, si victus fuisset Odoacar, pro merito laborum suorum loco eius, dum adveniret, tantum praeregnaret.*

48. Theoderic's initiative: Ennod. *Pan.* 14; 25; Ennod. *V. Epif.* 109; Jord. *Get.* 289–292. Zeno's initiative: Proc. *Bell.* 5, 1, 9; Eust. Epiph. *Frag.* 4 Müller = Evagr. *Hist.* 3, 27; Theoph. a. m. 5977; Jord. *Rom.* 348. Offer of 479: Malch. *Frag.* 18 Cresci, l. 259f. = *Frag.* 20 Blockley, l. 220f. Vengeance as *casus belli*: Ennod. *Pan.* 25; Joh. Ant. *Frag.* 214a Müller = *Frag.* 307 Roberto.

CHAPTER 5. THE PATH WEST

1. On the deposition of Romulus, see section 3 of this chapter. On the fall of Rome in Western thought, see Rehm 1930. The debates among historians are treated comprehensively by Demandt 2014. Börm 2008 studies failed attempts to restore the imperial monarchy in the West after 476.

2. Seeck 1895–1920 (see Leppin 1998); L. M. Hartmann 1910. Late Antiquity as a concept: Liebeschuetz 2003 and 2004; Meier 2012 and 2017; Wiemer 2013c. The art historian Alois Riegl (1858–1905) defined late Roman art as a distinct epoch but did not yet use the term "Late Antiquity"; see Elsner 2002; Liebeschuetz 2004, 3–5.

3. Dopsch 1918–1920; Pirenne 1937. The essays collected in Hübinger 1968a provide information about the debate over "cultural rupture or cultural continuity in the transition from Antiquity to the Middle Ages" that was ignited by Dopsch's magnum opus, but they do not include the posthumously published papers by the medievalist Marc Bloch (1886–1944): M. Bloch 1945a and 1945b. The reception of Pirenne is documented in Hübinger 1968b. Outstanding studies of more recent date include Claude 1985; McCormick 2001.

4. Christ 1970a collects important papers on this subject; see also Christ 1970b and 1983. Harper 2017 has again emphasized climate change (and plagues) as factors in the decline and fall. For a critical response, see Haldon et al. 2018. On the methodological problems of scientific, especially archeogenetic, historiography, see Sessa 2019; Meier and Patzold 2021.

5. Organic metaphors for history: Demandt 1978, 17–123.

6. Programmatic: P. Brown 1971; on Brown's oeuvre, see Vessey 1998; Markus 2009; Wiemer 2013c.

7. Goffart 1980, 35. For a more recent restatement of this position, see Goffart 2006, 23–39.

8. Heather 2005. Contemporary perceptions: Courcelle 1964.

9. Ward-Perkins 2005; Wickham 2005.

10. Historical narratives: Bury 1923, 395–565; Stein 1949, 476–565, and 1959, 284–476; Demandt 2007, 284–565. Western and Eastern Roman Empires: Stein 1925; Pabst 1986.

11. Border between the Eastern and Western Empires: Stein 1925, 347–364.

12. Erosion of the Western Roman Empire: Bleckmann 1996; Heather 2005, 193–250; Halsall 2007, 186–283.

13. *Magistri militum*: Demandt 1970. Generalissimos: O'Flynn 1983. *Magister militum et patricius*: Ensslin 1931. Child emperors: McEvoy 2013.

14. Flavius Constantius: Lütkenhaus 1998. Aëtius: Stickler 2002. Ricimer: MacGeorge 2002, 165–268; Anders 2010.

15. Ricimer's marriage to Alypia: Sid. *Ep.* 1, 5, 10f.; 1, 10, 1. Panegyric to Anthemius: Sid. *Carm.* 2. Expedition of 468: Stein 1959, 389–391; Henning 1999, 237f. Cost: Cand. *Frag.* 2; Joh. Lyd. *Mag.* 3, 43; Proc. *Bell.* 3, 6, 1; Theoph. a. m. 5961.

16. Ricimer's 6,000 soldiers: Joh. Ant. *Frag.* 207 Müller = *Frag.* 299 Roberto. Epiphanius as mediator: Ennod. *V. Epif.* 51–75. Fight for Rome, 471–472: Cass. *Chron.* a. 472, no. 1293; Malal. 14, 45, 373; Joh. Ant. *Frag.* 209, 1 Müller = *Frag.* 301 Roberto; Theoph. a. m. 5964; Paul. Diac. *Rom.* 15, 3f. Olybrius: Henning 1999, 47–50.

17. Diocletian's palace: Wilkes 1986. Spalatum was the name of a villa on the territory of Salona, from which the city of Spalato/Split developed during the Middle Ages. A sarcophagus from Salona bears a fragmentary inscription dated after Emperor Zeno: Gauthier, Marin, and Prévot 2010, no. 214.

18. Gundobad: *PLRE* II Gundobad. Return to the kingdom of the Burgundians: Malal. 14, 45. Glycerius: Henning 1999, 50f. Julius Nepos: Henning 1999, 51–55. *Magister militum Dalmatiae*: *CJ* 6, 61, 5. Orestes and Romulus: Henning 1999, 54–56.

19. Odoacer: Cesa 1994; Henning 1999, esp. 58–70, 178–187; MacGeorge 2002, 269–293; Caliri 2017. Elevation to king (*rex*): *Fasti Vind. pr.* a. 476, no. 619; *Pasch. Camp.* a. 476; *Auct. Haun. ord. pr.* a. 476; *Auct. Haun. ord. post.* a. 476, § 1. Orestes' death: Cass. *Chron.* a. 476, no. 1303; *Anon. Val.* 37; Jord. *Get.* 242; Jord. *Rom.* 344; Proc. *Bell.* 5, 1, 4–6. Paulus' death: *Fasti Vind. pr.* a. 476, no. 620; *Auct. Haun. ord. post. margo* a. 476, § 3. Romulus: Cass. *Var.* 3, 35; Jord. *Rom.* 344; Jord. *Get.* 242; Marc. Com. a. 476; cf. *Anon. Val.* 37 (*cum parentibus suis libere vivere*).

20. Odoacer's delegation: Malch. *Frag.* 10 Müller and Cresci, l. 1–10 (citation); discussed by Wiemer 2013a, 137–142.

21. Imperial insignia (*ornamenta palatii*): *Anon. Val.* 64; cf. Cass. *Chron.* a. 476, no. 1303: *cum tamen nec purpura nec regalibus uteretur insignibus* (sc. Odoacer).

22. On the significance of Odoacer's decision to abolish the position of the Western Roman emperor in the year 476: Croke 1983; Wiemer 2013a; Meier 2014.

23. Edica: *PLRE* II Edica. Edica at Attila's court: Prisc. *Frag.* 7 Müller and Cresci; *Frag.* 8 Müller and Cresci.

24. Battle of the Bolia: Jord. *Get.* 277f. Hunwulf: *PLRE* II Onoulphus. Hunwulf as Odoacer's general: Eug. *V. Sev.* 44, 4f.

25. Odoacer's mother: Malch. *Frag.* 8a Müller and Cresci. Odoacer and Severinus: Eug. *V. Sev.* 7. Adovacrius: Greg. Tur. *Hist.* 2, 18–19. Ricimer and Odoacer: Joh. Ant. *Frag.* 209, 1 Müller = *Frag.* 301 Roberto; Proc. *Bell.* 5, 1, 6.

26. Citation: Proc. *Bell.* 5, 1, 2–8; cf. Jord. *Get.* 242; Jord. *Rom.* 344; Ennod. *V. Epif.* 95.

27. On settlement, see in detail chap. 6, section 1, below.

28. Brachila: *Auct. Haun. ord. pr.* 477; *Auct. Haun. ord. post.* a. 477; *Auct. Haun. ord. post. margo* a. 477; *Fasti. Vind. pr.* a. 477; Marc. Com. a. 477; Jord. *Get.* 243. Adaric: *Auct. Haun. ord. pr.* a. 477; *Auct. Haun. ord. post.* a. 477; *Auct. Haun. ord. post. margo* a. 477.

29. Malch. *Frag.* 10 = *Frag.* 14 Blockley (quotation l. 26–30 Cresci = l. 22–25 Blockley).

30. Delegations of Odoacer and Julius Nepos: Malch. *Frag.* 10. Odoacer's titulature: P.Ital. 10–11, I, l. 1 (*dominus noster, praecellentissimus rex*); l. 10 (*rex*); II, l. 11f. (*praecellentissmus rex*); *Acta synodi* a. 502, § 4, MGH.AA XII, p. 445 (*praecellentissimus rex*); AE 1904, no. 148 = ILS 8955 = Fiebiger and Schmidt 1917, no. 194 (*dominus*); AE 1967, no. 7 = Orlandi 2004, 536–539, no. 35; cf. Cass. *Chron.* a. 476, no. 1303 (*nomenque regis adsumpsit*); Evagr. *Hist.* 2, 16 (*rhēga de proseipōn*). The assumption that Odoacer ruled in Julius Nepos' name until 480 (Kent 1966) is based on a questionable dating of gold coins minted for Nepos in Italy.

31. Death of Nepos: *Fasti Vind. pr.* a. 478, no. 626; Marc. Com. a. 480; *Auct. Haun. ord. pr.* a. 480; *Auct. Haun. ord. post.* a. 480; *Auct. Haun. ord. post. margo* a. 480; *Anon. Val.* 36. Glycerius and Nepos: Phot. *Cod.* 78 = Malch. *Test.* 2. Dating formula of the praetorian prefecture of Oriens: SEG 44, no. 909. Odoacer and Zeno: AE 1904, no. 148 = ILS 8955 = Fiebiger and Schmidt 1917, no. 194; AE 2010, no. 181.

32. Odoacer as a tyrant: Ennod. *Pan.* 23f.; 51f.; cf. 56–59; Ennod. *V. Epif.* 109; Cass. *Var.* 8, 17, 2; Arnold 2014, 11–56.

33. *Vicedominus*: P.Ital. †3; P.Ital. 10–11; Delmaire 1989a, 691–694. Only two officeholders are known; both were Romans.

34. *Caput senatus*: Mommsen 1889, 428–430; Stein 1920, 236–238. Seat inscriptions: Chastagnol 1966; corrected by Orlandi 2004. Some scholars (e.g., Chastagnol 1966, 53; Caliri 2017, 118) date copper coins bearing Zeno's portrait on the obverse and the abbreviation SC on the reverse to the year 477. These copper coins, however, were probably minted at Theoderic's behest ca. 490; see Wiemer 2021b, 50–59.

35. Tax policy: Cass. *Var.* 4, 38; Ennod. *V. Epif.* 107. Continuity in personnel: *PLRE* II Cassiodorus 3; *PLRE* II Liberius 3; *PLRE* II Opilio 3.

36. For details on the Acacian Schism, see chap. 10, section 2, below. Felix III on Emperor Zeno: Felix III *Ep.* 4, 1 Thiel = Schwartz 1934, 81f. no. 33 (*JK* 601 = *HJ* 1215).

37. Marc. Com. a. 476; see Croke 1983; Goltz 2008, 86–115. Watts 2011, however, plausibly argues that Odoacer's reign was regarded as a caesura much earlier in the Eastern Roman Empire. The anti-Chalcedonian author John Rufus argues (Joh. Ruf. *Pleroph.* 89) that the *Tomus Leonis* was the reason why Rome fell under barbarian rule, citing for this interpretation the Alexandrian patriarch Timothy Aelurus, who had died on July 31, 477.

38. Northern Italian chronicles: Wes 1967; Momigliano 1973. Felix III to Emperor Zeno: Felix III *Ep.* 1, 5 Thiel = Schwartz 1934, 69–73, no. 21 (*JK* 591 = *HJ* 1202). Senatorial

expectations: Malch. *Frag.* 10 Müller and Cresci; *Auct. Haun. ord. pr.* a. 476; *Auct. Haun. ord. post. margo* a. 476.

39. Cession of Provence: Proc. *Bell.* 5, 12, 20; Cand. *Frag.* 1 = Phot. *Cod.* 79, p. 165; *Chron. Gall.* a. 511, no. 657; *Auct. Haun. ord. pr.* a. 476, 1; Jord. *Get.* 244; Henning 1999, 321–324. Sicily: Vict. Vit. *Hist.* 1, 14. Dalmatia: Cass. *Chron.* a. 481, no. 1309; *Auct. Haun. ord. pr.* a. 482; *Fasti Vind. pr.* a. 482, no. 630.

40. Odoacer and Illus: Joh. Ant. *Frag.* 214, 2 Müller = *Frag.* 316, l. 6–10 Roberto. Severinus of Noricum: Thompson 1982, 113–136; Pohl 2001a. Rebaptism: Eug. *V. Sev.* 8, 1. Plundering of the monastery in Favianis: Eug. *V. Sev.* 44, 1f.

41. Odoacer's campaign against Feva: Cass. *Chron.* a. 487, no. 1316; *Auct. Haun. ord. pr.* a. 487; Eug. *V. Sev.* 44, 4; *Anon. Val.* 48. Hunwulf's campaign: Eug. *V. Sev.* 44, 4f. Evacuation of Noricum: Eug. *V. Sev.* 44, 5–7. Translation of St. Severinus: Eug. *V. Sev.* 45f.

42. Frideric and Theoderic: Eug. *V. Sev.* 44, 4. Odoacer and Zeno: Joh. Ant. *Frag.* 214, 7 Müller = *Frag.* 306 Roberto, l. 57–59; McCormick 1977.

43. The Stanford Geospatial Network Model of the Roman World (http://orbis.stanford. edu/) calculates the distance from Novae to Emona as 1,036 kilometers and the base travel time with oxcarts as eighty-six days. Thracian Goths who did not follow Theoderic: Proc. *Bell.* 5, 16, 2 (*PLRE* II Godigisclus). Goths serving in the armies of Anastasius and Justinian are on record: Theoph. a. m. 5997 (*stratia Gothōn te kai Bessōn kai heterōn Thrakiōn ethnōn*); Malal. 18, 14 (*Gothikē boētheia*); Proc. *Bell.* 1, 8, 3 (*PLRE* II Bessas); *CJ* 1, 5, 12, 17 (527). Goths in Edessa: Jos. Styl. 71 (*PLRE* II Ald), 93–96. Goths on the Crimea: Proc. *Aed.* 3, 7, 13; Vasiliev 1936, 3–69; Bierbrauer 2010.

44. Theoderic's army: Proc. *Bell.* 5, 1, 12; Ennod. *Pan.* 26. Route: Jord. *Get.* 292.

45. On the road route, see Miller 1916, 495–510.

46. Ulca = Vuka: Löwe 1961. L. Schmidt 1934, 294, and Ensslin 1959, 64, in contrast, identify the Ulca as the Sava. Thraustila: *PLRE* II Trapstila.

47. Citation: Ennod. *Pan.* 33f. According to Paul. Diac. *Rom.* 15, 15, the Gepid leader (whom he calls Trapstila) fell in the battle.

48. Ennod. *Pan.* 34f. mentions battles against Sarmatians.

49. Battle at the Isonzo: Ennod. *Pan.* 37f.; *Fasti Vind. pr.* a. 490, no. 639; Cass. *Chron.* a. 489, no. 1320; Jord. *Get.* 293; *Anon. Val.* 50.

50. Battle of Verona: Ennod. *Pan.* 39–47; Cass. *Chron.* a. 489, no. 1321; Jord. *Get.* 293; *Anon. Val.* 50.

51. Theoderic in Milan: Ennod. *V. Epif.* 109; *Anon. Val.* 51. Odoacer in Ravenna: *Anon. Val.* 50. The report that Odoacer fled to Rome but was turned away (Paul. Diac. *Rom.* 15, 15) cannot be accurate for chronological reasons. Tufa's treachery: Ennod. *V. Epif.* 111; *Anon. Val.* 51f.

52. Odoacer in Milan: Ennod. *Dict.* 1, 14f. Theoderic in Ticinum: Ennod. *V. Epif.* 111.

53. Thela: Joh. Ant. *Frag.* 214a Müller = *Frag.* 307 Roberto. Odoacer's coinage: Kraus 1928, 41–64; *RIC* X, 442; Ehling 1998; Metlich 2004, 11f., 25f., 35f.

54. Liguria: Ennod. *V. Epif.* 136–177; Ennod. *Pan.* 54; Cass. *Var.* 12, 28, 2f.; Paul. Diac. *Rom.* 15, 17. Sicily: Cass. *Chron.* a. 491, no. 1327; Ennod. *Pan.* 70; Cass. *Var.* 1, 3, 3. Visigoths: *Anon. Val.* 53. Vidimir: Jord. *Rom.* 347; Jord. *Get.* 283f. Battle of the Adda River: *Auct. Haun.* a. 491; Cass. *Chron.* a. 490, no. 1323; Jord. *Get.* 293; *Anon. Val.* 53.

Pierius: *Auct. Haun.* a. 491; *Anon. Val.* 53. Pierius' funerary inscription: *AE* 1993, no. 803a. Festus' diplomatic mission: *Anon. Val.* 53.

55. Camp *Ad Pinetum*: *Fasti Vind. pr.* a. 491, no. 640; *Auct. Haun.* a. 491; *Anon. Val.* 53f. Tufa and Frideric: *Fasti Vind. pr.* a. 493; *Auct. Haun.* a. 493; Ennod. *Pan.* 55. Dromones: *Fasti Vind. pr.* a. 493, no. 644; *Auct. Haun.* a. 493; Agn. 39.

56. Massacre: Ennod. *Pan.* 51; *Anon. Val.* 56. Proc. *Bell.* 5, 1, 25, mentions survivors. Hunwulf, Sunigilda, and Thela: Joh. Ant. *Frag.* 214a Müller = *Frag.* 307 Roberto; *Chron. Gall.* a. 511, no. 670. Odoacer's corpse: Joh. Ant. *Frag.* 214a Müller = *Frag.* 307 Roberto.

57. Devastation of Italy: Ennod. *Opusc.* 5, 20; Ennod. *V. Epif.* 138; Gelas. *Ep.* 6 Thiel (*JK* 621 = *HJ* 1255); Gelas. *Ep.* 14 Thiel (*JK* 636 = *HJ* 1270); *Frag.* 35 Thiel (*JK* 685 = *HJ* 1326); *Frag.* 9 Thiel (*JK* 706 = *HJ* 1364). Goths and Rugi in Ticinum: Ennod. *V. Epif.* 111–119. Famine in Rome: *Lib. pont.* 51, 3; Gelas. *Tract.* 6, 8 Thiel = *Avell.* 100, 8 (*JK* 627 = *HJ* 1260). Captives of the Burgundians: Ennod. *V. Epif.* 172. Captives of the Goths: Ennod. *V. Epif.* 115f.

58. Antichrist: *Pasch. Camp.* a. 493. Theoderic's first decree: Ennod. *V. Epif.* 122; Ensslin 1944a. Laurentius, Epiphanius, and Theoderic: Ennod. *V. Epif.* 123–135.

59. Victor, Epiphanius, and Gundobad: Ennod. *V. Epif.* 136–175. Ransoming of prisoners: Klingshirn 1985. Ostrogotho's engagement to Sigismund: Ennod. *V. Epif.* 163; Shanzer 1996–1997. Syagria: *PLRE* II Syagria.

60. Remission of taxes: Ennod. *V. Epif.* 182–189.

61. Theoderic as *patricius*: *Anon. Val.* 49; 51–54. First delegation of Festus: *Anon. Val.* 53. Festus: *PLRE* II 5. *Vestis regia*: Alföldi 1935, 29–31. The statement in Malal. 15, 9, that Theoderic's high officials were appointed by Zeno is confused and implausible. Delegation of Faustus Niger: *Anon. Val.* 57; Gelas. *Ep.* 10 Thiel = Schwartz 1934, 16–19, no. 7 (*JK* 622 = *HJ* 1256). Faustus Niger: *PLRE* II Faustus 9.

62. *Anon. Val.* 57; Jord. *Get.* 295; Claude 1978b. As the reference to § 294 shows, the words *tertioque, ut diximus, anno ingressus sui in Italiam* mean the third year of the siege of Ravenna.

63. Proclamation and *praesumptio regni*: Mommsen 1889, 248, n. 2 (legally inconsequential proclamation); Ensslin 1959, 70f. (expansion of Theoderic's kingship to encompass the entire army); A. H. M. Jones 1962, 129 (like Mommsen); Wolfram 1967, 45f.; Wenskus 1977, 484 (like Ensslin); Claude 1978b (expansion of kingship to Italy); Claude 1980, 155f.; Kohlhas-Müller 1995, 36 (like Ensslin); Heather 1996, 220f. ("proclaimed king" by the army); Wolfram 2009, 284–288 ("elevation to ruler of Goths and Romans on a par with the emperor").

CHAPTER 6. THE CONSOLIDATION OF POWER

1. On account of the absence of reliable data, the size of the population of ancient Italy is uncertain and controversial. I follow the low approach, which posits approximately six million inhabitants of Italy for the early imperial period, including approximately two million slaves; for a brief summary of the current state of research with further references, see Scheidel 2013a. Lower numbers must be presumed for Late Antiquity: Vera 2007, 498–500.

2. On Theoderic's governing strategy, see also Wiemer 2013b.
3. Rugi: Proc. *Bell.* 7, 2; Heather 1998; Steinacher 2017, 75–135. Breones: Cass. *Var.* 1, 11. Heruli: Cass. *Var.* 4, 10 + 4, 11. Gepids: Cass. *Var.* 5, 10; cf. Proc. *Bell.* 8, 32, 24.
4. Jews: cf. chap. 10, section 4, below.
5. Theoderic's dual state: cf. chap. 7 below.
6. Policy of fusion: C. Schäfer 2001; Spielvogel 2002. Alexander the Great: Wiemer 2015c, 158–162, 174–176.
7. Modalities of settlement in Italy: Porena 2012a (fundamental); Porena and Rivière 2012 (research discussion); Wiemer 2022a (succinct survey). Settlement of Vandals: Modéran 2002 and 2012.
8. Division of land: Porena 2012a and 2012b. Tax shares: Goffart 1980, 58–102; Durliat 1988 (refuted by Liebeschuetz 1997).
9. Quotation: Cass. *Var.* 2, 16, 5.
10. Ennodius to Liberius: Ennod. *Ep.* 9, 23, 5.
11. Liberius: *PLRE* II Liberius 3; O'Donnell 1981; Dumézil 2012. *Pittacia*: Cass. *Var.* 1, 18.
12. Gothic settlement areas: Bierbrauer: 1975, 25–41, and 1994, 140–152.
13. *Collatio glebalis*: Delmaire 1989a, 374–386; Barnish 1989. In the Eastern Roman Empire, the *gleba* was abolished by a law of Emperor Marcian: *CJ* 12, 2, 2 (455). Sicily: Proc. *Bell.* 7, 16, 16f.; Cracco-Ruggini 1980; Vera 1988. *Tertia* as a special tax: Cass. *Var.* 1, 14; 2, 18; P.Ital. 47–48.
14. *Patrimonium* of Amalafrida: Cass. *Var.* 9, 5. Theodahad: cf. chap. 9, section 3, below. The Gothic commander Uraias (cf. chap. 12, sections 2–3) was married to a very wealthy Gothic woman: Proc. *Bell.* 7, 1, 37. Gothic men with landed property: Matza (Cass. *Var.* 1, 15); Butila (Cass. *Var.* 2, 17); Tuluin (Cass. *Var.* 8, 10, 8); Tancan (Cass. *Var.* 8, 28); Aderit (P.Ital. 13). Gothic women with landed property: Ranilda (Cass. *Var.* 10, 26); Thulgilo (P.Ital. 30).
15. Procopius' terminology for the Gothic aristocracy: Proc. *Bell.* 5, 2, 11; 5, 2, 21; 5, 3, 11; 5, 4, 13; 5, 13, 26; 7, 8, 24; 7, 24, 27; 8, 35, 33 (*logimos*); 3, 8, 12; 6, 3, 36; 6, 20, 14; 6, 23, 8; 6, 29, 24 + 41; 7, 1, 1; 37, 8, 13; 7, 18, 26; 8, 23, 10; 8, 26, 4 + 21 (*dokimos*); 5, 13, 15; 6, 9, 8; 6, 20, 2; 6, 28, 29; 7, 1, 46 (*aristos*). These adjectives also occasionally appear in the superlative: Proc. *Bell.* 5, 2, 21 (*logimōtatos*); 8, 23, 1 (*dokimōtatos*). We also encounter expressions like "the foremost among the Goths" (Proc. *Bell.* 5, 7, 21); "very famous" (*ouk aphanē*) (Proc. *Bell.* 5, 18, 39; 1, 23, 9; 2, 7, 13); or "the unsullied among them" (*ei ti en autois katharon ēn*) (Proc. *Bell.* 5, 13, 17; 6, 29, 18; 6, 30, 4). It is often difficult to tell in a given example whether Procopius is emphasizing the aspect of excellence or honor. Cf. also Malch. *Frag.* 18 Cresci, l. 295–297 = *Frag.* 20 Blockley, l. 251f.; Jord. *Get.* 282; 304; Wiemer 2013b, 607f. Unfree Goths: Malchus *Frag.* 15 Cresci, l. 61f. = *Frag.* 18, 2 Blockley, l. 52f.; Proc. *Bell.* 3, 8, 12; Cass. *Var.* 5, 29; cf. Cass. *Var.* 5, 30 (*onera servilia*).
16. Dwelling places of the Goths: Bierbrauer 1975, 25–41; Christie: 2006, 357–364, 451–458, and 2020; Wiemer 2017.
17. Demilitarization of the Romans: Liebeschuetz 1996.
18. Arms and fighting style of the Goths: Wiemer and Berndt 2016.
19. Adulthood: Cass. *Var.* 1, 38. Muster: Cass. *Var.* 1, 24, 1 + 3. Quotation: Cass. *Var.* 5, 23.
20. Quotation: Ennod. *Pan.* 83f.

21. Respect for opponents: Proc. *Bell.* 5, 29, 40. Tuluin: Cass. *Var.* 8, 10, 7. Duels: Wiemer and Berndt 2016, 184–189.
22. *Millenarius*: Cass. *Var.* 5, 27; Wiemer and Berndt 2016, 182f. Quotation: Ennod. *Pan.* 69; cf. § 65.
23. *Comes Gothorum*: Tabata 2013, 71–95. *Formula comitivae Syracusanae*: Cass. *Var.* 6, 22. *Formula comitivae Neapolitanae*: Cass. *Var.* 6, 23; cf. 6, 24; Proc. *Bell.* 5, 3, 15. *Formula de comite insulae Curitanae et Celsinae*: Cass. *Var.* 7, 16.
24. *Formula comitivae Gothorum per singulas civitates*: Cass. *Var.* 7, 3. The *Formula comitivae diversarum civitatum* (Cass. *Var.* 7, 26), in contrast, appears to pertain to special officials appointed on a case-by-case basis who served as judges in a city, bearing the title of *comes*. The occupants of the *comitiva Romana* (Cass. *Var.* 7, 13) and the *comitiva Ravennas* (Cass. *Var.* 7, 14) apparently had purely administrative duties.
25. Quotation: Cass. *Var.* 7, 25, 1. Office of the *comes civitatis*: Cass. *Var.* 6, 25 (*princeps militum Syracusanae civitatis*); Cass. *Var.* 7, 28 (*Formula principis militum*). Recommendation letter for the *princeps* of a *comes*: Cass. *Var.* 7, 25. Office of a *comes provinciae*: Cass. *Var.* 7, 24 (*Formula principis Dalmatiarum*); cf. Cass. *Var.* 5, 14, 8 (*domestici comitis Dalmatiae*); Cass. *Var.* 6, 25 (*princeps officii comitis provinciae*).
26. Gildila: Cass. *Var.* 9, 14, 8. Florianus: Cass. *Var.* 1, 5. Marabad: Cass. *Var.* 4, 12; 4, 46 with Liebs 2002, 276–280. Theodegunda: Cass. *Var.* 4, 37.
27. Term of one year: Cass. *Var.* 6, 25. *Prior* in Reate and Nursia: Cass. *Var.* 8, 26. Wisibad: Cass. *Var.* 10, 29.
28. *Formula comitis provinciae*: Cass. *Var.* 7, 1.
29. *Formula tuitionis*: Cass. *Var.* 7, 39.
30. *Saiones*: Morosi 1981a; Maier 2005, 169–181. *Formula edicti ad quaestorem, ut ipse spondere debeat qui saionem meretur*: Cass. *Var.* 7, 42. *Saiones* and *comitiaci*: Cass. *Var.* 3, 20; 8, 27. On the *comitiaci*, cf. chap. 7, section 3, below.
31. *Sportulae*: Cass. *Var.* 9, 14, 4. Abuses: Cass. *Var.* 4, 27; 4, 28.
32. *Donativum*: Cass. *Var.* 4, 14, 2; 5, 26, 2; 5, 27, 1; 5, 36, 2; 7, 42, 3; 8, 26, 4.
33. *Fabricae*: Cass. *Var.* 7, 18 (*Formula de armifactoribus*); Cass. *Var.* 7, 19 (*Formula ad ppo de armifactoribus*); James 1988; Berndt and Wiemer 2016, 176–180.
34. Proc. *Bell.* 5, 11, 16 (stores of weapons in Provence and Venetia); Cass. *Var.* 1, 40, 2; 1, 24, 2.
35. Pitzia: Ennod. *Pan.* 12; Jord. *Get.* 300; *PLRE* II Pitzia. When Cass. *Var.* 5, 29, was written (between 523 and 526), the Pitzia mentioned there as *comes piae recordationis* was already dead. Petia: *Auct. Haun.* a. 514.
36. On Theoderic's foreign policy, cf. chap. 8 below.
37. Chastity (*pudicitia*) of Germanic women: Tac. *Germ.* 19.
38. Royal wedding mediation: Proc. *Bell.* 5, 11, 8 (Theodahad); Proc. *Bell.* 7, 1, 42f. (Ildebad).
39. Gothic law: Jord. *Get.* 68 (*belagines*); Agath. *Hist.* 1, 20, 1 (*patria nomima*). Theoderic's marriage legislation: *Ed. Theod. Var.* 36–39; Cass. *Var.* 5, 32; 5, 33; Wiemer 2017, 281–288. Late Roman marriage law: Arjava 1996, 193–205. Killing of an adulterer with impunity: Cass. *Var.* 1, 37.

40. Women in Theoderic's army: Malch. *Frag.* 15, l. 55–72; Proc. *Bell.* 6, 26, 34; cf. Ennod. *Pan.* 42–45. Women's names: Francovich Onesti 2007, 128–136; Haubrichs 2017; Wiemer 2017, 276–281.

41. Ostrogothic women: Wiemer 2017.

42. Weapons ban: *Anon. Val.* 83; *Nov. Just.* 85, 4 (539); Wiemer and Berndt 2016, 150f. Gothic beard: Ennod. *Carm.* 2, 57, with Liebeschuetz 2013, 158f.

43. Gothic: Proc. *Bell.* 3, 2, 5; 5, 10, 10; 6, 1, 15f.; Cass. *Var.* 5, 40, 5; 8, 21, 7; 11, 1, 6. Gothic onomastics: Amory 1997, 102–108; Wagner 1997. Homoean clergy: cf. chap. 10, section 1, below. Goths allegedly banned from attending school: Proc. *Bell.* 5, 2, 14f. Hildevara: P.Marini 85, new edition by Tjäder 1988. Hildevara was a *spectabilis femina*. Ranilo and Felithanc: P.Ital. 13. Both bore the title *sublimis*; moreover, Ranilo was the daughter of *vir gloriosus* Aderit (otherwise unknown).

44. Functional bilingualism: Francovich Onesti 2007, 9f. Bilingualism at Theoderic's court: cf. chap. 7, sections 1–3, below.

45. Quotation: Cass. *Var.* 8, 26, 3–4.

46. Theodahad: Proc. *Bell.* 5, 3, 2; Cass. *Var.* 4, 39; 5, 12; 10, 4, 4; cf. Cass. *Var.* 8, 28 (Tancan). Edict of Athalaric: Cass. *Var.* 9, 18, 2–6. Judicial deadlock in Samnium: Cass. *Var.* 3, 13.

47. Edict of Theoderic: Ubl 2020; Schmidt-Hofner and Wiemer 2022 (with a survey of older literature); for recent translations with commentary (superseding Dahn 1866), see Lafferty 2013 (reviewed critically by Liebs 2015); Licandro 2013; König 2018. Disciplinary problems: Cass. *Var.* 2, 8; 3, 38; 5, 10f.; 5, 26, 2; 6, 25; 7, 4, 3; 12, 5. Compensation: Cass. *Var.* 2, 8.

48. *Lex Burgundionum*: Nehlsen 1978; Liebs 2002, 163–166; Heather 2012; Schmidt-Hofner and Wiemer 2022. Dispute resolution in warrior societies: Schott 1995 and 1996. Oath of purgation: *L. Burg.* 8; 45; 80.

49. Cass. *Var.* 3, 24, 4. Trial by combat: Holzhauer 1986.

50. Blood feud: Proc. *Bell.* 5, 4, 26; 5, 11, 6–9; 7, 1, 37–42; 7, 1, 43–48; 7, 2, 6–13.

51. Liberius as *vir exercitualis*: Cass. *Var.* 11, 1. Military acculturation: Wiemer and Berndt 2016, 152, 156f., 175f.

52. Tuluin: *PLRE* II Tuluin; Cass. *Var.* 8, 10; 8, 11. Eutharic was consul in 519, but he apparently did not become a member of the senate.

53. Cyprianus: *PLRE* II Cyprianus 2; Cass. *Var.* 8, 21.

54. Barbara: *PLRE* II Barbara; Ennod. *Ep.* 8, 16. Amalasuintha: *PLRE* II Amalasvintha; Vitiello 2017, 46–54; Cass. *Var.* 11, 1 with Fauvinet-Ranson 1998. Amalaberga: *PLRE* II Amalaberga; Vitiello 2006b; Cass. *Var.* 4, 1, 2 (*litteris edoctam*). Cassiodorus' praise of Theoderic's granddaughter Matasuintha's virtues is too vague to shed light on her education: Cass. *Or.* 2, MGH.AA XII, p. 479. Theodahad: Cass. *Var.* 10, 3, 4f.; Proc. *Bell.* 5, 6, 10; 1, 6, 16; cf. chap. 11, section 1, and chap. 12, sections 1–2, below. Theoderic's interest in natural philosophy: Cass. *Var.* 9, 24, 8.

55. *Anon. Val.* 61: *Romanus miser imitatur Gothum et utilis Gothus imitatur Romanum.* The translation in the text is based on the interpretation suggested by Adams 1976, 108, which has been widely accepted, most recently by Festy and Vitiello 2020, 9. Adams has not, however, produced conclusive evidence for his contention that *utilis* in Late

Latin is synonymous to "rich." Perhaps one should, therefore, read *futilis* "worthless" (suggested by Zangemeister) or *vilis* "vile" (thus Ensslin 1959, 264, with 383, n. 4, following Gardthausen) instead of *utilis*. To take *utilis* in the sense of "respected" (thus König 1997, 151) makes nonsense of the antithesis between Roman and Goth. Festy and Vitiello 2020, 67f., unconvincingly refer to Isid. *Hist. Goth.* 16 (which is derived from Oros. *Hist.* 7, 41, 7) as evidence that the saying was transmitted by Cassiodorus.

56. Quotation: Sid. *Ep.* 1, 9, 2–4. Paulus: *PLRE* II Paulus 36. Gennadius Avienus: *PLRE* II Avienus 4. Caecina Decius: *PLRE* II Basilius 11.

57. Theodorus: Fulg. *Ep.* 6, 2f.; *PLRE* II Theodorus 62. Clients prepared to resort to violence: Cass. *Var.* 1, 27; *Lib. pont.* 53, 5. Cassiodorus' father: Cass. *Var.* 1, 3, 3f.; *PLRE* II Cassiodorus 3. Tullianus: Proc. *Bell.* 7, 18, 20–23; 7, 22, 1–5; 7, 22, 20–22; *PLRE* III Tullianus 1.

58. On local elites, cf. chap. 9, section 5, below.

59. Senate: La Rocca and Oppedisano 2016 (fundamental); cf. also Chastagnol 1992, 345–374. Senators and senatorial milieu: Eich 2020 (groundbreaking); cf. also Matthews 1981; Barnish 1988; C. Schäfer 1991; Heather 1998; Henning 1999. The prosopographies in C. Schäfer 1991 and Henning 1999 have been partly superseded by Orlandi 2004. Acclamations: Wiemer 2004a and 2013d.

60. Old and new families: Eich 2020. Episcopal see of Rome: cf. chap. 10, sections 2–3, below. Land disputes: Cass. *Var.* 1, 23. Trial for magic: Cass. *Var.* 4, 22f. In his *Encyclopedia*, Martianus Capella describes two sessions of the "senate of the gods" under the presidency of Jupiter; in the first one (Mart. Cap. 1, 94), Jupiter's proposal is passed by acclamation; in the second (Mart. Cap. 9, 888–898), a debate takes place; for analysis, see Barnish 1986.

61. Decii: *PLRE* II Stemma 26; Moorhead 1984; Al. Cameron 2012a, 150–153.

62. Symmachi: *PLRE* II Stemma 22. Anicii: Al. Cameron 2012a. Faustus Albus: *PLRE* II Faustus 4. Faustus Niger: *PLRE* II Faustus 9.

63. Quotations from Cass. *Var.* 3, 6.

64. *Devotio* of Decius Mus: Liv. 8, 9.

65. Acilii Glabriones: Herod. 2, 3, 4; Al. Cameron 2012a, 148–150. Corvini: Macr. *Sat.* 1, 6, 26; Al. Cameron 2012a, 150–153.

66. Senatorial landed property: cf. chap. 9, section 2, below. Urban houses of the fifth century: *V. Melaniae.gr.* 14; *V. Melaniae.lat.* 14, 2; Olymp. *Frag.* 1, 43 Müller = *Frag.* 41, 1 Blockley; *Gest. sen.* a. 438, § 1; Merob. *Carm.* 3; CIL XV 7420 (lead pipe from the Aventine). Urban houses of the sixth century: Proc. *Bell.* 7, 21, 26 (*patrikiōn oikiai*); Guidobaldi 1999; Machado 2012a, 2012b, and 2019. Symmachus: Cass. *Var.* 4, 51, 1f.; *PLRE* II Symmachus 9. Albinus: Cass. *Var.* 4, 30; *PLRE* II Albinus 9. *Philopolides Rhōmaioi*: Proc. *Bell.* 8, 22, 5.

67. Cost of the praetorship in the fifth century: Olymp. *Frag.* 1, 44 Müller = *Frag.* 41, 2 Blockley with Al. Cameron 1984. Cost of the consulship in the sixth century: Cass. *Var.* 3, 39; 5, 42, 11f.; 6, 1, 7f. Consular diptych of Boethius: R. Delbrück 1929, 103–106, no. 7; Volbach 1976, 32, no. 6 with pl. 3; Al. Cameron 2012a.

68. Leave from Rome: Cass. *Var.* 3, 21; 4, 48; 7, 36 (*formula commeatalis*). Seats in the theater and amphitheater: Cass. *Var.* 4, 42. Colosseum: Chastagnol 1966; Orlandi

2004. Spectacles: Fauvinet-Ranson 2006a, 379–440; Puk 2014. Patrons of the Greens: Cass. *Var.* 1, 20. Acclamations: Cass. *Var.* 1, 27; 1, 31, 4; Proc. *Bell.* 5, 6, 4; Al. Cameron 1976; Wiemer 2004a and 2013d.

69. Strife over the pantomime actor Helladius: Cass. *Var.* 1, 27; 1, 30–32; C. Piétri 1966; Fauvinet-Ranson 2006a, 319–323.

70. Ennodius and Boethius: Ennod. *Carm.* 2, 132; Di Rienzo 2005, 194–196. Education in sixth-century Italy: Riché 1995, 28–32. Chairs of rhetoric in Rome: Cass. *Var.* 9, 21; *Nov. Just.* Appendix 7, 22. Law: Liebs 1987, 70–75, 122f. Medicine: Cass. *Var.* 6, 19 (*Formula comitis archiatrorum*); Schulze 2005. Greek philosophy: Courcelle 1948.

71. Symmachus: Vitiello 2008. *Historia Romana: FHistLA* 15. On a visit to Constantinople, Symmachus discussed philological problems with the *grammaticus* Priscian (*PLRE* II Priscianus 2); Priscian wrote three minor works on antiquarian, metrical, and rhetorical subjects at his request, as we learn from the dedicatory epistle to Prisc. *Fig. num., GL* III, p. 405 Keil = p. 3 Passalacqua. Whether Cassiodorus also knew Priscian personally is unclear; he mentions him at the end of his long life in Cass. *Orth., GL* VII, p. 147, l. 15; p. 207, l. 13f. Cassiodorus as theologian: Schlieben 1974 and 1979; O'Donnell 1979, 131–176; Barnish 1987a. For a short introduction to Cass. *Anim.*, see Vessey 2004, 19–22. On Boethius: Matthews 1981; H. Chadwick 1981; Gruber 2011. Commentary on the *Categories*: Boeth. *In categ. comm.* 2, praef. Faustus Niger as versifier: Ennod. *Ep.* 1, 6; Ennod. *Carm.* 1, 7. Maximianus: Barnish 1990; Vitiello 2014b, 83f.

72. See Ennodius' recommendations for the study of the liberal arts in his *Paraenesis didascalica*: Ennod. *Opusc.* 6; Rallo Freni 1981. Ambrosius: Cass. *Var.* 8, 13; 8, 14; 11, 4; 11, 5; 12, 25; *PLRE* II Ambrosius 3. Beatus: *PLRE* II Beatus. Asterius: *PLRE* II Asterius 11. Felix: *PLRE* III Felix 2. Mavortius: *PLRE* II Mavortius 2.

73. Cass. *Lib.*; Ennod. *Libell.* 129–138, esp. 132f. (quotation). Lupercalia: Gelas. *Tract.* 6 Thiel = *Avell.* 97 (*JK* 627 = *HJ* 1260); McLynn 2008.

74. Theological interests of senators: Boeth. *Tract.* praef.; Joh. Diac. *Ep. ad Senarium; Ep. Johannis ad senatores,* in: ACO IV, 2, p. 206–210, no. 1 (*JK* 885 = *HJ* 1746); Sev. Ant. *C. imp. gram.* 3, pars posterior 29. Theodorus: Fulg. *Ep.* 6; *PLRE* II Theodorus 62; PCBE II Theodorus 12. Ascetic women of *illustris* rank: Fulg. *Ep.* 2 (Galla); Fulg. *Ep.* 3+4 (Proba); Fulg. *Ep.* 7 (Venantia); Dionys. Exig. *Praef.* 10. Cf. chap. 10, section 3, below.

75. Orestes' consular diptych: R. Delbrück 1929, 148–150, no. 32; Volbach 1976, 40f., no. 31 with pl. 16. *Libertas*: Moorhead 1987. *Romana libertas*: Ennod. *Ep.* 9, 30, 6; Cass. *Var.* 10, 33, 3; 11, 13, 1; Boeth. *Cons.* 1, 4, 26. *Dominus libertatis*: Cass. *Var.* 3, 11, 1; Ennod. *Ep.* 4, 26, 1. *Defensor libertatis*: Cass. *Var.* 3, 43, 2. *Custos libertatis*: CIL X 6850a, 6850b, and 6851 = *ILS* 827 = *ILCV* 35. *Atrium libertatis*: CIL VI 40807 = *ILS* 825. Crisis of 504–508: cf. chap. 8, sections 2–3.

76. Second delegation of Festus: *Anon. Val.* 64; Theod. Lect. 461; Theoph. a. m. 5993; cf. *Avell.* 102. The *terminus ante quem* is the death of Pope Anastasius II on November 19, 498. Olbrich 2013 argues that the senate played a constitutive part in Theoderic's elevation; his argument is based on a unique silver coin of unknown provenance that bears the name and portrait of Emperor Anastasius on the obverse and the mysterious abbreviation TSCR on the reverse, along with the defective legend VICRIA (instead of VICTORIA) and, in the exergue, the mint and (for silver, nonsensical) weight indi-

cator CONOR (instead of CONOB = *Constantinopoli obryzum*, "at Constantinople, 1/72 lb. gold"—i.e., a *solidus*). It is more than doubtful that this coin is a Roman issue, not least because the expansion of the abbreviation TSCR as *T*(*heodericus*) *S*(*enatus*) *C*(*onsulto*) *R*(*ex*) defies all titular conventions; it might be a barbarian imitation or a modern fake. I thank Reinhard Wolters for his expertise on this coin.

77. Coronation of Tzath I: Malal. 17, 9; *Chron. Pasch.* a. 522; Joh. Nik. 90; *PLRE* II Ztathius; Greatrex 1998, 133f. Cf. Agath. *Hist.* 3, 15, on the coronation of Tzath II in the year 555; Claude 1989.

78. Purple: Ennod. *Pan.* 89; Cass. *Var.* 1, 2; 6, 7, 6. Medallion of Morro d'Alba: see chap. 1, section 2, above. Theoderic's hair: Ennod. *Pan.* 91. Diadem and bald spot: Polem. *Brev.* 16. (I thank Bruno Bleckmann for this reference.) Justinian's portrait in Sant'Apollinare Nuovo: Agn. 86; Lorentz 1935; Baldini Lippolis 2000. Caesarius of Arles visits Theoderic: *V. Caes.* I, 36; cf. chap. 8, section 5, below.

79. Gothic royal costume: Jord. *Get.* 246; 278; 295; Agath. *Hist.* 1, 20, 10; Greg. Magn. *Dial.* 2, 14. Athalaric to Justin: Cass. *Var.* 8, 1, 5; cf. Cass. *Var.* 10, 22, 2; Wiemer 2020b, 275–279. For a convincing critique of Mommsen 1889, 465–484 (similarly, Ensslin 1959, 76–79), see A. H. M. Jones 1962; Prostko-Prostyński 2019, 33–62.

80. Theoderic's titulature: Prostko-Prostyński 2019, 56–62; Gillett 2002b, 98–100. Fictive kinship (*Ansippung*): Wolfram 1967, 56–62. Flavius: Keenan 1973–1974; Al. Cameron 1988; Prostko-Prostyński 2019, 63–74. Papyri: Bagnall, Cameron, Schwartz, and Worp 1987, 503. *Theodericus vict*(*or*) *ac triumf*(*ator*) *semper Aug*(*ustus*): *ILS* 827 = *ILCV* 35 = Fiebiger and Schmidt 1917, no. 193; cf. Cass. *Var.* 2, 33f. Basilius Decius: *PLRE* II Decius 2.

81. Anastasius to the senate: *Avell.* 113, 3f.; cf. *Avell.* 114, 7. Theoderic to Anastasius: Cass. *Var.* 1, 1, 2–5; the dating of the letter varies between 508 (thus Krautschick 1983, 50f.; Moorhead 1992, 45) and 510 or 511 (thus Ensslin 1959, 149f.; Prostko-Prostyński 2019, 238–241).

82. Treaty draft of 535: Proc. *Bell.* 5, 6, 2–5; Chrysos 1981. Treaty with Anastasius: Prostko-Prostyński 2019, 151–212; Wiemer 2020c, 275–279.

CHAPTER 7. THEODERIC'S DUAL STATE

1. Legitimacy discourse: Mommsen 1889; Ensslin 1940a and 1959; A. H. M. Jones 1962; Wolfram 1979 and 2009; Kohlhas-Müller 1995. Acceptance: Flaig 2019.

2. Monarchic rule in Antiquity: Rebenich 2012 (concise survey) and 2017 (broad panorama); Rebenich and Wienand 2017 (approaches and perspectives). The court: Winterling 1998. *Formula comitivae primi ordinis*: Cass. *Var.* 6, 12. *Adoratio purpurae*: Matthews 1989, 244–249. The *consistorium*: Delmaire 1995, 29–45.

3. Legislation on rank and elite competition: Schmidt-Hofner 2010.

4. Cass. *Var.* 6, 10 (*Formula qua per codicillos vacantes proceres fiant*); Cass. *Var.* 6, 11 (*Formula inlustratus vacantis*); Cass. *Var.* 7, 37 (*Formula spectabilitatis*); Cass. *Var.* 7, 38 (*Formula clarissimatus*).

5. Imperial traveling in Late Antiquity: Destephen 2016. Palace in Ticinum: *Anon. Val.* 71; Agn. 94. Palace in Verona: *Anon. Val.* 71. Palace in Monza: Paul. Diac. *Lang.* 4, 21. Galeata: *V. Hilari* 10–13; Deichmann 1989, 267–272; De Maria 2004. A magnificent

floor mosaic was discovered at this site in 2018. The physical location and internal organization of these central archives are unknown, but their existence is beyond doubt.

6. Palace in Ravenna: *Anon. Val.* 71; Agn. 94. Sant'Apollinare Nuovo as a "Palace Church": Agn. 86 = Fiebiger and Schmidt 1917, no. 181 = ILCV 1793. Theoderic's buildings in Ravenna: Deichmann: 1974, 125–190, 209–258; 1976, 326–329; and 1989; Deliyannis 2010, 114–136, 139–187; Jaeggi 2013, 154–217.

7. Building material: Cass. *Var.* 3, 9 (Sestinum?); Cass. *Var.* 3, 10 (*domus Pinciana* in Rome); Cass. *Var.* 5, 8 (Faenza); Deichmann 1989, 273–276 (capitals from Constantinople). Sant'Andrea dei Goti: Deichmann 1976, 326–329. Marble workers (*marmorarii*): Cass. *Var.* 1, 6. The king's garden: *ILS* 826 = Fiebiger and Schmidt 1917, no. 179 = ILCV 36; Jord. *Get.* 151; Ennod. *Carm.* 2, 111.

8. Rome and Ravenna: Gillett 2001; Wiemer 2015a; McEvoy 2017. Rome and Constantinople: Ward-Perkins 2012.

9. Main entrance to the palace: Agn. 94 with Duval 1960, 356–362. *Invicta Roma/Felix Ravenna*: Metlich 2004, 112–144, nos. 76–78 (Rome) and no. 81 (Ravenna). On Theoderic's copper coinage, see further in chap. 9, section 7, below.

10. City walls under Valentinian III: Agn. 40 with Jaeggi 2013, 75–77; *contra* Deliyannis 2010, 52–54 (under Honorius). Aqueduct: Cass. *Chron.* a. 502, no. 1342; *Anon. Val.* 71.

11. Population of Ravenna: Deichmann 1989, 114f. (5,000); Cosentino 2005 (10,000). Population of Rome in the fifth and sixth centuries: all estimates are based on the adaerated figures for the pork deliveries from Lucania for the *plebs Romana* given in Cass. *Var.* 11, 39; most recently, Lo Cascio 2013; cf. also Barnish 1987b, 160–164.

12. Constitution of Ravenna: Stein 1919, 59–71; Ausbüttel 1987; Deichmann 1989, 130–142. Oversight of the market: Cass. *Var.* 6, 6, 6; cf. Cass. *Var.* 11, 11. Importation of grain: Cass. *Var.* 1, 35; 2, 20. Sarcophagi: Cass. *Var.* 3, 19. *Comes Ravennatis*: Cass. *Var.* 7, 14. *Praefectus vigilum urbis Ravennatis*: Cass. *Var.* 7, 8.

13. *Cura palatii*: Cass. *Var.* 7, 5.

14. *Cubicularii*: Fiebiger and Schmidt 1917, no. 183 = ILCV 226; cf. Fiebiger and Schmidt 1917, no. 205 = ILCV 356. *Praepositus cubiculi*: Ensslin 1956a; Delmaire 1995, 151–160.

15. Triwa/Triggvila: Boeth. *Cons.* 1, 4, 10; *Anon. Val.* 82. Triggva: Ennod. *Ep.* 9, 21. For the name, see Francovich Onesti 2007, 100f., no. 314–316. He can hardly be identical with the *saio* Triwila, to whom Cass. *Var.* 3, 20, is addressed (*contra PLRE* II Triwila).

16. Audefleda: L. M. Hartmann 2008; Greg. Tur. *Hist.* 3, 31. Ereleuva: *PLRE* II Erelieva; Gelas. *Ep.* 4, MGH.AA XII, p. 390 = *Frag.* 36 Thiel (*JK* 683 = *HJ* 1312); Gelas. *Ep.* 5, MGH.AA XII, p. 390 (*JK* 721 = *HJ* 1376); Ennod. *Pan.* 42–45.

17. Ostrogotho: *PLRE* II Areagni. Betrothal to Sigismund: Ennod. *V. Epif.* 163. Thiudigotho: *PLRE* II Theodegotha. Amalafrida: *PLRE* II Amalafrida. Mother and daughter: Ennod. *Pan.* 42. Ostrogothic queens: L. M. Hartmann 2009, 25–36.

18. Amalaberga: *PLRE* II Amalaberga. Amalaberga as idealized young queen: Cass. *Var.* 4, 1. Amalasuintha: Ennod. *Ep.* 8, 16; Cass. *Var.* 11, 1, 6–8. Athalaric: Proc. *Bell.* 5, 2, 6–20. Tuluin: Cass. *Var.* 8, 10, 3.

19. Travels of the court: Cass. *Var.* 2, 20; 12, 18f. Grain from and for Liguria: Cass. *Var.* 2, 20, 2–3 (first quotation). Visitors at court: Cass. *Var.* 1, 20, 1 (second quotation); Cass. *Var.* 12,

19, 1. Grain from Calabria and Apulia: Cass. *Var.* 1, 35. Delicacies: Cass. *Var.* 6, 9, 7 (block quotation); Cass. *Var.* 12, 4, 2 (wine); Cass. *Var.* 12, 18, 1 (*regius apparatus*); Cass. *Var.* 12, 18, 3 (*mensa regia*). Judging from Anthimus' manual, the culinary standards at the Merovingian court were considerably lower: King Theuderic, a son of Clovis, was warned against eating meat and other foodstuffs raw (praet.) or to indulge in the Frankish passion for roasted bacon (§ 10); he was advised to drink beer, mead, or vermouth (§ 15).

20. Roman feasts: Vössing 2004, 265–539; Stein-Hölkeskamp 2005. The banquet of Emperor Majorian: Sid. *Ep.* 1, 11, 10–15. Goths at banquets: Proc. *Bell.* 7, 1, 45–47. Theoderic and Artemidorus: Cass. *Var.* 1, 43, 3. Theoderic and Cassiodorus: Cass. *Var.* 9, 24, 8.

21. Gothic shouting at a banquet: *Anth. Lat.* 285 Riese = 279 Shackleton-Bailey; Snædal 2009; Haubrichs 2012, 34f. The meaning of the fragments of Gothic is disputed; I follow the interpretation of Wolfgang Haubrichs. The epigram might refer to the Gothic retinue of Amalafrida (thus Zurli 2006). On proverbial Gothic drinking (*Biberunt ut Gothi*, "They drank like Goths"): Greg. Magn. *Dial.* 1, 9, 14. (I owe this reference to Mischa Meier.)

22. *Cithara* player: Cass. *Var.* 2, 40, 1; cf. Cass. *Var.* 2, 41, 4. The Vandalic king Gelimer himself sang while playing the harp: Proc. *Bell.* 3, 9, 6. Gothic tonalities: Boeth. *Mus.* 1, 1. Gothic songs: see chap. 3, section 2 (note 27), above.

23. Courtly culture: Deichmann 1989, 189–224; Hen 2007, 27–58. Wedding speech for Vitigis and Matasuintha: Cass. *Or.* 2 (MGH.AA XII, p. 477–484). Cassiodorus and Eutharic: Cass. *Chron.*, praef. *Comes archiatrorum*: Cass. *Var.* 6, 19. Anthimus, the author of the treatise *De observatione ciborum* (*PLRE* II Anthimus 3), wrote in Latin, identified as a Greek, and knew the Gothic word for polenta: Anthim. 64. If he is identical with the homonymous doctor who was banished from Constantinople in 478 for supporting Theoderic Strabo (Malch. *Frag.* 11 Cresci = 15 Blockley), he must have been an old man when he wrote the treatise. He might, however, have been a nephew or son of the former. Medical texts: Deichmann 1989, 218; Ieraci Bio 1994; Wiemer and Berndt 2016, 165f. with n. 164. Geography: Staab 1977.

24. *Evocatoriae*: Cass. *Var.* 7, 34f. Artemidorus: Cass. *Var.* 3, 22; further examples: Cass. *Var.* 2, 6 (Agapitus); Cass. *Var.* 3, 28 (Cassiodorus); Cass. *Var.* 5, 28 (Castinus).

25. The emperor and the circus: Al. Cameron 1976; Dagron 2011. *Adventus* ceremonial: MacCormack 1981, 17–91; Dufraigne 1994.

26. No hippodrome in Ravenna: Wiemer 2015a, 204–210. Amphitheater in Ticinum: Anon. *Val.* 71; *ILS* 829 = Fiebiger and Schmidt 1917, no. 203 = ILCV 39. Amphitheater in Ravenna: Agn. 2; 129; *Ep. Felicis* apud Agn. 60 (*JK* 877 = *HJ* 1711).

27. Municipal archives (*gesta municipalia*): Hirschfeld 1904; Classen 1977a. Curial landed property (*praedia curialium*): Cass. *Var.* 7, 47. The widespread view that Constantine the Great confiscated municipal lands is mistaken: Biundo 2006; Schmidt-Hofner 2006. Advocates: A. H. M. Jones 1964, 507–516; Wieling 1997; Barnish 2003.

28. Ruling style of Roman emperors: Bleicken 1982; Millar 1992; C. Kelly 2004; Wiemer 2006a; Schmidt-Hofner 2008.

29. *Res publica*: Suerbaum 1977, 247–267. *Rei publicae parere*: Cass. *Var.* 2, 24, 5. *Utilitas publica*: Gaudemet 1951. *Devotio*: Conti 1971, 83–121.

30. References to *pietas, iustitia, aequitas, temperantia, moderatio, mansuetudo, clementia, liberalitas, largitas,* and *munificentia* (and related terms) are so numerous that the index of Mommsen's edition of the *Variae* lists only a selection of them. On ruler's virtues: Wickert 1954, 2222–2253; Kohlhas-Müller 1995, 106–137. *Pietas:* Roesch 1978, 42f.; Kohlhas-Müller 1995, 121–126. *Iustitia* and *aequitas:* Kakridi 2005, 329–339.

31. *Civilitas* under Theoderic: Saitta 1993; Reydellet 1995; Amory 1997, 43–85 (misconceived); Kakridi 2005, 339–347; under the Principate: Wallace-Hadrill 1994; in Late Antiquity: Scivoletto 1970; Marcone 1985.

32. *Laus Gothorum est civilitas custodita:* Cass. *Var.* 9, 14, 8. Ennod. *Pan.* 11; 15; 56; 83; Ennod. *Ep.* 4, 5, 2; 9, 23, 6; Ennod. *Dict.* 13, 7.

33. *Libertas:* cf. chap. 6, section 3 (n. 75), above. *Libertas ruitura:* Ennod. *Dict.* 9, 6; Ennod. *Dict.* 10, 8. Severus and Paterius: Ennod. *Dict.* 13, 7. Ideology of restoration: La Rocca 1993; Fauvinet-Ranson 2006a, 267–274. Quotation: Cass. *Var.* 1, 28, 1; cf. Ennod. *Pan.* 56; 76f.

34. Forms and functions of late Roman legislation: Classen 1977b, 10–91; Van der Wal 1981; Riedlberger 2020, 26–131. Cassiodorus' edicts: Cass. *Var.* 11, 8; 11, 11; 11, 12; 12, 13. Edict of a *praefectus urbis Romae:* CIL VI 1711 (c. 488). Edicts of the Eastern Roman praetorian prefects from the late fifth and sixth centuries: SEG 44, no. 909 with Feissel 1994; *Nov. Just.* 166 (521); *Nov. Just.* 167 (548?); Goria and Sitzia 2013 (collection of all known prefectorial edicts with Italian translation and commentary). The edicts preserved in abridged form in Cod. Bodl. Roe 18 were first edited by Zachariae von Lingenthal 1842, 249–294; his edition (adopted by Goria and Sitzia 2013) has now been partly superseded by Schiavo 2018. Theoderic's edicts: *Ed. Theod.;* Cass. *Var.* 2, 25; 2, 36. Athalaric's edicts: Cass. *Var.* 9, 2; 9, 18. According to Proc. *Bell.* 6, 6, 17, Gothic envoys argued in 536 that Theoderic never issued "laws" (*nomoi*). Only under Athalaric did the royal chancellery call a ruling of the reigning king a *constitutio:* Cass. *Var.* 9, 15, 8. The inscription from Termoli (Apulia) on transhumance, which is known only from a copy (CIL IX 2826 = Fiebiger and Schmidt 1917, no. 286), contains the edict not of a Gothic king, as Mommsen thought, but of a praetorian prefect.

35. *Codex Theodosianus:* Matthews 2000a. *Novellae:* Liebs 1987, 188–190. *Lex Burgundionum:* cf. chap. 7, section 2, above. *Codex Euricianus:* d'Ors 1960; Nehlsen 1984; Liebs 2002, 157–163. *Breviarium Alaricianum* (also known as the *Lex Romana Visigothorum* = *L. Rom. Vis.*): Gaudemet 1965; Liebs 2002, 166–176; Matthews 2001.

36. On the *Edict of Theoderic* in detail, see Schmidt-Hofner and Wiemer 2022, where the earlier literature is discussed. Modern editions are based on the 1579 *editio princeps* by Pierre Pithou, who used one (or two?) now lost manuscripts: Bluhme 1889 (the basis of *FIRA* II, 676–710; König 2018 with German translation); Licandro 2013 (facsimile with Italian translation). Lafferty 2013 provides an English translation. Authorship: Nehlsen 1969; Liebs 1987, 191–194; Lafferty 2013, 22–46. Date: Ensslin 1959, 232f.; Lafferty 2013, 37–41; Schmidt-Hofner and Wiemer 2022. Nehlsen 1969 rightly refutes the attribution of the *Edict* to the Visigothic king Theoderic II, proposed by Vismara 1967. Sources: Ensslin 1959, 220–236; Lafferty 2013, 54–100 (for criticism, see Liebs 2015). Praetorian edict: Wieacker 1989, 462–485. The fundamental edition is Lenel 1927; the text is also reproduced in *FIRA* I 335–389.

37. Theoderic in Rome: cf. chap. 1, section 2, above. Confirmation of the laws of the Roman emperors: *Anon. Val.* 66. Publication of a legal collection as an edict in Rome: Malal. 15, 10 (*diataxis peri hekastou nomou*); followed by *Chron. Pasch.* a. 485. On the date: Ensslin 1959, 232f.; Lafferty 2013, 37–41; Schmidt-Hofner and Wiemer 2022. Legislation of the Burgundian kings: Heather 2012. Wood 2017, however, takes the view that the Burgundian kings issued laws as *magistri militum*.

38. Reception of the *Edict* in Gaul: Schmidt-Hofner and Wiemer 2022. A total of six manuscripts of Gallic and Italian provenance containing sections of the text is listed at http://www.leges.uni-koeln.de/lex/edictum-theoderici/. Ubl 2020 interprets the *Edict*, like Lafferty 2013, as a codification and fundamentally disputes its practical intention. Publication of edicts: Cass. *Var.* 9, 19, 3; 9, 20, 2. The quotation is from *Anon. Val.* 60: *a Gothis secundum edictum suum quem ei{u}s constituit rex fortissimus in omnibus iudicaretur.*

39. Theoderic's diplomatic correspondence: Gillett 2003, 174–190. *Patrius sermo*: Cass. *Var.* 4, 2, 4; cf. Cass. *Var.* 12, 9, 1 (*patrios sermones*).

40. Anduit: Cass. *Var.* 5, 29. Theodahad: Cass. *Var.* 3, 15.

41. Brandila and Patzen: Cass. *Var.* 5, 33f. with Wiemer 2017, 281–288, 297f.

42. *Formula de matrimonio confirmando et liberis legitimis faciendis*: Cass. *Var.* 7, 40. *Formula aetatis veniae*: Cass. *Var.* 7, 41. *Formula qua consobrinae matrimonium legitimum fiat*: Cass. *Var.* 7, 46.

43. Adila: Cass. *Var.* 2, 29. Diplomatic mission of Agnellus: Cass. *Var.* 1, 15; see more at the end of this chapter.

44. *Formula de competitionibus*: Cass. *Var.* 7, 44; Ward-Perkins 1984, 207f. Bronze statue in Como: Cass. *Var.* 4, 35. Theoderic publicized the award by edict in Cass. *Var.* 4, 36.

45. Tax evasion of senators: Cass. *Var.* 2, 24f. Tax evasion of Goths: Cass. *Var.* 4, 24 (*Picenum et Tusciae*); cf. Cass. *Var.* 1, 19 (*Adriana civitas*).

46. Trento: Cass. *Var.* 2, 17. *Formula qua census relevetur ei qui unam casam possidet praegravatam*: Cass. *Var.* 7, 45.

47. Cf. chap. 6, section 3, above.

48. Ticinum: Cass. *Var.* 4, 45. Noricum: Cass. *Var.* 3, 50. Venetia et Histria and Liguria: Cass. *Var.* 5, 10f. Tortona: Cass. *Var.* 1, 17. The *castellum* Verruca: Cass. *Var.* 3, 48. *Civitas* near Trento: Cass. *Var.* 5, 9. Field stones: Cass. *Var.* 2, 7. Repairs to the city walls of Catania, in contrast, were the result of the city's initiative (Cass. *Var.* 3, 49) but were apparently not carried out or completed: Proc. *Bell.* 7, 40, 21 (*polis ateichistos*).

49. Construction of a fleet: Cass. *Var.* 5, 16–20; cf. chap. 11, section 4, below.

50. Reactions to complaints from the province of Pannonia: Cass. *Var.* 3, 23f. (Colosseus). Siscia and Savia: Cass. *Var.* 4, 49 (Fridibad). Savia: Cass. *Var.* 5, 14f. (Severinus). Dalmatia et Savia: Cass. *Var.* 9, 8f. (Osuin and Severinus). Sicily: Cass. *Var.* 9, 10f. Complaints from the province of Hispania are the subject of a letter to Ampelius and Liwirit, the competent officials there: Cass. *Var.* 5, 39; cf. chap. 8, section 6, below.

51. *Formula comitivae primi ordinis*: Cass. *Var.* 6, 12. *Silentiarii*: Proc. *Hist. Arc.* 26, 28. *Formula notariorum*: Cass. *Var.* 6, 16; Delmaire 1995, 48–54. In 444, the *schola notariorum* numbered thirty members: *Nov. Val.* 6, 3.

52. *Referendarii*: Cass. *Var.* 6, 17; 8, 21, 6; 8, 25; *Anon. Val.* 85f.; Delmaire 1995, 48–54; Maier 2005, 140–142. Cyprianus: *PLRE* II Cyprianus 2. Quotations: Cass. *Var.* 5, 41, 2–4; 5, 40, 2 + 4.

53. *Maiores domus*: Maier 2005, 147–159. Ibba: *PLRE* II Ibba. On Pitzia and his potential identity with Petia, whom Theoderic killed in 514, see chap. 6, section 2, p. 148 with n. 35.

54. Arigern: *PLRE* II Arigernus. *Disciplina*: Cass. *Var.* 4, 16, 2; 4, 23, 1. Mission to Gaul and exhortation to the senators: Cass. *Var.* 4, 16.

55. Tuluin: *PLRE* II Tuluin. Quotation: Cass. *Var.* 8, 11, 3. In the *Variae*, this letter bears the inscription *Senatui urbis Romae Athalaricus rex*, but, as has long been recognized, it was clearly written in the name of Tuluin.

56. *Comitiaci*: Cass. *Var.* 6, 14 (*Formula magistri scrinii quae danda est comitiaco quando permilitat*); Morosi 1981b. According to Maier 2005, 186–196, the *comitiaci* belonged instead to the *officium* of the king.

57. *Magister officiorum*: Cass. *Var.* 6, 6; Clauss 1980; Delmaire 1995, 75–96. *Princeps officii*: Stein 1920, 195–239; Morosi 1979–1980; Clauss 1980, 30–39. Oversight and accountability of *officiales*: Haensch 2010.

58. Quotation: Cass. *Var.* 6, 5, 1–2.

59. *Quaestor (palatii)*: Cass. *Var.* 6, 5 (*formula*); Cass. *Var.* 5, 4, 3; 8, 13, 3–6; Ennod. *Carm.* 1, 2, 5; Ennod. *V. Epif.* 145; Harries 1988; Delmaire 1995, 57–63. In the *Variae*, Cassiodorus never adds *palatii* to the title *quaestor*. Letters of appointment: Cass. *Var.* 5, 3 + 5, 4 (Honoratus); Cass. *Var.* 8, 13 + 8, 14 (Ambrosius); Cass. *Var.* 8, 18 + 8, 19 (Fidelis); Cass. *Var.* 10, 6 + 10, 7 (Patricius). Draft and official copy: *Praeceptio regis*, MGH.AA XII, p. 424, no. 4; *Anagnosticum regis*, MGH.AA XII, p. 425f., no. 5; Ensslin 1949.

60. *Sacrae largitiones*: *CTh* 6, 30, 7 = *CJ* 12, 23, 7; Cass. *Var.* 6, 7; Delmaire 1989a (functional analysis), and 1989b (prosopography); concise summary in Delmaire 1995, 119–140. Letters of appointment: Cass. *Var.* 5, 40 + 5, 41 (Cyprianus); Cass. *Var.* 8, 16 + 8, 17 (Opilio).

61. *Collatio auri lustralis*: Cass. *Var.* 2, 26, 5; 2, 30, 3; Delmaire 1989a, 347–374. *Siliquaticum*: Delmaire 1989a, 299–301; *Nov. Val.* 15; Cass. *Var.* 2, 4; 2, 30, 3; 3, 25, 1; 3, 26, 1; 4, 19; 5, 31. *Comes siliquatariorum*: Cass. *Var.* 2, 12; 3, 25. *Collatio binorum et ternorum*: Cass. *Var.* 3, 8; 5, 16; 7, 20–22 (*Formulae binorum et ternorum*); Stein 1925, 388–394; Delmaire 1989a, 344f.

62. Minting of coinage: Wiemer 2021b. *Formula qua moneta committitur*: Cass. *Var.* 7, 32.

63. *Comes rei privatae*: Cass. *Var.* 6, 8; Delmaire: 1989a, 597–702, and 1995, 140–145. The inscription of the letter by which Senarius was appointed *comes patrimonii* (Cass. *Var.* 4, 3) wrongly styles him *comes privatarum*. Tancila: Ennod. *Ep.* 2, 23. Conflict of interests: Cass. *Var.* 1, 22. Incest and desecration of graves: Cass. *Var.* 6, 8, 3f.

64. *Comes patrimonii*: Cass. *Var.* 6, 9 (*formula*); cf. Cass. *Var.* 4, 3 and 4, 4 (letters of appointment for Senarius); Delmaire: 1989a, 691–694, and 1995, 145f.

65. The "Laterculus" of Polemius Silvius (Polem. *Lat.*), which was interpolated in the early sixth century, lists these fifteen provinces along with Corsica and Sardinia. The division into provinces may have varied in the Ostrogothic period, however, as was

often the case earlier. On the provinces of late antique Italy and their governors, see Chastagnol 1963 (with *fasti*, i.e., magistrate lists, for the years 284–536); Ausbüttel 1988, 95–104; Cecconi 1994 (with *fasti* covering ca. 200–476); Cecconi 1998. On the provincial administration under Gothic rule, see Arnold 2016; Gračanin 2016 (Dalmatia). The status and administration of Noricum Mediterraneum is uncertain: Cass. *Var.* 3, 50; Prostko-Prostyński 2002.

66. On the prefecture of Gaul, cf. chap. 8, section 5, below.

67. *Praefectus praetorio*: Cass. *Var.* 6, 3; Ensslin 1954, 2426–2502; Morosi 1975–1976. Quotation: Cass. *Var.* 6, 3, 3f. Letters of appointment: Cass. *Var.* 8, 20 (Avienus); Cass. *Var.* 9, 24 + 25 (Cassiodorus).

68. Edicts of prefects: Cass. *Var.* 11, 8; 11, 11; 11, 12; 12, 13; 12, 28. Advocates: A. H. M. Jones 1964, 507–516; Wieling 1997; Barnish 2003. Limitation on number of advocates: *Nov. Theod.* 10, 2; *CJ* 2, 7, 8.

69. Municipal tax collection: Cass. *Var.* 2, 17; 2, 25; 9, 4, 2f. *Exactores*: Cass. *Var.* 2, 24, 2; 5, 39, 13; 11, 7, 2; 11, 8, 4; 11, 16, 3; 12, 8, 2; 12, 14, 1; Delmaire 1996.

70. Assessment of the *annona*: Cerati 1975. *Horrea publica*: Proc. *Bell.* 6, 28, 25 (Ravenna); Cass. *Var.* 3, 41 (Marseille); Cass. *Var.* 10, 27 (Ticinum, Tortona, Trento, Treviso); Cass. *Var.* 12, 26 (Aquileia, Concordia, Forlì); Cass. *Var.* 12, 27 (Ticinum, Tortona); Vera 2008. *Coemptio*: Cass. *Var.* 1, 35, 2; 2, 26; 9, 14, 9; 10, 18, 2; 12, 4, 3; 12, 14, 6; 12, 22–24; 12, 26, 3. Complaints: Cass. *Var.* 9, 14, 9; Ennod. *V. Epif.* 104; Boeth. *Cons.* 1, 4, 12. In the Eastern Roman Empire, Emperor Anastasius regulated *coemptio* extensively in the year 498: *CJ* 10, 27, 2; Karayannopulos 1958, 96–99.

71. Tax assessment: Cass. *Var.* 2, 16, 4 (Liberius); Cass. *Var.* 4, 38, 1 (Faustus). *Supraindictiones*: Cass. *Var.* 1, 16, 2; 5, 14, 6; 9, 9, 3. Remission of taxes in the event of failed harvests caused by natural disasters: Cass. *Var.* 4, 50 (quotation § 7) with Leopold 1986; Cass. *Var.* 12, 26. Tax remission on account of enemy plundering: Cass. *Var.* 12, 7.

72. *Tertia*: Cass. *Var.* 1, 14; 2, 17; P.Ital. 47–48; Porena 2012a, 209–227. See chap. 6, section 1, above.

73. *Praefectura praetorio Orientis*: Joh. Lyd. *Mag.* 3, 1–43. *Praefectura praetorio Africae*: *CJ* 1, 27, 1.

74. Organization: Stein 1922; A. H. M. Jones 1964, 586–590; Morosi 1977.

75. *Esprit de corps*: C. Kelly 2004, 18–63. Model texts for the promotion of officers within the praetorian prefecture: Cass. *Var.* 11, 17–32.

76. Pay grades: Stein 1922, 74f.; A. H. M. Jones 1964, 590f.; Morosi 1977, 139.

77. *Sportulae*: A. H. M. Jones 1964, 602–605; C. Kelly 2004, 64–104; Haensch 2015.

78. Collective punishment: Noethlichs 1981, 222–228; Cass. *Var.* 2, 26, 3; *Ed. Theod.* 4; 55.

79. Governors' official duties: Cass. *Var.* 11, 9, 4f.

80. Faustus Niger: *PLRE* II Faustus 9; Cass. *Var.* 1, 35; 2, 26. In Cass, *Var.* 3, 20, 4, Cassiodorus calls him "that well-known schemer" (*notus ille artifex*).

81. Official designations and ranks of the governors of late antique Italy: Chastagnol 1963; Ausbüttel 1988, 107–115; Cecconi: 1994, 49–82, 209–224, and 1998, 172–179.

82. *Advocati*: A. H. M. Jones 1964, 507–516; Wieling 1997; Barnish 2003.

83. *Formula rectoris provinciae*: Cass. *Var.* 6, 21. Itinerary of provincial governors: *Nov. Maior.* 7, 17; Cass. *Var.* 5, 14, 7; 12, 15, 7. Governor's residence (*praetorium*): Haensch 1997; Lavan 1999 and 2001; Faber 2014. Repair of the *praetorium* of Syracuse: AE 1946, no. 207.

84. *Officia* of governors: *CJ* 1, 27, 13; 12, 57, 9; *Nov. Just.* 102, 2; A. H. M. Jones 1964, III, 175, n. 73; Palme 1999. *Commentariensis*: Haensch 1995. Governor's archives: Cass. *Var.* 5, 14, 9; 5, 39, 2 (*polypticha publica*); Haensch 1992 and 2013.

85. One-year term in office of provincial governors: Cass. *Var.* 7, 2; 9, 20, 1. Flavius Pius Maximus: CIL X 4859 with Cecconi 1994, 218.

86. The "epigraphic habit" of Late Antiquity: Smith and Ward-Perkins 2016, 43–55. Building inscriptions of the governors of Sicily in the late fifth or early sixth century: AE 1946, no. 207 (Syracuse, Flavius Gelasius Busiris); AE 1956, no. 259 (Catania, Merulus). Cassiodorus' father: Cass. *Var.* 1, 3, 3–5. Cassiodorus Senator: Cass. *Var.* 11, 39, 5 (the prefecture might also be meant here). Venantius: Cass. *Var.* 3, 8; 3, 46, 2; P.Ital. 47–48, A, l. 22. Tullianus: Proc. *Bell.* 7, 18, 20.

87. Prohibition on governing one's home province: Dio 71, 31, 1; *CJ* 1, 41, 9, 29, 3; Syn. *Ep.* 42; 73. Patronage of cities: Krause 1987b. Cassiodorus to Valerianus: Cass. *Var.* 12, 5, 2.

88. Governors' salaries: A. H. M. Jones 1964, III, 89f. with n. 65; Palme 1999, 112f.

89. *Cancellarii* and governors: Cass. *Var.* 11, 36; 12, 1; 12, 3; 12, 10. *Canonicarii* and governors: Cass. *Var.* 11, 38; 12, 4, 7.

90. *Dux Raetiarum*: Cass. *Var.* 7, 4. Servatus: Cass. *Var.* 1, 11. *Comes provinciae*: Cass. *Var.* 7, 1. *Comes Dalmatiae*: Cass. *Var.* 1, 40; 3, 26; 4, 9 (Osuin). *Comes Saviae*: Cass. *Var.* 4, 49 (Fridibad). *Comes Dalmatiarum et Saviae*: Cass. *Var.* 9, 8; 9, 9. *Comes Pannoniae Sirmiensis*: Cass. *Var.* 3, 23; 3, 24; 4, 23 (Colosseus). *Consularis Dalmatiae*: Cass. *Var.* 5, 24 (Epiphanius); 7, 24 (*princeps officii*). *Iudex Romanus* in the province of Savia: Cass. *Var.* 5, 14, 7.

91. Helping the poor as the bishops' responsibility: Cass. *Var.* 2, 30, 2 (*pauperes*); Cass. *Var.* 3, 37, 2 (quotation); Cass. *Var.* 9, 15, 6 (*pauperes*); Cass. *Var.* 11, 3, 5 (widows and orphans); Cass. *Var.* 12, 27, 2 (*egentes*); Gelas. *Frag.* 38 (*JK* 683 = *HJ* 1312); Finn 2006, 34–89; cf. chap. 10, section 2, below. On widows and orphans, see Krause 1995.

92. Distribution of income from Hispania: Proc. *Bell.* 5, 12, 47f. Gothic royal treasure: Proc. *Bell.* 5, 2, 26 with Stein 1949, 333; Hardt 2006, 35f. Reserves at the death of Emperor Anastasius: Proc. *Hist. Arc.* 19, 7 (320,000 pounds of gold). For further references, most of them later in date, see Hendy 1985, 224–227.

93. Quotation: Ennod. *Pan.* 58; cf. § 76f.; *Anon. Val.* 72f.; similarly, most recently, Arnold 2013, 175–294. Gatekeepers: Cass. *Var.* 7, 29. Grain prices in late antique Italy: *Nov. Val.* 13, 4; *Anon. Val.* 53; Cass. *Var.* 10, 27 (25 *modii* per *solidus*); 12, 27; 12, 28; (Cracco) Ruggini 1961, 361, 368–371.

94. The reading summarized here is that of Lafferty 2010 and 2013; for criticism, see Ubl 2020; Schmidt-Hofner and Wiemer 2022.

95. Provence: Cass. *Var.* 3, 17; cf. the *interpretatio* of *Nov. Val.* 32, 6. Pannonia Sirmiensis: Cass. *Var.* 3, 23f. Hispania: Cass. *Var.* 5, 39. Dalmatia et Savia: Cass. *Var.* 9, 8f. Sicily: Cass. *Var.* 9, 14. Theodahad: Cass. *Var.* 3, 15; cf. chap. 9, section 3, and chap. 11, section 1, below. Agnellus: Cass. *Var.* 1, 15; *PLRE* II Agnellus.

CHAPTER 8. RELUCTANT EXPANSION?

1. Clovis: Zöllner 1970, 44–73; Rouche 1996 (with a dossier of sources); Becher 2011. Tolosan kingdom of the Visigoths: Claude 1970, 28–53; Wolfram 2009, 178–248; Heather 1996, 181–215 (the best analysis); Delaplace 2015, 165–282.
2. Theoderic to Alaric II: Cass. *Var.* 3, 1; quotation: § 4 (*qui maligne gaudent alieno certamine*). Theoderic's foreign policy: Claude 1978a. Senarius: Ennod. *Ep.* 5, 15; 5, 16; *PLRE* II Senarius; Gillett 2003, 172–219, esp. 206–212; cf. section 4 of this chapter.
3. Theoderic to Gundobad: Cass. *Var.* 3, 2, 1f.
4. Theoderic to the kings of the Heruli, Warni, and Thuringians: Cass. *Var.* 3, 3. Steinacher 2017, 72–74, rightly disputes the existence of the so-called "western Heruli" (posited by L. Schmidt 1938–1941, 548–564, esp. 558–561). Only Sid. *Ep.* 8, 9, 31–33, mentions Heruli on the North Sea. Warni: Cass. *Var.* 5, 1; Proc. *Bell.* 8, 20, 1–41 (cf. 6, 15, 2; 7, 35, 15); L. Schmidt 1938–1940, 22–32; Springer 2006. Thuringians: L. Schmidt 1938–1940, 314–344; Springer 2005.
5. Theoderic to Clovis: Cass. *Var.* 3, 4. Quotation: § 3f. *Aliena malignitas*: § 5.
6. Battle of Vouillé: Proc. *Bell.* 5, 12, 33–45; *V. Caes.* I 28; Greg. Tur. *Hist.* 2, 37; *Chron. Caes.* a. 507; *Chron. Gall.* a. 511, nos. 688–691; Isid. *Hist. Goth.* 36f. On the location of the battlefield, see Mathisen 2013b.
7. Syagrius: Greg. Tur. *Hist.* 2, 18; 2, 27; *Lib. Hist. Franc.* 8f.; *PLRE* II Syagrius 2; Henning 1999, 293–303; MacGeorge 2002, 69–164. Whether Syagrius held the title of *rex Romanorum*, as Gregory of Tours suggests, is disputed.
8. Kingdom of the Vandals in North Africa: Merrills and Miles 2010; Vössing 2014; Steinacher 2016. L. Schmidt 1942 remains useful for the political history. Vandalic naval power: Courtois 1955, 205–209. Treaty (*pax*) between Gunthamund and Theoderic: Cass. *Chron.* a. 491, no. 1327; cf. Ennod. *Pan.* 70. Gunthamund's victory at sea: Drac. *Satisf.* 211–214. Francovich Onesti 2002, 58f., interprets *wentilseo* in the Old High German *Hildebrandslied* ("Song of Hildebrand") as "Vandal sea." This interpretation, however, should be rejected for contextual and linguistic-geographic reasons. (I thank Wolfgang Haubrichs for this reference.)
9. Marriage of Thiudigotho and Alaric: *Anon. Val.* 53; Jord. *Get.* 297; Proc. *Bell.* 5, 12, 22. Vidimir: Jord. *Rom.* 347; Jord. *Get.* 283f.
10. Theoderic and Audefleda: *Anon. Val.* 63; Jord. *Get.* 297; Greg. Tur. *Hist.* 2, 31; Becher 2011, 164–167. Clovis and Gundobad: *V. Eptadii* 8f. Clovis and Clotilde: Greg. Tur. *Hist.* 2, 28f.; Becher 2011, 167–173.
11. Kingdom of the Burgundians: Favrod 1997; Kaiser 2004a. Burgundians in Liguria: Ennod. *V. Epif.* 136–177; Ennod. *Pan.* 54; Cass. *Var.* 12, 28, 2f.; Paul. Diac. *Rom.* 15, 17. Engagement of Sigismund and Ostrogotho: Ennod. *V. Epif.* 163; Shanzer 1996–1997. Wedding: *Anon. Val.* 63; Jord. *Get.* 297; Greg. Tur. *Hist.* 3, 5.
12. Amalafrida and Thrasamund: *Anon. Val.* 68; Proc. *Bell.* 3, 8, 11–13. *Foedus* between Theoderic and Thrasamund: Ennod. *Pan.* 54; Vössing 2015, 26f.
13. Clovis vs. Alaric: Greg. Tur. *Hist.* 2, 27 (extradition of Syagrius); Greg. Tur. *Hist.* 2, 35 (peace of Amboise); *Auct. Haun.* a. 496 (Gothic reconquest of Saintes); *Auct. Haun.* a. 498 (Frankish capture of Bordeaux). Godegisel vs. Gundobad: Mar. Avent. a. 500;

Greg. Tur. *Hist.* 2, 32f.; *V. Sigismundi* 2; Kaiser 2004a, 59–63 (rightly critical of Favrod 1997, 322–360).

14. Frankish society in the sixth century: Grahn-Hoek 1976; Wickham 2005, 178–184. Frankish warrior society: Bodmer 1957; Jaeger 2017. *Campus Martius*: Greg. Tur. *Hist.* 2, 27.

15. Political status of the Alamanni in the late fifth century: Claude 1995 ("Großkönigtum"); contra Geuenich 2005, 72–77; intermediate, Drinkwater 2007, 334–363. Gibuld: Eug. *V. Sev.* 16; probably identical to the king of the Alamanni Gebavultus in *V. Lupi* 10.

16. Battle against the Alamanni and oath to receive baptism: Greg. Tur. *Hist.* 2, 31.

17. Battle of Zülpich: Greg. Tur. *Hist.* 2, 37. Geuenich, Grünewald, and Weitz 1996 is the catalogue of an exhibition organized on the occasion of the battle's fifteen hundredth anniversary.

18. Sources on the baptism of Clovis: Avit. *Ep.* 46 Peiper = *Ep.* 38 Malaspina; *Ep. Austr.* 8; Greg. Tur. *Hist.* 2, 30f. Important studies: von den Steinen 1933; Rouche 1996, 253–286; Schäferdiek 2004; Becher 2011, 174–203. In favor of the later dating: Weiss 1971 (contra Schäferdiek 1973); Wood 1985; Shanzer 1998. Clovis cannot, however, have been a Homoean before his baptism in Reims because the Catholic Church rejected anabaptism (see chap. 10, section 1, below). Remigius of Reims: Schäferdiek 1983; PCBE IV Remigius 2.

19. Theology of victory: McCormick 1987.

20. Quotations: Avit. *Ep.* 46 Peiper = *Ep.* 42 Malaspina, 1f. + 5 + 9 + 11. Avitus of Vienne: PCBE IV Avitus 2.

21. Cass. *Chron.* a. 505, no. 1344; Ennod. *Pan.* 60f.; Cass. *Var.* 8, 10, 4 (Tuluin); Jord. *Get.* 300. Ennodius had met (H)erduic, whom he styles as *vir illustris*, in Ticinum in 503 (Ennod. *Ep.* 2, 3). Pannonia Sirmiensis: Cass. *Var.* 3, 23, 3, 24; 4, 13. Thraustila: *PLRE* II Thrapstila. Thrasaric: *PLRE* II Thrasericus. Thrasaric's tombstone: SEG 59, no. 728. Colosseus: *PLRE* II Colosseus.

22. Emperor Valentinian III had formally surrendered Sirmium to the Eastern Roman Empire on the occasion of his marriage to Eudoxia (438): Cass. *Var.* 11, 1, 9f.; for context and date, see Stein 1925, 356f.; Ensslin 1948, 2236; Demougeot 1981. *Sirmiensis Pannonia quondam sedes Gothorum*: Cass. *Var.* 3, 23, 2.

23. War against Sabinianus: Ennod. *Pan.* 61–69; Marc. Com. a. 505; Jord. *Get.* 300f.; Jord. *Rom.* 387. As Croke 1982 has shown, *PLRE* II Mundo and *PLRE* IIIB Mundus are one and the same person. There is no evidence, however, for the claim that Attila's followers were called *Attilani* because the form *Attilanis* in Jord. *Get.* 301 should, following Mommsen, be taken as the genitive singular of the personal name Attila; cf. *Nov. Just.* 11, 1: *Attilanis temporibus*. Sabinianus: *PLRE* II Sabinianus 5.

24. Anastasius' Persian war: Greatrex 1998, 73–119.

25. Quotation: Cass. *Var.* 2, 41, 2.

26. Ennod. *Pan.* 72: *Alamanniae generalitas intra Italiae terminos sine detrimento Romanae possessionis inclusa est. Formula* of the *dux Raetiarum*: Cass. *Var.* 7, 1; cf. Cass. *Var.* 1, 11. Alamanni in Noricum: Cass. *Var.* 3, 50. Vitigis and the Alamanni: Agath. *Hist.* 1, 6. Stein 1949, 349, attributes the *incursio Sueborum* in Liguria mentioned by Cass. *Var.* 12, 7, 1 (written in 536 or 537) to the Alamanni, but Proc. *Bell.* 5, 12, 21, distinguishes between the two peoples.

27. Quotation: Cass. *Var.* 2, 41, 2.
28. Sources on the Battle of Vouillé: cf. n. 6 above. Amalaric's flight: Greg. Tur. *Hist.* 2, 37; *Lib. Hist. Franc.* 17. Battle for Provence: L. Schmidt 1938–1941, 154–158; Ewig 1952, 124–127 (with a different chronology); Favrod 1997, 395–404; Delaplace 2000. Survey of the sources in Sirago 1987.
29. Alaric's premature decision to do battle: Proc. *Bell.* 5, 12, 37–39.
30. Byzantine diplomacy: Meier 2009, 228–230. Clovis' arrival at Tours, 508: Greg. Tur. *Hist.* 2, 38 with Wiemer 2015a, 192–201. Client king: Becher 2011, 235–239; Mathisen 2013a.
31. Delegation to Carthage: Cass. *Var.* 1, 15. Rudolf: Jord. *Get.* 24; Cass. *Var.* 4, 2; cf. Proc. *Bell.* 6, 14, 11–22; *Origo gent. Lang.* 4; Paul. Diac. *Lang.* 1, 20.
32. Plundering of the Adriatic coast: Marc. Com. a. 508; Jord. *Rom.* 356; cf. Cass. *Var.* 1, 16; 1, 25; 2, 38. The expedition began in 507 and ended in 508: Krautschick 1983, 50f. Thrasamund and Anastasius: Proc. *Bell.* 3, 8, 14.
33. Siege of Arles: *V. Caes.* I 28–32; Cass. *Var.* 3, 32; 3, 44; 8, 10, 6f.; Klingshirn 1994, 106–110; Heijmans 2004, 76f. Victory over the Franks: Cass. *Chron.* a. 509, no. 1349; Jord. *Get.* 302. Mammo: Mar. Avent. a. 509.
34. Clovis' war propaganda: Greg. Tur. *Hist.* 2, 37; *Chlodowici regis ad episcopos ep.*, MGH. Cap. I, no. 1. Gallo-Roman senators: Greg. Tur. *Hist.* 2, 37; Schäferdiek 1967, 32–42.
35. Quotation: Caes. *Serm.* 70, 2.
36. Tax remission: Cass. *Var.* 3, 32 (Arles); Cass. *Var.* 3, 40 (all Gallic provinces); cf. Cass. *Var.* 4, 26 (Marseille). Ransom of prisoners: Avit. *Ep.* 10 Peiper = *Ep.* 7 Malaspina (to Eustorgius of Milan); Avit. *Ep.* 12 Peiper = *Ep.* 9 Malaspina (to Maximus of Ticinum); Avit. *Ep.* 35 Peiper = *Ep.* 31 Malaspina (to Liberius); *V. Eptadii* 12f.; *V. Caes.* I 32f. (Arles); *V. Caes.* I 36f. + 43 (Ravenna); *Lib. pont.* 53, 11; Graus 1961; Klingshirn 1985.
37. Avignon: Cass. *Var.* 3, 38. Grain imports for the army: Cass. *Var.* 3, 41; 3, 42; 3, 44. Narbonne: Cass. *Var.* 4, 17. *Siliquaticum*: Cass. *Var.* 4, 19. Arles: Cass. *Var.* 3, 44. Unigis: Cass. *Var.* 3, 43. *Postliminium*: Cass. *Var.* 3, 18.
38. Quotation: Cass. *Var.* 3, 17, 5. Gemellus: *PLRE* II Gemellus 2. His appointment letter is also preserved: Cass. *Var.* 3, 16.
39. Gesalec: Proc. *Bell.* 5, 12, 43; *Chron. Caes.* a. 508; Isid. *Hist. Goth.* 36; Vössing 2016a. Theoderic recognizes Gesalec: Cass. *Var.* 5, 43, 2. Goiaric: *Breviaricum Alarici* praef.; *Chron. Caes.* a. 510. Veila: *Chron. Caes.* a. 511.
40. Gesalec's escape and return: Cass. *Var.* 5, 43; *Chron. Gall.* a. 511, no. 690; *Chron. Caes.* a. 510; 513, § 2; Proc. *Bell.* 5, 12, 46; Isid. *Hist. Goth.* 36f. The *Laterculus regum Visigothorum* (*Lat. reg. Vand.*, MGH.AA XIII, p. 465) assigns Gesalec a reign of four years, one of which he spent in hiding; his demise thus falls in the year 511.
41. Theoderic as Amalaric's guardian: *Chron. Caes.* a. 513, 2; *Lat. reg. Vis.* (MGH.AA XIII, p. 465); Proc. *Bell.* 5, 12, 46. Fifteen regnal years for Theoderic in Hispania: *Chron. Caes.* a. 513; *Lat. reg. Vis.* (MGH.AA XIII, p. 465); Isid. *Hist. Goth.* 37. Proceedings of synods in Hispania: *Conc. Tarrac.* a. 516, CCH IV, p. 271, l. 28f. (= p. 34 Vives); *Conc. Gerun.* a. 517, CCH IV, p. 284, l. 22f. (= p. 39 Vives). Cf. n. 79 below.
42. Cass. *Var.* 5, 43, 1–3.

43. Theoderic to Thrasamund: Cass. *Var.* 5, 44. Hilderic: Proc. *Bell.* 3, 1, 9; Ferr. *V. Fulg.* 25; Vict. Tunn. a. 523, 1 + 2; Vössing 2019, 9–13.

44. Kings of the Rhenish Franks: Greg. Tur. *Hist.* 3, 40–42. Palace and Church of the Apostles in Paris: Brühl 1975, 6–33; Dierkens and Périn 2000. *Lex salica*: Ubl 2009, 2014, and 2017. Council of Orléans: *Conc. Aurel.* a. 511, CCL 148A, p. 3–19; for the royal veto of lay ordinations, see canon 4. Episcopal elections: *Conc. Aurel.* a. 549, CCL 148A, p. 147–161, canon 10.

45. Partitioning of 511: Ewig 1952, 114–128, and 2001, 31–33. Four residences: Greg. Tur. *Hist.* 4, 22.

46. *Infatigabilis triumphator*: Cass. *Or.* 1, MGH.AA XII, p. 466. Arcadius Placidus Magnus Felix: Mathisen 2003. The three letters: Cass. *Var.* 2, 1 (to Anastasius); 2, 2 (to Felix); 2, 3 (to the senate; quotation: § 1).

47. Marriage between Amalaberga and Hermanfrid: Cass. *Var.* 4, 1; cf. *Anon. Val.* 70; Jord. *Get.* 299; Proc. *Bell.* 5, 12, 22; 5, 13, 2; Greg. Tur. *Hist.* 3, 4. Hermanfrid and his brothers: Greg. Tur. *Hist.* 3, 4.

48. Gepids: Jord. *Get.* 113f.; Proc. *Bell.* 6, 14, 25–27; 6, 15, 36; L. Schmidt 1938–1941, 534f.; Pohl 1980, 276–278, and 1998c, 134f.; Sarantis 2016, 51–64; Steinacher 2017, 130–132, 161f. Fear of the Goths: Proc. *Bell.* 7, 34, 10. Gepids in Gaul: Cass. *Var.* 5, 10; 5, 11. Failed reconquest of Sirmium: Cass. *Var.* 11, 1, 10; Proc. *Bell.* 5, 3, 15f.

49. Heruli: Proc. *Bell.* 6, 14f.; 7, 33, 13f.; Jord. *Rom.* 364; Malal. 18, 6; 18, 14; Theoph. a. m. 6020; L. Schmidt 1938–1941, 548–564; Steinacher 2017, 139–160. Defeat and death of Rudolf: Proc. *Bell.* 6, 14, 11f.; *Origo gent. Lang.* 4; Paul. Diac. *Lang.* 1, 21; Stein 1949, 150f. (dating). Settlement within the borders of the empire: Marc. Com. a. 512, § 11; Proc. *Bell.* 6, 14, 28. Heruli in Ticinum: Cass. *Var.* 4, 32.

50. Lombards: Proc. *Bell.* 6, 14; 7, 33; *Origo gent. Lang.* 4; Paul. Diac. *Lang.* 1, 20f.; L. Schmidt 1938–1941, 565–626; Pohl 2001b. Wacho: *PLRE* III Vaces. Wives: *Origo gent. Lang.* 4; Paul. Diac. *Lang.* 1, 21; *PLRE* III Austrigusa, Ranicunda + Salinga. Palace of Wacho in Bohemia: *Chron. Gothan.* 2. Daughters: *PLRE* III Vuldetrada + Wisegardis. Alliance with the Byzantine emperor: Proc. *Bell.* 6, 22, 11f.

51. Diplomatic missions: Gillett 2003, 172–219, esp. 174–189; 231–238. Paean to Senarius: Cass. *Var.* 4, 3 (quotation: § 2); cf. Cass. *Var.* 4, 4. *Epitaphium Senarii*: MGH.AA XII, p. 499 = Fiebiger 1944, 10 no. 8; Gillett 2003, 194–198, 290. Inquiry concerning the baptismal liturgy: Joh. Diac. *Ep. ad Senarium*.

52. Scandinavia: Jord. *Get.* 10–26; Proc. *Bell.* 6, 15; Steinacher 2017, 149–152. Central places in Denmark: Høilund Nielsen 2014. Goths on the Crimea: Proc. *Bell.* 8, 4, 7–8; 5, 22; Proc. *Aed.* 3, 7, 13–17; Vasiliev 1936; Ajbabin and Chajredinova 2009, esp. 9–76 (burial ground of Lučistoe); Bierbrauer 2010; Mączyńska et al. 2016, esp. 1–18 (burial ground of Almalyk-Dere). Esti: Cass. *Var.* 5, 2; cf. Tac. *Germ.* 45; Jord. *Get.* 36; 120; Schmid 1973; Cristini 2021 (also on Cass. *Var.* 5, 1, a letter to the king of the Warni). Vitigis and the Persians: Proc. *Bell.* 2, 2, 1–12; 6, 22, 13–20. Persians at the court of Theoderic II in Toulouse: Sid. *Ep.* 8, 9, 5, v. 45ff.

53. Cass. *Var.* 3, 17, 1.

54. Prefecture of Gaul: Claude 1997b, esp. 361–379.

55. Provence in Late Antiquity: Buchner 1933; Guyon and Heijmans 2013. Cities: *Not. Gall.* XI, xv–xvii; Beaujard 2006. Long-distance trade: Claude 1985, 134–160; Wickham 2005, 746–759. Marseille: Loseby 1992; Bonifay and Piéri 1995.

56. Arles: Heijmans 2004. Chariot races: Sid. *Ep.* 1, 11, 10; Caes. *Serm.* 61, 3; Proc. *Bell.* 7, 33, 5; Heijmans 2004, 239–243. Theater and amphitheater: Klingshirn 1994, 174–176; Heijmans 2004, 238f. Cathedral: Guyon and Heijmans 2013, 173–179.

57. *Concilium septem provinciarum*: *Ep. Arel.* 8. Euric's death: *Chron. Gall.* a. 511, no. 666; Jord. *Get.* 245.

58. Gallic senators: Stroheker 1948. Education: Buchner 1933, 60–85; Riché 1995, 153–173.

59. Gallic isolationism: Matthews 1975; Mathisen 1992.

60. Arigern in Gaul: Cass. *Var.* 4, 16, 1. Letters to Liberius as *praefectus praetorio Galliarum*: Ennod. *Ep.* 9, 23; 9, 29; cf. Ennod. *Ep.* 8, 22; Avit. *Ep.* 35 Peiper = *Ep.* 31 Malaspina. Avignon: Cass. *Var.* 3, 38 (*comes* Wandil). Marseille: Cass. *Var.* 3, 34; 4, 12; 4, 46 (*comes* Marabad). Arles: *V. Caes.* I 48 (*comites civitatis*); Greg. Tur. *Glor. mart.* 77 (*dux* Ara).

61. Rebuilding support for rebuilding in Arles: Cass. *Var.* 3, 4 Immunities: Cass. *Var.* 4, 26 (Marseille); Ennod. *Ep.* 9, 29, 4 (*ad personam*). Theoderic appealed to the provincials of Gaul to "recover lawful ways" (*iuridici mores*; in essence, the rule of law): Cass. *Var.* 3, 17. *Fragmenta Gaudenziana*: MGH.LNG I 469–472; Buchner 1933, 25f.; Vismara 1968; Liebs 2002, 179–181. Schmidt-Hofner and Wiemer 2022 argue that the collection was authorized by the prefect Liberius.

62. Archotamia and Aetheria: Cass. *Var.* 4, 12; 4, 46; Liebs 2002, 276–280. Archotamia: *PLRE* II Archotamia; PCBE IV Archotamia. Aetheria: *PLRE* II Aetheria 2; PCBE IV Aetheria 1. Discipline problems: Cass. *Var.* 3, 38, 2; *V. Caes.* I 48. Archdeacon from Nîmes: Greg. Tur. *Glor. mart.* 77.

63. Caesarius of Arles: Klingshirn 1994; PCBE IV Caesarius 1. Narbonne: Cass. *Var.* 4, 17. Arles: *V. Caes.* I 20; Caes. *Test.* 8. Letter to a bishop in southern Gaul (Caesarius?): Ennod. *Ep.* 9, 3 = [Caes.] *Ep.* 1 with Hasenstab 1890, 21–26.

64. Accusation before Alaric II: *V. Caes.* I 21. Council of Agde: *Conc. Agath.* a. 506, CCL 148, p. 189–228; Caes. *Ep.* 3; Rur. *Ep.* 2, 33 = [Caes.] *Ep.* 4; Schäferdiek 1967, 55–65. Accusation of high treason: *V. Caes.* I 29. Convent in Arles: *V. Caes.* I 35.

65. Caesarius in Ravenna: *V. Caes.* I 36–41. Caesarius in Rome: *V. Caes.* I 42; Symm. pp. *Ep.* 14 Thiel = [Caes.], *Ep.* 6 = *Ep. Arel.* 25 (*JK* 765 = *HJ* 1461); Symm. pp. *Ep.* 15 Thiel = [Caes.], *Ep.* 7 = *Ep. Arel.* 27 (*JK* 764 = *HJ* 1460). Ennodius and Caesarius: Ennod. *Ep.* 9, 33, 1.

66. The claims to primacy of Arles: Caspar 1930, 440–452; Langgärtner 1964, 18–106; Schäferdiek 1967, 68–75; Mathisen 1989, 141–172; Klingshirn 1994, 65–69; L. Piétri 2001b, 238–243. Leo I vs. Hilary of Arles: Leo *Ep.* 10 (*JK* 407 = *HJ* 911); *Nov. Val.* 17. Partition of Viennensis as an ecclesiastical province: Leo *Ep.* 66 = *Ep. Arel.* 13 (*JK* 450 = *HJ* 971). Confirmation by Symmachus: Symm. pp. *Ep.* 3 Thiel (*JK* 754 = *HJ* 1423).

67. *Pallium*: *V. Caes.* I 39; Symm. pp. *Ep.* 15 Thiel = [Caes.] *Ep.* 7 = *Ep. Arel.* 26 (*JK* 764 = *HJ* 1460); cf. Symm. pp. *Ep.* 14 Thiel = [Caes.] *Ep.* 6 = *Ep. Arel.* 25 (*JK* 765 = *HJ* 1461).

68. Apostolic vicariate in Gaul and Hispania: Symm. pp. *Ep.* 16 = [Caes.] *Ep.* 8 = *Ep. Arel.* 28 (*JK* 769 = *HJ* 1466). Langgärtner 1964, 118–149; Schäferdiek 1967, 68–75; Klingshirn

1994, 127–132; L. Piétri 2001c, 386–390. Hispania ≠ Septimania: Schäferdiek 1967, 73f., n. 18; contra, e.g., Langgärtner 1964, 136–138.

69. Caesarius' reform program: Klingshirn 1994, 146–243; L. Piétri 2001c, 390–398. Synods: *Conc. Arel.* a. 524, CCL 148A, p. 42–46 (fourteen bishops); *Conc. Carp.* a. 527, CCL 148A, p. 47–52 (fifteen bishops); Felix IV *Ep.* 1 = [Caes.] *Ep.* 11 = *Ep. Arel.* 31 (JK 874 = HJ 1707); *Conc. Araus.* a. 529, CCL 148A, p. 53–76 (thirteen bishops); *Conc. Vas.* a. 529, CCL 148A, p. 77–81 (11 bishops); *Conc. Mass.* a. 533, CCL 148A, p. 84–97 (fourteen bishops).

70. Relationship of trust between Caesarius and Liberius: *V. Caes.* II 10–15. Apollinaris in Arles: *V. Apollinaris* 10; PCBE IV Apollinaris.

71. Council of Valence: *V. Caes.* I 60; PCBE IV Iulianus 9. Council of Orange: *Conc. Araus.* a. 529, CCL 148A, p. 53–76; Klingshirn 1994, 140–143. Gallic discussions of Augustine's doctrine of grace ("semi-Pelagianism"): Markus 1989.

72. Liberius in Gaul: O'Donnell 1981; Dumézil 2012. Consolidation of Athalaric's power and oath: Cass. *Var.* 8, 6; 8, 7; Wiemer 2020b, 274. *Patricius praesentalis*: Cass. *Var.* 11, 1; Const. Porph. *Cer.* 87. Liberius' funerary inscription: *CIL* XI 382 = ILCV 75. Agretia: *V. Caes.* II 12–15.

73. Amalaric: *PLRE* II Amalaricus. Adulthood among the Goths: Cass. *Var.* 1, 38: *Gothis aetatem legitimam virtus facit.*

74. Suebi: Claude 1970, 122–128; Thompson 1982, 161–187; Díaz 2011. Rechimund: Hyd. 226. Campaigns contemporary with Euric: *Chron. Gall.* a. 511, no. 651f.; Isid. *Hist. Goth.* 34; Fiebiger 1944, 12f., no. 13 = ILER 363 (Mérida); Stroheker 1937, 21–26, 70f.; Thompson 1982, 188–194; Kulikowski 2004, 203–209; Delaplace 2015, 268–279. Hispanic revolts against Alaric: *Chron. Caes.* a. 496f. (Burdulenus); a. 506 (Petrus). Gothic immigration to Hispania: *Chron. Caes.* a. 494; a. 497 (cf. *V. Vincentii* 6); Heather 1996, 198–210; Sasse 1997. Gothic exodus from Gaul after 531: Proc. *Bell.* 5, 13, 13. (The *Chronical of Zaragoza* is known in Latin as the *Chronica Caesaraugustana*.)

75. Visigoths in Spain: Thompson 1969; Claude 1970, 75–121; Heather 1996, 277–321; Collins 2001; Díaz and Valverde 2007, 259–612. Ostrogothic interregnum: García Iglesias 1975; Kulikowski 2004, 256–276; Díaz and Valverde 2007, 335–346. Suebian king: Hyd. 119; 137; *PLRE* II Rechila. *Comites civitatis*: C. *Eur.* 322. Dissemination of the *Breviarium Alaricianum*: *Commonitorium Alarici regis*, MGH.LNG I, p. 465–467. Theudis' "law on trial costs" of 546 is addressed to all *rectores* and *iudices*: MGH.LNG I, p. 467–469; Zeumer 1898. Visigothic *duces* in cities: Fiebiger 1944, 12f., no. 13 = ILER 363 (*dux* in Mérida); *Auct. Haun.* a. 498 (*dux* in Bordeaux).

76. Cities: Sanchéz Albornoz 1943 (municipal constitution); Kulikowski: 2004, esp. 209–255, and 2006b; Wickham 2005, 656–665; Eger and Panzram 2006; Panzram 2014 and 2015. The most important source for the agrarian history of sixth-century Hispania is a recently published collection of donations to the monastery of Asan in the Pyrenees; these are dated to 522 and 576: Tomás-Faci and Martín-Iglesias 2017, 277f., no. 1; 279f., no. 3; cf. the donation and testament of Bishop Vincentius of Huesca (dated 551 and ca. 576): Corcoran 2003 (with English translation). Trade: Wickham 2005, 741–758. Barcelona: Gurt and Godoy 2000; Bonnet and Beltrán de Heredia 2000. Tarragona: Gómez Fernández 2001; Panzram 2014, 466–471. Mérida: Mateos 2000; Gómez

Fernández 2003; Kulikowski 2004, 209–214; Panzram 2014, 463–466. Toledo: Velázquez and Ripoll López 2000; Panzram 2014, 471–476.

77. Theudis: Proc. *Bell.* 5, 12, 5–54; Jord. *Get.* 302; *PLRE* II Theudis. Ampelius and Liwirit: Cass. *Var.* 5, 35; 5, 39. According to Claude 1997b, 364–369, Ampelius was *praefectus (praetorio) Hispaniarum*; according to Mancinelli 2001, *vicarius Hispaniarum*. The first and only *praefectus Hispaniarum* attested was called Stephanus (*PLRE* III Stephanus 3); according to *Chron. Caes.* a. 529, he was dismissed in 529. Liwirit *vicedominus*: Mancinelli 2001. *Patrimonium*: Delmaire: 1989a, 691–694, and 1989b, 291–299.

78. Cass. *Var.* 5, 39, with detailed commentary by Mancinelli 2001.

79. *Episcopalis audientia*: *Conc. Tarrac.* a. 516, canon 4 + 10, *CCH* IV, p. 274 + 277f. (= p. 35 and 37 Vives). Provincial synods under Theoderic: *Conc. Tarrac.* a. 516, *CCH* IV, p. 269–281; *Conc. Gerun.* a. 517, *CCH* IV, p. 283–290. Prayer for Amalaric: *Conc. Tolet. II* a. 531, *CCH* IV, p. 354 (= p. 45 Vives). In a letter appended to these proceedings, the presiding metropolitan, Montanus of Toledo, threatens an influential layman named Toribius (not in *PLRE* III) with appeal to the king: *CCH* IV, p. 368f. (= p. 51f. Vives). On the date, cf. n. 81 below. Isid. *Hist. Goth.* 41 praises Amalaric's successor, Theudis, for permitting Catholic bishops to gather together in Toledo.

80. Caspar 1933, 765f.; Schäferdiek 1967, 75–81; Panzram 2015, 650–658. Hormisdas to John and all bishops of Hispania (517): Horm. *Ep.* 24 Thiel (*JK* 786 = *HJ* 1529); *Ep.* 25 Thiel (*JK* 787 = *HJ* 1530); *Ep.* 30 Thiel (*JK* 788 = *HJ* 1531). Both Elche (near Alicante) and Tarraco are mentioned as John's see in the sources. Hormisdas to John (519): Horm. *Ep.* 88 Thiel (*JK* 828 = *HJ* 1600); cf. *Avell.* 159; 160. Hormisdas to Sallustius of Seville and the bishops of the province of Baetica (521): Horm. *Ep.* 142 Thiel (*JK* 855 = *HJ* 1659); *Ep.* 143 Thiel (*JK* 856 = *HJ* 1660). Conferral of the apostolic vicariate on Zeno of Seville: Simpl. *Ep.* 21 Thiel (*JK* 590 = *HJ* 1193).

81. Visigothic nobility: Claude 1971a. Retinues: *C. Eur.* 310 f.; *L. Vis.* 5, 3, 1–4. The legislation distinguishes between *buccellarii* and *saiones*: Claude 1971a, 40–43; King 1972, 187–189. According to *V. Vincentii* 6, the Homoean *sacerdos* Wictharic was banished to Italy at the instigation of Gothic *principes* from Hispania.

82. Ostrogothic army in Hispania: Proc. *Bell.* 5, 12, 47–54. Mixed marriages: Proc. *Bell.* 5, 13, 6–8.

83. Isid. *Hist. Goth.* 39 claims that Amalaric had already become king in Theoderic's lifetime, and some modern scholars (e.g., Collins 2001, 41; Vössing 2016a, 249) follow him. Amalaric must have already been king in 522 if the second Council of Toledo, which took place in the fifth year of Amalaric's reign according to its introduction, should be dated to the year 527, as has been inferred from the year DLXV of the local era that is also mentioned there (on the Hispanic era, which began in 38 BCE, cf. Neugebauer 1981): *CCH* IV, p. 346 (= p. 42 Vives). The era year that was subsequently added cannot be correct, however, because all the sources attribute Amalaric, who died in 531, only five regnal years: Schäferdiek 1967, 84f. with n. 48. Amalaric's defeat and death: *Chron. Caes.* a. 531; Proc. *Bell.* 5, 13, 7–13; Jord. *Get.* 302; Greg. Tur. *Hist.* 3, 10; Isid. *Hist. Goth.* 40. Theudis: *PLRE* II Theudis.

CHAPTER 9. A "GOLDEN AGE"?

1. Palladius: R. Martin 1976, vii–xx; Vera 1999b; Grey 2007b, 364–367; Bartoldus 2014, 11–35. Palladius' full name was Rutilius Taurus Aemilianus Palladius (*PLRE* I Aemilianus 7); he went by the name Aemilianus in his lifetime: Cass. *Inst.* 1, 28, 6 with Al. Cameron 1985, 173f. The dating of Palladius' work varies between the early and late fifth century; currently, the later date has the most scholarly support (Martin, Vera, Bartoldus), but the evidence is inconclusive and a precise date is impossible to establish.

2. Mortality: Saller 1994, 9–69 (based on a model life-table "Level 3 West"). Checking the health of tenants before buying land: Pall. *Agric.* 1, 3f. Epidemics: Stathakopoulos 2004 (for criticism, see Wiemer 2004b); Harper 2017. Malaria in Italy: Sallares 2002. Plague in Rome and environs (under Pope Simplicius?): Gelas. *Tract.* 6, 23 = *Avell.* 100, 23 (*JK* 672 = *HJ* 1321). The "Plague of Justinian" reached Italy in 543 and broke out again ca. 569: Marc. Com. a. 543, 2; Mar. Avent. a. 569–571; Paul. Diac. *Lang.* 2, 4; 2, 26; its impact on Italy, however, is uncertain; see Leven 1987; Harper 2017, 218–235.

3. Four factors: Pall. *Agric.* 1, 2; cf. Cass. *Var.* 9, 3, 1. Regional diversity of Italy: Wickham 1981, 1–8; cf. Tichy 1985 (on modern Italy). Potter 1992 is an excellent introduction to the historical geography of Roman Italy, but *Italische Landeskunde*, by Heinrich Nissen (Nissen 1883–1902), is still indispensable because of the author's intimate familiarity with the country and unrivaled command of the textual sources. Pastoralism and transhumance: CIL IX 2826; Cass. *Var.* 12, 12, 1; *Nov. Just.* Appendix 7, 4 and 13; Volpe 1996, 276–280; Vera 2002; Crawford 2005. Fishermen: CIL VI 41382 (Rome, 400); Cass. *Var.* 5, 16, 5 (Po); Cass. *Var.* 5, 17, 6; 5, 20, 3; 12, 24, 5f. (Histria); cf. Cass. *Var.* 9, 6, 3f.; 12, 4, 1 (Bruttium). For textual evidence of regional specializations, see Hannestad 1962, 28–37.

4. Water mills: Pall. *Agric.* 1, 41; *CTh* 14, 15, 4; CIL VI 1711; Proc. *Bell.* 5, 19, 19; M. Bloch 1935; Marano 2015, 161–164. Quotation: Greg. Magn. *Ep.* 2, 38 (*JE* 1186 = *HJ* 2222), p. 139 Hartmann. The target of Gregory's rebuke, a *subdiaconus* of the Roman church named Petrus (PCBE II Petrus 70), was *rector patrimonii* and as such responsible for the administration of the papal possessions in all of Sicily.

5. Roads: Claude 1996, 49f. (too negative); Esch 1997 and 2011, esp. 13–16. Via Flaminia: Cass. *Var.* 11, 12; 12, 18. Via Appia: Proc. *Bell.* 5, 14, 6–11. Decemnovium: Cass. *Var.* 2, 32f.; CIL X 6850–6852 = *ILS* 827 = ILCV 35; Fauvinet-Ranson 2006a, 68–78; Giardina 2006, 73–100.

6. Transport costs: A. H. M. Jones 1964, 841f.; McCormick 2001, 64–122. Calabria: Cass. *Var.* 8, 31, 5; cf. Proc. *Bell.* 6, 20, 18; Joh. Lyd. *Mag.* 3, 61. Po: Cass. *Var.* 2, 20; 5, 18; 5, 20. Tiber: *Nov. Val.* 29 (450); Cass. *Var.* 5, 17, 6; 5, 20, 3; Proc. *Bell.* 5, 26, 7–13; 6, 7, 5. Mincio, Oglio, Serchio, and Arno Rivers: Cass. *Var.* 5, 17, 6; 5, 20, 3.

7. Settefinestre: Carandini and Ricci 1985. Roman agrarian authors: Flach 1990 (for criticism, see Jördens 1993).

8. Max Weber advanced his theory in 1896 in a lecture addressed to a non-specialist audience: Weber 1924. On its context and reception, see Deininger 1988.

9. Marc Bloch wrote the article during World War II but could not publish it himself, as he was executed by the Gestapo as a member of the Resistance on June 16, 1944: M. Bloch 1947.

10. Finley 1980, 123–149; de Ste. Croix 1981, 205–277. States of the discussion in Whittaker 1987, Whittaker and Garnsey 1998; Harper 2011, 3–32.

11. Slavery in late antique Italy: Nehlsen 1972, 123–127; Vera 1992–1993 and 2007; cf. Harper 2011, 33–200. Corvée: P.Ital. 3; Percival 1969; Vera 1986b, 425–430. Agrarian structural change: Wickham 1984; Vera 1995. Slaves in the rural economy: P.Ital. 10–11 (*inquilini sive servi*); P.Ital. 13 (*mancipia*); Cass. *Var.* 8, 33, 4 (*servi*); Proc. *Bell.* 7, 16, 25; Pelag. *Ep.* 84 (*JK* 956 = *HJ* 2008); V. *Caes.* I, 61 (*mancipia et clientes*); Greg. Magn. *Dial.* 1, 1 (*mancipium*); Greg. Magn. *Ep.* 4, 21 (*JE* 1293 = *HJ* 2340) (*mancipia*); Greg. Magn. *Ep.* 9, 10 (*JE* 1534 = *HJ* 2632) (*mancipia*); Greg. Magn. *Ep.* 9, 233 (*JE* 1760 = *HJ* 2879) (*pueri et alia mancipia*). Peasants bound to the soil: Ennod. *V. Epif.* 138 (*universa Italiae loca originariis viduata cultoribus; agricolae*); Ennod. *V. Epif.* 172; Greg. Magn. *Ep.* 9, 20 (*originarii*); Gelas. *Ep.* 20 Thiel (*JK* 651 = *HJ* 1297) (*homines suo iuri debitos*); Gelas. *Ep.* 22 Thiel (*JK* 658 = *HJ* 1302) (*originarii*); Greg. Magn. *Ep.* 5, 7 (*JE* 1323 = *HJ* 2374); Greg. Magn. *Ep.* 9, 203 (*JE* 1730 = *HJ* 2847). The many estates in Northeastern Hispania that were donated to the monastery of Asan in 522 and 576 were worked primarily by *mancipia* ("slaves"): Tomás-Faci and Martín-Iglesias 2017, 277f., no. 1; 279f., no. 3.

12. Peasant economy: Tschajanow 1923 and 1924; Chayanov 1966. For ancient Rome, Garnsey 1976 is fundamental.

13. Cass. *Var.* 6, 8, 1f. Slaves forbidden to be clergymen: Gelas. *Ep.* 10 Löwenfeld (*JK* 653 = *HJ* 1299).

14. Punishment for the enslavement of a free person: *Ed. Theod.* 78f. Legal status of the mother decisive: *Ed. Theod.* 65–67. Civil suit for the killing of a slave: *Ed. Theod.* 152; Nehlsen 1972, 132f.

15. The "fiscal" interpretation of the late Roman "colonate," pioneered by Carrié 1982 and 1983, has become the dominant view; a basically similar view was taken already by A. H. M. Jones 1958. Grey 2007b offers a good synthesis. Marcone 1985, Vera 2007, and Vera 2012b survey the scholarly debate. On the colonate under Justinian: Sirks 2008.

16. Quotation: *Ed. Theod.* 84; cf. *CJ* 6, 1, 4; Nehlsen 1972, 130f. The rule that hiding a fugitive *colonus* was a punishable offense had been laid down by *CTh* 5, 17, 2 (386), a reference I owe to John Noël Dillon.

17. Theft of crops: *Ed. Theod.* 146; cf. Paul. *Sent.* 2, 31, 30.

18. *Formula qua census relevetur ei qui unam casam possidet praegravatam*: Cass. *Var.* 7, 45. Peasant freeholders in Italy: Pall. *Agric.* 1, 6, 6; Cass. *Var.* 3, 14; 3, 20 (*praedium*); 3, 37; 4, 44 (*casa*); 8, 28 (*agellum*) 9, 5 (*mediocres*); Ennod. *Ep.* 6, 14; Pelag. *Ep.* 84 (*JK* 956 = *HJ* 2008); P.Ital. 35 (*agellarius*); Greg. Magn. *Ep.* 5, 38 (*JE* 1351 = *HJ* 2409). Curial landowners: Salv. *Gub.* 4, 20, 30f.; 5, 38f.; Caes. *Serm.* 154, 2; P.Ital. 35.

19. Royal landholdings: cf. chap. 7, section 3, above. Senatorial landholdings: Vera 1986b and 1988. Symmachus' landholdings: Vera 1986a. Melania the Younger's landholdings: *V. Melaniae.lat.* 18–21; Pall. *Hist. Laus.* 61, 5; Vera 2016. Sixty villages (*villae*):

V. Melaniae.lat. 18, 4; the Greek version has sixty-two *epoikia: V. Melaniae.gr.* 18. Ecclesiastical landholdings: cf. chap. 10, section 2, below.

20. Palladius' manor: Pall. *Agric.* 1, 7–42; Flach 1990, 204–215; Vera 1995. *Casae*: Cass. *Var.* 2, 12; 3, 43; 3, 52; 4, 14; 5, 14; 12, 8.

21. *Massa fundorum*: Vera 1999a (with a list of all references). Rent: Vera 1986b. Signia: P.Ital. 17. Via Appia: Greg. Magn. *Ep.* 14, 14 (*JE* 1991 = *HJ* 3080).

22. Lauricius: P.Ital. 1; *PLRE* II Lauricius.

23. Donation of Odoacer: P.Ital. 10–11. Pierius thereby acquired the palatial villa of Polače in the northeastern part of the island of Melite: Turkovic 2017.

24. Theodahad: Proc. *Bell.* 5, 3, 2f.; 4, 1–3; Cass. *Var.* 4, 39 (*homines*); 5, 12 (*homines*); 8, 23; Vitiello 2014b, 31–37. *Patrimonium Amalafridae*: Cass. *Var.* 8, 23. Theodosius: Cass. *Var.* 10, 5. Pension: Proc. *Bell.* 5, 6, 19; cf. Olymp. *Frag.* 1, 44 Müller = *Frag.* 41, 2 Blockley with Al. Cameron 1984.

25. Large leaseholders: Cass. *Var.* 1, 16; 5, 16f.; Ennod. *Ep.* 6, 10; Gelas. *Frag.* 28 Thiel (*JK* 738 = *HJ* 1395); Gelas. *Ep.* 3 Löwenfeld (*JK* 631 = *HJ* 1262); Pelag. *Ep.* 84 (*JK* 956 = *HJ* 2008). *Actores*: P.Ital. 10–11, I, l. 2; III, l. 2, 6; IV, l. 9; Gelas. *Ep.* 20 Thiel (*JK* 651 = *HJ* 1297); Gelas. *Ep.* 22 Thiel (*JK* 658 = *HJ* 1302); Gelas. *Ep.* 31 Thiel (*JK* 666 = *HJ* 1280); Cass. *Var.* 2, 21; 3, 29; 4, 35.

26. Slaves as leaseholders: Gelas. *Frag.* 28 Thiel (*JK* 738 = *HJ* 1395); Pelag. *Ep.* 84 (*JK* 956 = *HJ* 2008). Unfree property administrators: Krause 1987a, 148f. Favorite slaves: Pall. *Agric.* 1, 6, 18.

27. Supplying the army and court: Cass. *Var.* 10, 28 with Vera 2011. Leaseholders in Apulia: Cass. *Var.* 1, 16. For traders (*negotiatores*) in Apulia and Calabria: Cass. *Var.* 2, 26; cf. also traders in Sipontum: Cass. *Var.* 2, 38. Ship owners: Cass. *Var.* 4, 5.

28. Private granaries (*horrea*): Symm. *Ep.* 4, 68; P.Ital. 1, l. 34f.; ILCV 590; Cass. *Var.* 3, 29; 6, 11, 2; Vera 2008. Cf. also Olymp. *Frag.* 1, 44 Müller = *Frag.* 41, 2 Blockley.

29. Quotation: Cass. *Var.* 8, 33, 3. Rural fairs and markets: *Nov. Val.* 15, 5 (444 or 445); *Nov. Val.* 24 (447); Nollé 1982 (epigraphical sources from Asia Minor and North Africa); Ligt 1993.

30. Forms of rent: Krause 1987a, 100–112; Vera 1997.

31. Risk distribution: Grey 2007b, 363–367. Crop rotation and fallow fields: Ambr. *Virg.* 3, 16f.; Pall. *Agric.* 3, 1f.; 3, 6; 3, 10, 1; Caes. *Serm.* 6, 7. Feces as manure: Pall. *Agric.* 1, 33. Oxen: Pall. *Agric.* 4, 11; *Ed. Theod.* 150; Cass. *Var.* 3, 50 (Noricum); 12, 5, 5 (Bruttium); cf. Cass. *Var.* 5, 10 (Venetia and Liguria); Greg. Magn. *Ep.* 2, 38 (*JE* 1198 = *HJ* 2220) (Sicily); cf. Greg. Magn. *Ep.* 9, 233 (*JE* 1760 = *HJ* 2879) (oxen, cows, sheep). Crop sequencing: Pall. *Agric.* 2, 4 (January); 4, 3 (March); 10, 2 (September).

32. Crop failures and famines in Antiquity: Garnsey 1988. Case studies in Wiemer 1995 (Antioch in Syria, 362–363); 1997 (Antioch in Pisidia, 92–93); and 2006b (Edessa, 499–501).

33. Quotation: Cass. *Var.* 9, 5, 1.

34. Millet harvests: Pall. *Agric.* 10, 12. Crop failures and famines in late antique Italy: Ambrose, *On Duties*, 3, 37–41; Gaud. *Serm.* 13, 23; *C. Sirm.* 5 (419); *Nov. Val.* 31 (450); Petr. Chrys. *Serm.* 122; Ennod. *Opusc.* 5, 20; Cass. *Var.* 9, 5; 10, 27; 12, 26–28; (Cracco) Ruggini 1961, 466–489.

35. Quotation: *Ed. Theod.* 94.

36. Sale of children into slavery: Aug. *Ep.* 10*; Aug. *Ep.* 24*; *Nov. Val.* 31 (450); Cass. *Var.* 8, 33, 4 (quotation); Greg. Magn. *Ep.* 5, 38 (*JE* 1351 = *HJ* 2409); Greg. Magn. *Ep.* 8, 33 (*JE* 1522 = *HJ* 2611).

37. Anonymous tenant of the senator Venantius. Greg. Magn. *Dial.* 1, 1. Seasonal workers and day laborers: Ambr. *Ep.* 36, 12; 62, 3 (*mercennarius*); Paul. Nol. *Carm.* 20, 312f.; Petr. Chrys. *Serm.* 170, 8 (*operarii*). Distinctions of wealth: Greg. Magn. *Ep.* 1, 42 (*JE* 1112 = *HJ* 2128), p. 65 Hartmann (*pauperes* vs. *divites*); Greg. Magn. *Ep.* 13, 37 (*JE* 1902 = *HJ* 3049). Agricultural labor (*opus agrale*): Eug. *V. Sev.* 14.

38. Villages: Wickham 2005, 442–590 (fundamental); cf. also Grey 2011. Rural settlement forms: Volpe 1996, 147–196 (Apulia); Christie 2006, 401–441 (overview); Costambeys 2009, 102–107 (Tuscany, Latium, Lombardy, Abruzzi); De Vingo 2011 (Piedmont); Christie 2020 (northern Italy); Vaccaro 2020 (Sicily). "Estate-based identity": Wickham 2005, 470–473.

39. Slaves and *coloni* on the same estate: Symm. *Rel.* 38; P.Ital. 11; 13; *V. Caes.* I, 61 (*mancipia et clientes*); Greg. Magn. *Ep.* 9, 10 (*JE* 1534 = *HJ* 2632); Greg. Magn. *Ep.* 9, 233 (*JE* 1760 = *HJ* 2879).

40. *Coloni* of Jewish landlords: Greg. Magn. *Ep.* 4, 21 (*JE* 1293 = *HJ* 2340); cf. Rut. Nam. 378–386 (Jewish *conductor* in Campania).

41. Marriages between free persons and slaves: *Ed. Theod.* 64–68; Pelag. *Ep.* 64 (*JK* 1022 + 1023 = *HJ* 1976); *Nov. Just.* Appendix 7, 15.

42. Ennodius to Faustus: Ennod. *Ep.* 1, 7; 3, 19. Ennodius to Laconius: Ennod. *Ep.* 3, 16.

43. Harboring unfree persons: *Ed. Theod.* 84–87; Krause 1987a, 164–183. Unfree persons as clergy: Gelas. *Ep.* 20 Thiel (*JK* 651 = *HJ* 1297); Gelas. *Ep.* 21 Thiel (*JK* 653 = *HJ* 1299); Gelas. *Ep.* 22 Thiel (*JK* 658 = *HJ* 1302); Gelas. *Ep.* 4 Löwenfeld (*JK* 644 = *HJ* 1293). Church asylum for slaves: *Ed. Theod.* 70; Ennod. *Ep.* 1, 7; 3, 1.

44. Runaway slaves during the war in Provence: Cass. *Var.* 3, 43. Runaway slaves during Justinian's Gothic War: P.Ital. 13, l. 11f.; Proc. *Bell.* 7, 16, 14–15; 7, 22, 4 (Totila's speech). Prisoners of war in Italy: Avit. *Ep.* 10 Peiper = *Ep.* 7 Malaspina; Avit. *Ep.* 12 Peiper = *Ep.* 9 Malaspina; *V. Caes.* I 36 f. + 43 (Ravenna); *Lib. pont.* 53, 11. Pragmatic sanction: *Nov. Just.* Appendix 7, 15f.

45. Rural violence: Krause 2014, 58–78. Property boundaries: *Ed. Theod.* 104. Cattle rustling: *Ed. Theod.* 56–58; 88; Cass. *Var.* 4, 49; 7, 1, 3. Armed assaults: *Ed. Theod.* 16; 75. Arson: *Ed. Theod.* 77; 97. Bandits: Shaw 1984; Pottier 2006. Search for perpetrators: Cass. *Var.* 7, 3, 1; 8, 32, 5; 8, 33, 1–3; Krause 2014, 189–220. Collusion: *Ed. Theod.* 75; 77; 104; cf. Cass. *Var.* 8, 33, 2 (*aliquis rusticorum sive cuiuslibet loci homo*).

46. Patronage in the countryside: Krause 1987a, 88–202. Peasants on royal land: Cass. *Var.* 6, 9, 2. Goths as patrons: *Ed. Theod.* 43f.

47. Peasant unrest in Bruttium: Cass. *Var.* 12, 5, 3–5. Tullianus: Proc. *Bell.* 7, 18, 20–23; 7, 22, 1–5; 7, 22, 20–22; *PLRE* III Tullianus 1. Cassiodorus' father is claimed to have won Sicily for Theoderic in 493: Cass. *Var.* 1, 3, 3f.; *PLRE* II Cassiodorus 3.

48. Reggio di Calabria: Cass. *Var.* 12, 14, 1–3. Squillace: Cass. *Var.* 12, 15, 5; cf. Ennod. *Ep.* 1, 4, 3 (*laus terrae divitis*). Agricultural metaphors: Cass. *Var.* 5, 39, 1; 6, 11, 2; 6, 14, 2–3; 8, 31, 5; Gatzka 2019, 174, n. 16. Lexicon of snobbery: Cass. *Inst.* 1, 32, 2; cf. Cass. *Var.*

2, 13, 2 (*praesumptio truculentium rusticorum*); 6, 9, 2; 8, 31, 4 (*rusticitas*); 8, 32, 4 (*insidiae rusticorum*); 12, 5, 4 (*agreste hominum genus*); Ennod. *V. Ant.* 15 (*avari cultores*); Ennod. *Ep.* 6, 10 (*rustica temeritas*); Ennod. *Ep.* 9, 18, 1 (*rusticae voces*); Ennod. *Dict.* 6, 6 (*rusticitas*); Caes. *Serm.* 136, 2. Quotation: Sid. *Ep.* 4, 17, 2.

49. Landowners as church builders: C. Piétri 1981, 428–432; Krause 1987a, 119–126; Pack 1998, 1177–1182; Bowes 2012, 125–188. Foundation of Trygetius: Gelas. *Ep.* 35 Thiel (*JK* 680 = *HJ* 1357) with *PLRE* II Trygetius 3. Foundation of Faustus Albinus: *Lib. pont.* 53, 10. Further examples of private oratories: Gelas. *Ep.* 34 Thiel (*JK* 679 = *HJ* 1316); Gelas. *Ep.* 2 Löwenfeld (*JK* 630 = *HJ* 1276). Pelag. *Ep.* 36 Thiel (*JK* 995 = *HJ* 1935) mentions a basilica *in possessione filii et consiliari nostri viri magnifici Theodori* (*PLRE* III Theodorus 24). The *spectabilis femina* Magetia had people buried on her properties in Sora (Frosinone) and had requiem masses celebrated for them: Gelas. *Ep.* 33 Thiel (*JK* 709 = *HJ* 1315). San Vincenzo al Volturno: Sfameni 2006, 247–251. San Giusto: Sfameni 2006, 251–255. Papal approval for the consecration of churches: Gelas. *Ep.* 14 Thiel (*JK* 636 = *HJ* 1270), § 25; Gelas. *Ep.* 25 Thiel (*JK* 643 = *HJ* 1292).

50. Rustic religion in Noricum: Eug. *V. Sev.* 12 (locusts); 18 (blight). Sanctuary of Pan: *V. Floridi* 3f.; PCBE II Floridus. Benedict of Nursia: Greg. Magn. *Dial.* 2, 8 (temple of Apollo). Marcus' poem on Benedict, *Versus in Benedicti laudem*, ascribes the temple to Jupiter rather than Apollo (17–22). Rocca 1978 offers a new edition of this text, which may otherwise be found in the Patrologia Latina (PL 80, 183–186), printed under the title "Carmen de S. Benedicto." The poem is probably earlier than Gregory's largely fictitious biography. For the author (PCBE II Marcus 13), see also Paul. Diac. *Lang.* 1, 26.

51. Pagans on Sardinia: Greg. Magn. *Ep.* 5, 38 (*JE* 1351 = *HJ* 2409); cf. Greg. Magn. *Ep.* 4, 23 (*JE* 1295 = *HJ* 2342); Greg. Magn. *Ep.* 4, 25 (*JE* 1297 = *HJ* 2344); Greg. Magn. *Ep.* 4, 26 (*JE* 1298 = *HJ* 2345); Greg. Magn. *Ep.* 4, 27 (*JE* 1299 = *HJ* 2346); Greg. Magn. *Ep.* 4, 29 (*JE* 1302 = *JK* 2348); Greg. Magn. *Ep.* 9, 204 (*JE* 1731 = *HJ* 2848); Greg. Magn. *Ep.* 11, 12 (*JE* 1802 = *HJ* 2929). Paganism in Tyndaris (Sicily): Greg. Magn. *Ep.* 3, 59 (*JE* 1263 = *HJ* 2308).

52. Rustic religion in Provence: Klingshirn 1994, 201–243. Thursday (*dies Iovis*): Caes. *Serm.* 13, 5; 52, 2. Lunar eclipses and new moons: Caes. *Serm.* 13, 5; 52, 3. Diviners and healers: Caes. *Serm.* 13, 3–5; 52, 5 f.; 54, 3; 184, 4. New Year's: Caes. *Serm.* 192; 193; Arbesmann 1979.

53. Quotation: Caes. *Serm.* 53, 1. *Daemonium quod rustici Dianam appellant*: *V. Caes.* II, 18. Tree cult: Caes. *Serm.* 19, 4; 54, 5f.

54. Sorcerers and diviners: Caes. *Serm.* 54, 3.

55. Ritual bathing: Caes. *Serm.* 33, 1.

56. Groves: Cass. *Inst.* 1, 32, 2. Leucothea in Lucania: Cass. *Var.* 8, 33 with Barnish 2001a. Tree cult in Terracina: Greg. Magn. *Ep.* 8, 19 (*JE* 1507 = *HJ* 2595).

57. Warding off hail: Pall. *Agric.* 1, 35, 1 + 1, 35, 14f. Pest prevention: Pall. *Agric.* 1, 35 (quotation: § 16); cf. Pall. *Agric.* 4, 9, 14. Magic veterinary medicine: Pall. *Agric.* 14, 17; cf. Pall. *Agric.* 14, 65: in the event of diarrhea, one should affix a spell to the animal's tail.

58. *Aureum saeculum*: Ennod. *Pan.* 93. Quotation: § 56.

59. Ideology of restoration: La Rocca 1993; Fauvinet-Ranson: 2006a, 255–281, and 2006b. Quotations: Cass. *Var.* 1, 25, 1; 1, 28, 1; 3, 9, 1; Cass. *Chron.* s. a. 500, no. 1339.

60. Quotation: *Anon. Val.* 70f.
61. Building maintenance and infrastructure measures: Lenski 2002, 393–401 (catalogue for the reign of Emperors Valens und Valentinian I).
62. Consciousness of decline: Freund 1957, 1–40; Näf 1990. *Estuni*: Cass. *Var.* 3, 9. The identification with Sestino (Sestinum) (75 kilometers northeast of Arezzo) was first proposed by Mommsen; Histonium (Vasto) in the Abruzzi also comes into consideration. *Domus Pinciana*: Cass. *Var.* 3, 10.
63. Prosperity of Italy: L. Schmidt 1938–1941, 392; Ensslin 1959, 244; Johnson 1988, 74; Kohlhas-Müller 1995, 199–202; Hen 2007, 29; Deliyannis 2010, 111f.; Arnold 2013, 175–230.
64. Italy in Late Antiquity: Pack 1998; Humphries 2000. The cities of Italy in Late Antiquity and the early Middle Ages: Augenti 2006; Ghilardi, Goddard, and Porena 2006; Christie 2006, 183–280. Aosta, Aquileia, Brescia, Milan, and Verona: Haug 2003. Northern Italy: Ward-Perkins 1999; Witschel 2001 and 2020.
65. For discussion of the "end of the ancient city": Lepelley 1996b; Liebeschuetz 2001 (for criticism, see Lavan 2003); Haug 2003, 142–320; Krause and Witschel 2006; Liebeschuetz 2006b; Witschel 2008. Osimo: Proc. *Bell.* 6, 27, 2. Urbino: Proc. *Bell.* 6, 19, 2.
66. Urban network: Witschel: 2001, 113f., 143–149; 2008, 24f., 32–47; and 2020, 43–49. Leveling of municipal legal statuses: Lepelley 2001.
67. Grain exports from Calabria and Apulia: Cass. *Var.* 1, 34f. Export of grain, wine, and oil from Histria: Cass. *Var.* 12, 22, 2; cf. 12, 13. Export of grain to Gaul: Cass. *Var.* 4, 5, 2. Export of grain to North Africa: Cass. *Var.* 5, 35. Pork: Cass. *Var.* 2, 12. Timber: Cass. *Var.* 5, 16, 2; Greg. Magn. *Ep.* 6, 58 (*JE* 1442 = *HJ* 2517); Greg. Magn. *Ep.* 7, 37 (*JE* 1483 = *HJ* 2565); Greg. Magn. *Ep.* 8, 28 (*JE* 1517 = *HJ* 2606); Greg. Magn. *Ep.* 10, 21 (*JE* 1790 = *HJ* 2914). Slaves: *V. Caes.* 1, 21. Justinian's abolition of the *exceptio annalis Italici contractus*: *CJ* 7, 40, 1; Lenel 1906. Italic traders in Constantinople: Proc. *Hist. Arc.* 25, 8–10; Claude 1985, 149f.
68. Papyrus: Cass. *Var.* 11, 38. Architectural elements: Cass. *Var.* 10, 8, 2; 10, 9, 2. Warehouse in Classe: Malnati et al. 2007.
69. *Siliquatarii*: *Nov. Val.* 15 (444 or 445); Cass. *Var.* 2, 4; 2, 30, 3; 3, 25, 1; 3, 26, 1; 4, 19; 5, 31. *Comes siliquatariorum*: Cass. *Var.* 2, 12; 3, 25.
70. Regional ceramics: Wickham 2005, 708–741, esp. 728–741. Pig farming in Lucania: *Nov. Val.* 36 (452); Pall. *Agric.* 12, 13, 5f.; Cass. *Var.* 11, 39; Barnish 1987b; Volpe 1996, 297f. Royal lands: Gelas. *Ep.* 3 Löwenfeld (*JK* 633 = *HJ* 1263); Cass. *Var.* 1, 2; 1, 16; 5, 9; 5, 10; Volpe 1996, 351–356. Grain for Ravenna: Cass. *Var.* 1, 35; cf. 2, 26.
71. *Formula* for titular officeholders (*Quid enim fortunatius quam agrum colere et in urbe lucere*): Cass. *Var.* 6, 11, 2. Villas on Lake Como: Cass. *Var.* 11, 14, 3 (see Fauvinet-Ranson 2012–2013); Ennod. *Ep.* 1, 6, 4. Late antique villas in Italy: Sfameni 2006; Castrorao Barba 2020. End of villas in the West: Ripoll López and Arce Martínez 2000.
72. Quotation: Cass. *Var.* 8, 31, 7f.; see Lepelley 1990. "Game tokens of Palamedes" (*Palamedici calculi*): Isid. *Etym.* 18, 67. (I owe this reference to Rainer Thiel.)
73. Lib. *Or.* 11, 212–218 with Wiemer 2003; cf. also CIL III 352 = CIL III 7000 = *ILS* 6091 = MAMA VII 305 (Orcistus, Phrygia); CIL III 6866 = *ILS* 6090 = MAMA IV 236

(Tymandus, Pisidia); CIL XI 5265 = *ILS* 705 (Hispellum, Umbria); Proc. *Aed.* 6, 13–16; Witschel 2008, 24–31.

74. Urban elites: Liebeschuetz 2001, 124–127; Cecconi 2006b.

75. Presence of senatorial families in provincial cities prior to the fourth century: Eck 1980.

76. *Curiales esse nervos rei publicae ac viscera civitatum:* Nov. *Maior.* 7, princ.; quoted in Cass. *Var.* 9, 2, 6.

77. *Formula ad PPO ut sub decreto curialium praedia venundentur:* Cass. *Var.* 7, 47. Athalaric's edict: Cass. *Var.* 9, 2 (quotation: § 4) with Lepelley 1996a.

78. Falling to level of *possessores:* Cass. *Var.* 9, 4, 2f. *Quot curiales, tot tyranni:* Salv. *Gub.* 5, 18 with Lepelley 1983. Poor neighbor: Caes. *Serm.* 154, 2.

79. Curials and municipal magistrates: *Ed. Theod.* 52f.; P.Ital. 31 (540, Faenza); P.Ital. 4–5 (552, Ravenna); P.Vic., l. 17 (sixth century, Palermo). Ravenna: Ausbüttel 1987; Deichmann 1989, 130–142.

80. *Formula curatoris civitatis:* Cass. *Var.* 7, 12. Origin of the office: Burton 1979. *Curatores civitatis* in Gothic Italy: AE 2008, no. 524 (Tarquinia); CIL IX 268 (Ravenna, title supplemented); CIL IX 2074 (Beneventum).

81. *Defensor civitatis:* CTh 1, 29, 1–3; Frakes 2001; Schmidt-Hofner: 2011, 154–164 (fundamental), and 2014. The upper limit of 50 *solidi* is missing in the excerpt of the *Theodosian Code* (1, 29, 2) but appears in the *Justinian's Code*: 1, 55, 1. Justinian subsequently raised the upper limit to 500 *solidi:* Nov. *Just.* 15, 3 (535).

82. Nov. *Maior.* 3. Justinian formally declared the *defensor* the supreme municipal magistrate: Nov. *Just.* 15 (535).

83. *Formula defensoris cuiuslibet civitatis:* Cass. *Var.* 7, 11 (quotation: § 2).

84. *Defensores:* Cass. *Var.* 2, 17; 3, 9; 3, 49; 4, 45; 5, 14; 9, 10; P.Ital. 4–5, B, V, l. 11–13 (Ravenna, 552); P.Ital. 31, II, l. 6 (Ravenna, 539); P.Ital. 32, l. 1f. (Faenza, 540).

85. One-year term: Cass. *Var.* 7, 11, 2 (*per indictionem illam*). Justinian in 535 prohibited the holding of the office more than twice: Nov. *Just.* 15, 1. Tax collection by municipal officials: Cass. *Var.* 2, 17; 9, 4; 12, 8; Delmaire 1996. Tax liability: Cass. *Var.* 2, 25, 2.

86. Syracuse: Cass. *Var.* 9, 10f.; 9, 14. Como: Cass. *Var.* 2, 35; 2, 36. Catania: Cass. *Var.* 3, 49. Cf. Cass. *Var.* 9, 5 (*possessores* of an unnamed province); Cass. *Var.* 11, 14 (*possessores* of Como). Curial initiative: Cass. *Var.* 1, 19 (*Adriana civitas*). Velia: Cass. *Var.* 4, 11.

87. *Comes civitatis:* Cass. *Var.* 6, 24. *Comes* of Syracuse: Cass. *Var.* 7, 27. Feltre: Cass. *Var.* 5, 9. Forlì: Cass. *Var.* 4, 8; Cecconi 2006b, 62–64. Parma: Cass. *Var.* 8, 29f. Ravenna: Cass. *Var.* 5, 38; cf. 12, 17. Ticinum: Cass. *Var.* 4, 45.

88. Professional groups (*collegia*): Nov. *Sev.* 2 (465); *Ed. Theod.* 62 (*collegiati*). *Corporati* in Ravenna: AE 1977, no. 265b (membership list); cf. P.Ital. 36, l. 40 and 64 (*ex praeposito pistorum,* between 575 and 591). *Corporati* in Rome: CIL VI 9920 (*tabernarii,* membership list); CIL VI 1711 (*molendinarii*); Cass. *Var.* 6, 18 (*pistores* and *suarii*); Greg. Magn. *Dial.* 4, 56 (*tinctores*). *Corpora:* Cracco Ruggini 1971, esp. 134–193. Cf. Greg. Magn. *Ep.* 9, 113 (*JE* 1639 = *HJ* 2741) (*saponarii* in Naples). Patronage of craftsmen and tradesmen: Clemente 1972; Krause 1987a, 203–232.

89. Tax in gold: Cass. *Var.* 2, 26, 5; 2, 30, 3; cf. chap. 7, section 3. Specialization of late Roman trades: Petrikovits 1981.

90. Florentius (*pater pistorum regis Theoderici*): CIL XI 317 = Fiebiger and Schmidt 1917, no. 184; *Praefectus annonae*: Cass. *Var.* 6, 18; Vitiello 2002. Brickyards in Rome: Cass. *Var.* 1, 25 (*Portus Licinii*); Cass. *Var.* 2, 23. *Praepositus calcis*: Cass. *Var.* 7, 17. Building fund in Rome: Cass. *Var.* 1, 21; 2, 34; *Anon. Val.* 67. *Fabricae*: Cass. *Var.* 7, 19; James 1988, 281–287; Wiemer and Berndt 2016, 176–180. Purple dye: Cass. *Var.* 1, 2. Mining: Cass. *Var.* 9, 3. Salt: *Nov. Val.* 13, 1 (445); Cass. *Var.* 6, 7, 8; 12, 24, 6. Sarcophagi: Cass. *Var.* 3, 19; Kollwitz and Herdejürgen 1979 (Corpus of sarcophagi from Ravenna).

91. Army suppliers: Cass. *Var.* 10, 28 with Vera 2011.

92. Merchants and trade: Claude 1985, 167–244. Foreign traders in Gothic Italy: *Anon. Val.* 73; Proc. *Bell.* 5, 8, 21; 5, 8, 41; Cass. *Var.* 6, 23, 3f. (Naples); Cass. *Var.* 7, 9, 1; 7, 23 (Portus). Easterners and Jews: (Cracco) Ruggini 1959; Claude 1985, 175–193. Georgius: P.Ital. 4–5 B, V and VI (552). Antiochus: Proc. *Bell.* 5, 8, 21; 5, 8, 41. Julius "Argentarius" ("the banker"): Agn. 59; 77; Barnish 1985. Social stigma: Cass. *Ex. Ps.* 7, 15; cf. Caes. *Serm.* 43.

93. Cities of the high imperial period: Kolb 1984, 141–260; Ward-Perkins 1984, 1–13. Hippodromes in Italy (outside Rome): Humphrey 1986, 540–578.

94. Spolia: Ward-Perkins 1999. Transformation of the epigraphic habit: Witschel 2006 (Venetia et Histria); Smith and Ward-Perkins 2016, 43–55 (Italy) and 121–135 (Rome); Bolle 2017 (Tuscia et Umbria); Witschel 2020, 49–56.

95. Fortified cities in Procopius: Tabata 2013, 169–223 (list). Spectacles: Fauvinet-Ranson 2006a, 379–450; Puk 2014. Theaters: Malineau 2006. Amphitheaters: Ward-Perkins 1984, 111–116. Circuses: Ward-Perkins 1984, 92–118; Humphrey 1986, 613–625 (Milan, Aquileia). Aqueducts: Ward-Perkins 1984, 119–154, 250–255 (Rome); Marano 2015, 152–159. Baths: Ward-Perkins 1984, 127–129; Marano 2015, 159f.

96. Ravenna: cf. chap. 10, section 1, below. Church building in late antique Italy: Haensch 2017, 537f., n. 10 (comprehensive list of epigraphic attestations). Church building in northern Italy: Witschel 2001, 146–149, and 2020, 53–55. Aosta: Glaser 1997, 194–198. Como: Sannazaro 2015. Padua: CIL V 3100 = *ILS* 1297 = ILCV 1803 (*basilica vel oratoria S. Iustinae*); *PLRE* II Opilio 5. Tridentum (Doss Trento): Suppl. Ital. 6, 36; Glaser 1997, 156–160. Vicetia (Vicenza): AE 2011, no. 412 (*oratorium S. Mariae*). Tergeste (Trieste): Suppl. Ital. 10, 37f. Pola (Pula): Caillet 1993, 340–346. Parentium (Poreč): InscrIt X 2, 81; X 2, 87; Caillet 1993, 291–330. St. Peter im Holz (Noricum Mediterraneum): Caillet 1993, 347–351; Glaser 1997, 131–141; Prostko-Prostyński 2002.

97. De-urbanization: Ward-Perkins 1999 and 2005, 87–168; Witschel 2001, 113–118, 157f.; Christie 2006, 268–280; Brogiolo 2007, 117–127.

98. Theoderic's buildings in Ticinum: *Anon. Val.* 71; Agn. 94. *Sedes spectaculi*: CIL V 6418 = *ILS* 829 = Fiebiger and Schmidt 1917, no. 203. State of Ticinum: Cass. *Var.* 4, 45; 10, 29. Bridge over the Po: Proc. *Bell.* 6, 25, 8. Totila's royal treasure: Proc. *Bell.* 8, 33, 6; 8, 34, 19; Bullough 1966; Cracco Ruggini 1984; Ward-Perkins 1984, 115f.; Tabata 2013, 84f.

99. Milan: Ward-Perkins 1984, 226f.; Haug 2003, 65–85 (urban history) and 411–456 (catalogue); Leppin, Ristow, Breitenbach, and Weckwerth 2010; Tabata 2013, 242–244. Chariot races: Cass. *Var.* 3, 39; cf. 5, 25 (*tribunus voluptatum*). Siege and destruction in 538: Proc. *Bell.* 6, 7, 35–38; 6, 12, 26–41; 6, 21, 1–42; *Auct. Marcell.* a. 538, § 6; a. 539, § 3; Mar. Avent. a. 538.

100. Theoderic's buildings in Verona: *Anon. Val.* 71; Ward-Perkins 1984, 219f., 224–228; Haug 2003, 118–131 (urban development) and 457–484 (catalogue); Tabata 2013, 191–193. City walls: Cavallieri Manasse 1993. Theoderic in Verona: *Anon. Val.* 81f. Santo Stefano: *Anon. Val.* 83 with König 1986, 139–142.

101. Brescia: Brogiolo 1993 (fundamental); Haug 2003, 107–117 (urban development) and 382–410 (catalogue). Gothic garrison: Malal. 18, 140; Theoph. a. m. 6055. Brescia after the Gothic War: Greg. Magn. *Ep.* 4, 37 (*JE* 1309 = *HJ* 2356) (*episcopi et cives*); Greg. Magn. *Dial.* 4, 54 (*civitas*).

102. Aquileia: Jaeggi 1990 (urban development); Haug 2003, 86–106 (urban development) and 325–368 (catalogue); Sotinel 2006, esp. 244–248 (city history); Stella 2019, 123–176 (coin circulation in the fifth century). Wine and wheat: Cass. *Var.* 12, 26, 2. Grado: Paul. Diac. *Lang.* 2, 10; Sotinel 2006, 338–370; Tabata 2013, 288–294.

103. Baths and sewers of Parma: Cass. *Var.* 8, 29f. Baths in Spoleto: Cass. *Var.* 2, 37. Porticus in Spoleto: Cass. *Var.* 4, 24; *PLRE* II Helpidius 6; PCBE II Helpidius 4. Thermal baths in Abano: Cass. *Var.* 2, 39. Aqueduct of Vercelli: Cass. *Var.* 4, 31; PCBE II Aemilianus 2.

104. Arles: Cass. *Var.* 3, 44. Syracuse: Cass. *Var.* 9, 14, 1f. Catania: Cass. *Var.* 3, 49; Proc. *Bell.* 8, 40, 21 (*polis ateichistos*).

105. Line of fortifications along the Alps: Christie: 2006, 331–369, and 2020, 141–150; Brogiolo 2007, 114–117. Tortona: Cass. *Var.* 1, 17; Proc. *Bell.* 7, 23, 5 (*polis ateichistos*). Verruca: Cass. *Var.* 3, 48. City near Trento: Cass. *Var.* 5, 9. Theodericopolis: *Anon. Rav.* 4, 26. Identification with Curia (Chur): Schnetz 1925; Staab 1977, 51f. Localization near Lake Constance: Clavadetscher 1979, 159–162.

106. Quotation: Cass. Var. 11, 39, 1.

107. Rome in the sixth century: Witschel 2001, 125–129; Marazzi 2007; Behrwald 2020 (a comprehensive, up-to-date survey).

108. Quadratianus: CIL VI 1750 = *ILS* 5703; *PLRE* II Quadratianus 2; Henning 1999, 98 (dating). *Mons Caelius* and *Mons Oppius*: Witschel 2001, 124. Basilica Aemilia: CIL VI 36962; Machado 2006, 174f.; cf. Cass. *Var.* 10, 30 (broken elephants on the Via Sacra). Law of Majorian: *Nov. Maior.* 4 (458); cf. Janvier 1969 on building legislation in the *Theodosian Code*. Size of Rome's population ca. 500: Lo Cascio 2013.

109. *Comes formarum*: Cass. *Var.* 7, 6. *Comes Romanus*: Cass. *Var.* 7, 13. *Architectus in urbe Roma*: Cass. *Var.* 7, 15. *Praefectus vigilum*: Cass. *Var.* 7, 7. *Comes portus urbis Romae*: Cass. *Var.* 7, 9; Witschel 2001, 135–139. *Curator riparum et alvei Tiberis et cloacarum*: Chastagnol 1960, 46f. Johannes: Cass. *Var.* 3, 30; 3, 31.

110. Quotation: Cass. *Var.* 3, 30, 1; *PLRE* II Argolicus 1. Building fund: Cass. *Var.* 1, 21; 2, 34; *Anon. Val.* 67. Theatrum Pompeii: Cass. *Var.* 4, 51; *PLRE* II Symmachus 9; Fauvinet-Ranson 2000. *Portus Licini*: Cass. *Var.* 1, 25. *Figlinae regiae*: Cass. *Var.* 2, 23. Tile stamps: H. Bloch 1959; Westall 2014 (with the critical remarks by Behrwald 2020, 79–82). Tiles as building materials: Fauvinet-Ranson 2006a, 282–285. San Martino ai Monti (Titulus Silvestri): *Lib. pont.* 53, 8; Brandenburg 2013, 117f. Santi Cosma e Damiano: ILCV 1784; Krautheimer 1937, 137–143; Brandenburg 2013, 242–251.

111. Porticus Curva: Cass. *Var.* 4, 30; *PLRE* II Albinus 9. Granaries: Cass. *Var.* 3, 29; *PLRE* II Paulinus 11. Demolition instead of repair: Cass. *Var.* 3, 31, 5. *Domus Pinciana*: Cass. *Var.* 3, 10; *Lib. pont.* 60, 6 + 8.

112. Colosseum: *Anon. Val.* 60; Cass. *Chron.* a. 519, no. 1364 (*munera amphitheatralia*); Cass. *Var.* 5, 42; CIL VI 1716a-c = CIL VI 32094a-c = *ILS* 5635; *PLRE* II Basilius 13. Prohibition on intramural burials: *Ed. Theod.* 111; cf. *CTh* 9, 17, 6 (381) = *CJ* 1, 2, 2. Circus Maximus: *Anon. Val.* 67; Cass. *Var.* 3, 51; Proc. *Bell.* 7, 37; CIL VI 41388; Humphrey 1986, 126–131. Crypta Balbi. Manacorda 2001, 44–52; 129, no. 27 (= *AE* 2001, no. 508a); Fauvinet-Ranson 2006a, 246f. Curia: Cass. *Var.* 9, 7, 2; *AE* 1953, no. 68 = CIL VI 40807; cf. CIL 41420b = *AE* 2001, no. 219; Delmaire 1989b, 240f., no. 158 (dating).

113. *Praefectus annonae*: Cass. *Var.* 6, 18; Vitiello 2002. Professorial chairs for grammar, rhetoric, and law: Cass. *Var.* 9, 21; *Nov. Just.* Appendix 7, 22; Riché 1995, 28–32. Securus Memor Felix, who edited Horace in 527 and Martianus Capella in 534, is styled *orator urbis Romae*: *PLRE* III Felix 2. Patricius: Boeth. *In Cic. top.* 6 praef.; *PLRE* II Patricius 12; Vitiello 2014b, 83–88. Maximianus: Maxim. *Eleg.* 1, 9f.; *PLRE* II Maximianus 7.

114. *Ed. Theod.* 142; Nehlsen 1972, 125f.

115. Castorius and Faustus: Cass. *Var.* 3, 14. Complaint against Tancan: Cass. *Var.* 8, 28. Letters to bishops: Cass. *Var.* 3, 20; 3, 37; 4, 44. Letters to agents: Cass. *Var.* 2, 21; 3, 29; 4, 35.

116. State contracts for entrepreneurs: Cass. *Var.* 10, 28; Vera 2011.

117. The modern debate over the ancient economy received key impulses from Finley 1985, reviewed in Reden 2015 (disregarding Late Antiquity). Wickham 2005 is essential for the economic history of Late Antiquity (discussed by Haldon 2008). Economic growth in Antiquity: Saller 2002. Peace and growth: Cass. *Var.* 9, 10, 2.

118. Decemnovium: Cass. *Var.* 2, 32f.; CIL 6850 = *ILS* 827. Spoleto: Cass. *Var.* 2, 21. Theoderic's garden (*hortus regis*): CIL XI 10 = *ILS* 826 (with add. III, p. clxxii) = Fiebiger and Schmidt 1917, no. 179; Ennod. *Carm.* 2, 111; Jord. *Get.* 151.

119. Coinage reform of Theoderic: Wiemer 2021b (also on the dating of the copper coinage). The numismatic material may be consulted in Metlich 2004. *Solidus/nummus* ratio: *Nov. Val.* 16, 1 (1/7200). Gold/copper ratio (in pounds): *CTh* 11, 21, 2 (1/20); *CJ* 10, 29, 1 (1/25). The date of the introduction of large copper denominations is disputed: a date of ca. 490 appears, inter alia, in Hendy 1985, 488–490; Kent 1994, 218f.; Asolati 2013, 67. Against this, Grierson and Blackburn 1986, 31f.; Grierson and Mays 1992, 47; 186f.; and Metlich 2004, 47; 56–66, have declared in favor of dating its introduction to 477. The dating to 498 in Stahl 2012, 634–638, is unconvincing. Theoderic's coinage was imitated by Emperor Anastasius in 498: Marc. Com. a. 498; cf. Malal. 16, 12; *Chronicon ad annum 724* a. 824 (CSCO III, 4, p. 115); Metcalf 1969; Meier 2009, 126–128; Carlà 2009, 336–340; Hahn and Metlich 2013, 13–15.

120. Bankers (*argentarii*) in Ravenna: P.Ital. 12, II, l. 8 (Flavius Severus, 491); P.Ital. 29, l. 2 and 8 (Basilius, 504); P.Ital. 30, l. 109 (Iulianus, 539); P.Ital. 31, II, l. 1 and 14 (Paulus, *vir clarissimus*, 540); CIL XI 288 = ILCV 1795 + CIL XI 289 = ILCV 1796 + CIL XI 294 = ILCV 695 + CIL XI 295 with Deichmann 1974 and 1976, 3–33 (Iulianus "Argentarius"); P.Ital. 4–5 (four *argentarii*, three of them *clarissimi*, 552); CIL XI 350 (father and son, *viri clarissimi*, 581); P.Ital. 20 (ca. 600). Bankers in Rome: CIL VI 9162 = ILCV 3766 (Ioannes, 522); CIL VI 9157 = ILCV 3819 (Antoninus, 544); CIL VI 9163 = ILCV 696 (Iulianus, 557); Greg. Magn. *Ep.* 11, 16 (*JE* 1805 = *HJ* 2933, Ioannes, 601). Money lending and money changing: Sid. *Ep.* 1, 8, 2; Joh. Cass. *Coll.* 1, 20; Barnish 1985; Cosentino 2006. *Ratio temporis*: Cass. *Var.* 11, 11, 1; cf. Cass. *Var.* 7, 11, 2 (*qualitas temporum*).

121. Export ban on pork (*laridum*): Cass. *Var.* 2, 12. Priority of state needs: Cass. *Var.* 1, 34.

122. Ancient rulers' lack of an "economic policy": Wolters 1999, 234–258, 395–410; Schmidt-Hofner 2008, 209–216, 344–350. Development of law regarded as complete in the Gothic kingdom: Cass. *Var.* 11, 8, 1. Justinian's reform ideology: H. Jones 1988, 192–197; Krumpholz 1992; Noethlichs 2001, 703–752 (overview of legislation). On the perception of Justinian as a revolutionary, see Pazdernik 2005; Bjornlie 2013, 82–123. On the "other age of Justinian," see the groundbreaking work by Meier 2003.

CHAPTER 10. A HERETIC KING

1. Arian controversy: Hanson 1988. Homoeans prior to 381: Löhr 1986; Brennecke 1988.

2. Wulfila's creed: Aux. *Ep.* § 63, p. 308ʳ = Kinzig 2017, II, 3–4 § 186. Creed of the Council of Constantinople 360: Kinzig 2017, I, 423–425 § 160.

3. Nicene-Constantinopolitan Creed of 381: Kinzig 2017, I, 506–556 § 184. On Fritigern's Goths, see chap. 3, section 3, above. Conversion of the Tervingi: cf. chap. 3, section 4, above. Conversion of the Ostrogoths: Jord. *Get.* 133. Christian priests in Theoderic's army: Malch. *Frag.* 18 Cresci l. 163f. = *Frag.* 20 Blockley, l. 136f.

4. Outstanding overviews in Schäferdiek 1978 and 2014.

5. Quotation: Salv. *Gub.* 5, 9.

6. Quotation: Aux. *Ep.* § 49, p. 305ᵛ. "Synagogues of Satan": Aux. *Ep.* § 54, p. 306ᵛ.

7. Repeated baptism: Schäferdiek 1967, 159f. The Roman deacon John explained to the *vir illustris* Senarius (for him, see chap. 8, section 4, above) why "Arians" were not baptized again on returning to the Catholic Church: Joh. Diac. *Ep. ad Senarium* 9.

8. Gothic as the language of liturgy: Chrys. *Hom. habita in ecclesia Pauli*, in: PG 63, 499–510, here: 499f. with Schäferdiek 2007; *V. Marciani* 16; cf. Vict. *Vit. Hist.* 2, 3. Gothic sermon: Auer and de Vaan 2016; Falluomini 2017. Bilingual Bible editions: Stutz 1984. *Froja arme: Coll. Aug. c. Pasc.* 15 with Tiefenbach 1991; Reichert 2008.

9. Homoean liturgy: Greg. Tur. *Hist.* 6, 40; *Conc. Tolet. III* a. 589, anathema 16, *CCH* V, p. 49–159, here: p. 82f. (= p. 119 Vives); Joh. Bicl. *Chron.* a. 580, § 2.

10. Gothic feast calendar: Streitberg 2000, 472–474; Heather and Matthews 1991, 125–130 (with English translation); see Schäferdiek 1988. Theological literature: Schäferdiek 2014, 38–41. Between ca. 404 and 410, the Gothic monks Sunja and Fretela (who, however, accepted the Nicene Creed) were engaged in translating the Psalms into Latin: Jer. *Ep.* 106. Avoidance of Christological assertions: Ferr. *Ep. dogm.* 2.

11. Chaplains or military clergymen in the late Roman army: A. H. M. Jones 1953; Mathisen 2004. The structure of Homoean churches: Schäferdiek 1967; Heil 2011, 80–116; Mathisen 2014.

12. Wicthar: *V. Vincentii* 6 (where *generationis unius* should be read instead of *generationis unus*). Wicthar belonged to a Visigothic *generatio* (= fara?) that had seized land near Agen in Aquitania *sub hostilitatis sorte*. This adverbial phrase means "under conditions of hostile conquest"; cf. ThLL s.v. *hostilitas* 1b; differently, Goffart 1980, 95: "by virtue of the alien allotment." Wolfgang Haubrichs interprets the name Wicthar in Kampers 2014, 101f., n. 1, as "battle warrior."

13. Avitus of Vienne (*Ep.* 31 Peiper = *Ep.* 28 Malaspina) asked King Sigismund to prohibit annual assemblies of the "adversaries of the true faith" in Geneva, where Kings Godigisel and Sigismund (until 516) resided. According to Heil 2011, 80–85, the intended "adversaries" were the Homoeans; according to Schäferdiek 1985, 169f., however, he targeted the Bonosians. Synod of Agde (506): cf. chap. 8, section 5, above. Synod of Orléans (511): cf. chap. 8, section 4, above. Synod of Epao (517): cf. chap. 11, section 4, below.

14. Homoeans ("Arians") in the Roman Empire after 381: McLynn 1996; Snee 1998; Greatrex 2001. Catholics (pro-Nicene) = *Romani*: Greg. Tur. *Glor. mart.* 24; 78f.; Joh. Bicl. *Chron.* s. a. 580, § 2; Brennecke 1996.

15. Valentinian II and Ambrose: McLynn 1994, 158–219; Leppin 2003, 105. Sant'Agata dei Goti: Krautheimer 1937, 2–12; Mathisen 2009. Gothic churches in Rome: Greg. Magn. *Ep.* 3, 19 (*JE* 1223 = *HJ* 2256); Greg. Magn. *Ep.* 4, 19 (*JE* 1291 = *HJ* 2336); Greg. Magn. *Dial.* 3, 30; *Lib. pont.* 66, 4.

16. Catholics on Odoacer: Gelas. *Ep.* 26, 11 Thiel (*JK* 664 = *HJ* 1278); Ennod. *Pan.* 23; 36; 39; 52; Ennod. *V. Epif.* 101; 109.

17. The proclamation (*scriptura*) of Basilius survives because it was read at the synod of Rome of 502 and recorded in the proceedings: *Acta synhodi* a. 502, § 4f; 7f.; 10f., MGH. AA XII, p. 445–448. Pope Felix III: PCBE II Felix 28.

18. Favoring the Homoeans (called the *Arriana secta*): Anon. *Val.* 48. Odoacer and Severinus: Eug. *V. Sev.* 7; 32. Monastery of Severinus in Ravenna: Agn. 129; Deichmann 1974 and 1976, 371f. Cult of St. Severinus: Jenal 1995, 157–162.

19. Theoderic's Christian upbringing: Ennod. *Pan.* 80. Ereleuva: cf. chap. 7, section 1, above. Homoeans in Constantinople: Greatrex 2001. Theoderic's knowledge of the Bible: *Anagnosticum regis*, MGH.AA XII, p. 425f., no. 5; Ennod. *V. Epif.* 132–135. Constant prayer: Cass. *Var.* 9, 24, 2 (*divinae supplicationi semper assiduus*). Piety of Theoderic II: Sid. *Ep.* 1, 2. Euric's faith: Sid. *Ep.* 7, 6, 6 (*putat sibi tractatuum consiliorumque successum tribui pro religione legitima*). Thrasamund and Fulgentius: Ferr. *V. Fulg.* 21; Lapeyre 1929, 160–166. In the treatise *Contra Arianos* (Fulg. *Dicta reg. Thras.*), Fulgentius answers ten questions on the doctrine of the Trinity that King Thrasamund asked him; he continues the debate in the treatise *Ad Thrasamundum* (= Fulg. *Ad Thras.*). Gundobad and Avitus: Wood 2004; Heil 2013, 66f.

20. Homoean bishop in Rome: P.Ital. 49; Proc. *Bell.* 7, 9, 21. Stamped tiles at Sant'Agata dei Goti: information provided by Philipp von Rummel. Cass. *Var.* 2, 18, records a bishop Gudila of Sarsina; Cass. *Var.* 1, 26, records a bishop Unscila without indicating a location. There was a *Basilica barbarorum* in Vibo Valentia (Calabria): Gelas. *Frag.* 42 Thiel (*JK* 732 = *HJ* 1389).

21. Sant'Apollinare Nuovo: Agn. 86; 119; Deichmann 1974, 125–190; Deliyannis 2010, 146–174; Jaeggi 2013, 168–191. The *patrocinium* was transferred to St. Martin of Tours after the end of Gothic rule: Agn. 86.

22. Santo Spirito with baptistry: Agn. 86; Deichmann 1974, 245–258; Deliyannis 2010, 174–187; Jaeggi 2013, 191–200. Deichmann (1973; 1974 and 1976, 300–303) objects to the identification of this church with the *ecclesia S. Anastasiae* attested by P.Ital. 34 on the grounds that it was not yet common in the sixth century to name churches after saints, but this objection is hardly compelling. The *patrocinium* of the church was

transferred to St. Theodore of Ancyra after 540: Agn. 86. Anastasia in Sirmium: *AE*
2013, no. 1251 with Popović and Ferjancić 2013. Anastasia in Constantinople: Theoph.
a. m. 5950; *V. Marciani* 5; Snee 1998; Siebigs 2010, 500–509 (on the translation of her
relics from Sirmium to Constantinople).

23. Homoean churches in Ravenna: Agn. 70; 86; Deichmann 1974 and 1976, 243–245.
Bishop Hunimund: Agn. 86.

24. Document of 551: P.Ital. 34 with Schäferdiek 2009. *Codex argenteus*: Friesen 1927 (facsimile, also available online); Munkhammar 2011 (on the history of the codex). In
1970, another page of the *Codex argenteus* was discovered in Speyer: Thiebes 1987.

25. "Reconciliation" of 561: Agn. 85; P.Ital. 2. Conversions to the Roman Catholic faith:
Proc. *Bell.* 6, 6, 18; Cass. *Var.* 10, 26, 3 (Ranilda). The papyrus published by Tjäder 1988
(= P.Marini 85) records a donation made to the church of Ravenna in 523 by a *spectabilis femina* named Hildevara.

26. Church of the law of the Goths (*Ecclesia legis Gothorum*): P.Ital. 33, l. 1, 7f.; 10; P.Ital.
34, l. 109, 122. Gothic law (*Lex gotica*): V. *Sigismundi* 4, MGH.SRM II, p. 335 (*omnisque
gens Burgundionum legis Goticae videbantur esse cultores*). "Our law" (*lex nostra*):
P.Ital. 49, l. 14; cf. *Ep. Austr.* 45, MGH.Epp. III, p. 68: *ne se in eclesiae nostre praeiudicio, quippe velut aliene legis, inmisceat* (sc. Totila). "Others' law" (*lex aliena*): Avit. *Ep.*
7, p. 36, l. 13 Peiper = *Ep.* 4, 7 Malaspina; Avit. *Ep.* 38, p. 67, l. 8 Peiper = *Ep.* 34, 1
Malaspina.

27. Bishoprics in Italy: Sotinel 2006, 5, fig. 1.

28. *Cursus ecclesiasticus*: Joh. Diac. *Ep. ad Senarium* 10; C. Piétri 1976, 1:690–696.

29. Quadripartion of income: Simpl. *Ep.* 1 Thiel (*JK* 570 = *HJ* 1166); Gelas. *Ep.* 14, 27 Thiel
(*JK 636* = *HJ* 1270). Churches founded on private property (*Eigenkirchen*, "independent churches"): Gelas. *Ep.* 14, 25 Thiel (*JK* 636 = *HJ* 1270); Gelas. *Ep.* 25 Thiel (*JK* 643
= *HJ* 1292); Gelas. *Ep.* 34 Thiel (*JK* 679 = *HJ* 1316); Gelas. *Frag.* 21 Thiel (*JK* 681 = *HJ*
1324); Gelas. *Frag.* 22 Thiel (*JK* 687 = *HJ* 1328); Gelas. *Ep.* 33 Thiel (*JK* 709 = *HJ* 1315);
Gelas. *Ep.* 29 Löwenfeld (*JK* 704 = *HJ* 1362); L. Piétri 2002.

30. Milan: Cass. *Var.* 2, 29. Ravenna: P.Ital. 3 (dues in kind); Agn. 31 (*rector patrimonii
Siciliae*); Agn. 60 (12,000 *solidi*). Priests of the church of Ravenna seem to have earned
more than the bishop of a small town; Bishop John of Ravenna was advised to cede to
one of his priests the usufruct of an estate near Bologna that yielded thirty *solidi* per
annum: Simpl. *Ep.* 14 Thiel (*JK* 583 = *HJ* 1182).

31. Roman clergy: Eus. *Hist.* 6, 43, 11. Administration of church property: A. H. M. Jones
1964, 788–792; Richards 1979, 307–322; C. Piétri 1976, 1:696–728; Recchia 1978;
Moreau 2006 (*patrimonia*). Receipts: Gelas. *Ep.* 31 Thiel (*JK* 666 = *HJ* 1280); Gelas.
Ep. 32 Thiel (*JK* 667 = *HJ* 1281).

32. Episcopal elections: Gelas. *Frag.* 4 Thiel (*JK* 663 = *HJ* 1306); Gelas. *Frag.* 5 Thiel (*JK* 677
= *HJ* 1340); Gelas. *Ep.* 22 Löwenfeld (*JK* 720 = *HJ* 1376); Ennod. *Carm.* 1, 9, l. 37–125, esp.
85–87; Silva-Tarouca 1937, 3f., no. I; C. Piétri, Duval, and L. Piétri 1992; Norton 2007.

33. Simony: Gelas. *Ep.* 14, 21 Thiel (*JK* 636 = *HJ* 1270); Meier-Welcker 1952–1953.
Athalaric's decree on episcopal elections: Cass. *Var.* 9, 15. *Suffragium*: Gelas. *Ep.* 22
Löwenfeld (*JK* 720 = *HJ* 1376); Ennod. *Ep.* 3, 10, 3; 7, 1, 2; Cass. *Var.* 9, 15, 6f.; de Ste.
Croix 1954.

34. *Episcopalis audientia*: Selb 1967; Harries 1994, 191–202; Lenski 2001; Schmidt-Hofner 2011, 161–164.

35. Bishops as patrons of the poor: P. Brown: 1992, 71–117, and 2002. Alms and bishops: Finn 2006, 34–89.

36. Social position of bishops: Sotinel 1997 and 2006; contra Izdebski 2012. Epiphanius of Ticinum: Ennod. *V. Epif.* 79–94 (Euric); 106 (Odoacer); 122–135 (Theoderic); 136–177 (Gundobad); see Gillett 2003, 148–171. Bishops as dominant political power in Gaul (*Bischofsherrschaft*): Heinzelmann 1976; Baumgart 1995; for criticism, see Patzold 2014.

37. Quotation: Leo *Serm.* 4, 2 Chavasse = *Serm.* 95, 2 Dolle; on this, see Ullmann 1981, 61–87.

38. Text of the Henotikon: Kinzig 2017, III, 348–350 § 550; Evagr. *Hist.* 3, 14; Libt. *Brev.* 17, l. 54–138; Schwartz 1927, 52–56, no. 75; see Brennecke 1997.

39. Felix III *Ep.* 6 Thiel = *Ep.* 5 Schwartz (*JK* 599 = *HJ* 1214); Felix III *Ep.* 8 Thiel = *Ep.* 33 Schwartz (*JK* 601 = *HJ* 1215); Felix III *Ep.* 10 Thiel = *Ep.* 28 Schwartz (*JK* 602 = *HJ* 1216); cf. *Ep.* 7 Thiel = *Ep.* 26 Schwartz (*JK* 600 = *HJ* 1219). Acacian Schism: Caspar 1933, 10–81, 130–160; Schwartz 1934, 171–262; Maraval 2001; Kosiński 2010, esp. 177–197; Blaudeau 2012; Kötter 2013. John Talaia later became bishop of Nola: C. Piétri 1987; PCBE II Ioannes 9.

40. Two-Swords Theory: Gelas. *Ep.* 12, 1 Thiel (*JK* 632 = *HJ* 1277).

41. Roman synod of 495: Gelas. *Ep.* 30 Thiel (*HJ* *1279). Papal intervention: Ullmann 1981, 226–236; cf. also the English translation of the letters of Gelasius—with many mistakes—by Neil and Allen 2014.

42. Rome and Ravenna: Simpl. *Ep.* 14 Thiel (*JK* 583 = *HJ* 1182); Agn. 60 (*JK* 877 = *HJ* 1711).

43. Pelagianism: Gelas. *Ep.* 4 Thiel (*JK* 625 = *HJ* 1254); Gelas. *Ep.* 5 Thiel (*JK* 626 = *HJ* 1259); Gelas. *Ep.* 6 Thiel (*JK* 621 = *HJ* 1255); Gelas. *Tract.* 5 (*JK* 627 = *HJ* 1260); Joh. Diac. *Ep. ad Senarium* 9.

44. Hilary and Filotheus: Gelas. *Ep.* 26, 11 Thiel (*JK* 664 = *HJ* 1278). Filotheus is described as a *Macedonianus*—that is, he disputed the divine nature of the Holy Spirit (a doctrine named after bishop Macedonius of Constantinople, 342–346).

45. Euric: Sid. *Ep.* 7, 6; L. Piétri 2001b, 220–230. Alaric II: L. Piétri 2001c, 344–353. Persecution in North Africa: Modéran: 2001, 270–283, and 2003. Huneric's edict of persecution: Vict. Vit. *Hist.* 3, 12. Gunthamund: Gelas. *Ep.* 9, 2 Thiel (*JK* 628 = *HJ* 1261); Gelas. *Ep.* 26, 11 Thiel (*JK* 664 = *HJ* 1278); Proc. *Bell.* 3, 8, 6f.

46. Refugees: Gelas. *Ep.* 15, 1 Thiel (*JK* 675 = *HJ* 1338); Ennod. *Ep.* 2, 14 = Symm. pp. *Ep.* 11 Thiel (*JK* 762 = *HJ* 1458); Ferr. *V. Fulg.* 17–25. Persecution of the Manichaeans in Italy: Prosp. *Chron.* a. 443; Leo *Ep.* 7 (*JK* 405 = *HJ* 908); *Nov. Val.* 18 (445); Lepelley 1961, 137–144; Schipper and van Oort 2000 (sources and commentary). Reconciliation with those who had received second baptism: Felix III *Ep.* 13 Thiel (*JK* 487 = *HJ* 1021). Epiphanius in Toulouse: Ennod. *V. Epif.* 92 (*per sacerdotes suos polluta . . . convivia*); cf. Avit. *Ep.* 38, p. 67, l. 13f. Peiper = *Ep.* 34, 3 Malaspina.

47. Laurentius: PCBE II Laurentius 15. Laurentius and Odoacer: Ennod. *Dict.* 1, 12–19. Epiphanius, Odoacer, and Theoderic: Ennod. *V. Epif.* 113–114.

48. First embassy to Theoderic: Ennod. *V. Epif.* 122–135; Ensslin 1944a. Embassy to Gundobad: Ennod. *V. Epif.* 136–171. Second embassy to Theoderic: Ennod. *V. Epif.* 182–190.
49. Letters of recommendation: *Ep. Theod. Var.* no. I (*JK* 641 = *HJ* 1282); no. III (*JK* 652 = *HJ* 1298). Theoderic's titulature: Wiemer 2014, 323, n. 142.
50. Quotation: *Ep. Theod. Var.* no. II (*JK* 659 = *HJ* 1303).
51. Preservation of ecclesiastical privileges: *Ep. Theod. Var.* no. V (*JK* 721 = *HJ* 1377); no. VI (*JK* 722 = *HJ* 1378); no. VII (*JK* 723 = *HJ* 1379); no. VIII (*JK* 743 = *HJ* 1400).
52. Ennod. *Ep.* 9, 30 with Hasenstab 1890, 21–26. The quotation is from § 7.
53. Gelasius' ecclesiology: Ullmann 1981, 189–198; cf. 217–226. Elpidius of Volterra: Gelas. *Frag.* 7 Thiel (*JK* 735 = *HJ* 1392).
54. Grave robbery: Cass. *Var.* 4, 18. Church of Milan: Cass. *Var.* 2, 29; 2, 30. Germanus vs. Peter: Cass. *Var.* 3, 37. Julianus vs. Aurigena: Cass. *Var.* 3, 14. John vs. Januarius: Cass. *Var.* 3, 7. Stephanus vs. Antonius: Cass. *Var.* 4, 44.
55. Gudila: Cass. *Var.* 2, 18. Unscila: Cass. *Var.* 1, 26. Wicthar: *V. Vincentii* 6; cf. n. 12 above.
56. Aqueduct: Cass. *Var.* 3, 31. Damages payments: Cass. *Var.* 1, 8. Bishop of Turin: Cass. *Var.* 1, 9. Caesarius of Arles: *V. Caes.* I, 36; cf. chap. 8, section 5, above.
57. *Et vestrae et nostrae religionis episcopi*: Anagnosticum regis, MGH.AA XII, p. 425. *Religionem imperare non possumus*: Cass. *Var.* 2, 27, 2.
58. Pagan sacrifice and magic prohibited: *Ed. Theod.* 108; cf. Cass. *Var.* 9, 18, 9. Toleration required justification: Schmidt-Hofner 2016. Manichaeans in Rome: *Lib. pont.* 51, 1 (Gelasius I); *Lib. pont.* 53, 5 (Symmachus); *Lib. pont.* 54, 9 (Hormisdas); Lieu 1992, 206f.; Cohen 2015. Manichaeans in North Africa: Vict. Vit. *Hist.* 2, 1f.
59. Ereleuva: *Anon. Val.* 58. Helpidius: *PLRE* II Helpidius 6; *PCBE* II Helpidius 4. According to Theod. Lect. 463, Theoderic "the African" decapitated (*apekephalisen*) a Catholic deacon who had converted to the Homoean faith. The anecdote could, however, in fact be about Gaiseric's son of that name (*PLRE* II Theodericus 5): Ensslin 1944b.
60. Quotation: Cass. *Var.* 10, 26, 3–4.
61. "Your religion and ours" (*vestra et nostra religio*): Anagnosticum regis, MGH.AA XII, p. 425; Cass. *Var.* 10, 26, 4. "Others' religion" (*aliena religio*): Cass. *Var.* 8, 15, 1. *Christianae mentis vestrae pietas*: *Ep. Theod. Var.* no. I (*JK* 641 = *HJ* 1282). "Worshipper of almighty God" (*summi dei cultor*: Ennod. *Pan.* 80). "Other communion" (*altera communio*): Gelas. *Ep.* 9 Löwenfeld = *Ep. Theod. Var.* no. II (*JK* 650 = *HJ* 1310). *Propositum alienum*: Ennod. *Ep.* 9, 30, 7.
62. Pope Anastasius II: *Frag. Laur.*, MGH.GPR I, p. ix; Theod. Lect. 461. Laurentian Schism: Pfeilschifter 1896, 55–125; Duchesne 1925, 109–155; Caspar 1933, 88–118; Schwartz 1934, 230–237; Picotti 1958; Ensslin 1959, 113–127; C. Piétri: 1966, 128–139, and 1981, 444–467; Richards 1979, 69–113; Moorhead 1992, 114–139; Wirbelauer 1993, esp. 21–34. I consider all four "synods" attested in the proceedings as "sessions" of one and the same synod, which concluded with the *Quarta synodus habita Romae palmaris* on October 23, under the consul Rufius Magnus Faustus Avienus. The exact date is controversial because in both 501 and 502 the western consul was named Avienus. I accept the argument in favor of 502, which Pfeilschifter, Ensslin, Picotti, and Moorhead

support. Duchesne and Caspar, however, follow Mommsen's argument in his edition of Cassiodorus (MGH.AA XII, p. 416): according to him, sessions I–IV date to the year 501, and the fifth followed on November 6, 502. Wirbelauer 1993, 21–34, moves just this synod from the end to the beginning of the action by dating it to November 6, 501, and sessions I–V all to the year 502. His assumption, however, that the manuscripts present the proceedings in undisturbed chronological order is unwarranted.

63. Double election of 418: Caspar 1930, 360–365; Chantraine 1988.

64. Double election of 498: *Frag. Laur.*, MGH.GPR I, p. ix; *Lib. pont.* 53, 2; *Anon. Val.* 65. Bribe money: *Frag. Laur.*, MGH.GPR I, p. ix; Ennod. *Ep.* 3, 10; 6, 16; 6, 33.

65. Roman synod of 499: *Acta synodi a.* 499, MGH.AA XII, p. 391–415. Symmachus welcomes Theoderic: *Anon. Val.* 65. Cf. chap. 1, section 2, above.

66. *Lib. pont.* 53, 2; *Frag. Laur.*, MGH.GPR I, p. ix.

67. Audience with Theoderic: *Acta synodi palmaris*, MGH.AA XII, p. 426f.; Ennod. *Libell.* 12; 19. First session: *Relatio episcoporum ad regem*, MGH.AA XII, p. 422f and 423. Brawl: Ennod. *Libell.* 84. Marcellianus of Aquileia: PCBE II Marcellianus 3. Peter (Iunior) of Ravenna: PCBE II Petrus 30.

68. *Praeceptio regis III missa ad synodum*, MGH.AA XII, addit. II, no. 1, p. 419f.

69. *Praeceptio regis IIII missa ad synodum*, MGH.AA XII, addit. II, no. 2, p. 420f. (quotation p. 421, l. 24–p. 422, l. 5).

70. Report of the bishops: *Relatio episcoporum ad regem*, MGH.AA XII, addit. II, no. 3, p. 422f. (quotation p. 423, l. 21f.).

71. *Praeceptio regis*: MGH.AA XII, addit. II, no. 4, p. 424 (quotation l. 7–14).

72. *Anagnosticum regis*: MGH.AA XII, addit. II, no. 5, p. 425f.

73. *Quantum ad homines respicit*: MGH.AA XII, addit. II, no. 6, p. 431, l. 22.

74. Concluding protocol of the Palmary Synod: MGH.AA XII, addit. II, p. 432–435. 115 bishops: *Lib. pont.* 53, 4.

75. Quotation: *Lib. pont.* 53, 5.

76. Deposition of Laurentius: *Frag. Laur.*, MGH.GPR I, p. 410; cf. Theod. Lect. 462. Cassiodorus' attitude to Laurentius: Cass. *Chron.* a. 514, no. 1356.

77. Symmachian forgeries: Wirbelauer 1993 (with an edition and German translation). Marcellinus: Wirbelauer 1993, 284–301 (quotation on p. 301, l. 217–220). Xystus: Wirbelauer 1993, 262–271.

78. Festus: *PLRE* II Festus 5. Probinus: *PLRE* II Probinus 2. Faustus Niger: *PLRE* II Faustus 9. Symmachus: *PLRE* II Symmachus 9. Liberius, Ennodius, and Symmachus: Ennod. *Ep.* 5, 1 (previously attributed to Pope Symmachus: *JK* 752 = *HJ* *1418). Faustus and Symmachus: Avit. *Ep.* 34 Peiper = *Ep.* 30 Malaspina. Faustus, Symmachus, Festus, and Probinus: Ennod. *Opusc.* 6, 19f.

79. *Praeceptio regis Theoderici*: *Ep. Theod. Var.* no. 9, MGH.AA XII, p. 392. It is remarkable that Theoderic singles out strangers as recipients of ecclesiastical munificence. Inns (*xenodochia*) in Rome are not mentioned until the sixth century but may well be older: two of the three *xenodochia* mentioned by Gregory the Great bear the names of senatorial families: *Ep. Theod. Var.* 9, 8, p. 46, l. 20 Hartmann (*x. Anichiorum*, *JE* 1532 = *HJ* 2630); *Ep. Theod. Var.* 1, 42, p. 68, l. 19 Hartmann (*x. viae Novae*, *JE* 1112 = *HJ* 2128); *Ep. Theod. Var.* 9, 66, p. 86, l. 29–p. 87, l. 1 Hartmann (*x. quod Valeri nuncupatur*, *JE* 1591

= *HJ* 2793); *Ep. Theod. Var.* 9, 82, p. 97, l. 24f. Hartmann (*x. quod Valeri nuncupatur*; *JE* 1607 = *HJ* 2707). *Lib. pont.* 61, 2, records that Belisarius founded a hostel on the Via Lata; this was later known as S. Maria in Xenodochio.

80. Anastasius on Symmachus: Symm. pp. *Ep.* 10 Thiel (*JK* 761 = *HJ* 1451). *Dicis me esse Manichaeum*: § 6.

81. Quotation: Avit. *Ep.* 34, p. 64, l. 3–5 Peiper = *Ep.* 30, 8 Malaspina.

82. Letter from the East: [Symm.] *Ep.* 12 Thiel (*HJ* 1459). Symmachus' answer: Symm. pp. *Ep.* 13 Thiel = *Avell.* 104 (*JK* 763 = *HJ* 1457); see Caspar 1933, 121–123; Schurr 1935, 121–127, 233–235. Boethius was present when the letter from the eastern bishops was read in the senate and composed his treatise *Contra Eutychen et Nestorium* in response, which he dedicated to a Roman deacon named John, probably the future Pope John I: Boeth. *Tract.* 5, praef.; see Schurr 1935, 108–136; H. Chadwick 1981, 180–202. Recognition of the formula "of two natures" by John II: ACO IV, 2, p. 206–210 (*JK* 885 = *HJ* 1746).

83. Hormisdas: PCBE II Hormisda. Vitalianus: *PLRE* II Vitalianus 2. This Vitalianus has sometimes been identified as a Goth because Marc. Com. a. 514 + a. 519 (cf. Zach. *Hist.* 7, 13b; 8, 2a) gives him the surname Scytha. This epithet, however, does not refer to his ethnicity but rather his origin in the province of Scythia Minor (modern Dobruja). The same applies to the so-called Scythian monks and to John Cassian; cf. Marrou 1976. Anastasius to Hormisdas: *Avell.* 107 (*HJ* 1503). Hormisdas to Anastasius: Horm. *Ep.* 4 Thiel = *Avell.* 108 (*JK* 771 = *HJ* 1504).

84. Roman synod and authorization by Theoderic: *Lib. pont.* 54, 2 (from the Epitome Feliciana). Byzantine authors attribute the initiative to Theoderic, who allegedly supported Vitalianus: Theod. Lect. 511; Theoph. a. m. 6006; see Meier 2009, 310f. Hormisdas to Caesarius of Arles: Horm. *Ep.* 9 Thiel = [Caes.] *Ep.* 10 = *Ep. Arel.* 30 (*JK* 777 = *HJ* 1513); cf. Avit. *Ep.* 41 Peiper = *Ep.* 37 Malaspina. Instructions to the envoys: Horm. *Ep.* 7 Thiel = *Avell.* 116 + 116a (*JK* 774 = *HJ* 1508). The "formula of Hormisdas" is transmitted in different versions; see Caspar 1933, 764f. Hormisdas to Anastasius: Horm. *Ep.* 8 Thiel = *Avell.* 115 (*JK* 775 = *HJ* 1509).

85. Avitus to Senarius and Peter of Ravenna: Avit. *Ep.* 39 Peiper = *Ep.* 35 Malaspina; *Ep.* 40 Peiper = *Ep.* 36 Malaspina. Anastasius to Hormisdas: *Avell.* 111 (*HJ* 1517). Hormisdas' response: Horm. *Ep.* 13 Thiel = *Avell.* 112 (*JK* 779 = *HJ* 1518). Anastasius to the senate: *Avell.* 113. Response of the senate: [Horm.] *Ep.* 14 Thiel = *Avell.* 114. On these last two letters, see Clemente 2017, 134–139.

86. Anastasius to Hormisdas: [Horm.] *Ep.* 38 Thiel = *Avell.* 138 (*HJ* 1543).

87. Jews in Italy: Schürer 1986, 73–84; Noy 2000; Rutgers 2006; cf. Bachrach 1977, 27–33; Cohen 2016, 504–510; Brennecke 2020, 169–173. Cracco Ruggini 2011 is a collection of important studies on Italian Jewry in Late Antiquity. Jews in Late Antiquity: Linder 1987 (imperial laws from Constantine to Justinian with English translation and commentary); Rabello 1987–1988 (Jews in sixth-century imperial and ecclesiastical law). For overviews, see also Rabello 1987–1988, 45–150; de Lange 2005. Legal status of Jews since the time of Constantine the Great: Noethlichs 1996, 100–110; Lotter 2012. Cf. esp. *CTh* 16, 8, 24 (Honorius, 418); *CTh* 16, 8, 25 (Theodosius II, 423); *CTh* 16, 8, 26

(Theodosius II, 423); *CTh* 16, 8, 27 + 16, 10, 24 (Theodosius II, 423); *Const. Sirm.* 6 (Valentinian III, 425); *CTh* 16, 8, 28 (Valentinian III, 426).

88. Epitaph of Augusta: *AE* 1973, no. 218 = *JIWE* I 107. On the title *pater*, see Noy 2011, 322. Jewish inscriptions in the catacombs of Venusia: *JIWE* I 42–116; for an up-to-date inventory, see Laceenza 2019. For the late antique synagogue at Bova Marina, which was excavated in 1983–1987, see Costamagna 1991. According to a recently deciphered papyrus (P.Vic., l. 17) the Jew Assemori bought a house from the city council of Palermo. Jews and easterners in late antique northern Italy: (Cracco) Ruggini 1959. Rome: Cass. *Var.* 4, 43; cf. Cass. *Var.* 3, 45 (Samaritans). Ravenna: *Anon. Val.* 81–83; Joh. Ant. *Frag.* 214 Müller = *Frag.* 307, l. 11f. Roberto; cf. *CTh* 16, 9, 3 (Honorius, 415); *CTh* 16, 8, 23 (Honorius, 416), both issued in Ravenna and addressed to Annas *didascalus* and the *maiores Iudaeorum*. Milan: Cass. *Var.* 5, 37: *JIWE* I 1–2. Genua: Cass. *Var.* 2, 27; 4, 33. Naples: Proc. *Bell.* 5, 8, 41; 5, 10, 24–26; Greg. Magn. *Ep.* 6, 29 (*JE* 1409 = *HJ* 2480); Greg. Magn. *Ep.* 9, 105 (*JE* 1629 = *HJ* 2732); Greg. Magn. *Ep.* 13, 15 (*JE* 1879 = *HJ* 3017); *JIWE* I 27–37. For the Jewish community of Aquileia, see Cracco Ruggini 1977 (but the basilica at Monastero hardly was a synagogue). In the fifth century, the converted Jew Petrus qui Papario (PCBE II Petrus 38bis), who might have been from Aquileia, received the extraordinary honor of burial within the interior of a church in Grado: *AE* 1951, no. 104 = *JIWE* I 8.

89. End of the Jewish Patriarchate: *CTh* 16, 8, 29 (429, Theodosius II). Trilingualism of Jewish communities: *Nov. Just.* 146. Latin is predominant on the epitaphs from Venusia: Noy 1997, 309–311. On Jewish priests and synagogue officials, see Noy 2011.

90. Samaritans in Rome: Cass. *Var.* 3, 45. The idea that Theoderic pursued a "clearly defined pro-Jewish policy" (Bachrach 1977, 32) should be rejected. The *vir clarissimus* Telesinus, whom Pope Gelasius calls close to him (*noster*) in a letter, is sometimes cited as an example of a Jew of senatorial rank under Theoderic (Bachrach 1977, 27f.; Rutgers 2006, 505f.). Others, however, regard Telesinus as a convert from Judaism (e.g., *PLRE* II Telesinus; PCBE II Telesinus). The two opposing interpretations are based on differing editions of Gelasius' letter (*JK* 654 = *HJ* 1285), which is known only via the *Decretum* of Ivo of Chartres (d. 1115): the first on PL 59, 146 (reprinted in Linder 1998, p. 416, no. 700), the second on *Frag.* 46 Thiel; a critical edition does not as yet exist. In any case, the rank of *vir clarissimus* does not imply high office in the service of the king by this date; it could be held by members of the city council.

91. Theoderic to the Jews of Genua: Cass. *Var.* 2, 27, 2. Cf. Cass. *Ex. Ps.* 49, 23, l. 488f.: *Quid adhuc, Iudaei, desipitis? Cur vestrum interitum non timetis?*

92. Theoderic to the Jews of Milan: Cass. *Var.* 5, 37, 2.

93. Synagogue in Rome: Cass. *Var.* 4, 43. Christian slaves of Jewish masters: Gelas. *Frag.* 43 (*JK* 742 = *HJ* 1399); Greg. Magn. *Ep.* 3, 37 (*JE* 1242 = *HJ* 2276); Greg. Magn. *Ep.* 4, 9 (*JE* 1281 = *HJ* 2326); Greg. Magn. *Ep.* 9, 105 (*JE* 1629 = *HJ* 2732).

94. Synagogues in Vandal North Africa: *Nov. Just.* 37, 8. Jews in Naples: Proc. *Bell.* 5, 8, 41; 5, 10, 24–26.

95. Theodosius and Ambrose: Ambr. *Ep.* 74; McLynn 1994, 298–309; Leppin 2003, 138–143. A synagogue had been destroyed in Rome shortly beforehand: Ambr. *Ep.* 74, 23. Whether the synagogue that Ambrose would have wanted to burn, if it had not caught

fire "by act of god [*divino iudicio*]," stood in Aquileia or in Milan is unclear: Ambr. *Ep.* 74, 8 with Sotinel 2005, 174f.

96. Jews and "Arians" in Catholic polemic: Blumenkranz 1946, 194–198; Cracco Ruggini 1977, 359f. On anti-Jewish invective in Arator's *Historia apostolica*, dedicated to Pope Vigilius and recited "to great acclaim" in San Pietro in Vincoli before an audience of clerics and noblemen in 544 (Arat. *Ep. ad Vigilium; praef. cuiusdam de libro Aratori*, p. xxviiif. McKinley = p. 185f. Bruneau and Deproost), see Schwind 1990, 221–223; the dedicatory letter to Pope Vigilius and an anonymous report about the recitation are printed in all modern editions (but not in Schrader's translation) of Arat. *Hist. Apost.*: Arat. *Ep. ad Vigilium*, p. 3–5 McKinley = p. 1–3 Bruneau and Deproost; *praef. cuiusdam de libro Aratori*, p. xxviiif. McKinley = p. 185f. Bruneau and Deproost. Hellfire for Jews, heretics, and schismatics: Fulg. *De fide* 81.

97. Riots in Ravenna: *Anon. Val.* 81f. The verb *frustari* here, as often in late Latin, is used in the sense *fustari*: Adams 1976, 30. Legal basis: *Ed. Theod.* 97. The widespread assumption in the scholarly literature that riots had also broken out in Rome is based on an unwarranted emendation of the text; see Picotti 1956, 203f. *Symmachus scholasticus Iudaeus: Anon. Val.* 94. The title *scholasticus* denotes a man of letters, not the holder of a public office; it is often applied to advocates but not to jurisconsults. Jewish *scholastici* are attested in the late Roman east on inscriptions: in Larissa in Thessaly (SEG 29, no. 537 = *IJudOr* I Ach 5, fourth to sixth centuries), in Apamea in Syria (*IJudOr* III Syr 5, late fourth century), and in Sepphoris in Palestine (*IJudOr* III Syr 60, fifth century).

CHAPTER 11.　FROM COOPERATION TO CONFLICT

1. Quotation: Ennod. *Pan.* 93; cf. Ennod. *Ep.* 9, 30, 10 (from the year 511).
2. Wedding of Eutharic and Amalasuintha: Cass. *Chron.* a. 515, no. 1358; Jord. *Get.* 81; 251; 298. Athalaric born in 516: Jord. *Get.* 304; differently: Jord. *Rom.* 367; Proc. *Bell.* 5, 2, 1 (dating his birth to 518).
3. Theodahad: Vitiello 2014b, 41–58. *Vir spectabilis*: Cass. *Var.* 3, 15 (between 507 and 511). Reprimand by Theoderic: Cass. *Var.* 4, 39; 5, 12. Property in Tuscany: Proc. *Bell.* 5, 6, 19f.; *App. Maxim.* 3 + 4; Marc. Com. a. 536, § 6; *AE* 1928, no. 121 = Fiebiger 1939, no. 41 (lead water pipe bearing the name and title of the king, found at Rostalvecce [Viterbo] near Lake Bolsena).
4. Emperor Justin I: Stein 1949, 219–283; Vasiliev 1950; Croke 2007. Consuls for 519: Bagnall, Cameron, Schwartz, and Worp 1987, 518f.
5. Cass. *Chron.* a. 519, no. 1364; Cass. *Var.* 9, 25, 2f.; Cass. *Lib.*; *Anon. Val.* 80; *Lib. pont.* 54, 10 (gifts for St. Peter's); see Vitiello 2005, 71–80. Cassiodorus' panegyric to Eutharic: Cass. *Or.* 1.
6. Quotations: Cass. *Or.* 1, MGH.AA XII, p. 466 + p. 469f.
7. The references to Eutharic's age are vague: Jord. *Get.* 298 (*iuvenili aetate*); Cass. *Var.* 8, 1, 3 (*paene aequaevus* with Emperor Justin). The epithet "Cilliga" has not been clarified with certainty.
8. Theoderic and the Jews: chap. 10, section 4, above.

9. Consulship of Boethius' sons: Boeth. *Cons.* 2, 3, 8; Cass. *Lib.* (= MGH.AA XII, p. vi, l. 10f.); cf. Matthews 1981.

10. Execution of Boethius and Symmachus: *Anon. Val.* 87 (Boethius); 92 (Symmachus); Proc. *Bell.* 5, 1, 34; *Lib. pont.* 55, 5; Agn. 39. Confiscation: Boeth. *Cons.* 1, 4, 36; Proc. *Bell.* 5, 1, 34, **5, 2, 5**.

11. Quotation: *Anon. Val.* 85f.

12. The trial of Boethius has often been analyzed; important studies include Picotti 1931; Coster 1935; Barnish 1983; C. Schäfer 1991, 240–262; Moorhead 1992, 219–235; for a summary, see Goltz 2008, 355–399; more recently, Wojciech 2016. On the dates—trial in late 523 or early 524, execution in late 525 or early 526—see the convincing discussion in Festy and Vitiello 2020, 159–163.

13. Charges against Boethius: Boeth. *Cons.* 1, 4, 20–37; *Anon. Val.* 86f.; Proc. *Bell.* 5, 1, 34. An entry in the "Suda," a Byzantine lexicon from the late tenth century, mentions (s.v. Sebêros) a Severus who brought charges against the friends of an Albinus in the senate. This entry, however, refers to Septimius Severus and Clodius Albinus, as shown by Picotti 1931, 209–211 (pace Ensslin 1959, 308 with 387, n. 8).

14. Execution of Basilius: Greg. Magn. *Dial.* 1, 4; his trial: Cass. *Var.* 4, 22 + 4, 23.

15. Restitution of Boethius' property: Proc. *Bell.* 5, 1, 32; Greg. Magn. *Dial.* 4, 31; see also *Lib. pont.* 55, 5; *Fasti Vind. post.* a. 523; Mar. Avent. a. 525; Agn. 39.

16. Union between Rome and the imperial church: *Lib. pont.* 54, 5–7 (from the *Epitome Feliciana*); *Avell.* 159 (certificate of faith signed by John II on March 28, 519, and submitted to Hormisdas; *HJ* 1569); *Avell.* 160 (letter of Emperor Justin to Hormisdas, dated April 22, 519; *HJ* 1570); *Avell.* 167 (report of the pope's emissary Dioscorus; *HJ* 1577); the fundamental study is still Caspar 1933, 149–163; cf. Schwartz 1934, 258–262; Maraval 2001, 146–152; Blaudeau 2012, 146–148; Kötter 2013, 138–144. Consent of Theoderic: *Lib. pont.* 54, 8; cf. *Avell.* 147, 5; Cristini 2019c. Donation of Theoderic in St. Peter's: *Lib. pont.* 54, 10; cf. *Avell.* 147, 5. Pope John I: PCBE II Ioannes 26 + 28.

17. Quotation: *Anon. Val.* 88f. Marcellinus Comes, a contemporary close to the emperor's nephew Justinian, states in his "chronicle" that John made the trip to Constantinople on Theoderic's orders "to bring the Arians back to his [i.e., the king's] rite" (*pro Arrianis suae caerimoniae reparandis*): Marc. Com. a. 525 (adding *mittente* in the lacuna after *Theoderico rege sese*).

18. *Lib. pont.* 55, 5 (from the *Epitome Feliciana*): *omnem concessit petitionem propter sanguinem Romanorum, reddidit hereticis ecclesias suas.*

19. Composition of the embassy: *Lib. pont.* 55, 2 + 5 (from the *Epitome Feliciana*); Theoph. a. m. 6016.

20. Theoderic as protector of the Homoeans: Avit. *Ep.* 7 Peiper = *Ep.* 4, 7 Malaspina; see section 4 of this chapter. Avitus of Vienne: PCBE IV Avitus 2; Shanzer and Wood 2002.

21. "Arians" in the Eastern Roman Empire: Greatrex 2001. Permanent confiscation of "Arian" churches: Malal. 18, 84; Proc. *Hist. Arc.* 11, 16–20.

22. Pope John in Constantinople: *Lib. pont.* 55, 4; Marc. Com. a. 525; *Anon. Val.* 91; Greg. Magn. *Dial.* 3, 2; cf. also Ps.-Dorotheos in *Chron. Pasch.* II, App. VIII, p. 136; Theoph. a. m. 6016: Ensslin 1951; Löwe 1952b; Goltz 2008, 160–172, 403–424. "First papal coronation of the emperor": Demandt 2007, 233.

23. Imprisonment of all the envoys: *Lib. pont.* 55, 6. The fourth senatorial envoy, Agapitus "the patrician," had died in Greece on the way back from Constantinople: *Lib. pont.* 55, 6 (from the *Epitome Feliciana*).
24. Quotation: *Anon. Val.* 93.
25. Pope John as martyr: ILCV 985 = F. Schneider 1933, no. 8; *Lib. pont.* 55, 1–6; Greg. Magn. *Dial.* 4, 30; Greg. Tur. *Glor. mart.* 39.
26. Contested election of Felix IV: Cass. *Var.* 8, 15; *Lib. pont.* 56, 2 (from the *Epitome Feliciana*).
27. Sigismund: Kaiser 2004b. Conversion: Avit. *Ep.* 8 Peiper = *Ep.* 5 Malaspina. Pilgrimage to Rome: Avit. *Ep.* 29 Peiper = *Ep.* 26 Malaspina. St. Peter's in Geneva: Avit. *Ep.* 8 Peiper = *Ep.* 5 Malaspina; Avit. *Homiliae* 24 (MGH.AA VI, 2, p. 141–145). Relics: Avit. *Ep.* 29 Peiper = *Ep.* 26 Malaspina. Religious discussions: Heil 2011, 62–79. Easter: Avit. *Ep.* 76 Peiper = *Ep.* 72 Malaspina; *Ep.* 77 Peiper = *Ep.* 73 Malaspina.
28. Proceedings of the synod at Epao (*Concilium Epaonense*): CCL 148A, p. 20–37. Invitation letters: CCL 148A, p. 22–24. Banquets (*convivia*): *Conc. Epaon.* canon 15. Relapsed Catholics (*lapsi*): *Conc. Epaon.* canon 29. Churches of the heretics (*basilicae haereticorum*): *Conc. Epaon.* canon 33. Treatment of Homoean churches: Avit. *Ep.* 7 Peiper = *Ep.* 4 Malaspina.
29. Sigismund *patricius*: Avit. *Ep.* 9 Peiper = *Ep.* 6 Malaspina; *V. Abb. Acaun.* 3. Sigismund's letter to Anastasius: Avit. *Ep.* 93 Peiper = *Ep.* 88 Malaspina. Anastasius' letter to Sigismund: Avit. *Ep.* 94 Peiper = *Ep.* 89 Malaspina. Not *magister militum*: Demandt 1970, 691–699; Favrod 1997, 141–148.
30. Quotation: Avit. *Ep.* 94, p. 101, l. 26–32 Peiper = *Ep.* 89, 4f. Malaspina. It seems unwarranted to emend the transmitted phrase *series veritatis* to *species veritatis*.
31. Anastasius to the senate: *Avell.* 113, 3f.; cf. the senate's reply: *Avell.* 114, 7.
32. Murder of Sigeric: Greg. Tur. *Hist.* 3, 5 (*sicut novercarum mos est*); Greg. Tur. *Glor. mart.* 74; Mar. Avent. a. 522.
33. Sigismund's death: Greg. Tur. *Hist.* 3, 6; Mar. Avent. a. 523; *V. Sigismundi* 9.
34. Second Burgundian war: Proc. *Bell.* 5, 12, 23–32; Greg. Tur. *Hist.* 3, 6; Mar. Avent. a. 523 + a. 524; *V. Sigismundi* 8f. Ransom of the Brandobrici by Godomar: CIL XIII 2584 = Fiebiger and Schmidt 1917, no. 82 = RICG 15, no. 290. Chlodomer's defeat and death: Agath. *Hist.* 1, 3, 3; 1, 3, 5f.; Mar. Avent. a. 524. Tuluin: Cass. *Var.* 8, 10, 8. Favrod 1997, 439–443, argues that Gregory of Tours confused the Frankish king Theuderic with Theoderic the Great, but he fails to produce compelling reasons in his support.
35. Third Burgundian war: Cass. *Var.* 11, 1, 13; Proc. *Bell.* 5, 13, 3; Greg. Tur. *Hist.* 3, 11; Mar. Avent. a. 534. Godomar's reform policy: *L. Burg. Constitutiones extravagantes* 21.
36. Kingdom of the Vandals under Thrasamund and Hilderic: Vössing: 2014, 125–130, and 2019 (fundamental); Steinacher 2016, 289–292. Hilderic's oath: Vict. Tunn. a. 523, § 2. Amalafrida's flight and death: Cass. *Var.* 9, 1; Vict. Tunn. a. 523, § 1; Proc. *Bell.* 3, 9, 4. Through Cass. *Var.* 8, 23, Amalasuintha instructed the *comes patrimonii* Bergantinus to transfer to Theodahad part of the landholdings that had belonged to the private property of his deceased mother; the rest was supposed to follow later.

37. Fleet on the Po: Cass. *Var.* 3, 31; 4, 15. In 539, a rower (*dromonarius*) named Secundus and an overseer of rowers (*praepositus dromonariorum*) named Andreas are recorded as deceased landowners in the vicinity of Faenza: P.Ital. 30, l. 10–16.

38. Quotation: Cass. *Var.* 5, 16, 2.

39. Quotation: Cass. *Var.* 5, 16, 3–4. Theoderic's fleet-building program: (Cracco) Ruggini 1961, 548–552; Cosentino 2004. *Dromones*: Proc. *Bell.* 3, 11, 15f.; Joh. Lyd. *Mag.* 2, 14; Isid. *Etym.* 19, 1, 14; Pryor and Jeffreys 2006, 7–19, 123–161; Himmler 2011, 126–131.

40. Quotation: Cass. *Var.* 5, 17, 2f. Tax hike for Sicily: Cass. *Var.* 9, 10; (Cracco) Ruggini 1961, 296–301. Taxes for the indiction 525–526 could not be collected in full; the amount in excess of the usual rate was remitted after Theoderic's death. The report of the *Liber pontificalis* of Agnellus of Ravenna (§ 39) that Theoderic led an army from Ravenna to Sicily in his thirtieth regnal year (523? 500?), devastated the island, and brought it under his rule is chronologically confused and incompatible with the rest of our sources. The abundance of grain in Sicily: Proc. *Bell.* 7, 16, 17; cf. Jord. *Get.* 308; Vaccaro 2020.

41. According to Cass. *Var.* 5, 18; 5, 19; 5, 20. In 537 or 538, as praetorian prefect, Cassiodorus requisitioned horse-drawn boats to transport wine, oil, and grain from Histria to Ravenna: Cass. *Var.* 12, 24. The Goths did not build a navy again until 546: Proc. *Bell.* 7, 13, 4–6.

42. Fish weirs: Cass. *Var.* 5, 17, 6; 5, 20, 3.

43. Planned persecution: *Anon. Val.* 94f. Church of Santo Stefano in Verona: *Anon. Val.* 83. According to König 1986, Theoderic seized Santo Stefano for services for the Homoean community. Against this view, Haug 2003, 474, argues that the church was actually razed when the left bank of the Adige was incorporated within the city walls. There are no signs of destruction in the church, however, which is still standing today.

CHAPTER 12. THE GOTHIC KINGDOM IN ITALY AFTER THEODERIC

1. *Anon. Val.* 95; Agn. 39; Heidenreich and Johannes 1971 (critically reviewed by Krautheimer 1973); Deichmann 1974, 211–240; Deliyannis 2010, 124–136; Jaeggi 2013, 202–216. Imperial mausoleums: Johnson 2009.

2. Succession crisis: Wiemer 2020b; cf. Bonamente 2020. Sources: Cass. *Var.* 8, 2, 7; 8, 3, 3; 8, 4, 2; 8, 5, 1; 8, 6, 2; 8, 7, 3; Jord. *Get.* 304; Jord. *Rom.* 367; Proc. *Bell.* 5, 2, 1; *Anon. Val.* 96. The suggestion that Theoderic conferred the title *regina* on Amalasuintha, thus appointing her Athalaric's regent within his lifetime (as argued by Vitiello 2017, 29–38), runs counter to the evidence: Wiemer 2020b, 251–254.

3. Galla Placidia: Cass. *Var.* 11, 1, 9; Oost 1968; Sivan 2011; Busch 2015, 86–109.

4. Tuluin: Cass. *Var.* 8, 10–12; 8, 25; Ensslin 1936. Ambrosius: Cass. *Var.* 8, 13f.; *PLRE* II Ambrosius 3. Abundantius: Cass. *Var.* 9, 4; *PLRE* II Abundantius 3. Opilio: Cass. *Var.* 8, 16; *PLRE* II Opilio 4. Arator: Cass. *Var.* 8, 12; *PLRE* II Arator. Reparatus: Cass. *Var.* 9, 7; *PLRE* II Reparatus 1.

5. Athalaric's letter to Emperor Justin: Cass. *Var.* 8, 1 with Wiemer 2020b, 275–279. Coastal defense: Cass. *Var.* 9, 25, 8–10. Letters to subjects: Cass. *Var.* 8, 2–8 with

Wiemer 2020b, 246–263. Cf. Jord. *Get.* 304; Jord. *Rom.* 367; *Anon. Val.* 96; Proc. *Bell.* 5, 2, 1.

6. Quotation: Cass. *Var.* 8, 3, 4.

7. Separation between Ostrogoths and Visigoths: Proc. *Bell.* 5, 13, 4–8. These Ostrogoths potentially came from among the followers of Theudis. Marriages between a Visigoth man and an Ostrogoth woman were presumably rare.

8. Amalafrida's death: Cass. *Var.* 9, 1; Proc. *Bell.* 7, 9, 4. Friendship (*amicitia*) between Athalaric and Justinian: Cass. *Var.* 11, 1, 10f. (with Sarantis 2009, 21f.); Proc. *Bell.* 5, 3, 23.

9. Mundo: Cass. *Var.* 11, 1, 10f.; Cass. *Or.* 2 (MGH.AA XII, p. 473–479); Malal. 18, 46; Proc. *Bell.* 5, 3, 15 + 21; Theoph. a. m. 6032; Croke 1982; cf. chap. 8, section 2, above. Support against the Vandals: Proc. *Bell.* 3, 14, 5f.; 5, 3, 22–24. Gelimer's embassy: Malal. 18, 57. Justinian's complaint: Proc. *Bell.* 5, 3, 17; 5, 4, 19.

10. Amalasuintha's headgear: R. Delbrück 1929, I, 148, no. 32 (Phrygian cap); Volbach 1976, 40f., no. 31 (diadem); Rummel 2007, 263f. (bonnet, veil, or hairstyle).

11. Conflict over Athalaric's education: Proc. *Bell.* 5, 2, 5–18.

12. Athalaric's first edict: Cass. *Var.* 9, 2.

13. Beginning of construction of Santa Maria Maggiore: Agn. 57. San Vitale: Agn. 57; 59; 61; Sant'Apollinare in Classe: Agn. 63. The banker Julius ("Argentarius") appears as sponsor in all three cases; on him, see Barnish 1985. On the three churches in Ravenna, see Deichmann 1974 and 1976: 50–232 (San Vitale); 233–282 (Sant'Apollinare in Classe); and 343–348 (Santa Maria Maggiore); Deliyannis 2010, 222–250, 259–274; Jaeggi 2013, 224–227, 238–283.

14. Pope Felix IV: PCBE II Felix 48; *Lib. pont.* 56; ILCV 986 = F. Schneider 1933, no. 9 (epitaph). Arbitration in Ravenna: Agn. 60 (JK 877 = HJ 1711); cf. chap. 10, section 2, above. Exemption of the Roman clergy: Cass. *Var.* 8, 24 (to the church of Rome). Santi Cosma e Damiano: ILCV 1784; Krautheimer 1937, 137–143; Brandenburg 2013, 242–251.

15. Boniface II: PCBE II Bonifatius 20; *Lib. pont.* 57 (cf. 59, 1); ILCV 987 = F. Schneider 1933, no. 10 (epitaph); see Harnack 1924; Moreau 2015. Harnack 1924 calls Boniface the "first German pope" because his father bore the Germanic name Sigibuld; cf., however, *Lib. pont.* 57, 1: *Bonifatius, natione Romanus.* A Germanic name, however, need not entail Germanic ethnicity. See, e.g., Fiebiger 1944, no. 22 = JIWE II 550, for a Jew named Sigismund. In Boniface's pontificate, a synod took place at which the legitimacy of the consecration of the metropolitan Stephanus of Larissa (Thessaly) was debated; the fragments of its proceedings survive in the *Collectio Thessalonicensis* edited in Silva-Tarouca 1937; see Caspar 1933, 206–209. *Praeceptum papae Felicis*: Harnack 1924, 40f., no. III = ACO IV, 2, p. 96f. (JK 879a = HJ 1717). Decree of the senate of 530: Harnack 1924, 41, no. IV = ACO IV, 2, p. 97. Confession of guilt by the sixty supporters of Dioscorus: Harnack 1924, 41, no. V = ACO IV, 2, p. 97f. Vigilius: PCBE II Vigilius 6.

16. Athalaric's decree on episcopal elections: Cass. *Var.* 9, 15 (to John II; HJ 1737); cf. Cass. *Var.* 9, 16 (to Salventius); Meier-Welcker 1952–1953, 65–68. Pope John II: PCBE II Ioannes 30; *Lib. pont.* 58; ILCV 988 = F. Schneider 1933, no. 11 (epitaph). Justinian's edict on theopaschism: *CJ* 1, 1, 6. Theopaschite formula: Schurr 1935, 136–227;

Chadwick 1981, 174–222; Grillmeier and Hainthaler 1989, 333–359. Justinian to John II: *CJ* 1, 1, 8 = *Avell*. 84, 7–21. John II to Justinian: *Avell*. 84 (*JK* 884 = *HJ* 1740). John II to select senators: *ACO* IV, 2, p. 206–210 (*JK* 885 = *HJ* 1746); Caspar 1933, 219–221.

17. Amalaric's defeat and death: *Chron. Caes.* a. 531; Proc. *Bell.* 5, 13, 7–13; Jord. *Get.* 302; Greg. Tur. *Hist.* 3, 10; Greg. Tur. *Glor. conf.* 81. Thuringian war: L. Schmidt 1938–1940, 328–334. Amalaberga's flight: Proc. *Bell.* 5, 13, 2. Amalafridas came to Constantinople together with Vitigis in 540 and served Emperor Justinian as a general in a war against the Gepids in 551–552: Proc. *Bell.* 8, 25, 12–15; *PLRE* III Amalafridas. Burgundian war: Mar. Avent. a. 534; Proc. *Bell.* 5, 13, 1–3; Greg. Tur. *Hist.* 3, 11; Favrod 1997, 457–470; Kaiser 2004a, 72–74.

18. Assassination of Gothic leaders: Proc. *Bell.* 5, 2, 19–29.

19. Cassiodorus *praefectus praetorio Italiae*: Cass. *Var.* 9, 25. Liberius *patricius praesentalis*: Cass. *Var.* 11, 1, 16; Ensslin 1936. Athalaric's second edict: Cass. *Var.* 9, 18; cf. Cass. *Var.* 9, 19f. Cassiodorus' letters to Pope John II and the Catholic episcopacy: Cass. *Var.* 11, 2f.

20. Quotations: Cass. *Var.* 11, 1, 4 + 5–6 + 19; cf. Fauvinet-Ranson 1998.

21. Beginning of Amalasuintha's reign as queen: Cass. *Var.* 10, 1–4; Proc. *Bell.* 5, 4, 4–12; Jord. *Get.* 306; Evagr. *Hist.* 4, 19. According to Frye 1995, Athalaric died of diabetes.

22. Theodahad: Vitiello 2014b. Amalasuintha: Vitiello 2017.

23. Justinian: Stein 1949, 219–690 (still indispensable); Rubin 1960–1990 (extremely detailed but dated and unfinished); Evans 1996 (comprehensive but conventional); Meier 2003 (stressing the effects of the Justinianic Plague); Leppin 2011 (well balanced). Useful overview in Noethlichs 2001. The *Cambridge Companion to the Age of Justinian* (Maas 2005) offers an excellent introduction.

24. Gelimer seizes power: Proc. *Bell.* 3, 9, 8; 3, 17, 12; 4, 5, 8; Vict. Tunn. a. 531 with Vössing 2014, 129f.; Vössing 2016b.

25. Justinian's embassy: Proc. *Bell.* 5, 3, 10–29. Justinian's law: *CJ* 6, 51, 1.

26. Amalasuintha's deposition and death: Proc. *Bell.* 5, 4, 13–15; 25–31; *Auct. Marcell.* a. 534; Jord. *Get.* 306; Jord. *Rom.* 367f.; Agn. 62 (date of death). Embassy of Liberius and Opilio: Proc. *Bell.* 5, 4, 15; 5, 21, 21–25; Const. Porph. *Cer.* 87. Justinian's ambassador Peter went on to have a distinguished career, serving as *magister officiorum* from 539 to 565; he bears the surname "Patrician" as the author of three scholarly works (of which fragments survive): a history of the Roman Empire, a monograph on the office of *magister officiorum*, and a memoir of his diplomatic mission to Persia in 561 and 562; see *PLRE* III Petrus 6.

27. Byzantine war plan: Proc. *Bell.* 5, 5, 17–19.

28. Marriage alliance with Maximus: Cass. *Var.* 10, 11f.; *PLRE* II Maximus 20. Theodahad's oath: Cass. *Var.* 10, 16f. Gothic garrison: Cass. *Var.* 10, 18.

29. Embassies: Cass. *Var.* 10, 19–21; 10, 22–24; Vitiello 2014b, 119–138. Senate to Justinian: Cass. *Var.* 11, 13. Pope Agapetus: PCBE II Agapetus 11. Agapetus and Cassiodorus: Cass. *Inst.* praef. 1; ILCV 1898; Marrou 1931. Embassy of Pope Agapetus: Cass. *Var.* 12, 20; Libt. *Brev.* 21; *Auct. Marcell.* a. 535, § 2; a. 536, § 10; *Lib. pont.* 59, 2–5. Theodahad in Rome: Cass. *Var.* 12, 18f. On the copper coins minted for this occasion, see Wiemer 2021b, 61–63.

30. Draft treaty of 535: Proc. *Bell.* 5, 6, 1–5; Chrysos 1981.

31. Theodahad, Peter, and Justinian: Proc. *Bell.* 5, 6, 6–27; Cass. *Var.* 10, 15; 10, 19–26. On Athanasius, see *PLRE* III Athanasius 1. Both he and Peter were rewarded with high office after their return to Constantinople: Athanasius was appointed praetorian prefect of Italy; Peter, *magister officiorum* (Proc. *Bell.* 7, 22, 24).

32. Surrender of Gothic Provence: Proc. *Bell.* 5, 13, 14f.; Greg. Tur. *Hist.* 3, 31. Jordanes (Jord. *Get.* 305; Jord. *Rom.* 367) gives a different account. War in Dalmatia: Sarantis 2016, 89–100. Pope Silverius: PCBE II Silverius; *Lib. pont.* 60; *Auct. Marcell.* a. 536, § 5; Libt. *Brev.* 22; cf. Proc. *Bell.* 5, 11, 26; 5, 14, 4; Hildebrand 1922.

33. Byzantine advance and capture of Naples: Cass. *Var.* 12, 5; Proc. *Bell.* 5, 8–10; *Auct. Marcell.* a. 536, § 3; Jord. *Get.* 308f.; Jord. *Rom.* 370; *Lib. pont.* 60, 3.

34. Vitigis: *PLRE* III Vitigis. Proclamation as king: Cass. *Var.* 10, 31; Proc. *Bell.* 5, 11, 5; *Auct. Marcell.* a. 536, § 4; Jord. *Get.* 309f.; Jord. *Rom.* 372f. Theodahad's death: Proc. *Bell.* 5, 11, 6–9; *Auct. Marcell.* a. 536, § 6 (*iuxta fluvium Santernum*); Jord. *Get.* 309f.; Agn. 62 (*XV. miliario a Ravenna*). On the precise location, see Sgubbi 2005, who declares in favor of Bagnacavallo.

35. Vitigis in Rome: Proc. *Bell.* 5, 11, 6–10; Jord. *Get.* 309. Theudegisel: Proc. *Bell.* 5, 11, 10. Romans' oath of loyalty: Proc. *Bell.* 5, 11, 26. Theodenanda: Proc. *Bell.* 5, 8, 3; Jord. *Get.* 308; *Auct. Marcell.* a. 536, § 1. *ILS* 8990 = ILCV 40 = Fiebiger and Schmidt 1917, no. 204 with F. X. Zimmermann 1953 (epitaph for Fl. Amala Amalafrida Theodenanda).

36. Quotation: Cass. *Var.* 10, 31, 2.

37. Matasuintha: *PLRE* III Matasuentha. Marriage: Proc. *Bell.* 5, 12, 27; *Auct. Marcell.* a. 536, § 7; Jord. *Get.* 311; *Lib. pont.* 60, 2. Wedding speech: Cass. *Or.* 2 (MGH.AA XII, p. 477 484). Vitigis to Justinian: Cass. *Var.* 10, 32; cf. 10, 33–35. Copper coins of Vitigis. Metlich 2004, 118, no. 92 (10 *nummi*).

38. Mobilization: Proc. *Bell.* 5, 12, 28; cf. 5, 11, 16; 5, 13, 15. Alliance with Theudebert, Childebert, and Chlothar: Proc. *Bell.* 5, 13, 17–29; cf. 5, 11, 16f. Renunciation of the Alamannic protectorate: Agath. *Hist.* 1, 6; cf. 1, 4; Geuenich 2005, 89–94.

39. Loss of Rome: Proc. *Bell.* 5, 14, 4–6 + 12–15; *Auct. Marcell.* a. 536, § 8; Jord. *Get.* 311; *Lib. pont.* 60, 4. Fidelis: *PLRE* II Fidelis. Loss of Apulia et Calabria and Samnium: Proc. *Bell.* 5, 15, 1–4. Belisarius' army: Proc. *Bell.* 5, 5, 2–5; 5, 27, 1–3; *Auct. Marcell.* a. 537, § 2 (reinforcements).

40. First siege of Rome: Proc. *Bell.* 5, 17, 12–6, 10. 150,000 mounted Gothic warriors: Proc. *Bell.* 5, 16, 11. Length of the siege: Proc. *Bell.* 6, 10, 13. Sixty-nine skirmishes: Proc. *Bell.* 6, 2, 37. Silverius replaced by Vigilius: Proc. *Bell.* 5, 25, 13; Proc. *Hist. Arc.* 1, 14; 1, 27; Libt. *Brev.* 22; *Auct. Marcell.* a. 537, § 1; Vict. Tunn. a. 543; *Lib. pont.* 60, 6–9. Vigilius: PCBE II Vigilius 6. John's advance into Picenum: Proc. *Bell.* 6, 7, 27–34; 6, 10, 1–7; *Auct. Marcell.* a. 538, § 3.

41. Murder of the hostages by Vitigis: Proc. *Bell.* 5, 26, 1f.

42. Siege of Milan: Proc. *Bell.* 6, 7, 35–38; 6, 12, 26–41; 6, 21, 1–42; *Auct. Marcell.* a. 538, § 6; a. 539, § 3; Mar. Avent. a. 538.

43. Theudebert's plundering campaign: Proc. *Bell.* 6, 25; Jord. *Rom.* 375; *Auct. Marcell.* a. 539, § 4; Greg. Tur. *Hist.* 3, 32. Loss of Fiesole and Osimo: Proc. *Bell.* 6, 27, 25–34; *Auct. Marcell.* a. 539, § 2.

44. Frankish embassy: Proc. *Bell.* 6, 28, 7–15.

45. Justinian's proposed peace treaty: Proc. *Bell.* 6, 29, 1–3.

46. Quotation: Proc. *Bell.* 6, 29, 33f.

47. Vitigis' death: Jord. *Get.* 313. Matasuintha and Germanus: Jord. *Get.* 81; 251; 314; Proc. *Bell.* 7, 1, 2.

48. Proclamation of Hildebad: Proc. *Bell.* 6, 30, 16–30; *Auct. Marcell.* a. 540, § 5; Jord. *Rom.* 378. Hildebad's followers: Proc. *Bell.* 7, 1, 27.

49. Hildebad's death: Proc. *Bell.* 7, 1, 41–49. Proclamation of Eraric: Proc. *Bell.* 7, 2, 1–4; Jord. *Rom.* 379; *Auct. Marcell.* a. 541, § 2. Embassy to Justinian: Proc. *Bell.* 7, 2, 16–18.

50. Eraric's death: Proc. *Bell.* 7, 2, 18; *Auct. Marcell.* a. 542 § 2; Jord. *Rom.* 379; Paul. Diac. *Rom.* 16, 22.

51. Totila's proclamation as king: Proc. *Bell.* 7, 2, 10–18; 7, 4, 8f.; *Auct. Marcell.* a. 542 § 2; Jord. *Rom.* 379; *Lib. pont.* 61, 7; Paul. Diac. *Rom.* 16, 22. Five thousand followers of Totila: Proc. *Bell.* 7, 4, 1. On coins, Totila's name is always given as *d(ominus) n(oster) Baduila rex*: Kraus 1928, 178, n. 1; Metlich 2004, 110, no. 73; 119f., no. 97–99. The names Totila and Baduila appear together only in Jord. *Rom.* 380 (Totila qui Baduila). Only Marius of Avenches (Mar. Avent. a. 547, § 2; a. 553; a. 568) always calls the king Baduila. Reconquest of Italy: Proc. *Bell.* 7, 6, 3–5; Jord. *Rom.* 379; *Auct. Marcell.* a. 542, § 2. First recapture of Rome (December 546): Proc. *Bell.* 7, 18, 9 f. + 19f.; 7, 21, 1–17; *Auct. Marcell.* a. 547, § 5; *Lib. pont.* 61, 7; Malal. 18, 97; Theoph. a. m. 6039. Companions of Totila: Marc. Com. a. 542, § 2 (*duces suos*); Proc. *Bell.* 7, 5, 1 (*machimōtatoi*); Greg. Magn. *Dial.* 2, 14 (*comites*). The spelling of their names varies; for their meaning, see Francovich Onesti 2007, 40, no. 66; 82, no. 247; 103, no. 327.

52. For the ongoing debate on the mid-term effects of the Justinianic Plague, see Mordechai and Eisenberg 2019; Meier 2020. It seems clear, however, that the pandemic did not hit Italy as hard as the eastern Mediterranean. The only source that mentions the plague's effects on Italy is Marc. Com. a. 543, § 2: *mortalitas magna Italiae solum vastat, Orientem iam et Illyricum peraeque vastans.*

53. Totila's letter to the senate: Proc. *Bell.* 7, 9, 7–21. Demolition of city walls: Proc. *Bell.* 7, 6, 1 (Beneventum); 7, 8, 10f. (Naples); 7, 16, 22–24; 7, 22, 6f. (Rome); 7, 23, 3 (Spoleto); 7, 24, 32 (Tibur); 7, 25, 7–12; *Auct. Marcell.* a. 543, § 3 (Campania); Jord. *Rom.* 379. Cruelty and abuses: Proc. *Bell.* 7, 6, 26; 7, 10, 19–22; 7, 12, 19f.; 7, 15, 14f.; 7, 20, 34; 7, 26, 26f.; 7, 31, 20; *Auct. Marcell.* a. 545, § 1; Greg. Magn. *Dial.* 2, 15; 3, 11; cf. 1, 2; 2, 31; 3, 18; ILCV 1991 = F. Schneider 1933, no. 13 = Fiebiger and Schmidt 1917, no. 207.

54. Appropriation of rents by Totila: Proc. *Bell.* 7, 6, 5; 7, 9, 3; 7, 13, 1; 7, 22, 20. Flight of slaves: Proc. *Bell.* 7, 16, 14–15; 7, 22, 4; P.Ital. 13, l. 10–12; *Nov. Just.* Appendix 7, § 15f. "Social revolution": L. M. Hartmann 1897, 304–306; Stein 1949, 569–571; A. H. M. Jones 1964, 288f.; against Moorhead 2000.

55. Frankish conquests in northern Italy: Proc. *Bell.* 7, 33, 7f.; 8, 24, 6–10. Totila's coinage: Kraus 1928, 182–200; Metlich 2004, 33f., 37, 45, 53–55. Silver with Justinian's name on the obverse: Metlich 2004, 108f., nos. 66–69 (half-*siliqua*). Gold, silver, and copper with Anastasius' name on the obverse: Metlich 2004, 96f., nos. 38–40 (*solidus* and *tremissis*); 109f., nos. 70–72 (half-*siliqua*); 118f., nos. 94–96 (10 *nummi* and *minimus*). Copper with Totila's name on the obverse: Metlich 2004, 119f., nos. 97–99 (10 *nummi*

and *minimus*). Embassies to Justinian: first, anno 546: *Auct. Marcell.* a. 547, § 1; second, anno 547: Proc. *Bell.* 7, 21; third, anno 550: Proc. *Bell.* 7, 37, 6–8; cf. 8, 24, 4f.

56. Second recapture of Rome (January 550): *Ep. Arel.* 45 (*JK* 925 = *HJ* 1841); Proc. *Bell.* 7, 36; Jord. *Rom.* 382; *Exc. Sang.* 704. Rebuilding of Rome and chariot races: Proc. *Bell.* 7, 37, 1–3. Sicilian expedition: Proc. *Bell.* 7, 39, 2–5; 7, 40, 19–29; Jord. *Rom.* 382.

57. Western Roman senators in Constantinople: Proc. *Bell.* 7, 35, 9f.; Vigil. *Ep. ad Rusticum et Sebastianum*, in: ACO IV, 1, p. 188 (*JK* 927 = *HJ* 1846); Vigil. *Ep.* 1 Schwartz (*JK* 931 = *HJ* 1861); *Lib. pont.* 61, 7. Liberius sails to Sicily: Proc. *Bell.* 7, 39, 6; 8, 24, 1; Jord. *Rom.* 385. War preparations of Germanus: Proc. *Bell.* 7, 35, 9–10; 7, 37, 24–27; 7, 39, 2–9; Jord. *Get.* 251; Jord. *Rom.* 382; 385.

58. Narses: *PLRE* III Narses 1; Brodka 2018, esp. 122–163. His exact title as supreme commander is unknown. Narses' army: Proc. *Bell.* 8, 21, 19f.; 8, 26, 5–17.

59. Naval expeditions to Corcyra and Epirus: Proc. *Bell.* 8, 22, 17–32; Sarantis 2016, 293f. Sea battle off Ancona: Proc. *Bell.* 8, 23. Indulf (*PLRE* III Indulf), who had deserted from Belisarius to Totila, was later among the thousand men who refused to surrender after defeat at Mons Lactarius. Conquest of Corsica and Sardinia: Proc. *Bell.* 8, 24, 31–33.

60. Narses' march from Salona to Ravenna: Proc. *Bell.* 8, 26, 5; 8, 26, 18–25; 8, 28; Agn. 62.

61. Three hundred children (*paides*) as hostages: Proc. *Bell.* 8, 34, 7–8. Battle at Busta Gallorum (June 552): Proc. *Bell.* 8, 29–32; Mar. Avent. a. 553; Vict. Tunn. a. 554; *Lib. pont.* 61, 8; Agn. 62; Malal. 18, 116; Theoph. a. m. 6044; Rance 2005. Asbad kills Totila: Proc. *Bell.* 8, 32, 22–28; Asbad's epitaph: *Auct. Haun. Extrema* 2 (MGH.AA IX, 337, no. 2) = Suppl. It. 9, 15. Totila's garment and helmet (*kamelaukion*): Theoph. a. m. 6044 with Wiemer and Berndt 2016, 170f. Third recapture of Rome: Proc. *Bell.* 8, 33, 13–18, 34, 4. In an inscription erected in 565 (now lost), Narses claimed credit for restoring the Pons Salarius, two miles north of Rome, after he had defeated the kings of the Goths and restored the liberty of the city of Rome and the whole of Italy: CIL VI 1199 = *ILS* 832 = ILCV 776 = Fiebiger and Schmidt 1917, no. 217.

62. Teia's proclamation as king: Proc. *Bell.* 8, 33, 6; Agn. 62; Mar. Avent. a. 535. Murder of the 300 hostages: Proc. *Bell.* 8, 34, 8. Battle of Mons Lactarius (October 552): Proc. *Bell.* 8, 35.

63. Teia's death: Proc. *Bell.* 8, 35, 20–29. Treaty with the defeated Goths: Proc. *Bell.* 8, 35, 33–38; Agath. *Hist.* 1, 1.

64. Butilin and Leuthari: Agath. *Hist.* 1, 1; 1, 5–2, 13. Aligern: Agath. *Hist.* 1, 20. Capture of Verona: Malal. 18, 140; Theoph. a. m. 6055; Agn. 79; Paul. Diac. *Lang.* 2, 2 (Widin). A new study of the last Goths in Italy is a desideratum; L. Schmidt 1943 is dated but has not yet been superseded.

CHAPTER 13. THEODERIC THE GREAT

1. Quotation: Cass. *Orth.* praef. Vivarium: Courcelle 1938 and 1957; Klauser 1977; O'Donnell 1979, 177–222; Barnish 1989; Troncarelli 1998 (see the critical review by Halporn 2000).

2. Justinian's Pragmatic Sanction: *Nov. Just.* Appendix 7; L. M. Hartmann 1923, 344–348; Stein 1949, 612–618; Archi 1978 (fundamental); T. S. Brown 1984, 6–14. After the

Frankish invasion, Justinian suspended interest payments for five years in Italy and Sicily; if the security for a debt was destroyed, the debtor was to be freed of it: *Nov. Just.* Appendix 8. Devastation of Italy: Pelag. *Ep.* 4, 4 (*JK* 943 = *HJ* 1896); Pelag. *Ep.* 85 (*JK* 963 = *HJ* 2009); cf. Agn. 95: *provinciales Romani ubique ad nihilum redacti sunt.* Narses as ruler of Italy: Brodka 2018, 209–226.

3. Lombard conquest: L. M. Hartmann 1900, 34–55; Christie 1991; Brodka 2018, 226–242 (also on the dismissal of Narses). The praetorian prefecture of Italy continued to exist into the seventh century: T. S. Brown 1984, 10f.; Claude 1997b, 355–358; Brandes 2002, 58f. An *exarchus Italiae* is securely attested for the first time in 584 — by Pelagius II *Ep.*, MGH.Epp. II, App. II (*JE* 1052 = *HJ* 2047) — but the office might have been created at a considerably earlier date; cf. T. S. Brown 1984, 48–53; *PLRE* III Decius 2; *PLRE* III Smaragdus 2. Destruction of the original monastery of Monte Cassino: Greg. Magn. *Dial.* 2, 17; Paul. Diac. *Lang.* 4, 17; 6, 40; Leo Mars. *Chron.* 1, 2.

4. Three Chapters controversy: Caspar 1933, 234–305; Stein 1949, 623–690; Sotinel: 2001b and 2006, 295–370; Leppin 2011, 293–307; Battistella 2017.

5. Cassiodorus in Constantinople: Barnish 1987b; Amici 2005; van Hoof and van Nuffelen 2017, 283–290. Western Roman senators in Constantinople: cf. chap. 12, section 3 (n. 57) above. Vitigis' murder of the hostages: Proc. *Bell.* 5, 26, 1f. Cethegus: *PLRE* II Cethegus; PCBE II Cethegus; Proc. Bell. 7, 13, 12 (*caput senatus*). "Ordo generis Cassiodororum" (= Cass. *Lib.*): Krautschick 1983, 78–84; Al. Cameron 2012b, 159–164; Bjornlie 2013, 157–165. *Gothic History* of Cassiodorus available in Constantinople: Jord. *Get.* 1–2.

6. Epiphanius Scholasticus: PCBE IV Epiphanius 24; Brunhölzl 1975, 41f. *Historia tripartita*: Cass. Epiph. *Hist.* praef.; Cass. *Inst.* 1, 17, 2; on the date, see van Hoof and van Nuffelen 2017, 285–288. Pope Gregory the Great later warned others against reading this book: Greg. Magn. *Ep.* 7, 31 (*JE* 1477 = *HJ* 2558). Theodore of Mopsuestia: Cass. Epiph. *Hist.* 10, 34, 1 (after Sozomen). Praise of Facundus of Hermiane: Cass. *Ex. Ps.* 137. Dedication of his commentary on Psalms: Cass. *Ex. Ps.* praef. Cassiodorus, Cethegus, and the renegade deacons: Vigil. *Ep.*, *ad Rusticum et Sebastianum*, in: ACO IV, 1, p. 188 (*JK* 927 = *HJ* 1846); PCBE II Cethegus 1.

7. Commentary on Psalms: Schlieben 1974 and 1979; O'Donnell 1979, 131–176. *Institutions of Secular Learning* (*Institutiones saecularium litterarum*) as separate book: Troncarelli 1998, 12–21; Vessey 2004, 39–44.

8. Quotation: Cass. *Inst.* praef. Historiography: Cass. *Inst.* 1, 18. Geography: Cass. *Inst.* 1, 25. Medicine: Cass. *Inst.* 1, 31. Agronomy: Cass. *Inst.* 1, 28. Theoderic in Marcellinus Comes: Goltz 2008, 86–116. Boethius' translations of works by Porphyry and Aristotle: Cass. *Inst.* 2, 3, 18; cf. 2, 4, 7 (Nicomachus of Gerasa); Cass. *Inst.* 2, 6, 3 (Euclid). Boethius' philosophical works were known in Rome and Constantinople: the Roman deacon John owned a collection of Boethius' theological works: Boeth. *Tract.* 5 praef. In Constantinople, the copyist (*antiquarius*) Theodorus (*PLRE* II Theodorus 63) copied *De syllogismo hypothetico* for the western senator and *vir spectabilis* Renatus (*PLRE* II Renatus 1; PCBE II Renatus 3) in 527: Chadwick 1981, 254–257.

9. Quotation: Cass. *Inst.* 1, 30, 1; cf. 1, 15. Program of study: Vessey 2004, 42–79; Ferrari 2011.

10. Gregory the Great and Vivarium: Greg. Magn. *Ep.* 8, 30 (*JE* 1519 = *HJ* 2608); Greg. Magn. *Ep.* 8, 32 (*JE* 1521 = *HJ* 2610). Codex Amiatinus: Weitzmann 1977, 24, 126f., pl. 48; Vessey 2002, 67–92.

11. Theoderic's ruling concept: Wiemer 2013b and 2014; cf. chap. 6, section 1, above.

12. Disappearance of the Western senate: Stein 1939; T. S. Brown 1984, 21–37.

13. Machiavelli on Theoderic: *Istorie Fiorentine* (*Florentine Histories*, completed in 1525), book 1, chap. 4; cf. Costa 1977, 47–55; Pizzi 1994–1995, 262–266.

14. Moderation in victory: Cass. *Var.* 2, 41, 2: *illa mihi feliciter bella pervenerunt, quae moderato fine peracta sunt.* Roman ideology of world rulership: Rubin 1953; McCormick 1987.

15. Justinian's "Christian experiment": Leppin 2011, 335–354. Bodin on Theoderic: *Six livres de la République* (*Six Books of the Commonwealth*, 1576), book 4, chap. 6. Theoderic is also cited as a model of religious tolerance at the end of the dialogue *Colloquium heptaplomeres de rerum sublimium arcanis*, attributed to Bodin (edited by Ludwig Noack, Schwerin, 1857), manuscripts of which circulated in the seventeenth and eighteenth centuries. On Theoderic in Bodin and Isaac Casaubon, see Stone 1985, 157f. Voltaire on Theoderic: "Essai sur les mœurs et l'esprit des nations" (1756; published in English in 1759 as "An Essay on Universal History, the Manners, and Spirit of Nations"), chap. 12; *Dictionnaire philosophique* (*Philosophical Dictionary*, 1764), s. v. A comme Arianisme. Montesquieu, *De l'esprit des loix* (*The Spirit of the Laws*, 1748, book 30, chap. 12), declared that he intended to write a book about the Ostrogothic monarchy in Italy (but never did); cf. Wood 2013, 37–41. On Edward Gibbon, see section 4 in this chapter.

16. Synod of Toledo. Schäferdiek 1967, 192–194. Sacralization of the Visigothic monarchy: Ewig 1956, 24–37; Dartmann 2010. Anti-Jewish policy of the Visigothic kings: Bachrach 1977, 3–26.

17. Ensslin on Theoderic's "heroic" personality: Ensslin 1959, 332–338, esp. 334f. (quotation).

18. Theoderic in Asia Minor: Joh. Ant. *Frag.* 214, 6 Müller = *Frag.* 306, l. 25–28 Roberto; Evagr. *Hist.* 3, 17; Theoph. a. m. 5977. Theoderic in Byzantine chronicles: Goltz 2008, 542–586. Syriac chroniclers on Theoderic: Zach. *Hist. eccl.* 7, 12d; 9, 18a with Goltz 2009.

19. Gothic tradition in Hispania: Messmer 1960, 85–137; Teillet 1984, 459–644. Literature in Gothic Italy: Brunhölzl 1975, 25–47; Lozovsky 2016. Cassiodorus' reception in the Middle Ages: O'Donnell 1979, 239–255. Boethius' reception: Chadwick 1981, 254–257; Gruber 2011, 98–108. Dietrich saga: see section 3 of this chapter. Dietrich von Bern in the literature of the nineteenth and early twentieth centuries: Altaner 1912. The portrayal of Theoderic in historical novels has not yet been closely studied. On *Ein Kampf um Rom*, see section 6 of this chapter.

20. Awareness of different epochs: Cass. *Var.* 3, 5, 3 (*moderna saecula moribus ornabantur antiquis*); Cass. *Var.* 4, 51, 2 (*antiqui vs. moderni*); cf. Freund 1957, 1–40; Näf 1990; Moorhead 2006.

21. Charlemagne and Theoderic: Agn. 94; Hadrian I *Ep.* 81 MGH.Epp. 3, p. 614 (*JE* 2470 = *HJ* 4533); Einhard V. *Karoli* 26; Löwe 1952a, 397–399; Goltz 2008, 600–604; Tischler

2021. *De imagine Tetrici*: H. J. Zimmermann 1972, 148–152; Herren 1991 (text and translation); Lienert 2008, 52f., no. 48. The name "Tetricus" is a Latinization of the received German form of Theoderic's name, "Dietrich."

22. *Chronica Theodericiana*: H. J. Zimmermann 1972, 110–112, 256; Lienert 2008, 86, no. 102 + 262, no. B6. Giovanni de Matociis: H. J. Zimmermann 1972, 132–134, 236; Lienert 2008, 152f., no. 187; Festy and Vitiello 2020, xliii–xlv. A famous equestrian statue known as the "Regisole" (i.e., "Sun King") and believed to represent Theoderic stood in front of the cathedral of Pavia (ancient Ticinum) from the fourteenth century until it was destroyed as a symbol of monarchy in 1796. See Saletti 1997.

23. *Hildebrandslied*: Lienert 2008, 53f., no. 50. *Lament of Deor*: Lienert 2008, 55, no. 52. Rök runestone: H. J. Zimmermann 1972, 152–159; Lienert 2008, 51, no. 47; Düwel 2008, 114–118. Theoderic's battle with Odoacer: H. J. Zimmermann 1972, 111f.; Lienert 2008, 262, no. B6.

24. Heinzle 1999 provides a thorough introduction to the so-called Dietrich epics; for a brief overview, see Lienert 2015, 96–141. Dietrich Saga: Haubrichs 2000; Kragl 2020. No fewer than 315 Dietrich testimonia dating from the sixth to the sixteenth centuries are collected in Lienert 2008. A selection of 75 texts in Greek, Latin, and Middle High German are collected in H. J. Zimmermann 1972. The *Nibelungenlied* as German national epic: See 1994b, 83–134.

25. Dietrich von Bern as a figure of memory in medieval Europe: Graus 1975, 39–46.

26. Luther and Dietrich von Bern: Lienert 2008, 225f., no. 313. Court church of Innsbruck: Schleicher 1986; Lienert 2008, 267, no. B21. On "German antiquity" in the discourse of German humanists prior to the Reformation, see Borchardt 1971.

27. Cochlaeus and Cassiodorus: Cochlaeus 1529; Spahn 1898, 29f., 58f., 108f.; Stone 1985, 154–157. The first complete edition of the *Variae*, by the humanist Mariangelo Accursio (1489–1546), appeared in Augsburg in 1533. *Vita Theoderici*: Cochlaeus 1544; Cochlaeus and Peringskiöld 1699; cf. Spahn 1898, 295f.; Wiemer 2020b, 393f. Both editions were reviewed in detail by Hummel 1777, 428–454. Swedish Gothicism: Svennung 1967; Schmidt-Voges 2004; cf. Wiemer 2020b, 394. On German debates on Gothic language and culture from the sixteenth to the eighteenth centuries, see Brough 1985; on debates in England, see Kliger 1952, who also has an excursus (106–111) on North America.

28. On the importance of Cassiodorus for the Maurists, see Stone 1985, 160–163. Garet's edition of Cassiodorus is reprinted in volumes 69 and 70 of the *Patrologia Latina* (1865). Garet was missing only the *Complexiones in Epistulas Apostolorum*, which was were first published by Scipione Maffei in 1721.

29. Gibbon 1776–1788, chap. XXXIX. The quotations are taken from the Penguin edition by David Womersley (London, 1994), which gives the complete and unaltered text of the first edition.

30. On the image of Theoderic in European historiography, see Helbling 1954, esp. 59–84; Pizzi 1994–1995. For the "The Modern Origins of the Early Middle Ages," see Wood 2013.

31. Prize studies of the year 1810: Sartorius 1811a, esp. 237–246; Naudet 1811, esp. 188–196: "Jugement sur le système de Théodoric." Both books are discussed in Sartorius 1811b; cf. Wiemer 2020b, 398. The *Geschichte des ostgothischen Königs Theoderich und seiner*

Regierung (*History of the Ostrogothic King Theoderic and His Government*; Hurter 1807–1808), by the reformed pastor Friedrich Hurter (1787–1865) of Schaffhausen, who much later converted to Roman Catholicism, remained incomplete after the second volume and was largely ignored.

32. Valhalla as a German cultural monument: Nipperdey 1968. Hintze's memorandum: vom Brocke 2006 (including the text). Georg Pfeilschifter (1870–1936) was a Catholic priest who had earned his doctorate with a dissertation (still useful today) on relations between Theoderic and the Catholic Church (Pfeilschifter 1896); he was a professor of church history in Freiburg im Breisgau from 1903 to 1917 and from 1917 to 1935 in Munich.

33. Du Roure on Theoderic: Du Roure 1846, v–xxxi (discussed in detail and approvingly by the diplomat Émile de Langsdorff in 1847). "Germanic antiquity" in Italy from Machiavelli to Vico: Costa 1977; on Pietro Giannone (1676–1748) and Ludovico Muratori (1672–1750), see Pizzi 1994–1995, 266–274. Wood 2013, 113–136, covers Italian discourses on the Lombards in the first half of the nineteenth century. Pavirani on Gothic rule in Italy: Pavirani 1846–1847.

34. Gregorovius and Ranke on Theoderic: Gregorovius 1859, 277–327 (book 2, chap. 2); 455–463 (book 2, chapter 6: "Rückblick auf die Herrschaft der Goten in Italien"). Quotations are from the fifth, improved edition (Stuttgart–Berlin 1903). Gregorovius and Italy: Esch and Petersen 1993. Ranke on Theoderic: Ranke 1883, 370–445. Image of Theoderic in German historiography of the nineteenth century: Cesa 2003.

35. Hodgkin on Theoderic: Hodgkin 1885 and 1891. Hodgkin and Italy: Bullough 1968; Wood 2013, 217–220

36. Dahn on Theoderic: Dahn 1859, 1861, and 1866; on Dahn as a historian of the Goths, see Wiemer 2020b, 403–405. The quotations are from the 1880 reprint of Dahn 1859, the essay titled "Dietrich von Berne" (269). Racialized national thought in Germany from 1789 to 1914: See 2001, esp. 142–148.

37. *Ein Kampf um Rom*: Schwab 2003; Reemtsma 2004 (a misconceived rehabilitation); Wood 2013, 191–198. Dahn's novel, first published in Leipzig in 1876, was immediately translated into English (by Lily Wolffsohn); the translation came out in London under the title *A Struggle for Rome* in 1876–1878. A new translation by Herb Parker appeared under the same title in 2005. Quotations from the novel refer to book and chapter.

38. Mommsen and Late Antiquity: Croke 1990; Rebenich 1998; Wood 2013, 174–176. For Mommsen on Ostrogothic Italy, see also Wiemer 2020b, 405–407. The principles on which his edition of Jordanes was based have not gone uncontested but are defended with strong arguments by Galdi 2013.

39. Hartmann and Austrian historiography: Fellner 1985.

40. Pastor as a nationalist German author and critic: Wiwjorra 2001. The full title of Wangenheim's novel on Odoacer is *Das Ende West-Roms: Odoakar, ein Germanenschicksal* (Köslin 1925); the second edition was subtitled *Kulturgeschichtlicher Roman*. Wangenheim (1872–1959) joined the Nazi Party in 1922 and became director of the *Reichsbauernhochschule* in Goslar in 1934. Theoderic in pamphlets and papers of the Nazi era: Reier 1934; Prestel 1935; Eicke 1938; H. Neumann 1939. The Austrian painter Franz Jung-Ilsenheim (1883–1963) was popular during the Nazi era. The school

mural *Theoderich der Große. Nordisches Erbe am Mittelmeer* is available online at
https://www.deutsche-digitale-bibliothek.de (object number 2007SSM208.9). For his
novel *Theoderich. König des Abendlandes* (Munich, 1939), Wilhelm Schäfer used the
same title as the German translation of the novel *Théodoric, roi des Ostrogoths 454–526*
(Paris, 1935), by the French writer Marcel Brion (1895–1984), which appeared in 1936.
The Germanist Bayard Q. Morgan (1907–1964) from Stanford University praised
Schäfer's book as "an outstanding historical novel" with the laudable aim of "making
the German people acquainted with their national origins, familiar with the deeds of
past leaders, and conscious of a great tradition"; see his review in *Books Abroad* 13
(1939): 456.

41. Gerhard Vetter was a student of the influential ancient historian Wilhelm Weber (1882–
1948); his dissertation (Vetter 1938) was criticized by L. Schmidt 1939 and Ensslin 1940c.
Heinz-Eberhard Giesecke, also a student of Weber's, wanted to prove that "East-Germanic
Arianism" was a religion without a savior god and therefore "inherently compatible" (*art-gemäß*) with the "heroic essence" of the Germani (Giesecke 1939). The author was an
instructor for the SS at the "Ordensburg" Sonthofen (an educational facility for the Nazi
elite) since 1939. Theoderic's "Roman mission": Stauffenberg: 1938 (quotation p. 142) and
1949; Ensslin 1942; see Wiemer 2020b, 412–415. The ancient historian Alexander von
Stauffenberg (1905–1964) was a brother of Claus von Stauffenberg, the conspirator against
Hitler who was executed after the failed assassination attempt on July 20, 1944. Alexander
was then taken into *Sippenhaft* ("clan custody") and not released until shortly before the
end of the war; see Christ 2008 for more about him.

ANNOTATED BIBLIOGRAPHY

1. EDITIONS OF ANCIENT SOURCES

The bibliography below provides the reader with the most relevant editions, translations, and commentaries on classical, late antique, and early medieval authors that are cited in this book. For reasons of space, the information provided here has been limited to essentials: the work in question, the authors' surnames, and dates. I have not attempted to produce a comprehensive bibliography of every edition for every author.

This bibliography uses the abbreviations expanded in the "List of Abbreviations," along with "trans." to indicate translations and "comm." for commentaries. Arabic numbers following an abbreviation in roman (e.g., CFHB 2 below, under Agathias) indicate the number of a book in a series. Roman numerals after book titles indicate volume numbers; Arabic numbers that follow indicate parts of volumes and potentially also smaller divisions (e.g., MGH. GPR I 1 (under Agnellus, below) refers to volume 1, part 1, of MGH.GPR. A vertical line (|) is used to separate different editions of an ancient work.

Acta Conciliorum Oecumenicorum. Ed. E. Schwartz et al. 17 vols. 1914–1984. (Greek and Latin text.)

Agathias. *Historiae.* Ed. R. Keydell. CFHB 2. 1967. (Greek text.) | Trans. J. Frendo. CFHB 2A. 1975. (English trans.)

Agnellus. *Liber Pontificalis ecclesiae Ravennatis.* Ed. T. Mommsen. MGH.GPR I 1. 1898. (Latin text.) | Ed. A. Testi Rasponi. 1924. (Latin text, comm.) | Ed. & trans. C. Nauerth. FC 21. 1996. (Latin text, German trans., comm.) | Ed. D. M. Deliyannis. CCCM 199. 2006. (Latin text.) | Trans. D. M. Deliyannis. 2004. (English trans.)

Ambrose. *De spiritu sancto.* Ed. O. Faller. CSEL 79. 1964. (Latin text.)

———. *De Virginibus.* Ed. & trans. P. Dückers. FC 81. 2009. (Latin text, German trans., comm.)

———. *Epistulae.* Ed. O. Faller and M. Zelzer. CSEL 82, 1–4. 4 vols. 1968–1996. (Latin text.) | Trans. J. H. W. G. Liebeschuetz and C. Hill. TTH 43. 2005. (English trans.)

———. *On Duties.* Ed. and trans. I. J. Davidson. 2 vols. 2002. (Latin text, English trans., comm.)

Ammianus Marcellinus. *Res gestae.* Ed. W. Seyfarth. BT. 1978. (Latin text.) | Ed. & trans. E. Galletier et al. CUF. 5 vols. 1968–2002. (Latin text, French trans.)

Anonymus Valesianus. Ed. T. Mommsen. MGH.AA IX 306–328. 1892. (Latin text.) | Ed. J. Moreau. BT. 1968. (Latin text.) | Ed. & trans. I. König. 1997. (Latin text, German trans., comm.) | Ed. & trans. M. Festy and M. Vitiello. CUF. 2020. (Latin text, French trans., comm.)

Anthimus. *De observatione ciborum ad Theodoricum regem Francorum epistula.* Ed. & trans. E. Liechtenhain. 1963. (Latin text, German trans.)

Anthologia Latina. Ed. F. Buecheler et al. BT. 1895–1926. (Latin text.) | Ed. & trans. E. Wolff. 2016. (Latin text, French trans.)

Appendix Maximiani. Ed. & trans. W. C. Schneider. 2003. (Latin text, German trans.) | Trans. B. Goldlust. 2013. (French trans.) | Ed. & trans. A. Franzoi, P. Mastandrea, and L. Spinazzé. 2014. (Latin text, Italian trans., comm.) | Ed. & trans. A. M. Juster. 2018. (Latin text, English trans.)

Arator. *Historia Apostolica.* Ed. A. P. McKinlay. CSEL 72. 1951. (Latin text.) | Trans. R. J. Schrader et al. 1987. (English trans.) | Ed. A. P. Orbán. 2 vols. CCL 130 and 130A. 2006. (Latin text.) | Ed. & trans. B. Bruneau and P.-A. Deproost. 2017. (Latin text, French trans., comm.) | Trans. R. J. Hillier. TTH 73. 2020. (English trans.)

Auctarium Hauniense ordinis posterioris margo. Ed. T. Mommsen. MGH.AA IX, 307–311. 1892. (Latin text.)

Auctarium Hauniense ordo posterior. Ed. T. Mommsen. MGH.AA IX, 307–313. 1892. (Latin text.)

Auctarium Hauniense ordo prior. Ed. T. Mommsen. MGH.AA IX, 307–313. 1892. (Latin text.)

Auctarium Marcellini comitis. Ed. T. Mommsen. MGH.AA XI, 105–108. 1894. (Latin text.) | Ed. & trans. B. Croke. Byzantina Australiensia 7. 1995. (Latin text, English trans., comm.)

Auctarium Prosperi epitomae chronicon Hauniense. Ed. T. Mommsen. MGH.AA IX, 317–333. 1892. (Latin text.)

Auctarium Prosperi epitomae chronicon Vaticanae. Ed. T. Mommsen, MGH.AA IX, 491–493. 1892. (Latin text.)

Augustine. *De civitate dei.* Ed. B. Dombart and A. Kalb. BT. 5th ed. 1981. (Latin text.) | Ed. & trans. G. Bardy. BAug 33–37. 1959–1960. (Latin text, French trans., comm.)

———. *Epistulae.* Ed. A. Goldbacher. CSEL 34, 44, 57. 1895–1911. (*Ep.* 1–270.) (Latin text.) Ed. J. Divjak. CSEL 88. 1981. (*Ep.* 1*—29*.) (Latin text.) | Ed. & trans. J. Divjak et al. BAug 46B. 1987. (Latin text, French trans., comm.)

Auxentius. *Epistola.* Ed. & trans. R. Gryson. SC 267. 1980. (Latin text, French trans.)

Avitus. *Epistulae.* Ed. R. Peiper. MGH.AA VI 35–103. 1911. (Latin text.) | Trans. D. Shanzer and I. Wood. TTH 38. 2002. (English trans.) | Ed. & trans. M. Reydellet and E. Malaspina. CUF 411. 2016. (Latin text, French trans., comm.)

Boethius. *Consolatio Philosophiae.* Ed. L. Bieler. CCL 94. 1957. (Latin text.) | Ed. & trans. E. Gegenschatz and O. Gigon. 2nd ed. 1962. (Latin text, German trans.)

———. *In categorias Aristotelis commentarii.* Ed. J.-P. Migne. PL 64. 1891. (Latin text.)

——. *In Ciceronis topica commentarii.* Ed. J. C. Orelli and J. G. Baiter. 1833. (Latin text.) | Ed. J.-P. Migne, PL 64, 1039–1174. (Latin text.) | Trans. E. Stumpp. 1988. (English trans., comm.)

——. *De musica.* Ed. G. Friedlein. BT. 1867. (Latin text.) | O. Paul. 1872. (German trans.) | Trans. C. M. Bower and C. V. Palisca. 1989. (English trans.)

——. *Tractatus theologici.* Ed. & trans. M. Elsässer. 1988. (Latin text., German trans.) | Ed. C. Moreschini. BT. 2005. (Latin text.) | Ed. & trans. H. F. Stewart, E. K. Rand, and S. J. Tester. LCL. 1973. (Latin text. English trans.)

Caesarius of Arles. *Epistulae.* Ed. G. Morin. 1937–1942. (Latin text.)

——. *Sermones.* Ed. G. Morin. CCL 103–104. 1953–1954. (Latin text.) | Ed. & trans. M. J. Delage. SC 175, 243, 330. 1971–1986. (Latin text, French trans.)

——. *Testamentum.* Ed. G. Morin. 1937–1942. (Latin text.) | Trans. W. Klingshirn. TTH 19. 1994. (English trans.)

Candidus. *Fragmenta.* Ed. R. C. Blockley. *FCHLR* II 465–473. 1983. (Greek text, English trans.)

Cassiodorus. *Chronica.* Ed. T. Mommsen. MGH.AA XI 109–161. 1894. (Latin text.)

——. *De anima.* Ed. J. W. Halporn. CCL 96. 1973. (Latin text.) | Trans. J. W. Halporn. TTH 42. 2004. (English trans.) | Ed. & trans. A. Galonnier in: SC 585. 2017. (Latin text, French trans.)

——. *De orthographia.* Ed. H. Keil. *GL* VII. 1880. 143–210. (Latin text.)

——. *Expositio psalmorum.* Ed. M. Adriaen. CCL 97–98. 1958. (Latin text.) | Trans. P. G. Walsh. 3 vols. ACW 51. 1990. (English trans.)

——. *Institutiones divinarum et humanarum litterarum.* Ed. R. A. B. Mynors. OCT. 1937. (Latin text.) | Ed. & trans. W. Bürsgens. FC 39, 1+2. 2003. (Latin text, German trans., comm.) | Trans. J. W. Halporn and M. Vessey. TTH 42. 2004. (English trans., comm.)

——. *Libellus.* Ed. H. Usener. 1877. (Latin text, comm.) | Ed. T. Mommsen. MGH.AA XII, p. v–vi. 1894. (Latin text.) | Ed. & trans. A. Galonnier. 1991 (Latin text, French trans., comm.) | Trans. S. J. B. Barnish. TTH 12. 1992. (English trans.)

——. *Orationes.* Ed. L. Traube. MGH.AA XII 457–484. 1894. (Latin text.)

——. *Variae.* Ed. T. Mommsen. MGH.AA XII 1–385. 1894. (Latin text.) | Ed. A. Fridh. CCL 96. 1972. (Latin text.) | Ed. & trans. A. Giardina et al. 5 vols. 2014–2017 (Latin text, Italian trans., comm.) | Trans. M. S. Bjornlie. 2019. (English trans.)

Cassiodorus and Epiphanius. *Historia ecclesiastica tripartita.* Ed. W. Jacob and R. Hanslik. CSEL 71. 1952. (Latin text.)

Chronica (= Consularia) Caesaraugustana. Ed. T. Mommsen. MGH.AA XI 221–223. 1894. (Latin text.) | Ed. C. Cardelle de Hartmann. CCL 173A 1–55. 2001. (Latin text, comm.)

Chronica Gallica. Ed. T. Mommsen. MGH.AA IX 615–666. 1892. (Latin text.)

Chronicon ad annum 724. Ed. & trans. J.-B. Chabot. CSCO 3.3–4, p. 77–156 and 61–119. 1904. (Syriac text, Latin trans.)

Chronicon Paschale. Ed. L. Dindorf. CSHB 11–12. 2 vols. 1832. (Greek text.) | M. & M. Whitby. TTH 7. 1989. (English trans.)

Chrysostom, John. *Homiliae.* Ed. & trans. J.-P. Migne. PG 47–64. 1862–1863. (Greek text.) (Latin trans.)

Codex Euricianus. Ed. K. Zeumer. MGH.LNG I 1–32. 1902 (Latin text.) | Ed. & trans. E. Wohlhaupter. Germanenrechte 11. 1936. (Latin text, German trans.) | Ed. & trans. A. d'Ors. 1960. (Latin text, Spanish trans., comm.)

Codex Justinianus. Ed. P. Krüger. 1877. (Latin text.) | Ed. & trans. F. H. Blume and B. W. Frier. 2016. (Latin text, English trans.)

Codex Theodosianus. Ed. T. Mommsen. 1905. (Latin text.) | Trans. C. Pharr. 1952 (English trans.)

Collatio Augustini cum Pascentio. Ed. H. Müller et al. 2008. (Latin text, German trans.)

Collectio Avellana. Ed. O. Günther. CSEL 35. 1895–1898. (Latin text.)

Concilium Agathense a. 506 habitum. Ed. C. Munier. CCL 148 189–228. 1968. (Latin text.)

Concilium Arausicanum a. 529 habitum. Ed. C. de Clercq. CCL 148A 53–76. 1963. (Latin text.)

Concilium Arelatense a. 524 habitum. Ed. C. de Clercq. CCL 148A 42–46. 1963. (Latin text.)

Concilium Aurelianense a. 511 habitum. Ed. C. de Clercq. CCL 148A 3–19. 1963. (Latin text.)

Concilium Carpentocratense a. 527 habitum. Ed. C. de Clercq. CCL 148A 47–52. 1963. (Latin text.)

Concilium Epaonense a. 517 habitum. Ed. C. de Clercq. CCL 148A 20–37. 1963. (Latin text.)

Concilium Gerundense a. 517 habitum. Ed. G. Martínez Díez and F. Rodríguez. CCH 4 = MHS.SC 4, 283–290. 1984. (Latin text.)

Concilium Massiliense a. 533 habitum. Ed. C. de Clercq. CCL 148A 84–97. 1963. (Latin text.)

Concilium Tarraconense a. 516 habitum. Ed. G. Martínez Díez and F. Rodríguez. CCH 4 = MHS.SC 4, 269–281. 1984 (Latin text.)

Concilium Toletanum II a. 531 habitum. Ed. G. Martínez Díez and F. Rodríguez. CCH 4 = MHS.SC 4, 345–366. 1984. (Latin text.)

Concilium Toletanum III a. 589 habitum. Ed. G. Martínez Díez and F. Rodríguez. CCH 5 = MHS.SC 5, 49–159. 1992. (Latin text.)

Concilium Vasense a. 529 habitum. Ed. C. de Clercq. CCL 148A 77–81. 1963. (Latin text.)

Constantine Porphyrogenitus. *De Cerimoniis*. Ed. & trans. M. Moffat and M. Tall. Byzantina Australiensia 18. 2012. (Greek text, English trans.) | Ed. & trans. G. Dagron and B. Flusin. CFHB 52. 6 vols. 2020. (Greek text., French trans., comm.)

Constitutiones Sirmondianae. Ed. T. Mommsen. *CTh* I 2, p. 907–921. 1905. (Latin text.) | Trans. C. Pharr, 477–486. 1952. (English trans.)

Consularia Constantinopolitana. Ed. T. Mommsen. MGH.AA IX 197–247. 1892. (Latin text.) | Ed. & trans. R. W. Burgess. 1993. (Latin text, English trans.) | Ed. & trans. M. Becker et al. KFHist.G 1–4. 2016. (Latin text, German trans., comm.)

Cyril of Jerusalem. *Catecheses*. Ed. G. Röwekamp. FC 7. 1992. (Latin text, German trans.)

Damascius. *Vita Isidori*. Ed. C. Zintzen. 1967. (Greek text.) | Ed. & trans. P. Athanassiadi. 1999. (Greek text, English trans., comm.)

Dexippus. *Fragmenta*. Ed. & trans. G. Martin. 2006. (Greek text, German trans.) | Ed. & trans. L. Mecella. 2013. (Greek text, Italian trans., comm.)

Dio = Cassius Dio. *Historia Romana*. Ed. and trans. E. Cary. LCL. 9 vols. 1914–1927. (Greek text and English trans.)

Dionysius Exiguus. *Praefatio*. Ed. F. Glorie. CCL 85. 1972. (Latin text.)

Dracontius. *Satisfactio*. Ed. C. Moussy. CUF. 1988. (Latin text, French trans.)

Edictum Theoderici. Ed. F. Bluhme. MGH.LNG V 145–179. 1889. (Latin text.) | Ed. P. L. Falaschi. 1966. (Latin text.) | Ed. & trans. O. Licandro. 2013. (Latin text., Italian trans.) | Ed. & trans. I. König. 2018. (Latin text, German trans., comm.)

Einhard. *Vita Karoli Magni*. Ed. O. Holder-Egger. MGH.SRG 25, 1–41. 1911. (Latin text.) | Ed. & trans. R. Rau. AQDGMA 5, 165–211. 1955. (Latin text., German trans.) | Trans. D. Ganz. 2008. (English trans.)

Ennodius. *Carmina*. Ed. W. Hartel. CSEL 6, 507–608. 1882. (Latin text.) | Ed. F. Vogel. MGH.AA VII. 1885. (Latin text.)

——. *Dictiones*. Ed. W. Hartel. CSEL 6, 423–506. 1882. (Latin text.) | Ed. F. Vogel. MGH.AA VII. 1885. (Latin text.)

——. *Epistulae*. Ed. W. Hartel. CSEL 6, 1–260. 1882. (Latin text.) | Ed. F. Vogel. MGH. AA VII. 1885. (Latin text.) | Ed. & trans. S. Gioanni. CUF. 2006–2010. (Latin text, French trans.)

——. *Libellus adversus eos qui contra synodum scribere praesumpserint*. Ed. W. Hartel. CSEL 6, 287–330. 1882. (Latin text.) | Ed. F. Vogel. MGH.AA VII 48–67. 1885. (Latin text.)

——. *Opuscula*. Ed. W. Hartel. CSEL 6, 261–422. 1882. (Latin text.) | Ed. F. Vogel. MGH. AA VII. 1885. (Latin text.)

——. *Panegyricus*. Ed. W. Hartel. CSEL 6, 261–281. 1882. (Latin text.) | F. Vogel. MGH. AA VII 203–214. 1885. (Latin text.) | Ed. & trans. C. Rohr. 1995. (Latin text, German trans.) | Ed. & trans. S. Rota. 2002. (Latin text, Italian trans., comm.)

——. *Vita Antonii*. Ed. W. Hartel. CSEL 6, 383–393. 1882. (Latin text.) | Ed. F. Vogel. MGH.AA VII 185–190. 1885. (Latin text.)

——. *Vita Epiphanii*. Ed. W. Hartel. CSEL 6, 331–383. 1882. (Latin text.) | Ed. F. Vogel. MGH.AA VII 84–109. 1885. (Latin text.) | Trans. M. Cook. 1942. (English trans., comm.) | Trans. M. Cesa. 1986. (Italian trans., comm.)

Epistolae Austrasicae. Ed. W. Gundlach. MGH.Ep. III 110–153. 1898. (Latin text.) | Ed. & trans. E. Malaspina. 2001. (Latin text, Italian trans., comm.)

Epistulae Arelatenses. Ed. W. Gundlach. MGH.Ep. III 1–83. 1898. (Latin text.)

Epistulae Theodericianae Variae. Ed. T. Mommsen. MGH.AA XII 387–392. 1894. (Latin text.)

Eugippius. *Vita S. Severini*. Ed. H. Sauppe. MGH.AA I 1–30. 1877. (Latin text.) | Ed. T. Mommsen. MGH.SRG 26. 1898. (Latin text.) | Ed. & trans. R. Noll. 1963. (Latin text, German trans.) | Trans. L. Bieler and L. Krestan. FCPS 55. 1965. (English trans.) | Ed. & trans. F. Régerat. SC 374. 1991. (Latin text, French trans.)

Eunapius Sardianus. *Fragmenta*. Ed. & trans. R. C. Blockley. *FCHLR* II 1–150. 1983. (Latin text, English trans.)

Eusebius. *De vita Constantini*. Ed. F. Winkelmann. GCS 1, 1. 2nd ed. 1991. (Greek text.) | Trans. Av. Cameron and S. G. Hall. 1999. (English trans., comm.) | Ed. & trans. B. Bleckmann and H. Schneider. FC 83. 2007. (Greek text, German trans.)

———. *Historia Ecclesiastica*. Ed. E. Schwartz. 5th ed. 1952. (Greek text.) | Ed. & trans. H. J. Lawlor and J. E. L. Oulton. 1928. (English trans., comm.) | Ed. & trans. G. Bardy. SC 31, 41, 55, 73. 1952–1960. (Greek text, French trans.)

Eustathius of Epiphania. *Fragmenta*. Ed. and trans. C. Müller. *Fragmenta historicorum graecorum*. IV 138–142. 1868. (Greek text, Latin trans.)

Eutropius. *Breviarium*. Ed. H. Droysen. MGH.AA II 8–182. 1879. (Latin text.) | Ed. C. Santini. BT. 1979. (Latin text.) | Trans. H. W. Bird. TTH 14. 1993. (English trans., comm.) | Ed. & trans. J. Hellegouarc'h. CUF. 1999. (Latin text, French trans.)

Evagrius Scholasticus. *Historia ecclesiastica*. Ed. J. Bidez and L. Parmentier. 1898. (Greek text.) | Trans. M. Whitby. TTH 30. 2000. (English trans., comm.) | Ed. & trans. A. Hübner. FC 57. 2007. (Greek text, German trans.)

Excerpta Sangallensia. Ed. T. Mommsen. MGH.AA IX 274–336. 1892. (Latin text.)

Fasti Vindobonenses posteriores. Ed. T. Mommsen. MGH.AA IX 274–298. 1892. (Latin text.)

Fasti Vindobonenses priores. Ed. T. Mommsen. MGH.AA IX 274–334. 1892. (Latin text.)

Felix II (pope). *Epistulae*. Ed. A. Thiel. ERPG, 222–284. 1868. (Latin text.) | Trans. S. Wenzlowsky. BPS VI 201–329. 1878. (German trans.)

Felix IV (pope). *Epistulae*. Ed. J.-P. Migne. PL 65, 11–23. 1892. (Latin text.)

Ferrand of Carthage. *Epistula dogmatica adversus Arrianos aliosque haereticos*. Ed. A.-G. Hamman. PL Suppl. 4, 22–36. 1967. (Latin text.)

———. *Vita Fulgentii*. Ed. & trans. G. G. Lapeyre. 1929. (Latin text, French trans.) | Ed. A. Isola. CCL 91F. 2016. (Latin text.)

Fragmentum Laurentianum. Ed. L. Duchesne. *Lib. pont.* I 44–46. 1886. (Latin text.) | Ed. T. Mommsen. MCH.CPR I 1, IX–XI. 1898. (Latin text.) | Trans. R. Davies. TTH 6, 103–106. 2nd ed. 2000. (English trans.)

Fulgentius of Ruspe. *Ad Thrasamundum*. Ed. J. Fraipont. CCL 91, 95–185. 1968. (Latin text.)

———. *De fide sive de regula fidei*. Trans. L. Kozelka. BKV². 1934. (German trans.) | Ed. J. Fraipont. CCL 91A, 709–760. 1968. (Latin text.) | Trans. R. B. Eno. FCPS. 1997. (English trans.)

———. *Dicta regis Thrasamundi et contra eum responsionum liber unus*. Ed. J. Fraipont. CCL 91, 65–94. 1968. (Latin text.)

———. *Epistulae*. Ed. J. Fraipont. CCL 91, 187–444; CCL 91A, 445–629. 1968. (Latin text) | D. Bachelet. SC 487. 2004. (Latin text, French trans.)

Gaudentius of Brescia. *Sermones*. Ed. A. Glück. CSEL 68. 1936. (Latin text.) | Trans. S. L. Boehrer. 1965. (English trans., comm.) | Trans. C. Truzzi. 1996. (Italian trans., comm.)

Gelasius (pope). *Epistulae*. Ed. A. Thiel. ERPG, 284–483. 1868. (Latin text.) | Ed. G. Löwenfeld. 1885. (Latin text.) | Trans. S. Wenzlowsky. BPS VII 7–538. 1880. (German trans.) | Trans. B. Neil and P. Allen. 2014. (English trans.)

———. *Fragmenta*. Ed. A. Thiel. ERPG, 483–510. 1868. (Latin text.) | Trans. S. Wenzlowsky. BPS VII 7–538. 1880. (German trans.) | Trans. B. Neil and P. Allen. 2014. (English trans.)

———. *Tractatus*. Ed. A. Thiel. ERPG, 510–607. 1868. (Latin text.) | Trans. S. Wenzlowsky. BPS VII 7–538. 1880. (German trans.) | Trans. B. Neil and P. Allen. 2014. (English trans.)

Gerontius. *Vita Melaniae graeca*. Ed. M. Rampolla del Tindaro. 1905. (Greek text, Italian trans.) | Ed. & trans. D. Gorce. SC 90. 1962. (Greek text, French trans.)

——. *Vita Melaniae latina*. Ed. M. Rampolla del Tindaro. 1905. (Latin text, Italian trans.) | Ed. & trans. P. Laurence. 2002. (Latin text, French trans., comm.)

Gesta senatus Romani de Theodosiano publicano a. 438. Ed. T. Mommsen. *CTh* I 2, 1–4. 1905. (Latin text.)

Gregory the Great (pope). *Dialogi*. Ed. U. Moricca. FSI 57. 1924. (Latin text.) | Ed. & trans. A. de Vogüé and P. Autin. SC 251, 260, 265. 1978–1980. (Latin text, French trans.) | Trans. J. Funk, in BKV² 3. 1933. (German trans.)

——. *Epistulae*. Ed. P. Ewald and L. Hartmann. MGH.Ep. I–II. 1887–1899. (Latin text.) | Ed. & trans. P. Minard. 2 vols. in 3 (Livres I–IV). SC 370, 371, 520. 1991–2008. (Latin text, French trans., comm.) | Trans. M. R. C. Martyn. MST 40. 3 vols. 2004. (English trans.)

Gregory of Tours. *Liber in gloria confessorum*. Ed. W. Arndt and B. Krusch. MGH.SRM I 2, 744–820. 1885. (Latin text.) | Trans. R. van Dam. TTH 5. 2nd ed. 2004. (English trans.)

——. *Liber in gloria martyrum*. Ed. W. Arndt and B. Krusch. MGH.SRM I 2, 484–561. 1885. (Latin text.) | Trans. R. van Dam. TTH 4. 2nd ed. 2004. (English trans.)

——. *Historiae*. Ed. B. Krusch and W. Levison. MGH.SRM I 1². 1937–1951. (Latin text.) | Ed. & trans. R. Buchner. AQDGMA 1–2. 1955–1956. (Latin text, German trans.)

Gregory Thaumaturgus. *Epistula canonica*. Ed. J.-P. Migne. PG 10, 1019–1048. 1857. (Greek text.) | Trans. P. Heather and J. Matthews. TTH 11, 1–11. 1991. (English trans.)

Herodian. *Historiae*. Ed. C. M. Lucarini. BT. 2005. (Greek text.) | Ed. & trans. C. R. Whittaker. LCL. 2 vols. 1969–1970. (Greek text, English trans.)

Herodotus. *Historiae*. Ed. N. G. Wilson. OCT. 2015. (Greek text.)

Historia Langobardorum codicis Gothani. Ed. G. Waitz. MGH.SRL 1–7. 1878. (Latin text.)

Hormisdas (pope). *Epistulae*. Ed. O. Günther. CSEL 35, part 2, 495–742. 1898. (Latin text.)

Hydatius Lemicus. *Continuatio chronicorum Hieronymianorum*. Ed. T. Mommsen. MGH. AA XI 1–36. 1894. (Latin text.) | Ed. & trans. A. Tranoy. SC 218–219. 1974. (Latin text, French trans., comm.) | Ed. & trans. R. W. Burgess. 1993. (Latin text, English trans.) | Ed. & trans. J.-M. Kötter and C. Scardino. KFHist G 9–10. 2019. (Latin text, German trans., comm.)

Isidore of Seville. *Etymologiae*. Ed. W. M. Lindsay. OCT. 1911. (Latin text.) | Trans. S. A. Barney et al. 2006. (English trans.)

——. *Historia Gothorum Vandalorum et Sueborum*. Ed. T. Mommsen. MGH.AA XI 267–303. 1894. (Latin text.) | Ed. & trans. C. Rodríguez Alonso. 1975. (Latin text, Spanish trans., comm.)

Jerome. *Epistulae*. Ed. I. Hilberg. CSEL 54–56. 1910–1918. (Latin text.)

——. *Liber hebraicarum quaestionum in Genesim*. Ed. P. de Lagarde. CCL 72, 1–56. 1959. (Latin text.)

John of Antioch. *Fragmenta*. Ed. & trans. U. Roberto. 2005. (Greek text, Italian trans.) | Ed. & trans. S. Mariev. CFHB 47. 2008. (Greek text, English trans.)

John of Biclaro. *Chronica*. Ed. T. Mommsen. MGH.AA XI 211–220. 1894. (Latin text) | Ed. & trans. J. Campos. 1960. (Latin text, Spanish trans., comm.) | Trans. K. Baxter Wolf. TTH 9. 2nd ed. 1999. (English trans.)

John of Nikiu. *Chronicle*. Trans. R. H. Charles. 1916. (English trans.)

John the Deacon. *Epistula ad Senarium*. Ed. A. Wilmert. Studi e testi 59, 170–171. 1936. (Latin text.)

John the Lydian. *De magistratibus populi Romani*. Ed. R. Wünsch. BT. 1903. (Greek text.) | Ed. & trans. A. C. Bandy. 1983. (Greek text, English trans., comm.) | Ed. & trans. M. Dubuisson and J. Champs. CUF. 2006. (Greek text, French trans., comm.)

John Rufus. *Plerophoriae*. Ed. & trans. F. Nau. PO 8. 1912. (Syriac text, French trans.)

Jordanes. *De origine actibusque Getarum*. Ed. T. Mommsen. MGH.AA V 1, 53–138. 1882. (Latin text.) | Trans. C. C. Mierow. 2nd ed. 1915. (English trans., comm.) | Ed. F. Giunta and A. Grillone. FSI 117. 1991. (Latin text.) | Ed. & trans. A. Grillone. 2017. (Latin text, Italian trans., comm.) | Trans. L. van Hoof and P. van Nuffelen. TTH 75. 2020. (English trans., comm.)

——. *De summa temporum vel origine actibusque gentis Romanorum*. Ed. T. Mommsen. MGH.AA V 1, 1–52. 1882. (Latin text.) | Trans. L. van Hoof and P. van Nuffelen. TTH 75. 2020. (English trans., comm.)

Joshua the Stylite. *Chronicle*. Ed. & trans. W. Wright. 1882. (Syriac text, English trans.) | Trans. F. R. Trombley and J. W. Watt. TTH 32. 2000. (English trans., notes) | Trans. A. Luther. 1997. (German trans., comm.).

Laterculus regum Vandalorum et Alanorum. Ed. T. Mommsen. MGH.AA XIII 456–460. 1898. (Latin text.) | Ed. & trans. M. Becker and J.-M. Koetter. KFHist.G 6. 2016. (Latin text, German trans., comm.)

Laterculus regum Visigothorum. Ed. T. Mommsen. MGH.AA XIII 461–469. 1898. (Latin text.)

Leges Burgundionum (Liber Constitutionum). Ed. R. von Salis. MGH.LNG II 1, 29–116. 1892. (Latin text.) | Ed. & trans. F. Beyerle. Germanenrechte 10. 1936. (Latin text, German trans. | Trans. K. Fischer. 1949. (English trans.)

Leges Visigothorum. Ed. K. Zeumer. MGH.LNG I. 1902. (Latin text.) | Ed. & trans. K. Wohlhaupter. Germanenrechte 11. 1936. (Latin text, German trans.)

Leo Marsicanus. *Chronicon Casinense*. Ed. H. Hofmann. MGH.SRL SS 34. 1980. (Latin text.)

Leo the Great (pope). *Epistulae*. Ed. E. Ballerinie. PL 54, 593–1218. 1881. (Latin text.) | Trans. S. Wenzlowsky. BPS IV + V. 1878. (German trans.)

——. *Sermones*. Ed. A. Chavasse. CCL 138, 138A. 1973. (Latin text.) | Ed. & trans. R. Dolle. SC 22bis, 49bis, 74, 200. 2nd ed. 1976–2008. (Latin text, French trans.)

Lex Romana Visigothorum. Ed. G. Hänel. 1849. (Latin text.) | Trans. M. Conrat. 1903. (German trans.)

Libanius. *Orationes*. Ed. R. Förster. 4 vols. BT. 1903–1908. (Greek text.)

Liber Historiae Francorum. Ed. B. Krusch. MGH.SRM II 238–328. 1888. (Latin text.) | Ed. & trans. B. S. Bachrach. 1973. (Latin text, English trans.)

Liber Pontificalis ecclesiae Romanae. Ed. L. Duchesne. 2 vols. 1886–1892. (Latin text, comm.) | Ed. T. Mommsen. MGH.GPR I 1. 1898. (Latin text.) | Trans. R. Davies. TTH 6. 2nd ed. 2000. (English trans.)

Liberatus of Carthage. *Breviarium*. Ed. E. Schwartz. ACO II 5, 98–141. 1936. (Latin text.) | Trans. F. Carcione. 1989. (Italian trans.) | Ed. & trans. P. Blaudeau and F. Cassingena-Trévedy. SC 607. 2019. (Latin text, French trans., comm.)

Liv. = Livy (Titus Livius). *Ab urbe condita.* Ed. R. S. Conway and C. F. Walters. OCT. 1919. (Latin text.)

Macrobius. *Saturnalia.* Ed. J. Willis. BT. 1970. (Latin text.) | Ed. & trans. R. A. Kaster. LCL. 3 vols. 2011. (Latin text, English trans.)

Malalas, John. *Chronica.* Ed. E. Jeffreys et al. Byzantina Australiensia 4. 1986. (English trans.) | Ed. H. Thurn. CFHB 35. 2000. (Greek text.) | Trans. M. Meier. BGL 69. 2009. (German trans.)

Malchus. *Fragmenta.* Ed. & trans. L. R. Cresci. 1982. (Greek text, Italian trans., comm.) | Ed. & trans. R. C. Blockley. FCHLR II 404–455. 1983. (Greek text, English trans.)

——. *Testimonia.* Ed. & trans. L. R. Cresci. 1982. (Greek text, Italian trans., comm.) | Ed. & trans. R. C. Blockley. *FCHLR* II 402–404. 1983. (Greek text, English trans.)

Marcellinus Comes. *Chronicon.* Ed. T. Mommsen. MGH.AA XI 37–109. 1894. (Latin text.) | Ed. & trans. B. Croke. Byzantina Australiensia 7. 1995. (Latin text, English trans., comm.)

Marius of Avenches. *Chronicon.* Ed. T. Mommsen. MGH.AA XI 225–239. 1893. (Latin text.) | Ed. & trans. J. Favrod. 2nd ed. 1993. (Latin text, French trans., comm.)

Martianus Capella. *De nuptiis Mercurii et Philologiae.* Ed. J. Willis. BT. 1983. (Latin text.) | Trans. H. Zekl. 2005. (German trans.)

Maximianus. *Elegiae.* Ed. F. Spaltenstein. 1983. (Latin text, comm.) | Ed. & trans. W. C. Schneider. 2003. (Latin text, German trans.) | Trans. B. Goldlust. 2013. (French trans.) | Ed. & trans. A. Franzoi, P. Mastandrea, and L. Spinazzé. 2014. (Latin text, Italian trans., comm.) | Ed. & trans. A. M. Juster. 2018. (Latin text, English trans.)

Merobaudes. *Carmina.* Ed. MGH.AA XIV 1–4; 19f. 1905. (Latin text.) | Trans. F. M. Clover. 1971. (English trans., comm.)

Notitia Galliarum. Ed. T. Mommsen. MGH.AA IX 552–612. 1894. (Latin text.)

Novellae Justiniani. Ed. R. Schöll and G. Kroll. 5th ed. 1928. (Latin text.) | Trans. D. J. D. Miller and P. Sarris. 2018. (English trans., comm.)

Novellae Maioriani. Ed. T. Mommsen. CTh II 155–178. 1905. (Latin text.) | Trans. C. Pharr, 551–567. 1952. (English trans.)

Novellae Severi. Ed. T. Mommsen. CTh II 197–202. 1905. (Latin text.) | Trans. C. Pharr, 568–569. 1952. (English trans.)

Novellae Theodosii. Ed. T. Mommsen. CTh II 1–68. 1905. (Latin text.) | Trans. C. Pharr, 487–514. 1952. (English trans.)

Novellae Valentiniani. Ed. T. Mommsen. CTh II 69–154. 1905. (Latin text.) | Trans. C. Pharr, 515–550. 1952. (English trans.)

Olympiodorus. *Fragmenta.* Ed. R. C. Blockley. *FCHLR* II 151–220. 1983. (Greek text, English trans.)

Origo gentis Langobardorum. Ed. G. Waitz. MGH.SRL 1–6. 1878. (Latin text.) | Ed. & trans. A. Bracciotti. 1998. (Latin text, Italian trans., comm.)

Orosius. *Historia adversus paganos.* Ed. K. Zangemeister. 1882. (Latin text.) | Trans. A. Lippold. 2 vols. 1985–1986. (German trans.) | Ed. & trans. A. T. Fear. TTH 54. 2010. (Latin text, English trans.)

Palladius. *Opus agriculturae.* Ed. R. H. Rogers. BT. 1975. (Latin text.) | Ed. & trans. R. F. Martin et al. CUF. 1976–2010. (Latin text, French trans., comm.) | Ed. & trans. K. Brodersen. 2016. (Latin text, German trans.)

Palladius of Helenopolis. *Historia Lausiaca*. Ed. C. Butler. 1898. (Latin text, English trans., comm.)

Panegyrici Latini. Ed. & trans. E. Galletier. CUF. 3 vols. 1955. (Latin text, French trans.). | Ed. & trans. C. E. V. Nixon and B. Saylor Rodgers. 1994. (Latin text, English trans., comm.)

Papyri Italiae. Ed. J.-O. Tjäder. 1954–1982. (Latin text, German trans., comm.)

Paschale Campanum. Ed. T. Mommsen. MGH.AA IX 305–334. 1889. (Latin text.)

Passio S. Sigismundi regis. Ed. B. Krusch. MGH.SRM II 329–340. 1885. (Latin text.)

Passio S. Vincentii Aginnensis. Ed. B. de Gaiffier. *Analecta Bollandiana* 70: 160–181. 1952. (Latin text.)

Paul the Deacon. *Historia Langobardorum*. Ed. G. Waitz. MGH.SRL 12–187. 1878. (Latin text.) | Ed. & trans. W. F. Schwarz. 2009. (Latin text, German trans.)

———. *Historia Romana*. Ed. H. Droysen. MGH.AA II 183–224. 1879. (Latin text.)

Paulinus of Nola. *Carmina*. Ed. W. Hartel. CSEL 30. 1894. (Latin text.) | Trans. P. G. Walsh. ACW 40. 1975. (English trans.)

Paulus. *Sententiae*. Ed. S. Riccobono et al. FIRA II 317–417. 1940. (Latin text.)

Pelagius I (pope). *Epistulae*. Ed. P. Gassó. 1956. (Latin text.)

Petrus Chrysologus. *Sermones*. Ed. A. Olivar. CCL 24, 24A, and 24B. 1975–1982. (Latin text.) | Ed. & trans. G. Banterle et al. 3 vols. 1996–1997. (Latin text, Italian trans.) | Trans. W. B. Palardy. FCPS. 3 vols. 2004–2013. (English trans.)

Philostorgius. *Historia ecclesiastica*. Ed. J. Bidez and F. Winkelmann. GCS. 1972. (Latin text.) | Trans. P. R. Amidon. WGRW. 2007. (English trans.) | Ed. & trans. B. Bleckmann and M. Stein. KFHist.E 7. 2015. (Latin text, German trans., comm.)

Photius. *Codex*. Ed. & trans. R. Henry. CUF. 1959–1991. (Latin text, French trans., comm.)

Polemius Silvius. *Breviarium temporum*. Ed. T. Mommsen. MGH.AA IX 547. 1892. (Latin text.) | Ed. & trans. B. Bleckmann et al. KFHist.B 6. 2018. (Latin text, German trans., comm.)

———. *Laterculus*. Ed. T. Mommsen. MGH.AA IX 511–551. 1892. (Latin text.) | Ed. & trans. D. Paniagua. 2018. (Latin text, Italian trans.)

Priscian of Caesarea. *De figuris numerorum*. Ed. H. Keil. GL III 405–412. 1880. (Latin text.) | Ed. M. Passalacqua. 1987. (Latin text.)

Priscus of Panium. *Fragmenta*. Ed. P. Carolla. BT. 2010. (Greek text.) | Ed. & trans. R. C. Blockley. FCHLR II 221–400. 1983. (Greek text, English trans.)

Procopius. *De aedificiis*. Ed. J. Haury. BT. 1964. (Greek text.) | Ed. & trans. O. Veh. 1977. (Greek text, German trans.) | Trans. D. Roques. 2011. (French trans., comm.)

———. *Bella*. Ed. J. Haury. BT. 3 vols. 1962–1963. (Greek text.) | Ed. & trans. O. Veh. 3 vols. 1966. (Greek text, German trans.) | Trans. A. Kaldellis. 2014. (English trans.)

———. *Historia arcana*. Ed. J. Haury. BT. 1963. (Greek text.) | Ed. & trans. H. Leppin and M. Meier. 2004. (Latin text, German trans., comm.)

Prosper Tiro. *Epitoma chronicorum*. Ed. T. Mommsen. MGH.AA IX 385–485. 1892. (Latin text.) | Ed. & trans. M. Becker and J.-M. Kötter. KFHist.G 5. 2016. (Latin text, German trans., comm.)

Ptolemy. *Geographia*. Ed. A. Stückelberger and G. Graßhoff. 2 vols. 2006–2009. (Greek text, German trans.)

Ruricius of Limoges. *Epistulae.* Ed. R. Demeulenaere. CCL 64, 303–415. 1985. (Latin text.) | Trans. R. W. Mathisen. TTH 30. 1999. (English trans., comm.)

Rutilius Namatianus. *De reditu suo.* Ed. E. Doblhofer, 2 vols. 1972–1977. (Latin text, German trans., comm.) | Ed. & trans. E. Wolff. CUF. 2016. (Latin text, French trans., comm.)

Salvian of Marseille. *De gubernatione dei.* Ed. K. Halm. MGH.AA I 1–108. 1877. (Latin text.) | Ed. & trans. G. Lagarrigue. SC 176, 220. 1971 and 1975. (Latin text, French trans.)

Scriptores Historiae Augustae. Ed. E. Hohl. BT. 2nd ed. 1965. (Latin text.) | Trans. E. Hohl. 1976–1985. (German trans.) | Ed. & trans. A. Chastagnol. 1994. (Latin text, French trans.)

Severus Antiochensis. *Contra impium grammaticum.* Ed. J. Lebon, 6 vols. CSCO 93, 94, 101–102, 111–112. 1929–1965. (Syriac text, Latin trans.)

Sidonius Apollinaris. *Carmina.* Ed. F. Luetjohann. MGH.AA VIII 173–264. 1887. (Latin text.) | Ed. & trans. W. B. Anderson. LCL. 1936. (Latin text, English trans.) | Ed. & trans. A. Loyen. CUF. 1960. (Latin text, French trans.)

——. *Epistulae.* Ed. F. Luetjohann. MGH.AA VIII 1–172. 1887. (Latin text.) | Ed. & trans. W. B. Anderson. LCL. 1936. (Latin text, English trans.) | Ed. & trans. A. Loyen. CUF. 1970. (Latin text, French trans.) | Trans. H. Köhler. 2014. (German trans.)

Simplicius (pope). *Epistulae.* Ed. A. Thiel. ERPG, 175–214. 1868. (Latin text.) | Ed. O. Günther. CSEL 35. 124–155. 1895. (Latin text) | Trans. S. Wenzlowsky. BPS VI 99–200. 1878. (German trans.)

Socrates Scholasticus. *Historia ecclesiatica.* Ed. G. C. Hansen. GCS N.F. 1. 1995. (Greek text.) | Ed. & trans. P. Périchou and P. Maraval. SC 477, 493, 505–506. 2004–2007. (Greek text, French trans.)

Sozomen. *Historia ecclesiastica.* Ed. J. Bidez and G. C. Hansen. GCS N.F. 4. 1995. (Greek text.) | Ed. & trans. G. C. Hansen. FC 73. 2004. (Greek text, German trans.). | Ed. & trans. A. J. Festugière et al. SC 306, 418, 495, 516. 1983–2008. (Greek text, French trans.)

Strabo. *Geographia.* Ed. S. Radt. 10 vols. 2002–2011. (Greek text, German trans., comm.)

Symmachus (pope). *Epistulae.* Ed. A. Thiel. ERPG, 641–734. 1868. (Latin text.)

Symmachus, Quintus Aurelius. *Epistulae.* Ed. O. Seeck. MGH.AA VI 1, 1–278. 1883. (Latin text.) | Ed. & trans. J.-P. Callu. CUF. 1972–2002. (Latin text, French trans.)

——. *Relationes.* Ed. O. Seeck. MGH.AA VI 1, 279–317. 1883. (Latin text.) | Ed. & trans. R. H. Barrow. 1973. (Latin text, English trans.) | Ed. & trans. D. Vera. 1981. (Latin text, Italian trans., comm.)

Synesius. *Epistulae.* Ed. A. Garzya and D. Roques. CUF. 2nd ed. 2003. (Greek text, French trans.)

Tacitus. *Annales.* Ed. H. Heubner. BT. 1983. (Latin text.)

——. *Germania.* Ed. A. Önnerfors. BT. 1983. (Latin text.) | Ed. & trans. A. A. Lund. 1988. (Latin text, German trans., comm.) | Ed. & trans. G. Perl. GLQGM II. 1990. (Latin text, German trans., comm.)

Themistius. *Orationes.* Ed. H. Schenkl and G. Downey. BT. 1965–1974. (Greek text.) | Ed. & trans. R. Maisano. 1995. (Greek text, Italian trans.) | Trans. H. Leppin and W. Portmann (*or.* 1–19). BGL 46. 1988. (German trans.) | Trans. P. Heather and D. Moncur (selected speeches). TTH 36. 2001. (English trans., comm.)

Theodoret. *Historia ecclesiastica*. Ed. L. Parmentier. GCS N.F. 5. 1998. (Greek text.) | Ed. & trans. L. F. Bouffartigue et al. SC 501, 530. 2006–2009. (Greek text, French trans.)

Theodorus Lector. *Historia ecclesiastica*. Ed. G. C. Hansen. GCS. 1971. (Greek text.)

Theophanes. *Chronica*. Ed. C. de Boor. 1883. (Greek text.) | Trans. C. Mango and R. Scott. 1997. (English trans., comm.)

Victor of Tunnuna. *Chronica*. Ed. T. Mommsen. MGH.AA XI 163–206. 1894. (Latin text.) | Ed. & trans. A. Placanica. 1997. (Latin text, Italian trans., comm.) | Ed. C. Cardelle de Hartmann. CCL 173a. 2001. (Latin text.) | Trans. J. R. C. Martyn. 2008. (English trans.)

Victor Vitensis. *Historia persecutionis Africanae provinciae*. Ed. K. Halm. MGH.AA III 1–62. 1879. (Latin text.) | Trans. J. Moorhead. TTH 10. 1992. (English trans.) | Ed. & trans. S. Lancel. CUF. 2007. (Latin text, French trans., comm.) | Trans. J. R. C. Martyn. 2008. (English trans.) | Ed. & trans. K. Vössing. 2011. (Latin text, German trans., comm.)

Vigilius (pope). *Epistulae*. Ed. E. Schwartz. 1940. (Latin text.)

Vita Apollinaris Valentinensis. Ed. B. Krusch. MGH.SRM III 194–203. 1896. (Latin text.)

Vita Caesarii episcopi Arelatensis. Ed. B. Krusch. MGH.SRM III. 433–501. 1896.(Latin text.) | Trans. W. Klingshirn. TTH 19. 1994. (English trans.) | Ed. & trans. M.-J. Délage and M. Heijmans. SC 546. 2010. (Latin text, French trans., comm.) | Ed. & trans. F. Jung. 2018. (Latin text, German trans., comm.)

Vita Eptadii presbyteri Cervidunensis. Ed. B. Krusch. MGH.SRM III 186–194. 1896. (Latin text.)

Vita S. Floridi (BHS 3062). Ed. G. Spitzbart and W. Maaz. Analecta Bollandiana 106, 415–443. 1988. (Latin text, German trans.)

Vita Hilari abbatis Galeatensis. Ed. F. Zaghini. 2004. (Latin text, Italian trans., comm.)

Vita Lupi episcopi Trecensis. Ed. B. Krusch. MGH.SRM III 117–124. 1896. MGH.SRM VII 284–302. 1919. (Latin text.)

Vita Marciani Oeconomi. Ed. J. Wortley. *Byzantinische Zeitschrift* 103, 715–772. 2011. (Greek text, English trans.)

Vita Symeonis syriaca. Ed. A. S. E. Assemani. 1748. (Syriac text.) | Trans. H. Lietzmann. 1908. (German trans.) | Trans. R. Doran. 1992. (English trans.)

Vitae Abbatum Acaunensium. Ed. B. Krusch. MGH.SRM III 174–181. 1896. VII 322–336. 1919–1920. (Latin text.)

Zacharias Mytilenaeus. *Historia ecclesiastica*. Ed. E. W. Brooks. 1919–1924. (Syriac text, Latin trans.) | Trans. G. Greatrex. TTH 55. 2011. (English trans.)

Zonaras. *Epitome Historiarum*. Ed. T. Büttner-Wobst. BT. 1897. (Greek text.)

Zosimus. *Historia Nova*. Ed. L. Mendelsohn. BT. 1887. (Greek text.) | Ed. & trans. F. Paschoud. CUF. 1971–1989. (Greek text, French trans.)

2. SCHOLARLY LITERATURE

Scholarly literature is limited to works cited in the notes to this book. The format applied here has been adapted from the name/date system used in the German edition, which dispensed with authors' given names and the names of publishers.

Adams, J. N. 1976. *The Text and Language of a Vulgar Chronicle (Anonymus Valesianus II)*. London.

Ajbabin, A. I., and E. A. Chajredinova. 2009. *Das Gräberfeld beim Dorf Lucistoe*. Mainz.

Alföldi, A. 1926. *Der Untergang der Römerherrschaft in Pannonien*. Vol. 2. Berlin.

——. 1935. "Insignien und Tracht der römischen Kaiser." *Römische Mitteilungen* 50: 3–158.

Altaner, B. 1912. *Dietrich von Bern in der neueren Literatur*. Breslau.

Altheim, F. 1951. *Attila und die Hunnen*. Baden-Baden.

Amici, A. 2005. "Cassiodoro a Costantinopoli: Da 'magister officiorum' a 'religiosus vir.' " *Vetera Christianorum* 42: 215–231.

Amory, P. 1997. *People and Identity in Ostrogothic Italy, 489–554*. Cambridge, UK.

Anders, F. 2010. *Flavius Ricimer. Macht und Ohnmacht des weströmischen Heermeisters in der zweiten Hälfte des 5. Jahrhunderts*. Frankfurt.

Arbesmann, R. 1979. "The 'cervuli' and 'anniculae' in Caesarius of Arles." *Traditio* 35: 89–119.

Archi, G. G. 1978. "Pragmatica sanctio pro petitione Vigilii." In *Festschrift für Franz Wieacker zum 70. Geburtstag*, ed. O. Behrends et al., 11–36. Göttingen.

Arcuri, R. 2009. *Rustici e rusticitas in Italia meridionale nel VI sec. d.c. Morfologia sociale di un paesaggio rurale tardoantico*. Messina.

Arjava, A. 1996. *Women in Law in Late Antiquity*. Oxford.

Arnold, J. J. 2013. "Theoderic's Invincible Mustache." *Journal of Late Antiquity* 6: 152–183.

——. 2014. *Theoderic and the Roman Imperial Restoration*. Cambridge, UK.

——. 2016. "Ostrogothic Provinces: Administration and Ideology." In Arnold, Bjornlie, and Sessa 2016, 73–97.

——. 2017. "Theoderic and Rome: Conquered but Unconquered." *Antiquité Tardive* 25: 113–126.

Arnold, J. J., M. S. Bjornlie, and K. Sessa, eds. 2016. *A Companion to Ostrogothic Italy*. Leiden.

Asolati, M. 2012. *Praestantia nummorum: Temi e note di numismatica tardo antica e alto medievale*. Padua.

——. 2013. "La disponibilità della moneta enea nell'Italia ostrogota. Emissioni inedite." In *La monetazione di Taranto. Le monete degli Ostrogoti e dei Longobardi in Italia. Atti del 4° Congresso Nazionale di Numismatica. Bari, 16–17 novembre 2012*, 265–290. Bari.

Aubin, H. 1949. *Vom Altertum zum Mittelalter. Absterben, Fortleben und Erneuerung*. Munich.

Auer, A., and M. de Vaan, eds. 2016. *Le palimpseste gotique de Bologne: Études philologiques et linguistiques*. Lausanne.

Augenti, A., ed. 2006. *Le città italiane tra la tarda antichità e l'alto Medioevo: Atti del convegno, Ravenna, 26–28 febbraio 2004*. Florence.

Augenti, A., and C. Bertelli, eds. 2007. *Felix Ravenna. La croce, la spada, la vela: L'alto Adriatico fra V e VI secolo*. Milan.

Ausbüttel, F. M. 1987. "Die Curialen und Stadtmagistrate Ravennas im späten 5. und 6. Jh." *Zeitschrift für Papyrologie und Epigraphik* 67: 207–214.

——. 1988. *Die Verwaltung der Städte und Provinzen im spätantiken Italien*. Frankfurt.

Bachrach, B. S. 1977. *Early Medieval Jewish Policy in Western Europe*. Minneapolis, MN.

Badel, C. 2006. "Un chef germain entre Byzance et l'Italie: L'épitaphe d'Asbadus à Pavie (Suppl. It., 9, 15)." In Ghilardi, Goddard, and Porena 2006, 91–100.

Bagnall, R. S., Al. Cameron, S. R. Schwartz, and K. A. Worp. 1987. *Consuls of the Later Roman Empire*. Atlanta, GA.

Baldini Lippolis, I. 2000. "Il ritratto musivo nella facciata interna di S. Apollinare Nuovo a Ravenna." In *Atti del VI Colloquio dell'Associazione Italiana per lo studio e la conservazione del mosaico: Venezia 20–23 gennaio 1999*, 463–478. Ravenna.

Barnes, T. D. 1998. *Ammianus Marcellinus and the Representation of Historical Reality*. Ithaca, NY.

Barnish, S. J. B. 1983. "The Anonymous Valesianus II as a Source for the Last Years of Theodoric." *Latomus* 42: 572–596.

———. 1984. "The Genesis and Completion of Cassiodorus' Gothic History." *Latomus* 43: 336–361.

———. 1985. "The Wealth of Iulianus Argentarius: Late Antique Banking and the Mediterranean Economy." *Byzantion* 55: 5–38.

———. 1986. "Martianus Capella and Rome in the Late Fifth Century." *Hermes* 114: 98–111.

———. 1987a. "The Work of Cassiodorus after His Conversion." *Latomus* 48: 157–187.

———. 1987b. "Pigs, Plebeians and Potentes: Rome's Economic Hinterland, c. 350–600 A.D." *Papers of the British School at Rome* 54: 157–185.

———. 1988. "Transformation and Survival in the Western Senatorial Aristocracy, c. A.D. 400–700." *Papers of the British School at Rome* 56: 120–155.

———. 1989. "A Note on the *Collatio Glebalis*." *Historia* 38: 254–256.

———. 1990. "Maximian, Cassiodorus, Boethius, Theodahad: Literature, Philosophy and Politics in Ostrogothic Italy." *Nottingham Medieval Studies* 34: 16–31.

———. 2001a. "*Religio in stagno*: Nature, Divinity, and the Christianization of the Countryside in Late Antique Italy." *Journal of Early Christian Studies* 9: 387–402.

———. 2001b. "Sacred Texts of the Secular: Writing, Hearing, and Reading Cassiodorus' *Variae*." *Studia patristica* 38: 362–370.

———. 2003. "Liberty and Advocacy in Ennodius of Pavia: The Significance of Rhetorical Education in Late Antique Italy." In *Hommages à Carl Deroux*, ed. P. Defosse, 5:20–28. Brussels.

Barnish, S. J. B., and F. Marazzi, eds. 2007. *The Ostrogoths: From the Migration Period to the Sixth Century*. Woodbridge, UK.

Barth, F. 1969. *Ethnic Groups and Boundaries: The Social Organization of Culture Difference*. Bergen.

Bartoldus, M. J. 2014. *Palladius Rutilius Taurus Namatianus. Welt und Wert spätrömischer Landwirtschaft*. 2nd ed. Augsburg.

Battistella, F. 2017. *Pelagius I. und der Primat Roms. Ein Beitrag zum Drei-Kapitel-Streit und zur Papstgeschichte des 6. Jahrhunderts*. Hamburg.

Baumgart, S. 1995. *Die Bischofsherrschaft im Gallien des 5. Jahrhunderts. Eine Untersuchung zu den Gründen und Anfängen weltlicher Herrschaft der Kirche*. Munich.

Bazelmans, J. 1991. "Conceptualizing Early Germanic Political Structures: A Review of the Use of the Concept of *Gefolgschaft*." In *Images of the Past: Studies on Ancient Societies in Northwestern Europe*, ed. N. Roymans and F. Theuws, 91–130. Amsterdam.

Beaujard, B. 2006. "Les cités de la Gaule méridionale du IIIe au VIIe s." *Francia* 63: 11–23.

Becher, M. 2011. *Chlodwig I. Der Aufstieg der Merowinger und das Ende der antiken Welt.* Munich.

Beck, H., ed. 1986. *Germanenprobleme in heutiger Sicht.* Berlin.

Beck, H., D. Geuenich, H. Steuer, and D. Hakelberg, eds. 2004. *Zur Geschichte der Gleichung "germanisch-deutsch": Sprache und Namen, Geschichte und Institutionen.* Berlin.

Becker, A. 2013. *Les relations diplomatiques romano-barbares en Occident au Ve siècle: Acteurs, fonctions, modalités.* Strasbourg.

Behrwald, R. 2020. "Die gotischen Könige und die Stadtlandschaft Roms." In Wiemer 2020a, 63–88.

Behrwald, R., and C. Witschel, eds. 2012. *Rom in der Spätantike: Historische Erinnerung im städtischen Raum.* Stuttgart.

Bermond Montanari, G. 1972. "S. Maria di Palazzolo (Ravenna)." *Arheoloski Vestnik* 13: 212–221.

Berndt, G. M. 2011. "Beute, Schutzgeld und Subsidien." In *Lohn der Gewalt. Beutepraktiken von der Antike bis zur Neuzeit,* ed. H. Carl and H.-J. Bömelburg, 121–147. Paderborn.

———. 2013. "Aktionsradien gotischer Kriegergruppen." *Frühmittelalterliche Studien* 47: 7–52.

Berndt, G. M., and R. Steinacher, eds. 2014. *Arianism: Roman Heresy and Barbarian Creed.* Farnham.

Berschin, W. 1988. *Greek Letters and the Latin Middle Ages: From Jerome to Nicholas of Cusa.* Translated by J. C. Frakes. Revised and expanded edition. Washington, DC.

Bichler, R. 2000. *Herodots Welt. Der Aufbau der Historie am Bild der fremden Länder und Völker, ihrer Zivilisation und ihrer Geschichte.* Berlin.

Bierbrauer, V. 1975. *Die ostgotischen Grab- und Schatzfunde in Italien.* Spoleto.

———. 1994. "Archäologie und Geschichte der Goten vom 1.–7. Jahrhundert." *Frühmittelalterliche Studien* 28: 51–171.

———. 2007. "Neue ostgermanische Grabfunde des 5. und 6. Jahrhunderts in Italien." *Acta Praehistorica et Archaeologica* 39: 93–124.

———. 2010. "Goten im Osten und Westen: Ethnos und Mobilität am Ende des 5. und in der 1. Hälfte des 6. Jahrhunderts aus archäologischer Sicht." *Kölner Jahrbuch* 43: 71–111.

———. 2011. "Zum pannonischen Ostgotenreich (456/457–473) aus archäologischer Sicht." In Heinrich-Tamáska 2011, 361–380.

Biernacki, A. B. 2005. "A City of Christians: Novae in the 5th and 6th C AD." *Archeologia Bulgarica* 9: 53–74.

Biundo, R. 2006. "Le vicende delle proprietà municipali tra IV e V secolo d.C." In Ghilardi, Goddard, and Porena 2006, 37–51.

Bjornlie, M. S. 2013. *Politics and Tradition between Rome, Ravenna and Constantinople: A Study of Cassiodorus and the Variae, 527–554.* Cambridge, UK.

———. 2014. "Law, Ethnicity and Taxes in Ostrogothic Italy: A Case for Continuity, Adaptation and Departure." *Early Medieval Europe* 22: 138–170.

Blaudeau, P. 2012. *Le siège de Rome et l'Orient (448–536). Étude géo-ecclésiologique.* Rome.

Bleckmann, B. 1992. *Die Reichskrise des III. Jahrhunderts in der spätantiken und byzantinischen Geschichtsschreibung. Untersuchungen zu den nachdionischen Quellen der Chronik des Johannes Zonaras.* Munich.

———. 1996. "Honorius und das Ende der römischen Herrschaft in Westeuropa." *Historische Zeitschrift* 265: 561–595.

———. 2009. *Die Germanen. Von Ariovist bis zu den Wikingern.* Munich.

Bleicken, J. 1982. *Zum Regierungsstil des römischen Kaisers: Eine Antwort auf Fergus Millar.* Wiesbaden.

Bloch, H. 1959. "Ein datierter Ziegelstempel Theoderichs des Grossen." *Römische Mitteilungen* 66: 196–203.

Bloch, M. 1935. "Avènement et conquête du moulin à eau." *Annales d'histoire économique et sociale* 7: 538–563.

———. 1945a. "Sur les grandes invasions: Quelques positions et problèmes." *Revue de synthèse historique* 60: 55–81.

———. 1945b. "Une mise au point: Les invasions. Deux structures économiques." *Annales d'histoire sociale* 1: 33–46 and *Annales d'histoire sociale* 2: 13–28.

———. 1947. "Comment et pourquoi finit l'esclavage antique." *Annales: Économies, Sociétés, Civilisations* 2: 30–44, 161–170.

———. 1963. *Mélanges historiques.* 2 vols. Paris.

Blumenkranz, B. 1946. *Die Judenpredigt Augustins. Ein Beitrag zur Geschichte der jüdisch-christlichen Beziehungen in den ersten Jahrhunderten.* Basel.

Bodmer, J.-P. 1957. *Der Krieger der Merowingerzeit und seine Welt. Eine Studie über Kriegertum als Form der menschlichen Existenz im Frühmittelalter.* Zurich.

Bolle, K. 2017. "Spätantike Inschriften in Tuscia et Umbria. Materialität und Präsenz." In Bolle, Machado, and Witschel 2017, 147–212.

Bolle, K., C. Machado, and C. Witschel, eds. 2017. *The Epigraphic Cultures of Late Antiquity.* Stuttgart.

Bollmus, R. 2006. *Das Amt Rosenberg und seine Gegner. Studien zum Machtkampf im nationalsozialistischen Herrschaftssystem.* 2nd ed. Munich. (1st ed. 1970.)

Bona, I. 1991. *Das Hunnenreich.* Budapest.

Bonamente, G. 2020. "*Puer in regia civitate*: Atalarico e la difficile legittimazione del regno (Cassiod. *Variae* VIII 1–8)." *Occidente/Oriente* 1: 83–106.

Bonifay, M., and D. Piéri. 1995. "Amphores du Ve au VIIe s. à Marseille: Nouvelles données sur la typologie et le contenu." *Journal of Roman Archaeology* 8: 94–117.

Bonnet, C., and J. Beltrán de Heredia. 2000. "El primer grupo episcopal de Barcelona." In Ripoll López and Gurt 2000, 467–490.

Borchardt, F. L. 1971. *German Antiquity in Renaissance Myth.* Baltimore, MD.

Borhy, L. 2011. *Die Römer in Ungarn.* Mainz.

Börm, H. 2008. "Das weströmische Kaisertum nach 476." In *Monumentum et instrumentum inscriptum. Beschriftete Objekte aus Kaiserzeit und Spätantike als historische Zeugnisse. Festschrift für Peter Weiß zum 65. Geburtstag*, ed. H. Börm, N. Ehrhardt, and J. Wiesehöfer, 47–69. Stuttgart.

———. 2010. "Herrscher und Eliten in der Spätantike." In *Commutatio et contentio: Studies in the Late Roman, Sasanian, and Early Islamic Near East*, ed. H. Börm and J. Wiesehöfer, 159–198. Düsseldorf.

———. 2019. *Westrom. Von Honorius bis Justinian.* 2nd ed. Stuttgart. (1st ed. 2013.)

Boßhammer, S. 2021. *Wege zum Frieden im nachrömisch-gotischen Italien. Programmatik und Praxis gesellschaftlicher Kohärenz in den* Variae Cassiodors. Berlin.

Bowes, K. 2012. *Houses and Society in the Later Roman Empire.* London.

Bowra, C. M. 1952. *Heroic Poetry.* London.

Brandenburg, H. 2013. *Die frühchristlichen Kirchen in Rom vom 4. bis zum 7. Jahrhundert. Der Beginn der abendländischen Kirchenbaukunst.* 3rd ed. Regensburg. (1st ed. 2004.)

Brandes, W. 2002. *Finanzverwaltung in Krisenzeiten. Untersuchungen zur byzantinischen Administration im 6.–9. Jahrhundert.* Frankfurt.

Brather, S., ed. 2004. *Ethnische Interpretationen in der frühgeschichtlichen Archäologie. Geschichte, Grundlagen und Alternativen.* Berlin.

Brather, S., et al., eds. 2021. *Germanische Altertumskunde im Wandel. Archäologische, philologische und geschichtswissenschaftliche Beiträge aus 150 Jahren.* Berlin.

Brecht, S. 1999. *Die römische Reichskrise von ihrem Ausbruch bis zu ihrem Höhepunkt in der Darstellung byzantinischer Autoren.* Rahden, Germany.

Brennecke, H. C. 1988. *Studien zur Geschichte der Homöer. Der Osten bis zum Ende der homöischen Reichskirche.* Tübingen.

———. 1996. "Christianisierung und Identität—das Beispiel der germanischen Völker." In *Missionsgeschichte, Kirchengeschichte, Weltgeschichte. Christliche Missionen im Kontext nationaler Entwicklungen in Afrika, Asien und Ozeanien*, ed. U. van der Heyden and H. Liebau, 239–247. Stuttgart.

———. 1997. "Chalkedonense und Henotikon. Bemerkungen zum Prozess der östlichen Rezeption der christologischen Formel von Chalkedon." In *Chalkedon: Geschichte und Aktualität. Studien zur Rezeption der christologischen Formel von Chalkedon*, ed. J. van Oort and J. Roldanus, 24–53. Leuven.

———. 2000. "Imitatio—reparatio—continuatio. Die Judengesetzgebung im Ostgotenreich Theoderichs des Großen als *reparatio imperii*?" *Zeitschrift für antikes Christentum* 4: 133–148.

———. 2002. "Der sogenannte germanische Arianismus als 'arteigenes' Christentum. Die völkische Deutung der Christianisierung der Germanen im Nationalsozialismus." In *Evangelische Kirchenhistoriker im "Dritten Reich." Problembestimmung und Forschungsperspektiven*, ed. T. Kaufmann and H. Oelke, 310–329. Gütersloh.

———. 2007. *Ecclesia est in re publica. Studien zur Kirchen- und Theologiegeschichte im Kontext des Imperium Romanum.* Berlin.

———. 2014a. "Deconstruction of the So-Called Germanic Arianism." In Berndt and Steinacher 2014, 117–130.

———. 2014b. "Zwischen Byzanz und Ravenna. Das Papsttum an der Wende zum 6. Jahrhundert." In Meier and Patzold 2014, 217–238.

———. 2020. "*Ipse Haereticus favens Judaeis*. Homöer und Juden als religiöse Minderheiten im Ostgotenreich." In Wiemer 2020a, 155–174.

Brion, M. 1936. *Theoderich. König der Ostgoten*. Translated from French by F. Büchner. Frankfurt.

Brodka, D. 2009. "Einige Bemerkungen zum Verlauf der Schlacht bei Adrianopel (9. August 378)." *Millennium* 6: 265–280.

———. 2016. "Prokop von Kaisareia und seine Informanten: Ein Identifikationsversuch." *Historia* 65: 108–124.

———. 2018. *Narses. Politik, Krieg und Historiographie*. Berlin.

Brogiolo, G. P. 1993. *Brescia altomedievale: Urbanistica ed edilizia dal IV al IX secolo*. Mantua.

———. 1999. "Ideas of the Town in Italy during the Transition from Antiquity to the Middle Ages." In Brogiolo and Ward-Perkins 1999, 99–126.

———. 2007. "Dwellings and Settlements in Ostrogothic Italy." In Barnish and Marazzi 2007, 113–132.

———. 2011. "Dati archeologici e beni fiscali nell'Italia goto-longobarda." In Díaz and Martín Viso 2011, 87–106.

Brogiolo, G. P., and L. Castelletti. 1991 and 2001. *Archeologia a Monte Barro*. 2 vols. Lecco.

Brogiolo, G. P., and E. Possenti. 2000. "L'età gota in Italia settentrionale nella transizione tra tarda antichità e alto medioevo." In *Le invasioni barbariche nel Meridione dell'impero: Visigoti, Vandali, Ostrogoti*, ed. P. Delogu, 257–296. Soveria Mannelli.

Brogiolo, G. P., and B. Ward-Perkins, eds. 1999. *The Idea and Ideal of the Town between Late Antiquity and the Early Middle Ages*. Leiden.

Brokmeier, B. 1987. "Der große Friede 332. Zur Außenpolitik Konstantins des Großen." *Bonner Jahrbücher* 187: 80–100.

Brough, S. 1985. *The Goths and the Concept of Gothic in Germany from 1500 to 1750*. Frankfurt/Main.

Brown, P. 1971. *The World of Late Antiquity*. London.

———. 1992. *Power and Persuasion in the Later Roman Empire. Towards a Christian Empire*. Madison, WI.

———. 2002. *Poverty and Leadership in the Later Roman Empire*. Hanover, NH.

Brown, T. S. 1984. *Gentlemen and Officers: Imperial Administration and Aristocratic Power in Byzantine Italy* A.D. 554–800. London.

Browning, R. 1953. "Where Was Attila's Camp?" *Journal of Hellenic Studies* 73: 143–145.

Brühl, C. 1975. *Palatium und Civitas. Studien zur Profantopographie spätantiker Civitates vom 3. bis zum 13. Jahrhundert*. Vol. 1: *Gallien*. Cologne.

Brunhölzl, F. 1975. *Geschichte der lateinischen Literatur des Mittelalters*. Vol. 1: *Von Cassiodor bis zum Ausklang der karolingischen Erneuerung*. Munich.

Buchner, R. 1933. *Die Provence in merowingischer Zeit. Verfassung—Wirtschaft—Kultur*. Stuttgart.

Bullough, D. A. 1966. "Urban Change in Early Medieval Italy: The Example of Pavia." *Papers of the British School at Rome* 34: 82–130.

———. 1968. *Italy and Her Invaders (Inaugural Lecture)*. Nottingham.

Burton, G. P. 1979. "The *Curator Rei Publicae*. Towards a Reappraisal." *Chiron* 9: 465–487.

Bury, J. B. 1923. *History of the Later Roman Empire from the Death of Theodosius I to the Death of Justinian.* 2 vols. London.

Busch, A. 2015. *Die Frauen der theodosianischen Dynastie. Macht und Repräsentation kaiserlicher Frauen im 5. Jahrhundert.* Stuttgart.

Büsing-Kolbe, A., and H. Büsing. 2002. *Stadt und Land in Oberitalien.* Mainz.

Büsing, H., A. Büsing-Kolbe, and V. Bierbrauer. 1993 "Die Dame von Ficarolo." *Archeologia medievale* 20: 303–332.

Caillet, J.-P. 1993. *L'évergétisme monumental chrétien en Italie et à ses marges d'après l'épigraphie des pavements de mosaïques (IVe–VIIe s.).* Rome.

Caliri, E. 2017. Praecellentissimus Rex: *Odoacre tra storia e storiografia.* Messina.

Cameron, Al. 1976. *Circus Factions: Blues and Greens at Rome and Byzantium.* Oxford.

———. 1984. "Probus' Praetorian Games: Olympiodorus Fr. 4." *Greek, Roman, and Byzantine Studies* 25: 193–196.

———. 1985. "Polyonomy in the Late Roman Aristocracy: The Case of Petronius Probus." *Journal of Roman Studies* 75: 164–182.

———. 1988. "Flavius: A Nicety of Protocol." *Latomus* 47: 26–33.

———. 2012a. "Basilius and His Diptych Again: Career Titles, Seats in the Colosseum, and Issues of Stylistic Dating." *Journal of Roman Archaeology* 25: 513–530.

———. 2012b. "Anician Myths." *Journal of Roman Studies* 102: 133–171.

———. 2016. *Studies in Late Roman History and Literature.* Bari.

Cameron, Al., and D. Schauer. 1982. "The Last Consul: Basilius and His Diptych." *Journal of Roman Studies* 72: 126–143.

Cameron, Av. 1981. "Cassiodorus Deflated." *Journal of Roman Studies* 71: 183–186.

———. 1985. *Procopius and the Sixth Century.* London.

———. 2012. *The Mediterranean World in Late Antiquity, AD 395–700.* 2nd ed. London. (1st ed. 1993.)

Cameron, Av., and P. Garnsey, eds. 1998. *The Cambridge Ancient History.* 2nd ed. Vol. 13: *The Late Empire, A.D. 337–425.* Cambridge, UK.

Cameron, Av., B. Ward-Perkins, and M. Whitby, eds. 2000. *The Cambridge Ancient History.* 2nd ed. Vol. 14: *Late Antiquity: Empire and Successors, A.D. 425–600.* Cambridge, UK.

Carandini, A., and A. Ricci, eds. 1985. *Settefinestre: Una villa schiavistica nell'Etruria Romana.* 3 vols. Modena.

Carile, A., ed. 1995. *Teoderico il Grande fra Oriente e Occidente (Ravenna, 28 settembre–2 ottobre 1992).* Ravenna.

Carlà, F. 2009. *L'oro nella tarda antichità: Aspetti economici e sociali.* Turin.

Carolla, P. 2010. "Aspar, l'intrigo e il massacro: Una nuova lettura dell'exc. 39 di Prisco di Panio." *Mediterraneo antico* 13: 387–396.

Carrié, J.-M. 1982. "Le 'colonat du Bas-Empire': Un mythe historiographique?" *Opus* 1: 351–370.

———. 1983. "Un roman des origines: Les généalogies du 'colonat du Bas-Empire.' " *Opus* 2: 205–251.

Caspar, E. 1930. *Geschichte des Papsttums von den Anfängen bis zur Höhe der Weltherrschaft.* Vol. 1: *Römische Kirche und Imperium Romanum.* Tübingen.

———. 1933. *Geschichte des Papsttums von den Anfängen bis zur Höhe der Weltherrschaft.* Vol. 2: *Das Papsttum unter byzantinischer Herrschaft.* Tübingen.

Castrorao Barba, A. 2020. *La fine delle ville romane in Italia tra tarda antichità e alto medioevo (III–VIII secolo).* Bari.

Cavallieri Manasse, G. 1993. "Le mura teodericiane di Verona." In CISAM 1993, 633–644.

Cecconi, G. A. 1994. *Governo imperiale e élites dirigenti nell'Italia tardoantica. Problemi di storia politico-amministrativa.* Como.

———. 1998. "I governatori delle province italiche." *Antiquité Tardive* 6: 149–179.

———. 2006a. "Crisi e trasformazioni del governo municipale in Occidente tra IV e VI secolo." In Krause and Witschel 2006, 285–318.

———. 2006b. "*Honorati, possessores, curiales*: Competenze istituzionali e gerarchie di rango nella città tardoantica." In Lizzi Testa 2006, 41–64.

Cerati, A. 1975. *Caractère annonaire et assiette de l'impôt foncier au Bas-Empire.* Paris.

Cesa, M. 1994. "Il regno di Odoacre. La prima dominazione germanica in Italia." In *Germani in Italia,* ed. B. Scardigli and P. Scardigli, 307–332. Rome.

———. 2003. "Il regno di Teodorico nella valutazione della storiografia tedesca dell'Ottocento." In *Atti della Seconda Giornata Ennodiana,* ed. E. d'Angelo, 15–36. Naples.

Çetinkaya, H. 2009. "An Epitaph of a Gepid King at Vefa kilise camii in Istanbul." *Revue des Études byzantines* 67: 225–229.

Chadwick, H. 1981. *Boethius: The Consolations of Music, Logic, Theology, and Philosophy.* Oxford.

Chadwick, H. M. 1907. *The Origin of the English Nation.* Cambridge, UK.

Chantraine, H. 1988. "Das Schisma von 418/19 und das Eingreifen der kaiserlichen Gewalt in die römische Bischofswahl." In Kneissl and Losemann 1988, 79–94.

Chastagnol, A. 1960. *La préfecture urbaine à Rome sous le Bas-Empire.* Paris.

———. 1963. "L'administration du diocèse italien au Bas-Empire." *Historia* 12: 348–379.

———. 1966. *Le sénat romain sous le règne d'Odoacre. Recherches sur l'épigraphie du Colisée au Ve siècle.* Bonn.

———. 1992. *Le Sénat romain à l'époque impériale. Recherches sur la composition de l'Assemblée et le statut de ses membres.* Paris.

Chayanov, A. V. 1966. *The Theory of Peasant Economy.* Madison, WI.

Christ, K., ed. 1970a. *Der Untergang des Römischen Reiches.* Darmstadt.

———. 1970b. "Der Untergang des römischen Reiches in antiker und moderner Sicht. Eine Einleitung." In Christ 1970a, 1–31.

———. 1982. *Römische Geschichte und deutsche Geschichtswissenschaft.* Munich.

———. 1983. "Der Niedergang des römischen Reiches aus der Sicht der neueren Geschichtsschreibung." In *Römische Geschichte und Wissenschaftsgeschichte.* Vol. 2: *Geschichte und Geschichtsschreibung der römischen Kaiserzeit,* 199–233. Darmstadt.

———. 2008. *Der andere Stauffenberg: Der Historiker und Dichter Alexander von Stauffenberg.* Munich.

Christensen, A. S. 2002. *Cassiodorus, Jordanes and the History of the Goths: Studies in a Migration Myth*. Copenhagen.

Christie, N. J. 1991. "Invasion or Invitation? The Longobard Occupation of Northern Italy, AD 568–569." *Romanobarbarica* 11: 79–108.

———. 2006. *From Constantino to Charlemagne: An Archaeology of Italy, AD 300–800*. Aldershot.

———. 2011. *The Fall of the Western Empire: An Archaeological and Historical Perspective*. London.

———. 2020. "Ostrogothic Italy: Questioning the Archaeology of Settlement." In Wiemer 2020a, 125–154.

Chrysos, E. 1981. "Die Amaler-Herrschaft in Italien und das Imperium Romanum: Der Vertragsentwurf des Jahres 535." *Byzantion* 51: 430–474.

Chrysos, E. K., and A. Schwarcz, eds. 1989. *Das Reich und die Barbaren*. Vienna.

CISAM, ed. 1956. *I Goti in Occidente. Problemi. 29 marzo–5 aprile 1955*. Spoleto.

———. 1966. *Agricoltura e mondo rurale in occidente nell'alto medioevo*. Spoleto.

———. 1971. *Artigianato e tecnica nella società nell'alto medioevo occidentale*. Spoleto.

———. 1993. *Teoderico il Grande e i Goti d'Italia. Atti del XIII Congresso internazionale di studi sull'Alto Medioevo, Milano 2–6 novembre 1992*. 2 vols. Spoleto.

———. 1995. *La giustizia nell'alto medioevo (secoli V–VIII)*. Spoleto.

———. 2005. *Ravenna da capitale imperiale a capitale esarcale*. Spoleto.

Classen, P. 1977a. "Fortleben und Wandel spätrömischen Urkundenwesens im frühen Mittelalter." In *Recht und Schrift im Mittelalter*, ed. P. Classen, 13–54. Sigmaringen.

———. 1977b. *Kaiserreskript und Königsurkunde. Diplomatische Studien zum Problem der Kontinuität zwischen Altertum und Mittelalter*. Saloniki.

Claude, D. 1970. *Geschichte der Westgoten*. Stuttgart.

———. 1971a. *Adel, Kirche und Königtum im Westgotenreich*. Sigmaringen.

———. 1971b. "*Millenarius* und *thiuphadus*." *Zeitschrift für Rechtsgeschichte: Germanistische Abteilung* 88: 181–189.

———. 1978a. "Universale und partikulare Züge in der Politik Theoderichs des Großen." *Francia* 6: 19–58.

———. 1978b. "Zur Königserhebung Theoderichs des Großen." In *Geschichtsschreibung und geistiges Leben im Mittelalter. Festschrift für Heinz Löwe zum 65. Geburtstag*, ed. K. Hauck and H. Mordeck, 1–13. Cologne.

———. 1980. "Die ostgotischen Königserhebungen." In Wolfram and Daim 1980, 149–186.

———. 1985. *Der Handel im westlichen Mittelmeer während des Frühmittelalters*. Göttingen.

———. 1989. "Zur Begründung familiärer Beziehungen zwischen dem Kaiser und barbarischen Herrschern." In Chrysos and Schwarcz 1989, 25–56.

———. 1993. "Theoderich der Große und die europäischen Mächte." In CISAM 1993, 1:22–43.

———. 1995. "Zu Fragen des alemannischen Königtums an der Wende vom 5. zum 6. Jahrhundert." *Hessisches Jahrbuch für Landesgeschichte* 45: 1–16.

———. 1996. "Studien zu Handel und Wirtschaft im italischen Ostgotenreich." *Münstersche Beiträge zur antiken Handelsgeschichte* 15: 42–75.

——. 1997a. "Clovis, Théodoric et la maîtrise de l'espace entre Rhin et Danube." In *Clovis, histoire et mémoire. Actes du Colloque International d'Histoire de Reims, du 19 au 25 septembre 1996*, ed. M. Rouche (Paris), 1:409–419.

——. 1997b. "Niedergang, Renaissance und Ende der Praefekturverwaltung im Westen des römischen Reiches (5.–8. Jahrhundert)." *Zeitschrift für Rechtsgeschichte, Germanistische Abteilung* 114: 352–379.

Clauss, M. 1980. *Der magister officiorum in der Spätantike (4.–6. Jahrhundert)*. Munich.

Clavadetscher, O. P. 1979. "Churrätien im Übergang von der Spätantike zum Mittelalter nach den Schriftquellen." In *Von der Spätantike zum frühen Mittelalter. Aktuelle Probleme in historischer und archäologischer Sicht*, ed. J. Werner and E. Ewig, 159–178. Sigmaringen.

Clemente, G. 1972. "Il patronato nei *collegia* dell'impero Romano." *Studi Classici e Orientali* 21: 142–229.

——. 2017. "The Roman Senate and the Politics of Religion in the *Collectio Avellana* (IV–VI Century AD)." *Scripta Classica Israelica* 36: 123–139.

Coates-Stephens, R. 1998. "The Walls and Aqueducts of Rome in the Early Middle Ages." *Journal of Roman Studies* 88: 166–178.

——. 2003. "The Water-Supply of Rome from Late Antiquity to the Early Middle Ages." *Acta ad archaeologiam et artium historiam pertinentia* 17: 165–186.

Cochlaeus, J. 1529. *Antiqua regum Italiae Gothicae Gentis Rescripta, ex. 12. libris epistolarum Cassiodori ad Eutharicum*. Leipzig.

——. 1544. *Vita Theoderici Regis Quondam Ostrogothorum et Italiae*. Ingolstadt.

Cochlaeus, J., and J. Peringskiöld. 1699. *Vita Theoderici Regis Quondam Ostrogothorum et Italiae cum Additamentis & Annotationibus, quae Sueo-Gothorum ex Scandia Expeditiones & commercia illustrant opera Johannis Peringskiöld*. Stockholm.

Cohen, S. 2015. "Schism and the Polemic of Heresy: Manichaeism and the Representation of Papal Authority in the *Liber Pontificalis*." *Journal of Late Antiquity* 8: 195–230.

——. 2016. "Religious Diversity." In Arnold, Bjornlie, and Sessa 2016, 503–532.

Colafemmina, C. 1991. "Gli ebrei in Basilicata." *Bollettino Storico della Basilicata* 7: 9–32.

Collins, R. 2001. *Visigothic Spain 409–711*. Oxford.

Conti, P. M. 1971. *"Devotio" e "viri devoti" in Italia da Diocleziano ai Carolingi*. Padua.

Corcoran, S. 2003. "The Donation and Will of Vincent of Huesca: Latin Text and English Translation." *Antiquité Tardive* 11: 215–221.

Cosentino, S. 2004. "Re Teoderico costruttore di flotte." *Antiquité Tardive* 12: 347–356.

——. 2006. "Le fortune di un banchiere tardoantico: Giuliano argentario e l'economia di Ravenna nel VI secolo." In *Santi, banchieri, re. Ravenna e Classe nel VI secolo. San Severo il tempio ritrovato*, 43–48. Milan.

——. 2005. "L'approvvigionamento annonario di Ravenna dal V all'VIII secolo: L'organizzazione e i riflessi socio-economici." In CISAM 2005, 405–434.

Costa, G. 1977. *Le antichità germaniche nella cultura italiana da Machiavelli a Vico*. Naples.

Costamagna, L. 1991. "La sinagoga di Bova Marina nel quadro degli insediamenti tardoantichi della costa Ionica meridionale della Calabria." *Mélanges de l'École française de Rome: Moyen Âge* 103: 611–630.

Costambeys, M. 2009. "Settlement, Taxation and the Condition of the Peasantry in Post-Roman Central Italy." *Journal of Agrarian Change* 9: 92–119.

———. 2016. "The Legacy of Theoderic." *Journal of Roman Studies* 106: 249–263.

Coster, C. H. 1935. *The Iudicium quinquevirale*. Cambridge, MA.

Coumert, M. 2007. *Origines des peuples: Les récits du haut Moyen Âge occidental*. Paris.

Courcelle, P. 1938. "Le site du monastère de Cassiodore." *Mélanges d'Archéologie et d'Histoire de l'École française de Rome* 55: 259–307.

———. 1948. *Les lettres grecques en Occident: De Macrobe à Cassiodore*. 2nd ed. Paris. (1st ed. 1943.)

———. 1957. "Nouvelles recherches sur le monastère de Cassiodore." In *Actes du cinquième congrès d'archéologie chrétienne, Aix-en-Provence 13–19 septembre 1954*, 511–528. Vatican City.

———. 1964. *Histoire littéraire des grandes invasions germaniques*. 3rd ed. Paris. (1st ed. 1948.)

———. 1984. *Opuscula selecta: Bibliographie et recueil d'articles publiés entre 1938–1980*. Paris.

Courtois, C. 1955. *Les Vandales et l'Afrique*. Paris.

(Cracco-)Ruggini, L. 1959. "Ebrei e Orientali nell'Italia settentrionale fra il IV e il VI secolo d. Cr." *Studia et Documenta Historiae et Iuris* 25: 185–308.

———. 1961. *Economia e società nell' "Italia Annonaria." Rapporti fra agricoltura e commercio dal IV al VI secolo d.C.* Bari. Repr. 1995.

Cracco-Ruggini, L. 1971. "Le associazioni professionali nel mondo romano-bizantino." In CISAM 1971, 59–193.

———. 1977. "Il vescovo Cromazio e gli ebrei di Aquileia." In *Aquileia e l'Oriente mediterraneo. Atti della VII settimana di Studi Aquileiesi (24 aprile–1 maggio 1976)*, 353–381. Udine.

———. 1980. "La Sicilia e la fine del mondo antico (IV–VI secolo)." In *La Sicilia antica*. Vol. 2/2, ed. E. Gabba and G. Vallet, 483–524. Naples.

———. 1984. "Ticinum: Dal 476 d.C alla fine del Regno Gotico." In *Storia di Pavia*. Vol. 1: *L'età antica*, 271–312. Pavia.

———. 2011. *Gli ebrei in età tardoantica: Presenze, intolleranze, incontri*. Rome.

Crawford, M. H. 2005. "Transhumance in Italy: Its History and Its Historians." In *Noctes Campanae: Studi di storia antica ed archeologica dell'Italia preromana e romana in memoria di Martin W. Frederiksen*, ed. W. V. Harris and E. Lo Cascio, 159–179. Naples.

Cristini, M. 2018. "Eutarico Cillica successore di Teoderico." *Aevum* 92: 297–307.

———. 2019a. "Il patronato letterario nell'Italia Ostrogota." *Klio* 101: 276–322.

———. 2019b. " 'Graecia est professa discordiam.' Teoderico, Anastasio e la battaglia di Horreum Margi." *Byzantinische Zeitschrift* 112: 67–84.

———. 2019c. " 'In ecclesiae redintegranda unitate': Re Teoderico e la fine dello Scisma Acaciano." *Rivista di Storia della Chiesa in Italia* 73: 367–386.

———. 2021. "Diplomacy at the End of the World: Theoderic's Letters to the Warni and Hesti." *Klio* 103: 270–296.

Croke, B. 1982. "Mundo the Gepid: From Freebooter to Roman General." *Chiron* 12: 125–135.

———. 1983. "A.D. 476: The Manufacture of a Turning Point." *Chiron* 13: 81–119.

——. 1987. "Cassiodorus and the *Getica* of Jordanes." *Classical Philology* 82: 117–134.

——. 1990. "Theodor Mommsen and the Later Roman Empire." *Chiron* 20: 159–189.

——. 1992. *Christian Chronicles and Byzantine History, 5th–6th Centuries*. Aldershot.

——. 2005a. "Jordanes and the Immediate Past." *Historia* 54: 473–494.

——. 2005b. "Dynasty and Ethnicity: Emperor Leo I and the Eclipse of Aspar." *Chiron* 35: 147–204.

——. 2007. "Justinian under Justin: Reconfiguring a Reign." *Byzantinische Zeitschrift* 100: 13–56.

Dagron, G. 2011. *L'hippodrome de Constantinople: Jeux, peuple et politique*. Paris.

Dahn, F. 1859. "Dietrich von Berne (1859)." In F. Dahn, *Bausteine. Gesammelte Kleine Schriften*. Zweite Reihe, 249–271. Berlin, 1880.

——. 1861. *Die Könige der Germanen. Das Wesen des ältesten Königtums der germanischen Stämme. Zweiter Band: Die kleineren gotischen Völker—Die äußere Geschichte der Ostgoten*. Leipzig. (2nd ed. 1911.)

——. 1866. *Die Könige der Germanen. Das Wesen des ältesten Königthums der germanischen Stämme und seine Geschichte bis auf die Feudalzeit. Dritte Abtheilung: Verfassung des ostgotischen Reiches in Italien*. Würzburg.

——. 1876. *Ein Kampf um Rom. Historischer Roman*. Leipzig.

Daim, F., et al., eds. 1985. *Die Bayern und ihre Nachbarn. Berichte des Symposions der Kommission für Frühmittelalterforschung vom 25. bis 28. Oktober 1982 im Stift Zwettl, Niederösterreich*. 2 vols. Vienna.

Dartmann, C. 2010. "Die Sakralisierung König Wambas. Zur Debatte um frühmittelalterliche Sakralherrschaft." *Frühmittelalterliche Studien* 44: 39–58.

De Lange, N. 2005. "Jews in the Age of Justinian." In Maas 2005, 401–426.

De Maria, S., ed. 2004. *Nuove ricerche e scavi nell'area della Villa di Teodorico a Galeata: Atti della giornata di studi, Ravenna 26 marzo 2002*. Bologna.

De Ste. Croix, G. E. M. 1954. "*Suffragium*: From Vote to Patronage." *British Journal of Sociology* 5: 33–48.

——. 1981. *The Class Struggle in the Ancient Greek World. From the Archaic Age to the Arab Conquests*. London.

De Vingo, P. 2011. "Ländliche Gebiete im zentralen und südlichen Piemont zwischen Spätantike und Frühmittelalter." *Zeitschrift für Archäologie des Mittelalters* 39: 1–36.

Deichmann, F. W. 1973. "Ancora sulla 'ecclesia legis Gothorum S. Anastasiae.'" *Felix Ravenna* 105/106: 113–118.

——. 1974 and 1976. *Ravenna—Hauptstadt des spätantiken Abendlandes*. Vol. 2: *Kommentar, 1. und 2. Teil*. 2 vols. Stuttgart.

——. 1989. *Ravenna—Hauptstadt des spätantiken Abendlandes*. Vol. 2: *Kommentar, 3. Teil: Geschichte, Topographie, Kunst und Kultur, Indices zum Gesamtwerk*. Stuttgart.

Deininger, J. 1988. "'Die sozialen Gründe des Untergangs der antiken Kultur.' Bemerkungen zu Max Webers Vortrag von 1896." In Kneissl and Losemann 1988, 95–112.

Delaplace, C. 2000. "La 'Guerre de Provence' (507–511), un épisode oublié de la domination ostrogothique en Occident." In *Romanité et cité chrétienne: Permanences et mutations, intégration et exclusion du Ier au VIe siècle, Mélanges en l'honneur d'Yvette Duval*, 77–89. Paris.

———. 2003. "La Provence sous la domination ostrogothique (508–536)." *Les Annales du Midi* 244: 479–499.

———. 2015. *La fin de l'Empire romain d'Occident. Rome et les Wisigoths de 382 à 531.* Rennes.

Delbrück, R. 1929. *Die Consulardiptychen und verwandte Denkmäler.* 2 vols. Berlin.

Delehaye, H. 1912. "Saints de Thrace et de Mésie." *Analecta Bollandiana* 31: 161–301.

Deliyannis, D. M. 2010. *Ravenna in Late Antiquity.* Cambridge, UK.

Delmaire, R. 1989a. *Largesses sacrées et* res privata: *L'aerarium impérial et son administration du IVe au VIe siècle.* Rome.

———. 1989b. *Les responsables des finances impériales au Bas-Empire romain (IVe–VIe s.). Études prosopographiques.* Brussels.

———. 1995. *Les institutions du Bas-Empire romain de Constantin à Justinien. Les institutions civiles palatines.* Paris.

———. 1996. "Cités et fiscalité au Bas-Empire. À propos du rôle des *curiales* dans la levée des impôts." In Lepelley 1996b, 59–70.

Demandt, A. 1970. "Magister militum." In RE Suppl. XII, 553–790.

———. 1978. *Metaphern für Geschichte. Sprachbilder und Gleichnisse im historisch-politischen Denken.* Munich.

———. 2007. *Die Spätantike. Römische Geschichte von Diocletian bis Justinian. 284–565 n. Chr.* 2nd ed. Munich. (1st ed. 1989.)

———. 2014. *Der Fall Roms. Die Auflösung des Römischen Reiches im Urteil der Nachwelt.* 2nd ed. Munich. (1st ed. 1984.)

Demougeot, E. 1958. "Attila et les Gauls." *Mémoires de la Société d'agriculture, commerce, sciences et arts du département de la Marne* 73: 7–42.

———. 1981. "Le partage des provinces de l'Illyricum entre la pars Occidentis et la pars Orientis, de la tétrarchie au règne de Théodoric." In *La géographie administrative et politique, d'Alexandre à Mahomet. Actes du Colloque de Strasbourg (Juin 1979),* 229–253. Strasbourg.

———. 1988. *L'empire romain et les barbares d'Occident (IVe–VIIe siècles): Scripta varia.* Paris.

Destephen, S. 2016. *Le voyage impérial dans l'Antiquité tardive: Des Balkans au Proche-Orient.* Paris.

Di Rienzo, D. 2005. *Gli epigrammi di Magno Felice Ennodio.* Naples.

Díaz, P. C. 2011. *El reino suevo (411–585).* Madrid.

Díaz, P. C., and I. Martín Viso, eds. 2011. *Between Taxation and Rent: Fiscal Problems from Late Antiquity to Early Middle Ages.* Bari.

Díaz, P. C., and R. Valverde. 2007. "Goths Confronting Goths: Ostrogothic Political Relations in Hispania." In Barnish and Marazzi 2007, 353–386.

Díaz, P. C., C. Martínez Maza, and F. J. Sanz Huesma. 2007. *Hispania tardoantigua y visigoda.* Madrid.

Diefenbach, S., and G. M. Müller, eds. 2013. *Gallien in Spätantike und Frühmittelalter: Kulturgeschichte einer Region.* Berlin.

Dierkens, A., and P. Périn. 2000. "Les 'sedes regiae' mérovingiennes entre Seine et Rhin." In Ripoll López and Gurt 2000, 267–304.

Dopsch, A. 1918–1920. Wirtschaftliche und soziale Grundlagen der europäischen Kulturentwicklung. 2 vols. Vienna.

d'Ors, A. 1960. Estudios visigoticos II: El código de Eurico. Rome.

Drinkwater, J. F. 2007. The Alamanni and Rome, 213–496. Oxford.

Du Roure, L. M. 1846. Histoire de Théodoric-le-Grand, roi d'Italie, précédée d'une revue préliminaire de ses auteurs et conduite jusqu'à la fin de la monarchie ostrogothique. 2 vols. Paris.

Dubouloz, J. 2006. "Acception et défense des loca publica, d'après les Variae de Cassiodore: Un point de vue sur les cités d'Italie au VIe siècle." In Ghilardi, Goddard, and Porena 2006, 53–74.

Duchesne, L. 1925. L'Église au VIe siècle. Paris.

Dufraigne, P. 1994. Adventus Augusti, adventus Christi: Recherches sur l'exploitation idéologique et littéraire d'un cérémonial dans l'antiquité tardive. Paris.

Dumézil, B. 2012. "Le patrice Liberius: Développement et redéploiement d'un réseau dans la première moitié du VIe siècle." In Échanges, communications et réseaux dans le Haut Moyen Âge. Études et textes offerts à Stéphane Lebecq, ed. A. Gautier and C. Martin, 27–44. Turnhout.

Durliat, J. 1988. "Le salaire de la paix sociale dans les royaumes barbares (Ve–VIe siècles)." In Wolfram and Schwarcz 1988, 21–72.

Duval, N. 1960. "Que savons-nous du palais de Théoderic à Ravenne?" Mélanges d'Archéologie et d'Histoire de l'École française de Rome 72: 337–371.

Düwel, K. 2008. Runenkunde. 4th ed. Stuttgart. (1st ed. 1968.)

Eck, W. 1980. "Die Präsenz senatorischer Familien in den Städten des Imperium Romanum bis zum späten 3. Jahrhundert." In Studien zur antiken Sozialgeschichte. Festschrift Friedrich Vittinghoff, ed. W. Eck, H. Galsterer, and H. Wolff, 283–322. Cologne.

Eger, C., and S. Panzram. 2006. "Michael Kulikowski und die spätrömische Stadt in Spanien. Kritische Anmerkungen zum Fallbeispiel Munigua." Ethnographisch-Archäologische Zeitschrift 47: 267–280.

Ehling, K. 1998. "Wann beginnt die Eigenmünzung Odovacars?" Schweizer Münzblätter 190: 33–37.

Eich, P. 2020. "Quod prosperum nobis utile rei publicae sit: Senatorische Macht und Ressourcenkontrolle im Italien Theoderichs." In Wiemer 2020a, 193–222.

Eicke, H. 1938. Theoderich. König, Ketzer und Held. Leipzig.

Elsner, J. 2002. "The Birth of Late Antiquity: Riegl and Strzygowski in 1901." Art History 25: 358–379, 419f.

Ensslin, W. 1928. "Die Ostgoten in Pannonien." Byzantinisch-neugriechische Jahrbücher 6: 149–159.

———. 1931. "Zum Heermeisteramt des spätrömischen Reiches. Teil III: Der magister utriusque militiae et patricius des 5. Jahrhunderts." Klio 24: 467–502.

———. 1936. "Der Patricius Praesentalis im Ostgotenreich." Klio 29: 243–249.

———. 1940a. "Zu den Grundlagen von Odoakers Herrschaft." In Serta Hoffileriana, 381–388. Zagreb.

———. 1940b. "Rex Theodericus inlitteratus?" *Historisches Jahrbuch* 60: 391–396.

———. 1940c. Review of Vetter 1938. *Byzantinische Zeitschrift* 40: 168–175.

———. 1942. "Das Römerreich unter germanischer Waltung, von Stilicho bis Theoderich." In *Das neue Bild der Antike*. Vol. 2: *Rom*, ed. H. Berve, 421–432. Leipzig.

———. 1944a. "Der erste bekannte Erlass des Königs Theoderich." *Rheinisches Museum* 92: 266–280.

———. 1944b. "Theoderich 'der Afrikaner.' " *Philologische Wochenschrift* 64: 21–24.

———. 1947. "Aus Theoderichs Kanzlei." *Würzburger Jahrbücher für die Altertumswissenschaft* 2: 78–85.

———. 1948. "Flavius Placidus Valentinianus." In RE VIIA, 2232–2259.

———. 1949. "Zu dem Anagnosticum des Königs Theoderich des Grossen." *Annuaire de l'Institut de Philologie et d'Histoire Orientales et Slaves* 9: 233–245.

———. 1951. "Papst Johannes I. als Gesandter Theoderichs bei Kaiser Justinos I." *Byzantinische Zeitschrift* 44: 126–134.

———. 1953. "Zur Verwaltung Siziliens vom Ende des weströmischen Reiches bis zum Beginn der Themenverfassung." In *Atti dell'VIII congresso internazionale di studi bizantini, Palermo 3–10 aprile 1951*, 353–364. Rome.

———. 1954. "Praefectus praetorio." In RE XXII, 2391–2502.

———. 1956a. "Praepositis sacri cubiculi." In RE Suppl. VIII, 556–567.

———. 1956b. "Beweise der Romverbundenheit in Theoderichs des Großen Aussen- und Innenpolitik." In CISAM 1956, 509–536.

———. 1959. *Theoderich der Große*. 2nd ed. Munich. (1st ed. 1947.)

Errington, R. M. 1983. "Malchos von Philadelpheia, Kaiser Zenon und die beiden Theoderiche." *Museum Helveticum* 40: 82–110.

———. 1996. "Theodosius and the Goths." *Chiron* 26: 1–27.

———. 2006. *Roman Imperial Policy from Julian to Theodosius*. Chapel Hill, NC.

Esch, A. 1997. *Römische Straßen in ihrer Landschaft. Das Nachleben antiker Straßen um Rom mit Hinweisen zur Begehung im Gelände*. Mainz.

———. 2011. *Zwischen Antike und Mittelalter. Der Verfall des römischen Straßensystems in Mittelitalien und die Via Amerina*. Munich.

Esch, A., and J. Petersen, eds. 1993. *Ferdinand Gregorovius und Italien. Eine kritische Würdigung*. Tübingen.

Evans, J. A. S. 1996. *The Age of Justinian: The Circumstances of Imperial Power*. New York.

Ewig, E. 1952. "Die fränkischen Teilungen und Teilreiche (511–613)." In *Akademie der Wissenschaften in Mainz. Abhandlungen der geistes- und sozialwissenschaftlichen Klasse* 9: 651–715.

———. 1956. "Zum christlichen Königsgedanken im Frühmittelalter." In Mayer 1956, 7–74.

———. 1976. *Spätantikes und fränkisches Gallien. Gesammelte Schriften*. Vol. 1. Munich.

———. 2001. *Die Merowinger und das Frankenreich*. 4th ed. Stuttgart. (1st ed. 1988.)

Faber, E. 2014. *Von Ulfila bis Rekkared. Die Goten und ihr Christentum*. Stuttgart.

Falluomini, C. 2015. *The Gothic Version of the Gospels and Pauline Epistles: Cultural Background, Transmission and Character*. Berlin.

——. 2017. "Zum gotischen Fragment aus Bologna II: Berichtigungen und neue Lesungen." *Zeitschrift für deutsches Altertum und deutsche Literatur* 146: 284–294.

——. 2020. "Traces of Wulfila's Bible Translation in Visigothic Gaul." *Amsterdamer Beiträge zur Älteren Germanistik* 80: 5–24.

Fauvinet-Ranson, V. 1998. "Portrait d'une régente: Un panégyrique d'Amalasonthe (Cassiodore, Variae XI, 1)." *Cassiodorus* 4: 267–308.

——. 2000. "Une restauration symbolique de Théodoric: Le théatre de Pompée (Cassiodore, Variae IV, 51)." In *La mémoire de l'Antiquité dans l'Antiquité tardive et le haut Moyen Age*, ed. M. Sot, 37–54. Nanterre.

——. 2006a. Decor civitatis, decor Italiae: *Monuments, travaux publics et spectacles au VIe siècle d'après les* Variae de Cassiodore. Bari.

——. 2006b. "Le devenir du patrimoine monumental romain des cités d'Italie à l'époque ostrogothique." In Ghilardi, Goddard, and Porena 2006, 205–216.

——. 2012. "Le paysage urbain de Rome chez Cassiodore: Une christianisation passée sous silence." In Behrwald and Witschel 2012, 139–154.

——. 2012–2013. "L'éloge du lac de Côme par Cassiodore (*Variae* XI, 14): Lieux communs, réécriture, échos littéraires (Pline, Ammien Marcellin, Faustus, Ennode)." *Revue des études tardo-antiques* 2: 141–173.

Favrod, J. 1997. *Histoire politique du royaume burgonde (443–534)*. Lausanne.

Feissel, D. 1994. "L'ordonnance du préfet Dionysios inscrite à Mylasa en Carie (1er août 480)." *Travaux et Mémoires du Centre de Recherche d'Histoire et Civilisation de Byzance* 12: 263–298.

Fellner, G. 1985. *Ludo Moritz Hartmann und die österreichische Geschichtswissenschaft. Grundzüge eines paradigmatischen Konfliktes*. Vienna.

Ferrari, M. C. 2011. "*Manu hominibus praedicare*. Cassiodors Vivarium im Zeitalter des Übergangs." In *Bibliotheken im Altertum*, ed. E. Blumenthal and W. Schmitz, 223–249. Wolfenbüttel.

Festy, M., and M. Vitiello. 2020. *Anonyme de Valois: L'Italie sous Odoacre et Théodoric. Texte, traduction et commentaire*. Paris.

Fiebiger, O. 1939. "Inschriftensammlung zur Geschichte der Ostgermanen. Neue Folge." *Denkschriften der Akademie der Wissenschaften in Wien, philosophisch-historische Klasse* 70: 3.

——. 1944. "Inschriftensammlung zur Geschichte der Ostgermanen. Zweite Folge." *Denkschriften der Akademie der Wissenschaften in Wien, philosophisch-historische Klasse* 72: 2.

Fiebiger, O., and L. Schmidt. 1917. "Inschriftensammlung zur Geschichte der Ostgermanen." *Denkschriften der Akademie der Wissenschaften in Wien, philosophisch-historische Klasse* 60: 3.

Finley, M. I. 1980. *Ancient Slavery and Modern Ideology*. Cambridge, UK.

——. 1985. *The Ancient Economy*. 2nd ed. Cambridge, UK. (1st ed. 1973.)

Finn, R. 2006. *Almsgiving in the Later Roman Empire: Christian Promotion and Practice, 313–450*. Oxford.

Flach, D. 1990. *Römische Agrargeschichte*. Munich.

Flaig, E. 2019. *Den Kaiser herausfordern. Die Usurpation im Römischen Reich.* 2nd ed. Frankfurt am Main. (1st ed. 1992.)

Focke-Museum Bremen, ed. 2013. *Graben für Germanien. Archäologie unterm Hakenkreuz.* Stuttgart.

Fontaine, J. 1962. "Ennodius." In RAC V, 398–421.

Forlenza, R. 2017. "The Politics of the Abendland: Christian Democracy and the Idea of Europe after the Second World War." *Contemporary European History* 26: 261–286.

Frakes, R. 2001. Contra potentium iniurias: *The* Defensor civitatis *and Late Roman Justice.* Munich.

Francovich Onesti, N. 2002. *I Vandali: Lingua e storia.* Rome.

———. 2007. *I nomi degli Ostrogoti.* Florence.

———. 2013. *Goti e Vandali: Dieci saggi di lingua e cultura altomedievale.* Rome.

Freund, W. 1957. *Modernus und andere Zeitbegriffe des Mittelalters.* Cologne.

Friesen, O. von, ed. 1927. *Codex argenteus Upsalensis jussu Senatus Universitatis phototypice editus.* Uppsala.

Frye, D. 1995. "Athalaric's Health and Ostrogothic Character." *Byzantion* 65: 249–251.

Galdi, G. 2013. *Syntaktische Untersuchungen zu Jordanes. Beiträge zu den* Romana. Hildesheim.

Galonnier, A. 1996. "Anecdoton Holderi ou Ordo generis Cassiodororum: Introduction, édition, traduction et commentaire." *Antiquité Tardive* 4: 299–312.

García Iglesias, L. 1975. "El intermedio ostrogodo en Hispania (507–549 d.C.)." *Hispania antiqua* 5: 89–120.

Garnsey, P. 1976. "Peasants in Ancient Roman Society." *Journal of Peasants Studies* 3: 221–235.

———. 1988. *Famine and Food Supply in the Ancient World.* Cambridge, UK.

Gatzka, F. 2019. *Cassiodor, "Variae" 6. Einführung, Übersetzung und Kommentar.* Berlin.

Gaudemet, J. 1951. "Utilitas publica." *Revue historique de droit français et étranger* 29: 465–499.

———. 1965. *Le Bréviaire d'Alaric et les Epitome.* Milan.

Gaupp, E. T. 1844. *Die germanischen Ansiedlungen und Landtheilungen in den Provinzen des römischen Westreiches in ihrer völkerrechtlichen Eigenthümlichkeit und mit Rücksicht auf verwandte Erscheinungen der alten Welt und des späteren Mittelalters.* Breslau.

Gauthier, N., E. Marin, and F. Prévot, eds. 2010. *Salona IV: Inscriptions de Salone chrétienne IVe–VIIe siècles.* Rome.

Geary, P. J. 1983. "Ethnic Identity as a Situational Construct in the Early Middle Ages." *Mitteilungen der anthropologischen Gesellschaft in Wien* 113: 15–26.

Geiss, H. 1931. *Geld- und naturalwirtschaftliche Erscheinungsformen im staatlichen Aufbau Italiens während der Gotenzeit.* Breslau.

Gelzer, H., H. Hilgenfeld, and O. Cuntz, eds. 1898. *Patrum Nicaenorum nomina.* Leipzig.

Geuenich, D. 2005. *Geschichte der Alemannen.* Stuttgart.

Geuenich, D., T. Grünewald, and R. Weitz, eds. 1996. *Chlodwig und die Schlacht bei Zülpich. Geschichte und Mythos 496–1996.* Euskirchen.

Ghilardi, M., C. J. Goddard, and P. Porena, eds. 2006. *Les cités de l'Italie tardo-antique (IVe–VIe siècle): Institutions, économie, société, culture et religion.* Rome.

Giardina, A., ed. 1986. *Società romana ed impero tardoantico*. Vol. 1: *Istituzioni, ceti, econ-omie*. Rome.

———. 2006. *Cassiodoro politico*. Rome.

Gibbon, E. 1776–1788. *The History of the Decline and the Fall of the Roman Empire*. 6 vols. London. (New edition, ed. D. Womersley, 3 vols.; London, 1994.)

Giesecke, H.-E. 1939. *Die Ostgermanen und der Arianismus*. Leipzig.

Gillett, A. 1998. "The Purposes of Cassiodorus' *Variae*." In *After Rome's Fall: Narrators and Sources of Early Medieval History. Essays Presented to Walter Goffart*, ed. A. C. Murray, 37–50. Toronto.

———. 2001. "Rome, Ravenna, and the Last Western Emperors." *Papers of the British School at Rome* 69: 131–167.

———, ed. 2002a. *On Barbarian Identity: Critical Approaches to Ethnicity in the Early Middle Ages*. Turnhout.

———. 2002b. "Was Ethnicity Politicised in the Earliest Medieval Kingdoms?" In Gillett 2002a, 85–122.

———. 2003. *Envoys and Political Communication in the Late Antique West, 411–533*. Cambridge, UK.

Glaser, F. 1997. *Frühes Christentum im Alpenraum. Eine archäologische Entdeckungsreise*. Regensburg.

Goddard, C. J. 2006. "The Evolution of Pagan Sanctuaries in Late Antique Italy (Fourth–Sixth Centuries A.D.): A New Administrative and Legal Framework. A Paradox." In Ghilardi, Goddard, and Porena 2006, 281–308.

Goetz, H.-W., J. Jarnut, and W. Pohl, eds. 2003. *Regna and Gentes: The Relationship between Late Antique and Early Medieval Peoples and Kingdoms in the Transformation of the Roman World*. Leiden.

Goffart, W. 1980. *Barbarians and Romans: The Techniques of Accommodation AD 418–584*. Princeton, NJ.

———. 1988. *The Narrators of Barbarian History (AD 550–800): Jordanes, Gregory of Tours, Bede, and Paul the Deacon*. Princeton, NJ.

———. 2006. *Barbarian Tides: The Migration Age and the Later Roman Empire*. Philadelphia, PA.

Goltz, A. 2008. *Barbar—König—Tyrann. Das Bild Theoderichs des Großen in der Überlieferung des 5. bis 9. Jahrhunderts*. Berlin.

———. 2009. "Das 'Ende' des weströmischen Reiches in der frühbyzantinischen syrischen Historiographie." In Goltz et al. 2009, 169–198.

Goltz, A., and U. Hartmann. 2008. "Valerianus und Galerius." In Johne 2008, 223–296.

Goltz, A., H. Leppin, and H. Schlange-Schöningen, eds. 2009. *Jenseits der Grenzen. Beiträge zur spätantiken und frühmittelalterlichen Geschichtsschreibung*. Berlin.

Gómez Fernández, F. J. 2001. "Tarraco en el siglo V d. C.: Morfología y vitalidad urbana." *Hispania antiqua* 25: 371–392.

———. 2003. "Augusta Emerita en el transcurso del siglo V: Morfología y vitalidad urbana." *Hispania antiqua* 27: 263–279.

Gomolka-Fuchs, G., ed. 1999. *Die Sîntana de Mures-Cernjachov-Kultur. Akten des Internationalen Kolloquiums in Caputh vom 20. bis 24. Oktober 1995*. Bonn.

Goria, F., and F. Sitzia, eds. 2013. *Edicta praefectorum praetorio.* Cagliari.

Gorini, G. 1996. "Currency in Italy in the Fifth Century A.D." In *Coin Finds and Coin Use in the Roman World*, ed. C. E. King and D. G. Wing, 185–202. Berlin.

Gračanin, H. 2016. "Late Antique Dalmatia and Pannonia in Cassiodorus' *Variae.*" *Millennium* 13: 211–274.

Gračanin, H., and J. Škrgulja. 2014. "The Ostrogoths in Late Antique Southern Pannonia." *Acta Archaeologica Carpathica* 49: 165–205.

Grahn-Hoek, H. 1976. *Die fränkische Oberschicht im 6. Jahrhundert. Studien zu ihrer rechtlichen und politischen Stellung.* Sigmaringen.

Graus, F. 1959. "Über die sogenannte germanische Treue." *Historica* 1: 71–122.

———. 1961. "Die Gewalt bei den Anfängen des Feudalismus und die 'Gefangenenbefreiungen' der merowingischen Hagiographie." *Jahrbuch für Wirtschaftsgeschichte* 2: 61–156.

———. 1963. Review of Wenskus 1961. *Historica* 7: 185–191.

———. 1975. *Lebendige Vergangenheit. Überlieferung im Mittelalter und in den Vorstellungen vom Mittelalter.* Cologne.

———. 1986. "Verfassungsgeschichte des Mittelalters." *Historische Zeitschrift* 243: 529–589.

———. 2002. *Ausgewählte Aufsätze (1959–1989).* Sigmaringen.

Greatrex, G. B. 1998. *Rome and Persia at War, 502–532.* Leeds.

———. 2000. "Roman Identity in the Sixth Century." In *Ethnicity and Culture in Late Antiquity*, ed. G. Greatrex and S. Mitchell, 267–292. London.

———. 2001. "Justin I and the Arians." *Studia Patristica* 34: 73–81.

———. 2003. "Recent Work on Procopius and the Composition of Wars VIII." *Byzantine and Modern Greek Studies* 27: 45–67.

———. 2014. "Perceptions of Procopius in Recent Scholarship." *Histos* 8: 76–121, 121a–e (addenda).

———. 2018. "Procopius' Attitude towards Barbarians." In Greatrex and Janniard 2018, 327–354.

Greatrex, G. B., and S. Janniard, eds. 2018. *Le monde de Procope/The World of Procopius.* Paris.

Green, D. H. 1998. *Language and History in the Early Germanic World.* Cambridge, UK.

Greene, K. 1987. "Gothic Material Culture." In *Archaeology as Long-Term History*, ed. I. Hodder, 117–131. Cambridge, UK.

Gregorovius, F. 1859–1872. *Geschichte der Stadt Rom im Mittelalter. Vom V. bis zum XVI. Jahrhundert.* 8 vols. Stuttgart. (New edition in 4 vols. by C. H. Beck; Munich, 1988.)

Grey, C. 2007a. "Contextualizing Colonatus: The Origo of the Late Roman Empire." *Journal of Roman Studies* 97: 155–175.

———. 2007b. "Revisiting the Problem of *Agri Deserti* in the Late Roman Empire." *Journal of Roman Archaeology* 20: 362–382.

———. 2011. *Constructing Communities in the Late Roman Countryside.* Cambridge, UK.

Grierson, P. 1985. "The Date of Theoderic's Gold Medallion." *Hikuin* 11: 19–26.

Grierson, P., and M. Blackburn. 1986. *Medieval European Coinage, with a Catalogue of the Coins in the Fitzwilliam Museum, Cambridge.* Vol. 1: *The Early Middle Ages (5th–10th Centuries).* Cambridge, UK.

Grierson, P., and M. Mays. 1992. *Catalogue of Late Roman Coins in the Dumbarton Oaks Collection and in the Whittemore Collection: From Arcadius and Honorius to the Accession of Anastasius*. Washington, DC.

Grig, L., and G. Kelly, eds. 2012. *Two Romes: Rome and Constantinople in Late Antiquity*. Oxford.

Grillmeier, A., and T. Hainthaler. 1989. *Jesus der Christus im Glauben der Kirche*. Vol. 2/2: *Die Kirche von Konstantinopel im 6. Jahrhundert*. Freiburg.

Grillone, A. 2017. *Iordanes. Getica. Edizione, traduzione e commento*. Paris.

Grimm, J. 1828. *Deutsche Rechtsaltertümer*. Göttingen.

——. 1835. *Deutsche Mythologie*. Göttingen.

Grimm, W. 1829. *Die Deutsche Heldensage*. Göttingen.

Gruber, J. 2011. *Boethius. Eine Einführung*. Stuttgart.

Grünert, H. 2002. *Gustaf Kossinna (1858–1931). Vom Germanisten zum Prähistoriker. Ein Wissenschaftler im Kaiserreich und in der Weimarer Republik*. Rahden, Germany.

Grusková, J., and G. Martin. 2014a. "'Scythica Vindobonensia' by Dexippus (?): New Fragments on Decius' Gothic Wars." *Greek, Roman and Byzantine Studies* 54: 728–754.

——. 2014b. "Ein neues Textstück aus den 'Scythica Vindobonensia' zu den Ereignissen nach der Eroberung von Philippopolis." *Tyche* 29: 29–43.

——. 2015. "Zum Angriff der Goten unter Kniva auf eine thrakische Stadt (*Scythica Vindobonensia*, f. 195v)." *Tyche* 30: 35–53.

Gryson, R., ed. 1980. *Scolies ariennes sur le concile d'Aquilée: Introduction, texte latin, traduction et notes*. Paris.

Guerrini, P. 2011. "Theodericus rex nelle testimonianze epigrafiche." *Temporis Signa* 6: 133–174.

Guidobaldi, F. 1999. "Le domus tardoantiche di Roma come 'sensori' delle trasformazioni culturali e sociali." In *The Transformation of Urbs Roma in Late Antiquity*, ed. W. V. Harris, 53–68. Portsmouth, RI.

Gurt, J. M., and C. Godoy. 2000. "Barcíno, de sede imperial a *urbs regia* en época visigoda." In Ripoll López and Gurt 2000, 425–466.

Guyon, J., and M. Heijmans, eds. 2013. *L'Antiquité tardive en Provence (Ive–VIe siècle): Naissance d'une chrétienté*. Arles.

Hachmann, R. 1970. *Die Goten und Skandinavien*. Berlin.

Haehling, R. von. 1988. "*Timeo, ne per me consuetudo in regno nascatur*. Die Germanen und der römische Kaiserthron." In *Roma renascens: Beiträge zur Spätantike und Rezeptionsgeschichte Ilona Opelt zum 9.7.1988 gewidmet*, ed. M. Wissemann, 88–113. Frankfurt.

Haensch, R. 1992. "Das Statthalterarchiv." *Zeitschrift für Rechtsgeschichte, Romanistische Abteilung* 100: 209–317.

——. 1995. "*A commentariis* und *commentariensis*. Geschichte und Aufgaben eines Amtes im Spiegel seiner Titulaturen." In *La hiérarchie (Rangordnung) de l'armée romaine sous le Haut-Empire*, ed. Y. Le Bohec, 267–284. Paris.

——. 1997. Capita provinciarum. *Statthaltersitze und Provinzialverwaltung in der römischen Kaiserzeit*. Mainz.

———. 2010. "Kontrolle und Verantwortlichkeit von *Officiales* in Prinzipat und Spätantike." In *Die Verwaltung der kaiserzeitlichen römischen Armee. Studien für Hartmut Wolff,* ed. A. Eich, 177–186. Stuttgart.

———. 2013. "Die Statthalterarchive der Spätantike." In *Archives and Archival Documents in Ancient Societies,* ed. M. Faraguna, 333 349. Trieste.

———. 2015. "From Free to Fee? Judicial Fees and Other Litigation Costs during the High Empire and Late Antiquity." In *Law and Transaction Costs in the Ancient Economy,* ed. D. Kehoe, D. M. Ratzan, and U. Yiftach, 253–272. Ann Arbor, MI.

———, ed. 2016. *Recht haben und Recht bekommen im Imperium Romanum. Das Gerichtswesen der römischen Kaiserzeit und seine dokumentarische Evidenz.* Warsaw.

———. 2017. "Zwei unterschiedliche epigraphische Praktiken: Kirchenbauinschriften in Italien und im Nahen Osten." In Bolle, Machado, and Witschel 2017, 535–554.

Hahn, W., and M. Metlich. 2013. *Money of the Incipient Byzantine Empire: Anastasius I–Justinian I, 491–565.* 2nd ed. Vienna.

Haldon, J. 2008. "Framing Transformation, Transforming the Framework." *Millennium* 5: 327–352.

Haldon, J., et al. 2018. "Plagues, Climate Change, and the End of an Empire: A Response to Kyle Harper's *The Fate of Rome.*" *History Compass* 2018; e12505, e12506, e12507.

Halporn, J. W. 2000. Review of Troncarelli 1998. *The Medieval Review* 00.02.25. https://scholarworks.iu.edu/journals/index.php/tmr/article/view/14887/21005.

Halsall, G. 1999. "Movers and Shakers: The Barbarians and the Fall of Rome." *Early Medieval Europe* 8: 131–145.

———. 2007. *Barbarian Migrations and the Roman West, 376–568.* Cambridge, UK.

———. 2016. "The Ostrogothic Military." In Arnold, Bjornlie, and Sessa 2016, 173–199.

Hannestad, K. 1960. "Les forces militaires d'après la Guerre Gothique de Procope." *Classica & Medievalia* 21: 136–183.

———. 1962. *L'évolution des ressources agricoles de l'Italie du 4ème au 6ème siècle de notre ère.* Copenhagen.

Hanson, R. P. C. 1988. *The Search for the Christian Doctrine of God: The Arian Controversy, 318–381 A.D.* Grand Rapids, MI.

Hardt, M. 2006. *Gold und Herrschaft. Die Schätze europäischer Könige und Fürsten im ersten Jahrtausend.* Berlin.

Harhoiu, R. 1977. *The Fifth-Century Treasure from Pietroasa in the Light of Recent Research.* Oxford.

———. 1997. *Die frühe Völkerwanderungszeit in Rumänien.* Bucharest.

Harmatta, J. 1970. "The Last Century of Pannonia." *Acta Antiqua Academiae Scientiarum Hungaricae* 18: 361–369.

Harnack, A. von. 1924. "Der erste deutsche Papst (Bonifatius II., 530/32) und die beiden letzten Dekrete des römischen Senats." *Sitzungsberichte der Preußischen Akademie der Wissenschaften,* 24–42.

Harper, K. 2011. *Slavery in the Late Roman World, AD 275–425.* Cambridge, UK.

———. 2017. *The Fate of Rome: Climate, Disease, and the End of an Empire.* Princeton, NJ.

Harries, J. 1988. "The Roman Imperial Quaestor from Constantine to Theodosius II." *Journal of Roman Studies* 78: 148–172.

———. 1994. *Sidonius Apollinaris and the Fall of Rome, AD 407–485*. Oxford.

Hartmann, L. M. 1900. *Geschichte Italiens im Mittelalter*. Vol. 2: *Römer und Langobarden bis zur Teilung Italiens*. Gotha.

———. 1910. *Der Untergang der antiken Welt. Sechs volkstümliche Vorträge*. 2nd ed. Vienna. (1st ed. 1903.)

———. 1923. *Geschichte Italiens im Mittelalter*. Vol. 1: *Das italienische Königreich*. 2nd ed. Stuttgart–Gotha. (1st ed. 1897.)

———. 2008. "Gregor von Tours und arianische Königinnen oder: Hatte Chlodwig I. zwei oder drei Schwestern?" *Mitteilungen des Instituts für Österreichische Geschichtsforschung* 116: 130–137.

———. 2009. *Die Königin im frühen Mittelalter*. Stuttgart.

Hartmann, M. 2008. "Claudius Gothicus und Aurelianus." In Johne 2008, 297–323.

Hasenstab, B. 1890. *Studien zu Ennodius. Ein Beitrag zur Geschichte der Völkerwanderung*. Munich.

Haubrichs, W. 2000. "Ein Held für viele Zwecke. Dietrich von Bern und sein Widerpart in den Heldensagenzeugnissen des frühen Mittelalters." In *Theodisca. Beiträge zur althochdeutschen und altniederdeutschen Sprache*, ed. W. Haubrichs et al., 330–363. Berlin.

———. 2004. " 'Heroische Zeiten?' Wanderungen von Heldennamen und Heldensagen zwischen den germanischen *gentes* des frühen Mittelalters." In *Namenwelten. Orts- und Personennamen in historischer Sicht*, ed. A. van Nahl et al., 513–534. Berlin.

———. 2011. "Ethnizität zwischen Differenz und Identität. Sprache als Instrument der Kommunikation und der Gruppenbildung im frühen Mittelalter." *Zeitschrift für Literaturwissenschaft und Linguistik* 164: 10–38.

———. 2012. "Nescio latine! Volkssprache und Latein im Konflikt zwischen Arianern und Katholiken im wandalischen Afrika nach der *Historia persecutionis* des Victor von Vita." In *Geschichtsvorstellungen: Bilder, Texte und Begriffe aus dem Mittelalter. Festschrift für Hans-Werner Goetz zum 65. Geburtstag*, ed. S. Patzold et al., 13–42. Cologne.

———. 2017. "Krieg, Volk und Verwandtschaft. Zur Struktur und kulturellen Signifikanz ostgotischer Frauennamen." *Archiv für Kulturgeschichte* 99: 299–341.

Hauck, K., et al., eds. 1986. *Sprache und Recht. Beiträge zur Kulturgeschichte des Mittelalters. Festschrift Ruth Schmidt-Wiegand zum 60. Geburtstag*. Berlin.

Haug, A. 2003. *Die Stadt als Lebensraum. Eine kulturhistorische Analyse zum spätantiken Stadtleben in Norditalien*. Rahden, Germany.

Heather, P. J. 1986. "The Crossing of the Danube and the Gothic Conversion." *Greek, Roman and Byzantine Studies* 27: 289–318.

———. 1989. "Cassiodorus and the Rise of the Amals: Genealogy and the Goths under Hun Domination." *Journal of Roman Studies* 79: 103–128.

———. 1991. *Goths and Romans 332–489*. Oxford.

———. 1993. "The Historical Culture of Ostrogothic Italy." In CISAM 1993, 1:317–353.

———. 1994. "Literacy and Power in the Migration Period." In *Literacy and Power in the Ancient World*, ed. A. K. Bowman and G. Woolf, 177–197. Cambridge, UK.

——. 1995. "Theoderic, King of the Goths." *Early Medieval History* 4: 145–173.

——. 1996. *The Goths.* Oxford.

——. 1998. "Disappearing and Reappearing Tribes." In Pohl 1998a, 95–111.

——. 2003. " 'Gens' and 'Regnum' among the Ostrogoths." In Goetz, Jarnut, and Pohl 2003, 85–133.

——. 2005. *The Fall of the Roman Empire: A New History.* Oxford.

——. 2007. "Merely an Ideology? Gothic Identity in Ostrogothic Italy." In Barnish and Marazzi 2007, 31–59.

——. 2009. "Why Did the Barbarian Cross the Rhine?" *Journal of Late Antiquity* 2: 3–29.

——. 2010. "Liar in Winter: Themistius and Theodosius." In *From the Tetrarchs to the Theodosians: Essays on Later Roman History and Culture,* ed. S. Gill et al., 185–214. New York.

——. 2012. "Roman Law in the Post-Roman West: A Case Study in the Burgundian Kingdom." In *Das Vermächtnis der Römer. Römisches Recht und Europa,* ed. I. Fragnoli and S. Rebenich, 177–232. Bern.

——. 2016. Review of Bjornlie 2013. *Early Medieval Europe* 24 (2016): 369–372.

Heather, P. J., and J. F. Matthews. 1991. *The Goths in the Fourth Century.* Liverpool.

Heidenreich, R., and H. Johannes. 1971. *Das Grabmal Theoderichs zu Ravenna.* Wiesbaden.

Heijmans, M. 2004. *Arles durant l'Antiquité tardive: De la Duplex Arelas à l'Urbs Genesii.* Rome.

Heil, U. 2011. *Avitus von Vienne und die homöische Kirche im Reich der Burgunder.* Berlin.

Heinrich-Tamáska, O., ed. 2011. *Keszthely-Fenékpuszta im Kontext spätantiker Kontinuitätsforschung zwischen Noricum und Moesia.* Rhaden, Germany.

——. 2013. *Keszthely-Fenékpuszta. Katalog der Befunde und ausgewählter Funde sowie neue Forschungsergebnisse.* Budapest.

Heinzelmann, M. 1976. *Bischofsherrschaft in Gallien. Zur Kontinuität römischer Führungsschichten vom 4. bis zum 7. Jahrhundert. Soziale, prosopographische und bildungsgeschichtliche Aspekte.* Munich.

Heinzle, J. 1999. *Einführung in die mittelhochdeutsche Dietrichepik.* Berlin.

Helbling, H. 1954. *Goten und Vandalen. Wandlung der historischen Realität.* Zurich.

Hen, Y. 2007. *Roman Barbarians: The Royal Court and Culture in the Early Medieval West.* New York.

Hendy, M. F. 1985. *Studies in the Byzantine Monetary Economy, c. 300–1450.* Cambridge, UK.

Henning, D. 1999. *Periclitans res publica. Kaisertum und Eliten in der Krise des weströmischen Reiches 454/5–493 n. Chr.* Stuttgart.

Herren, M. W. 1991. "The 'De imagine Tetrici' of Walahfrid Strabo: Edition and Translation." *Journal of Medieval Latin* 1: 118–139.

Heschel, S. 2008. *The Aryan Jesus: Christian Theologians and the Bible in Nazi Germany.* Princeton, Oxford.

Hildebrand, P. 1922. "Die Absetzung des Papstes Silverius (537)." *Historisches Jahrbuch* 42: 213–249.

Himmler, F. 2011. *Untersuchungen zur schiffsgestützten Grenzsicherung auf der spätantiken Donau: 3.–6. Jh. n.Chr.* Oxford.

Hirschfeld, B. 1904. "Die Gesta municipalia in römischer und frühgermanischer Zeit." PhD diss. Marburg.

Hodgkin, T. 1885. *Italy and Her Invaders*. Vol. 3: *The Ostrogothic Invasion*. Oxford. (2nd ed., 1896; repr. 2001).

———. 1891. *Theoderic the Goth: The Barbarian Champion of Civilization*. New York.

Höfler, O. 1934. *Kultische Geheimbünde der Germanen*. Vol. 1. Frankfurt.

———. 1938. "Die politische Leistung der Völkerwanderungszeit." *Kieler Blätter*, 1: 282–297.

Høilund Nielsen, K. 2014. "Key Issues Concerning 'Central Places.' " In *Wealth and Complexity. Economically Specialised Sites in Late Iron Age Denmark*, ed. E. Stidsing, K. Høilund Nielsen, and R. Fiedel, 11–50. Aarhus.

Holzhauer, H. 1986. "Der gerichtliche Zweikampf. Ein Institut des Germanischen Rechts in rechtsethnologischer Sicht." In Hauck et al. 1986, 1:263–283.

Hübinger, P. E., ed. 1968a. *Kulturbruch oder Kulturkontinuität im Übergang von der Antike zum Mittelalter*. Darmstadt.

———. 1968b. *Bedeutung und Rolle des Islam beim Übergang vom Altertum zum Mittelalter*. Darmstadt.

Hummel, B. F. 1777. *Neue Bibliothek von seltenen und sehr seltenen Büchern und kleinen Schriften*. Vol. 2. Nuremberg.

Humphrey, J. H. 1986. *Roman Circuses: Arenas for Chariot Racing*. Berkeley and Los Angeles.

Humphries, M. 2000. "Italy, A.D. 425–600." In Av. Cameron et al. 2000, 525–551.

Hurter, F. von. 1807–1808. *Geschichte des ostgothischen Königs Theoderich und seiner Regierung*. 2 vols. Schaffhausen.

Huyse, P. 1999. *Die dreisprachige Inschrift Šābuhrs I. an der Kaʿba-i Zardušt (ŠKZ)*. 2 vols. London.

Iasiello, I. M. 2007. *Samnium: Assetti e trasformazioni di una provincia dell'Italia tardoantica*. Bari.

Ieraci Bio, A. M. 1994. "La cultura medica a Ravenna." *Atti dell'Accademia Pontaniana* 43: 279–308.

Iggers, G. G. 1984. *The German Conception of History: The National Tradition of Historical Thought from Herder to the Present*. 2nd ed. Middletown, CT.

Ioniţă, I. 2004. "Sântana-de-Mureş-Černjachov-Kultur." In RGA XXVI, 445–455.

Ivanov, R. 1997. "Das römische Verteidigungssystem an der unteren Donau zwischen Dorticum und Durostorum (Bulgarien) von Augustus bis Maurikios." *Bericht der Römisch-Germanischen Kommission* 78: 467–640.

Izdebski, A. 2012. "Bishops in Late Antique Italy: Social Importance vs. Political Power." *Phoenix* 66: 158–175.

Jaeger, D. 2017. *Plündern in Gallien 451–592. Eine Studie zur Relevanz einer Praktik für das Organisieren von Folgeleistungen*. Berlin.

Jaeggi, C. 1990. "Aspekte der städtebaulichen Entwicklung Aquileias in frühchristlicher Zeit." *Jahrbuch für Antike und Christentum* 33: 158–196.

———. 2013. *Ravenna. Kunst und Kultur einer spätantiken Residenzstadt. Die Bauten und Mosaiken des 5. und 6. Jahrhunderts*. Regensburg.

James, S. 1988. "The *fabricae*: State Arms Factories of the Later Roman Empire." In *Military Equipment and the Identity of the Roman Soldiers*, ed. J. C. Coulston, 257–331. Oxford.

Jankuhn, H., and D. Timpe, eds. 1989. *Beiträge zum Verständnis der Germania des Tacitus, Teil I*. Göttingen.

Janvier, Y. 1969. *La législation du Bas-Empire romain sur les édifices publics*. Aix-en-Provence.

Jarnut, J. 2004. "Germanisch: Plädoyer für die Abschaffung eines obsoleten Zentralbegriffes der Frühmittelalter-Forschung." In Pohl 2004, 107–113.

Jenal, G. 1995. *Italia ascetica atque monastica. Das Asketen- und Mönchtum in Italien von den Anfängen bis zur Zeit der Langobarden (ca. 150/250–604)*. 2 vols. Munich.

Johne, K.-P., ed. 2008. *Die Zeit der Soldatenkaiser. Krise und Transformation des Römischen Reiches im 3. Jahrhundert n. Chr.* 2 vols. Berlin.

Johnson, M. J. 1988. "Toward a History of Theoderic's Building Program." *Dumbarton Oaks Papers* 42: 73–96.

———. 2009. *The Roman Imperial Mausoleum in Late Antiquity*. Cambridge, UK.

Jones, A. H. M. 1953. "Military Chaplains in the Roman Army." *Harvard Theological Review* 46: 171–173.

———. 1958. "The Roman Colonate." *Past & Present* 13: 1–13.

———. 1962. "The Constitutional Position of Odoacer and Theodoric." *Journal of Roman Studies* 52: 126–130.

———. 1964. *The Later Roman Empire 284–602: A Social, Economic and Administrative Survey*. 3 vols. Oxford.

———. 1974. *The Roman Economy: Studies in Ancient Economic and Administrative History*. Oxford.

Jones, H. 1988. "Justiniani 'Novellae,' ou l'autoportrait d'un législateur." *Revue internationale des droits de l'antiquité* 35: 149–208.

Jördens, A. 1993. "Überlegungen zur römischen Agrargeschichte. Eine Besprechung des Handbuchs von Dieter Flach." *Archiv für Papyrusforschung* 39: 49–81.

Kaiser, R. 2004a. *Die Burgunder*. Stuttgart.

———. 2004b. "Sigismund († 523/524): Erster heiliger König des Mittelalters und erster königlicher Romfahrer, Bußpilger und Mönch." In *Päpste, Pilger, Pönitentiarie: Festschrift für Ludwig Schmugge zum 65. Geburtstag*, ed. Andreas Meyer et al., 199–210. Tübingen.

Kakridi, C. 2005. *Cassiodors Variae: Literatur und Politik im ostgotischen Italien*. Munich.

Kaldellis, A. 2004. *Procopius of Caesarea: Tyranny, History, and Philosophy at the End of Antiquity*. Philadelphia, PA.

Kampers, G. 2014. "Wictharius, *arrianae legis sacerdos*. Beobachtungen zu c. 6 der Passio S. Vincentii Aginnensis." *Millennium-Jahrbuch* 11: 101–120.

Karayannopulos, J. 1958. *Das Finanzwesen des frühbyzantinischen Staates*. Munich.

Kater, M. H. 2006. *Das "Ahnenerbe" der SS 1935–1945. Ein Beitrag zur Kulturpolitik des Dritten Reiches*. 4th ed. Munich. (1st ed. 1974.)

Katsarova, V. 2012. "Pautalia." In *Roman Cities in Bulgaria*, ed. R. Ivanov, 1:55–73. Sofia.

Kazanski, M. 1991. *Les Goths (Ier–VIIe s. ap. J.C.)*. Paris.

Keenan, J. G. 1973–1974. "The Names Flavius and Aurelius as Status Designations in Later Roman Egypt." *Zeitschrift für Papyrologie und Epigraphik* 11: 33–63 and 13: 283–304.

Kelly, C. 2004. *Ruling the Later Roman Empire.* Cambridge, MA.

———. 2008. *Barbarian Terror and the Fall of the Roman Empire.* London.

Kelly, G. 2008. *Ammianus Marcellinus: The Allusive Historian.* Cambridge, UK.

Kennell, S. A. H. 2000. *Magnus Felix Ennodius: A Gentleman of the Church.* Ann Arbor, MI.

Kent, J. P. C. 1966. "Julius Nepos and the Fall of the Western Empire." In *Corolla memoriae Erich Swoboda dedicata,* ed. R. M. Swoboda-Milenovic, 146–150. Graz.

———. 1971. "The Coinage of Theodoric in the Names of Anastasius and Justin." In *Mints, Dies and Currency: Essays Dedicated to the Memory of Albert Baldwin,* ed. R. A. G. Carson, 67–74. London.

———. 1994. *The Roman Imperial Coinage.* Vol. 10: *The Divided Empire and the Fall of the Western Parts 395–491.* London.

Kim, H. J. 2013. *The Huns, Rome and the Birth of Europe.* Cambridge, UK.

King, P. D. 1972. *Law and Society in the Visigothic Kingdom.* Cambridge, UK.

Kinzig, W. 2017. *Faith in Formulae: A Collection of Early Christian Creeds and Creed-Related Texts.* 4 vols. Oxford.

Kipper, R. 2002. *Der Germanenmythos im deutschen Kaiserreich. Formen und Funktionen historischer Selbstthematisierung.* Darmstadt.

Kiss, A. 1979. "Ein Versuch die Funde und das Siedlungsgebiet der Ostgoten in Pannonien zwischen 456–471 zu bestimmen." *Acta Archaeologica Academiae Scientiarum Hungaricae* 31: 329–339.

———. 1996. "Die Osthrogoten in Pannonien (456–473) aus archäologischer Sicht." *Zalai Múzeum* 6: 87–90.

Klauser, T. 1977. "War Cassiodors Vivarium ein Kloster oder eine Hochschule?" In *Bonner Festgabe Johannes Straub zum 65. Geburtstag,* ed. A. Lippold and N. Himmelmann, 413–420. Bonn.

Kliger, S. 1952. *The Goths in England: A Study in Seventeenth and Eighteenth Century Thought.* Cambridge, MA.

Klingshirn, W. E. 1985. "Caesarius of Arles and the Ransoming of Captives." *Journal of Roman Studies* 75: 183–203.

———. 1994. *Caesarius of Arles: The Making of a Christian Community in Late Antique Gaul.* Cambridge, UK.

Kneissl, P. 1969. *Die Siegestitulatur der römischen Kaiser. Untersuchungen zu den Siegerbeinamen des ersten und zweiten Jahrhunderts.* Göttingen.

Kneissl, P., and V. Losemann, eds. 1988. *Alte Geschichte und Wissenschaftsgeschichte. Festschrift für Karl Christ zum 65. Geburtstag.* Darmstadt.

———, eds. 1998. *Imperium Romanum: Studien zu Geschichte und Rezeption. Festschrift für Karl Christ zum 75. Geburtstag.* Stuttgart.

Knopf, R. 1929. *Ausgewählte Märtyrerakten.* Ed. G. Krüger. Tübingen.

Kohlhas-Müller, D. 1995. *Untersuchungen zur Rechtsstellung Theoderichs des Großen.* Frankfurt/Main.

Kolb, F. 1984. *Die Stadt im Altertum.* Munich.

Kollwitz, J., and J. Herdejürgen. 1979. *Die Sarkophage der westlichen Gebiete des Imperium Romanum. Zweiter Teil: Die ravennatischen Sarkophage.* Berlin.

König, I. 1986. "Theoderich d. Gr. und die Kirche S. Stefano zu Verona." *Trierer Theologische Zeitschrift* 95: 132–142.

———. 1997. *Aus der Zeit Theoderichs des Grossen. Einleitung, Text, Übersetzung und Kommentar einer anonymen Quelle.* Darmstadt.

———. 2018. *Edictum Theoderici regis. Das "Gesetzbuch" des Ostgotenkönigs Theoderich des Großen. Lateinisch und Deutsch.* Darmstadt.

Kosiński, R. 2010. *The Emperor Zeno: Religion and Politics.* Krakow.

Kossinna, G. 1912. *Die deutsche Vorgeschichte, eine hervorragend nationale Wissenschaft.* Würzburg.

Kötter, J.-M. 2013. *Zwischen Kaiser und Aposteln. Das Akakianische Schisma (484–519) als kirchlicher Ordnungskonflikt der Spätantike.* Stuttgart.

———. 2020. "Katholische Geistliche—homöischer König. Gedanken zu konfessioneller Differenz und politischer Kooperation." In Wiemer 2020a, 175–192.

Kragl, F. 2020. "(K)Ein Gote? Theoderich und die Heldensage der Germanen." In Wiemer 2020a, 369–392.

Kraus, F. F. 1928. *Die Münzen Odovacars und des Ostgotenreiches in Italien.* Halle.

Krause, J.-U. 1987a. *Spätantike Patronatsformen im Westen des Römischen Reiches.* Munich.

———. 1987b. "Der spätantike Städtepatronat." *Chiron* 17: 1–57.

———. 1995. *Witwen und Waisen im Römischen Reich.* 4 vols. Stuttgart.

———. 2014. *Gewalt und Kriminalität in der Spätantike.* Munich.

Krause, J.-U., and C. Witschel, eds. 2006. *Die Stadt in der Spätantike—Niedergang oder Wandel?* Stuttgart.

Krautheimer, R. 1937. *Corpus basilicarum christianarum Romae (IV–IX sec.).* Vol. 1. Vatican City.

———. 1973. Review of Heidenreich and Johannes 1971. *Art Bulletin* 55: 288–289.

Krautschick, S. 1983. *Cassiodor und die Politik seiner Zeit.* Bonn.

Krebs, C. B. 2012. *A Most Dangerous Book: Tacitus's* Germania *from the Roman Empire to the Third Reich.* New York.

Kroeschell, K. A. 1969. "Die Treue in der deutschen Rechtsgeschichte." *Studi medievali* (Ser. 3) 10: 465–490.

———. 1986. "Germanisches Recht als Forschungsproblem." In *Festschrift für Hans Thieme zu seinem 80. Geburtstag,* ed. K. A. Kroeschell, 3–19. Sigmaringen.

———. 1989. "Die *Germania* in der deutschen Rechts und Verfassungsgeschichte." In Jankuhn and Timpe 1989, 189–215.

———. 1995. *Studien zum frühen und mittelalterlichen Recht.* Berlin.

Krumpholz, H. 1992. *Über sozialstaatliche Aspekte in der Novellengesetzgebung Justinians.* Bonn.

Kulikowski, M. 2004. *Late Roman Spain and Its Cities.* Baltimore.

———. 2006a. "The Late Roman City in Spain." In Krause and Witschel 2006, 129–152.

———. 2006b. "Constantine and the Northern Barbarians." In *The Cambridge Companion to the Age of Constantine*, 2nd ed., ed. N. Lenski, 347–376. Cambridge, UK.

———. 2007. *Rome's Gothic Wars from the Third Century to Alaric.* Cambridge, UK.

———. 2017. "Urban Prefects in Bronze." *Journal of Late Antiquity* 10: 3–41.

La Rocca, C. 1993. "Una prudente maschera 'Antiqua': La politica edilizia di Teoderico." In CISAM 1993, 1:451–515.

La Rocca, A., and F. Oppedisano. 2016. *Il Senato romano nell'Italia ostrogota.* Rome.

Lacerenza, G. 2019. "Painted Inscriptions and Graffiti in the Jewish Catacombs of Venosa: An Annotated Inventory." *Annali Sezione Orientale* 79: 275–305.

Lackner, W. 1972. "Übersehene Nachrichten zur Kirchenpolitik Hunerichs und Odoakars im *Synaxarium ecclesiae Constantinopolitanae*." *Historia* 21: 762–764.

Lafferty, S. D. W. 2010. "Law and Society in Ostrogothic Italy: Evidence from the *Edictum Theoderici*." *Journal of Late Antiquity* 3: 337–364.

———. 2013. *Law and Society in the Age of Theoderic the Great. A Study of the* Edictum Theoderici. Cambridge, UK.

Lamma, P. 1951. *Teoderico.* Brescia.

Langgärtner, G. 1964. *Die Gallienpolitik der Päpste im 5. und 6. Jahrhundert, eine Studie über den apostolischen Vikariat von Arles.* Bonn.

Langsdorff, E. de. 1847. "Théodoric et Boëce." *Revue des Deux Mondes* 17: 827–860.

Laniado, A. 2015. "Aspar and His *phoideratoi*: John Malalas on a Special Relationship." In Roberto and Mecella 2015, 325–344.

Lapeyre, G. G. 1929. *Saint Fulgence de Ruspe: Un évêque catholique africain sous la domination vandale. Essai historique.* Paris.

Lavan, L. 1999. "Residences of Late Antique Governors: A Gazetteer." *Antiquité Tardive* 7: 135–164.

———. 2001. "The *praetoria* of Civil Governors in Late Antiquity." In *Recent Research in Late Antique Urbanism*, ed. L. Lavan, 39–56. Portsmouth, RI.

———. 2003. "Christianity, the City, and the End of Antiquity." *Journal of Roman Archaeology* 16: 705–710.

Lenel, O. 1906. "Zur exceptio annalis Italici contractus." *Zeitschrift für Rechtsgeschichte, Romanistische Abteilung* 27: 71–82.

———. 1927. *Das Edictum perpetuum. Ein Versuch zu seiner Wiederherstellung.* Leipzig.

Lenski, N. 1995. "The Date of the Gothic Civil War and the Date of the Gothic Conversion." *Greek, Roman and Byzantine Studies* 36: 51–87.

———. 1997. "*Initium mali Romano imperio*: Contemporary Reactions to the Battle of Adrianople." *Transactions of the American Philological Association* 127: 129–168.

———. 2001. "Evidence for the *audientia episcopalis* in the New Letters of Augustine." In *Law, Society and Authority in Late Antiquity*, ed. R. W. Mathisen, 83–97. Oxford.

———. 2002. *Failure of Empire: Valens and the Roman State in the Fourth Century A.D.* Berkeley, CA.

Leopold, J. W. 1986. "*Consolando per edicta*: Cassiodorus, *Variae*, 4, 50 and Imperial Consolations for Natural Catastrophes." *Latomus* 45: 816–836.

Lepelley, C. 1961. "Saint Léon le Grand et la cité romaine." *Revue des Sciences Religieuses* 35: 130–150.

——. 1983. "*Quot curiales, tot tyranni*: L'image du décurion oppresseur au Bas-Empire." In *Crise et redressement dans les provinces européennes de l'Empire (milieu du IIIe–milieu du IVe siècle): Actes du Colloque de Strasbourg (décembre 1981)*, ed. E. Frézouls, 143–156. Strasbourg.

——. 1990. "Un éloge nostalgique de la cité classique dans les *Variae* de Cassiodore." In *Haut Moyen Âge: Culture, éducation et société. Études offertes à Pierre Riché*, ed. M. Sot, 33–47. Nanterre.

——. 1996a. "La survie de l'idée de cité républicaine en Italie au début du VIe siècle, dans un édit d'Athalaric rédigé par Cassiodore (*Variae*, IX, 2)." In Lepelley 1996b, 71–83.

——, ed. 1996b. *La fin de la cité antique et le début de la cité médiévale de la fin du IIIe siècle à l'avènement de Charlemagne*. Bari.

——. 2001. "Le nivellement juridique du monde romain à partir du IIIe siècle et la marginalisation des droits locaux." *Mélanges de l'École française de Rome. Moyen Âge* 113: 839–856.

Leppin, H. 1998. "Ein 'Spätling der Aufklärung': Otto Seeck und der Untergang der antiken Welt." In Kneissl and Losemann 1998, 472–491.

——. 2003. *Theodosius der Große. Auf dem Weg zum christlichen Imperium*. Darmstadt.

——. 2010. "Truppenergänzungen in einer außergewöhnlichen Situation: Theodosius der Große und die Rekrutierungen nach Adrianopel." In *Die Verwaltung der kaiserzeitlichen römischen Armee. Studien für Hartmut Wolff*, ed. A. Eich, 188–201. Stuttgart.

——. 2011. *Justinian. Das christliche Experiment*. Stuttgart.

Leppin, H., S. Ristow, A. Breitenbach, and A. Weckwerth. 2010. "Mailand." In RAC XXIII, 1156–1202.

Leven, K.-H. 1987. "Die 'Justinianische' Pest." *Jahrbuch des Instituts für Geschichte der Medizin der Robert Bosch-Stiftung* 6: 137–161.

Licandro, O. 2013. *Edictum Theoderici: Un misterioso caso librario del Cinquecento*. Rome.

Liebeschuetz, J. H. W. G. 1993. *Barbarians and Bishops: Army, Church, and State in the Age of Arcadius and Chrysostom*. Oxford.

——. 1996. "The Romans Demilitarised: The Evidence of Procopius." *Scripta Classica Israelica* 15: 230–239.

——. 1997. "Cities, Taxes and the Accommodation of the Barbarians: The Theories of Durliat and Goffart." In *Kingdoms of the Empire: The Integration of Barbarians in Late Antiquity*, ed. W. Pohl, 135–151. Leiden.

——. 2001. *The Decline and Fall of the Roman City*. Oxford

——. 2003. "Late Antiquity, the Rejection of 'Decline,' and Multiculturalism." In *Atti del XIV Convegno Internazionale in memoria di Guglielmo Nocera*, ed. ARC, 639–652. Naples.

——. 2004. "The Birth of Late Antiquity." *Antiquité Tardive* 12: 253–261.

——. 2006a. *Decline and Change in Late Antiquity: Religion, Barbarians and Their Historiography*. Aldershot.

——. 2006b. "Transformation and Decline: Are the Two Really Incompatible?" In Krause and Witschel 2006, 463–484.

——. 2007. "The Debate about the Ethnogenesis of the Germanic Tribes." In *From Rome to Constantinople. Studies in Honour of Averil Cameron*, ed. H. Amirav and B. ter haar Romeny, 341–355. Leuven.

———. 2011a. "Making a Gothic History: Does the Getica of Jordanes Preserve Genuinely Gothic Traditions?" *Journal of Late Antiquity* 4: 185–216.

———. 2011b. "Why Did Jordanes Write the *Getica*?" *Antiquité Tardive* 19: 295–302.

———. 2013. "*Habitus Barbarus*: Did Barbarians Look Different from Romans?" In Porena and Rivière 2012, 13–28.

———. 2015. *East and West in Late Antiquity: Invasion, Settlement, Ethnogenesis and Conflicts of Religion*. Leiden.

Liebs, D. 1987. *Die Jurisprudenz im spätantiken Italien (260–640 n. Chr.)*. Berlin.

———. 2002. *Römische Jurisprudenz in Gallien (2. bis 8. Jahrhundert)*. Berlin.

———. 2015. Review of Lafferty 2013. *Zeitschrift für Rechtsgeschichte, Romanistische Abteilung* 132: 560–570.

Lienert, E., ed. 2008. *Dietrich-Testimonien des 6. bis 16. Jahrhunderts*. Tübingen.

———. 2015. *Mittelhochdeutsche Heldenepik. Eine Einführung*. Berlin.

Lieu, S. N. C. 1992. *Manichaeism in the Later Roman Empire and Medieval China*. 2nd ed. Tübingen. (1st ed. 1985.)

Ligt, L. de. 1993. *Fairs and Markets in the Roman Empire: Economic and Social Aspects of Periodic Trade in a Pre-Industrial Society*. Amsterdam.

Lillington-Martin, C., and E. Turquois, eds. 2017. *Procopius of Caesarea: Literary and Historical Interpretations*. Abingdon.

Linder, A. 1987. *The Jews in Roman Imperial Legislation*. Detroit, MI.

———. 1998. *Jews in the Legal Sources of the Early Middle Ages*. Detroit, MI.

Lippold, A. 1973. "Theodosius I." In RE Suppl. XIII, 837–961.

Lizzi Testa, R., ed. 2006. *Le trasformazioni delle élites in età tardoantica: Atti del Convegno Internazionale Perugia, 15–16 marzo 2004*. Rome.

———. 2016a. "Bishops, Ecclesiastical Organization and the Ostrogothic Regime." In Arnold, Bjornlie, and Sessa 2016, 451–479.

———. 2016b. "Mapping the Church and Asceticism in Ostrogothic Italy." In Arnold, Bjornlie, and Sessa 2016, 480–502.

Lo Cascio, E. 2013. "La popolazione di Roma prima e dopo il 410." In *The Sack of Rome in 410 AD: The Event, Its Context and Its Impact*, ed. J. Lipps, C. Machado, and P. von Rummel, 411–422. Wiesbaden.

Löhlein, G. 1932. *Die Alpen- und Italienpolitik der Merowinger im VI. Jahrhundert*. Erlangen.

Löhr, W. A. 1986. *Die Entstehung der homöischen und der homöusianischen Kirchenpartei. Studien zur Synodalgeschichte des 4. Jahrhunderts*. Bonn.

Lorentz, F. von. 1935. "Theoderich—nicht Iustinian." *Römische Mitteilungen* 50: 339–347.

Loseby, S. T. 1992. "Marseille: A Late Antique Success Story?" *Journal of Roman Studies* 82: 165–185.

Lotter, F. 2012. "Die kaiserzeitliche Judengesetzgebung von Konstantin bis zur Veröffentlichung von Justinians Novelle 146 (553)." *Aschkenas* 22: 247–390.

Löwe, H. 1948. "Cassiodor." *Romanische Forschungen* 60: 420–446.

———. 1952a. "Von Theoderich dem Großen bis zu Karl dem Großen." *Deutsches Archiv für Erforschung des Mittelalters* 9: 353–401.

———. 1952b. "Theoderich der Große und Papst Johann I." *Historisches Jahrbuch* 72: 83–100.

———. 1961. "Theoderichs Gepidensieg im Winter 488/489. Eine historisch-geographische Studie." In *Historische Forschungen und Probleme. Festschrift für Peter Rassow*, ed. K. E. Born, 1–16. Wiesbaden.

———. 1991. "Vermeintlich gotische Überlieferungsreste bei Cassiodor und Jordanes." In *Ex ipsis rerum documentis. Beiträge zur Mediävistik. Festschrift für Harald Zimmermann zum 65. Geburtstag*, ed. K. Herbers et al., 17–30. Sigmaringen.

Lozovsky, N. 2016. "Intellectual Culture and Literary Practices." In Arnold, Bjornlie, and Sessa 2016, 316–349.

Lund, A. A. 1995. *Germanenideologie im National sozialismus*. Heidelberg.

Lütkenhaus, W. 1998. *Constantius III. Studien zu seiner Tätigkeit und Stellung im Westreich 411–421*. Bonn.

Maas, M., ed. 2005. *The Cambridge Companion to the Age of Justinian*. Cambridge, UK.

MacCormack, S. 1981. *Art and Ceremony in Late Antiquity*. Berkeley, CA.

MacGeorge, P. 2002. *Late Roman Warlords*. Oxford.

Machado, C. 2006. "Building the Past: Monuments and Memory in the *Forum Romanum*." In *Social and Political Life in Late Antiquity*, ed. W. Bowden, A. Gutteridge, and C. Machado, 157–194. Leiden.

———. 2012a. "Aristocratic Houses and the Making of Late Antique Rome and Constantinople." In Grig and Kelly 2012, 136–158.

———. 2012b. "Between Memory and Oblivion: The End of the Roman *domus*." In Behrwald and Witschel 2012, 111–138.

———. 2016a. "Italy." In Smith and Ward-Perkins 2016, 43–55.

———. 2016b. "Rome." In Smith and Ward-Perkins 2016, 121–135.

———. 2019. *Urban Space and Aristocratic Power in Late Antiquity, AD 270–535*. Oxford.

Mączyńska, M. 2007. "Wielbark-Kultur." In RGA XXXIV, 1–20.

Mączyńska, M., et al. 2016. Das frühmittelalterliche Gräberfeld Almalyk-Dere am Fusse des Mangup auf der Südwestkrim. Mainz.

Maenchen-Helfen, O. J. 1978. *Die Welt der Hunnen. Eine Analyse ihrer historischen Dimension. Deutschsprachige Ausgabe besorgt von R. Göbl*. Vienna.

Maier, G. 2005. *Amtsträger und Herrscher in der Gothia Romana. Vergleichende Untersuchungen zu den Institutionen der ostgermanischen Völkerwanderungsreiche*. Stuttgart.

Malineau, V. 2006. "Le théâtre dans les cités de l'Italie tardo-antique." In Ghilardi, Goddard, and Porena 2006, 187–203.

Mallan, C., and C. Davenport. 2015. "Dexippus and the Gothic Invasions: Interpreting the New Vienna Fragment (Codex Vindobonensis Hist. gr. 73, ff. 192v–193r)." *Journal of Roman Studies* 105: 203–226.

Malnati, L., et al. 2007. "Nuovi scavi archeologici a Classe: Campagne 2004–2005." In Augenti and Bertelli 2007, 33–38.

Manacorda, D. 2001. *Crypta Balbi: Archeologia e storia di un paesaggio urbano*. Milan.

Mancinelli, A. 2001. "Sul centralismo amministrativo di Teodorico: Il governo della Spagna in età ostrogota." In *XII Convegno Internazionale in memoria di André Chastagnol*, ed. ARC, 217–263. Naples.

Manso, J. K. F. 1824. *Geschichte des Ost-Gothischen Reiches in Italien.* Breslau.

Marano, Y. A. 2015. " 'Watered . . . with the Life-Giving Wave': Aqueducts and Water in Ostrogothic Italy." In *Ownership and Exploitation of Land and Natural Resources in the Roman World,* ed. P. Erdkamp, K. Verboven, and A. Zuiderhoek, 150–169. Oxford.

Maraval, P. 2001. "Die Rezeption des Chalcedonense im Osten." In L. Piétri 2001a, 120–157.

Marazzi, F. 2007. "The Last Rome: From the End of the Fifth to the End of the Sixth Century." In Barnish and Marazzi 2007, 279–302.

———. 2016. "Ostrogothic Cities." In Arnold, Bjornlie, and Sessa 2016, 98–120.

Marcone, A. 1985. "A proposito della 'civilitas' nel tardo impero: Una nota." *Rivista Storica Italiana* 97: 969–982.

Marini, G. 1805. *I papiri diplomatici, raccolti ed illustrati.* Rome.

Markus, R. A. 1989. "The Legacy of Pelagius: Orthodoxy, Heresy and Conciliation." In *The Making of Orthodoxy: Essays in Honour of Henry Chadwick,* ed. R. Williams, 214–234. Cambridge, UK.

———. 2009. "Between Marrou and Brown: Transformations of Late Antique Christianity." In Rousseau 2009, 1–14.

Marrou, H.-I. 1931. "Autour de la bibliothèque du pape Agapit." *Mélanges d'archéologie et d'histoire* 48: 124–169.

———. 1976. "La patrie de Jean Cassien." In H.-I. Marrou, *Patristique et humanisme: Mélanges,* 345–361. Paris.

Martin, G. 2006. *Dexipp von Athen. Edition, Übersetzung und begleitende Studien.* Tübingen.

Martin, R. 1976. "Introduction." In *Palladius, Traité d'agriculture.* Vol. 1: *Livres I et II,* vii–lxvii. Paris.

Martindale, J. R. 1980. *The Prosopography of the Later Roman Empire.* Vol. 2: AD 395–527. Cambridge, UK.

———. 1992. *The Prosopography of the Later Roman Empire.* Vol. 3: AD 527–641. Cambridge, UK.

Martínez Jiménez, A. J. 2011. "Monte Barro: An Ostrogothic Fortified Site in the Alps." *Assemblage* 11: 34–46.

Martus, S. 2009. *Die Brüder Grimm. Eine Biographie.* Berlin.

Marušič, B. 1967. *Das spätantike und byzantinische Pula.* Pula.

Mateos, P. 2000. "*Augusta Emerita,* de capital de la *diocesis Hispaniarum* a sede temporal visigoda." In Ripoll López and Gurt 2000, 491–520.

Mathisen, R. W. 1989. *Ecclesiastical Factionalism and Religious Controversy in Fifth-Century Gaul.* Washington, DC.

———. 1992. "Fifth-Century Visitors to Italy: Business or Pleasure?" In *Fifth-Century Gaul: A Crisis of Identity?,* ed. J. F. Drinkwater and H. Elton, 228–238. Cambridge, UK.

———. 1993. *Roman Aristocrats in Barbarian Gaul: Strategies for Survival in an Age of Transition.* Austin, TX.

———. 1997. "Barbarian Bishops and the Churches 'in barbaricis gentibus' during Late Antiquity." *Speculum* 72: 664–697.

———. 2003. " '*Qui genus, unde patres?*' The Case of Arcadius Placidus Magnus Felix." *Medieval Prosopography* 24: 56–73.

———. 2004. "Emperors, Priests, and Bishops: Military Chaplains in the Roman Empire." In *The Sword of the Lord: Military Chaplains from the First to the Twenty-First Century*, ed. D. L. Bergen, 29–43. Notre Dame, IN

———. 2009. "Ricimer's Church in Rome: How an Arian Barbarian Prospered in a Nicene World." In *The Power of Religion in Late Antiquity*, ed. A. Cain and N. Lenski, 307–326. Farnham.

———. 2013a. "Clovis, Anastasius, and Political Status in 508 C.E.: The Frankish Aftermath of the Battle of Vouillé." In Mathisen and Shanzer 2013, 79–110.

———. 2013b. "Vouillé, Voulon, and the Location of the Campus Vogladensis." In Mathisen and Shanzer 2013, 43–62.

———. 2014. "Barbarian 'Arian' Clergy, Church Organization, and Church Practices." In Berndt and Steinacher 2014, 145–192.

Mathisen, R. W., and D. Shanzer, eds. 2013. *The Battle of Vouillé: Where France Began.* Berlin.

Matthews, J. F. 1975. *Western Aristocracies and Imperial Court A.D. 364–425.* Oxford.

———. 1981. "Anicius Manlius Severinus Boethius." In *Boethius: His Life, Thought and Influence*, ed. M. Gibson, 15–43. Oxford.

———. 1989. *The Roman Empire of Ammianus.* London.

———. 2000a. *Laying Down the Law: A Study of the Theodosian Code.* New Haven, CT.

———. 2000b. "Roman Law and Barbarian Identity in the Late Roman West." In *Ethnicity and Culture in Late Antiquity*, ed. S. Mitchell and G. Greatrex, 31–44. London.

———. 2001. "Interpreting the *Interpretationes* of the *Breviarium*." In *Law, Society, and Authority in Late Antiquity*, ed. R. Mathisen, 11–33. Oxford.

———. 2010. *Roman Perspectives: Studies in the Social, Political and Cultural History of the First to Fifth Centuries.* Swansea.

Mayer, T., ed. 1956. *Das Königtum. Seine geistigen und rechtlichen Grundlagen.* Sigmaringen.

McCormick, M. 1977. "Odoacer, Emperor Zeno and the Rugian Victory Legation." *Byzantion* 47: 212–222.

———. 1987. *Eternal Victory: Triumphal Rulership in Late Antiquity, Byzantium, and the Early Medieval West.* New York.

———. 2001. *Origins of the European Economy: Communications and Commerce, A.D. 300–900.* Cambridge, UK.

McEvoy, M. A. 2013. *Child Emperor Rule in the Late Roman West, AD 367–455.* Oxford.

———. 2016. "Becoming Roman? The Not-So-Curious Case of Aspar and the Ardaburii." *Journal of Late Antiquity* 9: 483–511.

———. 2017. "Shadow Emperors and the Choice of Rome (455–476 AD)." *Antiquité Tardive* 25: 95–112.

McLynn, N. 1994. *Ambrose of Milan: Church and Court in a Christian Capital.* Berkeley, CA.

———. 1996. "From Palladius to Maximinus: Passing the Arian Torch." *Journal of Early Christian Studies* 4: 477–493.

———. 2008. "Crying Wolf: The Pope and the Lupercalia." *Journal of Roman Studies* 98: 161–175.

Mecella, L. 2013. *Dexippo di Athene: Testimonianze e frammenti*. Rome.

Meier, M. 2003. *Das andere Zeitalter Justinians. Kontingenzerfahrung und Kontingenzbewältigung im 6. Jahrhundert n. Chr*. Göttingen.

———. 2009. *Anastasios I. Die Entstehung des byzantinischen Reiches*. Stuttgart.

———. 2012. "Ostrom—Byzanz, Spätantike—Mittelalter. Überlegungen zum 'Ende' der Antike im Osten des Römischen Reiches." *Millennium* 9: 187–254.

———. 2014. "Nachdenken über 'Herrschaft.' Die Bedeutung des Jahres 476." In Meier and Patzold 2014, 143–216.

———. 2017. "Die Spätantike, zeitlich und räumlich neu gefasst. Eine Zwischenbilanz aktueller Suchbewegungen." *Historische Zeitschrift* 304: 686–706.

———. 2019. *Geschichte der Völkerwanderung. Europa, Asien und Afrika vom 3. bis zum 8. Jahrhundert n. Chr*. Munich.

———. 2020. "The Justinianic Plague: An 'Inconsequential Pandemic'? A Reply." *Medizinhistorisches Journal* 55: 172–199.

Meier, M., and F. Montinaro, eds. 2022. *A Companion to Procopius*. Leiden.

Meier, M., and S. Patzold, eds. 2014. *Chlodwigs Welt. Organisation von Herrschaft um 500*. Stuttgart.

———. 2021. *Gene und Geschichte. Was die Archäogenetik zur Geschichtsforschung beitragen kann*. Stuttgart.

Meier-Welcker, H. 1952–1953. "Die Simonie im frühen Mittelalter." *Zeitschrift für Kirchengeschichte* 64: 61–93.

Merrills, A., and A. Miles. 2010. *The Vandals*. Oxford.

Messmer, H. 1960. *Hispania-Idee und Gotenmythos. Zu den Voraussetzungen des traditionellen vaterländischen Geschichtsbilds im spanischen Mittelalter*. Zurich.

Metcalf, D. M. 1969. *The Origins of the Anastasian Currency Reform*. Amsterdam.

Metlich, M. A. 2004. *The Ostrogothic Coinage in Italy from A.D. 476*. London.

Millar, F. 1992. *The Emperor in the Roman World (31 BC–AD 337)*. 2nd ed. London. (1st ed. 1977.)

Miller, K. 1916. *Itineraria Romana. Römische Reisewege an der Hand der Tabula Peutingeriana dargestellt*. Stuttgart.

Millet, V. 2008. *Germanische Heldendichtung im Mittelalter. Eine Einführung*. Berlin.

Mirković, M. 2007. *Moesia Superior. Eine Provinz an der mittleren Donau*. Mainz.

Mirković, M., A. Milošević, and V. Popović. 1971. *Sirmium—Its History from the 1st Century A.D. to 582 A.D.* Belgrade.

Mitthoff, F., G. Martin, and J. Grusková, eds. 2020. *Empire in Crisis: Gothic Invasions and Roman Historiography. Beiträge zu einer Internationalen Tagung zu den Wiener Dexipp-Fragmenten (Dexippus Vindobonensis), Wien, 3.–6. Mai 2017*. Vienna.

Mócsy, A. 1974. *Pannonia and Upper Moesia: A History of the Middle Danube Provinces of the Roman Empire*. London.

Modéran, Y. 2001. "Afrika und die Verfolgung durch die Vandalen." In L. Piétri 2001a, 264–299.

——. 2002. "L'établissement territorial des Vandales en Afrique." *Antiquité Tardive* 10: 87–122.

——. 2003. "Une guerre de religion: Les deux Églises d'Afrique à l'époque vandale." *Antiquité Tardive* 11: 21–44.

——. 2012. "Confiscations, expropriations et redistributions foncières dans l'Afrique vandale." In Porena and Rivière 2012, 129–156.

Momigliano, A. 1955. "Cassiodorus and Italian Culture." *Proceedings of the British Academy* 41: 207–245.

——. 1973. "La caduta senza rumore di un impero nel 476 d. C." *Annali della Scuola Normale Superiore di Pisa*. Serie 3, vol. 3, fasc. 2: 397–418.

——. 1978. "Cassiodoro." In *Dizionario Biografico degli Italiani*. Vol. 21: *Caruso–Castelnuovo*, ed. L. Agnello et al., 494–504.

Mommsen, T., ed. 1882. *Iordanis Romana et Getica*. Berlin.

——. 1889. "Ostgothische Studien." *Neues Archiv* 14: 225–249 and 453–544.

——. 1910. *Gesammelte Schriften*. Vol. 6: *Historische Schriften*. Berlin.

Moorhead, J. 1983a. "The Last Years of Theoderic." *Historia* 32: 106–120.

——. 1983b. "Italian Loyalties during Justinian's Gothic War." *Byzantion* 53: 575–596.

——. 1984. "The Decii under Theoderic." *Historia* 33: 107–115.

——. 1987. "*Libertas* and *Nomen Romanum* in Ostrogothic Italy." *Latomus* 46: 161–168.

——. 1992. *Theoderic in Italy*. Oxford.

——. 1999. "Cassiodorus on the Goths in Ostrogothic Italy." *Romanobarbarica* 16: 241–259.

——. 2000. "Totila the Revolutionary." *Historia* 49: 382–386.

——. 2006. "The Word *modernus*." *Latomus* 65: 425–433.

Mordechai, L., and M. Eisenberg. 2019. "Rejecting Catastrophe: The Case of the Justinianic Plague." *Past & Present* 244: 3–50.

Moreau, D. 2006. "Les patrimoines de l'église romaine jusqu'à la mort de Grégoire Le Grand: Dépouillement et réflexions préliminaires à une étude sur le rôle temporel des évêques de Rome durant l'antiquité la plus tardive." *Antiquité Tardive* 14: 79–93.

——. 2015. " 'Ipsis diebus Bonifatius, zelo et dolo ductus': The Root Causes of the Double Papal Election of 22 September 530." In *The Bishop of Rome in Late Antiquity*, ed. G. D. Dunn, 177–195. Farnham.

Morosi, R. 1975–1976. "L'attività del 'Praefectus Praetorio' nel Regno Ostrogoto attraverso le 'Variae' di Cassiodoro." *Humanitas* 27–28: 71–94.

——. 1977. "L'*officium* del prefetto del pretorio nel VI secolo." *Romanobarbarica* 2: 104–148.

——. 1979–1980. "Il *princeps officii* e *la schola agentum in rebus*." *Humanitas* 31–32: 23–70.

——. 1981a. "I 'Comitiaci,' funzionari romani nell'Italia ostrogota." *Quaderni catanesi di studi classici e medievali* 3: 77–111.

——. 1981b. "I *saiones*, speciali agenti di polizia presso i Goti." *Athenaeum* 59: 150–165.

Morton, C. 1982. "Marius of Avenches, the *Excerpta Valesiana*, and the Death of Boethius." *Traditio* 38: 107–136.

Muhlack, U. 1989. "Die 'Germania' im deutschen Nationalbewusstsein vor dem 19. Jahrhundert." In Jankuhn and Timpe 1989, 128–154.

Müllenhoff, K. 1870–1908. *Deutsche Altertumskunde*. 5 vols. Berlin.

Müller, H., D. Weber, and C. Weidmann. 2008. *Collatio Augustini cum Pascentio. Einleitung, Text, Übersetzung*. Vienna.

Müller, K. E. 1968–1980. *Geschichte der antiken Ethnographie und ethnologischen Theoriebildung*. 2 vols. Wiesbaden.

Munkhammar, L. 2011. *The Silver Bible: Origins and History of the* Codex Argenteus. Uppsala.

Näf, B. 1990. "Das Zeitbewusstsein des Ennodius und der Untergang Roms." *Historia* 39: 100–123.

———. 1995. *Senatorisches Standesbewußtsein in spätrömischer Zeit*. Fribourg.

———. 2017. "Wilhelm Ensslin und die Spätantike." In *In solo barbarico . . . Das Seminar für Alte Geschichte der Philipps-Universität Marburg von seinen Anfängen bis in die 1960er Jahre*, ed. V. Losemann and K. Ruffing, 187–211. Münster.

Nagy, T. 1971. "The Last Century of Pannonia in the Judgement of a New Monograph." *Acta Antiqua Academiae Scientiarum Hungaricae* 19: 299–345.

Naudet, J. 1811. *Histoire de l'établissement, des progrès et de la décadence de la monarchie des Goths en Italie*. Paris.

Neckel, G. 1944. *Vom Germanentum. Ausgewählte Aufsätze und Vorträge*. Leipzig.

Nehlsen, H. 1969. Review of Vismara 1967. *Zeitschrift für Rechtsgeschichte, Germanistische Abteilung* 86: 246–260.

———. 1972. *Sklavenrecht zwischen Antike und Mittelalter. Germanisches und römisches Recht in den germanischen Rechtsaufzeichnungen*. Vol. 1: *Ostgoten, Westgoten, Franken, Langobarden*. Göttingen.

———. 1978. "Lex Burgundionum." In HRG II, 1901–1915.

———. 1984. "Codex Euricianus." In RGA V, 42–47.

Neugebauer, O. 1981. "On the Spanish 'Era.'" *Chiron* 11: 371–380.

Neumann, G., and H. Seemann, eds. 1992. *Beiträge zum Verständnis der Germania des Tacitus. Teil II*. Göttingen.

Neumann, H. 1939. *Theoderich der Große. Der Herr Italiens*. Bad Langensalza.

Nicolet, C. 2003. *La fabrique d'une nation: La France entre Rome et les Germains*. Paris.

Nipperdey, T. 1968. "Nationalidee und Nationaldenkmal in Deutschland im 19. Jahrhundert." *Historische Zeitschrift* 206: 529–585.

Nissen, H. 1883–1902. *Italische Landeskunde*. 2 vols. Berlin.

Noble, T. F. X. 1993. "Theoderic and the Papacy." In CISAM 1993, 395–423.

Noethlichs, K. L. 1981. *Beamtentum und Dienstvergehen. Zur Staatsverwaltung in der Spätantike*. Wiesbaden.

———. 1996. *Das Judentum und der römische Staat. Minderheitenpolitik im antiken Rom*. Darmstadt.

———. 2001. "Iustinianus (Kaiser)." In RAC XIX, 668–763.

Nollé, J. 1982. *Nundinas instituere et habere. Epigraphische Zeugnisse zur Einrichtung und Gestaltung von ländlichen Märkten in Afrika und in der Provinz Asia*. Hildesheim.

Norton, P. 2007. *Episcopal Elections 250–600: Hierarchy and Popular Will in Late Antiquity*. Oxford.

Noy, D. 1997. "Writing in Tongues: The Use of Greek, Latin and Hebrew in Jewish Inscriptions from Roman Italy." *Journal of Jewish Studies* 48: 300–311.

——. 2000. "The Jews in Italy in the First to Sixth Centuries C.E." In *The Jews of Italy: Memory and Identity*, ed. B. D. Cooperman and B. Garvin, 47–64. Bethesda, MD.

——. 2011. "Jewish Priests and Synagogue Officials in the Greco-Roman Diaspora of Late Antiquity." In *Priests and State in the Roman World*, ed. J. Richardson and F. Santangelo, 313–332. Stuttgart.

O'Donnell, J. J. 1979. *Cassiodorus*. Berkeley, CA.

——. 1981. "Liberius the Patrician." *Traditio* 37: 31–72.

Offergeld, T. 2001. Reges pueri. *Das Königtum Minderjähriger im frühen Mittelalter*. Munich.

O'Flynn, J. M. 1983. *Generalissimos of the Western Roman Empire*. Edmonton.

Olbrich, K. 2013. "Theodoricus Senatus Consulto Rex. Münzprägung zwischen römischer und deutscher Rechtsgeschichte." *Jahrbuch für Numismatik und Geldgeschichte* 63: 187–197.

Oost, I. 1968. *Galla Placidia Augusta: A Biographical Essay*. Chicago.

Orlandi, S. 2004. *Epigrafia anfiteatrale dell'occidente romano*. Vol. 6: *Roma: Anfiteatri e strutture annesse con una nuova edizione e commento delle iscrizioni del Colosseo*. Rome.

Pabst, A. 1986. Divisio regni. *Der Zerfall des Imperium Romanum in der Sicht der Zeitgenossen*. Bonn.

Pack, E. 1998. "Italia (landeskundlich)." In RAC XVIII, 1049–1202.

Palme, B. 1999. "Die *officia* der Statthalter in der Spätantike. Forschungsstand und Perspektiven." *Antiquité Tardive* 7: 85–133.

Panzram, S. 2014. "Die Iberische Halbinsel um 500—Herrschaft 'am Ende der Welt.' Eine Geschichte in neun Städten." In Meier and Patzold 2014, 449–486.

——. 2015. " 'Hilferufe' aus Hispaniens Städten. Zur Ausbildung einer Metropolitanordnung auf der Iberischen Halbinsel (4.–6. Jahrhundert)." *Historische Zeitschrift* 301: 626–661.

Pastor, W. 1920. *Theoderich, im Leben, in der Kunst, im Ruhm*. Berlin.

Patzold, S. 2014. "Bischöfe, soziale Herkunft und die Organisation lokaler Herrschaft um 500." In Meier and Patzold 2014, 523–544.

Pavirani, P. 1846–1847. *Storia del regno dei Goti in Italia*. 2 vols. Ravenna.

Pazdernik, C. 2005. "Justinianic Ideology and the Power of the Past." In Maas 2005, 185–212.

Peachin, M. 1990. *Roman Imperial Titulature and Chronology, A.D. 235–284*. Amsterdam.

Percival, J. 1969. "P. Ital. 3 and Roman Estate Management." *Latomus* 102: 607–615.

Petrikovits, H. 1981. "Die Spezialisierung des römischen Handwerks II (Spätantike)." *Zeitschrift für Papyrologie und Epigraphik* 43: 285–306.

Pfeilschifter, G. 1896. *Der Ostgotenkönig Theoderich der Große und die katholische Kirche*. Münster.

——. 1910. *Theoderich der Große*. Mainz.

Picotti, G. B. 1931. "Il senato romano e il processo di Boezio." *Archivio storico italiano*, ser. 7, vol. 15: 205–228.

———. 1956. "Osservazioni su alcuni punti della politica religiosa di Teodorico." In CISAM 1956, 173–226.

———. 1958. "I sinodi romani nello scisma laurenziano." In *Studi storici in onore di Gioacchino Volpe per il suo 80 compleanno*, 2:743–786. Florence.

Piétri, C. 1966. "Le Sénat, le peuple chrétien et les partis du cirque à Rome sous le Pape Symmaque (498–514)." *Mélanges de l'École française de Rome* 78: 123–139.

———. 1976. *Roma Christiana: Recherches sur l'Eglise de Rome, son organisation, sa politique, son idéologie de Miltiade à Sixte III (311–440)*. 2 vols. Rome.

———. 1978. "Évergétisme et richesses ecclésiastiques dans l'Italie du IVe à la fin du Ve s.: L'exemple romain." *Ktèma* 3: 317–337.

———. 1981. "Aristocratie et société cléricale dans l'Italie chrétienne au temps d'Odoacre et de Théodoric." *Mélanges de l'École française de Rome* 93: 417–467.

———. 1983. "Les pauvres et la pauvreté dans l'Italie de l'Empire chrétien (IVe siècle)." In *Miscellanea historiae ecclesiasticae: Actes du VIe Colloque de Varsovie 1978*, 267–300. Brussels.

———. 1987. "Jean Talaïa, émule d'Athanase au Ve siècle." In *Alexandrina: Hellénisme, judaïsme et christianisme à Alexandrie. Mélanges offerts à Claude Mondésert*, 277–295. Paris.

———. 1997. *Christiana respublica: Éléments d'une enquête sur le christianisme antique*. 3 vols. Rome.

Piétri, C., Y. Duval, and L. Piétri. 1992. "Peuple chrétien ou *Plebs*: Le rôle des laïcs dans les élections ecclésiastiques en Occident." In *Institutions, société et vie politique dans l'empire romain au IVe siècle ap. J.-C. Actes de la table ronde autour de l'œuvre d'André Chastagnol: Paris, 20–21 janvier 1989*, ed. M. Christol et al., 373–395. Rome.

Piétri, L., ed. 2001a. *Die Geschichte des Christentums. Religion — Politik — Kultur*. Vol. 3: *Der lateinische Westen und der byzantinische Osten (431–642)*. Freiburg.

———. 2001b. "Die wechselvolle Geschichte der Kirchen im westlichen Abendland. B. Gallien." In L. Piétri 2001a, 222–263.

———. 2001c. "Die Durchsetzung des nizänischen Bekenntnisses in Gallien." In L. Piétri 2001a, 343–398.

———. 2002. "Évergetisme chrétien et fondations privées dans l'Italie de l'Antiquité tardive." In *Humana sapit: Études d'Antiquité tardives offerts à Lellia Cracco Ruggini*, ed. J.-M. Carrié and R. Lizzi Testi, 253–263. Turnhout.

Pilhofer, P. 1990. Presbyteron kreitton. *Der Altersbeweis der jüdischen und christlichen Apologeten und seine Vorgeschichte*. Tübingen.

Pirenne, H. 1937. *Mahomet et Charlemagne*. Paris.

Pizzi, A. 1994–1995. "Teoderico nella grande storiografia europea." *Romanobarbarica* 13: 259–282.

Pohl, W. 1980. "Die Gepiden und die *gentes* an der unteren Donau nach dem Zerfall des Attilareiches." In Wolfram and Daim 1980, 239–305.

———, ed. 1998a. *Strategies of Distinction: The Construction of Ethnic Communities 300–800*. Leiden.

——. 1998b. "Telling the Difference: Signs of Ethnic Identity." In Pohl 1998a, 17–69.

——. 1998c. "Gepiden § 3: Historisch." In RGA II, 131–140.

——, ed. 2001a. *Eugippius und Severin. Der Autor, der Text und der Heilige.* Vienna.

——. 2001b. "Langobarden II. Historisches." In RGA XVIII, 61–69.

——. 2001c. "The *Regia* and the *Iring*—Barbarian Places of Power." In *Topographies of Power in the Early Middle Ages*, ed. M. de Jong and F. C. W. Theuws, 439–466. Leiden.

——. ed. 2004. *Die Suche nach den Ursprüngen. Von der Bedeutung des frühen Mittelalters.* Vienna.

——. 2005. *Die Völkerwanderung. Eroberung und Integration.* 2nd ed. Stuttgart. (1st ed. 2002.)

——. 2010. *Die Germanen.* 2nd ed. Munich. (1st ed. 2004.)

——. 2013. "Introduction—Strategies of Identification. A Methodological Profile." In *Strategies of Identification: Ethnicity and Religion in Early Medieval Europe*, ed. W. Pohl and G. Heydemann, 1–64. Turnhout.

——. 2014. "Romanness: A Multiple Identity and Its Changes." *Early Medieval Europe* 22: 406–418.

——. 2018. "Von der Ethnogenese zur Identitätsforschung." In *Neue Wege der Frühmittelalterforschung. Bilanz und Perspektiven*, ed. W. Pohl et al., 9–34. Vienna.

——. 2020. "Gotische Identitäten." In Wiemer 2020a, 315–340.

Popa, A. 1997. "Die Siedlung Sobari, Kr. Soroca (Republik Moldau)." *Germania* 75: 119–131.

Popović, I. 2007. "Sirmium (Sremska Mitrovica)—Residenzstadt der Römischen Kaiser und Stätte der Frühen Christen." In *Roms Erbe auf dem Balkan. Spätantike Kaiservillen und Stadtanlagen in Serbien*, ed. U. Brandl and M. Vasić, 17–32. Mainz.

Popović, I., and S. Ferjancić. 2013. "A New Inscription from Sirmium and the Basilica of St. Anastasia." *Starinar* 63: 101–114.

Porena, P. 2012a. *L'insediamento degli ostrogoti in Italia.* Rome.

——. 2012b. "Voci e silenzi sull'insediamento degli Ostrogoti in Italia." In Porena and Rivière 2012, 227–278.

Porena, P., and Y. Rivière, eds. 2012. *Expropriations et confiscations dans les royaumes barbares: Une approche régionale.* Rome.

Potter, T. W. 1992. *Roman Italy.* 2nd ed. London.

Pottier, B. 2006. "Entre les villes et les campagnes: Le banditisme en Italie du IVe au VIe siècle." In Ghilardi, Goddard, and Porena 2006, 251–266.

Prestel, J. 1935. *König Theoderich.* Berlin.

Prinz, F. 1992. "Cassiodor und das Problem christlicher Aufgeklärtheit in der Spätantike." *Historische Zeitschrift* 254: 561–580.

Prostko-Prostyński, J. 2002. "Ursus: Ein ostgotischer Statthalter in Binnen-Norikum?" *Zeitschrift für Papyrologie und Epigraphik* 139: 297–302.

——. 2008. "Novae in Times of Theodoric the Amal." In *Novae: Legionary Fortress and Late Antique Town. A Companion to the Study of Novae*, ed. T. Derda, P. Dyczek, and J. Kolendo, 141–157. Warsaw.

——. 2019. *Utraeque res publicae: The Emperor Anastasius I's Gothic Policy.* 3rd ed. Posen. (1st ed. 1994.)

Pryor, J., and E. Jeffreys. 2006. *The Age of the Dromon: The Byzantine Navy ca. 500–1204.* Leiden.

Puk, A. 2014. *Das römische Spielewesen in der Spätantike.* Berlin.

R.-Alföldi, M. 1978. "Il medaglione d'oro di Teodorico." *Rivista italiana di numismatica* 80: 133–142. German version in R.-Alföldi 2001, 204–210.

———. 1988. "Das Goldmultiplum Theoderichs des Großen. Neue Überlegungen." *Rivista Italiana di Numismatica* 90: 367–372.

———. 2001. *Gloria Romanorum: Schriften zur Spätantike, zum 75. Geburtstag der Verfasserin am 6. Juni 2001.* Ed. H. Bellen and H. M. von Kaenel. Stuttgart.

Rabello, A. M. 1987–1988. *Giustiniano, ebrei ed samaritani alla luce delle fonti storico letterarie, ecclesiastiche e giuridiche.* 2 vols. Milan.

Rallo Freni, R. A. 1981. *La Paraenesis didascalica di Magno Felice Ennodio con il testo latino e la traduzione.* 2nd ed. Messina. (1st ed. 1970.)

Rance, P. 2005. "Narses and the Battle of Taginae (Busta Gallorum) 552: Procopius and Sixth Century Warfare." *Historia* 54: 424–472.

Ranke, L. von. 1883. *Weltgeschichte. 4. Teil: Das Kaiserthum in Konstantinopel und der Ursprung romanisch-germanischer Königreiche.* Leipzig.

Rebenich, S. 1998. "Otto Seeck, Theodor Mommsen und die 'Römische Geschichte.'" In Kneissl and Losemann 1998, 582–607.

———. 2012. "Monarchie." In RAC XXIX, 1113–1196.

———, ed. 2017. *Monarchische Herrschaft im Altertum.* Berlin.

Rebenich, S., and J. Wienand. 2017. "Monarchische Herrschaft im Altertum. Zugänge und Perspektiven." In Rebenich 2017, 1–42.

Recchia, V. 1978. *Gregorio Magno e la società agricola.* Rome.

Reden, S. von. 2015. *Antike Wirtschaft.* Berlin.

Reemtsma, J. P. 2004. "Untergang. Eine Fußnote zu Felix Dahns 'Kampf um Rom.'" *Rechtsgeschichte* 5: 76–105.

Rehm, W. 1930. *Der Untergang Roms im abendländischen Denken. Ein Beitrag zur Geschichtsschreibung und zum Dekadenzproblem.* Leipzig. (Repr. Darmstadt, 1966.)

Reichert, H. 2008. "Die Sprache der Wandalen in Afrika und 'Auch Römer dürfen *froia arme* für *domine miserere* sagen.'" In H. Müller, Weber, and Weidmann 2008, 145–172.

Reier, H. 1934. *Theoderich der Große. Heldische Geisteshaltung im Spiegel römischer Geschichtsschreibung.* Leipzig.

Reinerth, H., ed. 1940. *Vorgeschichte der deutschen Stämme.* 3 vols. Leipzig.

Reydellet, M. 1995. "Théoderic et la *civilitas.*" In Carile 1995, 285–296.

Richards, J. 1979. *The Popes and the Papacy in the Early Middle Ages 456–752.* Boston.

Riché, P. 1995. *Éducation et culture dans l'Occident barbare, VIe–VIIIe siècles.* 4th ed. Paris. (1st ed. 1962.)

Riedlberger, P. 2020. *Prolegomena zu den spätantiken Konstitutionen. Nebst einer Analyse der erbrechtlichen und verwandten Sanktionen gegen Heterodoxe.* Stuttgart.

Ripoll López, G., and J. Arce Martínez. 2000. "The Transformation and End of Roman 'Villae' in the West (Fourth–Seventh Centuries): Problems and Perspectives." In *Towns and Their Territories between Late Antiquity and the Early Middle Ages,* ed. G. P. Brogiolo, N. Gauthier, and N. J. Christie, 63–114. Leiden.

Ripoll López, G., and J. M. Gurt, eds. 2000. *Sedes regiae (a. 400–800)*. Barcelona.

Roberto, U., and L. Mecella, eds. 2015. *Governare e riformare l'impero al momento della sua divisione: Oriente, Occidente, Illirico*. Rome.

Rocca, S. 1978. "Versus in Benedicti laudem." *Romanobarbarica* 3: 335–364.

Roesch, G. 1978. ΟΝΟΜΑ ΒΑΣΙΛΕΩΣ. *Studien zum offiziellen Gebrauch der Kaisertitel in spätantiker und frühbyzantinischer Zeit*. Vienna.

Rohr, C. 1995. *Der Theoderich-Panegyricus des Ennodius*. Hannover.

Rosen, K. 1982. *Ammianus Marcellinus*. Darmstadt.

———. 2016. *Attila. Der Schrecken der Welt*. Munich.

Rota, S. 2002. *Magno Felice Ennodio: Panegyricus dictus clementissimo regi Theoderico (opusc. 1)*. Rome.

Rouche, M. 1996. *Clovis: Suivi de vingt-et-un documents traduits et commentés*. Paris.

Rousseau, P., ed. 2009. *Transformations of Late Antiquity: Essays for Peter Brown*. Farnham.

Rubin, B. 1953. *Theoderich und Iustinian. Zwei Prinzipien der Mittelmeerpolitik*. Munich.

———. 1960–1995. *Das Zeitalter Justinians*. 2 vols. Munich and Berlin.

Rummel, P. von. 2007. Habitus barbarus. *Kleidung und Repräsentation spätantiker Eliten im 4. und 5. Jahrhundert*. Berlin.

Rutgers, L. V. 2006. "The Jews of Italy, c. 235–638." In *The Cambridge History of Judaism*. Vol. 4: *The Late Roman-Rabbinic Period*, ed. S. Katz, 492–508. Cambridge, UK.

Sainte Marthe, D. de. 1694. *La vie de Cassiodore, chancelier et premier ministre de Théodoric le Grand et de plusieurs rois d'Italie*. Paris.

Saitta, B. 1993. *La* civilitas *di Teoderico: Rigore amministrativo, "tolleranza" religiosa e recupero dell'antico nell'Italia ostrogota*. Rome.

Saletti, C. 1997. *Il regisole di Pavia*. Como.

Sallares, R. 2002. *Malaria and Rome: A History of Malaria in Ancient Italy*. Oxford.

Saller, R. 1994. *Patriarchy, Property and Death in the Roman Family*. Cambridge, UK.

———. 2002. "Framing the Debate over Growth in the Ancient Economy." In *The Ancient Economy*, ed. W. Scheidel and S. von Reden, 251–269. Edinburgh.

Sanchéz Albornoz, C. 1943. *Ruina y extinción del municipio romano en España e instituciones que le reemplazan*. Buenos Aires.

Sannazaro, M. 2015. "Ceti sociali a Como nella produzione epigrafica di V e VI secolo." *Rivista archeologica dell'antica provincia e diocesi di Como* 197: 34–44.

Sarantis, A. 2009. "War and Diplomacy in Pannonia and the Northwest Balkans during the Reign of Justinian: The Gepid Threat and Imperial Responses." *Dumbarton Oaks Papers* 63: 15–40.

———. 2016. *Justinian's Balkan Wars: Campaigns, Diplomacy and Development in Illyricum, Thrace and the Northern World A.D. 527–65*. Liverpool.

———. 2019. "Justinian's Novella 11: Memory and Imperial Propaganda in the Buildup to the Gothic War." *Early Medieval Europe* 27: 494–520.

Sarnowski, T. 2012. *Novae, an Archaeological Guide to a Roman Legionary Fortress and Early Byzantine Town on the Lower Danube*. Warsaw.

Sartorius, G. 1811a. *Versuch über die Regierung der Ostgothen während ihrer Herrschaft in Italien, und über die Verhältnisse der Sieger zu den Besiegten im Lande*. Hamburg.

———. 1811b. Review of Wolfe-Tone 1810, Naudet 1811, and Sartorius 1811a. *Göttingische Gelehrte Anzeigen* 111: 1097–1112.

Šašel Kos, M., and P. Scherrer, eds. 2002. *Die autonomen Städte in Noricum und Pannonien/NORICUM*. Ljubljana.

———, eds. 2003a. *Die autonomen Städte in Noricum und Pannonien/PANNONIA I.* Ljubljana.

———, eds. 2003b. *Die autonomen Städte in Noricum und Pannonien/PANNONIA II.* Ljubljana.

Sasse, B. 1997. "Die Westgoten in Südfrankreich und Spanien. Zum Problem der archäologischen Identifikation einer wandernden *gens.*" *Archäologische Informationen* 20, 1: 29–48.

Savino, E. 2005. "Ebrei a Napoli nel VI secolo d.C." In *Hebraica hereditas: Studi in onore di Cesare Colafemmina*, ed. G. Lacerenza, 299–314. Naples.

Schäfer, C. 1991. *Der weströmische Senat als Träger antiker Kontinuität unter den Ostgotenkönigen (490–540 n. Chr.).* Sankt Katharinen, Germany.

———. 2001. "Probleme einer multikulturellen Gesellschaft. Zur Integrationspolitik im Ostgotenreich." *Klio* 83: 182–197.

Schäfer, W. 1939. *Theoderich. König des Abendlandes.* Munich.

Schäferdiek, K. 1967. *Die Kirche in den Reichen der Westgoten und Suewen bis zur Errichtung der westgotischen katholischen Staatskirche.* Berlin.

———. 1973. "Ein neues Bild der Geschichte Chlodwigs? Kritische Erwägungen zu einem chronologischen Versuch." *Zeitschrift für Kirchengeschichte* 84: 270–277.

———. 1978. "Germanenmission." In *RAC* X, 492–548.

———. 1979a. "Zeit und Umstände des westgotischen Übergangs zum Christentum." *Historia* 28: 90–97.

———. 1979b. "Wulfila. Vom Bischof von Gotien zum Gotenbischof." *Zeitschrift für Kirchengeschichte* 90: 253–292.

———. 1983. "Remigius von Reims. Kirchenmann einer Umbruchszeit." *Zeitschrift für Kirchengeschichte* 94: 256–278.

———. 1985. "Bonosus von Naissus, Bonosus von Serdika und die Bonosianer." *Zeitschrift für Kirchengeschichte* 96: 162–178.

———. 1988. "Das gotische liturgische Kalenderfragment—Bruchstück eines Konstantinopler Martyrologs." *Zeitschrift für die neutestamentliche Wissenschaft* 79: 116–137.

———. 1993. "Märtyrerüberlieferungen aus der gotischen Kirche des vierten Jahrhunderts." In *Logos: Festschrift für Luise Abramowski zum 8. Juli 1993*, ed. H.-C. Brennecke et al., 328–360. Berlin.

———. 1996. *Schwellenzeit. Beiträge zur Geschichte des Christentums in Spätantike und Frühmittelalter.* Berlin.

———. 2004. "Chlodwigs Religionswechsel. Bedingungen, Ablauf und Bewegkräfte." In *Patristica et oecumenica. Festschrift für Wolfgang A. Bienert zum 65. Geburtstag*, ed. P. Gemeinhardt, 105–121. Marburg.

———. 2007. "Johannes Chrysostomos und die ulfilanische Kirchensprache." *Zeitschrift für Kirchengeschichte* 117: 289–296.

———. 2009. "Die Ravennater Papyrusurkunde Tjäder 34, der *Codex argenteus* und die ostgotische arianische Kirche." *Zeitschrift für Kirchengeschichte* 120: 215–231.

———. 2014. "Ulfila und der sogenannte gotische Arianismus." In Berndt and Steinacher 2014, 21–44.

Scheidel, W. 2013a. "Explaining the Maritime Freight Charges in Diocletian's Prices Edict." *Journal of Roman Archaeology* 26: 464–468.

———. 2013b. "Italian Manpower." *Journal of Roman Archaeology* 26: 678–687.

Schiavo, S. 2018. *Ricerche sugli editti dei prefetti del pretorio del Cod. Bodl. Roe 18. Processo e documento*. Naples.

Schildt, A. 1999. *Zwischen Abendland und Amerika. Studien zur westdeutschen Ideenlandschaft der 50er Jahre*. Munich.

Schipper, H. G., and J. van Oort. 2000. *St. Leo the Great: Sermons and Letters against the Manichaeans. Selected Fragments*. Turnhout.

Schleicher, E. 1986. "Das Grabmal Kaiser Maximilians I. in der Innsbrucker Hofkirche." In *Österreichische Kunsttopographie*. Vol. 47: *Die Kunstdenkmäler der Stadt Innsbruck. Die Hofbauten*, 359–426. Vienna.

Schlesinger, W. 1953. "Herrschaft und Gefolgschaft in der germanisch-deutschen Verfassungsgeschichte." *Historische Zeitschrift* 176: 225–275.

———. 1956. "Über germanisches Heerkönigtum." In Mayer 1956, 105–141.

———. 1963. "Randbemerkungen zu drei Aufsätzen über Sippe, Gefolgschaft und Treue." In *Alteuropa und die moderne Gesellschaft. Festschrift für Otto Brunner*, ed. Das Historische Seminar der Universität Hamburg, 11–59. Göttingen.

Schlieben, R. 1974. *Christliche Theologie und Philologie in der Spätantike: Die schulwissenschaftlichen Methoden der Psalmenexegese Cassiodors*. Berlin.

———. 1979. *Cassiodors Psalmenexegese. Eine Analyse ihrer Methoden als Beitrag zur Untersuchung der Geschichte der Bibelauslegung der Kirchenväter und der Verbindung christlicher Theologie mit antiker Schulwissenschaft*. Göppingen.

Schmid, W. P. 1973. "Aisten." In RGA I, 116–118.

Schmidt, K. D. 1939. *Die Bekehrung der Ostgermanen zum Christentum*. Vol. 1: *Der ostgermanische Arianismus*. Göttingen.

Schmidt, L. 1934. *Geschichte der deutschen Stämme bis zum Ausgang der Völkerwanderung*. Vol. 1: *Die Ostgermanen*. 2nd ed. Munich. (1st ed. 1904–1910.)

———. 1938–1941. *Geschichte der deutschen Stämme bis zum Ausgang der Völkerwanderung*. Vol. 2: *Die Westgermanen*. 2nd ed. Munich. (1st ed. 1911–1918.)

———. 1939. "Theoderich, römischer Patricius und König der Goten." *Zeitschrift für schweizerische Geschichte* 19: 404–414.

———. 1942. *Geschichte der Wandalen*. 2nd ed. Munich. (1st ed. 1901.)

———. 1943. "Die letzten Ostgoten." *Abhandlungen der Preußischen Akademie der Wissenschaften, philosophische-historische Klasse* 10: 1–15.

Schmidt-Hofner, S. 2006. "Die städtische Finanzautonomie im spätrömischen Reich." In Wiemer 2006a, 209–248.

———. 2008. *Reagieren und Gestalten. Der Regierungsstil des spätrömischen Kaisers am Beispiel der Gesetzgebung Valentinians I*. Munich.

———. 2010. "Ehrensachen. Ranggesetzgebung, Elitenkonkurrenz und die Funktionen des Rechts in der Spätantike." *Chiron* 40: 209–243.

———. 2011. "Staatswerdung von unten. Justiznutzung und Strukturgenese im Gerichtswesen der römischen Kaiserzeit." In *Der wiederkehrende Leviathan. Staatlichkeit und Staatswerdung in Spätantike und Früher Neuzeit*, ed. P. Eich, S. Schmidt-Hofner, and C. Wieland, 139–179. Heidelberg.

———. 2014. "Der *Defensor civitatis* und die Entstehung des städtischen Notabelnregiments in der Spätantike." In Meier and Patzold 2014, 487–522.

———. 2016. "Toleranz braucht Rechtfertigung. Zur Funktion des Mailänder Edikts und verwandter Texte des früheren 4. Jh. n. Chr." In *Religiöse Toleranz: 1700 Jahre nach dem Edikt von Mailand*, ed. M. Wallraff, 159–192. Berlin.

Schmidt-Hofner, S., and H.-U. Wiemer. 2022. "Die Politik der Form: Das 'Edictum Theoderici,' das Prätorische Edikt und die Semantiken königlicher Rechtsetzung im postimperialen Westen." In *Chiron* 52: 335–411.

Schmidt-Voges, I. 2004. "De antiqua claritate et clara antiquitate Gothorum." *Gotizismus als Identitätsmodell im frühneuzeitlichen Schweden*. Frankfurt.

Schneege, G. 1894. "Theoderich der Grosse in der kirchlichen Tradition des Mittelalters und in der Deutschen Heldensage." *Deutsche Zeitschrift für Geschichtswissenschaft* 11: 18–45.

Schneider, F. 1933. *Die Epitaphien der Päpste und andere stadtrömische Inschriften des Mittelalters (IV.–XII. Jahrhundert)*. Rome.

Schneider, H. 1928–1934. *Germanische Heldensage*. 3 vols. Berlin.

———, ed. 1951. *Germanische Altertumskunde*. 2nd ed. Munich. (1st ed. Tübingen, 1938.)

Schnetz, J. 1925. "Theodericopolis." *Zeitschrift für Schweizerische Geschichte* 5: 346–350.

Schott, C. 1995. "Traditionelle Formen der Konfliktlösung in der Lex Burgundionum." In *La giustizia nell'alto medioevo, secoli V–VIII*, ed. CISAM 1995, 933–961. Spoleto.

———. 1996. "*Lex Burgundionum*. Titel 52—Der Aunegilde-Skandal." In *Alles was Recht war. Rechtsliteratur und literarisches Recht. Festschrift für Ruth Schmidt-Wiegand zum 70. Geburtstag*, ed. H. Höfinghoff et al., 25–36. Essen.

Schramm, P. E. 1954. *Herrschaftszeichen und Staats symbolik. Beiträge zu ihrer Geschichte vom dritten bis zum sechzehnten Jahrhundert*. Vol. 1. Munich.

Schröder, B.-J. 2005. "Ein falsches Argument in der Diskussion über den Anlass von Ennodius' Theoderich-Panegyricus (zu Ennod. opusc. 1, §22)." *Historia* 54: 499–500.

———. 2007. *Bildung und Briefe im 6. Jahrhundert. Studien zum Mailänder Diakon Magnus Felix Ennodius*. Berlin.

Schulze, C. 2005. *Medizin und Christentum in Spätantike und frühem Mittelalter. Christliche Ärzte und ihr Wirken*. Tübingen.

Schürer, E. 1986. *The History of the Jewish People in the Age of Jesus Christ (175 B.C.–A.D. 135): A New English Version Revised and Edited by G. Vermes, F. Millar and M. Goodman*. Vol. 3, part 1. Edinburgh.

Schurr, V. 1935. *Die Trinitätslehre des Boethius im Licht der "skythischen Kontroversen."* Paderborn.

Schwab, H.-R. 2003. "Helden, hoffnungslos. Felix Dahns 'Ein Kampf um Rom' als gründerzeitliche Schicksalstragödie." In *Ein Kampf um Rom. Historischer Roman*, by F. Dahn (Munich), 1065–1129. Originally published 1876.

Schwartz, E. 1927. *Codex Vaticanus gr. 1431. Eine antichalkedonische Sammlung aus der Zeit Kaiser Zenos.* Munich.

———. 1934. *Publizistische Sammlungen zum Acacianischen Schisma.* Munich.

Schwind, Johannes. 1990. *Arator-Studien.* Göttingen.

Scivoletto, N. 1970. "La *civilitas* del IV secolo e il significato del *Breviarium* di Eutropio." *Giornale Italiano di Filologia Classica* 22: 14–45.

———. 1986. "Cassiodoro e la 'retorica della città.' " *Giornale Italiano di Filologia* 38: 3–24.

See, K. von. 1970. *Deutsche Germanen-Ideologie. Vom Humanismus bis zur Gegenwart.* Frankfurt.

———. 1978. "Was ist Heldendichtung?" In *Europäische Heldendichtung,* ed. K. von See, 1–40. Darmstadt.

———. 1981. *Germanische Heldensage. Stoffe, Probleme, Methoden; eine Einführung.* 2nd ed. Wiesbaden. (1st ed. 1971.)

———. 1994a. "Germanenbilder." In See 1994c, 9–30.

———. 1994b. "Das Nibelungenlied—ein Nationalepos?" In See 1994c, 83–134.

———. 1994c. *Barbar, Germane, Arier. Die Suche nach der Identität der Deutschen.* Heidelberg.

———. 2001. *Freiheit und Gemeinschaft. Völkisch-nationales Denken in Deutschland zwischen Französischer Revolution und Erstem Weltkrieg.* Heidelberg.

See, K. von, and J. Zernack. 2004. *Germanistik und Politik in der Zeit des Nationalsozialismus. Zwei Fallstudien. Hermann Schneider und Gustav Neckel.* Heidelberg.

Seebold, E. 1986. "Die Konstituierung des Germanischen in sprachlicher Sicht." In Beck 1986, 168–182.

Seeck, O. 1895–1920. *Geschichte des Untergangs der antiken Welt.* 6 vols. Stuttgart.

Selb, W. 1967. "Episcopalis audientia von der Zeit Konstantins bis zur Nov. XXXV Valentinians III." *Zeitschrift für Rechtsgeschichte, Romanistische Abteilung* 84: 162–217.

Sessa, K. 2012. *The Formation of Papal Authority in Late Antique Italy: Roman Bishops and the Domestic Sphere.* Cambridge, UK.

———. 2019. "The New Environmental Fall of Rome: A Methodological Consideration." *Journal of Late Antiquity* 12: 211–255.

Sfameni, C. 2006. *Ville residenziali nell'Italia tardoantica.* Bari.

Sgubbi, G. 2005. "Sulla località Quinto dove nel 536 d.C. fu ucciso il re dei Goti Teodato." *Historia* 54: 227–232.

Shanzer, D. 1996–1997. "Two Clocks and a Wedding: Diplomatic Relations with the Burgundians." *Romanobarbarica* 14: 225–258.

———. 1998. "Dating the Baptism of Clovis: The Bishop of Vienne vs. the Bishop of Tours." *Early Medieval Europe* 7: 29–57.

Shanzer, D., and I. Wood. 2002. "Introduction." In *Avitus of Vienne. Letters and Selected Prose,* ed. D. Shanzer and I. Wood, 1–85. Liverpool.

Shaw, B. D. 1982–1983. "Eaters of Flesh, Drinkers of Milk: The Ancient Mediterranean Ideology of the Pastoral Nomad." *Ancient Society* 13–14: 5–31.

———. 1984. "Banditry in the Roman Empire." *Past & Present* 105: 3–52.

Siebigs, G. 2010. *Kaiser Leo I. Das oströmische Reich in den ersten drei Jahren seiner Regierung (457–460 n. Chr.).* Berlin.

Silva-Tarouca, C. 1937. *Epistularum Romanorum pontificum ad vicarios per Illyricum aliosque episcopos Collectio Thessalonicensis.* Rome.

Sirago, V. A. 1987. "Gli Ostrogoti in Gallia secondo le *Variae* di Cassiodoro." *Revue des Études Anciennes* 89: 63–77.

Sirks, A. J. B. 2008. "The Colonate in Justinian's Reign." *Journal of Roman Studies* 98: 120–143.

Sitzmann, A., and F. E. Grünzweig. 2008. *Die altgermanischen Ethnonyme. Ein Handbuch zu ihrer Etymologie.* Vienna.

Sivan, H. 2011. *Galla Placidia: The Last Roman Empress.* Oxford.

Smith, R. R. R., and B. Ward-Perkins, eds. 2016. *The Last Statues of Antiquity.* Oxford.

Snædal, M. 2009. "The 'Vandal Epigram.'" *Filologia Germanica* 1: 181–214.

Snee, R. 1985. "Valens' Recall of the Nicene Exiles and Anti-Arian Propaganda." *Greek, Roman and Byzantine Studies* 26: 395–419.

———. 1998. "Gregory Nazianzen's Anastasia Church: Arianism, the Goths, and Hagiography." *Dumbarton Oaks Papers* 52: 158–164.

Soproni, S. 1985. *Die letzten Jahrzehnte des pannonischen Limes.* Munich.

Sotinel, C. 1989. "Arator, un poète au service de la politique du pape Vigile?" *Mélanges de l'École française de Rome* 101: 805–820.

———. 1995. "Les ambitions d'historien d'Ennode de Pavie: La *Vita Epiphanii.*" In *La narrativa cristiana antica: Codici narrativi, strutture formali e schemi retorici*, 585–605. Rome.

———. 1996. "L'évergetisme dans le royaume gothique: Le témoignage d'Ennode de Pavie." In *Homenatge a Francesco Giunta: Committenza e committenti tra antichità e alto medioevo*, ed. M. Mayer Olivé and M. Miró Vinaia, 213–222. Barcelona.

———. 1997. "Le recrutement des évêques en Italie aux IVe et Ve siècles: Essai d'enquête prosopographique." In *Vescovi e pastori in epoca teodosiana: XXV incontro di studiosi dell'antichità cristiana (Roma, 8–11 maggio 1996)*, 192–202. Rome.

———. 1998. "Le personnel épiscopal: Enquête sur la puissance de l'évêque dans la cité." In *L'évêque dans la cité: Image et autorité*, ed. E. Rébillard and C. Sotinel, 105–126. Rome.

———. 2001a. "Rom und Italien am Übergang vom Römischen Reich zum Gotenreich." In L. Piétri 2001a, 300–342.

———. 2001b. "Das Dilemma des Westens. Der Drei-Kapitel-Streit." In L. Piétri 2001a, 462–490.

———. 2005. *Identité civique et christianisme: Aquilée du IIIe au VIe siècle.* Rome.

———. 2006. "Les évêques italiens dans la société de l'Antiquité tardive: L'émergence d'une nouvelle élite?" In Lizzi Testa 2006, 377–404.

———. 2010. *Church and Society in Late Antique Italy and Beyond.* Aldershot. (Includes English translations of Sotinel 1989, 1997, 1998, and 2006.)

Spahn, M. 1898. *Johannes Cochläus. Ein Lebensbild aus der Zeit der Kirchenspaltung.* Berlin.

Spielvogel, J. 2002. "Die historischen Hintergründe der gescheiterten Akkulturation im Ostgotenreich." *Historische Zeitschrift* 214: 1–24.

Springer, M. 2005. "Thüringer § 2: Historisch." In RGA XXI, 521–530.

———. 2006. "Warnen." In RGA XXXIII, 274–281.

Staab, F. 1977. "Ostrogothic Geographers at the Court of Theodoric the Great: A Study of Some Sources of the Anonymous Cosmographer of Ravenna." *Viator* 7: 27–64.

Stadermann, C. 2020. "*Restitutio Romanarum Galliarum.* Theoderichs des Großen Intervention in Gallien (507–511)." *Frühmittelalterliche Studien* 54: 1–67.

Stahl, M. 2012. "The Transformation of the West." In *The Oxford Handbook of Greek and Roman Coinage*, ed. W. E. Metcalf, 633–654. Oxford.

Stathakopoulos, D. C. 2004. *Famine and Pestilence in the Late Roman and Early Byzantine Empire: A Systematic Survey of Subsistence Crisis and Epidemics.* Aldershot.

Stauffenberg, A. Graf Schenk von. 1938. "Theoderich der Große und seine römische Sendung." *Würzburger Studien zur Altertumswissenschaft* 13: 115–129.

——. 1940. "Theoderich und Chlodwig." In *Gestalter deutscher Vergangenheit*, ed. P. R. Rohden, 39–53. Potsdam.

——. 1948. *Das Imperium und die Völkerwanderung.* Munich.

Stein, E. 1919. "Beiträge zur Geschichte von Ravenna in spätrömischer und byzantinischer Zeit." *Klio* 16: 40–71.

——. 1920. "Untersuchungen zum Staatsrecht des Bas-Empire." *Zeitschrift für Rechtsgeschichte, Romanistische Abteilung* 41: 195–251.

——. 1922. *Untersuchungen über das Officium der Prätorianerpräfektur seit Diokletian.* Vienna.

——. 1925. "Untersuchungen zur spätrömischen Verwaltungsgeschichte." *Rheinisches Museum* 74: 347–394.

——. 1939. "La disparition du sénat de Rome à la fin du VIe siècle." *Bulletin de la Classe des Lettres de l'Académie de Belgique* 25: 308–322.

——. 1949. *Histoire du Bas-Empire.* Vol. 2: *De la disparition de l'empire d'occident à la mort de Justinien.* Brussels.

——. 1959. *Histoire du Bas-Empire.* Vol. 1: *De l'état romain à l'état byzantin (284–476).* Edited by J.-R. Palanque. Paris.

Stein-Hölkeskamp, E. 2005. *Das römische Gastmahl. Eine Kulturgeschichte.* Munich.

Steinacher, R. 2016. *Die Vandalen. Aufstieg und Fall eines Barbarenreichs.* Stuttgart.

——. 2017. *Rom und die Barbaren: Völker im Alpen und Donauraum (300–600).* Stuttgart.

Stella, A. 2019. *Aquileia tardoantica: Moneta, storia ed economia.* Trieste.

Steuer, H. 1987. "Helm und Ringschwert. Prunkbewaffnung und Rangabzeichen germanischer Krieger." *Studien zur Sachsenforschung* 6: 190–236.

——, ed. 2001. *Eine hervorragend nationale Wissenschaft. Deutsche Prähistoriker zwischen 1900 und 1995.* Berlin.

Stickler, T. 2002. *Aëtius. Gestaltungsspielräume eines Heermeisters im ausgehenden weströmischen Reich.* Munich.

——. 2007. *Die Hunnen.* Munich.

——. 2015. "Aspar und die westlichen Heermeister. Ein Vergleich." In Roberto and Mecella 2015, 289–306.

——. 2020. "Römische Identität(en) im gotischen Italien." In Wiemer 2020a, 295–314.

Stöber, F. 1886. "Quellenstudien zum Laurentianischen Schisma (498–514)." *Sitzungsberichte der kaiserlichen Akademie der Wissenschaften in Wien, philosophische-historische Klasse* 112: 269–347.

Stone, H. 1985. "The Polemics of Toleration: The Scholars and Publishers of Cassiodorus' *Variae.*" *Journal of the History of Ideas* 46: 147–165.

Straub, J. 1943. "Die Wirkung der Niederlage bei Adrianopel auf die Diskussion über das Germanenproblem in der spätrömischen Literatur." *Philologus* 95: 255–286.

Streitberg, W. 2000. *Die gotische Bibel.* 2 vols. 7th ed. Edited by P. Scardigli. Heidelberg. (1st ed. 1908–1910.)

Stroheker, K. F. 1937. *Eurich. König der Westgoten.* Stuttgart.

———. 1948. *Der senatorische Adel im spätantiken Gallien.* Tübingen.

———. 1965. *Germanentum und Spätantike.* Zurich.

Stutz, E. 1984. "Codices Gotici." In RGA V, 52–60.

Suerbaum, W. 1977. *Vom antiken zum frühmittelalterlichen Staatsbegriff. Über Verwendung und Bedeutung von* res publica, regnum, imperium *und* status *von Cicero bis Jordanis.* 3rd ed. Münster. (1st ed. 1961.)

Sundwall, J. 1919. *Abhandlungen zur Geschichte des ausgehenden Römertums.* Helsingfors.

Svennung, J. 1967. *Zur Geschichte des Goticismus.* Stockholm.

Swain, B. 2016. "Goths and Gothic Identity in the Ostrogothic Kingdom." In Arnold, Bjornlie, and Sessa 2016, 203–233.

Tabata, K. 2013. *Città dell'Italia nel VI secolo D.C.* Rome.

Teillet, S. 1984. *Des Goths à la nation gothique: Les origines de l'idée de nation en Occident du Ve au VIIe siècle.* Paris.

Thiebes, B. 1987. *Das Speyer-Fragment des Codex Argenteus, Bibel des Ulfilas in Uppsala.* Speyer.

Thompson, E. A. 1945. "The Camp of Attila." *Journal of Hellenic Studies* 65: 112–115.

———. 1965. *The Early Germans.* Oxford.

———. 1966. *The Visigoths in the Time of Ulfila.* Oxford.

———. 1969. *The Goths in Spain.* Oxford.

———. 1982. *Barbarians and Romans: The Decline of the Western Empire.* Madison, WI.

———. 1996. *The Huns.* Revised ed. by P. J. Heather. Oxford. (1st ed. 1948.)

Tichy, F. 1985. *Italien. Eine geographische Landeskunde.* Darmstadt.

Tiefenbach, H. 1991. "Das wandalische *Domine miserere.*" *Historische Sprachforschung* 104: 251–268.

Timpe, D. 1986. "Ethnologische Begriffsbildung in der Antike." In Beck 1986, 22–40.

———. 1995. *Romano-Germanica. Gesammelte Studien zur Germania des Tacitus.* Stuttgart.

———. 1998. "Gefolgschaft." In RGA X, 533–554.

Tischler, M. M. 2021. "Remembering the Ostrogoths in the Carolingian Empire." In *Historiography and Identity III: Carolingian Approaches,* ed. R. Kramer et al., 65–122. Turnhout.

Tjäder, J.-O. 1954–1982. *Die nichtliterarischen lateinischen Papyri Italiens aus der Zeit 445–700.* 3 vols. Lund.

———. 1988. "Der verlorene Papyrus Marini 85." In *Scire litteras. Forschungen zum mittelalterlichen Geistesleben,* ed. S. Krämer and M. Bernhard, 364–375. Munich.

Tomás-Faci, G., and J. C. Martín-Iglesias. 2017. "Cuatro documentos inéditos del monasterio visigodo de San Martín de Asán (522–586) = Four Unpublished Documents from Visigothic Monastery of San Martín de Asán (522–586)." *Mittellateinisches Jahrbuch* 52: 261–85.

Tönnies, B. 1989. *Die Amalertradition in den Quellen zur Geschichte der Ostgoten. Untersuchungen zu Cassiodor, Jordanes, Ennodius und den* Excerpta Valesiana. Hildesheim.

Troncarelli, F. 1998. *Vivarium: I libri, il destino.* Turnhout.

Tschajanow, A. V. 1923. *Die Lehre von der bäuerlichen Wirtschaft. Versuch einer Theorie der Familienwirtschaft im Landbau.* Berlin. (Repr. Düsseldorf, 1999.)

———. 1924. "Zur Frage einer Theorie der nichtkapitalistischen Wirtschaftssysteme." *Archiv für Sozialwissenschaft und Sozialpolitik* 51: 577–613.

Turkovic, T. 2017. "The Late Antique 'Palace' in Polače Bay (Mljet) — Tetrarchic 'Palace'?" *Hortus Artium Mediaevalium* 17: 211–233.

Ubl, K. 2009. "L'origine contestée de la loi salique: Une mise au point." *Revue de l'Institut français d'histoire en Allemagne* 1: 208–234.

———. 2014. "Im Bann der Traditionen. Zur Charakteristik der Lex Salica." In Meier and Patzold 2014, 423–445.

———. 2017. *Sinnstiftungen eines Rechtsbuchs. Die Lex Salica im Frankenreich.* Ostfildern.

———. 2020. "Das Edikt Theoderichs des Großen. Konzepte der Kodifikation in den post-römischen Königreichen." In Wiemer 2020a, 223–238.

Ullmann, W. 1981. *Gelasius I. (492–496). Das Papsttum an der Wende der Spätantike zum Mittelalter.* Stuttgart.

Ungern-Sternberg, J. von, and H. Reinau, eds. 1988. *Vergangenheit in mündlicher Überlieferung.* Stuttgart.

Urlacher-Becht, C. 2014. *Ennode de Pavie, chantre officiel de l'Église de Milan.* Paris.

Vaccaro, E. 2020. "Landscapes, Townscapes and Trade in Sicily AD 400–600." In Wiemer 2020a, 89–124.

Van der Wal, N. 1981. "Edictum und lex edictalis. Form und Inhalt der Kaisergesetze im spätrömischen Reich." *Revue internationale des droits de l'antiquité*, ser. 3, 28: 277–313.

van Hoof, L. 2016. "Maximian of Ravenna *Chronica,*" *Sacris Erudiri* 55: 259–276.

van Hoof, L., and P. van Nuffelen. 2017. "The Historiography of Crisis: Jordanes, Cassiodorus and Justinian in Mid Sixth-Century Constantinople." *Journal of Roman Studies* 107: 275–300.

———. 2020. *Jordanes: Getica et Romana.* Liverpool.

Vansina, J. 1985. *Oral Tradition as History.* Madison, WI.

Várady, L. 1969. *Das letzte Jahrhundert Pannoniens 376–476.* Amsterdam.

Vasiliev, A. A. 1936. *The Goths in the Crimea.* Cambridge, MA.

———. 1950. *Justin the First: An Introduction to the Epoch of Justinian the Great.* Cambridge, MA.

Velázquez, I., and G. Ripoll López. 2000. "Toletum, la construcción de *una urbs regia.*" In Ripoll López and Gurt 2000, 521–578.

Vera, D. 1986a. "Simmaco e le sue proprietà: Strutture e funzionamento di un patrimonio aristocratico del IV secolo d.C." In *Colloque genevois sur Symmaque à l'occasion du mille six centième anniversaire du conflit de l'autel de la victoire,* ed. F. Paschoud, 231–276. Paris.

———. 1986b. "Forme e funzioni della rendita fondiaria nella tarda antichità." In Giardina 1986, 367–447, 723–760.

———. 1988. "Aristocrazia romana ed economie provinciali nell'Italia tardoantica: Il caso siciliano." *Quaderni catanesi di studi classici e medievali* 10: 115–172.

——. 1992–1993. "Schiavitù rurale e colonato nell'Italia imperiale." *Scienze dell'antichità. Storia archeologia antropologia* 6–7: 291–339.

——. 1993. "Proprietà terriera e società rurale nell'Italia gotica." In CISAM 1993, 1:133–166.

——. 1995. "Dalla 'villa perfecta' alla villa di Palladio: Sulle trasformazioni del sistema agrario in Italia fra principato e dominato." *Athenaeum* 83: 189–212, 331–356.

——. 1997. "Padroni, contadini, contratti: *Realia* del colonato tardoantico." In *Terre, proprietari e contadini dell'impero romano: Dall'affitto agrario al colonato tardoantico*, ed. E. Lo Cascio, 185–224. Rome.

——. 1999a. "*Massa fundorum*: Forme della grande proprietà e poteri della città in Italia fra Costantino e Gregorio Magno." *Mélanges de l'Ecole française de Rome, Antiquité* 111: 991–1026.

——. 1999b. "I silenzi di Palladio e l'Italia: Osservazioni sull'ultimo agronomo romano." *Antiquité Tardive* 7: 283–297.

——. 2002. "*Res pecuariae* imperiali e concili municipali nell'Apulia tardoantica." In *Ancient History Matters: Studies Presented to Jens Erik Skydsgaard on His Seventieth Birthday*, ed. K. Ascani, 245–257. Rome.

——. 2007. "Essere 'schiavi della terra' nell'Italia tardoantica: Le razionalità di una dipendenza." *Studia historica. Historia antigua* 25: 489–505.

——. 2008. "Gli horrea frumentari dell'Italia tardoantica: Tipi, funzione, personale." *Mélanges de l'Ecole française de Rome, Antiquité* 120: 323–336.

——. 2011. "Dalla liturgia al contratto: Cassiodoro, *Variae* X, 28 e il tramonto della città curiale." In Díaz and Martín Viso 2011, 51–70.

——. 2012a. "Stato, fisco e mercato nell'Italia gotica secondo le *Variae* di Cassiodoro: Fra ideologia politica e realtà." In *Agoranomes et édiles: Institutions des marchés antiques*, ed. C. Hasenohr and L. Capdetrey, 245–258. Bordeaux.

——. 2012b. "Questioni di storia agraria tardoromana: Schiavi, coloni, villae." *Antiquité Tardive* 20: 115–122.

——. 2016. "La *Vita Melaniae iunioris*, fonte fondamentale per la storia economica e sociale della tarda antichità." In *"Libera curiositas": Mélanges d'histoire romaine et d'antiquité tardive offerts à Jean-Michel Carrié*, ed. C. Freu, S. Janniard, and A. Ripoll, 217–228. Turnhout.

——. 2019. *I doni di Cerere: Storie della terra nella tarda antichità.* Turnhout.

——. 2020. *Fisco, annona, mercato: Studi sul Tardo impero Romano.* Bari.

Vessey, M. 1998. "The Demise of the Christian Writer and the Remaking of 'Late Antiquity': from H.-I. Marrou's 'Saint Augustine' (1938) to Peter Brown's 'Holy Man' (1983)." *Journal of Early Christian Studies* 6: 377–411.

——. 2002. "From 'cursus' to 'ductus': Figures of Writing in Western Later Antiquity (Augustine, Jerome, Cassiodorus, Bede)." In *European Literary Careers: The Author from Antiquity to the Renaissance*, ed. P. G. Cheney and F. A. De Armas, 47–103. Toronto.

——. 2004. "Introduction." In Cassiodorus, *Institutions of Divine and Secular Learning and On the Soul*, translated by J. W. Halporn, 1–101. Liverpool.

Vetter, G. 1938. *Die Ostgoten und Theoderich.* Stuttgart.

Vidén, G. 1984. *The Roman Chancery Tradition: Studies in the Language of Codex Theodosianus and Cassiodorus' Variae*. Gothenburg.

Vismara, G. 1967. *Edictum Theoderici*. Milan.

———. 1968. *Fragmenta Gaudenziana*. Milan.

Vitiello, M. 2002. "Fine di una magna potestas: La prefettura dell'annona nei secoli quinto e sesto." *Klio* 84: 491–525.

———. 2004. "Teoderico a Roma: Politica, amministrazione e propaganda nell'*adventus* dell'anno 500 (Considerazioni sull' 'Anonimo Valesiano II')." *Historia* 53: 73–120.

———. 2005. *Momenti di Roma ostrogota: Adventus, feste, politica*. Stuttgart.

———. 2006a. " 'Cassiodoriana': Gli *Excerpta Valesiana*, l'*aduentus* e le *laudes* del principe Teoderico." *Chiron* 86: 113–134.

———. 2006b. " 'Nourished at the Breast of Rome': The Queens of Ostrogothic Italy and the Education of the Roman Elite." *Rheinisches Museum* 149: 398–412.

———. 2008. "Last of the Catones: A Profile of Symmachus the Younger." *Antiquité Tardive* 16: 297–315.

———. 2014a. "Theoderic and the Italic Kingdom in Cassiodorus' Gothic History: A Hypothesis of Reconstruction." *Klio* 96: 665–683.

———. 2014b. *Theodahad: A Platonic King at the Collapse of Ostrogothic Italy*. Toronto.

———. 2017. *Amalasuntha: The Transformation of Queenship in the Post-Roman World*. Philadelphia, PA.

———. 2020. " 'Anthologizing Their Successes': Visions of the Past in Gothic Italy." In Wiemer 2020a, 341–368.

Volbach, W. F. 1976. *Elfenbeinarbeiten der Spätantike und des Frühen Mittelalters*. 3rd ed. Mainz. (1st ed. 1916.)

Volpe, G. 1996. *Contadini, pastori e mercanti nell'Apulia tardoantica*. Bari.

vom Brocke, B. 2006. "Über den Beinamen 'der Große' von Alexander dem Großen bis zu Kaiser Wilhelm 'dem Großen.' Annotationen zu Otto Hintzes Denkschrift 'Die Bezeichnung 'Kaiser Wilhelm der Große' für Friedrich Althoff (1901)." In *Das Thema "Preußen" in Wissenschaft und Wissenschaftspolitik des 19. und 20. Jahrhunderts*, ed. W. Neugebauer, 231–267. Berlin.

von den Steinen, W. 1933. "Die Taufe Chlodwigs. Eine quellenkritische Studie." *Mitteilungen des Österreichischen Instituts für Geschichtsforschung, Ergänzungsbände* 12: 417–501. Also published separately: 3rd ed., Darmstadt, 1969.

Vössing, K. 2004. *Mensa regia. Das Bankett beim hellenistischen König und beim römischen Kaiser*. Munich.

———. 2014. *Das Königreich der Vandalen. Geiserichs Herrschaft und das Imperium Romanum*. Darmstadt.

———. 2015. "Vandalen und Goten. Die schwierigen Beziehungen ihrer Königreiche." In *Littérature, politique et religion en Afrique vandale*, ed. É. Wolff, 11–38. Paris.

———. 2016a. "König Gesalechs Sturz (510/511 n. Chr.) und der Anfang vom Ende der ostgotisch-vandalischen Allianz." *Historia* 65: 244–255.

———. 2016b. "König Gelimers Machtergreifung in Procop. Vand. 1,9,8." *Rheinisches Museum* 159: 416–428.

———. 2019. *Das Vandalenreich unter Hilderich und Gelimer (523–534 n. Chr.). Neubeginn und Untergang.* Paderborn.

Wagner, N. 1967. *Getica. Untersuchungen zum Leben des Jordanes und zur frühen Geschichte der Goten.* Berlin.

———. 1986. "Der völkerwanderungszeitliche Germanenbegriff." In Beck 1986, 130–154.

———. 1997. "Ostgotische Personennamengebung." In *Nomen et gens. Zur historischen Aussagekraft frühmittelalterlicher Personennamen,* ed. D. Geuenich, W. Haubrichs, and J. Jarnut, 41–57. Berlin.

Wahle, E. 1941. *Zur ethnischen Deutung frühgeschichtlicher Kulturprovinzen. Grenzen der frühgeschichtlichen Erkenntnis.* Heidelberg.

Wallace-Hadrill, A. 1994. "*Civilis Princeps*: Between Citizen and King." *Journal of Roman Studies* 72: 32–48.

Ward-Perkins, B. 1984. *From Classical Antiquity to the Middle Ages: Urban Building in Northern and Central Italy AD 300–800.* Oxford.

———. 1997. "Continuitists, Catastrophists and the Towns of Post-Roman Northern Italy." *Papers of the British School at Rome* 65: 157–176.

———. 1999. "Re-using the Architectural Legacy of the Past, *entre idéologie et pragmatisme.*" In Brogiolo and Ward-Perkins 1999, 225–244.

———. 2000. "Land, Labour and Settlement." In Av. Cameron, Ward-Perkins, and Whitby 2000, 315–345.

———. 2005. *The Fall of Rome and the End of Civilization.* Oxford.

———. 2010. "Where Is the Archaeology and Iconography of Germanic Arianism?" In *Religious Diversity in Late Antiquity,* ed. D. Gwynn and S. Bangert, 265–289. Leiden.

———. 2012. "Old and New Rome Compared: The Rise of Constantinople." In Grig and Kelly 2012, 53–78.

Watts, E. 2011. "John Rufus, Timothy Aelurus, and the Fall of the Western Roman Empire." In *Romans, Barbarians, and the Transformation of the Roman World. Cultural Interaction and the Creation of Identity in Late Antiquity,* ed. R. W. Mathisen and D. Shanzer, 97–106. Aldershot.

Weber, M. 1924. "Die sozialen Gründe des Untergangs der antiken Kultur (1896)." In *Gesammelte Aufsätze zur Sozial- und Wirtschaftsgeschichte,* 289–311. Tübingen.

———. 1976. *Wirtschaft und Gesellschaft. Studienausgabe.* 5th ed. Tübingen. (1st ed. 1922.)

Weiss, R. 1971. *Chlodwigs Taufe: Reims 508. Versuch einer neuen Chronologie für die Regierungszeit des ersten christlichen Frankenkönigs unter Berücksichtigung der politischen und kirchlich-dogmatischen Probleme seiner Zeit.* Bern.

Weitzmann, K. 1977. *Late Antique and Early Christian Book Illumination.* London.

Wenskus, R. 1977. *Stammesbildung und Verfassung. Das Werden der frühmittelalterlichen gentes.* 2nd ed. Cologne. (1st ed. 1961.)

———. 1986. "Über die Möglichkeit eines allgemeinen interdisziplinären Germanenbegriffs." In Beck 1986, 1–21.

Wes, M. A. 1967. *Das Ende des Kaisertums im Westen des Römischen Reichs.* The Hague.

Westall, R. 2014. "Theoderic Patron of the Churches of Rome?" *Acta ad archaeologiam et artium historiam pertinentia* 27: 119–138.

Whittaker, C. R. 1987. "Circe's Pigs: From Slavery to Serfdom in the Later Roman World." In *Classical Slavery*, ed. M. I. Finley, 88–122. London.

Whittaker, C. R., and P. Garnsey. 1998. "Rural Life in the Later Roman Empire." In Av. Cameron and Garnsey 1998, 277–311.

Wickert, L. 1954. "Princeps." In RE XXII, 1998–2296.

Wickham, C. 1981. *Early Medieval Italy: Central Power and Local Society 400–1000.* London.

——. 1984. "The Other Transition: From the Ancient World to Feudalism." *Past & Present* 103: 3–36.

——. 1988. "Marx, Sherlock Holmes, and Late Roman Commerce." *Journal of Roman Studies* 78: 183–193.

——. 2005. *Framing the Early Middle Ages: Europe and the Mediterranean 400–800.* Oxford.

Wieacker, F. 1989. *Römische Rechtsgeschichte. Erster Abschnitt: Einleitung, Quellenkunde, Frühzeit und Republik.* Munich.

Wieling, H. J. 1997. "Advokaten im spätantiken Rom." In *Atti del XI Convegno Internazionale in onore di Felix B. J. Wubbe*, ed. ARC, 419–463. Naples.

Wiemer, H.-U. 1995. *Libanios und Julian. Studien zum Verhältnis von Rhetorik und Politik im vierten Jahrhundert n. Chr.* Munich.

——. 1997. "Das Edikt des L. Antistius Rusticus. Eine Preisregulierung als Antwort auf eine überregionale Versorgungskrise?" *Anatolian Studies* 47: 195–215.

——. 2003. "Vergangenheit und Gegenwart im *Antiochikos* des Libanios." *Klio* 85: 442–468.

——. 2004a. "Akklamationen im spätrömischen Reich. Zur Typologie und Funktion eines Kommunikationsrituals." *Archiv für Kulturgeschichte* 86: 27–73.

——. 2004b. Review of Stathakopoulos 2004. *sehepunkte* 4, no. 6. http://www.sehepunkte. de/2004/06/5822.html

——, ed. 2006a. *Staatlichkeit und politisches Handeln im Römischen Reich.* Berlin.

——. 2006b. "Kaiser und Katastrophe. Zur Bewältigung von Versorgungskrisen im spätrömischen Reich." In Wiemer 2006a, 249–282.

——. 2009. "Kaiserkritik und Gotenbild bei Malchos von Philadelpheia." In *Jenseits der Grenzen. Beiträge zur spätantiken und frühmittelalterlichen Geschichtsschreibung*, ed. A. Goltz et al., 25–60. Berlin.

——. 2013a. "Malchos von Philadelpheia, die Vandalen und das Ende des Kaisertums im Westen." In *Fragmentarisch erhaltene Historiker des 5. Jahrhunderts n. Chr.*, ed. B. Bleckmann and T. Stickler, 121–159. Stuttgart.

——. 2013b. "Die Goten in Italien. Wandlungen und Zerfall einer Gewaltgemeinschaft." *Historische Zeitschrift* 296: 593–628.

——. 2013c. "Late Antiquity 1971–2011. Positionen der angloamerikanischen Forschung." *Historische Zeitschrift* 296: 114–130.

——. 2013d. "*Voces populi*. Akklamationen als Surrogat politischer Partizipation im spätrömischen Reich." In *Genesis und Dynamiken der Mehrheitsentscheidung*, ed. E. Flaig, 173–202. Munich.

——. 2013e. Review of Bjornlie 2013. *Sehepunkte* 13, no. 11. http://www.sehepunkte. de/2013/11/22995.html.

———. 2014. "Odovakar und Theoderich. Herrschaftskonzepte nach dem Ende des Kaisertums im Westen." In Meier and Patzold 2014, 157–211.

———. 2015a. "Rom—Ravenna—Tours. Rituale und Residenzen im poströmischen Westen." In *Raum und Performanz. Rituale in Residenzen von der Antike bis 1815*, ed. D. Boschung et al., 167–218. Stuttgart.

———. 2015b. Review of Arnold 2014. *Sehepunkte* 15, no. 10. http://www.sehepunkte. de/2015/10/25443.html

———. 2015c. *Alexander der Große*. Munich. (1st ed. 2005.)

———. 2017. "Keine Amazonen. Frauen in ostgotischen Kriegergruppen." *Archiv für Kulturgeschichte* 99: 265–298.

———, ed. 2020a. *Theoderich der Große und das gotische Italien*. Berlin.

———. 2020b. "Von Theoderich zu Athalarich. Das gotische Königtum in Italien." In Wiemer 2020a, 239–294.

———. 2020c. "Statt eines Nachworts: Theoderich und die Goten in Italien, 1544–2018." In Wiemer 2020a, 393–444.

———. 2021. "Coinage and Currency in Ostrogothic Italy." *Chiron* 51: 37–75.

———. 2022. "Procopius and the Barbarians in the West." In Meier 2021.

———. Forthcoming. "Ansiedlung." In *Das Römische Reich und die Barbaren*, ed. M. Becher, J. Bemman, and K. Vössing (Der Neue Pauly, Supplement 14).

Wiemer, H.-U., and G. Berndt. 2016. "Instrumente der Gewalt. Bewaffnung und Kampfesweise gotischer Kriegergruppen." *Millennium* 10: 141–210.

Wilkes, J. J. 1986. *Diocletian's Palace, Split: Residence of a Retired Roman Emperor*. Oxford.

Winterling, A., ed. 1998. *Comitatus. Beiträge zur Erforschung des spätantiken Kaiserhofes*. Berlin.

Wiotte-Franz, C. 2001. *Hermeneus und Interpres. Zum Dolmetscherwesen in der Antike*. Saarbrücken.

Wirbelauer, E. 1993. *Zwei Päpste in Rom. Der Konflikt zwischen Laurentius und Symmachus (498–514)*. Munich.

Witschel, C. 2001. "Rom und die Städte Italiens in Spätantike und Frühmittelalter." *Bonner Jahrbücher* 201: 113–162.

———. 2006. "Der 'epigraphic habit' in der Spätantike. Das Beispiel der Provinz *Venetia et Histria*." In Krause and Witschel 2006, 359–412.

———. 2008. "Sterbende Städte? Betrachtungen zum römischen Städtewesen in der Spätantike." In *Schrumpfende Städte. Ein Phänomen zwischen Antike und Moderne*, ed. A. Lampen and A. Ozawar, 17–78. Cologne.

———. 2013. "Die spätantiken Städte Galliens. Transformationen von Stadtbildern als Ausdruck einer gewandelten Identität?" In Diefenbach and Müller 2013, 153–200.

———. 2020. "Die Städte Nord- und Mittelitaliens im 5. und 6. Jahrhundert n. Chr." In Wiemer 2020a, 37–62.

Wiwjorra, I. 2001. "Willy Pastor (1867–1933). Ein völkischer Vorgeschichtspublizist." In "*. . . trans Albim fluvium.*" *Forschungen zur vorrömischen, kaiserzeitlichen und mittelalterlichen Archäologie. Festschrift für Achim Leube zum 65. Geburtstag*, ed. M. Meyer, 11–24. Rahden, Germany.

——. 2006. *Der Germanenmythos. Konstruktion einer Weltanschauung in der Altertumsforschung des 19. Jahrhunderts.* Darmstadt.

Wojciech, K. 2016. "Die Gerichtsbarkeit des *Praefectus urbis Romae* über Senatoren zur Zeit Theoderichs. Verfahrensrechtliche Kontinuität und politischer Pragmatismus." In Haensch 2016, 265–298.

Wolfe-Tone W. T. 1810. *Etat civil et politique d'Italie sous la domination des Goths.* Paris.

Wolfram, H. 1967. *Intitulatio I. Lateinische Königs- und Fürstentitel bis zum Ende des 8. Jahrhunderts.* Graz.

——. 1975a. "Gotische Studien I. Das Richtertum Athanarichs." *Mitteilungen des Instituts für Österreichische Geschichtsforschung* 83: 1–32.

——. 1975b. "Gotische Studien II. Die terwingische Stammesverfassung und das Bibelgothische." *Mitteilungen des Instituts für Österreichische Geschichtsforschung* 83: 289–324.

——. 1976 "Gotische Studien III. Die terwingische Stammesverfassung und das Bibelgothische (II)." *Mitteilungen des Instituts für Österreichische Geschichtsforschung* 84: 239–261.

——. 1977. "Theogonie, Ethnogenese und ein kompromittierter Großvater im Stammbaum Theoderichs des Großen." In *Festschrift für Helmut Beumann zum 65. Geburtstag,* ed. K.-U. Jäschke and R. Wenskus, 80–97. Sigmaringen.

——. 1979. "Gotisches Königtum und römisches Kaisertum von Theodosius dem Großen bis Justinian I." *Frühmittelalterliche Studien* 13: 1–28.

——. 2004. "Die dauerhafte Ansiedlung der Goten auf römischem Boden. Eine endlose Geschichte." *Mitteilungen des Instituts für Österreichische Geschichtsforschung* 112: 11–35.

——. 2005. *Gotische Studien. Volk und Herrschaft im frühen Mittelalter.* Munich.

——. 2009. *Die Goten. Von den Anfängen bis zur Mitte des sechsten Jahrhunderts. Entwurf einer historischen Ethnographie.* 5th ed. Munich. (1st ed. 1979.)

Wolfram, H., and F. Daim, eds. 1980. *Die Völker an der unteren und mittleren Donau im fünften und sechsten Jahrhundert.* Vienna.

Wolfram, H., and A. Schwarcz, eds. 1988. *Anerkennung und Integration. Zu den wirtschaftlichen Grundlagen der Völkerwanderungszeit 400–600.* Vienna.

Wolters, R. 1999. *Nummi Signati. Untersuchungen zur römischen Münzprägung und Geldwirtschaft.* Munich.

Wood, I. N. 1985. "Gregory of Tours and Clovis." *Revue belge de philologie et d'histoire* 63: 249–272.

——. 2003. Review of Christensen 2002. *Historisk Tidsskrift* 103: 465–484.

——. 2004. "The Latin Culture of Gundobad and Sigismund." In *Akkulturation. Probleme einer germanisch-romanischen Kultursynthese in Spätantike und frühem Mittelalter,* ed. D. Hägemann, 367–380. Berlin.

——. 2013. *The Modern Origins of the Early Middle Ages.* Oxford.

——. 2017. "Burgundian Law Making, 451–534." *Italian Review of Legal History* 3: 1–27.

Wulf-Rheidt, U. 2017. "Die schwierige Frage der Nutzung des Römischen Kaiserpalastes auf dem Palatin in Rom in der Spätantike." *Antiquité Tardive* 25: 127–148.

Wyss, U. 1983. *Die wilde Philologie. Jacob Grimm und der Historismus.* Munich.

Zachariae von Lingenthal, K. E. 1842. *Anekdota. Theodori scholastici breviarium novella-rum* [. . .] *edicta praefectorum praetorio* [. . .] *edidit, prolegomenis, versione Latina et adnotationibus illustravit.* Leipzig.

Zelzer, K. 1993. "Das Mönchtum in Italien zur Zeit der Goten." In CISAM 1993, 1:425–449.

Zeumer, K. 1898. "Das Processkostengesetz des Königs Theudis vom 24. November 546." *Neues Archiv* 23: 73–103.

Zeuß, J. K. 1837. *Die Deutschen und die Nachbarstämme.* Munich.

Zimmermann, F. X. 1953. "Der Grabstein der ostgotischen Königstochter Amalafrida Theodenanda in Genazzano bei Rom." In *Beiträge zur älteren europäischen Kulturgeschichte. Festschrift für Rudolf Egger,* ed. G. Moro, 2:330–354. Klagenfurt.

Zimmermann, H. J. 1972. "Theoderich der Große—Dietrich von Bern. Die geschichtli-chen und sagenhaften Quellen des Mittelalters." PhD diss. Bonn.

Zöllner, E. 1970. *Geschichte der Franken bis zur Mitte des 6. Jahrhunderts.* Munich.

Zuckerman, C. 1991. "Cappadocian Fathers and the Goths." *Travaux et mémoires du Centre de recherche d'histoire et civilisation de Byzance* 11: 473–486.

———. 1994. "L'Empire d'Orient et les Huns: Notes sur Priscus." *Travaux et mémoires du Centre de recherche d'histoire et civilisation de Byzance* 12: 159–182.

Zurli, L. 2006. " 'De conviviis barbaris' (285–285a Riese = 279–280 Shackleton Bailey): Una rivisitazione." *Giornale Italiano di Filologia* 58: 335–340.

INDEX

Figures and notes are indicated by f and n following the page number. The traditional abbreviation cos. indicates "consul." A slash indicates two forms of a name that are both used. Names in parentheses are either modern forms of ancient names or vice versa.